# ACCOUNTING
## A Management Approach

*THE*
*WILLARD J. GRAHAM SERIES*
*IN ACCOUNTING*

CONSULTING EDITOR    **ROBERT N. ANTHONY**
*Harvard University*

# ACCOUNTING
# A Management Approach

**MYRON J. GORDON**, Ph.D.
*Professor of Finance*
*Faculty of Management Studies*
*University of Toronto*

**GORDON SHILLINGLAW**, Ph.D.
*Professor of Accounting*
*Graduate School of Business*
*Columbia University*

FIFTH EDITION • 1974

**RICHARD D. IRWIN, INC.** *Homewood, Illinois* 60430

*Irwin-Dorsey Limited Georgetown, Ontario* L7G 4B3

© RICHARD D. IRWIN, INC., 1951, 1959, 1964, 1969, and 1974

Fifth Edition

11 12 13 14 15 16 17 18 MP 5 4 3 2 1 0 9 8

ISBN 0-256-01542-2
Library of Congress Catalog Card No. 74–75089

*Printed in the United States of America*

LEARNING SYSTEMS COMPANY—
a division of Richard D. Irwin, Inc.—has developed a
PROGRAMMED LEARNING AID
to accompany texts in this subject area.
Copies can be purchased through your bookstore
or by writing PLAIDS,
1818 Ridge Road, Homewood, Illinois 60430.

*To Betty and Barbara*

# PREFACE

A TEXTBOOK should be more than an annotated guide to current knowledge or practice. It should pose problems, identify issues, and above all encourage thought. Our objective has been to provide a sound, thorough overview of accounting information for the managers, investors, and others who need it.

Our emphasis throughout is on the *interpretation* of accounting figures rather than on the process of preparing them, because we are convinced that this is the only way that the introductory accounting course should be taught. For those who will go no farther in the study of accounting than this introduction, knowledge of the accounting process is unimportant except insofar as it is necessary to an appreciation of the meaning of accounting figures. For the future accountant, an initial emphasis on process at the expense of meaning is likely to lend an aura of sanctity to existing methods that will inhibit the later search for meaning. For this reason we offer this book, without apology, as an appropriate introduction to accounting for the future accountant as well as for others.

This book has three parts. Part I establishes the basic concepts and structure of accounting and provides an introduction to the mechanics of double-entry bookkeeping. The most important aspects of this material are contained in Chapters 2, 3, 4, and 5, which explain how the accountant uses the accounting process to derive financial statements from the data available to him. The next three chapters deal primarily with techniques of statement preparation and data processing.

Part I closes with a chapter on the elements of financial statement analysis, designed to provide an initial understanding of how companywide financial statements are used. We regard this as a transitional chapter, a point of reference to return to from time to time during the study of the material in Part II.

Most of Part II is devoted to an examination of the alternatives available to accountants in the measurement of income, assets, liabilities, and owners' equity for external financial reporting. We have not taken the easy route, avoiding controversial issues by limiting ourselves to a statement of a set of rules that are or should be observed in practice. Instead, we have tried to present alternative solutions to measurement problems, together with their supporting arguments and some indication of their probable effects on the meaning of the information provided by the firm's financial statements. Whenever appropriate, we cite accepted practice and authoritative rulings, along with a brief summary of our evaluation of these positions.

Some may be surprised to find in Part II material that is often reserved for more advanced courses. This reflects our conviction that no student should complete an introductory course in accounting without some appreciation of most of the practices to be encountered in the financial statements published by corporations. This has forced us to take up the accounting and economics of such topics as declining-charge depreciation, deferred income taxes, pension plans, stock options, and pooling of interests. While the treatment of these topics is not as thorough as we might like and does not absolve the future accountant from the need for further study, it does, we hope, assure that the user of financial statements will not find the terminology and accounting practices used in published statements completely unfamiliar.

Part III deals with the use of accounting information by the firm's own management. The first five chapters examine the use of accounting data in various kinds of planning activities, while the final three chapters explore the accountants' methods of reporting detailed operating data to management.

This book may be used in a one-semester, two-quarter, or one-year introductory course, or as the basic text in a liberal arts college course in accounting. It can also be used, as previous editions have been, in executive development programs of various lengths. If dealt with thoroughly, Parts I and II provide ample material for a full semester or even longer. Those instructors who want to take up some of the chapters from Part III in a one-semester course, however, will find it possible to pass over

Chapters 6, 7, 8, and 9 without serious loss of continuity. They will also find that many of the chapters in Part II begin with fundamental and comparatively simple topics and progress to more difficult material. To save time, the final sections of these chapters can be treated less thoroughly or passed over entirely without loss of continuity. Finally, if the length of the course prevents complete coverage of Part III, Chapters 21, 22, and 25 can be omitted without sacrificing the basic objective of providing the student with a management-oriented introduction to cost accounting.

The inclusion of an appendix containing solutions to selected practice problems from most of the chapters has proven to be highly useful and is retained in this edition. The purpose is two-fold: (1) to permit students to test their comprehension of the text material before starting on the problems assigned by the instructor; and (2) to provide material that students can use independently to increase their facility in problem solving. We have not included solutions to give the student a model for solving every problem in the book, however, because we feel that the experience of coping with unfamiliar problem formats is more conducive to learning than routine memorization of a standardized solution format.

We should like to emphasize to the reader that learning accounting requires effort. We have made every effort to make this book clear and readable, but it is not a novel. We assume that the student is a mature individual, able to understand and apply conceptual material. The best course to follow is to study the illustrations in the text carefully, verifying each figure and perhaps even duplicating the calculations on scratch paper. The next step is to work some of the practice problems to be found at the end of each chapter. Once this has been done, the student should try to summarize the concepts or principles underlying the solutions.

Much of whatever merit this book may have can be attributed to those who have taught us, criticized our work, and worked with us over the years. The links that go back farthest in time are those with our former colleague and co-author, Thomas M. Hill, with Frank P. Smith, and with William Cooper. Charles Bastable reviewed the fourth edition with his usual meticulous care, and his comments and suggestions were extremely useful as we set to work on the present edition. Lloyd Heath also deserves our thanks for reviewing the entire manuscript for the publisher just prior to copy-editing. Our responses to his efforts are clearly evident in the text.

We are also grateful to many others who have written or spoken to us about specific points in the text or problem material, in particular George Benston, Joel Berk, John Burton, John A. Elliott, Calvin Engler, Haim Fellman, Dennis Gordon, Adolph Matz, Philip Myers, Charles R. Purdy, Michael Schiff, Russell Taussig, Gerard A. von Dohlen, A. Tobey Yu, Zenon Zannetos, and Stephen Zeff. Thanks, also, to Norman Berman and Joseph Greco for reviewing the problem solutions so carefully and constructively. Our memory being what it is, we apologize in advance to others who belong on this list but whom we have neglected to mention.

Our greatest thanks must go to Carl L. Nelson, who read at least one draft of every chapter and several of some. His incisive, often caustic comments added more grey to our hair and more clarity and consistency to the text. Most of the improvements in this edition would have been impossible or incomplete without his help and guidance.

Finally, we should like to express our gratitude to John Burton, Charles Bastable, and Carl Nelson for their permission to use or adapt a number of their pet problems, and to the IMEDE management development institute in Lausanne, Switzerland, for its permission to reproduce a number of cases from its collection. Whether the figures are stated in dollars, in lire, or in francs, the accounting problems are basically the same, and we'd like to think that the presence of these cases will make this a little more obvious.

*May 1974*                              MYRON J. GORDON
                                        GORDON SHILLINGLAW

# CONTENTS

xiii

## Part II   EXTERNAL FINANCIAL REPORTING

## Part III    ACCOUNTING DATA FOR MANAGEMENT PLANNING AND CONTROL

# Part I

# Basic Accounting Concepts

# 1

# INTRODUCTION

ACCOUNTING is a systematic means of writing and interpreting the economic history of individual organizations. Its main purpose is to provide information, first to the organization's management and second to outsiders. It also provides a conceptual framework which can be used to express and test management's plans for the organization's future.

Although this view of accounting applies to all kinds of organizations, including governments, fraternal societies, and educational institutions, our main focus will be on business enterprises that are owned by private individuals. This chapter has two purposes: (1) to examine the background against which today's business accounting takes place; and (2) to introduce the fundamental principles of financial accounting measurement.

## THE ROLE OF ACCOUNTING

Present-day accounting can trace its origins to the Renaissance, when a new class of merchants needed a means of organizing their records of such things as the amounts owed by and to various outsiders, the payment and collection of bills, and the nature, quantity, location, and cost of their property.

Important as these records were, information summaries derived from them were even more important. The merchant entrusted his capital to ship captains and other agents, often operating at great distances from home base. The Renaissance accountant prepared *financial statements* which showed the capital employed in each venture and how effectively the agent had used it.

The emergence of financial statements of this kind was occasioned by the shift from feudalism to a market-oriented economic system. In feudal society wealth was used to produce goods for current consumption. Since wealth was not used to produce wealth, borrowed money could be paid back only if the borrower could take it from someone else. The feudal lord borrowed money so that he could live or fight beyond his means; he repaid, if at all, from the fruits of battle, the favors of his liege lord, or the proceeds of a good marriage. In most cases, credit placed strains on the borrower that endangered the stability of the feudal system.

By contrast, the medieval merchant's wealth was capital to be employed for profit, and profit and credit were means for the further accumulation of capital. The new accounting system was well suited to meet the needs of these merchants. The great 19th-century economic historian Werner Sombart wrote,

> One can scarcely conceive of capitalism without double-entry bookkeeping: they are related as are form and content. It is difficult to decide, however, whether in double-entry bookkeeping capitalism provided itself with a tool to make it more effective, or whether capitalism derives from the "spirit" of double-entry bookkeeping.[1]

The modern business firm is a far cry from the merchant firms of the Renaissance. One big difference is that most business today is conducted by corporations rather than by one-man firms ("individual proprietorships") or partnerships. The corporate form of organization makes it possible to bring large numbers of people together as the owners of business firms, thereby making large-scale enterprises financially feasible. Since most of these owners have no direct contact with corporate management, they must rely on financial statements as their primary source of information on the economic status and performance of the business.

Furthermore, the corporations that account for the lion's share of business activity today are so large and so widely diversified that management cannot plan and control current operations on the basis of direct personal observation or by working with the financial statements of the company as a whole. For planning

---

[1] W. Sombart, *Der Moderne Kapitalismus*, as quoted in A. C. Littleton and B. S. Yamey, *Studies in the History of Accounting* (Homewood, Ill.: Richard D. Irwin, Inc., 1956), p. 4. See also R. H. Tawney, *Religion and the Rise of Capitalism* (New York: Harcourt, Brace & World, 1926); and Robert L. Heilbroner, *The Making of Economic Society* (New York: Prentice-Hall, Inc., 1962).

and control, management needs detailed information on the performance of subordinate managers and the cost and profitability of the firm's many activities. It gets this information primarily from accounting.

These two sets of information needs provide the basis for a two-way classification of accounting information outputs: *financial accounting* and *managerial accounting*. Providing information to investors and others outside the company's management is the domain of financial accounting or enterprise accounting. Information provided for internal use, mostly dealing with individual segments of the company's business, is the province of managerial accounting.

## ACCOUNTING PRACTITIONERS

Most of the people who work in accounting are employed directly by business firms and other organizations. They prepare payrolls, record purchases and sales, and keep track of their employers' property. They prepare financial statements that summarize the effects on the organization of activities and events that have already taken place, and help management develop budgetary plans for the future. They participate in the design of systems to do all this, and help management understand the meaning of the figures that emerge from these systems.

The skills required by these activities vary widely. By far the largest number of people perform largely routine clerical functions for which high school or technical school education is adequate preparation. At the top of the pyramid, in contrast, is the chief accounting officer or *controller*, performing duties that in the large organization require extensive formal education and many years of practical experience.

The second group of accounting practitioners are the public accountants who provide services to their clients for a fee. Some of this is "write-up" work, in which the public accountant prepares financial statements for clients who don't have employees to do this. Some of it is helping the client develop information for use in resolving income tax questions. Some is "management services," helping the client design record-keeping systems and planning and control systems or analyzing the client's business problems and opportunities.

None of these activities is unique to public accounting. The unique role of public accountants is to *audit* the financial statements of business corporations and other organizations. No matter how competent and honest the company's own accountants are, the investor and other outsiders need an independent representative who will state that:

1. The figures representing the organization's financial status and performance are complete and are measured on the basis of agreed-upon measurement principles; and
2. The organization has provided adequate safeguards to protect itself from fraud or embezzlement.

The public accounting profession has developed to meet these needs.[2] The importance of integrity and professional standards of conduct was well stated by one of the great figures in the development of public accounting in this country, George O. May:

> The work of the financial accountant involves the assumption of responsibility to persons other than the immediate client in matters which require the exercise of judgment in the selection and application of appropriate rules or principles and the adherence thereto, if need be in the face of opposition from the client. It is clearly of a professional character. It gives the independent accountant that just ground for pride in his work which is essential to the establishment of a profession on a high ethical level.[3]

The importance of the public accountant is evidenced by the fact that practically all corporate bylaws and extended-loan contracts require periodic audits of the corporation's accounts by an independent certified public accountant. Auditing has been defined as "an exploratory, critical review by a public accountant of the underlying internal controls and accounting records of a business enterprise or other economic unit, precedent to the expression by him of an opinion of the propriety of its financial statements."[4]

Upon completion of the audit, the public accountant writes a letter (known as an *opinion*) which the corporation attaches to its financial statements. A typical opinion reads:

> We have examined the balance sheet of XYZ, Inc., at December 31, 19x1, and December 31, 19x0, and the related statements of income, retained earnings, and changes in financial position for the

---

[2] For a history of the development of public accounting, see James Don Edwards, *History of Public Accounting in the United States* (East Lansing, Mich.: Michigan State University Press, 1960), and Stephen A. Zeff, *Forging Accounting Principles in Five Countries: A History and Analysis of Trends* (Champaign, Ill.: Stipes Publishing Co., 1972).

[3] George O. May, *Financial Accounting* (New York: The Macmillan Co., 1943), p. 64. Public accountancy exhibits the usual characteristics of a profession in that admission, or "certification," is controlled by experience and examination requirements (in this case established by state laws), and in that accepted standards of professional conduct exist.

[4] Eric L. Kohler, *A Dictionary for Accountants* (New York: Prentice-Hall, Inc., 1957), pp. 44–45.

years then ended. Our examination was made in accordance with generally accepted auditing standards, and accordingly included such tests of the accounting records and such other auditing procedures as we considered necessary in the circumstances.

In our opinion, the accompanying balance sheets and statements of income, retained earnings, and changes in financial position present fairly the financial position of XYZ, Inc., at December 31, 19x1, and December 31, 19x0, the results of its operations and the changes in financial position for the years then ended, in conformity with generally accepted accounting principles applied on a basis consistent with that of the preceding year.

Although couched in technical language, this is intended to assure the reader that the auditor has done his job. He has used professionally recognized methods to verify that the financial statements are consistent with the available factual evidence and that when the company's accountants have had to use their judgment they have followed accounting principles that are widely accepted by the accounting profession.

Most audits of the financial statements of publicly-owned corporations in the United States are performed by large and medium-sized public accounting firms. These firms are organized as partnerships, and the largest among them have hundreds of partners and branch offices or affiliates throughout the United States and in many foreign countries.

All of the partners and most of the professional staff in these firms are *certified public accountants*. The CPA is an individual who has satisfied the educational, experience, and examination requirements that have been established by the state in which he wishes to qualify.

## ENTERPRISE FINANCIAL STATEMENTS

With these preliminaries behind us, we can take our first look at the kinds of information the accountant prepares to represent the economic status and performance of individual business enterprises.

The accountant regards the business enterprise as a collection of resources subject to a common control and employed for profit. The firm's resources are summarized in a *balance sheet* or *statement of financial position*. Economic performance, on the other hand, is summarized in the *income statement*. Our purpose in the next few paragraphs will be to examine the basic structure of these statements and the bases on which the figures in them are prepared.

## Assets and Asset Measurement

The statement of financial position consists of a list of the measurable assets owned or controlled by the firm on a specific date, together with a list of the liabilities and owners' equities in the firm at that time. *Assets* are things that have value to the firm, such as those in the left-hand column of Exhibit 1–1.

*Exhibit 1–1*

XYZ Company

STATEMENT OF FINANCIAL POSITION

December 31, 19x1

| *Assets* | | *Liabilities and Owners' Equity* | |
|---|---|---|---|
| Cash | $ 30,000 | Accounts payable | $ 50,000 |
| Accounts receivable | 50,000 | Notes payable | 20,000 |
| Inventories | 100,000 | Bonds payable | 80,000 |
| Plant and equipment | 160,000 | Owners' equity | 190,000 |
| Total Assets | $340,000 | Total Equities | $340,000 |

Certain assets, such as cash and the amounts receivable from customers, are measured directly in monetary terms. Cash is the amount of money the firm has on hand or in the bank. Accounts receivable are measured by the value of these customers' obligations to the company.

For nonmonetary assets such as the items of merchandise which comprise the inventory and the various machines which comprise the firm's equipment, arriving at a money amount is not as simple. Since an asset is a thing of value, it might seem reasonable to measure each asset by the amount of money for which it can be sold—*market value.* Laymen therefore are often shocked to learn that market value is not the basis of measurement, or what the accountant calls the "basis of valuation," for most assets.

Many accountants prefer to pass over the basis of measurement as quickly and quietly as possible in an introductory discussion of accounting. We believe that shock and disillusionment with accounting are thereby only compounded, and therefore we admit this terrible truth as clearly and forcefully as possible at the outset. Accountants measure only a few kinds of assets— most notably cash and short-term accounts receivable—at amounts approximating their current values. For all other assets accountants base their measurements on the amounts the firm has expended to acquire them. This is called the *historical cost basis* of measurement.

To illustrate the distinction between market value and historical cost, let us assume that the Lucky Land Development Company bought 200 acres of farm land in 19x1 for $100,000. The company still owned the land four years later, and by that time its market value had risen to $250,000 due to its potential use in suburban housing. The company's financial statements, however, still listed the land at its $100,000 historical cost.

Market value is only one of several measures by which value can be defined. Some of these measures are in fact used in conventional financial accounting, and we shall discuss them at a later time. We shall also examine a set of value-based financial statements in Chapter 10 and find them wanting. Until then, however, we shall concentrate wholly on the development of the historical cost basis of accounting.

### Liabilities and Owners' Equity

Individuals may be endowed by nature or other benefactors with various assets. Business firms are ordinarily not so fortunate. The firm's assets are provided by its owners and its creditors, who thereby acquire owners' or creditors' equities in the firm. The statement of financial position includes a list of these, as in the right side of Exhibit 1-1.

A creditor is someone from whom the company has acquired assets or services for which the company is legally required to make payment or provide services in the future. A creditor's equity in a business is commonly called a *liability*. Liabilities typically arise because other businesses supply goods or services in advance of payment (*accounts payable*), banks or others lend the firm money for short periods of time (*notes payable*), and others lend money to the firm for long periods of time (*bonds payable* or *long-term debt*).

Owners are distinguished from creditors in that the firm is under no legal obligation to repay the amounts the owners have invested in the firm. The owners, in other words, have a *residual* interest in the firm. If the firm is ever liquidated—that is, if it goes out of business and its assets are all distributed among the owners and creditors—the owners are legally entitled to all of the assets that are left after the creditors' claims have been satisfied in full. This may be either more or less than the owners have invested in the firm. Creditors, on the other hand, can initiate legal action if the company fails to make timely payment of any amount due them under the terms of the agreement under which they have lent assets to the firm.

At first glance it might seem reasonable to measure each liability by the amount the firm is legally obliged to pay the creditor.

Similarly, the money figure for the ownership equity could be the amount the owners might obtain by liquidating the firm or by selling their interest in it.[5] In fact, the money amount reported for each equity is the amount *invested in the firm,* not the amount the creditor or owner will or may *get out of the firm.* The reasons for this choice will become apparent as we proceed.

### The Accounting Equation

The equality between the asset and equity totals in Exhibit 1–1 is no coincidence. The fundamental *accounting equation*

$$\text{Total Assets} = \text{Total Liabilities} + \text{Owners' Equity}$$

holds for all balance sheets at all points in time. The equation holds because the assets on one side and the liabilities and owners' equity on the other side merely represent two ways of looking at the same set of resources. The equity side represents the resources provided to the firm, classified according to their source, while the asset side represents these same resources classified according to their use.

This way of viewing the equity side may not always seem to fit the facts. For example, a liability may arise from a court order to pay someone who has taken and won a legal action against the firm. Since none of the firm's resources came from this creditor, our description of the meaning of the accounting equation would seem to be invalid. Not so. Between the date on which the liability became definite enough to justify recognizing it in the financial statements and the date on which it is liquidated, the firm is using resources that really belong to someone else – that is, the creditor provides funds by not insisting on immediate payment. In many situations, management may find that deferral of payments is a much more convenient way of obtaining resources than any other action it can take.

### Working Capital

Unlike the simple statement in Exhibit 1–1, published statements of financial position group the assets and liabilities into classes on the basis of their closeness to cash. The assets, for example, are divided between current assets and noncurrent assets. *Current assets* are "cash and other assets that are reason-

---

[5] In accordance with this notion, the owners' equity was at one time called the *net worth.* Since the reported figure does not represent what the owners could obtain by selling their equity and since the two figures may differ by a very wide margin, the term net worth should not be used.

ably expected to be realized in cash or sold or consumed during the normal operating cycle of the business or within one year if the operating cycle is shorter than one year."[6]

Liabilities are also classified as either current or noncurrent, *current liabilities* being those that are expected to be eliminated by the use of assets that are classified as current in the same balance sheet. In any case, current liabilities include all liabilities that will become payable during the next 12 months, no matter how short the operating cycle may be. For example, if a company has a liability that will be paid off in installments spread over several years, the portion that will have to be paid during the next 12 months will be classified as a current liability.

An organization's current assets less its current liabilities constitute its *working capital*. This figure is seldom presented on the balance sheet itself, but it is widely cited by bankers and other users of the financial statements.

The statement of financial position in Exhibit 1–2 identifies three categories of current assets and two current liabilities. This leaves plant and equipment as the only noncurrent asset, and bonds payable as the only noncurrent liability. Working capital in this case amounted to $110,000, the difference between total current assets ($180,000) and total current liabilities ($70,000).

Exhibit 1–2

XYZ Company

STATEMENT OF FINANCIAL POSITION

December 31, 19x1

| Assets | | Liabilities and Owners' Equity | |
|---|---:|---|---:|
| Current assets: | | Current liabilities: | |
| Cash | $ 30,000 | Accounts payable | $ 50,000 |
| Accounts receivable | 50,000 | Notes payable | 20,000 |
| Inventories | 100,000 | Total current liabilities | $ 70,000 |
| Total current assets | $180,000 | Bonds payable | 80,000 |
| Plant and equipment | 160,000 | Total liabilities | $150,000 |
| | | Owners' equity | 190,000 |
| | | Total Liabilities and | |
| Total Assets | $340,000 | Owners' Equity | $340,000 |

## The Income Statement

The social purpose of the resources invested in a business is to produce goods and services that are demanded by other organizations or by individual consumers. The private purpose is to pro-

---

[6] American Institute of Certified Public Accountants, *APB Accounting Principles, Current Text* (New York: Commerce Clearing House, Inc., 1972), Sec. 1027.25.

duce *income* — that is, to increase the owners' equity in the business. Income therefore measures the economic productivity of the resources that the owners have invested in the firm.

In economic theory the income of a firm during some period of time is the amount the owners could take out of the business and still leave it as well off at the end of the period as at the beginning.[7] To illustrate the idea in terms of the 200 acres of land discussed earlier, if that land were the only asset of the Lucky Land Development Company its income for the period 19x1 to 19x5 would be $150,000, the difference between the value of the land at the start of the period and its value at the end. Income defined in this way includes *all* changes in value, regardless of their source, on the grounds that they all represent changes in the owners' well-being.

This definition of income has some intuitive merit. The accountant's measure of income is slightly different, however. The accountant uses the term *net income* to refer to the excess of revenues over the expenses incurred, plus or minus any gains or losses that are recognized during the period. These are summarized in an income statement like the one illustrated in Exhibit 1–3. Revenues and expenses are defined as follows:

> Revenues consist of the resources received by the business in exchange for the products or services it provides to outsiders. These resources usually are monetary assets — cash or customers' promises to pay cash in the future — for which values can be determined fairly easily. Revenues therefore are measured by the *value* of the resources received. Expenses are the resources consumed in the creation of revenues, measured at amounts equal to their *cost*.

Exhibit 1–3

XYZ Company

INCOME STATEMENT

For the Year Ended December 31, 19x1

| | | |
|---|---:|---:|
| Sales revenue................... | | $900,000 |
| Less expenses: | | |
| Cost of goods sold............ | $600,000 | |
| Wages and salaries ........... | 200,000 | |
| Other operating costs ......... | 40,000 | |
| Interest...................... | 15,000 | 855,000 |
| Net Income.................... | | $ 45,000 |

---

[7] The underlying definition can be found in J. R. Hicks, *Value and Capital* (London: Oxford University Press, 1939), p. 172. Further examination of this concept can be found in our Chapter 10 and also in Robert K. Jaedicke and Robert T. Sprouse, *Accounting Flows, Income, Funds, and Cash* (Englewood Cliffs, N.J.: Prentice-Hall, Inc., 1965), chap. ii.

Gains and losses are more difficult to define, and we shall limit ourselves to a simple example at this point. Suppose that fire destroys uninsured inventories that have cost the company $2,000. This will be recognized as a loss because resources have been consumed without an offsetting benefit. It will be reported on the income statement for the period in which the fire occurred.

## Accounting Principles and Standards

The development of a company's financial statements is not the self-evident, pedestrian clerical exercise that accounting is sometimes pictured to be. Alternative accounting measurements, each quite plausible, can produce radically different results. This kind of diversity is not a desirable state of affairs, however, because it makes different statements difficult to compare and interpret. The most interesting and important part of accounting is the development and application of principles to achieve uniformity in accounting measurement and guide the exercise of judgment whenever uniformity is not possible.

On a most general level we can identify seven principles that accountants believe should govern the measurement rules they employ. These principles are: (1) relevance, (2) verifiability, (3) objectivity, (4) consistency, (5) comparability, (6) materiality, and (7) disclosure. These words alone convey considerable meaning, and their more precise definition at this point would not add much to their understanding.

Even without further explanation of their meaning, it should be clear that these principles are not always mutually compatible, and they do not lead unambiguously to one solution for each measurement problem. Their function is to guide accountants in the development of principles that are more concrete and operational. An accounting principle which can be derived from those stated above and which is considerably less general is the historical cost basis of asset measurement. Principles such as historical cost are still quite broad, however, and to resolve issues in applying them to various classes of transactions accountants have developed further guidelines known as *accounting standards.*

Accounting standards for external financial reporting in the United States have been developed by the accounting profession itself, first informally and then through the activities of committees and boards of the American Institute of Certified Public Accountants, the major professional association in the public accounting field. Responsibility for further development of accounting standards is now vested in the Financial Accounting Standards Board, created in 1973 by the AICPA with the cooperation and financial support of the other major United States professional associations of accountants and financial executives.

## MANAGEMENT'S INTEREST IN ACCOUNTING

The preparation of accounting information for management's use draws on many of the same concepts that have been developed for external financial reporting. Management's requirements are different enough, however, to call for the application of a number of additional concepts, unique to managerial accounting. Furthermore, the accounting principles that are followed in managerial accounting have never been codified to the same extent as those underlying external statements. Each company's accountants are more or less free to design systems to meet the needs of that company's management. Unlike the distant owner, management can question the accountant directly whenever the meaning or validity of accounting information is unclear.

We shall postpone any further discussion of these issues to the chapters in Part III, but this does not mean that management has no interest in financial statements prepared for the enterprise as a whole. For one thing, the image which the company presents to those outside the management is fashioned in large part by the financial statements. The company's executives cannot be indifferent to how their actions are to be presented to the owners and others.

Second, every major management decision and many minor ones can be made intelligently only with knowledge of the past performance and current status of the firm as a whole and an evaluation of what they imply for the firm's future.

An understanding of enterprise financial statements is also a necessary prerequisite to any analysis of such matters as proposals to acquire or merge with other companies, to expand into new markets, or to withdraw from old ones. In fact, the accounting system can be regarded as a model of the firm, and a manager who understands this model can visualize his decisions as accounting transactions and evaluate their consequences for the financial statements and for the welfare of the company.

## THE INFLUENCE OF GOVERNMENT

The role of government in the development of accounting systems has been largely indirect, except in industries under direct governmental regulation. One important influence has been the income tax on personal and corporate incomes. Published financial statements in the United States need not be identical to the statements that are submitted to the United States Internal Revenue Service and other taxing authorities. Indeed, differences are both frequent and substantial. Taxation does influence accounting measurements, however, at least partly because differences between accounting measurements and tax measurements increase the cost of operating accounting systems.

A governmental body that exerts a great deal of influence on published corporate financial statements is the Securities and Exchange Commission. Created in 1933, the SEC has wide powers to specify the form and content of the financial statements that must be filed by corporations within its jurisdiction. Although conflicts do arise, the accounting profession is unlikely to adhere to positions that it cannot persuade the Commission to accept.

Government has had a relatively minor influence on accounting for internal use. Statistical reporting requirements on such matters as employees' wages and hours have undoubtedly affected the information base that is available to management, but otherwise the government's influence has been felt mainly by companies with substantial government contracts. Many of these contracts relate the contract price to cost, and contractors have designed their systems to meet the government's demands for cost data. Such systems are often very different from those that otherwise might have been adopted. The government body that now has the responsibility of prescribing accounting standards for this purpose is the Cost Accounting Standards Board, established in 1972.

### SUMMARY

Accounting is the primary means of organizing and reporting information, mostly in financial terms, for the use of an organization's management and outsiders. Accounting designed for outsiders is known as financial accounting; measurement and reporting for internal consumption is the domain of managerial accounting.

From an accounting standpoint, an organization can be viewed as a set of resources assembled and used to carry out one or more activities to achieve one or more objectives. Accounting summaries of an organization's resources, generally known as statements of financial position or balance sheets, do not pretend to measure the organization's economic value. Instead, they list as assets the resources which can be measured readily in monetary terms. They also show the sources of these assets, divided into two categories—liabilities and owners' equities. Since the list of assets and the list of liabilities and owners' equities merely measure two aspects of the same set of resources, the two lists have identical totals. This equality is the basis of the accounting equation.

Accountants also report on the economic productivity of an organization's resources. In the business firm, the accountant's measure of productivity is known as net income. In general, net income is the difference between the value of the resources the firm receives for its goods and services and the costs of the resources it consumes in the process.

Accounting measurements for external financial reporting must follow the prescriptions laid down in financial accounting standards. Many of these standards provide only very broad guidelines, and the accountant must use his judgment in applying them. Even so, the standards underlying published financial statements are intended to apply to all companies in like situations, and the certified public accountants who audit the statements must see that they have been followed.

The company's accountants are subject to no such external constraints for internal managerial accounting. Accounting measurements for managerial use can take any form as long as they give management the information it wants at a price it is willing to pay.

## QUESTIONS AND PROBLEMS

1. When a company applies for a bank loan, what information will the bank probably require? What is the company accountant's part in providing this information? What is the independent public accountant's part?

2. The public accountant is engaged by the board of directors of the company whose statements he is to audit, and paid from company funds. How can this practice be reconciled with the public accountant's responsibilities to the investing public, to government, and to other interested parties?

3. What contributions can the independent public accountant make to the design of accounting systems? In what ways does he have an advantage over the company's own accountants? What advantages does the company accountant have?

4. The annual audit of a corporation's financial statements is performed largely to satisfy certain needs of outside investors. In what ways can it also be of service to management?

5. The owner of a farm suddenly found that a rich oil field that had just been discovered nearby extended into his property. His title to the land included title to any mineral wealth it contained.

a) Did the discovery lead to an immediate increase in the known assets of this farm? Did it lead to income immediately? Is it likely that the farm's market value increased as a result of the discovery?

b) Would the accountant report an immediate increase in assets on the farm's balance sheet? On the income statement for the period in which the discovery was made?

6. An item that is Smith's asset may be Brown's liability, or owners' equity on the books of Smith's Drug Store. For each of the following items on the balance sheet of Carter's Feed Store, indicate in which section, if any, of someone else's balance sheet it would appear:

a) Accounts receivable.
b) Merchandise inventory.
c) Cash in bank.
d) Notes receivable.
e) Prepaid insurance.
f) Investments in government securities.
g) Land.
h) Wages payable.
i) Carter, owner's equity.

*7. The following items, arranged in alphabetical order, comprise the assets, liabilities, and owners' equity of a small business. Organize these data in the form of a balance sheet.

| | |
|---|---:|
| Accounts payable to creditors | $12,300 |
| Accounts receivable from customers | 6,900 |
| Building | 24,000 |
| Cash on hand and in bank | 9,000 |
| Delivery equipment | 9,600 |
| Furniture | 4,200 |
| Inventory of merchandise | 29,100 |
| Land | 2,500 |
| Long-term debt | 16,500 |
| Notes payable to bank | 8,000 |
| Notes receivable from customers | 3,900 |
| Owners' equity | 52,400 |

8. George Johnson invested $10,000 of his own money in a small service business and borrowed another $5,000 from a bank, also for

---

* Solutions to problems marked with an asterisk (*) are found in Appendix B.

business use. At the end of his first year of operations, he found that there was $17,000 in the enterprise's bank account. He owed his suppliers $3,000 and had not repaid the bank loan. His business assets other than cash were negligible. During the year he had paid himself a salary of $6,000.

a)  What conclusions would you draw about his first year's operations?
b)  For what decisions would this information be used? What additional information would the decision makers be likely to call for in making these decisions?
c)  What problems do you foresee if Mr. Johnson's only business record is his checkbook?

9. The assets, liabilities, and owners' equity of the Brandon Company on December 31 were as follows:

| | |
|---|---:|
| Accounts payable | $13,300 |
| Accounts receivable | 8,120 |
| Buildings | 35,760 |
| Cash on hand and in bank | 6,600 |
| Equipment | 4,450 |
| Interest payable | 180 |
| Inventory of merchandise | 11,200 |
| Land | 18,000 |
| Long-term debt | 10,200 |
| Notes payable | 9,000 |
| Owners' equity | To be derived |
| Prepaid insurance | 2,000 |
| Wages payable | 1,770 |

Prepare a statement of financial position.

*10.  On January 21, 19x4, three young bachelors, Mr. Robinson, Mr. Griffiths, and Mr. Thorndike, formed a partnership to operate a small bar. Each partner contributed $1,500 cash, for a total of $4,500. On the day the partnership was formed, the Dingy Dive Bar was purchased for $14,500. This price included land valued at $2,000, improvements to land at $2,000, buildings at $9,500, and bar equipment at $1,000. The partnership made a down payment of $3,000 (from its $4,500 cash) and signed a note for the balance of the $14,500.

After operating the bar for one month, the partners found that despite withdrawing $200 each in cash from the business, $1,000 in cash remained; in addition, there was inventory on hand amounting to $300 and accounts receivable of $150. They still owed $11,500 on the note, and now had accounts payable of $200. They also owed $50 in wages to one of their bartenders.

a)  Draw up a balance sheet for the Dingy Dive Bar as of January 21, 19x4, taking into account the above data.
b)  Draw up a second balance sheet as of February 21, 19x4.

c)   From the information given, what can you say of the success of the venture to date?

**11.**  Stanley Throckmorton, who sells popcorn at public events, has no capital invested in his business other than the cash he keeps in his "business" wallet and a pushcart he bought five years ago for $200. This pushcart contains a corn popping machine, storage space for materials (unpopped corn, butter, and salt), and a compartment in which the popped corn can be kept warm until a customer buys it.

One morning, Mr. Throckmorton left home with $100 in cash in his business wallet. Contemplating an unusually busy day, he bought materials (corn, butter, and salt) costing $120. Although he usually paid cash for his purchases, this was an exceptionally large one for him. Being a regular customer of his supplier, he was permitted to charge $50 of the total amount and pay cash for the rest.

He then attended a baseball game where he sold three quarters of his purchases for $135, all in cash. At the end of the day, he returned home with his unsold stock, planning to replenish his inventory, pay his bill, and obtain fuel for his corn popper on the following morning. (He normally bought fuel on alternate business days at a cost of about $4. A purchase of this size was enough for two days' operation of the corn popper.)

a)   How would you measure the results of Mr. Throckmorton's operations for this day? Quantify your answer as much as possible, and list the items, if any, which you found difficult to quantify.

b)   Why should Mr. Throckmorton be interested in a measure of his operating results, defined as in (a)? How might knowledge of operating results affect his business actions?

c)   What other information might Mr. Throckmorton want to be able to get from his accounting records?

**12.**  Angus MacTavish scratched his head in bewilderment. "I can't figure it out," he said. "I've been running this business for almost a year and I have more customers by far than I had expected when I started. I have had to hire a new bookkeeper just to get out the bills to my customers and to record their payments when they come in. Yet here I am, just before Christmas, and I don't have enough cash in the bank to pay for that new coat I promised to buy my wife if the business did well. I wonder what has gone wrong."

Mr. MacTavish went into business for himself on January 1, 19x1. He took $30,000 from his savings, rented a store, bought a stock of merchandise from a wholesaler, hired a shop assistant, and opened his doors for business. The store proved to be in an excellent location, and Mr. Mac-Tavish quickly earned a reputation of being an honest merchant with good-quality merchandise and favorable prices. As the year wore on, his store became more and more crowded with customers and he had to add an extra clerk to handle the business.

During the year, he bought one additional display cabinet to display his stock of a new line of products that a manufacturer's representative offered to him. Other than this, he didn't recall any major purchases of furniture or equipment. It seemed to him, however, that the better his business became, the less cash he had in the bank.

Mr. MacTavish was confident that his December business would bring in enough cash so that he needn't worry about not being able to meet the payroll at the end of December, but even so he would have a good deal less cash in the bank at the end of the year than he had when he started in business. This disturbed him because as he put it, "I have sunk everything I have into this business, given up a good steady job with a strong company, and have worked day and night to make a go of it. If it's not going to pay off, I'd like to know it soon so that I can sell out and go back to work with someone else. I've made a lot of sacrifices this past year to go into business for myself, and I'd like to know whether it was all worthwhile."

This statement was made by Mr. MacTavish to Mr. Thomas Carr, a local public accountant to whom he had turned for advice. Mr. Carr replied that the first thing that he would have to do would be to try to draw up a set of financial statements for the MacTavish store that would summarize the results of the first year's operations to date.

a) To what extent does the decline in Mr. MacTavish's cash balance indicate the success or failure of his business operations during this period? What other explanations can you offer for this change? How would you measure the degree of success achieved by the store during its first year?

b) If you were Mr. MacTavish, what kinds of information would you need before you could decide whether to stay in business or to sell out? How much of this information would you expect Mr. Carr to be able to supply?

c) Assuming that Mr. MacTavish decides to stay in business and decides that he needs a bank loan to provide him with additional cash, what kinds of information do you think that the banker would want to have before approving the loan? Would this necessarily be the same as the information needed by Mr. Carr?

13. "We can't do business if you don't give me any more to go on than that," said Claude Montrone. After 15 years on the marketing staff of a large manufacturer of office supplies and equipment, Mr. Montrone was thinking of going into business for himself. A small inheritance, added to the accumulated savings of the past 15 years, gave him approximately $70,000 to invest. His older brother had indicated that he would be willing to invest up to $15,000 if he felt that the business venture was sound. Mr. Montrone also hoped to borrow from his bank additional amounts as needed. These amounts would be repaid during the first five years of the new venture. The manager of his bank had said that the bank would be happy to consider a loan application, but of course the actual granting

of the loan would depend on the bank's appraisal of the ability of the business to generate enough funds to pay back the loan plus interest.

The statement quoted at the beginning of this case was directed to Paul Alain, owner of a store in Nutley, New Jersey. Mr. Alain owned several enterprises, and as he approached retirement age he found it increasingly difficult to do an adequate management job in each one. Therefore, he had decided to sell his most important business, the Alain Stationery Store, and he was offering to sell the store's assets for $100,000. The buyer would also have to accept the obligation to pay the amounts owed to the store's suppliers (accounts payable), amounting to about $10,000.

Mr. Montrone thought that he might be able to persuade Mr. Alain to spread some of the purchase price over a five-year period, but he doubted that Mr. Alain would come down in his price as a result of bargaining. The purchaser would receive a five-year renewable lease on the store itself, the goods in inventory, and the amount owed to the store by some of its customers. If he bought the store, Mr. Montrone would have Mr. Alain's list of customers, and he saw no reason why he would not be able to keep the two store clerks who had been working in the store for more than five years.

Mr. Montrone had inspected the store and had toured the area in and around Nutley to get some idea of the location of his customers and potential customers, and of the quality of the competition. He was generally familiar with the competitive situation in the area and felt that he could develop a considerable amount of business with small and medium-sized commercial and industrial companies in the area. Mr. Alain gave him the names of several of his larger customers but was unwilling to show Mr. Montrone any details on his business with these customers.

The only data that Mr. Montrone had were the following, all supplied to him by Mr. Alain:

| Year | Sales to Customers | Salaries and Dividends Paid to Paul Alain |
|---|---|---|
| 1964 ......... | 105,000 | 15,000 |
| 1965 ......... | 100,000 | 15,000 |
| 1966 ......... | 110,000 | 15,000 |
| 1967 ......... | 130,000 | 16,000 |
| 1968 ......... | 125,000 | 17,000 |
| 1969 ......... | 120,000 | 12,000 |
| 1970 ......... | 130,000 | 18,000 |
| 1971 ......... | 140,000 | 18,000 |
| 1972 ......... | 135,000 | 20,000 |
| 1973 ......... | 150,000 | 20,000 |

a) What additional information would Mr. Montrone want to have before deciding whether to buy this business? How much of this information would you expect to find in the accounting records of Alain Stationers, Inc.?

*b)* If you were Mr. Montrone's banker, what information would you want to have to assist you in evaluating a loan request from Mr. Montrone? Would this information be any different from the information that Mr. Montrone would want for the purpose of deciding whether to buy the business?

*c)* To what extent would you expect accounting data to have entered into Mr. Alain's decision to sell the store and to set the price at $100,000? What kind of data should be looked for in making these decisions?

*d)* If you were Mr. Montrone, what services would you expect an independent accountant—that is, an accountant not in Mr. Alain's employ—to render in connection with this acquisition?

# 2

# DERIVING FINANCIAL
# STATEMENTS FROM
# TRANSACTIONS ANALYSES

THE ACCOUNTANT'S USUAL MEASURES of a business firm's income
and financial position are based on his analysis of the economic
effects of individual *transactions* – that is, the actions and events
the firm participates in directly. Our task in this chapter is to
show how an accountant might analyze a series of typical transactions and summarize the results of these analyses in a set of
simple financial statements.

## TRANSACTIONS ANALYSIS

Even a small business enterprise engages in a wide variety of
transactions. It receives and pays cash, buys and sells merchandise, and participates in many related activities. By examining
the accountant's analyses of the transactions arising from the
formation and operation of one of these, a small retail store, we
can illustrate the fundamentals of accounting transactions analysis generally.

### Investment Transactions

In June of 19x0, the sales manager of the Ajax Manufacturing
Company offered Charles Erskine the exclusive dealership rights
in his community for the Ajax line of refrigerators, radios, and
other electrical appliances. Mr. Erskine, a salesman for a wholesale distributor of a competing line of appliances, decided that he
had a good chance of succeeding; and so he resigned his job and
began to organize his own business, The Erskine Appliance Store.

On June 30, Mr. Erskine formalized his decision to go into business by depositing $20,000 in a checking account for The Erskine Appliance Store. This was an investment transaction, providing the new business with its first asset, $20,000 in cash. It also gave Mr. Erskine an owner's interest in the firm. Since accounting systems measure owners' equities by the amounts invested by the owners in the business, this transaction can be said to have created an owner's equity of $20,000. The full analysis of the transaction therefore can be written as follows:

(1)

| Asset Increase | Accompanied | Owner's Equity Increase |
|---|---|---|
| Cash................... $20,000 | by | Erskine's Investment... $20,000 |

Notice that this analysis shows what happened to the assets and equities of the business as a separate entity. If we were to analyze its immediate effect on Mr. Erskine's personal fortune, the results would be quite different. A $20,000 decrease in one asset, cash, would be just offset by a $20,000 increase in another, Mr. Erskine's investment in the store. Our focus here is on the business itself, however, and we shall not concern ourselves further with Mr. Erskine's personal transactions.

### Purchase and Payment Transactions

Immediately after opening the new bank account, Mr. Erskine signed the Ajax franchise agreement and took a two-year lease (starting July 1) on a store containing ample office, storage, and display space. The rent was $800 a month and he paid the rent for three months in advance. By this transaction, the firm acquired for $2,400 the right to use the space for three months. Since such a right was clearly something of value owned by the business, it was classified as an asset and the transaction was analyzed as follows:

(2)

| Asset Increase | Accompanied | Asset Decrease |
|---|---|---|
| Prepaid Rent............ $2,400 | by | Cash .................... $2,400 |

Since one asset was exchanged for another with no change in the equities in this transaction, the total assets remained unchanged at $20,000. The accounting equation showed the following figures after this transaction was completed:

| Cash | | Prepaid Rent | | Erskine's Investment |
| $17,600 | + | $2,400 | = | $20,000 |

Mr. Erskine also took delivery at this time on merchandise for which he agreed to pay $8,000 sometime during the next 30 days. By this transaction the firm acquired an asset, merchandise, costing $8,000. No other asset was given up immediately, however, because the supplier was willing to wait a short while for his money. That is, the supplier made a short-term investment in The Erskine Appliance Store. This investment gave him a creditor's rights rather than the ownership rights that Mr. Erskine acquired by his initial investment in the firm. In other words, the firm assumed a liability in exchange for an asset, as follows:

(3)

| Asset Increase | Accompanied | Liability Increase |
| Inventory............... $8,000 | by | Accounts Payable ....... $8,000 |

Next, Mr. Erskine bought secondhand equipment, paying $6,000 in cash from the store's bank account. He felt that this was a bargain price, much less than the equipment was worth. The only unambiguous fact, however, was that the cost of this equipment was $6,000. Mr. Erskine felt that for the moment, at least, he wanted his accounting records to show how his original investment in the business had been used — that is, assets purchased from outsiders were to be measured at their cost to the store. His analysis of this transaction, therefore, was that one asset, cash, had simply been exchanged for another asset, equipment:

(4)

| Asset Increase | Accompanied | Asset Decrease |
| Equipment ............. $6,000 | by | Cash .................... $6,000 |

This left the total asset figure at $28,000, and the accounting equation remained in balance.

Mr. Erskine's final act on June 30 was to hire an assistant at a salary of $680 a month. The assistant was to start work the next morning. This had no effect on the assets and equities, however. Because the assistant would be paid only if he actually showed up for work, the firm owed him nothing on June 30. No asset was created either, because the firm had no ownership right in the assistant's future services.

## Maintaining the Accounting Equation

Transactions analysis is governed by one restriction — the accounting equation must always remain balanced. This means that the accounting analysis of *each* transaction must also be balanced — that is, a change in one item must be accompanied by a change in one or more other items so that the total of the assets remains equal to the total of the liabilities and owners' equity.

These specifications are met by the table in Exhibit 2–1, which shows the effects of The Erskine Appliance Store's first four transactions. Notice particularly that the accounting equation remained balanced after each transaction was analyzed. The total of the amounts shown for the store's four assets at the end of June was $28,000, and the amounts shown for the liabilities and owners' equity added up to the same total. Of this, $20,000 had been supplied by Mr. Erskine and $8,000 by a creditor, the supplier of merchandise.

*Exhibit 2–1*

The Erskine Appliance Store

ASSETS, LIABILITIES, AND OWNER'S EQUITY

June 30, 19x0

|  | Cash | + | Inventory | + | Equipment | + | Prepaid Rent | = | Accounts Payable | + | Erskine's Investment |
|---|---|---|---|---|---|---|---|---|---|---|---|
| (1) | +20,000 | | | | | | | | | | 20,000 |
| (2) | − 2,400 | | | | | | + 2,400 | | | | |
| Bal. | 17,600 | | | | | | + 2,400 | = | | | 20,000 |
| (3) | | | + 8,000 | | | | | | + 8,000 | | |
| Bal. | 17,600 | + | 8,000 | | | | + 2,400 | = | 8,000 | + | 20,000 |
| (4) | − 6,000 | | | | + 6,000 | | | | | | |
| Bal. | 11,600 | + | 8,000 | + | 6,000 | + | 2,400 | = | 8,000 | + | 20,000 |

## Sale Transactions: Revenues and Expenses

Nothing that Mr. Erskine did during June produced measurable income for the firm. When the store opened for business in July, however, Mr. Erskine hoped that the events of that month would produce net income immediately.

The effect of income is to increase the owner's equity. For example, suppose that The Erskine Appliance Store sold merchandise to its customers for $8,930. Of this, $1,880 was in cash and the remaining $7,050 was sold on credit.[1] The merchandise cov-

---

[1] The terms "on credit" and "on account" are used interchangeably to mean that payment for goods or services purchased or sold is to be made at some date later than the date of the delivery of the goods or the performance of the service.

ered by these sales was part of the first shipment that Mr. Erskine had received from his supplier on June 30. It had cost $6,420.

Notice what happened: Mr. Erskine exchanged one group of assets (merchandise) for another (cash and accounts receivable). As a result of these exchanges, his total assets increased by $2,510. Since the liabilities went neither up nor down, the owner's equity must have increased by $2,510 as well. This analysis can be summarized as follows:

(5)

| Asset Increases | | Accompanied | Asset Decrease | |
|---|---|---|---|---|
| Cash | $1,880 | by | Inventory | $6,420 |
| Accounts Receivable | 7,050 | | | |
| | | | Owner's Equity Increase | |
| | | | Erskine, Proprietor | 2,510 |

This is a correct analysis of the effects of these sales transactions on the store's assets and equities so long as no asset other than the $6,420 in merchandise is given up to make the sales. Even if this assumption is true, however, this analysis of the sales transactions does not provide all the information needed to prepare an income statement for the month's operations. To meet this need, the transactions analysis must identify both the revenues from the sales and the expenses, i.e., the cost of the assets given up to obtain the sales.

Accordingly, Mr. Erskine's accountant made the following analysis of the sales transactions:

(5a)

| Asset Increases | | Accompanied | Owner's Equity Increase | |
|---|---|---|---|---|
| Cash | $1,880 | by | Sales Revenue | $8,930 |
| Accounts Receivable | 7,050 | | | |

The left-hand column lists the assets the store received from its customers during the month; the right-hand column shows that these transactions increased the owner's equity.

We know, of course, that owner's equity did not increase by the full $8,930. To obtain this amount, Mr. Erskine had to deliver merchandise which had cost the store $6,420. Since this removed the particular merchandise from the company's inventory, that asset decreased in size and so did the owner's equity. This analysis can be summarized as follows:

(5b)

| Owner's Equity Decrease | | Accompanied | Asset Decrease | |
|---|---|---|---|---|
| Cost of Goods Sold | $6,420 | by | Inventory | $6,420 |

These two analyses show the same changes in assets, liabilities, and owner's equity as analysis (5) above; the only difference is that two figures, +$8,930 and −$6,420, have been substituted for the +$2,510 figure in analysis (5).

## Cost versus Expense

Notice the distinction between cost and expense. Cost measures the amount of resources that are sacrificed to obtain something, and the accountant uses cost to measure nonmonetary assets. Hence, assets can be referred to as costs. Expenses, on the other hand, are the costs of assets given up to obtain sales revenue. Assets, therefore, are costs or resources that the firm still has, while expenses are costs or resources that the firm has given up during a particular period of time.

## Operating Expense Transactions

Subtracting the cost of the merchandise sold from sales revenues does not yield the net income figure. Many other goods and services are consumed each period to create the period's revenues. This means that their costs are also expenses of the current period. Because few of them can be identified clearly with individual revenue transactions, however, the net income from any specific sale cannot be measured.

Mr. Erskine had few of these other expenses during July. The first consisted of his assistant's wages for the month, amounting to $680. Some people find it helpful to think of this sort of expenditure as a three-stage phenomenon: first, the acquisition of valuable services (an asset); second, the consumption of those services in the creation of revenue (an expense); and third, the payment for the services. Mr. Erskine took the intermediate course, however, of recognizing the first two of these stages as one, leaving the payment to be handled separately later. The first-stage analysis showed the following:

(6)

| Owner's Equity Decrease | Accompanied | Liability Increase |
|---|---|---|
| Wages Expense ........... $680 | by | Wages Payable ........... $680 |

This shows the entire amount of the wages as a current operating expense, a reduction in the owner's equity, because Mr. Erskine saw no reason why his assistant's work this month would benefit any period other than the present. The same amount had to be recognized as a liability because Mr. Erskine had a legal obligation to pay his assistant for the services he had rendered in July.

Electricity, telephone, and other miscellaneous operating costs of the month amounted to $600. Since these costs related to current operations, they must be regarded as having been consumed in the creation of revenues — in other words, treated as expense:

(7)

| *Owner's Equity Decrease* | *Accompanied* | *Liability Increase* |
|---|---|---|
| Miscellaneous Expense.... $600 | *by* | Accounts Payable......... $600 |

Notice that in classifying these costs as expense we need not know whether any cash payments were made during the month. The services were consumed in creating July's revenues, and this is all we need to know. The timing of the cash payments should have no effect on the timing of expense recognition.

## Other Transactions

A number of other transactions took place during July. First, additional merchandise was purchased on credit at a total cost of $4,300:

(8)

| *Asset Increase* | *Accompanied* | *Liability Increase* |
|---|---|---|
| Inventory............... $4,300 | *by* | Accounts Payable ....... $4,300 |

The owner's equity was not affected by this set of transactions. Acquisition of the assets was financed temporarily by an increase in a liability.

Second, collections from customers on credit sales (see transaction 5) totaled $1,680. These were pure exchange-of-asset transactions and had no effect on the owner's equity. The analysis was:

(9)

| *Asset Increase* | *Accompanied* | *Asset Decrease* |
|---|---|---|
| Cash .................... $1,680 | *by* | Accounts Receivable .... $1,680 |

Third, payments were made to the store's suppliers and to its employees. In other words, assets were surrendered to liquidate some of the store's liabilities, and these transactions were analyzed as follows:

(10)

| Liability Decreases | Accompanied | Asset Decrease |
|---|---|---|
| Accounts Payable ....... $8,370 | by | Cash .................... $9,050 |
| Wages Payable .......... 680 | | |

Payment of the employee's salary canceled the liability that we identified in our analysis of transaction (6).

Finally, Mr. Erskine withdrew $1,200 in cash for his personal use. This reduced both the assets and the owner's equity by $1,200 and was analyzed as follows:

(11)

| Owner's Equity Decrease | Accompanied | Asset Decrease |
|---|---|---|
| Erskine, Withdrawals.... $1,200 | by | Cash .................... $1,200 |

Mr. Erskine was in doubt whether this reduction in owner's equity should be regarded as a salary expense or as a partial repayment of his investment in the business (a "disinvestment"). His accountant promised to discuss this question with him at the end of the month; meanwhile, he identified it separately from the expenses.

### End-of-Period Analyses

The data for each of the transactions analyses described above were found in documents that were prepared or received by The Erskine Appliance Store as a matter of routine. Data for the analysis of merchandise purchases, for example, came from the bills or *invoices* received from the store's suppliers.

Not all of the facts relevant to the preparation of periodic financial statements were contained in documents of this sort, however. For example, a portion of the asset prepaid rent was consumed during the month, but the landlord had no reason to send Mr. Erskine a document conveying this information. Mr. Erskine's accountant had to be alert to make sure that the cost of the store rental for July was not overlooked.

Going back to the documents underlying transactions (2), the accountant found that the rental payment of $2,400 had covered a period of three months in advance from July 1, at a rental of $800 a month. Since one month had gone by, one third of the total prepayment, or $800, had been consumed by July 31 as Mr. Erskine used the store premises to conduct his business. The $800 therefore was an operating expense of the month; both the assets and the owner's equity had been reduced by $800. This analysis can be summarized succinctly as follows:

(12)

| Owner's Equity Decrease | Accompanied | Asset Decrease |
|---|---|---|
| Rent Expense............. $800 | by | Prepaid Rent............. $800 |

The life of the equipment was more uncertain, but at the time he bought it Mr. Erskine estimated that it would have a useful life of 5 years (60 months) and that one sixtieth of its $6,000 cost should be considered a cost of producing revenue in July. Accordingly, $100 of *depreciation* had to be subtracted both from the asset and from the owner's equity:

(13)

| Owner's Equity Decrease | Accompanied | Asset Decrease |
|---|---|---|
| Depreciation Expense..... $100 | by | Equipment...............:. $100 |

The process of transferring costs from asset to expense in this way is known as *cost amortization*.

## THE FINANCIAL STATEMENTS

After these transactions had been analyzed, the assets, liabilities, and owner's equity of The Erskine Appliance Store appeared as in Exhibit 2–2. The numbers in parentheses refer to the transaction numbers in the discussion above. The plus and minus signs alongside the various owner's equity elements identify them as positive or negative components of the total owner's equity.

Mr. Erskine's accountant prepared three financial statements from this exhibit: an income statement; a statement of changes in owner's equity; and a statement of financial position (balance sheet).

### The Income Statement

The usefulness of identifying the revenues and expenses separately becomes very apparent when the time comes to prepare an income statement. All that Mr. Erskine's accountant had to do was to arrange these elements in some suitable order. Exhibit 2–3 illustrates one such format.

*Exhibit 2–2*

## The Erskine Appliance Store
## ASSETS, LIABILITIES, AND OWNER'S EQUITY
### Month Ended July 31, 19x0

### Assets

#### *Cash*

| | |
|---|---|
| Bal. 7/1 | 11,600 |
| (5a) | + 1,880 |
| (9) | + 1,680 |
| (10) | − 9,050 |
| (11) | − 1,200 |
| Bal. 7/31 | 4,910 |

#### *Accounts Receivable*

| | |
|---|---|
| Bal. 7/1 | − |
| (5a) | + 7,050 |
| (9) | − 1,680 |
| Bal. 7/31 | 5,370 |

#### *Inventory*

| | |
|---|---|
| Bal. 7/1 | 8,000 |
| (5b) | −6,420 |
| (8) | +4,300 |
| Bal. 7/31 | 5,880 |

#### *Prepaid Rent*

| | |
|---|---|
| Bal. 7/1 | 2,400 |
| (12) | − 800 |
| Bal. 7/31 | 1,600 |

#### *Equipment*

| | |
|---|---|
| Bal. 7/1 | 6,000 |
| (13) | − 100 |
| Bal. 7/31 | 5,900 |

### Liabilities

#### *Accounts Payable*

| | |
|---|---|
| Bal. 7/1 | 8,000 |
| (7) | + 600 |
| (8) | +4,300 |
| (10) | −8,370 |
| Bal. 7/31 | 4,530 |

#### *Wages Payable*

| | |
|---|---|
| (6) | + 680 |
| (10) | − 680 |
| Bal. 7/31 | − |

### Owner's Equity

#### *Erskine's Investment (+)*

| | |
|---|---|
| Bal. 7/1 | 20,000 |

#### *Sales Revenue (+)*

| | |
|---|---|
| (5a) | 8,930 |

#### *Cost of Goods Sold (−)*

| | |
|---|---|
| (5b) | 6,420 |

#### *Wages Expense (−)*

| | |
|---|---|
| (6) | 680 |

#### *Rent Expense (−)*

| | |
|---|---|
| (12) | 800 |

#### *Depreciation Expense (−)*

| | |
|---|---|
| (13) | 100 |

#### *Miscellaneous Expense (−)*

| | |
|---|---|
| (7) | 600 |

#### *Erskine, Withdrawals (−)*

| | |
|---|---|
| (11) | 1,200 |

All expenses are decreases in owner's equity. These amounts are therefore subtracted from the revenues to find the *net* increase in owner's equity that resulted from the operations of the period. This is the net income. If the expenses exceed the revenues, then the difference is a net *loss*. In this case, however, a small net income of $330 was reported for the month.

Exhibit 2–3

The Erskine Appliance Store

INCOME STATEMENT

For the Month Ended July 31, 19x0

| | | |
|---|---:|---:|
| Sales revenue................................ | | $8,930 |
| Expenses: | | |
| Cost of goods sold........................ | $6,420 | |
| Wage expense ............................ | 680 | |
| Rent expense ............................ | 800 | |
| Miscellaneous expense................... | 700 | |
| Total expense........................... | | 8,600 |
| Net Income............................... | | $  330 |

## Treatment of Owner's Withdrawals

Although Mr. Erskine regarded the $1,200 that he withdrew from the business during July as a reasonable payment by the store for his services and for the use of the $20,000 that he had invested in it, the income statement in Exhibit 2–3 did not list this amount among the expenses.

One reason for this omission is that since owners have no contracts entitling them to specified payments for the use of their money, the accountant would have to estimate what a reasonable charge would be. This would inject his judgment farther into the measurement process than he is now willing to go.

The same difficulty applies to charges for the owner's personal services to the business. Unless the business is a corporation, the law recognizes no distinction between the firm and its owners. That is, an owner cannot enter a contract with his own unincorporated business. In the absence of contractual evidence, accountants have been unwilling to recognize withdrawals by owners as salary expenses.

These arguments were not very impressive to Mr. Erskine. He knew that he had given up a job in which he had been earning about $1,000 a month. Furthermore, the securities that he had sold to get the $20,000 that he had invested in the store had been bringing him earnings of close to $200 a month. While acknowledging that the first month's operations were likely to be a poor test of the store's profitability, he knew that he couldn't afford to keep the store going indefinitely if it continued to show a loss after his personal salary and interest on his investment were deducted.

The accountant agreed to give Mr. Erskine the income statement that he wanted, reflecting these deductions.[2] He suggested, however, that Mr. Erskine keep this statement for his private use only. Since most people do not expect owners' salaries and interest on owners' investments to be treated as expenses, statements that do this may be misinterpreted.

### Statement of Changes in Owner's Equity

Mr. Erskine's accountant brought the net income and personal withdrawal figures together in the statement of changes in owner's equity, shown in Exhibit 2–4. This statement shows the beginning and ending balances and all of the changes in the owner's equity that were recorded during the month.

Exhibit 2–4

The Erskine Appliance Store

STATEMENT OF CHANGES IN OWNER'S EQUITY

For the Month Ended July 31, 19x0

| | |
|---|---:|
| Owner's Equity, July 1, 19x0 | $20,000 |
| Add: Net income for the month | 330 |
| | $20,330 |
| Less: Withdrawals | 1,200 |
| Owner's Equity, July 31, 19x0 | $19,130 |

It should be apparent that a similar statement could be constructed for any balance sheet item or group of items. For example, a statement could show the beginning-of-year cash balance, the amounts of cash received from various sources, the amounts of cash paid out for various purposes, and the ending cash balance. The published statements of companies in France, Italy, and some other countries often provide a summary of the additions to and subtractions from *each* balance sheet item, but United States companies never go this far.

---

[2] Measurements of this kind are sometimes made by economists for statistical or analytical purposes, Starting with accounting net income, the economist deducts "imputed wages" for any managerial services provided by the owner-managers and "imputed interest" on the owners' invested capital, leaving a residual that he calls profit.

## The Statement of Financial Position

The final statement that Mr. Erskine's accountant prepared at the end of July was a statement of financial position, more commonly referred to as a balance sheet. Exhibit 2–5 shows statements for both the beginning and the end of the month. The beginning figures are a repetition of those given on the last line of Exhibit 2–1; the July 31 amounts have been drawn from Exhibit 2–2 except for the owner's equity figure which came from Exhibit 2–4.

*Exhibit 2–5*

The Erskine Appliance Store

COMPARATIVE STATEMENTS OF FINANCIAL POSITION
July 31 and June 30, 19x0

ASSETS

|  | *July 31* | *June 30* |
|---|---|---|
| Current Assets: | | |
| Cash | $ 4,910 | $11,600 |
| Accounts receivable | 5,370 | . . . |
| Inventory | 5,880 | 8,000 |
| Prepaid rent | 1,600 | 2,400 |
| Total current assets | $17,760 | $22,000 |
| Equipment | 5,900 | 6,000 |
| Total Assets | $23,660 | $28,000 |

LIABILITIES AND OWNER'S EQUITY

| | *July 31* | *June 30* |
|---|---|---|
| Current Liabilities: | | |
| Accounts payable | $ 4,530 | $ 8,000 |
| Owner's Equity: | | |
| Erskine, proprietor | 19,130 | 20,000 |
| Total Liabilities and Owner's Equity | $23,660 | $28,000 |

It should be noted that the income statement, a statement of *performance,* together with the statement of changes in owner's equity, constitute a connecting link between these two statements of *status.* The income and owner's equity statements summarize the operating transactions that took place *during* the period, while the balance sheet shows the company's position at the *end* of the period.

## OMISSIONS FROM FINANCIAL STATEMENTS

As our earlier discussion of basic accounting measurement concepts showed, the balance sheet does not list all of the resources at the firm's disposal, nor does the income statement list all of the changes that take place in the value of these resources.

Mr. Erskine was particularly aware of some of these omissions because he planned to approach the bank for a loan and was anxious that his balance sheet present every justifiable evidence of financial strength. With this objective in mind, he was concerned that his statements ascribed no value to what he considered his most important assets: his dealership franchise and his customer following in the trade.

His accountant agreed that these items were important and suggested that their existence be pointed out to the bank in a letter accompanying the firm's financial statements. He explained that they did not belong in the balance sheet because he could not verify the evidence on which measurements of these assets would have to be based.

He also pointed out that although the statements reflected the rent that had been paid, they ignored the fact that Mr. Erskine had signed a two-year lease. This contract was also an important factor, one which would be favorable if property values went up and unfavorable if they went down or if the space became unsuitable to the needs of the business. The accountant then said, however, that the accounting profession did not regard the signing of a lease as an exchange of assets that should be recognized in the statements. Only a prepayment of rent could be recognized at that time.

Finally, he noted that Mr. Erskine had apparently intuitively accepted the cost basis of measurement in developing data for his own use. For example, although Mr. Erskine had believed that his equipment was worth more than he had paid for it, he had not considered reporting any amount other than the actual purchase price.

## NET INCOME VERSUS TAXABLE INCOME

Throughout this chapter we have gone on the implicit assumption that the net income figure ought to be the best possible estimate of the difference between the amount of resources earned during the period and the amount of resources sacrificed to obtain them. Unfortunately, the term "income" is often applied to an entirely different measure, *taxable income*, and this can lead to a good deal of confusion.

Taxable income is the figure that fiscal authorities use in computing the firm's income taxes. It is what the legislature says it is, subject only to review by the judiciary.

Since the legislature often uses income taxation as a way of influencing the actions of business managers and investors, taxable income often differs substantially from accounting income before taxes.

For example, a business firm may pay a registered lobbyist to present its point of view on legislative matters. This is a legitimate cost of doing business and should be reported as a current expense. It is not deductible for tax purposes, however, presumably because Congress considers it socially desirable to discourage lobbying.

Accounting figures are undeniably influenced by the desire to reduce taxes, as we shall demonstrate in later chapters, but the basic objectives of accounting measurement differ completely from the objectives underlying the income tax return. Taking this into consideration we shall at least begin by assuming that the accountant's only thought in drawing up an income statement is to measure the firm's economic performance as impartially as possible.

## SUMMARY

Accounting measures of income and financial position are based on summaries of the accountants' analyses of individual transactions. The analysis of a transaction consists of the identification of its effects on the firm's assets, liabilities, and owners' equities.

Each transaction affects at least two kinds of assets, liabilities, or owners' equities. If the accountant's work is done properly, the accounting equation will be in balance both before and after each transaction is analyzed.

At the end of each period, the accountant lists the revenues and expenses on the income statement for the period and the assets, liabilities, and owners' equity on the balance sheet. These statements do not necessarily reflect all of the available information about the financial status and productivity of the firm, because the accountant is generally unwilling to use estimates that he cannot verify readily.

This means that both management and outsiders must be alert, ready to recognize situations in which information on unmeasured quantities is vital to an understanding of the firm and its operations.

## QUESTIONS AND PROBLEMS

**1.** Under what circumstances does a particular cash outlay result in an asset? An expense? Give two other possible effects of a cash outlay.

**2.** "All business assets eventually become expenses." Defend or criticize.

**3.** Explain why an increase in an asset is always accompanied by a decrease in some other asset, or by an increase in a liability, or by an increase in the owners' equity.

**4.** Why is it not possible to measure the net income on any one sale transaction?

**5.** "Although the accountant chooses to derive the net income figure by measuring changes in the owners' equity, net income in reality consists of an increase in the firm's net assets (total assets minus total liabilities)."

Does this statement add anything to your understanding of accounting? Is it true? Describe a transaction that increases net assets without producing income. Does this disprove the statement quoted above?

**6.** Explain why owners' withdrawals are not classified as expenses.

**7.** Andrew Jenkins worked 100 hours in the Acme Hardware Store during June. He was paid $450 during July for these services. How much of this amount was an expense in June? How much was an expense in July? Explain.

**8.** State whether each of the following is true, false, or doubtful. Give reasons.
a) The total assets of a business are increased by the purchase of goods on credit.
b) Cash and owners' equity are the same.
c) The total of a firm's assets occasionally may exceed the total of its liabilities and owners' equities.
d) Since long-term debt and owners' investments are both sources of long-term capital, they may be considered as essentially identical.
e) Income is a source of capital.
f) When a firm owes taxes to a governmental body, that governmental body is, in effect, providing some of the capital used by the firm.

**9.** The following appeared on the financial statements of a retail store:

| | |
|---|---|
| Sales | $100,000 |
| Expenses other than cost of goods sold | 30,000 |
| Net income | 5,000 |
| Cost of purchases | 80,000 |
| Ending inventory | 30,000 |

What was the beginning inventory?

**10.** Merchandise costing $4,000 is sold for $5,200.

a) Analyze the effects of this transaction on the assets, liabilities, and owners' equity.

b) Explain the purpose of each change which appears in your analysis.

c) What expenses connected with this transaction are known at the time the sale takes place? What expenses are not known?

d) How and when will the profit or loss resulting from this transaction be determined?

**\*11.** Prepare an income statement and balance sheet from the following (no owner investments or withdrawals were made during the period):

| | |
|---|---:|
| Accounts payable | $ 250 |
| Accounts receivable | 300 |
| Cash | 100 |
| Cost of goods sold | 700 |
| Furniture | 600 |
| Inventories | 380 |
| Note payable | 350 |
| Prepaid rent | 40 |
| R. A. Copake, Capital | To be derived |
| Revenue from sales | 1,000 |
| Salaries and wages expense | 120 |
| Sundry expenses | 60 |
| Taxes expense | 20 |
| Taxes payable | 5 |
| Wages payable | 50 |

**12.** From the following financial data for four business firms, determine the amount of all items for which the amount is not given:

| | A | B | C | D |
|---|---|---|---|---|
| Assets 1/1/x0 | $ 60,000 | $100,000 | $ 80,000 | $500,000 |
| Liabilities 1/1/x0 | 25,000 | 36,000 | 20,000 | 100,000 |
| Assets 12/31/x0 | 70,000 | 103,000 | 88,000 | 600,000 |
| Liabilities 12/31/x0 | 26,000 | 29,000 | 16,000 | 180,000 |
| Owners' equity 1/1/x0 | 35,000 | 70,000 | 60,000 | 400,000 |
| Owners' equity 12/31/x0 | 44,000 | 74,000 | 72,000 | 420,000 |
| Revenue 19x0 | 350,000 | 500,000 | 400,000 | 1,535,000 |
| Expense 19x0 | 337,000 | 494,000 | 380,000 | 1,500,000 |
| Withdrawals 19x0 | 4,000 | 5,000 | 8,000 | 15,000 |

$\Delta OE = 9000 = NI - W.D$
$= 13000 - W.D$

$4000$
$= NI - 5000$

$NI = 20,000$
$W = 8000$
$\Delta OE = 12000$

$\Delta OE = 20,000$
$W = 15000$
$NI = 35,000$

**13.** All accounts receivable of the Borman Company arise from the sale of merchandise. On January 1, the accounts receivable amounted to $35,000; on January 31, they were $42,000. During January the amount of cash received from customers on account was $32,000. The only other change in accounts receivable was caused by the sale of merchandise. What was the amount of sales during January?

---

\* Solutions to problems marked with an asterisk (\*) are found in Appendix B.

14. The Carlton Company buys merchandise for resale to its customers. From the following data determine the amount of the company's purchases of merchandise during 19x0 and the cost of goods sold:

|  | 1/1/x0 | 12/31/x0 | 19x0 |
|---|---|---|---|
| Accounts payable arising from merchandise purchases | $19,000 | $21,000 | – |
| Inventory of merchandise | 24,000 | 19,000 | – |
| Payments to suppliers of merchandise | – | – | $30,000 |
| Sales | – | – | 52,000 |

15. The financial records of Charles Fox's automobile shop showed the following amounts on December 31, 19x6:

| | |
|---|---|
| Accounts payable | $ 2,210 |
| Accounts receivable | 4,100 |
| Buildings | 12,000 |
| Cash | 640 |
| Equipment | 12,130 |
| C. Fox, cash withdrawn for personal use during 19x0 | 6,000 |
| C. Fox, owner's equity | ? |
| General expenses | 3,140 |
| Inventory of repair parts | 4,250 |
| Repair parts used during 19x6 | 3,560 |
| Revenues | 28,940 |
| Wages expense | 15,090 |
| Wages payable | 380 |

a) Prepare an income statement for 19x6 and a balance sheet as of December 31, 19x6.

b) Explain why the amounts shown for wages expense and wages payable are not identical.

c) What was Mr. Fox's equity in the business on January 1, 19x6 (the beginning of the year)?

*16. How much should be charged to expense in 19x3 as a result of each of the following events?

(1) Purchased office furniture on July 1, 19x3, $4,200; office furniture has a 12-year life in this company.

(2) Hired a salesman on October 1 at a salary of $700 a month; salaries are paid on the 15th of each month. The salesman worked at this job until January 31, 19x4, when he left the company.

(3) Sold merchandise costing $220,000.

(4) Paid a supplier $24,000 for merchandise received in 19x2.

(5) Paid $22,500 for store rental on November 1, 19x3, covering the period from October 1, 19x3, through March 31, 19x4.

17. Indicate the effects, if any, of each of the following events on the assets, liabilities, and owners' equity of a hardware store. Each of these events took place this month. (Assume that all transactions of previous months were analyzed correctly and that no transactions analyses have been made this month.)

(1) Perform services and bill customer for $700. *Acct. Rec. ↑ D (A);* *Sale Revenue ↑ C (O.E.)*

(2) Order an electric typewriter for the office, to be delivered two months from now, price $420 to be paid at delivery. *no effect*

(3) Purchase and pay for a two-year supply of office stationery, price $380. *(A no change) office supp. ↑ D + decrease assets later, and credit to expense acct* *(cash ↓) C*

(4) Repay the $1,000 borrowed from a bank on the last day of last month, plus $9 interest. *L (Debt) ↓ D $1000   Interest Exp. ↑ D (OE ↓)* *A (cash) ↓ C $1009*

(5) Hire a new secretary on the last day of this month, salary $600 a month. *no effect*

(6) Pay a salesman $750 for services he performed last month. *A (cash) ↓ C   L (Acct. pay) ↓ D*

(7) Pay the owner's salary for this month, $1,200 (the business is organized as an individual proprietorship). *A (cash) ↓ C   Withdrawal – owner salary ↑ D*

(8) Collect cash from customer, $1,500, for services performed last year. *A (cash) ↑ D   A (acct Rec) ↓ C*

(9) Depreciation for this month was $360. *↓ (Less on Assets side)* *A (Accumulated Depreciation Acct) ↑ D* *↓ (Depreciation Expense) ↑ C*

**18.** The owners of the M Wholesale Company prepared the following lists of their company's assets and liabilities:

|  | December 31 | |
|---|---|---|
|  | 19x8 | 19x9 |
| Cash | $ 2,000 | $ 4,200 |
| Merchandise inventory | 12,300 | 15,000 |
| Accounts receivable | 7,000 | 5,000 |
| Accounts payable for merchandise | 8,000 | 10,100 |
| Furniture and fixtures (net after deduction of depreciation) | 3,000 | 2,600 |

All 19x9 expenses except depreciation and the cost of goods sold were paid in cash during 19x9. A further analysis of the company's checkbook for 19x9 shows two more groups of transactions: (1) deposits of all amounts received from customers during the year, $50,000; and (2) payments to suppliers for merchandise amounting to $33,000. No other receipts or payments occurred during 19x9.

For 19x9, what were the:

a) Sales revenues?
b) Purchases of merchandise?
c) Cost of merchandise sold?
d) Other expenses?

e) Net income?
f) Owners' equity (12/31/x8)?
g) Owners' equity (12/31/x9)?

**19.** The McIntyre Company is engaged in a variety of mining and manufacturing operations in the United States. The following are just a few of the many events that took place in this company last year:

(1) A machine was purchased from the Mining Machinery Company; payment was deferred until this year, but the machine was delivered and installed in one of McIntyre's mines.

(2) The company borrowed $10,000,000 from a life insurance company. Interest payments on this loan will amount to $800,000 a

year for 20 years; the amount borrowed will be repaid at the end of that time.

(3) A bookkeeper was hired, employment to begin on January 2 of this year. One month's salary was paid in December of last year to help the bookkeeper pay off some outstanding personal debts; the advance will be deducted from this year's salary payments.

(4) The market value of the owners' equity in this company increased by 20 percent.

(5) Completion of a highway interchange doubled the market value of a parcel of land owned by the company.

(6) A routine audit revealed that the company's cash balance was $250,000 less than the amount shown in the company's records, and that no insurance was carried against such cash shortages.

(7) A machine was leased from the Rothwell Service Company; payments are to be made annually for five years, the first payment to be made this year. At the end of the five-year period, the machine will be returned to Rothwell where it will be scrapped.

(8) One of the company's research engineers was finally able to solve a difficult miniaturization problem, after several weeks of work on McIntyre Company time. McIntyre patented the solution last year, and is now preparing to offer it commercially in exchange for annual royalty payments. A substantial number of royalty agreements are anticipated.

What immediate effect, if any, did each of these events have on the accountant's measurements of the company's assets, liabilities, and owner's equity last year? If the event had no such effect, explain why.

*20. Earl Holt decides to operate a hot dog stand near a football stadium during the football season. The following transactions describe the financial effects of his activities in setting up the business and operating it for one week:

(1) He deposits $300 in the Second National Bank.

(2) He rents a site, paying $45 for the right to use the location on the following three Saturdays.

(3) A tent and other equipment are purchased from a bankrupt concern for $110; a check is issued in payment.

(4) Merchandise is purchased from the Hill Wholesale Company, $305; Holt pays $100 down (by check), and promises to pay the balance on Monday after the first game.

(5) All of the merchandise is sold for cash on the first Saturday, and the total receipts, $650, are deposited in Mr. Holt's bank account.

(6) Holt decides that one third of the rent payment is applicable to the business done at the first game, and that the tent and equipment will have a cash value of $47 at the end of the third Saturday, the last game of the season. After that game Mr. Holt will go out of this business.

(7) On Monday, the balance due the Hill Wholesale Company is paid in full.

a) Summarize the effects of these transactions on the assets, liabilities and owner's equity of Mr. Holt's hot dog business, using the format illustrated in Exhibit 2–2. Be sure to indicate clearly which are the assets, which are the liabilities, and which are the owner's equities.

b) Prepare a balance sheet as of Monday night, after all the above information has been collected.

c) Prepare an income statement for the period that ended Monday night.

**21.** A merchandise company was formed on January 1 of last year. It had the following transactions during January:

*January 1*

(1) A cash investment of $60,000 is made in the business by the owner, Mr. John Doe.

(2) A building, $60,000, and equipment, $24,000, are purchased. Cash in the amount of $59,000 is paid for these items. The balance is owed on a 5-year note payable.

*January 2–31*

(3) Merchandise costing $40,000 is purchased on credit.

(4) Merchandise costing $30,000 is sold for $50,000. Of this amount, $21,000 is for cash and the balance is sold on credit.

(5) Salaries and wages total $13,500 for the month and are paid in cash.

(6) Miscellaneous expenses amount to $4,200. Of this amount, $3,300 is paid in cash; the rest will be paid in February.

(7) The depreciation for the month is $150 on the building and $200 on the equipment.

(8) Mr. Doe will have to pay interest on the note payable in the amount of $200 a month. His first payment will be due for payment in cash on April 1.

a) Analyze each of these transactions, identifying their effects on the following assets, liabilities, and owners' equities, using the format illustrated in Exhibit 2–2:

| | |
|---|---|
| Cash | Equipment |
| Accounts receivable | Accounts payable |
| Inventory | Notes and interest payable |
| Buildings | J. Doe, Owner |

Label each of these to identify it as either an asset (A), a liability (L), or an owners' equity (O.E.).

b)  Prepare an income statement for the month.
c)  Prepare a balance sheet as of January 31.

22. James Westbridge buys and sells iron pipe. On January 1, his business had the following assets, liabilities, and owners' equity:

Cash, $3,000; Receivables, $50,000; Inventories, $136,000; Store Equipment, $74,800; Prepaid Insurance, $816; Accounts Payable, $33,800; J. Westbridge, Prop., $221,516; Taxes Payable, $9,300.

During January, merchandise costing $78,800 was purchased on account. Merchandise with a cost of $82,100 was sold on account for $106,300. Tax expense applicable to the month of January was estimated to be $2,000, but no taxes were paid during January.

At the end of the month, $790 of insurance remained prepaid. Depreciation of store equipment for the month was $300. Miscellaneous expenses paid in cash amounted to $16,200. During the month, customers paid bills amounting to $125,100, and Mr. Westbridge paid $109,700 to his suppliers of merchandise.

a)  List the January 1 figures for the various assets, liabilities, and owner's equity, using the format illustrated in Exhibit 2–2. Then show the financial effects of the month's transactions, using only these eight categories.
b)  Prepare an income statement for the month of January and a balance sheet as of January 31.

23. On December 31, George Harvey completed his first year as proprietor of a men's clothing store. The following data summarize his first year's transactions.

(1)  He invested $14,000 cash in the business. *cash ↑D / O.E.(capital) C*
(2)  In January he borrowed $6,000 cash from a bank. *A(cash) ↑D / L(note pay.) ↑C*
(3)  In January he secured a five-year lease on shop space, rental charges to be based on sales volume in the store. Rent for the twelve months that ended on December 31 amounted to $2,292, paid entirely in cash. *A(cash) ↓C / (rent) D*
(4)  He bought furniture and store equipment for $7,500 cash. *A (cash) ↓ C / A(equip) ↑ D*
(5)  He bought merchandise on credit for $28,585. *A(Inv) ↑D / L(Acct. pay) ↑C*
(6)  During the year he sold some of the merchandise described in (5). The cost of the merchandise sold was $21,690, and he sold it for $32,200, of which $17,100 was cash and $15,100 was on credit. *(a) Cost of goods sold ↑ 21690 D (i → O.E. ↓) / Inv. ↓ 21690 C   (b) A(cash) ↑ 17,100 D / Acct. rec. ↑ 15,100 D / Sales Rev. C*
(7)  He paid himself a "salary" of $6,000, paid $642 as wages to part-time employees, and paid $2,022 for other expenses, all in cash. *withdrawal 6000 / wage exp 642 / other exp 2022 ↑ D / cash ↓ C*

(8) He returned defective merchandise to a supplier for full credit, $881. Payment for this merchandise had not been made to the supplier.

(9) He collected $4,426 owed him by customers who had bought merchandise on credit.

(10) During the year, he made payments to suppliers on account, totaling $21,520.

(11) A shoplifter stole merchandise which had cost $82.

(12) On December 31, Mr. Harvey repaid $300 of the amount borrowed plus an additional $480, representing one year's interest on the amount borrowed.

(13) He decided to depreciate his furniture and equipment evenly over a five-year period. He did not believe that there would be any salvage value at the end of that time.

a) Analyze the effects of the above transactions on the assets, liabilities, and owner's equity of Mr. Harvey's business, using the format illustrated in Exhibit 2–2. Identify the various revenues, expenses, and other owner's equity items separately from each other.

b) Prepare an income statement for the year and a year-end balance sheet. What further information would you want to have before you could tell Mr. Harvey whether his business venture was a success from a financial viewpoint?

**24.** In January, Mr. Alan Bucknell opened a retail grocery store. The following list summarizes the transactions of his first year of business:

(1) Mr. Bucknell invested $25,000 in cash.

(2) He bought a store building and equipment for $9,000, paying $8,000 cash and borrowing the remaining $1,000 from a bank.

(3) He bought on account merchandise costing $22,125.

(4) He sold merchandise which had cost him $18,910 for $23,725, of which $12,550 was for cash and the balance on credit.

(5) He paid his employees' wages in cash, $4,245.

(6) He paid $1,575 cash for other operating expenses.

(7) He received $150 cash for rent of storage space in his store loft during the year.

(8) He suffered an uninsured loss by fire of merchandise costing $1,000 and equipment which had cost him $520.

(9) He paid $19,750 of his accounts payable, $17,250 with cash and $2,500 with notes payable.

(10) His customers paid him $10,750 of the amounts they owed him.

(11) At the end of the year he owed an employee $50 for wages earned by the employee during the last few days of December.

(12) During the year he withdrew for his own use $1,200 in cash and merchandise which had cost $525.

(13) Bills for expenses incurred in December but unpaid on December 31 amounted to $110.

(14) The depreication of building and equipment during the period was estimated to be $200.

(15) On December 31 he paid the bank $90 interest on the bank loan, covering the period from the time of the loan to the end of the year.

a) Analyze the effects of the above transactions on the assets, liabilities, and owner's equity of Mr. Bucknell's business, using the format illustrated in Exhibit 2–2. Identify the various revenues, expenses, and other owner's equity items separately from each other.

b) Prepare an income statement for the year and a balance sheet as of December 31.

# *3*

# THE MECHANICS OF
# TRANSACTIONS ANALYSIS

In any firm which enters into a significant number of transactions, the accountant has to develop a set of formal procedures to translate the analyses of these transactions into financial statements and other usable information. The purpose of this chapter is to describe the basic elements of the methods used for this purpose. In the process, we shall try to explain a number of technical terms that the accountant uses to communicate with others.

## THE BOOKKEEPING PROCESS

The means by which the accounting analyses of transactions are recorded in a formal way is known as *bookkeeping*. We shall discuss the following five aspects or components of bookkeeping systems:

1. Accounts.
2. Documents, journals and ledgers.
3. Double-entry bookkeeping.
4. Debit/credit notation.
5. Closing entries.

### Accounts

An account is simply a place in which to record the effects of the firm's transactions on one of its assets, liabilities, or elements of owners' equity. The *balance* in an account on any date is the cumulative difference between the increases and the decreases that have been recorded in the account since it was created.

47

For example, The Erskine Appliance Store's *Cash* account was used to accumulate the effects on the company's cash position of all cash receipt and cash payment transactions. The following figures appeared in this account as a result of the first three transactions affecting cash, as described in Chapter 2:

| | | | | |
|---|---|---|---|---|
| | | *Cash* | | |
| *Date* | *Description* | *Increase* | *Decrease* | *Balance* |
| June 30 | Investment by owner | 20,000 | | 20,000 |
| 30 | Prepayment of rent | | 2,400 | 17,600 |
| 30 | Equipment purchase | | 6,000 | 11,600 |

The $11,600 balance in this account at the end of June showed how much of Mr. Erskine's original bank deposit was still on hand when the store opened for business on July 1.

Before analyzing any transactions, the accountant has to decide what accounts will be necessary to provide the information that is to be made available to management or outsiders. A list of the titles of these accounts is known as the *chart of accounts.* When Mr. Erskine opened his store, for example, his accountant established the chart of accounts shown in Exhibit 3–1. Because the store's operations were likely to be quite simple for the time being, its chart of accounts was quite short.

*Exhibit 3–1*

The Erskine Appliance Store

**INITIAL CHART OF ACCOUNTS**

|  |  |
|---|---|
| Assets | Cash<br>Accounts receivable<br>Inventory<br>Prepaid rent<br>Equipment |
| Liabilities | Accounts payable<br>Wages payable |
| Owner's Equity | Erskine, Investment<br>Sales revenue<br>Cost of goods sold<br>Wages expense<br>Rent expense<br>Depreciation expense<br>Miscellaneous expense<br>Erskine, Withdrawals |

Bookkeeping method depends in the first instance on the way the accounts are constructed. The accounts that are used to implement the concepts that we have been developing may take many forms, but they can all be represented schematically by accounts drawn in the shape of the letter T. A *T-account* representing the Cash account, for example, looks like this:

| Cash | |
| --- | --- |
| (+) | (−) |
| Beginning balance ...... $$$ | Disbursements .......... $$$ |
| Receipts................. $$$ | |

The left side of this account is used to show the balance of cash on hand at any time and to record cash receipts; the right side of the T is used to record cash disbursements.

By tradition and common agreement, T-accounts representing asset accounts show positive balances on the left side; T-accounts for liabilities and owners' equities are just the reverse, with balances on the right side. One way to remember this is to think of the balance sheet as a large T-account, in which the assets appear on the left and the liabilities and owners' equities appear on the right.

### Documents, Journals, and Ledgers

Data usually enter the accounting system on documents that are prepared or received at the time the transactions take place. Analysis of these documents reveals which assets and equities have been affected and which accounts should be used to record these effects.

These analyses are typically assembled ("entered") first in a *journal,* a chronological record of the transactions represented by the documents. A journal is a book, file of papers, reel of magnetic tape, or other medium in which the accounting analysis of each transaction is recorded *in its entirety.* In some cases, a file of the documents themselves may serve as a journal. The record of a transaction in a journal is known as a *journal entry.*

Each figure in a journal eventually must be transferred or *posted* to the accounts in the ledger. Since every transaction affects at least two categories of asset, liability, or owners' equity, each journal entry of necessity leads to two or more entries in the ledger. In the ledger, the individual transaction no longer appears as a complete entity; instead, its component parts are scattered among the accounts. The sequence of these data flows is summarized in the following diagram:

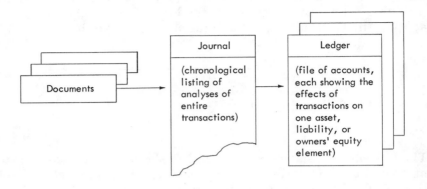

## Double-Entry Bookkeeping

The bookkeeping system that is implicit in the transactions analyses that we discussed in Chapter 2 is known as double-entry bookkeeping. Rather than repeat that entire series, let us illustrate the double-entry approach by examining the first four transactions that a new business entered into during its first month of operations:

1. The owners invested $20,000 cash in the business.
2. The firm bought merchandise on credit at a total cost of $10,000.
3. The firm paid its trade creditors $8,000 in cash.
4. The firm exchanged merchandise that had cost $4,000 for $6,000 in cash.

Accounts showing the record of these transactions in plus-and-minus form might appear as follows:

|  | *Cash* | + | *Inventory* | = | *Accounts Payable* | + | *Owners' Equity* |
|---|---|---|---|---|---|---|---|
| (1) | +20,000 | | | | | | +20,000 |
| (2) | | | +10,000 | | +10,000 | | |
| (3) | − 8,000 | | | | − 8,000 | | |
| (4) | + 6,000 | | − 4,000 | | | | $\begin{cases} + \ 6,000 \\ - \ 4,000 \end{cases}$ |
| Ending Balance | 18,000 | + | 6,000 | = | 2,000 | + | 22,000 |

The same accounts and transactions in T-account form are shown in Exhibit 3–2. Notice that each transaction is recorded by an entry on the left side of one account and an entry, equal in amount, on the right side of another. This is the essence of double-entry bookkeeping: the accounting record of each transaction has at least one left-side entry and one right-side entry, and the total of the amounts entered on the left side must equal the total of the amounts entered on the right.

Exhibit 3–2

TRANSACTIONS ANALYSES IN T-ACCOUNT FORMAT

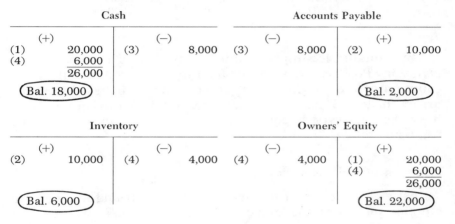

Since positive balances in asset accounts appear on the left, then entries recording increases in assets should also appear on the left. Conversely, an entry recording a decrease in an asset should be placed in the right side of the T-account for that asset. Just the reverse holds true for the liabilities and the owners' equities — an increase is entered on the right, a decrease on the left. The end-of-period account balance in any account can be calculated by subtracting the total of the figures shown in one side of the account from the total of the amounts shown in the other side.

These conventional rules governing the use of T-accounts may be summarized as follows:

1.   An *increase* in an *asset* is entered on the *left* side of the T, as is the balance in the asset account.
2.   A *decrease* in an *asset* is entered on the *right* side of the T.
3.   An *increase* in an *equity* is entered on the *right* side of the T, as is the balance in the equity account.
4.   A *decrease* in an *equity* is entered on the left side of the T.

The main advantage of this right-left arrangement is that the nature of account balances and the effects of transactions are indicated clearly by the *positions* of the figures, without need for further verbal description. When we list the final account balances, for example, we find that the total of the left-side balances equals the total of the right-side balances:

|  | *Left* | *Right* |
|---|---|---|
| Cash.................. | $18,000 | |
| Inventory.............. | 6,000 | |
| Accounts payable...... | | $ 2,000 |
| Owners' equity......... | | 22,000 |
| Total............ | $24,000 | $24,000 |

This equality is simply another expression of the accounting equation. Positive balances in liability and owners' equity accounts are on the right side; positive balances in asset accounts are on the left. Since total assets must equal the total of the liabilities and the owners' equity, the left-side total must equal the right-side total.

### Debit and Credit Notation

Just as it is not precise to use the terms plus and minus without also specifying the kind of account, so is it also a bit cumbersome to use the terms left side and right side repeatedly. A more concise and general notation has had to be found. The accountant says:

> *Debit* (abbreviated as *Dr.*) for an entry on the *left* side, meaning by this an increase in an asset *or* a decrease in a liability or owners' equity; and
> *Credit* (abbreviated as *Cr.*) for an entry on the *right* side, meaning by this an increase in a liability or owners' equity *or* a decrease in an asset.

Thus, increase in cash is the event that is recorded by a debit to Cash. Similarly, to credit Cash means to record a cash disbursement.

All this can be summarized in schematic terms very simply, as in the following diagram:

| Asset | | Liability | | Owners' Equity | |
|---|---|---|---|---|---|
| + | − | − | + | − | + |
| Dr. | Cr. | Dr. | Cr. | Dr. | Cr. |

The format that was used to represent the analysis of transactions in earlier chapters can now be replaced by a more compact form of notation. For example, the analysis of a $10,000 purchase of merchandise on credit can be presented in the following way:

| Accounts | Debit | Credit |
|---|---|---|
| Inventory .................................... | 10,000 | |
|     Accounts Payable ........................ | | 10,000 |

In this form, debits are invariably written first; credits are written underneath, with both the account titles and amounts *indented to the right*. This is a journal entry, written in what is called *general journal form*.

## Revenue and Expense Accounts

The Owners' Equity account in our illustration showed two additions to owners' equity and one subtraction:

Owners' Equity

| | (−) | | (+) | |
|---|---|---|---|---|
| (4) | 4,000 | (1) | | 20,000 |
| | | (4) | | 6,000 |

As we pointed out in Chapter 2, to prepare income statements the accountant has to separate the revenues and expenses from other elements of the owners' equity. In this case, three accounts would be used to record the three figures shown in the T-account above: one for the initial investment, one for the revenues, and one for the cost of goods sold.

These three accounts can be pictured as subdivisions of the owners' equity, as in the following diagram:

Owners' Equity

| (−) Cost of Goods Sold | | (+) Owners' Investment | |
|---|---|---|---|
| Dr. | Cr. | Dr. | Cr. |
| (4) 4,000 | | | (1) 20,000 |

| | | Revenue from Sales | |
|---|---|---|---|
| | | Dr. | Cr. |
| | | | (4) 6,000 |

The two accounts at the right are designed to accumulate the amounts *added* to the owners' equity: the Owners' Investment account accumulates the increases resulting from the owners' investments of funds in the firm; the Revenue from Sales account accumulates the gross increases in owners' equity that result from sales of goods and services during the period. As additions to owners' equity, the amounts are shown in the right-hand column.

Cost of Goods Sold is an expense account. Expenses *reduce* the owners' equity. Therefore, a positive balance in an expense account is a subtraction from owners' equity. Since subtractions from owners' equity are shown by debits, entered on the left side of owners' equity accounts, expenses are entered in the left side of expense accounts. Expense accounts have debit balances.

Transaction (4) can now be written in debit/credit form. The first entry records the increases in cash and owners' equity resulting from the month's sales:

(4a)

| | | |
|---|---:|---:|
| Cash ............................................. | 6,000 | |
|     Revenue from Sales ....................... | | 6,000 |

A second entry is necessary to record the cost of securing these revenues:

(4b)

| | | |
|---|---:|---:|
| Cost of Goods Sold............................ | 4,000 | |
|     Inventory....................................... | | 4,000 |

The debit to Cost of Goods Sold records the expense (decrease in owners' equity); the credit to Inventory records the accompanying decrease in assets.

### Inventory Bookkeeping

The sale of merchandise requires the removal of the cost of this merchandise from the Inventory account. The amount to be removed can be determined either by the *perpetual inventory method* or by the *periodic inventory method.* Under the periodic inventory method, no entry is made to record the cost of goods sold until the end of the accounting period. At that time, the remaining inventories are counted and their costs are determined. The cost of goods sold is then measured by subtracting the costs of the ending inventory from the total cost of the beginning inventory and the costs of the goods received in inventory during the period:

Cost of Goods Sold = Opening Inventory + Purchases −
                                          Ending Inventory.

The perpetual inventory method, in contrast, requires that the cost of purchased goods be added (debited) to the Inventory account at the time they are received and that the costs of goods sold be credited to the Inventory account when the goods leave the storeroom. Barring error, theft, or delay, the balance in the Inventory account should always equal the cost of the goods on hand.

The periodic inventory method is cheaper than a perpetual inventory system. The costs of purchases are simply debited to a Purchases account or to the Inventory account itself; daily or weekly transfers to the Cost of Goods Sold account are avoided, and this account retains a zero balance until the inventory count is taken at the end of the period.

Perpetual inventory records offer substantial advantages, however. First, they provide an independent check on the reliability of the inventory control system. In periodic systems, the costs of inventory shortages cannot be separated from the cost of goods sold. Second, they allow the preparation of financial statements quarterly or more often without the burden of taking a physical count each time. Third, they provide a measure of the dollar investment in inventory at all times, a feature that is especially important in financial control.

## Closing Entries

Revenue and expense accounts are temporary owners' equity accounts, used to accumulate the results of operations *for one accounting period only*. Before the next year's transactions can be posted, therefore, the existing balances in these accounts must be removed. This is accomplished by closing entries.

In this case, a single closing entry would be enough. The credit balance in the Revenue from Sales account is canceled by debiting that account for an amount equal to the account balance. Similarly, the debit balance in Cost of Goods Sold is eliminated by crediting that account for an amount equal to the account balance. The $2,000 difference is added to the balance in the Owners' Investment account:

(5)

| | | |
|---|---|---|
| Revenue from Sales | 6,000 | |
|     Cost of Goods Sold | | 4,000 |
|     Owners' Investment | | 2,000 |

This shows that the owners' equity in the business has been increased by $2,000 by the operations of this period. The owners' equity accounts now show the following:

| Cost of Goods Sold | | Revenue from Sales | | Owners' Investment |
|---|---|---|---|---|
| (4)  4,000 | (5)  4,000 | (5)  6,000 | (4)  6,000 | (1) 20,000 |
| | | | | (5)  2,000 |
| | | | | 22,000 |

This, of course, is exactly where we ended up before we complicated the example by adding revenue and expense accounts.

## ACCOUNTING FOR DEPRECIABLE ASSETS: CONTRA ACCOUNTS

The first part of this chapter introduced some new terminology and a new form of notation for transactions analyses, but no new kinds of accounts. The usual method of accounting for depreciation, however, ordinarily requires the creation of accounts of a kind that we have not yet encountered, known as *contra accounts*. To see what these are, how they are used, and what purposes they serve, we shall devote the remainder of this chapter to a brief examination of the methods used to account for depreciable assets.

### Recording Depreciation

Land, buildings, equipment, and other physical assets that provide operating capacity for a number of accounting periods are usually called *fixed assets, long-lived assets*, or *property*. Those that lose their usefulness due to deterioration or obsolescence are known as *depreciable assets.*

When we introduced the concept of depreciation in Chapter 2, we analyzed its effects in the following way:

| Owners' Equity Decrease (Depreciation Expense) | accompanied by | Asset Decrease (Equipment) |
|---|---|---|

This translates in debit and credit terms into an entry of the following form:

Depreciation Expense ............................. xxx
    Equipment .......................................     xxx

If we were to repeat this procedure for three years, the accounts would show the following amounts at the end of three years (assuming equipment costing $8,000 and depreciation of $1,000 a year):

### Equipment

| Original cost of | | Depreciation, year 1 .......... 1,000 |
|---|---|---|
| equipment purchased ........ 8,000 | | Depreciation, year 2 .......... 1,000 |
| | | Depreciation, year 3 .......... 1,000 |
| (Bal. 5,000) | | 3,000 |

### Depreciation Expense

| Depreciation, year 3 .......... 1,000 | |
|---|---|

The $5,000 balance in the Equipment account would show the portion of original cost that had not yet been charged to expense —in other words, *unexpired cost.* The balance shown in the Depreciation Expense account for the third year would be only the cost expiring during that year, of course, because expense accounts accumulate costs for one accounting period only and are closed out at the end of each period.

Although this method in no way violates accounting theory, it makes it impossible to identify the original cost of equipment without complete access to the company's records, and then only after a good deal of work. Because this kind of information is generally thought to be useful (and is often required by law), a more common treatment is to use a separate account in which to accumulate the figures reflecting the expired portion of original cost. This account is called *Accumulated Depreciation, Allowance for Depreciation,* or *Depreciation to Date* and is really a subdivision of the related property account:[1]

| Furniture and Equipment | | Accumulated Depreciation | |
|---|---|---|---|
| Original cost of | | Depreciation, year 1  1,000 | |
| equipment pur- | | Depreciation, year 2  1,000 | |
| chased    $8,000 | | Depreciation, year 3  1,000 | |
| | | (Bal. $3,000) | |

---

[1] This account is sometimes referred to as the Reserve for Depreciation, a title which unfortunately gives the misleading idea that it represents a reserve supply of funds accumulated for the replacement of the assets. There is no reason why the firm should have idle funds equal to the balance in this account, and therefore the use of the term reserve in this connection has been discouraged.

The entry to record depreciation for the third year would be:

Depreciation Expense ......................... 1,000
    Accumulated Depreciation ................              1,000

As before, the debit serves to record the reduction in the owners' equity, while the credit to Accumulated Depreciation records the consumption of the asset.

The Accumulated Depreciation account is our first example of a contra account. A contra account is always paired with some other account and serves to accumulate some or all of the negative effects of transactions on the asset or equity item to which it is coupled. For example, the Accumulated Depreciation account is a deduction-from-asset contra account, or *contra asset* account. Since the parent asset account has a debit balance, the contra account has a credit balance. In financial reporting, the balance in the contra account should always be deducted from the balance in its parent account, as follows:

Equipment, at original cost ............................. $8,000
    Less: Accumulated depreciation ....................... 3,000
Equipment, net ......................................... $5,000

The net figure is usually referred to as the asset's *book value*.

It should be emphasized that although the Accumulated Depreciation account normally carries a credit balance, it is neither a liability nor an owners' equity account. As we have just seen, it is inseparable from the account in which the asset's original cost is recorded. As such, it belongs in the asset section of the chart of accounts.

The amount shown in the Accumulated Depreciation account can be used as a rough index of the age of the company's equipment—the older the equipment, the higher the ratio of accumulated depreciation to original cost. An increase in this ratio usually means that the company is riding on its past investments in facilities; a reduction in the ratio is likely to signal a modernization or expansion program.

### Sale of Depreciable Assets

When depreciable assets are *retired* (in most cases, this means when they are sold), their original cost and accumulated depreciation must be removed from the accounts. Such sales lead to recognition of gains or losses if the sale prices are greater or less than the book value of the assets sold.

For example, suppose that one of the machines included in the $8,000 recorded in the Equipment account above was sold for $300 in cash at the beginning of year 4. Information in the equipment files revealed that this machine had cost $1,600 originally and that depreciation of $600 had been accumulated on it during the first three years. The book value of this machine therefore was $1,000 ($1,600 minus $600) and the company suffered a $700 loss on the sale, computed as follows:

| | |
|---|---|
| Proceeds from sale of machine | $  300 |
| Less: Book value of machine sold | 1,000 |
| Loss on Sale of Machine | $ (700) |

In this case, the loss resulted from an incorrect estimate of life at the time the equipment was acquired. If life had been forecasted correctly, a total of $1,300 would have been charged as depreciation during the first three years, just enough to bring the book value down to the ultimate $300 sale price at the beginning of the fourth year. On these grounds it can be argued that the proper treatment of the loss would be to go back and restate the company's earnings for the first three years. Unfortunately, the income statements of prior years are past history, and repeated correction of prior years' earnings figures could be most confusing. In conformance with common practice, therefore, the company would report the entire loss on its income statement for year 4, with no attempt to prorate any portion of it to earlier years.

The entry to record a sale like this is straightforward. Because the machine was no longer owned by the company, its balances in both the asset and the contra-asset accounts had to be removed. The entry to accomplish this was:

| | | |
|---|---|---|
| Cash | 300 | |
| Accumulated Depreciation | 600 | |
| Loss on Sale of Equipment | 700 | |
| Equipment | | 1,600 |

In this entry, the credit of $1,600 removed the original cost of the machine from the accounts, while the debit of $600 did the same for the accumulated depreciation applicable to it. The debit to cash recorded the inflow of this asset, and the debit to the loss account recorded the decrease in the owners' equity that was recognized at the time of the sale.

## CORPORATE OWNERS' EQUITY ACCOUNTS

It will be recalled from Chapter 2 that when Charles Erskine opened The Erskine Appliance Store he did so with as few formalities as possible. The legal form of organization he selected was the *individual proprietorship,* an organization that can be created by anyone as one of his or her rights under the common law. No official permission need to be obtained; from a legal point of view, the activities of the business unit are regarded as simply one portion of the activities of the proprietor, or owner.[2]

Most business activity is carried out by corporations, however. A corporation is established by the issuance of a corporate charter by a governmental agency.[3] The property of the corporation is legally separate from that of its owner(s); if an owner dies, the corporation lives on. Furthermore, the corporation, not its owner(s), is liable for the corporation's debts. This *limited liability* feature makes investment in the business feasible for many people who have confidence in its future but do not wish to become active in its management.

In exchange for their investment, the owners of a corporation receive shares of *capital stock,* entitling them to vote on such questions as the election of members of the board of directors. The board appoints the company's top managers and establishes the basic policies that management is expected to observe in operating the business.

When a business is incorporated, the accountant establishes an account or accounts to record the amounts paid to the corporation by the purchasers of shares of stock. The following entry would be an appropriate way to record the exchange of 10,000 shares of a company's stock for $350,000 in cash:

Cash .................................... 350,000
    Capital Stock ..........................          350,000

The debit records the increase in the corporation's assets; the credit to Capital Stock records the increase in the shareowners' equity.

Another function of the board of directors is to declare *cash dividends,* payments to the shareowners for the use of their

---

[2] Another form of organization that can be formed under the common law is the general partnership, created by pooling the resources of two or more persons under a formal agreement or contract among the partners.

[3] In the United States, corporate charters are almost invariably granted by individual states. State incorporation laws vary considerably, and firms engaged in interstate operations usually organize under whichever state law is regarded as most suitable for their particular operations.

funds.[4] Like proprietor withdrawals, corporate dividends are not expenses. Instead, they are regarded as distributions of funds earned by corporate operations. Thus they are not deducted from revenues in the calculation of net income. The entry to record the declaration of $15,000 in dividends is:

```
Dividends Declared ......................... 15,000
    Dividends Payable ...,...................         15,000
```

The Dividends Declared account is a temporary owners' equity account, used to identify the reductions in owners' equity due to dividend declarations during the year. The Dividends Payable account is a liability account; dividends declared but not yet paid are liabilities of the corporation.

One other account, Retained Earnings, is necessary to present the shareholders' equity on a corporate balance sheet. The balance in the Retained Earnings account measures the difference between total net income and the total amount of dividends declared since the date of incorporation. For example, if a corporation has had net income of $25,000 since it was incorporated and has declared dividends of $15,000, the balance in Retained Earnings will be $10,000. The owners' equity section of the balance sheet will appear as follows:

```
Capital stock ............................................. $350,000
Retained earnings ........................................   10,000
    Total Shareowners' Equity ...........................  $360,000
```

At the end of each year all revenue, expense, and dividend declared accounts are closed into the Retained Earnings account, thereby restoring revenue, expense, and dividend declared account balances to zero.

## SUMMARY

Accountants have developed a concise form of notation to discuss the results of transactions analyses with each other. The term *debit* is used to describe an increase in an asset or a decrease in a liability or in an element of owners' equity. The term

---

[4] In the United States, the power to declare dividends is vested in the board of directors. The directors of companies in which shares are owned by the general public ordinarily meet to declare dividends four times a year. In Europe and in much of the rest of the world, dividends are declared once each year by a formal vote of the shareholders at the annual shareholders' meeting. The vote is usually on a dividend proposal formulated by the directors, however.

*credit* describes a decrease in an asset or an increase in a liability or owners' equity.

If the accountant wishes to summarize a transactions analysis in written form, he merely has to write the names and amounts of the items affected in a table, with the debits first and the credits below them and indented to the right. This same format is sometimes used to record transactions analyses in an organization's formal accounting records.

Consistent with this notation, accounts are generally represented schematically by diagrams in the shape of the letter T. Debits are entered on the left side of the T, credits on the right. When the amounts credited to an account exceed the amounts debited to it, the account is said to have a credit balance; an excess of debits over credits produces a debit balance.

This system provides a basis for subdividing some accounts into positive and negative components. If the account normally has a debit balance, then its companion, known as a contra account, will have a credit balance. The Accumulated Depreciation account, for example, is a contra-asset account with a credit balance, representing the portion of the cost of depreciable assets that has been transferred out of the property accounts since the asset was originally acquired.

## QUESTIONS AND PROBLEMS

1. Explain why asset and expense accounts both have debit balances even though expenses are not assets.

2. Explain the nature and function of a contra account.

3. Explain the distinction between paid-in capital and retained earnings.

4. "Net income arises because the company receives more assets from its operations than it has to use to obtain them." If this is so, why are the income measurement accounts part of owners' equity instead of among the assets.

5. Is the Allowance for Depreciation account an asset, liability, or owners' equity account? Explain.

6. Is the Dividends Declared account an asset, a liability, or an owners' equity account? Explain its function.

7. Does a substantial balance in Retained Earnings indicate the presence of large cash balances?

8. The salary of the owner-manager of a corporation is considered an expense while the salary of the owner-manager of an individual proprietorship is regarded as a withdrawal of part of the owner's investment. What sense, if any, does this make?

9. Indicate whether each of the following would result in an entry to the left- or right-hand side of a T-account.

a) Liability increase.    R , C
b) Asset decrease.    R , L
c) Expense increase.    L , D
d) Ownership equity decrease.    L , D
e) Revenue increase.    R , C

10. What is a closing entry, and what is its purpose?

11. Describe the relationship between journal and ledger.

12. A company uses an Accumulated Depreciation account. One of its machines was scrapped last month. This machine cost $1,000 initially and had a book value of $200 at the time it was scrapped. Someone has suggested that the following entry be made to record the disposition of the machine:

Loss on Equipment Retirement ..................... 200
    Equipment ..................................... 200

Why would this be wrong?

13. The Wiley Company uses the periodic inventory method. It is now the end of the year, but the annual inventory count has not yet been taken. What is the balance in the Merchandise Inventory account likely to measure? Is the balance in the Cost of Goods Sold account likely to be close to the amount that will be reported on the annual income statement as the cost of goods sold during the period?

14. The balance in a Merchandise Inventory account is $160,000. The company uses the perpetual inventory method. A physical count reveals that the balance in this account should be $142,000. The Cost of Goods Sold account has a balance of $1,200,000. To what kinds of events or actions might you attribute the difference between $160,000 and $142,000?

15. The Lamay Company uses the periodic inventory method to account for the costs of the merchandise it has available for sale in any one year. The inventory was counted on December 31, 19x1, and the cost of the merchandise on hand at that time was found to be $146,000. Before this information was entered in the accounts, the inventory account had a balance of $1,460,000. Sales revenues for the year totaled $2,000,000. Calculate the cost of goods sold for the year.

*16. Given the following information, compute net income for the year 19x1:

|  | 1/1/x1 | 12/31/x1 |
|---|---|---|
| Assets...................... | $120,000 | $140,000 |
| Liabilities ................. | 24,000 | 28,000 |

During 19x1, the owners invested an additional $6,000 in the business through the purchase of additional shares of common stock from the company. Dividends of $24,000 were declared and paid during the year.

17. The opening balance in an Equipment account was $300, with accumulated depreciation totaling $100 shown in a separate account.

Depreciation for the year is $50, equipment purchases during the year amount to $250, and items originally costing $75 are sold for $20, resulting in a retirement loss of $40.

What is the correct ending balance in the Accumulated Depreciation account?

*18. You are given the following partial list of account balances for a retail store that uses the periodic inventory method:

|  | Debit | Credit |
|---|---|---|
| Inventory ......................................... | $ 80,000 |  |
| Purchases of merchandise .......................... | 760,000 |  |
| Freight cost of merchandise purchased ............. | 70,000 |  |
| Sales revenues...................................... |  | $1,200,000 |

You are told that the cost of the items on hand at the end of the year is $92,000.

a) Explain the difference between the two figures given for the inventory, $80,000 and $92,000.
b) Calculate the cost of goods sold during the period.

19. The XYZ Company balance sheet on January 1, 19x1, listed assets of $1,100,000, liabilities of $100,000, and capital stock for which the company had received $300,000.

During the year, $140,000 was received from the sale of additional capital stock, and dividends of $40,000 were declared and paid. The balance sheet on December 31, 19x1, showed assets of $1,500,000 and liabilities of $350,000.

Calculate the following (label all your calculations):

a) Retained earnings, January 1, 19x1.
b) Retained earnings, December 31, 19x1.
c) Net income for the year 19x1.

---

* Solutions to problems marked with an asterisk (*) are found in Appendix B.

**20.** After all transactions for the year had been recorded, the following balances were found in the owners' equity accounts of a small corporation (the sequence of the accounts in the list below is alphabetical and has no other significance):

|  | Debit | Credit |
|---|---|---|
| Capital stock ........................ |  | $ 20,000 |
| Cost of goods sold .................. | $70,000 |  |
| Dividends declared ................. | 6,000 |  |
| Other expenses..................... | 21,000 |  |
| Retained earnings.................. |  | 1,000 |
| Sales revenue ...................... |  | 100,000 |

*a)* What does the $6,000 figure opposite "dividends declared" mean? Were these dividends paid in cash during the year?
*b)* What does the $1,000 figure opposite "retained earnings" mean?
*c)* What balance would you show opposite "retained earnings" on the year-end balance sheet?

\*21. The Alpha Company bought a truck on January 1, 19x7, for $4,000. It was decided to charge depreciation on the basis of a five-year life and salvage value of $800 at the end of five years, equal amounts to be charged as depreciation expense for each of the five years. The truck was placed in service immediately and used for three years, at the end of which time it was sold for $1,100 cash.
Prepare journal entries to record:

*a)* The purchase of the truck.
*b)* Depreciation for 19x7.
*c)* Sale of the truck.

**22.** Balance sheet information:

|  | 1/1/xx | 12/31/xx |
|---|---|---|
| Equipment ................................ | $800,000 | $900,000 |
| Allowance for depreciation ................. | 130,000 | 160,000 |

Income statement information:

Depreciation on equipment, $80,000.
Loss on sale of equipment,  $ 5,000.

Other information:

Expenditures for the purchase of new equipment, $157,000.

What were the proceeds from the sale of equipment?

**23.** The Sturdy Shoe Company operates a chain of retail shoe stores. The company buys all its shoes from a large producer who brands them with the Sturdy name. The cost of shoes purchased is debited at the time of purchase to the Inventory account. The company's December 31 account balances were as follows:

| | | |
|---|---:|---:|
| Cash | $    20,119 | |
| Accounts receivable | 232,684 | |
| Inventory | 1,058,888 | |
| Prepaid rent and insurance | 22,156 | |
| Furniture and equipment | 116,621 | |
| Trucks | 51,460 | |
| Accounts payable | | $    66,980 |
| Notes payable | | 100,000 |
| Allowance for depreciation | | 48,918 |
| Common stock | | 300,000 |
| Retained earnings | | 128,189 |
| Sales | | 1,428,160 |
| Administrative expenses | 64,892 | |
| Selling expenses | 215,782 | |
| Rent expense | 181,603 | |
| Other operating expenses | 107,215 | |
| Other revenues | | 13,387 |
| Interest expense | 14,214 | |
| | $2,085,634 | $2,085,634 |

The year-end physical inventory count indicated that the cost of the items on hand at the end of the year was $269,821.

Prepare a year-end balance sheet and an income statement for the year.

24. On January 2, 19x1, Company X bought an electric typewriter for office use, paying $540 in cash. The company expected to sell this typewriter for $90 after using it for six years. Depreciation was to be charged in equal amounts each year.

a)  Assuming that all journal entries for the year have been made correctly but that no closing entries have been made:

(1)  What balance would you expect to find in the Allowance for Depreciation account as of December 31, 19x3?
(2)  What balance would you expect to find in the Depreciation Expense account as of December 31, 19x3?
(3)  What was the "book value" of the typewriter as of December 31, 19x3?

b)  What entry would be required on December 31, 19x6, if the typewriter were sold on that date for $90, cash?
c)  What entry would be required on December 31, 19x4, if the typewriter were sold on that date for $80, cash?

25. The bookkeeper for the Auld Sod Company recorded the following events:

(1)  Purchased on credit a three-year policy from Casualty Insurers, Inc., for $732.

(2)   Purchased office supplies for $99. Payment was made in cash.
(3)   Paid cash, $167, for bunting, banners, displays, and refreshments provided for guests entertained two days earlier.
(4)   Sold linens on credit to Talbot Textile Company for $850. The linens had cost $650.

The entries he made are shown below:    $OE = A - L$    $A = OE + L$

*Prepaid Insurance*
(1)   ~~Insurance Expense~~ ............................ 732                    O.E. ↓
          Accounts Payable ......................                    732    L ↑

(2)   Office Supplies .............................. 99                    A ↑
          *cash* ~~Accounts Payable~~ ........................                    99    A ↓

(3)   Advertising Expense ........................ 167                    O.E. ↓
*Cash*    Inventories .................................                    167    A ↓

(4)   Accounts Receivable ........................ 850                    A ↑
*Cost of goods sold*    Inventories .............................. 650                    850  650    O.E. ↓
                                              *Sales Rev.*                                                    850    A ↓
                                                                                              850    O.E ↑

For each of the above entries that was made incorrectly, indicate the correct entry and your reasons for believing that the bookkeeper's entry was made incorrectly.


**26.** You have the following balance sheets for last year for a small retail store:

|  | January 1 | December 31 |
|---|---|---|
| Cash............................................. | $ 10 | $ 12 |
| Accounts receivable from customers ............. | 20 | 25 |
| Merchandise inventory.......................... | 30 | 32 |
| Current assets ................................ | $ 60 | $ 69 |
| Plant and equipment, net ...................... | 50 | 52 |
| Total Assets ............................. | $110 | $121 |
|  |  |  |
| Accounts payable to suppliers of merchandise ... | $ 15 | $ 22 |
| Shareowners' equity: |  |  |
| Capital stock ................................ | 60 | 60 |
| Retained earnings ............................ | 35 | 39 |
| Total Liabilities and Owners' Equity ....... | $110 | $121 |

You are given the following additional data on the year's transactions:

(1)   Collections from customers, $145
(2)   Payments to suppliers of merchandise, $95
(3)   Purchases of equipment (all paid in cash) $6
(4)   Dividends to shareowners (all paid in cash), $5
(5)   Plant and equipment retired or sold during the year, none.

*a)*   Compute sales revenues for the year.
*b)*   Compute the cost of merchandise sold during the year.
*c)*   Compute depreciation for the year.
*d)*   Compute net income for the year.

**27.** Two successive balance sheets showed the following amounts:

|  | End of Year 1 | End of Year 2 |
|---|---|---|
| Property, plant and equipment (cost) | $10,000 | $11,200 |
| Less: Accumulated depreciation | 4,000 | 4,500 |
| Property, plant and equipment (net) | $ 6,000 | $ 6,700 |

The income statements for the two years included the following items:

|  | Year 1 | Year 2 |
|---|---|---|
| Depreciation | $1,000 | $ 900 |
| Gain (loss) on the sale of property, plant and equipment | 100 | (200) |

The notes to the financial statements reported that the original cost of property, plant, and equipment retired amounted to $800 in year 1 and $700 in year 2.

Describe the transactions that led to changes in the Property, Plant and Equipment and Accumulated Depreciation accounts *during year* 2. Quantify the effects of these transactions on the company's accounts. (If you decide to do this by means of journal entries, give a brief verbal explanation of the meaning of each entry line.)

*28. Analyze the following transactions and prepare journal entries to record their effects on the company's accounts. Use revenue and expense accounts. The business is organized as a corporation.

(1) The company purchases merchandise for $5,000; the supplier accepts, as payment for this purchase, the company's written promise (its *note*) to pay this amount next month.

(2) The company receives $4,000 from customers to pay for goods purchased by them during the previous month.

(3) The company pays accounts payable of $6,000.

(4) The company pays salaries of $1,000 earned by employees in the current month.

(5) The company borrows $50,000 on a long-term note.

(6) The company sells merchandise on account for $8,000; the cost of this merchandise, purchased in a previous period, was $6,000.

(7) The company purchased a piece of land at a cost of $7,000, cash.

(8) The board of directors declared a dividend of $3,000, which the company paid in cash to its shareholders.

(9) Office stationery costing $60 was purchased on credit for current use.

(10) Someone stole $100 in cash from the company. The loss is fully covered by insurance, but nothing has yet been received from the insurance company.

**29.** Prepare journal entries in debit and credit form for each of the following transactions. For each debit and each credit, indicate (*a*) whether it represents an increase or a decrease in assets, liabilities, or ownership, and (*b*) whether the amount would appear in full on the income statement for the current year. The business is organized as an individual proprietorship. These transactions are completely independent of each other and do not represent all the year's transactions of this company.

   (1)  Purchase of merchandise on extended-payment contract, $2,100; one third of price paid at time of purchase, the remainder to be paid in installments after the first of next year.

   (2)  Payment of $15,000 to suppliers on account.

   (3)  A three-year insurance policy was taken out last year, and the three-year premium of $1,800 was paid in cash at that time. Record the amount applicable to the current year.

   (4)  Sale of merchandise, $8,300 for cash and $13,700 on account; cost of merchandise sold, $16,400.

   (5)  Purchase of land and building, $12,000 for the land and $40,000 for the building; $30,000 was paid in cash and the remainder in the form of a 20-year mortgage payable.

   (6)  Collection of $18,300 on customers' accounts.

   (7)  Use of office supplies, $800; these supplies had been debited to the Office Supplies Inventory account at the time of purchase.

   (8)  Depreciation on delivery equipment, $1,550.

   (9)  Payment of employee salaries for current period, $700.

  (10)  Withdrawal of $560 cash by Mr. N. R. Gee, owner.

**30.** Prepare journal entries in debit and credit form for each of the following transactions. For each debit and each credit, indicate (*a*) whether it represents an increase or a decrease in assets, liabilities, or ownership; and (*b*) whether the amount would appear in full on the income statement for the current month. The business is organized as a corporation. The company prepares a separate income statement for each month's operations. These transactions are completely independent of each other and do not represent all the month's transactions of this company.

   (1)  Purchased office equipment for cash, $4,700.

   (2)  Received bill from plumbing contractor for repairs performed this month, $225.

   (3)  Sold merchandise on account, $22,400; cost of this merchandise was $16,700.

   (4)  Issued 100 shares of the company's capital stock for $5,000 cash.

   (5)  Hired clerk to start work the first of next month, salary $560 a month.

   (6)  Collected $26,200 from customers on account.

   (7)  Borrowed $1,000 cash from bank.

   (8)  Ordered carload of bagged charcoal for sale to customers, $24,000.

   (9)  Recorded $1,400 depreciation and $2,200 expiration of prepaid rent.

  (10)  Paid $1,500 salary to Mr. N. A. Woods, owner of 75 percent of the corporation's capital stock.

  (11)  Received and paid bills, as follows:
       For new delivery truck, $2,600.
       For insurance policy to be effective the first of next month, $220.
       For this month's telephone service, $85.

*31. The Handyman Tool Shop is an unincorporated retailer of home hardware supplies. The shop's balance sheet as of August 31, 19x1, is shown below:

Handyman Tool Shop

**BALANCE SHEET**

As of August 31, 19x1

| ASSETS | | | LIABILITIES AND OWNER'S EQUITY | | |
|---|---|---|---|---|---|
| Current assets: | | | Liabilities: | | |
| Cash | | $ 2,510 | Accounts payable | | $ 5,180 |
| Accounts receivable | | 3,060 | Salaries payable | | 140 |
| Merchandise inventory | | 7,200 | Total liabilities | | $ 5,320 |
| Total current assets | | $12,770 | | | |
| Equipment | $22,140 | | Owner's Equity: | | |
| Less: Depreciation | | | T. Square, proprietor | | 22,470 |
| to date | 7,120 | 15,020 | Total Liabilities and | | |
| Total Assets | | $27,790 | Owner's Equity | | $27,790 |

    The store's transactions for the month of September are summarized in the items below:

   (1)  Sold merchandise at an aggregate sales value of $11,700. Of this amount, $2,700 was for cash and $9,000 on credit. The cost of the merchandise sold was $6,700.

   (2)  Purchased merchandise from suppliers on account at a cost of $4,630.

   (3)  Made cash payments for the following:

| | |
|---|---|
| September store rental | $ 500 |
| Purchase of secondhand delivery truck | 1,800 |
| Salaries (See note, top of page 71) | 1,480 |
| Miscellaneous expenses for September | 700 |

   (4)  Paid $5,300 to suppliers of merchandise.

   (5)  September depreciation on equipment amounted to $160.

   (6)  Mr. Square, owner of the shop, invested an additional $2,000 of his own funds in the business.

   (7)  Collected $3,500 from customers.

NOTE: Since salaries are paid on a weekly basis, the cash *disbursed* during a month for salaries seldom equals the amount of salary *earned* by employees during the month. Thus, $140 of the cash salary payment made during the month was to pay off the liability that existed at the end of August. Mr. Square himself received no salary for working in the store.

*a)* Analyze each transaction, using journal entries in debit and credit form.

*b)* Enter in T-accounts the September 1 balances given above, set up revenue and expense accounts plus any others required by your analysis in (*a*), and post your analyses of the transactions to these T-accounts.

*c)* Prepare an income statement for the month of September and a balance sheet as of September 30. (Ignore income taxes.)

**32.** The balance sheet of the Freemont Hardware Store as of March 31, 19xx, was as shown below:

Freemont Hardware Store, Inc.

BALANCE SHEET

As of March 31, 19xx

| ASSETS | | | LIABILITIES AND OWNERS' EQUITY | | |
|---|---|---|---|---|---|
| Current assets: | | | Liabilities: | | |
| Cash | | $11,000 | Accounts payable | | $15,800 |
| Accounts receivable | | 24,100 | Notes payable | | 3,000 |
| Merchandise inventory | | 21,700 | Total current liabilities | | $18,800 |
| Total current assets | | $56,800 | Long-term debt | | 12,000 |
| Building | $30,000 | | Total Liabilities | | $30,800 |
| Equipment | 10,800 | | Shareholders' equity: | | |
| Total | $40,800 | | Capital stock | | $40,000 |
| Less: Depreciation | | | Retained earnings | | 17,800 |
| to date | 9,000 | 31,800 | Total shareholders' equity | | $57,800 |
| | | | Total Liabilities and | | |
| Total Assets | | $88,600 | Owners' Equity | | $88,600 |

The following items summarize the company's transactions for the month of April:

(1) Purchased merchandise on account from suppliers at a total cost of $13,500.

(2) Purchased on account an electric warehouse truck at a cost of $800.

(3) Sold on account for $18,200 merchandise costing $11,500.

(4) Collected $15,000 on accounts receivable.

(5) Paid $17,200 on accounts payable.

(6) Depreciation charges were:

| | |
|---|---|
| Office and warehouse equipment | $70 |
| Automotive equipment | 80 |
| Building | 50 |

(7)  On April 1, a two-year general coverage insurance policy was purchased for $120 cash.

(8)  On April 1, paid rent of $660 for the use of additional storage space for six months, beginning April 1, 19xx.

(9)  Made other cash payments for the following:

Salaries of employees .................................... $2,800
Miscellaneous operating expenses for April ............. 1,140
Interest for April on notes payable and long-term debt ...  75

*Retained Earning Acct.*

(10)  The board of directors declared a dividend in the amount of $500, to be paid to shareholders in cash on May 15.

a)  Analyze each transaction, using journal entries in debit and credit form.

b)  Enter in T-accounts the April 1 balances given above, set up revenue and expense accounts plus any others required by your analysis in (a), and post your analyses of the transactions to these T-accounts.

c)  Prepare an income statement for the month of April and a balance sheet as of April 30. (Ignore income taxes.)

33. The Greeley School, a private preparatory day school for boys, accepted its first students and held its first classes in September, 19x1. The school was founded by Jonathan Greeley, the former senior tutor of a large eastern preparatory school.

Mr. Greeley was anxious to try out a new system of instruction and had persuaded a group of wealthy businessmen to supply most of the capital he needed to finance the new venture. He intended to operate the school for profit, partly to demonstrate that it could be done, and partly because this seemed to him the best basis on which to attract the required capital.

As expected, enrollment was below capacity during the first year, but by May 19x2 applications for September enrollment were so numerous that Mr. Greeley believed his classes would be filled during the second year.

His backers were impressed by the file of admission applications and pleased by the competence Mr. Greeley seemed to have shown in administering the school, but they were anxious to find out how much money the school had lost during its initial year of operations. As one of the shareholders said, "The enrollment figures are impressive, but so are those at the university, and they have to tap us alumni every year just to meet the payroll. I don't expect we'll show a profit at Greeley this year, but if the loss is much larger than we had expected we ought to think seriously of closing up shop or selling our shares for whatever we can get for them."

The school started its formal existence on July 1, 19x1, with the issuance of a corporate charter. The following transactions took place during its first 12 months:

(1)  Two hundred shares of capital stock were issued on July 1, 19x1, for $30,000, cash.

(2)  At the same time, the shareholders deposited an additional $10,000 in the corporation's bank account, receiving in exchange notes payable in this amount.

(3)  A two-year lease was signed, giving the school the right to use a large mansion and its grounds from July 1, 19x1, to June 30, 19x3. The monthly rental was $2,000. An initial cash payment of $6,000 was made on July 1, 19x1, and cash payments of $2,000 each were made on the first of each succeeding month, through June 1, 19x2.

(4)  A set of classroom blackboards was purchased on credit for $3,600. Other private schools in the area estimated that, on the average, blackboards could be used for 12 years before replacement became necessary.

(5)  Classroom furniture costing $9,000 was purchased from the Tower Seating Company, which accepted a down payment of $4,000 in cash and a note payable for the balance. Classroom furniture was expected to have an eight-year life, on the average.

(6)  Equipment of various kinds, with an expected average life of five years, was purchased for $7,000, cash.

(7)  Students' tuition and other fees amounted to $78,000. Of this amount, $6,000 had not yet been collected by June 30, 19x2, but Mr. Greeley was confident that this amount would be received before the new school year began in September.

(8)  Salaries were paid in cash:
Teaching staff, $54,000.
Office staff, $11,000.

(9)  On June 15, 19x2, two parents paid tuition for the 19x2–x3 school year, amounting to $3,400.

(10)  Various school supplies were bought on credit for $4,100. Of these, $200 were still in the school's storeroom, unused, on June 30, 19x2.

(11)  Utility bills and other miscellaneous operating costs applicable to the year ending June 30, 19x2, were paid in cash, $3,800.

(12)  Payments amounting to $4,500 were made on account to suppliers of items referred to in items 4 and 10 above.

(13)  The holders of the school's notes were paid interest of $900. In addition, the Tower Seating Company was paid $1,500 of the amount borrowed (item 5, above).

a)  Prepare a list of account titles that you think would be useful for recording these transactions, including revenue and expense accounts and an allowance for depreciation account. Then analyze the above transactions in debit and credit form. For each debit and each credit, indicate (1) whether the effect is to increase or to decrease an asset (A), a liability (L), or the shareholders' equity (O.E.); and (2) whether the amount would appear in full on the income statement for the current year. For example:

Cash.......................................... xxx
    Capital Stock ............................. xxx
(Increase A; increase O.E.; no effect on current income.)

Do not forget to record depreciation for the year.

b) Post these amounts to T-accounts.

c) Prepare an income statement for the year and a balance sheet as of June 30, 19x2.

d) Upon seeing your figures, Mr. Greeley objected to the depreciation charge. "We just can't afford to write off any of those costs this year," he said. "Next year our tuition will be up, and we can start recovering depreciation." Do you agree with Mr. Greeley, or do you have a different concept of depreciation? Defend your position.

e) If you were a shareholder, how would you use the financial statements in your evaluation of the financial success or failure of this new enterprise? Assuming that your decision to retain your shares or sell them would be based on your forecast of future financial statements, would the financial statements of a period already in the past be of any relevance to you?

# 4

# INCOME AND CASH FLOWS FROM MANUFACTURING OPERATIONS

JUST AS MOLIERE'S BOURGEOIS GENTLEMAN was delighted to learn that he had been talking prose all of his life, it may be a pleasure to discover that while we were learning the fundamentals of transactions analysis in the preceding chapter, we were actually practicing accrual accounting. The purpose of this chapter is to examine more thoroughly the basic concepts of accrual accounting as they might be applied in two small firms that create income by producing goods or performing services.

## ACCRUAL BASIS ACCOUNTING

Accrual basis accounting ignores the timing of cash receipts and disbursements completely for income measurement. Under accrual accounting, a cost is *capitalized*—entered in an asset account—if it seems likely to produce future benefits (revenues or cost reductions) and is *expensed* when the benefits materialize. The timing of cash disbursement has no bearing on these questions.

By the same token, in accrual accounting revenue recognition may come either before or after the receipt of cash. The question is whether the revenue is earned, not whether it has been evidenced by the receipt of cash.

For example, Mr. John Appleby operates a small management consulting business under the name of Appleby Associates. On January 2, he agreed to carry out an assignment for the Jones

Company. On January 22 he purchased and received materials costing $1,000 for use on this assignment. He paid for the materials on February 9 and started to work on the assignment on March 5. The project was completed on March 28, and the Jones Company was billed for the contract price of $12,000 on that date. Salaries of employees who worked on the assignment during March totaled $4,000, and this amount was paid on March 31.

This series of transactions is summarized in Exhibit 4–1. An expenditure in January was followed by a cash disbursement of

Exhibit 4–1

APPLEBY ASSOCIATES: TIMING OF EVENTS

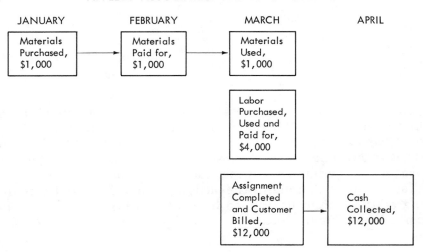

$1,000 in February, another disbursement of $4,000 in March, and a cash receipt of $12,000 in April. This does not mean, however, that the company lost $1,000 in February, lost $4,000 in March, and earned $12,000 in April. In this situation, accrual accounting would bring all of these figures together in the income statement for March, when all of the work was done and the customer was billed. Income of $7,000 on this contract would be recognized at that time.

## MANUFACTURING COST FLOWS

The linkage between accrual-basis income and the flow of cash is perhaps the most indirect in firms that manufacture tangible products in one period for delivery to customers in some later period. Manufacturing processes are designed to add value to purchased materials by using labor and machinery to convert them to new asset forms. They therefore lengthen the interval between the acquisition of resources and the delivery of finished products to customers.

To illustrate the relationships between manufacturing costs and company financial statements, let us look at the first six months' operations of Strong Cabinets, Inc., a small woodworking firm. This company was founded on July 1, 19x1, by David Strong, a dealer in high-fidelity sound systems, to manufacture wooden cabinets in which his customers could install system components. The company began operations with $20,000 in cash, provided by Mr. Strong in exchange for shares of capital stock.

### Preproduction Transactions

Mr. Strong began by renting factory space in a building adjoining his store, buying a secondhand set of cabinet-making tools and equipment, and hiring a skilled cabinetmaker. The rental on the factory space amounted to $8,400 a year, payable in advance. The entry to record this on July 1, 19x1, showed the acquisition of one asset in exchange for another:

$$(1)$$

| | | |
|---|---|---|
| Prepaid Rent ..................................... | 8,400 | |
| Cash......................................... | | 8,400 |

The tools and equipment were bought on account for $10,000, and their cost was entered in a new asset account, Factory Equipment. The accompanying liability was also recognized at this time by an addition to the Accounts Payable account. The record of this transaction therefore showed the following changes:

$$(2)$$

| | | |
|---|---|---|
| Factory Equipment............................ | 10,000 | |
| Accounts Payable .......................... | | 10,000 |

Most of a retailer's or wholesaler's purchases are of merchandise bought for resale to the company's customers. A manufacturer's purchases, in contrast, consist mainly of materials and parts that are to be used in the manufacturing process. Strong Cabinets, for instance, purchased lumber and other materials for use in the cabinet shop, as the factory was called, but had no intention of selling those materials without converting them into finished cabinets.

The materials purchased during 19x1 were obtained from suppliers on credit, at a total cost of $22,000. The entries recording these purchases showed that both assets and liabilities had increased:

(3)

Materials Inventory ............................ 22,000
    Accounts Payable ...........................         22,000

## Recording Issuance of Materials

Up to now, the only thing to distinguish this illustration from one for a retail store has been the title of the inventory account. Materials cost accounting differs from merchandise cost accounting in a more fundamental way, however. When production materials are *issued*—that is, when they are taken from the materials stock room and delivered to factory operating personnel— they are merely transferred from one asset category to another.

The cost of the materials issued to the cabinet shop during 19x1 totaled $14,000. The entries that the accountants made to record these transactions showed increases in the work in process inventory and decreases in the quantity of raw materials on hand:

(4)

Work in Process Inventory...................... 14,000
    Materials Inventory ........................         14,000

The Work in Process Inventory account was used to accumulate all of the costs assigned to the products being manufactured. It was an asset account, not an expense account, because the products to which these costs related had not yet been used to produce revenues.

## Recording Factory Payrolls

Payroll costs for factory employees are recorded just as for office and store employees, with one difference: the cost is charged to a factory cost account such as Work in Process Inventory rather than to an expense account. Shop labor is used to create an asset, in this case work in process, and the costs of such labor do not become expense until the revenues from cabinet sales appear on the income statement.

During the second half of 19x1 (the first six months of shop operations), wages and salaries in the cabinet shop amounted to $20,000. The entries recording these payrolls showed the inventory increase accompanied by an increase in payroll liabilities:

(5)

Work in Process Inventory........................ 20,000
    Wages and Salaries Payable ................            20,000

## Recording Depreciation

Depreciation is another example of a cost that is ordinarily treated as a current expense when it relates to facilities used for administrative or marketing activities but is treated as an asset when it relates to manufacturing facilities. Once again, the argument is that the asset has merely been converted from one form to another – the services formerly embodied in a machine have now been embodied in the goods manufactured during the period. Thus factory depreciation does not become an expense until revenues from the goods to which it has been charged have been recognized on the income statement.

Depreciation on shop facilities in the cabinet shop during the second half of 19x1 amounted to $800; the entry to record this treated it as a conversion of one asset (equipment) into another (inventory):

(6)

Work in Process Inventory........................... 800
    Accumulated Depreciation ......................        800

The credit to Accumulated Depreciation served to record the decrease in the company's equipment assets. This account was a contra-asset account, as explained in Chapter 3. The balance in this account appeared on the balance sheet as a deduction from the original cost of the equipment.

## Other Factory Costs

Factory utilities and other miscellaneous shop costs not recorded in any of the entries above amounted to $7,200 during 19x1. The entries to record these transactions had the following effects on the account balances:

(7)

Work in Process Inventory ........................ 7,200
    Accounts Payable ............................        7,200

As this shows, the costs that were incurred to help create salable goods were added to an asset account; the liability to pay for the cost-originating services was recognized by the addition to the Accounts Payable account.

Finally, six months' rent on the cabinet shop itself had to be charged to shop operations. Rent of $8,400 was paid on July 1, 19x1 (entry [1] above), covering the next 12 months. Six months' rent therefore had to be treated as a cost of factory operations for the last six months of 19x1. The accountant's analysis showed the following asset changes:

(8)

| Work in Process Inventory | 4,200 | |
|---|---|---|
| Prepaid Rent | | 4,200 |

Once again, only the *form* of the asset was changed; the asset total remained the same after this transaction was recorded as it had been before.

### The Cost of Goods Finished

Putting the various costs incurred in the manufacture of the cabinets in the Work in Process Inventory account resulted in the following:

Work in Process Inventory

| (4) Materials | 14,000 | |
|---|---|---|
| (5) Wages | 20,000 | |
| (6) Depreciation | 800 | |
| (7) Miscellaneous | 7,200 | |
| (8) Rent | 4,200 | |
| | 46,200 | |

Some of the cabinets for which these costs were incurred were still unfinished at the end of 19x1. Others, however, with a total factory cost of $36,600, had been completed and transferred to the merchandise stock room for sale to customers. These costs had to be transferred from the Work in Process Inventory account to a new inventory account called Finished Goods Inventory:

(9)

| Finished Goods Inventory | 36,600 | |
|---|---|---|
| Work in Process Inventory | | 36,600 |

Both of these accounts were asset accounts; the transfer of costs merely indicated the change in the inventory from an unfinished to a finished form. This left $9,600 in the Work in Process Inventory account as the cost of the unfinished cabinets in the factory on December 31, 19x1.

## The Cost of Goods Sold

The Finished Goods Inventory account plays the same role in a manufacturing organization as the Merchandise Inventory account does for a wholesaler or retailer. It keeps the costs of salable products on the balance sheet until the goods themselves are sold. In this case, the cabinets sold during 19x1 had a total manufacturing cost of $28,000. The delivery of these cabinets to the company's customers reduced both the inventory asset and the owners' equity. The entries to record these changes can be summarized as follows:

(10)

Cost of Goods Sold .............................. 28,000
    Finished Goods Inventory ...................    28,000

This left a balance of $8,600 in the Finished Goods Inventory account, the cost of the finished cabinets still on the storeroom shelves at the end of 19x1:

Finished Goods Inventory

| (9) | 36,600 | (10) | 28,000 |
|---|---|---|---|
| Bal. 12/31 | 8,600 | | |

## The Manufacturing Cost Statement

This completes the so-called *operating cycle* of a manufacturing company. This cycle consists of purchasing materials, processing them into finished goods, and selling them to customers. The flow of manufacturing costs through the accounts is diagrammed in Exhibit 4–2. Notice that inventories are found at three stages – unprocessed, partly processed, and finished. Each of the dollar amounts identified with a cost flow in this diagram came from one of the ten entries that we used in the illustration.

The diagram can be converted very simply to T-account form by inserting a large T in place of each of the rectangular boxes. Costs flowing into an account would be represented by debits at the left; costs leaving an account would be shown as credits, at the right of the account.

*Exhibit 4–2*

## MANUFACTURING COST FLOWS

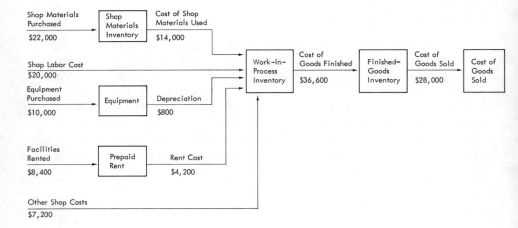

These cost flows can also be summarized in tabular form, as in the manufacturing cost statement in Exhibit 4–3. This

*Exhibit 4–3*

### Strong Cabinets, Inc.

## STATEMENT OF MANUFACTURING COSTS AND COST OF GOODS SOLD
### For the Six Months Ended December 31, 19x1

Materials cost:
Materials purchased ......................................... $22,000
    Less: Materials on hand, December 31, 19x1 ................. 8,000
    Cost of materials used ..................................... $14,000
Labor costs ................................................... 20,000
Depreciation .................................................. 800
Rent on factory ............................................... 4,200
Other factory costs ........................................... 7,200
    Total Factory Cost ........................................ $46,200
Less: Work in process inventory, December 31, 19x1 ............. 9,600
    Cost of goods finished..................................... $36,600
Less: Finished cabinets inventory, December 31, 19x1 ........... 8,600
Cost of Goods Sold ............................................ $28,000

shows that of the $46,200 in costs actually applicable to factory operations during 19x1, only $28,000 was transferred to expense on the income statement for the year. The remaining $18,200 was divided between the Work in Process Inventory and Finished

Goods Inventory accounts. In addition, materials inventories showed a year-end balance of $8,000, factory equipment costs of $9,200 remained on the balance sheet, and rent prepayments amounted to $4,200 at the end of the year.

Notice that nowhere in this illustration was reference made to the payment of cash. The timing of cash payment has no bearing on the apportionment of costs among the various categories of assets and expenses. Eliminating cash transactions from the illustration therefore interfered in no way with our ability to trace the manufacturing cycle through the accounts.

## Nonmanufacturing Costs and the Income Statement

Every manufacturer incurs many costs for activities other than manufacturing. Advertising costs, the president's salary, and expenditures on research and development are only a few examples of costs that are incurred for purposes other than the conversion of raw materials into finished products.

All such costs are accounted for just as they would be in a retailing or wholesaling concern. Sales office rental costs and advertising costs are recognized as expense when the space and advertising services are provided, whether products have been sold or not. They are not part of the cost of manufacturing products and therefore they do not enter the factory cost accounts in any way. They go directly to expense without passing through the Work in Process Inventory and Finished Goods Inventory accounts along the way.

Mr. Strong and a part-time clerical assistant constituted the entire selling and administrative work force at Strong Cabinets during 19x1. Their salaries for this period amounted to $7,000. The entries to accrue these payrolls can be summarized as follows:

(11)
Selling and Administrative Salary Expense ........ 7,000
    Wages and Salaries Payable ...................         7,000

The effect of these transactions, in other words, was to decrease the owners' equity and increase the company's liabilities.

Other selling and administrative expenses had the same effect. They amounted to $3,100 and can be summarized as follows:

(12)
Other Selling and Administrative Expenses ........ 3,100
    Accounts Payable ............................         3,100

To complete the illustration, we need to recognize the revenues earned during the period. Finished cabinets were sold on account for a total of $40,000, thereby increasing the firm's assets and its owners' equity:

(13)

| | | |
|---|---|---|
| Accounts Receivable .......................... | 40,000 | |
| Sales Revenue .............................. | | 40,000 |

The income statement derived from the revenue and expense accounts appears in Exhibit 4–4. (The figures in this statement can be verified by posting transactions (10) through (13) to the accounts.)

Exhibit 4–4

Strong Cabinets, Inc.

INCOME STATEMENT

For the Six Months Ended December 31, 19x1

| | | |
|---|---|---|
| Sales revenue ......................................... | | $40,000 |
| Expenses: | | |
|   Cost of goods sold ................................. | $28,000 | |
|   Selling and administrative salaries ................. | 7,000 | |
|   Other selling and administrative expenses .......... | 3,100 | |
|     Total expenses ................................. | | 38,100 |
| Net Income ......................................... | | $ 1,900 |

## INCOME VERSUS CASH FLOW

The income statement is intended to measure the economic performance of the firm. While this is important, management also needs information that will help it plan and evaluate its success in keeping its liquid resources at desired levels. A firm may be profitable yet unable to pay its debts because its assets are not in liquid form. Similarly, the firm's ability to pay dividends or buy new equipment hinges on the availability of cash rather than the availability of income.

Information for these purposes can be found in statements of cash flows. For decision making, these should summarize the company's forecasts of future cash flows; for evaluating past performance, historical statements are appropriate. Both can take the same form.

An historical cash flow statement can be derived from an analysis of the entries that have been made in the company's cash account. For example, the following entries were made in Strong Cabinets' cash account during 19x1:

Cash

| | | |
|---|---|---|
| Balance, June 30, 19x1 ..................................... | | --- |
| (0) Investment by Mr. Strong ............................... | +$20,000 | |
| (1) Payment of rent.......................................... | − 8,400 | |
| (14) Collection of accounts receivable......................... | + 34,000 | |
| (15) Payments to suppliers .................................... | − 25,000 | |
| (16) Bank loan ................................................ | + 15,000 | |
| (17) Payments of wages and salaries.......................... | − 26,500 | |
| (18) Payment of equipment purchased ........................ | − 8,000 | |
| Balance, December 31, 19x1 ............................. | $ 1,100 | |

These cash flows can be rearranged to distinguish between those that arose in connection with the routine operation of the business and those that arose in other ways. One such arrangement is shown in Exhibit 4–5. Although the operations for the

Exhibit 4–5

Strong Cabinets, Inc.

STATEMENT OF CASH FLOWS

For the Six Months Ended December 31, 19x1

| | | |
|---|---|---|
| Cash flow from operations: | | |
| Received from customers....................... | | $34,000 |
| Less: Paid to suppliers ......................... | $25,000 | |
| Paid to employees ........................ | 26,500 | |
| Paid to landlord ......................... | 8,400 | 59,900 |
| Net cash flow from operations (outflow) ........ | | ($25,900) |
| Nonoperating cash inflows: | | |
| Initial investment ............................ | $20,000 | |
| Bank loan ..................................... | 15,000 | 35,000 |
| Nonoperating cash outflow: | | |
| Paid for equipment............................ | | (8,000) |
| Net increase in cash balance .................... | | $ 1,100 |

period generated a net income of $1,900, they also resulted in a cash outflow of $25,900, and the purchase of equipment consumed another $8,000. The company was able to meet these demands for cash only as a consequence of the investment by Mr. Strong and the bank loan, which came through at the very end of the year, just in time to cover the last batch of payments to suppliers and employees.

This statement reflected a series of events that either would not or should not be repeated in the following year. For one thing, Mr. Strong had no more money to put into the business and his bank was unwilling to increase the size of its loan. Fortunately, no further expenditures for equipment would be necessary, so the key to the future lay in preventing a repetition of the $25,900 cash outflow from operations.

Analysis of the account balances reveals that the first six months' operations required a buildup of inventory and accounts receivable. In this, it was like most new businesses. In the absence of additional outside investment, however, Mr. Strong had to prevent a further buildup of these assets in 19x2 to insure a positive cash flow from operations. This probably meant curtailing the firm's growth. Growth creates great demands for cash, and so long as the rate of profit and the terms of purchase and sale remain unchanged, operating cash outflows can be halted only by reducing the rate of growth.

Further discussion of this problem and of the construction and use of statements patterned after the one in Exhibit 4–5 must wait until we have learned more about the analysis of accounting transactions, a task that will occupy us in the next few chapters. For the moment we must content ourselves with observing that cash flow and income are not the same thing, and that statements focusing on one will not answer questions that relate to the other.

## SUMMARY

The accounting structure introduced in the last three chapters is known as accrual accounting and is the dominant method of financial accounting, except for the very smallest firms. In accrual accounting, costs are recognized as expenses when the related revenues are recognized, even if the related cash disbursements are made earlier or later. A cost is capitalized (added to an asset account) if it can reasonably be expected to contribute directly or indirectly to future income. A cost is expensed if the resources it represents were consumed directly or indirectly in producing the current year's revenues.

Manufacturing costs provide an excellent illustration of the application of the accrual concept. Accounting views manufacturing as a process of adding the costs of manufacturing labor and other manufacturing services to the cost of purchased materials. The costs of manufacturing follow the flow of the goods themselves, from raw materials inventory to work in process to finished goods and finally to goods sold. The costs of the goods at all of these stages except the last are regarded as costs of assets and thus rest appropriately in the inventory section of the balance sheet. Only when the goods are sold do these costs become expenses as the cost of goods sold. Costs of administering the company and of selling and distributing its products, of course, are taken directly to expense, just as in a wholesaling or retailing concern.

Information on the firm's cash flows is necessary to an understanding of its financial condition and prospects. Net income is a measure of the productivity of the firm's resources, not an index of the adequacy or composition of the firm's cash flows. A good income record can easily be jeopardized if the cash inflows are inadequate to support it. Conversely, a poor earnings record may be accompanied by a rich and continuing flow of cash. For these reasons, preparation of cash flow statements is an essential part of accounting.

## QUESTIONS AND PROBLEMS

1. Under what circumstances is depreciation cost not depreciation expense?

2. What is the logical justification for assigning factory labor costs to asset accounts, while salemen's salaries are treated as expenses?

3. What difference does it make whether factory maintenance and repair cost is considered a cost of a product or a cost of a period?

4. What kind of information can a statement of cash flows provide?

5. Explain how the problems of accounting for manufacturing activities differ from those encountered in connection with trading activities. How are they similar?

6. Company X is a "growth company" — that is, its sales, earnings, and capital resources show a sharp upward trend from year to year. Is the amount of cash flow from operations likely to be greater than, less than, or equal to net income?

7. What courses of action are open to a profitable company if its cash flows from operations are inadequate to finance its current rate of growth?

8. Why is the payment of cash not regarded by accountants as valid evidence that resources have been consumed?

9. Which of the following costs of the current month are also expenses of the current month?

a)  Depreciation on office equipment.
b)  Production superintendent's salary.
c)  Raw materials purchased for the factory.

*d)*  Factory labor on work shipped to customers this month.
*e)*  Depreciation on factory machinery.
*f)*  Materials used this month to package finished products.
*g)*  Cartons used this month to ship products to customers.
*h)*  Sales brochures purchased for use during the next six months.
*i)*  Wages of raw materials stockroom clerk.
*j)*  Wages of shipping department manager.
*k)*  Freight charge on materials received.
*l)*  Freight charge on materials shipped.
*m)*  Factory labor used to build new storage cabinets in sales room.
*n)*  Factory labor used to repair office water cooler.
*o)*  Factory labor used to repair factory water cooler.
*p)*  Outside contractor's fee for repairing factory machine.

**10.** Manufacturing costs for a period totaled $300,000, the work in process inventory increased from $250,000 at the beginning of the period to $280,000 at the end, and the cost of goods sold during the period amounted to $310,000.

*a)*  Calculate the cost of goods finished during the period.
*b)*  By how much did the cost of finished goods on hand increase or decrease during the period?

**11.** The following data were taken from the ledger accounts of the Abcess Manufacturing Company for the most recent month:

| | |
|---|---:|
| Factory materials inventory, beginning of month | $      0 |
| Work in process inventory, beginning of month | 0 |
| Finished goods inventory, beginning of month | 5,000 |
| Purchases of factory materials | 360,000 |
| Depreciation on factory and factory equipment | 15,000 |
| Factory materials placed in production | 290,000 |
| Depreciation on office equipment | 2,000 |
| Sales and administrative salaries | 59,000 |
| Factory labor | 140,000 |
| Sundry selling and administrative expense | 29,000 |
| Sundry production costs for the month | 135,000 |
| Revenue from sales | 525,000 |
| Income taxes on taxable income for the month | 24,000 |
| Dividends declared during the month | 35,000 |
| Work in process inventory, end of month | 115,000 |
| Finished goods inventory, end of month | 85,000 |
| Retained earnings, beginning of month | 40,000 |

Compute the following figures:

*a)*  Total production costs for the month
*b)*  Total cost of goods finished during the month
*c)*  Cost of goods sold during the month
*d)*  Net income for the month
*e)*  Retained earnings, end of month
*f)*  Raw materials inventory, end of month

**12.** The Albatross Corporation is engaged in the manufacture and sale of plastic water toys. Its inventory accounts showed the following balances:

|  | January 1 | June 30 |
|---|---|---|
| Raw materials .................... | $10,000 | $16,000 |
| Work in process ................. | 40,000 | 50,000 |
| Finished goods ................... | 20,000 | 10,000 |

The following costs were incurred between these two dates:

| | |
|---|---|
| Factory raw materials purchased ......... | $90,000 |
| Factory labor ............................ | 40,000 |
| Factory depreciation ..................... | 7,000 |
| Factory utilities and other costs ........... | 13,000 |
| Salesmen's salaries ...................... | 5,000 |
| Office salaries ........................... | 8,000 |
| Other selling and office costs ............. | 4,000 |

Prepare a statement showing (*a*) the cost of goods finished during this period, and (*b*) the cost of goods sold.

*13. The Buildmore Company had the following inventories on September 1:

| | |
|---|---|
| Raw materials ................... | $20,000 |
| Work in process ................. | 30,000 |
| Finished goods ................... | 12,000 |

During the month of September: the cost of raw materials purchased was $60,000; labor cost incurred was $80,000; and other costs applicable to production totaled $30,000.

On September 30 inventories were:

| | |
|---|---|
| Raw materials ................... | $25,000 |
| Work in process ................. | 20,000 |
| Finished goods ................... | 20,000 |

Show all journal entries necessary to record the above transactions.

**14.** Prepare debit and credit analyses of the following set of related transactions of the Goodhue Chemical Company.

(1) Ordered from a supplier 30 55-gallon drums of chemicals at $65 a drum. Of this price, $5 applied to the drum, which was returnable when empty.
(2) Received 27 of the drums ordered above.
(3) Paid freight charges of $108 for delivery of the 27 drums.
(4) Returned two drums of chemicals to the supplier for full credit as defective merchandise.
(5) Paid the bill due to the supplier after deducting the amount paid for incoming freight charges on the two defective drums.

---

* Solutions to problems marked with an asterisk (*) are found in Appendix B.

(6)  Bought 5,500 empty quart tins which cost a total of $295, delivered and labeled.

(7)  Paid five temporary employees $25 each per day for two days' work to fill the tins with chemicals and put them on the shelves.

(8)  Sold 4,500 quarts of chemicals on account at $0.50 each.

(9)  Collected $1,450 from customers.

(10)  Returned 24 empty drums to the supplier. The remaining drum had been lost from the pile at the rear of the store.

**15.** The Central Department Store purchased a large quantity of unfinished and unassembled wooden kitchen cabinets at a bankruptcy sale with the intention of retailing these units "as is" at a very low price. The management soon discovered, however, that the units were too complicated for the average householder to assemble without great difficulty. The company then decided to assemble and finish the cabinets and offer them at a price sufficiently above that originally intended to cover the costs of these operations. The following transactions took place:

(1)  Purchase of 2,100 unassembled units for cash at $10 each.

(2)  Sale of 100 unassembled units on credit at a unit price of $16.

(3)  Payment of one month's wages to employees for assembling and finishing the remaining 2,000 units: four carpenters at $900 each and six painters at $750 each.

(4)  Payment of one month's wages to two regularly employed warehouse men who acted as material handlers, $660 each. Because this activity occurred during a slack period, this actually entailed no extra cost to the company. For the same reason, adequate work space was available in the company's warehouse.

(5)  Purchase of paint and other supplies on credit, $900. When the operation was finished, supplies estimated to have cost $60 remained on hand. These could all be used in the company's normal maintenance operations.

*a)*  Analyze these transactions in debit and credit form.

*b)*  In line with the company's original objective of increasing the retail price just enough to cover assembly and finishing costs, what would you set as the new selling price? Support your conclusion.

*c)*  Assuming that the company has set the price at the figure you selected in (*b*), prepare all of the journal entries that would be necessary to record the changes in the assets, liabilities, and owners' equity resulting from a credit sale of 200 finished cabinets.

*16.** The Illumino Corporation manufactures lighting fixtures. On the first of April, the company had on hand raw materials which had cost $17,200, finished fixtures costing $34,000, and partially completed fixtures on which $23,400 in raw materials and other costs had already been incurred.

During April, additional materials costing $35,000 were purchased, and materials costing $48,400 were put into process. April factory labor costs were $26,000, and other manufacturing costs totaled $15,600. At the end of April, incomplete fixtures on hand represented $2,200 in materials, $1,400 in labor applied, and $800 of other costs. Finished fixtures costing $97,000 were shipped to customers during the month.

Prepare journal entries for the month of April.

*17. A company's annual report showed the following income statement for the year 19x1:

| Sales | | $500,000 |
|---|---|---|
| Less: Cost of goods sold | $300,000 | |
| Depreciation | 20,000 | |
| Other expenses | 100,000 | 420,000 |
| Net Income | | $ 80,000 |

The company's balance sheets at the beginning and end of the year were as follows:

| | January 1 | | December 31 | |
|---|---|---|---|---|
| Cash | | $ 40,000 | | $ 50,000 |
| Accounts receivable | | 80,000 | | 100,000 |
| Merchandise inventory | | 60,000 | | 70,000 |
| Plant equipment: | | | | |
| Original cost | $200,000 | | $260,000 | |
| Less: Accumulated | | | | |
| depreciation | 70,000 | 130,000 | 90,000 | 170,000 |
| Total Assets | | $310,000 | | $390,000 |
| | | | | |
| Accounts payable | | $ 50,000 | | $ 30,000 |
| Capital stock | | 110,000 | | 140,000 |
| Retained earnings | | 150,000 | | 220,000 |
| Total Liabilities and | | | | |
| Owners' Equity | | $310,000 | | $390,000 |

All accounts payable arose out of the purchase of merchandise or the purchase of other goods and services for immediate consumption. All accounts receivable arose out of sales of merchandise to customers.

a) How much cash was received from customers during the year?
b) What was the total cost of goods purchased during the year?
c) How much cash was paid to suppliers, employees, and others during the year for goods or current services?
d) How much cash was provided by the company's operations during the year?
e) What were the company's other sources and uses of cash during the year?

**18.** A retailer had the following transactions during the month of December:

(1) Bought merchandise on account for $100,000 and paid merchandise suppliers $80,000 on account.

(2) Sold merchandise on account for $120,000 and collected $105,000 on account from its customers. The cost of the merchandise sold was $70,000.

(3) Had miscellaneous operating expenses of $30,000. Of this, $28,000 was paid in cash; the remaining $2,000 was purchased on account.

(4) Declared and paid cash dividends of $10,000.

(5) Borrowed $8,000 from a bank.

(6) Paid $3,000 for office equipment that had been bought and installed during the preceding month. Depreciation on office equipment amounted to $1,000 a month.

*a)* Prepare an income statement for the month.

*b)* Prepare a statement of cash flows for the month.

**19.** The Poirot Manufacturing Company has a very simple bookkeeping system, using only the following 13 accounts:

| | |
|---|---|
| Cash | Accounts payable |
| Accounts receivable | Wages and salaries payable |
| Materials and supplies inventory | Sales |
| Work in process | Cost of goods sold |
| Finished goods inventory | Selling and administrative |
| Machinery and equipment |    expense |
| Depreciation to date – | Dividends declared |
|    Machinery and equipment | |

The company completed the following transactions during the month of September:

(1) Materials and supplies purchased on account and received during September, $34,000.

(2) Materials and supplies issued to factory production departments, $36,000.

(3) Wage and salary costs, paid in cash:

Factory labor ................................. $20,000
Selling and administrative salaries ............    4,000

(4) Depreciation for September:

Factory machinery .............................. $500
Administrative office equipment.................    300

(5) Sundry manufacturing costs, paid in cash, $8,000.

(6) Miscellaneous selling and administrative expenses incurred and paid in cash, $3,800.

(7) Products completed and transferred to finished goods inventories, $62,000.

(8) Sales on account, $78,000.

(9) The balance in the Finished Goods Inventory account was $1,000 greater on September 30 than on September 1, after all appropriate entries for September were recorded.

(10) Cash dividends declared and paid, $20,000.

a) Prepare journal entries to record each of the foregoing items, using only the thirteen accounts listed above. (Note: some of these accounts had opening balances on September 1, but since these do not enter into the solution of the problem they have been omitted.)

b) Compute net income for the month of September.

**20.** As vice president in charge of operations at the Velting Corporation, you have studied the sales forecast for the coming year that your company's economists have prepared. After correcting some inconsistencies in their projections, you have asked the controller to estimate the cost of goods sold for the coming year. He is to make his computations on the basis of the following information:

(1) Your company manufactures and sells only one product, and you expect that 200,000 units of this product will be sold during the coming year.

(2) Each unit of the product requires approximately 4 pounds of material A and 0.1 pounds of material B.

(3) The company has no inventory of material A, which is highly perishable and is delivered to the factory daily in quantities sufficient for the day's production. Purchase prices during the coming year are expected to average 60 cents a pound.

(4) The company will have 25,000 pounds of material B on hand at the beginning of the year and will buy no more until this stock has been exhausted. The material now in stock was purchased at a cost of $4 a pound. The market price of material B is now $4.50 a pound and is expected to hold constant at that level throughout the coming year.

(5) It is estimated that two hours of labor at $5 an hour will be required to produce each finished unit.

(6) Annual depreciation on factory buildings and equipment will be $136,000.

(7) Other factory costs are expected to total $40,000 plus an additional $2,000 for every 10,000 units finished.

(8) Production is of such a nature that there will be no opening or closing inventories of goods in process.

(9) The company will have 20,000 units of finished products in inventory at the beginning of the year, at a cost of $13 each.

(10) A partially completed inventory study by a professional team of operations research persons leads you to feel that the final in-

ventory at the close of the year should consist of 40,000 finished units.

You know that the controller has had no formal training in accounting and you have some reservations about his ability. You have decided, therefore, to prepare your own estimate of the cost of goods sold as a check against his figures. So that he will be able to follow your calculations easily, you have decided to perform them in the sequence listed below. Show all of the steps in your calculations in a logical format, labeling each figure clearly.

a)  Compute the number of finished units to be produced next year.
b)  Compute the estimated cost of the raw materials to be used for the desired production.
c)  Compute the estimated cost of goods to be manufactured next year.
d)  Compute the estimated cost of goods to be sold next year. (Due to a design change, the units produced during the year will be slightly different from those in stock at the beginning of the year. For this reason, the units in the opening inventory will be sold before any units produced during the coming year are placed on sale.)
e)  Compute the estimated cost of all materials and finished goods that will remain in inventory at the end of the coming year.

21.  On February 1, the Paltry Corporation's accounts showed the following balances (all accounts not shown had zero balances):

| | | |
|---|---:|---:|
| Cash | 9,200 | |
| Accounts receivable | 13,000 | |
| Raw materials | 3,500 | |
| Work in process | 5,000 | |
| Finished goods | 6,200 | |
| Prepaid insurance | 1,000 | |
| Plant and equipment | 62,000 | |
| Allowance for depreciation | | 22,000 |
| Accounts payable | | 13,900 |
| Capital stock | | 34,000 |
| Retained earnings | | 30,000 |

The following transactions took place during February:

(1)  Purchased raw materials on account, $42,000.
(2)  Issued raw materials to factory for use on month's production, $38,500.
(3)  Sold merchandise: for cash, $10,000; on credit, $90,000.
(4)  Collected $93,000 on accounts receivable.
(5)  Paid rent on office equipment for February, March, and April, $900.
(6)  Purchased factory equipment on account, $9,000.
(7)  Purchased office furniture on account, $1,000.
(8)  Paid employees' wages: factory, $20,000; office and sales force, $8,000.
(9)  Paid suppliers on account, $35,000.

(10)   Recognized depreciation for February: factory, $300; office, $100.

(11)   Paid salesmen and executives: for travel and entertainment expenses during month, $2,000; as advances against March expenses, $1,050.

(12)   Paid bills for miscellaneous factory costs, $25,200; miscellaneous office and sales costs, $15,000.

(13)   Sold a piece of factory equipment for $500 cash; its original cost was $3,000 and it had accumulated depreciation of $2,100 at the date of sale.

(14)   Noted expiration of insurance premiums: on office, $50; on factory, $250.

(15)   Finished and transferred to warehouse goods costing $68,000.

(16)   Declared cash dividend to shareholders, $2,000, payable on March 15.

(17)   Counted inventories on February 28; cost of finished goods on hand was $5,800.

a)   Prepare journal entries to record all of the above information.

b)   Enter the February 1 account balances in T-accounts and post the journal entries to these accounts (note: you may find it helpful to post each entry as soon as you journalize it).

c)   Prepare an income statement for February and a balance sheet as of February 28.

**22.** On May 1, the Deppe Company's accounts had the following balances (all accounts not listed had zero balances):

| | | |
|---|---:|---:|
| Cash ...................................... | 25,600 | |
| Accounts receivable ....................... | 11,800 | |
| Materials and supplies .................... | 7,200 | |
| Work in process .......................... | 6,500 | |
| Finished goods ........................... | 12,900 | |
| Prepaid insurance......................... | 1,200 | |
| Plant and equipment....................... | 156,000 | |
| Accumulated depreciation.................. | | 76,000 |
| Accounts payable ......................... | | 15,400 |
| Capital stock ............................. | | 80,000 |
| Retained earnings......................... | | 49,800 |

The following transactions took place during May:

(1)   Materials and supplies purchased on account, $30,300.

(2)   Wages and salaries earned by employees during month: factory labor, $29,700; factory supervision, $4,900; sales and office salaries, $23,400. (Note: Cash payments occasioned by employee payrolls are described in item [9] below.)

(3)   Materials put into production, $18,800.

(4)   Equipment purchased on contract, $10,000, payments to be made in four quarterly installments of $2,500 each.

(5)   Goods sold on account for $110,000.

(6) Supplies used: factory, $3,200; office, $2,700.

(7) Collections from customers, $106,000.

(8) Sale of capital stock for cash, $10,000.

(9) Payments made:

To materials suppliers, on account, $32,500.

To equipment manufacturer, on contract (see [4] above), $2,500.

To employees, $57,740.

Office rental for May, $2,300.

Repairs of factory equipment, $600.

Electricity and other utilities for May: factory, $3,600; office, $500.

Other costs for May: factory, $8,660; office, $13,100.

(10) Equipment sold, $300 cash (original cost, $5,000; book value, $800).

(11) Dividends declared, $3,000, to be paid on June 15.

(12) Insurance premiums expired: factory, $200; office, $100.

(13) Depreciation: factory, $4,000; office, $800.

(14) Bills received during May but unpaid as of May 31:

For May newspaper advertising, $300.

For taxes on factory, May 1 through October 31, $1,200.

(15) Cost of goods finished, $64,200.

(16) Finished goods on hand, May 31, $11,800.

a) Prepare journal entries to record all of the above information in accrual basis accounts. You will need to open accounts in addition to those listed at the beginning of this problem.

b) Set up T-accounts, enter the May 1 account balances, and post your journal entries to these accounts.

c) Prepare an income statement for May and a balance sheet as of May 31. Ignore any income taxes that might be levied on the Deppe Company's income for the month.

**23.** John Q. Wixon, sole owner and chief executive of the Wixon Widget Company, operating a very simple business. He made widgets at a cost of $.80 each and sold them for $1.00. He had no other expenses, and the Wixon Widget Company's income therefore amounted to $.20 for each widget that he sold.

All production costs were paid in cash; suppliers in this industry were unwilling to provide credit to their customers. Mr. Wixon tried to keep his inventory at the end of each month equal to the number of units sold during that month. Inventory turnover, therefore, was 12 times a year when sales were constant; this was better than any of Mr. Wixon's competitors had been able to achieve.

All sales were made on 30-day credit—that is, customers were required to pay cash one month after receiving their widgets. These terms were strictly enforced, even though Mr. Wixon's competitors granted more liberal terms.

The Wixon Widget Company had no liabilities. It had the following assets at the beginning of last year:

Cash ................................ $1,075
Accounts receivable .................. 1,000
Inventory ........................... 800

During January, Mr. Wixon produced 1,000 widgets, sold 1,000 widgets, and collected $1,000 in cash from his customers. The company's net income was $200 and its end-of-month assets were:

Cash ................................ $1,275
Accounts receivable .................. 1,000
Inventory ........................... 800

In February, sales increased to 1,500 widgets (500 widgets more than in January). The company produced 2,000 widgets during the month and collected $1,000 from customers. Net income was $300.

Mr. Wixon sold 2,000 widgets in March, produced 2,500 and collected $1,500. The company's net income jumped to $400.

Sales continued to increase in April and seemed likely to continue to increase by 500 units a month indefinitely. In fact, the sales picture looked so good that Mr. Wixon went on vacation on April 20. On May 1 he received a telegram from home: "Return immediately. We're overdrawn at the bank." Returning to the office, he found that production, sales, and collections had gone according to plan but that the company's bank account was overdrawn by $225. Extremely puzzled, he rushed to the bank, asking for a loan and an explanation of what had gone wrong.

a)  Prepare a table showing revenues, expenses, and net income for each month, January through December.
b)  Prepare a table showing cash receipts, cash disbursements, and net cash flow for each month.
c)  Prepare a list of the firm's assets as of the end of each month. (The firm had no liabilities at the beginning of the year. If your figures indicate that cash disbursements will reduce the cash balance to less than zero, show the deficiency as a negative amount on the "Cash" line rather than as a liability. Ignore interest costs on any such amounts.)
d)  Using the figures in the tables above, prepare an answer to Mr. Wixon's question. What were the factors that determined the size of the monthly cash flows? What actions could Mr. Wixon take to solve the problem that had arisen? (Suggestion: examine the effects on cash flows of actions that might be taken to influence each of the factors that you have identified as a determinant of cash flow.)

# 5

# THE TIMING OF REVENUE
# AND EXPENSE RECOGNITION

ACCRUAL ACCOUNTING REQUIRES that the costs of obtaining revenues be shown as expenses of the period in which the revenues
are recognized. The timing of revenue recognition therefore can
be a highly important determinant of reported net income. The
purpose of this chapter is to examine the implications of the
criteria by which the accountant decides when to recognize
revenue.

## CRITERIA FOR REVENUE RECOGNITION

In all of the illustrations used in the preceding chapters, revenues were recognized when customers were billed for the company's products or services. Billing thereby became the signal for
recognizing costs as expenses.

This is not the only possible signal for revenue-expense recognition, however. In fact, at least five distinct events can be found
in the operating cycle, any one of which might be taken as the
signal that revenues have been earned:

1. Acquisition of resources.
2. Receipt of customer orders.
3. Production.
4. Delivery of goods or performance of services.
5. Collection of cash.

An economist might even argue that *each* of the productive activities of the firm adds value in some measure to the goods or merchandise purchased. On these grounds, a portion of the ultimate sale price ought to be recognized as revenue as each activity is performed. The difficulty is that the ultimate sale price is the joint product of all activities and it is impossible to say with certainty how much is attributable to any one activity. *For this reason, the accountant selects one event as the signal for revenue recognition and ignores the others. His problem is to decide which one to select.*

For public reporting, revenues are generally recognized at the first point in the operating cycle at which *all* of the following conditions are satisfied:

1. The principal revenue-producing service has been performed.
2. Any costs that are necessary to create the revenue but have not yet been incurred are either negligible or can be predicted with a reasonable degree of accuracy.
3. The amount ultimately collectible in cash or its equivalent can be estimated with a reasonable degree of accuracy.

The argument for the second and third of these criteria is that recognition of revenue and expense before these conditions are met would introduce too great an element of subjectivity into the income statement.[1]

In applying these criteria to specific situations, the accountant most often concludes that revenues should be recognized at the time of delivery of goods or performance of services. For this reason, we shall examine this possibility first, and then turn to a brief examination of the four alternatives listed above.

## REVENUE RECOGNITION AT TIME OF DELIVERY

Although cash is often received before the performance of service or the shipment of goods, the more common case is the *credit sale* in which shipment or service precedes collection. In most such cases, it is deemed proper to recognize revenue at the time the service is performed or the goods are delivered.[2]

---

[1] It can be argued that the accountant's usual standard of verifiability is too rigid and that less precise evidence should be accepted. How far the standard could be relaxed without impairing the credibility of the financial statements is not clear.

[2] This is often referred to as recognition *at the time of sale,* but this begs the question because a sale may be said to take place at any one of several points in the cycle. The salesman, for example, believes that he has made a sale when he books an order from a customer. For reasons cited in the next section, the accountant chooses not to recognize the sale when the order is received.

## Reasons for Prevalence of Delivery Basis

The justification of the delivery basis is simple. In most cases, it is the first point in the cycle at which all three criteria are met. The seller's economic role has been performed for the most part when the goods are delivered or the services provided. Few if any costs remain to be incurred in the future, and those that remain can be predicted accurately. While the amount that eventually will be collected from customers is *unknown*, it is usually highly *predictable*. Defaults (*credit losses*), customer discounts, and other future leakages from the stated price of the goods delivered are generally small and predictable.

To illustrate how this works and the problems that it creates, let us see how the delivery basis might be applied to Marsden-Brown, Inc., an engineering firm specializing in the installation of lighting systems. Marsden-Brown agreed on October 18, 19x0, to design and install a new lighting system in the Granco Department Store. The contract price was $200,000, and the following events took place subsequent to the signing of the contract:

*19x0*
1. Granco paid Marsden-Brown a cash advance of $40,000 on October 22.
2. Marsden-Brown began work on the contract and spent $50,000, all paid in cash, for materials, labor, and other services used on the contract.

*19x1*
3. Marsden-Brown spent an additional $110,000 on the contract; of this, $85,000 was paid in cash and $25,000 was to be paid to suppliers in 19x2.
4. The installation was completed on August 13, and Granco accepted delivery.
5. Granco paid Marsden-Brown $115,000 in cash. The remaining $45,000 of the contract price was to be paid in 19x2 after the system had been tested extensively in practice and necessary modifications had been made by Marsden-Brown.

*19x2*
6. Marsden-Brown paid $9,500 in cash to make necessary modifications in the Granco system.
7. Granco paid Marsden-Brown the final $45,000 portion of the contract price and released Marsden-Brown from all further obligations.

8. Marsden-Brown paid the $25,000 in accounts payable that had been created in 19x1.

The receipts and disbursements over the three-year period 19x0 to 19x2 resulted in a total net income of $30,500, as shown in the right-hand column of Exhibit 5–1.

Exhibit 5–1

Marsden-Brown, Inc.

RECEIPTS AND DISBURSEMENTS ON GRANCO CONTRACT

|  | 19x0 | 19x1 | 19x2 | Total |
|---|---|---|---|---|
| Receipts . . . . . . . . . . . . . . . | $40,000 | $115,000 | $45,000 | $200,000 |
| Disbursements. . . . . . . . . . | 50,000 | 85,000 | 34,500 | 169,500 |
| Net receipts . . . . . . . . . . | −$10,000 | +$ 30,000 | +$10,500 | +$ 30,500 |

Unfortunately, the last of this information did not become available until 19x2. This does not mean that 19x2 was the best year to recognize the income from this contract, however. Applying the three criteria discussed earlier points clearly to 19x1 as the year for revenue recognition. First, almost all of the work to be done under the terms of the contract had been done by 19x1. Second, a total of $155,000 had been received and collection of the remaining $45,000 was practically certain. Third, all of the costs of the contract were known in 19x1 except for the system modification costs. These were small and could be estimated with a margin of error that was very small in relation to the total costs of the contract.

The same tests indicate that 19x0 was too early for income recognition. The total contract price was known with a high degree of certainty at that time, but little work had been done and the costs of completing the contract were quite uncertain.

For these reasons the company decided to recognize the revenue, expense, and income on the Granco contract in 19x1. To do this, it had to include in the expenses for that year an estimate of the outlays that would have to be made for system modifications in 19x2. The estimate in this case was $10,000, and the 19x1 income statement included the following:

| | | |
|---|---|---|
| Revenue . . . . . . . . . . . . . . . . . . . . . . . . . . . . . . . | | $200,000 |
| Expenses: | | |
| Design and installation. . . . . . . . . . . . . . . . . . | $160,000 | |
| System modifications. . . . . . . . . . . . . . . . . . . | 10,000 | |
| Total expenses . . . . . . . . . . . . . . . . . . . . . | | 170,000 |
| Profit Margin. . . . . . . . . . . . . . . . . . . . . . . . . . . | | $ 30,000 |

The use of estimates of this kind introduces errors into the income measurement process in that the actual outlays undoubtedly will be either larger or smaller than the amounts estimated. When these errors are small, however, the accountant accepts them rather than exclude income entirely from the current income statement. In this case, it would have been a far more serious error to postpone income recognition to 19x2. This contract was one of the company's accomplishments in 19x1, and its performance record for that year should show the results of this work. By recognizing income in 19x1, the accountant limited the error in the 19x1 income statement to only $500. The error from not including it would have been $30,500, a much larger figure.

### Transactions Analysis

Having adopted the delivery basis for income recognition in this case, the accountant could analyze the individual transactions that took place. First, Granco's initial $40,000 payment increased Marsden-Brown's cash assets and its liabilities by that amount:

(1)

| | | |
|---|---|---|
| Cash | 40,000 | |
| Liability for Advance Payments | | 40,000 |

Second, Marsden-Brown's expenditure of $50,000 on this contract in 19x0 decreased the cash balance but created another asset, very much like factory work in process:

(2)

| | | |
|---|---|---|
| Contracts in Progress | 50,000 | |
| Cash | | 50,000 |

Expenditures in 19x1 increased the size of this contract "inventory," while decreasing the cash balance and increasing the company's liabilities for later payments to suppliers:

(3)

| | | |
|---|---|---|
| Contracts in Progress | 110,000 | |
| Cash | | 85,000 |
| Accounts Payable | | 25,000 |

Upon completion of the installation, Marsden-Brown recognized the full contract price as revenue. This eliminated the liability that was created when the advance payment was received, and created a receivable for the remaining $160,000. The entry was:

(4)

| | | |
|---|---|---|
| Accounts Receivable | 160,000 | |
| Liability for Advance Payments | 40,000 | |
| Sales Revenue | | 200,000 |

Recognition of the full contract price as revenue also required the accountant to remove the contract costs from the list of assets and recognize them as expenses:

(5)

| | | |
|---|---|---|
| Contract Expenses | 160,000 | |
| Contracts in Progress | | 160,000 |

The second payment from Granco then reduced the receivable and increased the amount of cash on hand by $115,000:

(6)

| | | |
|---|---|---|
| Cash | 115,000 | |
| Accounts Receivable | | 115,000 |

Next, in order not to overstate reported income for 19x1, the expense account was also charged with the estimated costs to be incurred on the contract in 19x2:

(7)

| | | |
|---|---|---|
| Contract Expenses | 10,000 | |
| Liability for Contract Guarantee | | 10,000 |

The final entry in this series was made in 19x2, when $9,500 was spent on modifying the system and Marsden-Brown was relieved of all further responsibility for its performance. Fulfilment of the company's contract obligations at this time eliminated its liability to the customer. The $500 difference between the liability that had been recognized earlier and the actual cost of system modification was treated as a gain, to be reported as income in 19x2. The entry was:

(8)

| | | |
|---|---|---|
| Liability for Contract Guarantee | 10,000 | |
| Cash | | 9,500 |
| Gains and Losses on System Modifications | | 500 |

If the company's estimates are unbiased, the gains and losses on various system modification projects should just about cancel each other in time.


### Customer Defaults

A more common estimation problem arises whenever revenues are recognized before customers pay their accounts in full. Since the dollar amount that customers promise to pay generally exceeds the dollar amount that eventually will be received, revenue, income, and assets will be overstated unless some adjustment is made.

One adjustment method is to estimate ultimate defaults by customers by applying a predetermined default percentage to the volume of credit sales. At the time of delivery, the seller cannot know which *specific* customers will not meet their obligations in full; he can only predict the *aggregate amount* of defaults by these customers. If experience indicates that a percentage *r* of all credit sales S will produce accounts that will ultimately prove uncollectible (sometimes called *bad debts*), the total amount of customer defaults will be *r*S and net revenues will be (1 − *r*) S.

To illustrate, let us assume credit sales of $1 million, collections of $800,000, and an anticipated default ratio of 1 percent. The sales transactions would be recorded as follows:

Accounts Receivable...................... 1,000,000
    Sales Revenue.........................      1,000,000

The collections would affect the asset accounts only, as follows:

Cash ........................................ 800,000
    Accounts Receivable .....................      800,000

Estimated defaults should be deducted from gross revenues to yield a *net* revenue figure that represents the amount of cash that the company will receive as a direct result of the period's sales.[3] On sales of $1 million, a 1 percent default estimate could be shown in the revenue section of the income statement as follows:

Gross Sales ......................................... $1,000,000
    Less: Estimated defaults by customers .............      10,000
Net Sales ........................................... $  990,000

A similar amount would have to be deducted from accounts receivable to avoid overstating the value of this asset on the balance sheet.

Both of these results could be achieved by the following entry:

Customer Defaults.............................. 10,000
    Allowance for Uncollectible Accounts........      10,000

---

[3] When collection is to be deferred for a substantial period, net revenues should be stated at the *present value* of the amounts the company expects to collect. AICPA, *APB Accounting Principles: Current Text* (New York: Commerce Clearing House, 1972), Sec. 4111.11. The calculation of present value is explained in Chapter 10 below.

Here we meet two new accounts which need explanation. The balance in the Customer Defaults account is a negative component of the owners' equity. It is not an expense, because expenses are all costs of resources that have been consumed in the creation of revenues. Although it is often listed among the expenses, it should be shown as a deduction from gross revenues, as in the illustration above.

The Allowance for Uncollectible Accounts, on the other hand, is our second example of a deduction-from-asset contra account. The purpose of the credit to this account is to recognize the fact that the amounts entered in the Accounts Receivable account overstate the value of that asset. The credit cannot be made directly to Accounts Receivable, however, because the company does not know which specific accounts will be uncollectible.

The Allowance for Uncollectible Accounts provides a means of reducing the reported value of the receivables without crediting Accounts Receivable directly. The allowance account normally has a credit balance, which is shown on the balance sheet as a deduction from gross receivables. A credit to this account, as in the entry above, increases the account balance, thereby reducing the amount at which the receivables are reported on the balance sheet. If the calculation has been made correctly this should reduce the book value of the receivables to the amount management expects to collect in the future.

### Write-off of Uncollectible Accounts

When management decides that a particular receivable is in fact uncollectible, it should be removed from the file of current receivables. In addition, since the amounts in the Allowance for Uncollectible Accounts have been put there specifically because some receivables will eventually prove uncollectible, the balance in this account should be reduced whenever the receivables themselves are written off.

In our example, the entry to record the write-off of a $1,000 account would be as follows:

Allowance for Uncollectible Accounts . . . . . . . . . . . . . . 1,000
    Accounts Receivable . . . . . . . . . . . . . . . . . . . . . . . . . .          1,000

The credit to Accounts Receivable reduces the balance in this account, and the debit to the allowance reduces its balance by the same amount. The entry does not record a reduction in the asset, however, because the value of the receivables as a whole has not fallen. All that the entry has done is to identify a *specific* account for which a *general* allowance was made when revenues were recorded and the probable defaults were recognized.

### Aging the Accounts

Percentage estimates of the kind described above are useful in planning, but they are subject to error and should be checked periodically. Some companies even keep the percentage estimates out of the formal accounts altogether, preferring to record estimates of customer defaults at the end of the year.

The technique that is used for this purpose is known as *aging the accounts*. This consists of classifying the individual customer balances by age groups and evaluating each of these in the light of the proposition that the older the claim, the less likely it is to be collected. Loss experience rates are applied to the amounts in each age category to arrive at an estimate of the total dollar amount of uncollectible claims. The required end-of-period entry is whatever amount is necessary to bring the balance in the contra account up to or down to the indicated level.

For example, suppose that the allowance account in our illustration showed the following:

Allowance for Uncollectible Accounts

| Write-offs | 1,000 | Bal. 1/1 | 14,000 |
| | | Additions | 10,000 |
| | | Bal. 12/31 23,000 | |

The open accounts receivable were then classified by age. Matching the amount in each age group with estimates of uncollectibility, derived from the company's past experience, produced the following table:

| (1) | (2) | (3) | (4) |
|---|---|---|---|
| Age | Amount | Estimated Percentage Uncollectible | Estimated Amount Uncollectible (2) × (3) |
| 0–30 days | $400,000 | 0.1 | $    400 |
| 31–60 days | 80,000 | 2.0 | 1,600 |
| 61–90 days | 60,000 | 5.0 | 3,000 |
| 91 days and older | 40,000 | 40.0 | 16,000 |
| Total | $580,000 | | $21,000 |

This showed that the balance in the Allowance for Uncollectible Accounts account should have been $21,000, just $2,000 less than the actual account balance. This meant that the company's experience with customer defaults in this year was better than it had expected. The entry to correct this error is shown here as:

Allowance for Uncollectible Accounts.............. 2,000
 Customer Defaults............................     2,000

The debit brought the balance in the allowance account down to $21,000; the credit to Customer Defaults brought its balance down to $8,000, representing the net amount of customer defaults applicable to the current period's revenues.

### Collection Costs

In most cases, the only expenditures to be made after the goods are delivered are the costs of collecting the amounts due. Although these can be substantial, the customary practice is to recognize them as expenses when the expenditures are made rather than when revenues are recognized.

This violation of the matching principle ordinarily can be overlooked because the amounts are small in relation to gross revenue and net income. If the amounts are felt to be material, however, they should be treated in exactly the same way as estimated customer defaults.

### Managerial Implications of Customer Defaults

While customer defaults in most businesses are inevitable, management has a great deal to say about how large they will be. Its main instrument for this purpose is credit policy – that is, the criteria on which decisions to extend credit are based. Credit policy is to some extent dictated by the customary practice in individual industries or markets, but every seller has some leeway in deciding how much credit risk he will bear.

A liberal credit policy usually leads to larger sales volumes but greater collection costs and more customer defaults. A tight credit policy, implemented by careful investigation of the creditworthiness of prospective customers and refusal to deal with any but the best credit risks, can reduce customer defaults and collection costs, but at the cost of lower sales volume and increased costs of credit investigation. Management must decide how far to go in trading increased customer defaults for greater sales, and different companies in the same line of business will find different answers to this question.

The key accounting problem in connection with this managerial interest in credit policy is not the method of recognizing customer defaults in the financial accounts but rather the means employed for estimating their amount. Although treatment of this subject is beyond the scope of an introductory text, the techniques of statistical inference can be used to get more effective estimates of default rates on receivables in various age brackets directly from the firm's past accounting data.[4] The next step is to develop from these data estimates of the changes in default rates consequent on changes in credit policy, which is the question relevant to the business decision that must be made.

## REVENUE RECOGNITION AT TIME OF SALES ORDERS

Another possible point for revenue recognition is the point at which the sales order is received. The order is a highly significant event in the operating cycle. Most companies which experience significant lags between the date of the order and the date of the shipment will record orders received so that the amount of orders on hand for future delivery (the backlog) can be reported periodically to management. In these circumstances the performance of the sales force probably should be judged more on the basis of orders received than on goods shipped.

Order and backlog information is sometimes also reported to creditors and stockholders to guide them in their appraisals of the company's future prospects, but revenues and receivables are never recognized in externally published reports on the basis of orders received during the period. The reason is simply that the criteria for revenue recognition are not met at the time the order is received—the goods have not yet been produced, the costs of producing them are not adequately predictable, or order cancellations are frequent and variable.

## REVENUE RECOGNITION AT TIME OF PRODUCTION

An alternative to the delivery basis that is sometimes feasible is to recognize revenue at the time goods are produced. The pro-

---

[4] See R. M. Cyert, H. J. Davidson, and G. L. Thompson, "Estimation of the Allowance for Doubtful Accounts by Markov Chains," *Management Science*, April, 1962, pp. 287–303; and R. M. Trueblood and R. M. Cyert, *Sampling Techniques in Accounting* (Englewood Cliffs, N.J.: Prentice-Hall, Inc., 1957).

duction basis will provide a more useful measure of income than the delivery basis whenever production precedes delivery by a substantial or widely varying time interval and production is the last major value-creating activity.

For example, consider a mining company that produces ore and sells it under a long-term contract at $12 a ton. During the first three quarters of 19x1 it produced 600,000 tons at a total cost of $6,300,000. Using the production basis, it recognized sales revenue of $7,200,000 (600,000 tons × $12) and net income of $900,000.

Another 180,000 tons of ore were produced during the final quarter of the year, at a total cost of $1,800,000. Although a transportation strike prevented the delivery of this ore until 19x2, the production basis required the company to recognize revenue of $2,160,000 (180,000 tons × $12) and net income of $360,000 in 19x1. In contrast, recognition of the sale at the time of delivery would have reduced 19x1 income by $360,000 and raised 19x2 income by the same amount.

This situation clearly calls for the production basis. The nature of the firm's business is such that delivery is not the critical event. With a contract under which the customer takes all of the firm's production at an agreed-upon price, and with all costs known when production is completed, production rather than delivery is the appropriate basis for revenue and expense recognition.

## Meeting the Recognition Criteria

Accountants are generally unwilling to recognize revenues at the time of production because two key conditions have not been met by then: (a) not all of the significant value-adding services have been performed; and (b) the amount of cash ultimately collectible is too uncertain at that point.

If these objections can be overcome, then no fundamental barrier arises to recognizing revenue on the principle that income arises through changing the form, time, or place of an asset rather than through its exchange. In fact, the production basis is used when no significant amount of services is required subsequent to production, when the amount of ultimate collection is reasonably certain, and when the timing of deliveries is more volatile than the timing of production. Application of this method is most common in shipbuilding and other industries in which the production cycle is very long and production is initiated only on receipt of a firm order at a specific price. It is also used by the producers of certain raw materials when the sales price is known at the time of production as in the previous illustration.

### Percentage-of-Completion Accounting

The most widely used version of the production basis is the *percentage-of-completion* method of revenue recognition. For example, Marsden-Brown, Inc., decided to adopt the production basis for recognizing revenues from its design and installation contracts. In mid-19x4 the firm obtained a contract to install the lighting for the Arkwright County Sports Arena, a job that was to take six months. The contract price was $200,000, and the estimated total cost was $160,000. Marsden-Brown was to bill the customer at the end of each quarter for 80 percent of the sales value of the work done to date.

Work began on October 18, 19x4, and the actual costs charged to the job prior to December 31, 19x4 amounted to $80,000. Progress on the contract was reviewed at the end of the year, and the job was found to be 45 percent completed. Production basis accounting therefore required recognition of revenue of $90,000 for 19x4 (45 percent of the $200,000 contract price), and the customer was billed for *progress payments* of $72,000 (80 percent of $90,000).

In practice, the account structure to record this information would be relatively complex. In essence, however, Marsden-Brown's income statement showed a gross margin of $10,000:

| | |
|---|---:|
| Contract Revenue ....................................... | $90,000 |
| Less: Cost of Work Performed ......................... | 80,000 |
| Gross Margin on Contract Work Performed .............. | $10,000 |

The balance sheet showed:

| | | |
|---|---:|---:|
| Accounts receivable........................... | | $72,000 |
| Inventory (market value of contract work | | |
| performed to date) ........................ | $90,000 | |
| Less: Progress billings ...................... | 72,000 | |
| Inventory (net).......................... | | 18,000 |

The only novel element here is the method used to measure the inventory. By subtracting the amounts already billed from the total value of the progress achieved on the contract to date,

Marsden-Brown treated the inventory as a kind of deferred receivable, the portion of the total that although earned was not yet billable. The amount billed during 19x4 had no effect on the amount of revenue recognized during the period. When the job was completed in 19x5, the revenue for that year was $110,000 — that is, the full contract price ($200,000) minus the $90,000 recognized in 19x4.

This approach has substantial managerial significance. It shows management at an early date that earnings on this contract are accruing at a rate of only $12\frac{1}{2}$ percent of cost instead of the anticipated 25 percent. If management is given this information at this early date, the company may be able to take action that will prevent excessive costs on the remainder of the job.

The same information presumably would be significant to the outside investor, but the progress percentage and amount of future collections for the work done may not be predictable with enough accuracy to permit inclusion of this information in the company's published financial statements. It can and should be reported to management, however.

### Estimating the Percentage of Completion

Estimating the percentage of completion is not easy. Most authorities agree that it should be based on the amount of progress achieved rather than the amount of cost actually incurred, but how to measure progress is not at all clear. For example, should the purchase of materials to be used on the job be regarded as progress?

Probably the best solution is to decide in advance how much of the contract price is to be assigned to each phase of the contract, with most if not all of the weight assigned to labor and other services that are intended to add value to purchased materials. If the available evidence points to the probability of substantial cost overruns on remaining portions of the contract, however, the profit margin on the contract as a whole should be reestimated and a new allocation prepared.

## REVENUE RECOGNITION AT TIME OF COLLECTION

One other basis for revenue recognition is sometimes used: the time of collection. It is appropriate only if the amount of cash to be collected or the amount of cost yet to be incurred is not readily predictable at the time of production or delivery.

The collection basis has its widest practical application in recording revenues and expenses from installment sales. Land development companies are now the most notable users of the so-called *installment method* of revenue and expense recognition because collections and costs are typically too difficult to predict at the time of sale. The method is not applicable to most installment sales of merchandise, however, because customer defaults ordinarily can be predicted quite accurately for this kind of installment contract.[5]

Because the method is rarely used and because the procedures used are both highly variable among firms and quite complicated, no attempt will be made here to illustrate it in detail. Essentially, it requires the measurement of receivables at cost. If selling costs have been incurred, they should be capitalized as part of the cost of the receivables. Revenues are measured by the amounts of cash collected from customers; the costs of the goods sold, including selling costs, are transferred from the receivables account to expense accounts at that time. Collection costs are expensed as they are incurred.

Accounting practice usually departs slightly from this description. Selling costs are usually expensed as they are incurred and not incorporated in the asset, because they are too difficult to identify clearly with specific sales transactions. There is no logical reason, however, why sales commissions or other readily identifiable costs should not be deferred until the company recognizes the revenues they have produced.

## SUMMARY

In most companies, revenues are *recognized* at the time of delivery of goods or at the time of performance of an intangible service for an outside customer or client. The justification for this rule is that this is the first point in the operating cycle at which the revenue is both *earned* and *quantifiable* with a sufficient degree of accuracy. Under certain circumstances, revenues should be recognized prior to delivery if they are both earned and quantifiable earlier, or deferred to a later point if quantification is subject to too great a degree of uncertainty at the time of delivery.

The amount shown as revenue in any period should be the value of products or services at the time revenues are recognized. If customer defaults are anticipated, an estimate of their amount must be deducted from gross revenues in computing net income

---

[5] *APB Accounting Principles*, Sec. 4020.

and from the balance of outstanding customer accounts in computing the value of the receivables.

The timing of expense recognition in each case depends on the timing of revenue recognition. As revenues are recognized, all costs applicable to these revenues should be expensed. The expenses of any given period, in other words, should include both the costs of resources used in the past and costs to be incurred in the future, to the extent that these relate to the revenues of the current period. Until the point of revenue recognition, the inventory or account receivable should be measured at cost.

## QUESTIONS AND PROBLEMS

1. What income measurement problems are raised by revenue recognition at the time of delivery of goods to customers, and what solutions has the accountant devised to deal with these problems?

2. Corporations which sell products which carry guarantees against defective parts and so forth are now required for tax purposes to report the entire sale price of the products as revenue of the period in which the products are sold. What is wrong with this treatment as far as income measurement is concerned? Under what conditions would this treatment be satisfactory?

3. Discuss the problem of defining the "time of sale."

4. Explain the nature and the purpose of the account Allowance for Uncollectible Accounts. When would this account be debited? Credited? What other accounts would be affected by each of these entries?

5. Would you expect to find an Allowance for Uncollectible Accounts on the balance sheet of a company that recognizes revenue at the time of collection? Would use of the collection basis eliminate the need to estimate any of the determinants of current net income?

6. Why is the delivery basis of revenue recognition used far more often than any other?

7. Individuals and small businesses often measure income on a cash basis. Revenues of a period are measured by the amount of cash received from customers during the period; expenses are measured, for the most part, by the amount of cash paid out during the period. How different is this from accrual-basis accounting with revenue recognition at the time of collection?

8. Does the recording of customer defaults on the basis of estimates reflect extreme conservatism?

9. The deductions from revenues for estimated customer defaults are measured by the amounts due from defaulting customers. The real loss to the seller, however, is the cost of the merchandise or services that have been provided to the customer, plus any related handling and selling costs. How can existing practice be justified in the face of this fact?

10. On what consistent basis can the following three practices in revenue recognition be justified? In other words, state the recognition principle that might be used to justify all three; also state the conditions that must be met if the practice is not to violate the principle.

a) Recognition at time of shipment by a wholesaler of grocery products.
b) Recognition at time of production by a highway contractor.
c) Recognition at time of collection by a retail installment seller of household appliances.

11. An economist would argue that income is created or earned by a wide variety of the firm's activities (e.g., production, sale, delivery, etc.), yet the accountant in the typical case selects one of these activities to signal the time at which all revenues are to be recognized.

a) Assuming that the economist's view is correct, under what circumstances would the accountant's method lead to an undistorted measure of periodic income?
b) What are the obstacles to a practical implementation of the economist's concept?

12. Merrill Productions, Inc., has just produced a new Broadway musical which has been acclaimed by theater critics and audiences alike. Orders for tickets for the next six months' performances are now being filled at the box office. The company prepares financial statements only once a year, after the close of its "fiscal year," which begins on July 1 and ends on the following June 30.

a) Prepare a journal entry to record the sale on October 28 of two $6.60 tickets for the evening performance on the following February 25.
b) Would you record this sale any differently if the accounting period were one month instead of one year? Explain.
c) If the procedure that you used in your answer to (a) is followed for all ticket sales, what kind of an entry would have to be made on June 30 each year? How would you obtain the data necessary to make this entry?

13. The balance sheet of a shipbuilding company shows among the current assets the following:

Contracts in process (Note A).................. $5,352,494.74

Note A to the balance sheet reads as follows:

Note A — The balance sheet amount for contracts in process is the accumulated cost plus or minus the portion (based on percentage of completion) of estimated final gross profit or estimated final loss, less billings (exclusive of collections against future costs); except, that unless (*a*) progress thereon has reached a point, generally, of not less than 50 percent of completion, and (*b*) experience is deemed sufficient to establish estimates as reasonably indicative of final results, no recognition has been taken of possible profit on work which, though substantially advanced, had not reached such a stage of completion. Accumulated billings on contracts, in respect of which no net profit has been taken up into income by reason of such policy, amounted to $21,605,440.00. All estimates of final contract profits or losses as of the close of any period are subject to revision as contracts progress toward completion. The amount of gross profit, or loss, taken up in any accounting period in respect of any contract is the amount accrued to the date of closing of such period less the total of amounts taken up in prior periods.

*a*)   Restate Note A in the form of a table, with a separate line for each item that entered into the derivation of the $5,352,494.74 figure. Place an X in the amount column for any item for which a numerical figure is not supplied in the note.

*b*)   Explain how, if at all, differences in the amounts billed to customers will affect the amount of net income reported for the year, all other things being equal.

*c*)   Why did this company differentiate between contracts that were less than 50 percent completed and those that had reached or exceeded that level? Do you agree that this was a valid distinction? State your reasons.

*d*)   Do financial statements prepared on this basis serve the investing public better than those prepared on other possible bases? Justify your position. As part of your answer, you should compare this company's basis of revenue recognition with some other basis that it might reasonably have used. Your comparison should indicate how the choice between these two bases would affect the company's reported net income.

*14. The Reilly Company recognizes revenues at the time of delivery. Customer defaults are expected to average 1 percent of gross sales. You have the following information for the month of June:

(1)   Opening balances:
       Accounts receivable, $950,000.
       Allowance for Uncollectible Accounts, $25,000.
(2)   Gross sales, $500,000.
(3)   Collections from customers, $510,000.
(4)   Write-offs of specific uncollectibles, $8,000.

---

*a*) Prepare journal entries to record your analyses of the effects of items (2), (3), and (4).

*b*) What was the net amount of the company's accounts receivable at the end of the month?

*c*) What amount should be shown on the monthly income statement for customer defaults?

*15. The following is a summary of the "aging" schedule for accounts receivable of Billerica Trading Company as of the end of the fiscal year:

| Total | 0–30 Days | 31–45 Days | 46–60 Days | Over 60 Days |
|-------|-----------|------------|------------|--------------|
| $348,788 | $283,615 | $52,110 | $12,552 | $511 |

According to past experience, bills over 60 days old were likely to be completely uncollectible, those in the third category about 4 percent uncollectible, those in the second category about 1 percent uncollectible, and those in the first category about 0.2 percent uncollectible.

At this time, the Allowance for Uncollectible Accounts has a balance of $1,816. What adjustment, if any, should be made?

16. The Flintop Company was organized and commenced business on January 1. Management decided to recognize revenue at the time of delivery. Although it had no prior experience as to the collectibility of its receivables, it decided to use 1½ percent of sales as its estimate of customer defaults until better information became available.

During the year the company delivered products to customers at an aggregate selling price of $200,000, and collected $150,596 on account from these customers.

*a*) Prepare journal entries to record your analyses of the effects of these transactions on the company's assets, liabilities, and owners' equity.

*b*) On December 1, the Elk Products Company, one of Flintop's customers, was declared bankrupt, with no assets to satisfy creditors' claims. At that time Elk Products owed Flintop $404. Prepare the necessary entry.

*c*) On December 31, an analysis of accounts receivable showed the following:

| Age of Accounts | Amount Receivable |
|-----------------|-------------------|
| 0–30 days........................... | $30,000 |
| 31–60 days........................... | 11,000 |
| 61–120 days......................... | 6,000 |
| More than 120 days................. | 2,000 |

The Company's auditors suggested that the following percentages be used to compute the amounts that would probably prove uncollectible: 0–30 days, ¼ of 1 percent; 31–60 days, 1 percent; 61–120 days, 10 percent; more than 120 days, 50 percent. Prepare a journal entry to implement this suggestion.

1%/4    17. A company prepares a set of interim financial statements each month and an annual financial report once a year. Its fiscal year ends on December 31. On November 30, after all entries for the month had been made, the following balances were found in the accounts relating to credit sales and accounts receivable:

|  | Debit | Credit |
|---|---|---|
| Accounts receivable | 500,000 |  |
| Allowance for uncollectible accounts |  | 15,000 |
| Bad Debt Estimated customer defaults | 12,800 |  |
| Recovery of overdue accounts |  | 300 |
| Revenues from credit sales |  | 2,560,000 |

Bookkeeping entries during the first 11 months of the year had been based on the assumption that customer defaults would average 0.5 percent of credit sales.

During December, credit sales totaled $250,000, specific accounts receivable in the amount of $1,700 were recognized as uncollectible, and $1,000 of accounts previously written off as uncollectible were collected. Collections of other accounts receivable during the month totaled $270,000. An examination of the accounts receivable outstanding at the end of the year indicated that $11,000 of these accounts would eventually prove uncollectible.

Recoveries of overdue accounts in this company are treated as miscellaneous income of the period in which recovery is made — no attempt being made to adjust the estimate of customer defaults to reflect these recoveries.

a) Explain briefly what each of the five November 30 account balances represents.
b) Present journal entries to record the December transactions.
c) What are the balances in each of the above five accounts as of December 31 prior to the year-end examination of the quality of the accounts receivable?
d) Was the company's experience with customer defaults during this year normal, high, or low? If high or low, by how much?
e) Show the accounts receivable section of the December 31 sheet, in good form and with the correct account balances.

*18. The Joplin Manufacturing Company guarantees its products against product defects that are detected during the first year after the products are delivered to customers. Past experience indicates that the cost of correcting any such defects will average 2 percent of Joplin's selling prices. Revenues are recognized at the time of delivery. You have the following information for the year 19x1:

(1) Opening balance in Liability under Product Guarantees account, $25,000.

(2)  Gross sales revenue for the year, $3,000,000, all on credit; collections from customers, $2,800,000.

(3)  Expenditures made to correct defects discovered and reported by customers during the year, $53,000, all paid in cash.

a)  Analyze the effects of these transactions on the firm's assets, liabilities, and owners' equity. Then prepare journal entries in general journal form to record your analyses.

b)  Set up a T-account for the Liability under Product Guarantees account, enter the opening balance, post the entry or entries that you assigned to this account as a result of your analyses in (a), and compute the balance in this account at the end of the year. What does this balance measure?

19.  The Herklion Company purchased a large quantity of used industrial equipment and shipped it to a foreign country for use in the government's industrialization program. Herklion paid $800,000 for the equipment and an additional $30,000 to transport it to the foreign country.

By the time the equipment arrived at its destination, the customer government had no foreign exchange to pay for it. Instead, it offered to give Herklion $100 of its own 7 percent bonds for every $95 due on the shipment of equipment. At that time, these bonds had a market value of $91 for every $100 of bonds.

Herklion accepted the offer and received $1,000,000 in bonds which it kept for two years and then sold at a price of $90 for every $100 of bonds. During this two-year period, the foreign government paid interest promptly and regularly on these bonds at the prescribed interest rate of 7 percent a year.

a)  Did the contractor make a profit or a loss on the equipment transaction? When and how much?

b)  How, if at all, would your answer to (a) have differed if the bonds had been sold immediately?

c)  How, if at all, would your answer have differed if the bonds had been held until their maturity date and then collected in full?

*20.  The Burfran Manufacturing Company has just been formed to produce a new product at a cost of $12 a unit, which will be paid in cash at the time of production. It will cost $6 a unit to sell the product, and this amount will be paid for at the time of shipment. The sale price is to be $25 a unit; all sales will be on credit.

The following results are expected during the first two years of the company's operations:

|  | Units Produced | Units Shipped | Cash Collected from Customers |
|---|---|---|---|
| First year | 100,000 | 70,000 | $1,500,000 |
| Second year | 80,000 | 90,000 | 1,875,000 |

a)  State the effect on the various assets and owners' equities of producing one unit, shipping one unit, and collecting $25, if revenue is recognized at the time of production.

b) What total income would the company report in each year if revenue were recognized at the time that cash is collected from the customer? (For this purpose, assume that general administrative expenses amount to $200,000 a year and that income taxes are zero.)

21. The Swazy Construction Company has secured a contract with the state of Iowa for the construction of 15 miles of highway at a contract price of $100,000 a mile. Payments for each mile of highway are to be made according to the following schedule:

(1)  40 percent at the time the concrete is poured.
(2)  50 percent at the time all work on that mile is completed.
(3)  10 percent when all 15 miles of highway have been completed, inspected, and approved.

At the end of the first period of operation, five miles of highway have been entirely completed and approved, concrete has been poured and approved on a second stretch of five miles, and preliminary grading has been done on the third five-mile stretch.

The job was originally estimated to cost $80,000 a mile. Costs to date have coincided with these original estimates and have totaled the following amounts: (1) on the completed stretch, $80,000 a mile; (2) on the second stretch, $64,000 a mile; and (3) on the third stretch, $10,000 a mile. It is estimated that each unfinished stretch will be completed at the costs originally estimated.

a) How much should the state of Iowa have paid Swazy during or at the end of the first period of operation under the terms of the contract? Show computations.

b) How much profit would you report for this period? Show your calculations and justify your method.

22. A farmer keeps pigs. Each year his sows give birth to piglets, which he raises for eventual sale to meat-packers. Each year he buys feed for the pigs and pays a hired man to feed them. Some years when pig prices are high, he sells more pigs than are born; in other years, he sells fewer pigs than are born, resulting in an increase in the total number and weight of his herd. Sales are always for cash and quotations of prices from hog auctions are published daily in the newspapers.

a) What basis of revenue and expense recognition would be most meaningful to the farmer in this case? Explain your reasoning.

b) Asssume that feed and labor costs average $2 per pig per month. A pig born on July 1 weighs 80 pounds in December when hog prices are 30 cents a pound. It is sold the following March for $40. Using the method of revenue recognition you selected in (a) above, compute the cumulative effect of these transactions on the figures shown as total assets and total owners' equity on the December 31 and March 31 balance sheets.

10/4    **23.** The Saranac Company produces a single product at a cost of $6 each, all of which is paid in cash when the unit is produced. Selling expenses of $3 a unit are paid at the time of shipment. The sale price is $10 a unit; all sales are on account. No customer defaults are expected, and no costs are incurred at the time of collection.

During 19x1, the company produced 100,000 units, shipped 76,000 units, and collected $600,000 from customers. During 19x2, it produced 80,000 units, shipped 90,000 units, and collected $950,000 from customers.

a)   Determine the amount of net income that would be reported for each of these two years:
    (1)   If revenue and expense are recognized at the time of production.
    (2)   If revenue and expense are recognized at the time of shipment.
    (3)   If revenue and expense are recognized at the time of collection.
b)   Would the asset total shown on the December 31, 19x2, balance sheet be affected by the choice among the three recognition bases used in (a)? What would be the amount of any such difference?

**24.** The Naive Manufacturing Company produces a product at a cost of $7.50 a unit, all of which is paid at the time of production. It costs $2 a unit to sell the product, all of which is paid at the time the product is shipped to the customer. The sale price is $10 a unit. All sales are on account. Collection costs are 2 percent of the amount collected, all paid during the period of collection. No customer defaults are expected.

During the first year of operation, the company expects to produce 20,000 units, to ship 18,000 units, and to collect $170,000 from its customers.

During the second year it expects to produce 30,000 units, to ship 29,000 units, and to collect $280,000 from its customers.

a)   Suppose that the company recognizes revenue (and hence income) at the time of production:
    (1)   State the effect on the various assets and equities of producing one unit and incurring the related production costs.
    (2)   State the effect on the various assets and equities of shipping one unit and incurring the related selling costs.
    (3)   State the effect on the various assets and equities of collecting $10 and incurring the related collection costs.
    (4)   What net income will be reported for the first year?
    (5)   What net income will be reported for the second year?
b)   Repeat the calculations called for in (a), but on the assumption that the company recognizes revenue (and hence income) at the time of shipment.
c)   Repeat the calculations called for in (b), but on the assumption that the company recognizes revenue (and hence income) at the time of collection.

d) Companies that recognize revenue at the time of shipment ordinarily treat collection costs as an expense of the period of collection. Using this procedure, what is the net income for each year?

e) Companies that recognize revenue at the time of collection ordinarily treat selling costs as an expense of the period in which they are incurred. Using this procedure, what is the net income for each year?

25. Ward Sales, Inc., sells and installs air conditioning equipment. As soon as equipment is installed on a customer's premises, an invoice is prepared and the full price of the equipment is recorded in the Accounts Receivable account.

Although Ward's installers try to install the equipment to meet the needs of those who will be living or working in the air conditioned space, adjustments often have to be made after the equipment has been in operation for some time. Ward recognizes an obligation to make these adjustments without charge to the customer.

The following data have been derived from the company's records for the month of June:

(1) Beginning balances in selected accounts:

| | |
|---|---:|
| Cash | $ 50,000 |
| Accounts receivable | 88,000 |
| Air conditioner inventories | 125,000 |
| Accounts payable (to air conditioner manufacturers) | 110,000 |
| Wages payable to equipment installers | 500 |
| Wages payable to equipment adjusters | 300 |
| Liability for product adjustments | 2,500 |
| (2) Cash collected from customers | 135,000 |
| (3) Payments to air conditioner manufacturers, on account | 85,000 |

(4) The cost of making post-installation adjustments of customers' air conditioners is expected to average 3 percent of the selling price of the equipment.

(5) Wage payments to employees:

| | |
|---|---:|
| To installers | 8,500 |
| To equipment adjusters | 1,400 |
| To sales and administrative employees | 11,000 |

(6) Other operating costs, all paid in cash:

| | |
|---|---:|
| Installation of air conditioning equipment | 800 |
| Adjustment of air conditioning equipment | 100 |
| Selling and administrative activities | 3,700 |

(7) Ending balances in selected accounts:

| | |
|---|---:|
| Accounts receivable | 103,000 |
| Air conditioner inventories | 105,000 |
| Accounts payable | 95,000 |
| Wages payable to equipment installers | 1,000 |
| Wages payable to equipment adjusters | 300 |

a) Compute sales revenues for the month.

b) Calculate the cost of air conditioners purchased during the month.

c) Determine the expenses for the month and calculate net income.

d) What should be the June 30 balance in the Liability for Product Adjustments account?

e) Prepare journal entries to record your analyses of all of the above transactions.

**26.** For a number of years, the Wagner Company deferred recognition of revenues until the time of collection on the grounds that bad debts were too unpredictable to record on an estimated basis. The company was 100 percent owned by members of the Wagner family until December 30, 19x2, when a few hundred shares of stock were sold to outsiders. The following information relates to the year 19x3:

(1)  Amounts due from customers on January 1 for goods shipped by the Wagner Company prior to that date, $300,000; the cost of the goods represented by these receivables was $180,000.

(2)  Goods shipped: price, $800,000; merchandise cost, $600,000.

(3)  Collections, $900,000; merchandise costs applicable to amounts collected, $650,000.

(4)  Specific customer defaults, $18,000; merchandise costs applicable to these amounts, $11,000; the affected merchandise could not be repossessed or otherwise recovered.

(5)  One customer who had defaulted early in 19x2 and whose account had been written off at that time paid his account in full, $1,200. At the time of the default, Wagner had recognized a loss of $950, which was the cost of the merchandise shipped to this customer.

(6)  Selling and administrative expenses, paid in cash, $182,000.

(7)  Merchandise purchased on account, $630,000.

(8)  Payments to suppliers of merchandise, $660,000.

*a*)  At what amount did the Wagner Company report its receivables in its balance sheet at the *beginning* of the year? Set up a T-account and enter this figure.

*b*)  Analyze the transactions for the year, using the collection basis of revenue recognition, and state these analyses in general journal form.

*c*)  Prepare an income statement for the year, based on your analyses of the year's transactions.

**27.** To meet its responsibilities to its new stockholders, the board of directors of the Wagner Company (problem 26) engaged the firm of Wachum and Krey, independent public accountants, to audit the company's accounts and accounting procedures as of the end of 19x3. As a result of its investigation, Wachum and Krey became convinced that the company's revenue recognition practice was providing a misleading income statement and recommended an immediate change to a delivery basis of revenue recognition.

The staff of Wachum and Krey reviewed the list of receivables that had been outstanding on January 1, 19x3 and estimated that $30,000 of these would never be collected. (In other words, the Allowance for Uncollectible Accounts account should have had a $30,000 balance at the beginning of the year.)

Wachum and Krey also analyzed the Wagner Company's past experience and found that uncollectible accounts had averaged 3 percent of sales, although this had been partially offset to varying amounts by recoveries of accounts written off in years prior to the year of recovery.

a) Prepare a journal entry or entries to convert the opening balances in the company's accounts to the delivery basis. (Note: this will require the recognition of a greater asset total on that date than the company had reported previously. The net amount of this write-up should be credited to a special adjustment account. The balance in the adjustment account should be shown on the income statement as a single item entitled, "Cumulative effect on prior years of changing to a different revenue recognition basis," to be included as the final figure in the determination of net income for 19x3.)

b) Reanalyze the transactions for the year, using the delivery basis for revenue recognition, and state these analyses in general journal form.

c) Prepare an income statement for the year, based on your analyses in (b).

d) Is the delivery basis likely to give management and investors a better or poorer indication of the firm's current performance than the collection basis? Illustrate your answer with figures from this problem and problem 26.

28. The Better Bottom Boatyard was organized early in 19x0 to manufacture small, high-quality pleasure boats for weekend sailors. Mr. Eben Hartley, the proprietor of the yard, estimated that the boats would cost $21,000 each to manufacture, including his own salary as an element of manufacturing cost. Actual manufacturing costs departed from this figure over the years, but Mr. Hartley remained convinced that this was a good estimate.

The customer was required to make a deposit of $5,000 when he placed his order, another $10,000 when the boat was placed in production, and the remainder of the $30,000 purchase price when the finished boat was delivered. A number of Mr. Hartley's acquaintances agreed to act as salesmen on a part-time basis. They received no salaries, but earned a $1,000 commission whenever they took an order. Because Mr. Hartley was short of cash, each of the salesmen agreed to wait to receive his commission until the boat was delivered.

Manufacturing costs were accumulated separately for each boat. At the end of each year, Mr. Hartley estimated for any unfinished boats the percentage of the total work that had already been done. This percentage completion was measured in terms of the ratio of the *estimated* costs for the work done to date to the total estimated cost of $21,000 for the completed boat. Thus if the work done to date on a boat should have cost $7,000 according to the estimates, Mr. Hartley would say that the boat was one-third finished, even if actual costs incurred on that boat so far amounted to $10,000.

The following events took place during the first six years of the boatyard's operations:

(1)   Orders, production starts, and deliveries were:

| Year | No. of Orders Received | No. of Boats Started | No. of Boats Delivered |
|------|------------------------|----------------------|------------------------|
| 19x0 | 3 | 3 | 0 |
| 19x1 | 1 | 1 | 3 |
| 19x2 | 5 | 5 | 2 |
| 19x3 | 2 | 2 | 4 |
| 19x4 | 4 | 4 | 2 |
| 19x5 | 1 | 1 | 4 |

As soon as each boat was completed, it was delivered to the customer.

(2)   The following progress and manufacturing costs were reported during these years:

| Year | Boat Number | Percent of Work Performed during Year | Manufacturing Cost Incurred during Year |
|------|-------------|----------------------------------------|-----------------------------------------|
| 19x0 | A–1 | 66$^2$/$_3$% | $16,000 |
|      | A–2 | 50 | 11,000 |
|      | A–3 | 33$^1$/$_3$ | 8,200 |
| 19x1 | A–1 | 33$^1$/$_3$ | 8,000 |
|      | A–2 | 50 | 11,000 |
|      | A–3 | 66$^2$/$_3$ | 15,000 |
|      | A–4 | 50 | 11,500 |
| 19x2 | A–4 | 50 | 10,200 |
|      | A–5 | 100 | 23,000 |
|      | A–6 | 75 | 14,000 |
|      | A–7 | 50 | 10,000 |
|      | A–8 | 25 | 5,000 |
|      | A–9 | 0 | — |
| 19x3 | A–6 | 25 | 6,000 |
|      | A–7 | 50 | 12,100 |
|      | A–8 | 75 | 14,000 |
|      | A–9 | 100 | 23,000 |
|      | A–10 | 50 | 11,300 |
|      | A–11 | 50 | 11,000 |
| 19x4 | A–10 | 50 | 8,000 |
|      | A–11 | 50 | 10,400 |
|      | A–12 | 75 | 15,000 |
|      | A–13 | 50 | 11,000 |
|      | A–14 | 25 | 5,100 |
|      | A–15 | 0 | — |
| 19x5 | A–12 | 25 | 5,000 |
|      | A–13 | 50 | 11,000 |
|      | A–14 | 75 | 16,000 |
|      | A–15 | 100 | 20,000 |
|      | A–16 | 0 | — |

(3)   Miscellaneous selling and administrative expenses amounted to
$8,800 each year.

*a*)   Compute net income each year on each of three bases of revenue
recognition: (1) orders received, (2) percentage of completion, and
(3) delivery. State whatever assumptions you had to make to prepare
these figures.

*b*)   Which of these three bases would provide the income statement that
you, as a nonmanagement stockholder, would find most meaningful? Explain, indicating the advantages of the basis you have selected, its shortcomings, and why you have selected it rather than
one of the other two?

†29.   Smith & Wells, Ltd., manufactures a variety of machined parts
which it sells to customers in the automotive and transportation industries. About half of the company's sales are of products listed in the company's regular catalog. The remainder of the annual sales is in custom
items. Sales revenues for both types of products are recognized at the
time the goods are shipped to the customers.

Deliveries of catalog items, except for very large orders, are made
from warehouse inventories, which are allowed to fluctuate from month
to month to help stabilize production levels.

Custom items, often designed to the customer's own specifications,
are manufactured only upon receipt of a firm order. Cancellations of
orders on which production operations have commenced are extremely
rare, and Smith & Wells, Ltd., can always recover its costs on any such
cancelled orders.

During 1966 the company's sales force turned in a gratifying 20 percent increase in new orders over their 1966 level, almost all of the increase being for custom products. To meet this increased demand, the
rate of production in the company's factory was increased twice during
the year, once in July and once again in October. Because the production
cycle for custom items averages four to six months, however, the increase in the rate of production did not lead to any marked rise in
revenue.

In mid-January of 1967, Mr. T. E. S. Evans, the managing director of
Smith & Wells, Ltd., received a preliminary set of financial statements
for 1966 from his chief accountant, Mr. J. B. Burke. Excerpts from these
statements are shown in Exhibit 1. Mr. Evans was very much concerned
by the decline in reported income from the 1965 level and asked Mr.
Burke for an explanation to be presented to the top management group
at their January meeting.

*a*)   Did the income reported for 1966 give a reasonably accurate mea-

---

† Copyright 1967 by l'Institut pour l'Etude des Méthodes de Direction de l'Entreprise,
(IMEDE), Lausanne, Switzerland. Reproduced by permission.

sure of the operating performance of Smith & Wells, Ltd., during the year?

b) What changes, if any, would you recommend making in the company's method of income measurement? Indicate why changes are or are not necessary, using figures from Exhibit 1 to illustrate your argument.

*Exhibit 1*

Smith & Wells, Ltd.

SELECTED FINANCIAL DATA FOR 1964–66

(000 omitted)

| | 1964 | 1965 | 1966 |
|---|---|---|---|
| Net revenue from goods shipped: | | | |
| Catalog items | £xxx | £ 960 | £ 970 |
| Custom products | xxx | 990 | 1,030 |
| Total | £xxx | £1,950 | £2,000 |
| | | | |
| Cost of goods shipped | £xxx | £1,170 | £1,240 |
| Selling and administrative expenses | xxx | 600 | 620 |
| Net operating income before taxes and special charges | £xxx | £ 180 | £ 140 |
| | | | |
| New orders received, net of cancellations (at sale prices): | | | |
| Catalog items | £xxx | £ 980 | £1,000 |
| Custom products | xxx | 1,020 | 1,400 |
| Total | £xxx | £2,000 | £2,400 |
| | | | |
| Inventories on 31 December (at cost): | | | |
| Materials | £100 | £ 100 | £ 150 |
| Work in process: | | | |
| Catalog items | 45 | 50 | 50 |
| Custom products | 148 | 155 | 230 |
| Finished goods (catalog items only) | 470 | 500 | 480 |
| | | | |
| Details of custom products work in process on 31 December: | | | |
| Total contract sale prices | £480 | £ 500 | £ 625 |
| Estimated total production cost | 290 | 300 | 375 |
| Production costs incurred to date | 148 | 155 | 230 |
| % of work completed to date | 50% | 50% | 60% |
| | | | |
| Orders on hand but not yet put into production on 31 December, custom products (at contract sale prices) | £810 | £ 800 | £1,025 |

xxx—Data not available.

# 6

# PURCHASES, SALES, AND PAYROLL TRANSACTIONS

MOST TRANSACTIONS in any given firm fall into a few well-defined categories. Most of these are familiar to us already, from the illustrations in previous chapters, but they are not always as simple as these illustrations may seem to imply. The purpose of this chapter is to outline some of the complexities that may be encountered and to see how they affect the analysis of the transactions.

To accomplish this purpose, we shall examine a group of representative transactions in the following categories:

1. Purchases and payments.
2. Sales and collections.
3. Payrolls.

By way of illustration, we shall analyze a number of the transactions of a small merchandising corporation, Erskine Enterprises, Inc., during the year 19x7. The president and principal shareholder in this corporation is Mr. Charles Erskine, who founded the business in 19x1. The corporation's business in 19x7 was conducted through a single retail store, selling household appliances and related merchandise.

## PURCHASE TRANSACTIONS

The amounts shown on the invoices accompanying the merchandise purchased by Erskine Enterprises during 19x7 totaled $1,000,000. The suppliers of this merchandise gave the company 30 days to pay, with a 2 percent discount if it paid cash within 10 days after the invoice date. (These terms are abbreviated as 2/10, n/30, which is read as, two ten, net thirty.) The invoice price is known as the *gross price* of the merchandise; the amount due after deducting the discount is the *net price*.

### Cash Discounts

In offering this cash discount, Mr. Erskine's suppliers expected him to take advantage of it. In fact, they worked out the terms so that he would find it very expensive to pass up the discount. If he failed to take advantage of the discount by the tenth day, he had only 20 additional days before the invoice became overdue and his credit rating became impaired. Two percent interest for a 20-day loan is very expensive.

For example, on a $100 order the net price of the merchandise was $98. By not paying promptly, Erskine Enterprises would pay $2 for the use of this $98 for 20 days, about one eighteenth of a year. This was equivalent to an annual interest charge of 36.7 percent:

$$\text{Interest rate} = \frac{\text{Interest for one year}}{\text{Amount borrowed}} = \frac{\$2 \times 18}{\$98} = 36.7 \text{ percent}$$

This is a very high interest rate, and Mr. Erskine was willing to pay it only when he was desperately short of cash and unable to borrow it anywhere else.

Many companies record purchases at their gross price, on the grounds that this is simpler and less confusing to their clerical employees. Mr. Erskine decided to record his purchases at their net price, however, on the grounds that this was a better measure of their cost. After all, this was the amount that he actually expected to pay his suppliers.

With $20,000 in cash discounts available on gross purchases of $1 million, the net price of the merchandise bought during 19x7 was $980,000. This amount was debited to the Merchandise Inventory account to reflect the increase in that asset. The same amount was credited to Accounts Payable to show a corresponding increase in that liability:

Merchandise Inventory ...................... 980,000
    Accounts Payable .........................     980,000

### Purchase Discounts Lost

The invoices paid during the year had a total net price of $1,144,000; the amount actually paid was slightly greater,

$1,145,000. The reason for the $1,000 difference is that several invoices were paid late through carelessness and the applicable discounts were lost.

These lost discounts were not really part of the cost of the merchandise. They were the cost of mistakes made during the year, and a burden on the current year's revenues – that is, an expense. Whenever Erskine Enterprises failed to take advantage of a discount, the additional cost was charged to Purchases Discounts Lost, an expense account, rather than to Merchandise Inventory. The entries to record the year's payments to trade creditors therefore had the following effects:

```
Accounts Payable ........................ 1,144,000
Purchases Discounts Lost ................     1,000
    Cash .................................             1,145,000
```

The debit to Accounts Payable recognized the reduction in this liability, the debit to Purchases Discounts Lost recorded the expense due to late payment, and the credit to Cash brought the balance in this asset account down to its correct level.

## Using the Gross Price Method

It should be noted that if the company had recorded purchases at their gross price, it would have credited a Purchases Discounts account for the amount of any discounts actually taken when the invoices were paid. A $20 discount on payment of a $1,000 invoice would have been recorded as follows:

```
Accounts Payable.................................. 1,000
    Purchases Discounts...........................          20
    Cash..........................................         980
```

The amount of any discounts lost would not be identified in the accounts. In principle, the balance in the Purchases Discounts account should be deducted in statement preparation from the gross cost of merchandise purchased; in practice, it is usually carried directly to the income statement. The difference in reported income in any one year is unlikely to be material.

## SALES TRANSACTIONS

Purchases discounts also have their counterpart in sales transactions. The accounting problem is very similar, but the apparent differences are great enough to call for a brief illustration.

## Merchandise Sales

Erskine Enterprises sold both to retail customers and to commercial, industrial, and institutional buyers. Retail customers were generally required to pay cash, and local financial institutions provided credit to many of these customers to enable them to do so. Until 19x6 the store's commercial, industrial, and institutional customers were given straight 30-day purchase terms, but as the company expanded this part of its business it found that these buyers expected to receive discounts for prompt payment. Accordingly, in 19x7 Mr. Erskine began offering a 2 percent discount to his nonretail customers if they paid cash within 10 days after the invoice date, the same terms that he received from his own suppliers.

The significant figure here again is the net price. Because Mr. Erskine wanted his Accounts Receivable account to provide a continuing record of the total amounts owed by customers, however, all credit sales were recorded at their gross price. Credit sales in 19x7 totaled $1,340,000; cash sales (paid for in cash at the time of delivery) brought in $480,000. The entries to record these transactions can be summarized as follows:

| | | |
|---|---|---|
| Cash | 480,000 | |
| Accounts Receivable | 1,340,000 | |
| Sales Revenues | | 1,820,000 |

This showed increases in two assets and an increase in owners' equity in the amount of $1,820,000.

## Sales Discounts

This entry overstated both the value of the accounts receivable at the date of sale and the sales revenues for the period. Customers generally take advantage of any discounts offered to them, for the reasons cited earlier. During 19x7, for example, Erskine Enterprises received $1,158,000 in full payment of customer account balances amounting to $1,180,000. The analyses of these transactions can be summarized in the following entry:

| | | |
|---|---|---|
| Cash | 1,158,000 | |
| Sales Discounts | 22,000 | |
| Accounts Receivable | | 1,180,000 |

The debit to Cash shows the increase in the cash balance resulting from these transactions, while the credit to Accounts Receivable shows the reduction in that asset. The difference was recorded in the Sales Discounts account, a contra account to

Sales Revenues. The debit entries to this account in effect corrected the overstatement of revenue that resulted from the recording of sales at their gross price. The revenue section of the income statement, in other words, should show the following:

Gross sales.................................................. xxx
　　Less: Discounts allowed customers ........................ xxx
Net Sales .................................................... xxx

Net sales is the significant figure for management and outsiders as well.

### Returns and Allowances

Collections are also reduced in many cases by the allowances granted to customers for returned or damaged merchandise. These allowances are typically treated in the same way as sales discounts except that the debits are to Sales Returns and Allowances instead of to Sales Discounts. Because of the similarities, discussion of sales discounts should serve to illustrate the concepts underlying the accounting for returns and allowances as well.

## PAYROLL TRANSACTIONS

Aside from the cost of merchandise, the largest cost incurred by Erskine Enterprises is its payroll cost. This comes in two parts: the gross pay of the company's employees; and payroll taxes and other payroll-related costs.

### Recording Gross Pay

Payrolls prepared during 19x7 amounted to $400,000 for store employees and $100,000 for executive and office personnel. These amounts were treated as current expenses because they were incurred to produce current sales revenues. The entries to record these payrolls divided the expense into two categories:

Administrative Expenses ..................... 100,000
Selling Expenses............................. 400,000
　　Salaries and Wages Payable ..............         500,000

The administrative payrolls in this case included Mr. Erskine's $50,000 salary for 19x7. This was treated as an expense because he was an employee of a corporation. Corporations are legally separate from their owners, and any salary paid by a corporation to an owner for services rendered is assumed to be paid to an independent party. Since this assumption is clearly invalid for the closely held corporation, owners' salaries should be identified separately, if not in the ledger at least in a supporting schedule.

### Recording Payroll Taxes

The amounts recorded in entry (10) were the employees' gross pay, the amounts the corporation had agreed to pay the employees themselves. Not all of this was to be paid in cash to the employees, however. Like other organizations, Erskine Enterprises was obligated to withhold $65,000 for income taxes and $25,000 for F.I.C.A. taxes levied on the employees.[1] These amounts were to be paid to government tax collectors on the employees' behalf.

Before paying the employees, therefore, Erskine Enterprises' accountants had to compute the amount that would be payable to the tax collector. These payroll deductions amounted to $90,000 on all of the payrolls prepared during the year.

The tax deductions from employees' gross pay are taxes on the employee, not on the employer. The employer is also subject to certain taxes based on the size of his payrolls. For example, an employer whose employees are subject to F.I.C.A. taxes is required to match the amounts deducted for this purpose from the employees' gross pay. This means that Erskine Enterprises had to pay $50,000 to the federal government, just twice the amount deducted from employees' paychecks.[2] The additional $25,000 represented operating expenses for the year, recorded by debits of $5,000 for taxes on the administrative payrolls and $20,000 for taxes on the store payrolls. The full entry was:

Administrative Expenses ........................ 5,000
Selling Expenses .............................. 20,000
    Taxes Payable..............................            25,000

The credit to Taxes Payable recorded the company's liability to make these payments.

Most employers are also required to pay unemployment com-

---

[1] F.I.C.A. stands for Federal Insurance Contributions Act; the tax is popularly referred to as the social security tax, although it is actually only one of a number of taxes supporting social security benefits.

[2] The F.I.C.A. tax is levied on the wages and salaries of all employees in occupations covered by the law. The amount of an individual's wages or salary that is subject to this tax and the tax rate are set by Congress and are likely to change from year to year. To keep the arithmetic simple, in this illustration, we are using an arbitrary rate of 10 percent of the entire gross payroll, half levied on the employees and half on the employer.

pensation taxes and workmen's compensation insurance premiums, and many firms have pension plans, health plans, or other programs which require additional payments by the employer to separate funds. All of these additional charges are known as *fringe benefits*. To keep the illustration as simple as possible, let us assume that the total cost of these fringe benefits to Erskine Enterprises in 19x7 amounted to 3 percent of the employees' gross pay. This amounted to $3,000 on the administrative payrolls and $12,000 on the store payrolls. Let us also assume that this entire amount was payable to government agencies and could be classified as taxes. This means that the company needed to use only one account, Taxes Payable, to record the liability for payment of the fringe benefits. The costs were split as before, between two expense accounts:

| | | |
|---|---|---|
| Administrative Expenses | 3,000 | |
| Selling Expenses | 12,000 | |
| Taxes Payable | | 15,000 |

## Payroll Payments

Payments against payroll liabilities offer few surprises and need little discussion. Erskine Enterprises paid its employees the full $410,000 due them on the 19x7 payrolls. The $90,000 difference between this amount and the gross payroll was credited to the Taxes Payable account. The entries can be summarized as follows:

| | | |
|---|---|---|
| Salaries and Wages Payable | 500,000 | |
| Taxes Payable | | 90,000 |
| Cash | | 410,000 |

The debit recorded a decrease in the company's liability to its employees, while the credit to Taxes Payable recognized its liability to the government for the taxes withheld from its employees' pay.

The company also paid $126,000 during the year against its tax liabilities. This amount was less than the recorded liability because December taxes were not paid prior to the end of 19x7. The entries to record these payments can be summarized as follows:

| | | |
|---|---|---|
| Taxes Payable | 126,000 | |
| Cash | | 126,000 |

This reflected the simultaneous reductions in the company's liabilities and in its assets.

## SUMMARY

The main task of this chapter has been to examine the accounting analyses of three common groups of transactions — purchases, sales, and payrolls.

Purchases and sales can be recorded either at their gross price or at their net price, after deducting all allowable discounts. In either case, the significant figure to management and investors is the net cost or net price of the goods or services bought or sold.

This chapter has also directed attention to some of the problems met in accounting for the costs of work done by employees. The main managerial problem in analyzing payroll transactions is to identify payroll costs with various company programs, departments, and activities. In addition, the accountant must classify the liabilities arising from work done by employees, distinguishing between amounts payable to the employees themselves and amounts withheld for payment to governmental agencies and other third parties.

## QUESTIONS AND PROBLEMS

1. Should purchases discounts lost be regarded as part of the cost of merchandise purchased? Give your reasons.

2. Are sales discounts expenses? Are the credits given to customers for returned or damaged merchandise expenses? Explain your reasoning, including a definition of expense that supports the positions you have taken.

3. Are payroll taxes that are levied on the employer always expenses of the current period? If not, give at least one example of a situation in which they would be treated otherwise.

4. Are sales discounts forfeited by customers revenues? If so, would you classify them as part of the company's sales revenues or in some other revenue category?

5. Suppose that a manufacturer sells his products to wholesalers at the retail list price less a "trade discount" of 40 percent. How, if at all, does this differ from the cash discount? Would you expect this manufacturer to record sales at list price or at net price? Explain.

6. A company uses the gross price method in recording both purchases and sales.

   a) What possible objections can you see to this practice as pertains to *purchases*?

*b*) What kind of adjustment, if any, will this practice make necessary at the time of statement preparation?

7. In deciding from which supplier to purchase materials, how would you define "materials cost"? Would this have any bearing on your choice between the net price and gross price methods of recording purchases? Explain.

8. Why are quantity and cash discounts often recorded differently? Are there any fundamental differences in the nature of the two types of discounts that provide a conceptual basis for this differentiation in book-keeping treatment? Should they be handled any differently in annual financial reporting? Explain.

9. Payroll liabilities must be classified into separate categories, show-ing the amounts payable to governments, the amounts payable to the employees, and the amounts payable to others. The accountant does not use this classification scheme in classifying the cost side of payroll transactions.

Is this correct, or should the amounts charged to, say, selling expense be subdivided to indicate the amounts paid directly to employees and the amounts withheld for payment to others?

10. By granting discounts for prompt payment, a seller is likely to receive payment from his customers much earlier than he would with-out the discounts. This will reduce his need to obtain funds from other sources, and the granting of discounts therefore may be regarded as a source of funds.

The calculations in this chapter indicate that this is likely to be a fairly expensive way of obtaining funds. What explanation can you offer for the prevalence of cash discounts in many lines of business?

11. The costs of fringe benefits in the Acme Company average 30 percent of the employees' gross pay. The gross pay of salesmen is classi-fied as selling expense, but all fringe benefit costs are classified as ad-ministrative expenses. Would you recommend that fringe benefits earned by the salesmen be classified as part of selling expense, or would you be content to continue the company's present system? What differ-ence would it make?

12. The Dripple Corporation classifies the costs of its wage payrolls into two categories: factory wages and office wages. The gross pay of factory employees amounts to $10,000 each week; the gross pay of em-ployees in the company's administrative and sales offices is $2,000 a week.

The company is required to withhold 15 percent of its employees' gross pay for their personal income taxes. F.I.C.A. taxes amount to 13 percent of gross pay, one half to be deducted from employees' paychecks, the other half to be contributed by the employer. The company is also subject to an unemployment compensation insurance tax of 3 percent of gross pay.

a) How much should be charged to factory work in process each week?
b) Prepare journal entries to record: (1) accrual of one week's payrolls and payroll taxes; and (2) one week's payments to employees.

*13. The Northumberland Company is a distributor of textiles in southern New England. Salaries and wages are paid by the month. Operating expenses are broken down by departments. Record the following data for March in journal form:

| Department | Cash Payments to Employees | Income Tax Withheld | F.I.C.A. Tax Withheld | Insurance Premiums Withheld | F.I.C.A. Taxes on the Company | Unemployment Taxes on the Company |
|---|---|---|---|---|---|---|
| Office......... | $ 7,740 | $1,500 | $ 500 | $260 | $ 500 | $ 300 |
| Sales ......... | 14,988 | 3,500 | 1,000 | 512 | 1,000 | 600 |
| Warehouse.... | 10,016 | 1,200 | 600 | 184 | 600 | 360 |
| Total...... | $32,744 | $6,200 | $2,100 | $956 | $2,100 | $1,260 |

14. The Farnsworth Company has two salesmen, Green and Harris. Green is on a salary of $10,000 a year and gets a 1½ percent commission on the sales for which he is responsible. Harris's annual salary is $9,000 plus 2 percent commission. Commissions and salaries are recorded in separate accounts.

Last year, Green achieved sales of $200,000, while Harris sold $150,000. Income taxes withheld amounted to 20 percent of total salaries and commissions, and the F.I.C.A. tax was 14 percent, half levied directly on the company and half to be deducted from employee wages. In addition, the company had to pay unemployment taxes of 2 percent of the gross payroll.

Prepare a summary entry or entries to record the payroll costs and liabilities for the year, recording first the accrual of the payrolls and related costs and then recording the payments of cash.

15. The Chadwick Company had the following balances in its liability accounts on August 31:

Wages payable...................... $ 5,000
Taxes payable .................... 48,000
Accounts payable ................. 65,000

It had the following payroll-related transactions during September:

---

* Solutions to problems marked with an asterisk (*) are found in Appendix B.

(1)  Gross pay earned by employees:
    Factory ............................................ $40,000
    Sales.............................................. 10,000
    Administration ..................................... 12,000
(2)  Amounts withheld from gross pay:
    Federal income taxes ............................. 9,000
    F.I.C.A. taxes ..................................... 4,650
    Medical insurance premiums........................ 1,750
(3)  Amounts paid:
    To employees ..................................... 45,000
    To government agencies:
        For income taxes withheld ...................... 8,200
        For F.I.C.A. taxes .............................. 9,000
        For unemployment compensation
          insurance taxes ............................... 1,800
    To medical insurance company .................... 1,850
(4)  Unemployment compensation insurance tax: $2\frac{1}{2}$ percent of gross pay.

Prepare journal entries to record all of these transactions. Label each account as an asset (A), a liability (L), or an expense (E).

**16.** On January 18 the Sanford Plumbers Supply Corporation purchased six laundry tubs on credit from the Stone Manufacturing Company at a gross price of $27 each. The terms were 2/10, n/30.

The tubs arrived on January 25 and three of them were immediately reshipped, in the original crates, to the Lowe Plumbing Company at a gross price of $36 each. The terms of sale were 1/10, n/30.

The following day, Lowe Plumbing notified Sanford that the tubs were defective. Sanford agreed to allow Lowe to deduct $6 a tub, or a total of $18, from the net amount payable to Sanford. Sanford inspected the three tubs that remained in its own inventory and found that they were undamaged. Sanford then contacted the Stone Manufacturing Company, which agreed to deduct $18 from the sum due from Sanford.

On February 4, Lowe paid Sanford $88.92 for the tubs. On February 20, Sanford paid Stone $144.

a)  Prepare journal entries to record each of these events on the books of the Sanford Plumbers Supply Corporation, using the gross price method to record both purchases and sales.
b)  Repeat this process, using the net price method to record purchases and sales.
c)  Prepare a comparative statement showing gross sales, net sales, gross margin, and the contribution of these transactions to the company's net income for the year, as these figures would emerge from accounts kept under (1) the gross price method, and (2) the net price method.
d)  At what amounts would the three remaining tubs be shown on Sanford's balance sheet under these two methods?

*17. The Pacific Company purchased, on February 12, 20 radio sets at $50 each from the Amsterdam Radio Company, terms: 2 percent, 10 days; net, 30 days. On February 14, 10 of the sets were sold to the Jones Electric Company for $60 each, terms: 2 percent, 10 days; net, 30 days.

On February 16, five sets were returned by Jones for full credit because the cabinets were scarred. The Pacific Company appraised the returned sets at $30 each, wholesale value, and the Amsterdam Company agreed to deduct the difference between the original gross price and this appraised value from the gross amount due from Pacific.

The Pacific Company paid its bill to Amsterdam immediately on receipt of this credit allowance. Jones Electric, however, failed to pay its bill to Pacific until February 28, and therefore lost the cash discount.

a) Using the gross price method for both purchases and sales, analyze these transactions in debit and credit form, first for Pacific, second for Jones Electric.

b) In what way or ways did the accounts of these two companies present an inaccurate picture of company performance during February or of its financial position as of February 28? What corrections should be made before the financial statements are prepared?

18. The Bartoli Company buys some of its merchandise subject to discounts for prompt payment. Merchandise inventories on March 31 had cost $75,000 less cash discounts of $900, and accounts payable on that date amounted to $40,000 at gross prices, against which cash discounts of $600 were still applicable.

During April, the company bought merchandise on account at a gross price of $50,000, subject to a 2 percent discount for prompt payment. A portion of the month's purchases, with a gross price of $2,500, was returned to suppliers for credit.

During the month the company paid all of its April 1 accounts payable plus $12,000 of the April purchases (measured at gross prices). The company took all available cash discounts on the April purchases, but lost $100 of the discounts available to it on the April 1 accounts payable because it failed to pay some of these accounts within the discount period. All discounts on the rest of the April purchases would be taken early in May.

The gross price of the merchandise inventory on hand on April 30 was $45,000. All of this inventory can be assumed to have consisted of goods purchased during April.

a) If you were the sales manager of the Bartoli Company and were interested in measuring the profitability of the month's sales, what figure representing the cost of goods sold would you use? Show your calculations and explain your reasoning.

b) At what amount should accounts payable be listed on the April 30 balance sheet?

*c*) How much was actually paid on account to suppliers during the month?

**19.** The firm of Granville Associates performs consulting services and develops new products for its clients. On consulting projects, revenues are recognized when the work is performed; on development projects, revenues are recognized when the projects are completed.

On successful product development projects — that is, those that yield a product or products that the client decides to add to its product line — Granville Associates is obligated to help the client with problems that will arise in putting the new product into production. This "project warranty" is expected to cost 5 percent of the amount billed the client for the product development work. Granville Associates recognizes this expense when it completes each successful development project.

All costs except those classified as executive and administrative expenses are charged to some project, either product development or consulting services or project warranty work. The following payroll-related events took place during April:

(1) Payrolls (all employees were paid monthly, on the last day of the month):

| Employee Category | Gross Pay | Federal Tax Withheld | State Tax Withheld | F.I.C.A. Tax Withheld | Health Insurance Premiums | Net Pay (Paid in Cash) |
|---|---|---|---|---|---|---|
| Consulting associates ... | $ 40,000 | $ 7,000 | $ 2,400 | $ 2,600 | $ 400 | $ 27,600 |
| Engineers............... | 120,000 | 18,000 | 6,000 | 7,800 | 2,400 | 85,800 |
| Secretarial.............. | 20,000 | 2,600 | 600 | 1,300 | 500 | 15,000 |
| Executive and administrative........ | 36,000 | 6,400 | 3,000 | 2,340 | 300 | 23,960 |
| Total.............. | $216,000 | $34,000 | $12,000 | $14,040 | $3,600 | $152,360 |

(2) Employees' time distributions:

| | Consulting Services | Product Development | Project Warranty | Executive and Administrative |
|---|---|---|---|---|
| Consulting associates ..... | 60% | 35% | 1% | 4% |
| Engineers................. | 18 | 80 | 2 | — |
| Secretarial............... | 65 | 20 | — | 15 |
| Executive and administrative.......... | — | — | — | 100 |

(3) An unemployment tax of 2½ percent of gross pay was levied on the employer. The only other payroll tax was the employer's portion of F.I.C.A. tax, equal to the amounts withheld from employee payrolls for this purpose.

(4) Paid in cash:
 Federal income taxes withheld, $35,000.
 State income taxes withheld, $12,500.
 F.I.C.A. taxes, $29,380.
 Unemployment taxes, $5,650.

*a*) Prepare journal entries to record the effects of all of the above transactions. Label each account in each entry as an asset (A), a liability (L), or an expense (E).

*b*) Explain why the payments described in item (4) differed from the taxes summarized in items (1) and (3).

**20.** The Foundation Retail Company: (1) issues monthly financial statements; (2) uses perpetual inventory records; and (3) uses the *gross* price method in recording sales and the *net* price method in recording purchases. Some of the firm's transactions for the month of February were as follows:

Feb. 3 Purchase of goods on account from A&M Company for $50,000, terms 2/5, n/30.

7 Payrolls for the week ended February 7: gross pay, $2,000; income taxes withheld, $300; F.I.C.A. taxes withheld, 6.5 percent; remainder paid in cash.

8 Sale of goods to L. Ward on account for $1,000, terms 2/5, n/10. Foundation Retail always sells at a 25 percent markup on cost.

10 Sale of goods to G. Rankin for $5,000, terms 2/5, n/10. Markup is 25 percent on cost.

11 Payment of $3,000 to government agencies, covering income taxes withheld, F.I.C.A. taxes, and unemployment compensation insurance taxes on January payrolls.

12 Receipt of check for $1,000 from L. Ward in payment for goods purchased on the 8th of the month.

13 Receipt of check from G. Rankin for $4,458 in payment for goods purchased on February 10. He explains that he is returning goods from this shipment with a gross invoice price of $400. Some of these items were damaged in shipment and some were not the items he had ordered. He also says that he has paid a trucking company $50 to return the merchandise to Foundation Retail. He asks for a credit of $450 against the gross balance in his account.

14 Payrolls for the week ended February 14: same amounts as on February 7.

18 Payment of $50,000 is made to A&M Company for the purchase of February 3.

20 L. Ward writes that he forgot to deduct his discount from his payment of February 12. He asks Foundation Retail to credit his account.

21 Payrolls for the week ended February 21: same amounts as on February 7.

24 The goods sent by Rankin are received. (See February 13.) Upon inspection, it is found that goods with a gross sale price of $300 were spoiled through faulty packing by Foundation Retail and must be thrown away; the remainder are in good condition and are placed back on the stockroom shelves. Full credit is extended to Mr. Rankin.

28 Payrolls for the week ended February 28: same amounts as on February 7.

28 Accrual of employers' share of the month's payroll taxes: F.I.C.A. tax, matching employees' share; unemployment compensation, 3 percent of gross payrolls.

Prepare journal entries in debit/credit form to record each of these transactions. For each line in each entry indicate whether the amount represents an increase or a decrease in an asset, a liability, or the owners' equity.

# 7

# PREPARING THE STATEMENTS

THE ACCOUNTANT'S WORK is far from completed when the effects of routine transactions have been recorded in the accounts. In fact, his task is just beginning, because clerical employees have done most of the routine work, simply following instructions that the accountant was able to issue in advance.

The accountant's work at the end of the accounting period begins with the preparation of a *trial balance*, or list of the balances in the general ledger accounts. Second, he must make a number of *adjusting entries*, embodying the results of transactions analyses that have not been made part of the clerical routine. Once the adjusting entries have been made, the accountant can prepare the financial statements from the adjusted account balances. His final task is then to prepare the accounts to receive the record of the next period's transactions.

The purpose of this chapter is to see what the accountant has to do at each of these four stages. Since this introduces few concepts that we have not already discussed, the chapter can also serve as a means of reviewing the main ideas of accrual accounting that we covered earlier.

## TRIAL BALANCE

The main purpose of the trial balance is to bring the figures in the general ledger together in a compact format. Exhibit 7–1, for example, shows Erskine Enterprises' trial balance as of December 31, 19x7, drawn from the ledger accounts. Notice that this shows both balance sheet and income statement accounts, with-

Exhibit 7–1

Erskine Enterprises, Inc.

UNADJUSTED TRIAL BALANCE

December 31, 19x7

| Account | Debit | Credit |
|---|---|---|
| Cash......................................... | $   64,000 | $ |
| Accounts receivable........................... | 319,000 | |
| Allowance for uncollectible accounts........... | | 9,000 |
| Notes receivable ............................. | 90,000 | |
| Merchandise inventory........................ | 180,000 | |
| Prepaid insurance ........................... | 6,000 | |
| Furniture and equipment ..................... | 144,000 | |
| Accumulated depreciation ..................... | | 39,000 |
| Accounts payable ............................ | | 182,000 |
| Taxes payable ............................... | | 4,000 |
| Dividends payable ........................... | | 20,000 |
| Notes payable................................ | | 30,000 |
| Capital stock................................ | | 385,000 |
| Retained earnings ........................... | | 50,000 |
| Sales revenues............................... | | 1,820,000 |
| Sales discounts ............................. | 22,000 | |
| Cost of goods sold ........................... | 960,000 | |
| Administrative expenses ...................... | 148,000 | |
| Selling expenses ............................. | 582,000 | |
| Purchases discounts lost ..................... | 1,000 | |
| Loss on retirement of equipment............... | 3,000 | |
| Dividends declared........................... | 20,000 | |
| Total.................................. | $2,539,000 | $2,539,000 |

out segregation. The only aspects of an account that have any relevance at this point are the amount of its balance and whether this is a debit or a credit balance.

## COST AMORTIZATIONS

Financial statements drawn directly from the account balances at this stage would be incomplete because certain kinds of facts have not yet been reflected in the accounts. For example, Erskine's bookkeeping routine included no procedure for amortizing the costs of prepaid insurance and furniture and fixtures — that is, transferring costs out of these accounts as the assets' services were consumed. This task was left to the accountants.

### Amortizing Prepaid Insurance Costs

The balance in Erskine Enterprises' Prepaid Insurance account was $6,000 at the end of 19x7. A review of the insurance policy file revealed that this amount could be traced back to five insurance policies that had been in force for all or part of 19x7. The file showed the following:

| (1) Policy No. | (2) Effective Date | (3) Expiration Date | (4) Un-adjusted Balance | (5) Monthly Premium Cost | (6) Months this Year | (7) Premiums Expired (5) × (6) | (8) Un-expired Premiums (4) − (7) |
|---|---|---|---|---|---|---|---|
| AB 406-721 | 1/1/x4 | 12/31/x7 | $ 540 | $ 45 | 12 | $ 540 | – |
| CD 492-881 | 4/1/x6 | 3/31/x7 | 60 | 20 | 3 | 60 | – |
| XL 172-008 | 7/1/x5 | 12/31/x8 | 2,400 | 100 | 12 | 1,200 | $1,200 |
| CD 712-654 | 4/1/x7 | 3/31/x8 | 300 | 25 | 9 | 225 | 75 |
| PL 202-903 | 1/1/x7 | 12/31/x9 | 2,700 | 75 | 12 | 900 | 1,800 |
| Total..... | | | $6,000 | | | $2,925 | $3,075 |

The total at the bottom of column (4) is the balance in the ledger account; the amounts shown in column (7) represent the cost of insurance coverage for 19x7. These amounts had to be transferred from the Prepaid Insurance account to an expense account or accounts.

A close study of the insurance policies revealed that $2,400 of the expiring premiums applied to store facilities and operations, and that the remaining $525 provided insurance coverage for the office and central administration. The adjusting entry was:

(a)

Selling Expenses................................... 2,400
Administrative Expenses.......................... 525
    Prepaid Insurance ............................ 2,925

This reduced the balance in the Prepaid Insurance account to $3,075, representing the unexpired premiums on the three policies still in force on January 1, 19x8. It also recognized two categories of expense.

## Amortizing Furniture and Equipment Costs

Erskine Enterprises' ledger showed furniture and equipment on hand at the end of 19x7 with a total original cost of $144,000, of which $39,000 had been amortized in previous years. Depreciation on these assets amounted to $10,000 in 19x7. Of this, $6,000 applied to equipment used in the store; the remaining $4,000 was on office furniture and equipment. The entry to record depreciation therefore was:[1]

---

[1] The expense accounts would be subdivided in practice to permit ready isolation of the depreciation component. This kind of detail is omitted to avoid expanding the illustration unnecessarily.

(b)

Selling Expenses ................................. 6,000
Administrative Expenses ........................ 4,000
  Accumulated Depreciation....................         10,000

The two debits served to recognize the decrease in owners' equity resulting from the effect of the passage of time on the company's furniture and equipment. The credit to Accumulated Depreciation represented an asset reduction, reflecting the reduction in the remaining usefulness of this group of assets.

## REVENUE ADJUSTMENTS

A company's revenue accounts may also need adjusting at the end of the period. Erskine Enterprises, for example, made one pair of entries to bring the balance in the Allowance for Uncollectible Accounts to its correct level, entries that we first encountered in Chapter 5. In this case, the company's bookkeepers made no entries for probable customer defaults as part of the bookkeeping routine in 19x7. Instead, the company's accountant examined the outstanding receivables at the end of the year to estimate how much of the gross amount would be uncollectible. His first discovery was that $8,000 of the receivables shown in the ledger were worthless and should be written off. The entry was:

(c)

Allowance for Uncollectible Accounts.............. 8,000
  Accounts Receivable.........................         8,000

As we saw in Chapter 5, this reduced the balance both in the Accounts Receivable account and in the contra-asset account, leaving the book value of the receivables unchanged.

The accountant's next step was to age the remaining receivables. The aging analysis in this case showed the following:

| (1) Number of Days since Invoice Date | (2) Amount Receivable | (3) Estimated Percentage Uncollectible | (4) Estimated Amount Uncollectible (2) × (3) |
|---|---|---|---|
| 0–30 days............... | $150,000 | 0.2% | $    300 |
| 31–60 days.............. | 80,000 | 1.0 | 800 |
| 61–90 days.............. | 50,000 | 3.6 | 1,800 |
| 91 days and older........ | 31,000 | 30.0 | 9,300 |
| Total .............. | $311,000 | | $12,200 |

After entry (c) had been posted, the account balance was only $1,000. The table, however, shows that the balance in the allowance at the end of the year should have been $12,200. The following entry therefore was necessary to restore the account balance to its proper level:

(d)

Customer Defaults ............................. 11,200
    Allowance for Uncollectible Accounts .......        11,200

The Customer Defaults account, it will be remembered, is another deduction-from-revenues contra account. A debit to this account records a reduction in the owners' equity. A credit to the Allowance for Uncollectible Accounts records a diminution in the company's assets. After entry (d) was made, therefore, the balance in the allowance account was $12,200, indicating that current receivables were actually worth $12,200 less than their face value as a result of expected collection difficulties.

### Recognizing Cash Discounts on Outstanding Receivables

As we saw in Chapter 6, Erskine Enterprises in 19x7 started giving a 2 percent cash discount to its nonretail customers who paid their bills within 10 days. Some of the invoices outstanding on December 31, 19x7, were still entitled to this discount, and the Erskine accountants estimated that $2,800 in discounts would be taken on these accounts in 19x8.

This amount is likely to be immaterial and in practice it probably would be ignored in statement preparation. In concept, however, it arose out of 19x7 sales and therefore should be reflected in the 19x7 financial statements. Since the Erskine accountant did not know whether $2,800 would be a material amount, he decided to make the entry:

(e)

Sales Discounts ................................... 2,800
    Allowance for Sales Discounts .................        2,800

Sales Discounts is a deduction-from-revenues contra account, and the debit to this account showed the reduction in owners' equity that the discounts occasioned. The Allowance for Sales Discounts account is a deduction-from-asset contra account, similar to the Allowance for Uncollectible Accounts. The credit to this account reduced the net receivable balance to its correct level.[2] (Because Erskine Enterprises only began granting cash

---

[2] The Sales Discounts and Allowance for Sales Discounts accounts would have been unnecessary if Erskine Enterprises had recorded its sales at their *net* price. Collection of the full gross price after the expiration of the discount period would then have required a credit to Miscellaneous Revenue for the difference between the gross and net prices. The net price method is conceptually superior but slightly more difficult to implement.

discounts in 19x7, this allowance had never been necessary before. A new account had to be added to the chart of accounts to accommodate this entry.)

## INTEREST AND PAYROLL ACCRUALS

A third type of adjusting entry is the *accrual*, defined as the recognition of part or all of a revenue or expense, together with its related asset or liability, when the accounting period ends before the asset or liability would be recorded as part of the ordinary bookkeeping routine. To illustrate this rather complex definition, let us look at two of the most common accruals, the accrual of interest and the accrual of wages.

### Accruing Interest Expense

For many business concerns, an important source of funds, particularly to finance seasonal peaks of activity, is short-term borrowing from commercial banks. The instrument most commonly used for this purpose is called a *promissory note*, and it is a promise to pay a specified amount on a specified date, known as the *maturity date*. The amount borrowed is termed the *proceeds;* the amount paid for the use of the proceeds is called *interest;* and the amount to be repaid to the lender on the maturity date is known as the *maturity value.*

Erskine Enterprises' trial balance at the end of 19x7 listed notes payable amounting to $30,000. This amount was the proceeds of a bank loan that the company had taken out on December 1, 19x7, giving in exchange a 90-day, 6 percent promissory note. The period between the borrowing and maturity dates, in this case 90 days, is the *life* or *term* of the loan. The 6 percent figure is the *interest rate.* Unless some other period is explicitly specified, interest rates are always stated as *annual* rates, regardless of the term of the loan.

It is accepted financial practice to compute interest on short-term loans on the basis of a 360-day year. Therefore, a 90-day note would require interest at 90/360, or 1/4 of the annual rate. Erskine Enterprises, in other words, agreed to pay the bank $30,000 plus interest of $450 (1/4 × 6 percent × $30,000) on March 1, 19x8, exactly 90 days from the date of the loan.[3]

[3] The maturity date is computed on the basis of actual elapsed days, not on the basis of the 360-day year. In computing the maturity date, the day the loan is made is not counted. Thus a loan made on November 15 gives rise to interest for 15 days during November, starting with November 16. Debts maturing on a day on which the banks are closed are payable on the next banking day. In this case, the term of the loan covered 30 days in December, 31 days in January, 28 days in February, and 1 day in March, for a maturity date of March 1.

In the normal bookkeeping routine the next part of this transaction to be recorded would be the repayment of the loan, plus interest, on March 1, 19x8. No entry would be made until that date. Erskine Enterprises had to prepare financial statements for 19x7, however, and this required an entry to accrue interest expense for the period from December 1 through December 31. After all, the company had used the bank's money for 30 days during 19x7, and the cost of using it for this period was a cost of doing business during 19x7, even though the interest payment would not have to be made until March 1, 19x8. This meant that 30/90 of the $450 total interest cost, or $150, was a 19x7 expense. The entry to record this was:

(f)

Interest Expense ...................................... 150
    Accrued Interest Payable..........................     150

The debit to the expense account recorded the reduction in the owners' equity that this occasioned; the credit to Accrued Interest Payable recorded the liability for future payment of this amount.

It should be pointed out here that companies sometimes borrow by *discounting* their own promissory notes or notes that they have received from their customers. In discounting a note, the lender calculates the amount due at the maturity date and then deducts interest on this amount to determine the sum that he will make available to the borrower. For example, Erskine Enterprises might have given a note to a bank, promising to pay $30,000 90 days later. If the bank had discounted this note at 6 percent, it would have deducted $450 interest in advance, giving Erskine only $29,550. The interest accrual for the first 30 days would still have been $150.

### Accruing Interest Revenue

Business firms occasionally accept promissory notes from their customers if payment is to be deferred beyond the normal credit period. For example, Erskine Enterprises took a note for $90,000 from one of its customers on November 15, 19x7. The entry made at that time was:

Notes Receivable ............................... 90,000
    Accounts Receivable .......................     90,000

The trial balance at the end of the year still showed a balance of $90,000 in the Notes Receivable account.

This was a 90-day note, bearing interest at a rate of 8 percent a year, payable at the maturity date. Erskine Enterprises earned interest on this note for 46 days in 19x7, but none of this was recorded as part of the bookkeeping routine. Interest for these 46 days amounted to $920, computed as follows:

$$\$90,000 \times 0.08 \times 46/360 = \$920$$

The adjusting entry in this case was an exact counterpart of entry (f), which accrued interest on the company's note payable. The entry here was:

(g)

| | | |
|---|---|---|
| Accrued Interest Receivable | 920 | |
|     Interest Revenue | | 920 |

This entry served to recognize both the asset and the increase in the owners' equity. (Interest revenue is more commonly referred to as "interest income," but for the sake of clarity we prefer to reserve the word "income" for measures of the *net income* of the firm.)

## Payroll Accruals

Another kind of accrual, the accrual of payroll liabilities, also arises because completion of the regular bookkeeping cycle does not always take place on the final day of the accounting period. Salaries and wages are often paid weekly, while the accounting period is a year or a month.

For example, Erskine Enterprises' last weekly payroll period of 19x7 ended on December 28. Monday and Tuesday, December 30 and 31, were full working days, which means that some wages were *earned by employees in 19x7 but were not recorded* in the accounts until the next year. These amounts were paid as part of the first weekly wage payroll of 19x8, but part of that payroll was really a cost applicable to 19x7.

Employees in the store and office earned $5,000 and $1,000, respectively, on the two working days between the end of the last weekly payroll period and the end of the year. The entry to accrue these costs was:

(h)

| | | |
|---|---|---|
| Selling Expenses | 5,000 | |
| Administrative Expenses | 1,000 | |
|     Salaries and Wages Payable | | 6,000 |

The credit to Salaries and Wages Payable recognized the company's liability to pay its employees in 19x8 for work done in 19x7.

Notice that the payroll liability was not classified into the amounts that would eventually be paid to the employees and the amounts that would be paid on their behalf to others. It was the *amount* of the liability rather than its distribution that was significant at this point.

Liability for wages also creates a liability for the employer's share of payroll taxes. Payroll taxes applicable to the wages accrued for the last two working days of 19x7 were at a combined rate of 8 percent. The accrual was calculated by multiplying this rate by the figures in entry (*h*) above:

(*i*)

| | | |
|---|---|---|
| Selling Expenses | 400 | |
| Administrative Expenses | 80 | |
| Taxes Payable | | 480 |

## OTHER ADJUSTMENTS

Four other adjusting entries had to be made before the 19x7 financial statements could be prepared. These offer few surprises and can be dealt with fairly quickly.

### Inventory Shrinkage

Erskine Enterprises used the perpetual inventory method to record transfers from the inventory account to Cost of Goods Sold, as described in Chapter 3. This produced an end-of-year balance of $180,000 in the inventory account.

Inventory balances in perpetual inventory systems should be verified periodically by a physical count of the items on hand. Any discrepancy between the book value of the inventory and the cost of the actual quantity on hand on the inventory date has to be taken to the income statement, either as a separate item or as an adjustment to the cost of goods sold figure.

To reduce the clerical load and minimize interference with everyday operations, most companies count only part of their inventory at any one time. Erskine's inventories consisted mainly of a few large items, however, making it feasible to count the entire inventory at one time. The tally on December 31, 19x7, located merchandise with a total cost of only $173,400. The $6,600 difference between this and the $180,000 book value was attributable to theft, carelessness, errors in cost bookkeeping, or even errors in the annual count. Lacking any way of separating the amounts due to these various causes, Erskine's accountants charged off the entire amount by means of the following entry:

(j)

```
Inventory Shrinkage Expense ....................... 6,600
        Merchandise Inventory .......................        6,600
```

The credit to Merchandise Inventory recognized the reduction in this asset that was revealed by the annual count; the debit to Inventory Shrinkage Expense recorded the accompanying reduction in owners' equity. If the count had exceeded the book value of the merchandise on hand, the account would have been credited. In published statements the account is ordinarily closed out to cost of goods sold.


## Bookkeeping Corrections

Clerical employees are no less likely to make mistakes than anyone else, and one of the auditor's jobs is to look for various kinds of bookkeeping errors. Common errors are incorrect transcription of dollar amounts, incorrect classifications leading to debits or credits to the wrong accounts, and failure to record transactions in their entirety.

Erskine Enterprises' auditors found only one error large enough to require correction at the end of 19x7. A $10,000 payment had been received in advance from a customer, covering merchandise that had not yet been delivered by the end of 19x7. When the payment was received, the credit was made to Sales Revenue rather than to Advances from Customers. To correct this error and to avoid overstating sales and understating the firm's liabilities, the following adjusting entry was made:

```
Sales Revenues.................................. 10,000
        Advances from Customers..................        10,000
```

This reduced the reported revenue figure and recorded the year-end liability of $10,000.


## Income Tax Accrual

One more accrual remained to be made, the accrual of the income tax on the year's income. This entry had to be made last, because many of the earlier accruals affected the amount of taxable income.

To estimate the tax, the accountants computed revised balances in all of the income statement accounts, and from these, the before-tax earnings for the year. The amounts shown in the company's tax return differed to some extent from those in the accounts, but the overall difference in this case was not great.

The estimated tax for the year amounted to $23,000. These figures were summarized in the following entry:

(l)

| | | |
|---|---|---|
| Income Tax Expense | 23,000 | |
| Taxes Payable | | 23,000 |

The first figure in this entry recorded the impact of income taxes on the owners' equity; the credit to Taxes Payable recorded the liability.

## STATEMENT PREPARATION AND PRESENTATION

Once the adjusting entries have been figured out, the accountant is in a position to prepare the financial statements for the period. Exhibit 7–2 presents the T-accounts representing Erskine Enterprises' ledger for 19x7, showing the unadjusted balances and the year-end adjusting entries. The adjusted balances in these accounts can be used to construct the company's financial statements for the year.

Exhibit 7–2

Erskine Enterprises, Inc.

**LEDGER ACCOUNTS INCLUDING ADJUSTING ENTRIES**
December 31, 19x7

**Cash**

| Bal. 64,000 | |
|---|---|

**Notes Receivable**

| Bal. 90,000 | |
|---|---|

**Accrued Interest Receivable**

| (g) | 920 | |
|---|---|---|

**Accounts Receivable**

| Bal. 319,000 | (c)  8,000 |
|---|---|
| Bal. 311,000 | |

**Allowance for Uncollectible Accounts**

| (c)  8,000 | Bal.  9,000 |
|---|---|
| | (d)  11,200 |
| | Bal. 12,200 |

**Notes Payable**

| | Bal.  30,000 |
|---|---|

**Accrued Interest Payable**

| | (f)  150 |
|---|---|

**Accounts Payable**

| | Bal. 182,000 |
|---|---|

**Salaries and Wages Payable**

| | (h)  6,000 |
|---|---|

**Taxes Payable**

| | Bal.  4,000 |
|---|---|
| | (i)  480 |
| | (l)  23,000 |
| | Bal. 27,480 |

**Sales Revenues**

| (k) 10,000 | Bal. 1,820,000 |
|---|---|
| | Bal. 1,810,000 |

**Customer Defaults**

| (d)  11,200 | |
|---|---|

**Sales Discounts**

| Bal.  22,000 | |
|---|---|
| (e)  2,800 | |
| Bal. 24,800 | |

**Interest Revenue**

| | (g)  920 |
|---|---|

**Cost of Goods Sold**

| Bal. 960,000 | |
|---|---|

*Exhibit 7–2 — Continued*

| Allowance for Sales Discounts | | Advances from Customers | | Administrative Expenses | |
|---|---|---|---|---|---|
| | (e)    2,800 | | (k)    10,000 | Bal. 148,000 | |
| | | | | (a)         525 | |
| | | | | (b)      4,000 | |
| | | | | (h)      1,000 | |
| | | | | (i)           80 | |
| | | | | Bal. 153,605 | |

| Merchandise Inventory | | Dividends Payable | | Selling Expenses | |
|---|---|---|---|---|---|
| Bal. 180,000 | (j)    6,600 | | Bal.   20,000 | Bal. 582,000 | |
| Bal. 173,400 | | | | (a)      2,400 | |
| | | | | (b)      6,000 | |
| | | | | (h)      5,000 | |
| | | | | (i)           400 | |
| | | | | Bal. 595,800 | |

| Prepaid Insurance | | Capital Stock | | Purchases Discounts Lost | |
|---|---|---|---|---|---|
| Bal.    6,000 | (a)    2,925 | | Bal. 385,000 | Bal.    1,000 | |
| Bal. 3,075 | | | | | |

| Furniture and Equipment | | Retained Earnings | | Interest Expense | |
|---|---|---|---|---|---|
| Bal. 144,000 | | | Bal.   50,000 | (f)         150 | |

| Accumulated Depreciation | | Dividends Declared | | Income Tax Expense | |
|---|---|---|---|---|---|
| | Bal.   39,000 | Bal.   20,000 | | (l)    23,000 | |
| | (b)   10,000 | | | | |
| | Bal. 49,000 | | | | |

| Loss on Retirement of Equipment | |
|---|---|
| Bal.    3,000 | |

| Inventory Shrinkage Expense | |
|---|---|
| (j)    6,600 | |

## The Income Statement

The income statements of, United States business firms consist of three parts: ordinary income from continuing operations, income from discontinued operations, and income from extraordinary events. Most companies have only the first of these in most years.

Erskine Enterprises, for example, prepared the income state-

ment shown in Exhibit 7–3 to cover its operations for the year
19x7. This is known as a single-step statement, in that all revenue
items are grouped together at the top and net income is determined by subtracting the expenses from this total in one single
step.

Exhibit 7–3

Erskine Enterprises, Inc.

INCOME STATEMENT

For the Year Ended December 31, 19x7

| | | |
|---|---:|---:|
| Gross revenues from sales ......................... | | $1,810,000 |
| Less: Cash discounts on sales................... | $ 24,800 | |
| Customer defaults ....................... | 11,200 | 36,000 |
| Net revenue from sales ........................... | | $1,774,000 |
| Interest revenues ................................. | | 920 |
| Total revenues............................. | | $1,774,920 |
| Less: Cost of merchandise sold ................. | $960,000 | |
| Selling expenses ........................... | 595,800 | |
| Administrative expenses.................. | 153,605 | |
| Inventory shrinkage expense ............. | 6,600 | |
| Purchases discounts lost ................. | 1,000 | |
| Loss on retirement of equipment.......... | 3,000 | |
| Interest expense ......................... | 150 | |
| Income taxes ........................... | 23,000 | 1,743,155 |
| Net Income........................................ | | $    31,765 |

Some companies use a different format, preferring to segment
the ordinary income portion of their income statements. A simple
segmented structure would show the following (including hypothetical figures to illustrate the concept):

| | |
|---|---:|
| Sales revenue....................................... | $100 |
| Less: Cost of goods sold........................... | 60 |
| Gross margin ...................................... | $ 40 |
| Less: Operating expenses......................... | 28 |
| Income before income taxes ...................... | $ 12 |
| Less: provision for income taxes .................. | 5 |
| Net Income........................................ | $  7 |

The purpose of segmentation is to highlight key relationships,
such as the relationship between gross margin and sales revenues. We prefer the single-step statement because it is simpler
to read. It leaves it to the reader to select the relationships that
he wishes to emphasize and study.

In practice, operating expenses are ordinarily classified somewhat differently. Instead of reporting functional totals for such
functions as sales or administration, most companies divide their

expenses into such categories as salaries, purchased services, depreciation, and so forth. Although many companies disclose such items as research and development costs on a functional basis, the general feeling is that disclosure of functional totals would reveal relationships that should be concealed from competitors.

### Income from Discontinued Operations and Extraordinary Events

The income statement of a United States business firm may also include income from two other types of income sources. The first of these is income from major operations which have been discontinued during the year. The other is income from events which are clearly unusual and unexpected, referred to as *extraordinary items*. This means that the income statement of a company with both discontinued operations and extraordinary items will show the following segmentation at the bottom of the statement (with hypothetical numbers inserted for illustrative purposes):

| | | |
|---|---:|---:|
| Income from continuing operations | | $7 |
| Discontinued operations: | | |
| Income (loss) from operations of discontinued Division X (less applicable income taxes of $3) | $(5) | |
| Gain (loss) on disposal of Division X, including provision of $1 for operating losses during phase-out period (less applicable income taxes of $2) | 2 | (3) |
| Income before extraordinary items | | $4 |
| Extraordinary item: earthquake damage (less applicable income taxes of $1) | | (1) |
| Net Income | | $3 |

At one time, an item such as Erskine Enterprises' 19x7 loss on equipment retirement would have been treated as an extraordinary item, either reported at the bottom of the income statement or charged directly against retained earnings.[4] To qualify for recognition as an extraordinary item today, however, a gain or loss must be of a type that occurs infrequently and is unusual in the circumstances in which the company operates. Thus losses due to strikes would not be classified as extraordinary; they may be infrequent, but they are not really unusual. Gains and losses

---

[4] The staff of the American Institute of Certified Public Accountants found that 204 out of a sample of 600 annual reports for 1971 reported extraordinary items in the income statement. Slightly more than one-third of the extraordinary items represented gains or losses on discontinued operations, which are now treated differently, as described above. AICPA, *Accounting Trends and Techniques, 1972* (26th ed.; New York: AICPA, 1972), p. 253.

on the sale of plant and equipment are specifically classified as ordinary income, and only three items are specifically accepted as extraordinary — major casualties (such as earthquakes), expropriations, or prohibitions under newly enacted laws or regulations.[5]

## Statement of Changes in Retained Earnings

Changes in the Retained Earnings account are summarized each year in the retained earnings statement. In most cases, the only changes will be those on Erskine Enterprises' 19x7 statement shown in Exhibit 7–4: net income and dividends. In fact, when this is the case a single statement is typically used to show both the income statement and the changes in retained earnings.

*Exhibit 7–4*

**Erskine Enterprises, Inc.**
**STATEMENT OF CHANGES IN RETAINED EARNINGS**
**For the Year Ended December 31, 19x7**

| | |
|---|---:|
| Retained earnings at beginning of year | $50,000 |
| Add: Net income | 31,765 |
| | $81,765 |
| Less: Cash dividends declared | 20,000 |
| Retained earnings at end of year | $61,765 |

Most of the charges and credits to retained earnings other than income and dividends arise from events such as mergers with other businesses which we are not yet prepared to discuss. For the moment we shall mention only two events that lead to direct charges or credits to retained earnings: (1) the effects of lawsuits relating to prior years' events; and (2) the recalculation of income tax expenses of previous years. A statement including these would be constructed as follows, again using numbers created for the illustration:

| | |
|---|---:|
| Retained earnings, beginning of year, as previously stated | $120 |
| Prior period adjustment resulting from settlement of lawsuit | (11) |
| Prior period adjustment resulting from restatement of income taxes for 19xx | 4 |
| Retained earnings, beginning of year, as restated | $113 |
| Add: Net income | 3 |
| Less: Dividends declared | (2) |
| Retained earnings, end of year | $114 |

---

[5] *Opinion No. 30, Reporting the Results of Operations* (New York: AICPA, 1973).

The argument for this treatment is that including these adjustments in current income would be misleading because they arose from events that clearly took place in a previous year or years. The major argument against it is that the series of net income figures no longer serves as a summary of the firm's income. If prior period adjustments do not cancel each other over a period of time, a summary based on the income figures alone will either overstate or understate the firm's past profit performance.

## Statement of Financial Position

The third financial statement is the statement of financial position, or balance sheet. Erskine Enterprises' year-end balance sheet is shown in Exhibit 7–5. The asset and liability balances in this statement were copied from the T-accounts in Exhibit 7–2. They were divided between current and noncurrent items, as defined in Chapter 1. In this case, the company had no noncurrent liabilities.

*Exhibit 7–5*

Erskine Enterprises, Inc.

**STATEMENT OF FINANCIAL POSITION**

December 31, 19x7

ASSETS

*Current Assets:*

| | | |
|---|---|---|
| Cash.......................................... | | $ 64,000 |
| Notes and interest receivable ................... | | 90,920 |
| Accounts receivable ........................... | $311,000 | |
| Less: Allowance for uncollectible accounts..... | (12,200) | |
| Allowance for sales discounts........... | ( 2,800) | 296,000 |
| Merchandise inventory......................... | | 173,400 |
| Prepaid insurance ............................. | | 3,075 |
| Total Current Assets ........................ | | $627,395 |
| Furniture and equipment ......................... | $144,000 | |
| Less: Accumulated depreciation ................ | 49,000 | 95,000 |
| Total Assets ............................. | | $722,395 |

LIABILITIES AND SHAREOWNERS' EQUITY

*Current Liabilities:*

| | | |
|---|---|---|
| Notes and interest payable...................... | | $ 30,150 |
| Accounts payable .............................. | | 182,000 |
| Salaries and wages payable..................... | | 6,000 |
| Taxes payable ................................. | | 27,480 |
| Dividends payable ............................. | | 20,000 |
| Advances from customers ...................... | | 10,000 |
| Total Current Liabilities .................... | | $275,630 |
| *Shareowners' Equity:* | | |
| Capital stock ................................. | $385,000 | |
| Retained earnings ............................. | 61,765 | |
| Total Shareowners' Equity .................. | | 446,765 |
| Total Liabilities and Shareowners' Equity.. | | $722,395 |

The retained earnings figure on this balance sheet differs from the balance in the Retained Earnings account in the trial balance. The latter figure, it will be remembered, was the balance in this account at the *beginning* of the year. The year-end balance was obtained by adding the net income for the year and subtracting the dividends — in other words, the figures summarized in the statement of changes in retained earnings (Exhibit 7–4).

## CLOSING ENTRIES

The accounting cycle for the year can be said to be completed when the various temporary owners' equity accounts are closed out. This brings the balance in the Retained Earnings account to its proper level and prepares the temporary owners' equity accounts to receive the record of the next year's transactions.

Erskine Enterprises made two closing entries at the end of 19x7, one to transfer the balances in revenue and expense accounts to retained earnings, and the other to close out the Dividends Declared account. The first of these was as follows:

(I)

| | | |
|---|---:|---:|
| Sales Revenues | 1,810,000 | |
| Interest Revenue | 920 | |
| Customer Defaults | | 11,200 |
| Sales Discounts | | 24,800 |
| Cost of Goods Sold | | 960,000 |
| Selling Expenses | | 595,800 |
| Administrative Expenses | | 153,605 |
| Purchases Discounts Lost | | 1,000 |
| Inventory Shrinkage Expense | | 6,600 |
| Loss on Retirement of Equipment | | 3,000 |
| Income Tax Expense | | 23,000 |
| Interest Expense | | 150 |
| Retained Earnings | | 31,765 |

Because the Sales Revenues and Interest Revenue accounts had credit balances prior to closing, the debit entries had the effect of reducing the balances in these accounts to zero. Similarly, the credits to the contra-revenue and expense accounts restored the balances in those accounts to zero. The final credit entry, to Retained Earnings, was the net income for the year.

Finally, the balance in Dividends Declared was closed into Retained Earnings:

(II)

| | | |
|---|---:|---:|
| Retained Earnings | 20,000 | |
| Dividends Declared | | 20,000 |

The debit to Retained Earnings recognized that the distribution of dividends reduced the owners' equity permanently. The credit to Dividends Declared restored this account to a zero balance so that it could start 19x8 with a clean slate, ready to accumulate the 19x8 dividend information.

Once the closing entries were posted, the accountant could prepare a *post-closing trial balance.* If the closing entries have been recorded properly, the only accounts with non-zero balances will be the permanent balance sheet accounts, as in Exhibit 7–6. All of the temporary accounts will have zero balances.

Exhibit 7–6

Erskine Enterprises, Inc.

POST-CLOSING TRIAL BALANCE

December 31, 19x7

|  | Debits | Credits |
|---|---|---|
| Cash | $ 64,000 | |
| Notes receivable | 90,000 | |
| Accrued interest receivable | 920 | |
| Accounts receivable | 311,000 | |
| Allowance for uncollectible accounts | | $ 12,200 |
| Allowance for sales discounts | | 2,800 |
| Merchandise inventory | 173,400 | |
| Prepaid insurance | 3,075 | |
| Furniture and equipment | 144,000 | |
| Accumulated depreciation | | 49,000 |
| Notes payable | | 30,000 |
| Accrued interest payable | | 150 |
| Accounts payable | | 182,000 |
| Salaries and wages payable | | 6,000 |
| Taxes payable | | 27,480 |
| Advances from customers | | 10,000 |
| Dividends payable | | 20,000 |
| Capital stock | | 385,000 |
| Retained earnings | | 61,765 |
| Total | $786,395 | $786,395 |

## SUMMARY

Most bookkeeping is designed not to facilitate the preparation of financial statements but to prepare such action documents as payrolls, customer invoices, and materials requisitions. Data for information purposes is derived as a by-product of these important but routine activities.

In this situation it is probably not surprising that the bookkeeping routine fails to take account of all of the data that have a bearing on accrual basis financial statements. These data must be reflected in end-of-period adjusting entries, initiated by the accountant for the sole purpose of deriving financial statements. This chapter has illustrated a number of the more common types of adjusting entries.

Once the adjusting entries have been made, the accountant can translate the adjusted account balances into income statements, balance sheets, and statements of changes in retained earnings. After he has finished preparing these statements, the accountant can then close the temporary owners' equity accounts, setting the stage for the next accounting cycle.

## QUESTIONS AND PROBLEMS

1. If the routine bookkeeping work has been done correctly during the year, why is it necessary to make adjusting entries at the end of the year?

2. What is an "adjusting entry"? Give some common examples.

3. What is a "trial balance," and what purpose does it serve? Explain the difference between a trial balance and a balance sheet. What kinds of accounts are found on the post-closing trial balance?

4. What does the amount shown for retained earnings on an unadjusted trial balance measure?

5. Are adjusting entries to revenue or contra-revenue accounts likely to be necessary if the firm recognizes revenue at the time of collection?

6. Comment on the differences and similarities between depreciation and insurance expense.

7. What is meant by "discounting a note"?

8. Do you agree that a loss on the sale of a delivery truck should not be reported as an "extraordinary item" on the income statement for the period? Would you prefer to charge it directly to retained earnings? Explain your position on these questions.

9. An error in calculating depreciation in previous years, discovered when a long-life asset is sold at a loss, must be reported on the current year's income statement as a determinant of income before extraordinary items. An additional tax liability arising from a government audit of a prior year's tax return is charged directly to retained earnings, without appearing on the current year's income statement. On what grounds can this apparent inconsistency be justified? Cite an argument for reporting both of these on the income statement.

10. The Deeping Company employed approximately 2,000 workers. The payroll was accumulated on a weekly basis. The amount due each

employee for his day's work was entered daily in the payroll book. At the end of the week these daily amounts were added and the resulting total for each employee constituted his wages. At the time of payment, the total payroll was posted to the company's accounts as wage expense.

The company's fiscal year ended November 30. One year, this date fell on Wednesday, midway between paydays. In closing his books and making up statements for the year, the bookkeeper included among the operating expenses the total amount of wages shown in the accounts as having been paid. On examining the books later, the company's auditor remarked that in his opinion the statements drawn up therefrom were inaccurate in that the amount of wages applicable to the period between November 26, the last previous payday, and November 30, the end of the fiscal year, had not been included in the figures shown on the statements. The bookkeeper replied that since a similar condition had existed at the end of the previous fiscal year, any errors involved—if they did exist—would offset each other. What was more, he did not agree that the accounting was incorrect, since the cash had not yet been paid out. Payroll expense, he said, was incurred with the payment of cash.

Discuss this matter with reference both to the company's balance sheet and to its income statement.

*11. On February 1, the Ready Service Company's balance sheet showed accrued wages payable of $300. The gross wages shown on the four weekly payrolls paid during February, covering wages up to and including February 25, totaled $4,200. Employee wages for the period February 26 to February 28 amounted to $500.

*a)* What was the total wages expense for the month of February?
*b)* What was the correct balance in Accrued Wages Payable as of the close of business on February 28?

*12. On September 15, Calhoun borrowed $6,000 from the bank, promising to pay the bank $6,000 plus accrued interest at 6 percent 60 days from the date of the note. On November 14 he paid the accrued interest and renewed the note for an additional 30 days. At the second maturity, on December 14, Calhoun paid $4,000 in cash and gave a new 30-day, 6 percent note for the remaining amount due. This last note was paid in full when due.

Journalize the entries for these transactions on Calhoun's books. Include an accruing entry for December 31, Calhoun's balance sheet date. Date all entries.

13. The Peterson Company borrowed $20,000 from a bank on January 21, giving in exchange a 90-day, 9 percent note.

*a)* Prepare an entry to record the borrowing.
*b)* Prepare whatever entry this transaction would make necessary on January 31 if the Peterson Company wished to prepare a set of ac-

---

* Solutions to problems marked with an asterisk (*) are found in Appendix B.

crual basis financial statements as of the close of business on that date.

c) What entry would be necessary on January 31 if the Peterson Company prepared financial statements quarterly instead of monthly, the first quarter of the year ending on March 31? What entry would be made on February 28? On March 31?

**14.** The Crown Company uses the periodic inventory method. The annual inventory count was made at the end of 19x1 and reflected in the ledger. Subsequently, the following bookkeeping errors were discovered:

(1) A purchase of merchandise for $4,200 was incorrectly debited to Furniture and Fixtures.

(2) Cash of $1,300 received from a customer on account was incorrectly credited to Sales.

(3) A $400 payment to a vendor on account was incorrectly debited to Merchandise Inventories.

(4) A sales invoice for $400 was not recorded; payment was not received from the customer before the end of the year, but Crown's management anticipated no difficulty in collecting it early in 19x2.

(5) A $100 telephone bill was incorrectly charged to Entertainment Expense instead of to Telephone Expense.

a) For each of these, construct the adjusting entry that would have been made if the error had been discovered before the financial statements were prepared and before the year-end closing entries were made.

b) Construct the adjusting entries that would have been made if these errors had been discovered after the closing entries had been made and the financial statements for the year had been published.

**15.** The following figures appeared in the Prepaid Rent account of a motion picture theater during 19x1:

Prepaid Rent

| | | | |
|---|---|---|---|
| Bal. 1/1 | 10 | (2) | 55 |
| (1) | 55 | | |
| Bal. 12/31 | 10 | | |

The debit and the credit shown here summarize the many debits and the many credits that were actually entered in this account during the year.

Investigation shows that the balance in this account on December 31, 19x1 should have been $5.

a) How much money was paid to the landlord in 19x1?

b) What was the rent expense for 19x1?

c) What adjusting entry had to be made before the books could be closed at the end of 19x1?

d) How did the credits to this account arise during the year?

**16.** The following figures appeared in the Accrued Salaries Payable account of an advertising firm during 19x2:

Accrued Salaries Payable

| (2) | 1,360 | Bal. 1/1 | 50 |
| | | (1) | 1,400 |
| | | Bal. 12/31 90 | |

The debit and the credit shown here represent the many debits and the many credits that were actually entered in this account during the year.

All of these figures were correct and no further adjustments were necessary. Payroll taxes were zero, and all salary costs passed through this account.

*a)* Calculate salary expense for the year.
*b)* How much of the salaries earned by employees in 19x2 were paid in cash during the year?
*c)* How much was paid to employees during 19x2 for work done in 19x1?
*d)* How much will be paid to employees in 19x3 for work done in 19x2?

*17. The accounts of the James Dandy Sales Company showed the following balances at the end of 19x3:

| | Debit | Credit |
|---|---|---|
| Accounts payable | | $ 70,000 |
| Accounts receivable | $ 50,000 | |
| Accrued wages | | 2,000 |
| Allowance for bad debts | | 1,000 |
| Allowance for depreciation | | 62,000 |
| Capital stock | | 73,000 |
| Cash | 20,000 | |
| Cost of goods sold | 480,000 | |
| Depreciation | 21,000 | |
| Dividends | 3,000 | |
| Fire loss | 34,000 | |
| Furniture and fixtures | 200,000 | |
| Income taxes | 3,000 | |
| Insurance expired | 1,000 | |
| Interest expense | 4,000 | |
| Inventories | 80,000 | |
| Mortgage payable (due in 19x6) | | 50,000 |
| Notes payable (due in 19x4) | | 30,000 |
| Office supplies used | 5,000 | |
| Other expenses | 9,000 | |
| Prepaid insurance | 2,000 | |
| Refund of prior years' taxes | | 8,000 |
| Rent expense | 22,000 | |
| Retained earnings | | 48,000 |
| Sales | | 700,000 |
| Sales returns and allowances | 14,000 | |
| Taxes payable (due in 19x4) | | 4,000 |
| Wages and salaries | 100,000 | |
| Total | $1,048,000 | $1,048,000 |

Prepare a year-end balance sheet in good form, an income statement for the year, and a statement of changes in retained earnings. (No entries were made in the Retained Earnings account during the year.)

18. The following figures constituted the trial balance of a wholesale distributor as of December 31, 19x1:

|  | Debit | Credit |
|---|---|---|
| Accounts payable, current | | $ 206 |
| Accounts receivable, current | $ 762 | |
| Accumulated depreciation | | 1,109 |
| Allowance for doubtful current accounts | | 8 |
| Bonds payable (due May 1, 19x9) | | 192 |
| Building | 1,138 | |
| Capital stock | | 918 |
| Cash | 227 | |
| Depreciation | 129 | |
| Dividends declared | 198 | |
| Dividends payable to shareowners | | 50 |
| Furniture and equipment | 660 | |
| Income taxes | 221 | |
| Interest expense | 8 | |
| Inventories | 821 | |
| Investments in capital stock of other companies | 330 | |
| Loans to suppliers and customers, long-term | 48 | |
| Loans and advances to employees, short-term | 5 | |
| Loss on sale of equipment | 26 | |
| Marketable securities | 53 | |
| Merchandise sold | 2,142 | |
| Miscellaneous expenses | 147 | |
| Noncurrent accounts payable | | 82 |
| Notes payable, short-term | | 1 |
| Prepaid insurance | 11 | |
| Prepaid taxes | 4 | |
| Retained earnings | | 1,181 |
| Salaries payable | | 92 |
| Sales revenues | | 4,941 |
| Taxes payable | | 225 |
| Wages and salaries expense | 2,075 | |
| Total | $9,005 | $9,005 |

Prepare an income statement for the year, a balance sheet as of December 31, and a statement of changes in retained earnings. (No entries were made in the Retained Earnings account during the year.)

19. Financial statements for the Columbia Lumber Company are to be prepared from the balances in the accounts on October 31. The balance in the Cash account is correct, but the bookkeeper has made mistakes in recording a number of the transactions that took place during the month.

The incorrect entries are presented below. For each of these, prepare a journal entry to correct the error. (The bookkeeper's entries have already been posted to the ledger accounts.)

a) An outside contractor built a new truck loading platform:

Wage Expense.............................. 13,251
Cash .................................    13,251

b)  The bookkeeper accrued employees' wages for the last three days of
the month:

Wages Payable ................................. 437
Wage Expense...............................    437

c)  A three-year liability insurance policy was purchased on October 1,
but payment was not made during the month. The insurance coverage was effective immediately:

Insurance Expense .............................. 756
Accounts Payable ..........................    756

d)  A damaged truck was repaired early in October at a cost of $290.
This amount was charged to the Maintenance of Vehicles account.
A check for this amount was then received from an insurance com-
pany, and the bookkeeper made the following incorrect entry:

Cash ............................................ 290
Accident Losses ............................    290

e)  New posture chairs were purchased for the secretarial staff:

Office Expense ................................. 282
Accounts Receivable .......................    282

f)  A check for $78 was accepted in full settlement of a recent $80 invoice to Windlass Industries, Inc.:

Cash............................................. 78
Accounts Receivable............................. 2
Sales Revenue .............................    80

g)  A power saw with an original cost of $560 and accumulated depre-
ciation of $480 was sold for $90:

Cash............................................. 90
Equipment.................................    90

20. The Club Company was formed to provide meals and entertainment for its members. It started its operations on January 1, 19x6. The
club's board of directors wants an income statement for the first nine
months of 19x6. Make journal entries to bring the books up to date, reflecting the following information:

(1)  Beverages costing $1,000 were purchased in January, at which
time an account "Beverage Expense" was debited. A count of
beverages on hand on September 30 indicated that one quarter
of the January purchase had not been consumed as of that date.
(2)  Kitchen and bar equipment was purchased on January 1. The
amount of $40,000 was debited to an account, "Equipment." No
depreciation was charged. It was estimated that the equipment

would last for 16 years from date of purchase, with no salvage value at the end of that time.

(3)  On August 31, the club borrowed $5,000 from a member. The club gave the member a note, promising to repay the $5,000 within 90 days plus interest on this note at a rate of 9 percent per year. No interest payment was made prior to September 30.

(4)  The club's weekly payroll amounted to $1,470, of which $210 was for bar service, $150 was for the building custodian, $180 was for secretarial help, and $930 was for dining room employees. The club was open three days a week – Friday, Saturday, and Sunday. Employees were paid regularly on Saturday, each weekly paycheck covering the preceding Saturday, Sunday, and Friday. The Saturday, September 29 payroll, which was recorded correctly, covered the week that ended Friday, September 28. Employer payroll taxes of 10 percent were applicable to these payrolls.

(5)  The account "Prepaid Insurance" had been debited for all insurance premiums paid. The balance in this account on September 30 was $480. Analysis showed that this represented $120 paid on January 1, 19x6, for fire insurance covering the calendar years 19x6 and 19x7, and $360 for workmen's compensation and general liability insurance covering the calendar year 19x6.

(6)  On June 1, 19x6, the Club Company received $360 from employees of a neighboring store in payment for parking privileges in the club's lot. The payment covered one year's parking fees to May 31, 19x7, and was entered in an account titled "Miscellaneous Rental Income."

(7)  Local property taxes on the club's building, covering the period July 1, 19x6, through June 30, 19x7, amounting to $2,400, had not been paid and were not due until November 30, 19x6.

(8)  The club's cigar counter and checkroom were operated by two young college students as a concession; they paid the club $10 a week for the privilege. The last payment received covered the period up to and including Sunday, September 2.

**21.** In each of the following, prepare the journal entry that is necessary to adjust the accounts as of the end of the fiscal year. *Each part of this question is independent of the others.* In each case, assume that the company is engaged in wholesaling, that its fiscal year ended on December 31, 19x1, and that *the books for 19x1 have not yet been closed.* (If no entry is necessary, write "no entry.")

(1)  Local property taxes covering the period October 1, 19x1, through September 30, 19x2, are expected to amount to $30,000. These will be paid in July, 19x2.

(2)  Bills are received on January 10, 19x2, covering electric service for the month of December, 19x1, totaling $1,000.

(3)  The perpetual inventory records indicate that the cost of merchandise on hand on December 31, 19x1, was $50,500. A physical count has revealed that the amount actually on hand originally cost $48,500.

(4) The last weekly payroll period of 19x1 ended on December 27. The next weekly payroll covered the period December 27, 19x1, through January 2, 19x2. This included three working days in 19x1 and two working days in 19x2, holidays being counted as "working days" for this purpose. The total January 2 payroll was $25,000, of which $5,000 was for office employees and $20,000 was for store employees. (Employer payroll taxes may be ignored.)

(5) In 19x0 the company purchased merchandise for inventory amounting to $10,000, but at the time of acquisition the purchase was incorrectly debited to "Office Supplies Expense." The merchandise itself was placed in the storeroom, however, and was counted properly in the annual physical inventory taken at the end of 19x0. In reviewing certain records now, just after the end of 19x1, the earlier error has been discovered.

(6) A machine that had cost $11,000 when new, was sold during 19x1 for $5,000. At the time of the sale, its "book value" was $3,000. To record the sale, a bookkeeper debited Cash and credited Other Income.

(7) The company uses the gross price method of recording sales. On December 31, 19x1, the balance in Accounts Receivable was $40,000. The company grants a 2 percent cash discount for prompt payment, and it is expected that all of the amounts receivable on December 31, 19x1, will be paid during the cash discount period.

22. The Tabor Supply Company sells scientific instruments to the trade. After all entries in the company's journals for 19x0 had been posted to the ledger accounts, the journals were destroyed by fire. The company's accountants have been able to reconstruct most of the journal entries from the basic documents, but in each of the following accounts *one* entry is still unexplained. In each case, reconstruct the complete journal entry that was *most probably* made during the year and which will account for the unexplained portion of the change in the account balance. Each problem is independent of the other problems. You should assume that the balances are correct and therefore that no correcting entries are required:

*Example:*
    Given: Capital Stock account:

| | |
|---|---|
| Beginning balance | $ 40,000 |
| Ending balance | 65,000 |

Answer:

| | | |
|---|---|---|
| Cash | 25,000 | |
|     Capital Stock | | 25,000 |

*a)* Retained Earnings account:

| | |
|---|---|
| Beginning balance | $ 95,000 |
| Ending balance | 100,000 |
| Net income for year, transferred by closing | 12,000 |

*b)* Prepaid Insurance account:

| | | |
|---|---|---|
| Beginning balance | $ | 2,400 |
| Expired during period | | 2,600 |
| Ending balance | | 1,900 |

*c)* Wages Payable account:

| | | |
|---|---|---|
| Beginning balance | $ | 1,100 |
| Wages paid | | 10,500 |
| Ending balance | | 1,400 |

*d)* Accounts Receivable account (at gross):

| | | |
|---|---|---|
| Beginning balance | $ | 100,000 |
| Written off as bad | | 2,000 |
| Cash received | | 200,000 |
| Discounts allowed | | 4,000 |
| Ending balance | | 110,000 |

*e)* Patents account:

| | | |
|---|---|---|
| Ending balance | $ | 20,000 |
| Purchased for cash | | 10,000 |
| Beginning balance | | 14,500 |

*f)* Accounts Payable account:

| | | |
|---|---|---|
| Beginning balance | $ | 50,000 |
| Ending balance | | 70,000 |
| Purchases | | 90,000 |
| Returns | | 2,000 |

*g)* Buildings account:

| | | |
|---|---|---|
| Beginning balance | $ | 200,000 |
| New building purchased | | 50,000 |
| Ending balance | | 230,000 |

Building—Accumulated Depreciation account:

| | | |
|---|---|---|
| Net increase in account balance | $ | 35,000 |
| Depreciation expense | | 42,000 |
| Note: There were no cash receipts from sale of buildings. | | |

*23. On December 31, the unadjusted trial balance of the Robant Hardware Company showed the following accounts and balances:

| | | |
|---|---|---|
| Cash | $ | 56,000 |
| Accounts receivable | | 170,000 |
| Inventory | | 525,000 |
| Furniture and fixtures | | 200,000 |
| Allowance for depreciation—furniture and fixtures | | 125,000 |
| Prepaid insurance | | 2,000 |
| Prepaid rent | | 1,000 |
| Accounts payable | | 100,000 |
| Capital stock | | 200,000 |
| Retained earnings | | 117,000 |
| Sales | | 500,000 |
| Wage expense | | 20,000 |
| Rent expense | | 11,000 |

| | |
|---|---:|
| Miscellaneous expenses | 55,000 |
| Dividends declared | 2,000 |

The following additional information is available:

(1) Depreciation for the year, equal to 12 percent of the original cost of the furniture and fixtures, had not yet been recorded.
(2) The correct balance in the Prepaid Insurance account at the end of the year was $1,200.
(3) The company had no prepaid rent on December 31.
(4) The company owed $4,000 to employees on December 31 for work done during the year.
(5) The annual physical inventory showed that goods costing $225,000 were on hand on December 31.

a) Set up T-accounts, enter the figures from the trial balance, and make any necessary adjusting entries. Insurance expense is classified as a miscellaneous expense.
b) Prepare in good form an income statement for the year and a statement of financial position as of December 31.

*24. The December 31, 19x3, unadjusted trial balance of the Guyton Company is shown below:

### The Guyton Company
#### TRIAL BALANCE
#### As of December 31, 19x3

| | Debit | Credit |
|---|---:|---:|
| Cash | $ 28,800 | |
| Temporary investments | 17,700 | |
| Accounts receivable | 91,600 | |
| Allowance for uncollectible accounts | | $ 1,500 |
| Inventory of merchandise, January 1, 19x3 | 89,000 | |
| Prepaid insurance | 1,900 | |
| Other prepaid expenses | 1,340 | |
| Land | 16,000 | |
| Building and equipment | 45,800 | |
| Allowance for depreciation, building, and equipment | | 8,100 |
| Accounts payable | | 18,800 |
| Mortgage on real estate | | 45,000 |
| Capital stock | | 150,000 |
| Retained earnings | | 53,720 |
| Sales | | 412,000 |
| Sales discounts, returns, and allowances | 12,000 | |
| Estimated customer defaults | 2,100 | |
| Interest income | | 480 |
| Purchases | 344,500 | |
| Advertising | 1,200 | |
| Salaries and wages | 16,400 | |
| Miscellaneous selling expense | 5,800 | |
| Property taxes | 3,300 | |
| Insurance expense | 525 | |
| Miscellaneous general expenses | 8,435 | |
| Interest expense | 3,200 | |
| Total | $689,600 | $689,600 |

Information for adjustments:

(1) Accrued interest payable on mortgage,
    December 31, 19x3 ............................... $    400
(2) Insurance expired (last quarter).....................    175
(3) Accrued wages payable, December 31, 19x3 ........    240
(4) Depreciation expense, building and equipment......  1,240
(5) Inventory of merchandise, December 31, 19x3 ...... 86,440
(6) Merchandise received, December 31, 19x3, but not
    recorded in the accounts or included in the inventory
    count .........................................    975
(7) Cash discounts available to customers,
    December 31, 19x3 ...............................    890
(8) Estimated uncollectible receivables,
    December 31, 19x3 ...............................  2,150

Set up T-accounts, enter the figures from the trial balance, and make any necessary adjusting entries. Then prepare: (a) a balance sheet as of December 31, 19x3; and (b) an income statement for the period ended December 31, 19x3.

**25.** The preliminary trial balance of the Blackstone Machine Company taken on December 31 is shown below:

**Blackstone Machine Company**
**PRELIMINARY TRIAL BALANCE**
December 31

| *Debit* | | *Credit* | |
|---|---|---|---|
| Cash........................$ | 60,000 | Accounts payable...........$ | 50,000 |
| Accounts receivable........ | 197,500 | Notes payable.............. | 140,000 |
| Inventories................. | 370,000 | Accrued payroll ............ | 3,000 |
| Land....................... | 40,000 | Accrued interest............ | 2,000 |
| Buildings .................. | 150,000 | Accrued taxes.............. | 5,000 |
| Machinery and equipment... | 400,000 | Mortgage on real estate..... | 100,000 |
| Dividends declared ......... | 36,000 | Allowance for depreciation: | |
| Sales returns and allowances | 26,000 | Buildings ................ | 30,000 |
| Discounts allowed customers | 17,000 | Machinery and equipment | 90,000 |
| Cost of goods sold........... | 785,000 | Common stock ............. | 600,000 |
| Administrative expense..... | 45,000 | Retained earnings.......... | 165,000 |
| Interest expense ............ | 14,000 | Sales...................... | 1,080,000 |
| Selling expense ............. | 132,000 | Interest income ............ | 500 |
| | | Discounts received ......... | 7,000 |
| Total...................$2,272,500 | | Total..................$2,272,500 | |

The auditors' investigation has disclosed the following facts:

(1) The physical inventory count, taken on December 31, was accurate. The balance in the Inventories account has already been corrected to reflect the quantities revealed by this count.

(2) $1,500 should be added to the Accrued Taxes account because

a dispute as to the proper income tax for a previous year has been settled in favor of the government.

(3) Merchandise shipped back for credit by a customer on December 29 has not been recorded. This merchandise cost $1,400 and had been sold to the customer at a price of $2,100. The merchandise is in salable condition and will be placed back in the merchandise stockroom as soon as it is received.

(4) A purchase of equipment for $2,000 was debited to the Inventories account at the time of purchase.

(5) On December 1 the company gave its bank a 60-day note with a face value of $140,000. The bank discounted this note at 9 percent and the company debited the interest of $2,100 to Discounts Allowed Customers.

(6) The cash amount shown on the trial balance is the sum of the balances in three accounts: Cash on Hand, Cash in Bank, and Petty Cash. Petty Cash includes $2,600 advanced to salesmen for travel and entertainment expenses. December expense statements received from salesmen early in January amount to $1,700.

(7) Machinery costing $17,000 has been sold and the proceeds of $2,000 debited to cash and credited to Sales, no other record being made. The book value of these assets at the time of sale was $4,800.

(8) An invoice for raw materials received on December 29 has been recorded at $5,290 instead of $5,920, the bookkeeper having transposed the 9 and the 2.

(9) No provision has been made for the 2 percent discounts offered for payment within 10 days on $100,000 of sales made subsequent to December 21.

(10) The board of directors on December 15 declared a quarterly dividend to shareholders, amounting to $12,000, payable on the following January 5. This action has not been recorded.

a) Prepare any journal entries that are necessary to reflect this additional information.

b) Prepare an income statement for the year, together with a statement of changes in retained earnings.

c) Prepare a statement of financial position at the end of the year.

d) Prepare all entries necessary to close the accounts at the end of the year.

26. The Caron Corporation operates an appliance store and repair shop. It has four kinds of inventory: merchandise, store supplies, office supplies, and repair supplies. Purchases of merchandise and repair supplies are charged initially to separate purchase accounts; purchase of store and office supplies are entered directly in inventory accounts. The company does not keep perpetual inventory records; instead it counts the inventories on hand at the end of each quarter. The fiscal year begins each year on January 1. The company's trial balance on March 31, 19x4, was as follows:

|  | Debit | Credit |
|---|---|---|
| Cash ............................................. | $ 22,372 | |
| Accounts receivable ............................. | 67,840 | |
| Allowance for uncollectible accounts .............. | | $   1,830 |
| Merchandise inventory ........................... | 61,180 | |
| Prepaid insurance ............................... | 2,000 | |
| Store equipment................................. | 28,600 | |
| Allowance for depreciation − store equipment ....... | | 8,150 |
| Office equipment ................................ | 10,200 | |
| Allowance for depreciation − office equipment....... | | 3,870 |
| Repair equipment ............................... | 20,400 | |
| Allowance for depreciation − repair equipment ...... | | 7,010 |
| Store supplies .................................. | 330 | |
| Office supplies.................................. | 1,260 | |
| Accounts payable................................ | | 49,700 |
| Notes payable .................................. | | 20,000 |
| Common stock .................................. | | 80,000 |
| Retained earnings ............................... | | 29,840 |
| Revenue from sale of merchandise ................. | | 185,130 |
| Repair department revenues....................... | | 17,440 |
| Purchases of merchandise......................... | 97,330 | |
| Repair supplies purchased ........................ | 800 | |
| Salaries, store employees ......................... | 40,100 | |
| Payroll taxes, store ............................. | 2,807 | |
| Sundry store expenses ........................... | 7,600 | |
| Salaries and wages, repair employees.............. | 11,900 | |
| Payroll taxes, repair department................... | 833 | |
| Sundry repair department expenses................. | 2,030 | |
| Salaries, office employees......................... | 18,400 | |
| Payroll taxes, office ............................. | 1,288 | |
| Sundry office expenses........................... | 5,700 | |
| Total ....................................... | $402,970 | $402,970 |

The following additional information is available:

(1)  An inventory count at the end of March revealed the following balances: merchandise, $58,920; store supplies, $140; office supplies, $660; repair supplies, $350.

(2)  The balance in Notes Payable on the trial balance represents a 90-day, 9 percent promissory note dated March 16, 19x4, and due on June 14, 19x4. Interest on this note had not yet been recorded in the accounts; it was to be paid along with the face value of the note on June 14, 19x4.

(3)  Depreciation is calculated at the following rates: store equipment, 10 percent of original cost per year; office equipment, 20 percent per year; and repair equipment, 8 percent per year. No purchases or sales of equipment were made between January 1 and March 31.

(4)  Wages earned during March but unpaid as of March 31 were as follows: store, $1,500; office, $600; repair department, $400. These wages were subject to employer payroll taxes totaling 10 percent.

(5)  Uncollectible accounts in this company average 0.5 percent of merchandise sales.

(6)  The balance in Prepaid Insurance reflects the January 1 unexpired premiums on the following three policies: (a) a three-year

fire insurance policy expiring March 31, 19x5, three-year premium $2,160; (b) a one-year workmen's compensation policy, expiring December 31, 19x4, annual premium $800; and (c) a one-year comprehensive liability policy, expiring June 30, 19x4, annual premium $600.

(7)  Dividends amounting to $1,500 were declared on March 20, payable on April 15, 19x4.

(8)  Property taxes amount to $6,000 a year; taxes for the calendar year 19x4 were payable on August 1, 19x4.

a)  Adjust the account balances to reflect the additional information provided above. You will probably find it useful to set up T-accounts, enter the figures from the trial balance, and then enter your analyses of the facts given above.

b)  Prepare an income statement for the three months that ended on March 31, 19x4. In this statement separate, insofar as possible, the results of operations of the company's sales and repair departments.

c)  Prepare a statement of financial position as of March 31, 19x4.

27.  Barclay Distributors, Inc., was organized on January 1, 19x0. During its first four years of operation, only cash receipts and cash disbursements were recorded as part of the daily bookkeeping routine. Revenues were recognized at the time of collection; purchases were recognized at the time of payment. At the end of each year, a physical count of merchandise inventories was made (all goods on hand or in transit were included in the count, regardless of whether cash payment had been made), and the cost of goods sold was determined by subtracting this amount from the sum of the January 1 merchandise inventory and the cash purchases of merchandise during the year. A depreciation charge was also computed at the end of each year. No other departures were made from a strict cash basis of accounting.

The unadjusted trial balance of this company on December 31, 19x3, showed the following items:

|  | Debit | Credit |
|---|---|---|
| Cash | $ 2,230 | |
| Merchandise | 15,000 | |
| Furniture and equipment | 30,000 | |
| Accumulated depreciation | | $ 9,000 |
| Notes payable | | 10,000 |
| Common stock | | 30,000 |
| Retained earnings | 3,000 | |
| Dividends declared | 0 | |
| Sales | | 117,000 |
| Merchandise purchases | 66,700 | |
| Cost of goods sold | 0 | |
| Wages and salaries | 33,000 | |
| Payroll taxes | 2,970 | |
| Rent | 6,700 | |
| Utilities | 1,300 | |
| Depreciation | 0 | |
| Interest expense | 400 | |
| Other expense | 4,700 | |
| Total | $166,000 | $166,000 |

At the end of 19x3, Mr. Dennis Barclay, the president of the company, engaged an accounting firm to review his accounting system and to draw up financial statements for the year. The accountants' first recommendation, to adopt the accrual basis of accounting, was accepted by Mr. Barclay. Investigation by the accountants then revealed the following facts:

(1)   Depreciation of 10 percent of original cost had not yet been recorded for 19x3.

(2)   Merchandise on hand on December 31, 19x3, amounted to $12,700; the comparable January 1, 19x3, figure was listed on the trial balance opposite Merchandise.

(3)   Amounts payable for merchandise on hand but not yet paid for totaled $6,000 on January 1, 19x3, $4,500 on December 31, 19x3.

(4)   Amounts due from customers for goods shipped were $14,200 on January 1, 19x3, and $19,600 on December 31, 19x3.

(5)   Accrued interest on notes payable amounted to $300 on January 1, 19x3, and $200 on December 31, 19x3.

(6)   Wages earned but unpaid totaled $800 on January 1, 19x3, and $1,200 on December 31, 19x3; employer's payroll taxes averaging 9 percent were applicable to these amounts.

(7)   Unpaid utilities bills were $150 on January 1, 19x3, and $175 on December 31, 19x3.

(8)   Rent was paid monthly until September, when a new lease was negotiated. Rent of $4,000 for one year in advance was paid on October 1, 19x3.

(9)   Two employees had expense advances of $250 each, an amount that had not changed during the year. When these sums were originally advanced in 19x1, the debit was to Other Expense. On January 4, 19x4, the two employees submitted December, 19x3, expense statements totaling $140 and checks were drawn to restore the cash advances to the full amount.

(10)   A check in the amount of $1,000, dated December 31, 19x3, and in payment for two new electric typewriters for the office, was incorrectly debited to Merchandise Purchases.

(11)   The balance in the Cash account represented the company's bank balance. The accountants found that an additional $150 was in the change drawer in the cash register.

(12)   An additional $3,500 in undeposited checks was found in the back of Mr. Barclay's desk on January 1, 19x4. It was Mr. Barclay's custom to let the checks accumulate for a week or so until his bookkeeper told him that the bank balance was dangerously low. Then he would send all the undeposited checks to the bank for deposit. One such deposit had been made on December 31, 19x2.

(13)   A check in the amount of $136, payable to the Jones Plumbing Company for plumbing repairs and dated December 18, 19x3, was incorrectly recorded in the cashbook and ledger at $163.

a)   Establish T-accounts, enter the amounts from the trial balance, and make whatever adjustments are necessary to bring the accounts up to date on an accrual basis as of December 31, 19x3.
b)   Prepare a balance sheet in good form as of December 31, 19x3.
c)   Prepare an income statement for the year 19x3. The adjustment necessary to convert the balance in Retained Earnings from the cash basis to an accrual basis as of the beginning of 19x3 should be entered directly in the Retained Earnings account. It should not be shown on the income statement for 19x3.
d)   Compare the net income figure for 19x3 with the figure that would have been reported for Barclay Distributors, Inc., if the company had remained on a cash basis.

28.  (Review Problem) The income statement for Crestmore Stores, Inc., for last year and the company's statement of financial position as of the end of the year were as follows:

Crestmore Stores, Inc.
### STATEMENT OF FINANCIAL POSITION
At the End of Last Year
(000 omitted)

ASSETS

| | | |
|---|---|---|
| *Current assets:* | | |
| Cash ................................................... | | $   321 |
| Accounts receivable ($235 gross, less allowance for | | |
| uncollectible amounts, $21) ........................... | | 214 |
| Merchandise inventory ................................. | | 578 |
| Prepaid rent........................................... | | 14 |
| Total current assets ................................ | | $1,127 |
| Furniture and equipment ............................... | $660 | |
| Less: Accumulated depreciation........................ | 279 | 381 |
| Total Assets ........................................ | | $1,508 |

LIABILITIES AND SHAREOWNERS' EQUITY

| | | |
|---|---|---|
| *Current liabilities:* | | |
| Accounts payable ..................................... | | $     64 |
| Accrued salaries and wages ........................... | | 16 |
| Accrued income taxes payable ......................... | | 87 |
| Total current liabilities ........................... | | $   167 |
| *Shareowners' equity:* | | |
| Capital stock (480,000 shares)........................ | $460 | |
| Retained earnings..................................... | 881 | |
| Total shareowners' equity ........................... | | 1,341 |
| Total Liabilities and Shareowners' Equity ......... | | $1,508 |

Crestmore Stores, Inc.
INCOME STATEMENT
For Last Year

| | | |
|---|---:|---:|
| Gross sales | | $2,776 |
| Less: Cash discounts | $ 53 | |
| Estimated customer defaults | 22 | 75 |
| Net sales | | $2,701 |
| Expenses: | | |
| Cost of goods sold | $1,221 | |
| Salaries and wages | 920 | |
| Rent | 122 | |
| Depreciation | 46 | |
| Lost and stolen merchandise | 12 | |
| Other operating expenses | 133 | |
| Interest | 7 | |
| Income taxes | 96 | |
| Total expenses | | 2,557 |
| Net Income | | $  144 |

You have the following figures from the company's operating budget for the current year (in thousands of dollars):

(1)  Gross sales, $3,595.
(2)  Cash discounts on sales, $68.
(3)  Estimated customer defaults, $18 (0.5% of gross sales).
(4)  Write-offs of specific customer accounts as uncollectible, $14.
(5)  Accounts receivable (gross) at end of year (after write-offs of specific uncollectible accounts), $350.
(6)  Purchases of merchandise for resale, $1,857.
(7)  Payments to suppliers of merchandise, $1,612.
(8)  Cost of merchandise lost or stolen, $20.
(9)  Merchandise inventory at end of year (as determined by physical count), $1,040.
(10)  Salaries and wages paid, $1,199.
(11)  Accrued salaries and wages at end of year, $30.
(12)  Rental payments, $171.
(13)  Prepaid rent, balance at year-end, $26.
(14)  Other operating expenses, paid in cash, $201.
(15)  Depreciation on furniture and equipment, $78.
(16)  Income tax payments, $103.
(17)  Income tax expense, $163. (The company will benefit for one final year from special tax advantages, and for this reason the tax rate is lower than the normal rate.)

The following additional information is available from the capital expenditure and finance budgets for the year (in thousands of dollars):

(18)  Quarterly dividends to be declared March 20, June 20, September 20, and December 20, for cash payment 60 days later, $12 each quarter.
(19)  Proceeds of bank loan, carrying interest at 9 percent, to be re-

ceived on July 1, $400. Interest will be payable to the bank semi-annually, the first payment falling due on January 1 of next year. Management does not intend to borrow any other money during the year.

(20)  Proceeds from sale of additional shares of common stock to be issued on December 24 to company officers under stock option plan, 10,000 shares, $27 ($2.70 a share).

(21)  Purchases of store and office furniture and equipment for cash, $628.

(22)  Retirement and disposal of worn and obsolete furniture and store equipment: original cost, $235, accumulated depreciation, $146, cash proceeds from sale, $76.

a)  Prepare an estimated income statement for the current year and an estimated end-of-year balance sheet. (Probably the most efficient way to proceed is to set up accounts, enter the year-beginning balances, and then enter the information provided above.)

b)  Prepare a statement of the estimated cash flows for the year, consisting of three sections: (1) the net cash flow (receipts minus disbursements) from ordinary operations; (2) other cash receipts; and (3) other cash disbursements.

c)  Be ready to comment briefly on the apparent profitability, liquidity, and financial policies of Crestmore Stores, Inc., insofar as you can determine them from the information provided above.

d)  Prepare a rough estimate of the effects that achieving a sales level of only 90 percent of the budgeted amount would have on net income and cash. What assumptions did you make in preparing this estimate? How might management use this additional information?

# 8

# PROCESSING
# ACCOUNTING DATA

RECORDING ACCOUNTING DATA is a much more complicated process than the preceding chapters may have implied. The years since the end of the World War II have witnessed an unparalleled growth both in the number of business transactions and in the speed and variety of the equipment available for processing them. Consequently, the design of the working details of data processing systems requires a great deal of technical knowledge, far more than this chapter can hope to provide. Its objective is more modest: to provide an understanding of the basic elements of similarity in processing systems and of some of the ways in which a few simple problems may be solved.

## GENERAL CHARACTERISTICS OF DATA PROCESSING SYSTEMS

Accounting data processing is only one kind of data processing, but it shares a number of basic elements with systems designed to process other kinds of data, such as scientific data or election data. A brief look at the characteristics of data processing systems in general is therefore a useful prelude to a discussion of accounting data processing.

### Basic Elements of Data Processing Systems

Every data processing system consists of inputs, files, a processor, and output. The principal inputs are various kinds of *data.* These data may be either factual or hypothetical, depending on the purpose of the system. The processor serves to convert these data into various forms of *output*, using data and instructions previously stored in the files to effect this result.

These relationships are shown graphically in Exhibit 8–1. In processing routine financial transactions, the data inputs are generally contained in documents; the information output is customarily in the form of a report or reports, although in very advanced systems it may also be in the form of direct instructions governing some element of the company's operations, the result of building a decision-making routine into the processor. There are also output documents, such as bank checks or invoices. Processing is the connection between inputs and outputs. It consists primarily of *classifying* the data, *sorting* them, *reading* them into the processing unit, *performing arithmetic* operations, *updating* files of data, and *preparing output* reports and documents.

Exhibit 8–1

BASIC ELEMENTS OF A DATA PROCESSING SYSTEM

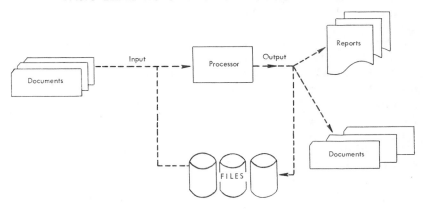

For example, in a bank the incoming checks (the documents) must first be classified by depositor account number, sorted on this basis, and read into the processor where they are merged with the day's deposits for each account. New account balances must then be prepared, and the results summarized to show the total of the day's transactions and the new balances in all accounts (files). Reports issued periodically to depositors and to various executives of the bank provide each with information useful for the decisions he has to make.

The sequence need not always be the same—sorting, for example, may be the second, third, or fourth step—but most processing programs will include all six steps at some time. Nor is it necessary that the processor be an electronic computer; a clerk with pencil and piece of paper performs the same function, and he may be able to do some of the preliminary steps more quickly than the auxiliary units of an electronic system, thus offsetting the computer's speed in performing arithmetic operations.

### Characteristics of Business Data Processing

Business data processing creates some difficult problems for the manufacturers of equipment and the designers of systems. Whereas in scientific work, relatively long and complex mathematical operations must be performed, business data processing is characterized by:

1. Large quantities of input data.
2. Extensive data files.
3. Large quantities of output documents and reports.
4. Few and simple computational operations.

For example, payroll preparation requires the extraction of basic data from each employee's attendance and work records, from records showing the number of dependents he claims for tax purposes and the other deductions he has authorized, and from tables of withholding tax rates, and so forth. The only computations required are simple arithmetic to find gross pay, deductions, and net pay for each employee. Output then consists of (1) a paycheck for each man, (2) account entries, and (3) updating of the files of employee earnings and deductions to date.

These characteristics place a premium on systems that can handle input and output rapidly; speed of arithmetic operations is important but is far less crucial than it is for scientific work. If documents can be fed into a computer at a rate of only 200 per minute, for example, it is of little relevance that the internal processor is capable of performing the arithmetic operations at a rate of 10,000 documents a minute. Consequently, progress in equipment design from a business data processing point of view is measured to a large extent in terms of the speed of input and output devices.

Business data processing also requires a large filing capacity easily accessible to the processor. A file drawer of accounts receivable cards, for example, might be located at the desk of the accounts receivable clerk. In processing either a credit sale or a collection, the clerk would remove the card from the file and make the appropriate entry, either by hand or on some kind of bookkeeping machine. The access time to any single account would be relatively short.

The greater the storage requirements, the more space is needed and the more difficult it is to secure rapid access to all parts of the file simultaneously. One clerk can no longer handle the entire job, and means must be provided for the larger processing task. A large department store with 50,000 accounts receivable, for example, might find it more economical to store accounts receivable data on reels of magnetic tape which can be connected to an electronic computer for updating. The continuing increase in the quantities of data contained in the files places increasing emphasis on cheap, compact storage capacity, readily accessible to the processor. Increasing capacity and accessibility of data storage units, therefore, is a second dimension of progress in equipment design for business data processing purposes.

## PROCESSING ROUTINE COMMERCIAL TRANSACTIONS

The largest single set of inputs to any financial information system almost inevitably must be provided by the multitude of routine commercial transactions, such as purchases and sales, payments and collections. It is not possible in these few pages to describe an actual data processing system of any complexity. Instead, the illustration that follows is intended to highlight some of the concepts underlying all or most data processing systems. To avoid obscuring this fundamental objective, discussion of the details of how computers or any other kinds of equipment work will be kept to a minimum.

### The Chart of Accounts

The Graham Company is a regional distributor of industrial supplies. The data processing equipment it uses is relatively simple and inexpensive, in line with the small size of its business. All systems entail some combination of people and equipment, but in the Graham Company very little equipment is used.

The first step in describing the company's system is to examine its chart of accounts. The adoption of a chart of accoutns or the alteration of an existing chart reflects crystallization of a policy decision as to the types of data to be collected and the manner in which such data are to be classified.

Data from a given transaction can be classified in many ways. For example, the revenue from the sale of merchandise might be identified as to the type of product, the department in which the sale took place, the salesman, and the type of customer. Some companies may make none of these classifications; others may make even more. The problem in each case is to try to anticipate the demands for data that will be made in the future and to design the chart of accounts to meet these demands. The problem is important. For example, if sales revenues are not classified by geographical region when they are recorded initially, a regional breakdown can be obtained later only at considerable cost.

The structure and content of the chart of accounts thus depend to a great extent on the kinds of information management and others will want to obtain. It is not surprising, therefore, that even relatively similar companies will have quite different charts of accounts. Most charts of accounts, nevertheless, have two kinds of classification in common: (1) classification by nature of the element, and (2) classification by organization unit.

As to the first of these, it is common practice to group all the asset accounts together, followed by liability, ownership, revenue, and expense accounts, in that order. Thus a representative list of accounts might be as follows:

| Account Numbers | Kind of Accounts |
|---|---|
| 100–199 | Assets |
| 200–299 | Liabilities |
| 300–399 | Owners' equities |
| 400–499 | Revenues |
| 500–599 | Cost of goods sold |
| 600–699 | Selling expenses |
| 700–799 | Administrative expenses |
| 800–899 | Financial expenses |
| 900–999 | Noncurrent income |

The numbering system used and the amount of detail provided in each category vary considerably, but it is from some such base that the account structure is built.

The second element common to most charts of accounts is organizational breakdown of manufacturing costs, revenues, and expenses. Most companies are organized in a network of subdivisions that might be referred to as departments. Each element of cost or revenue or expense can be traced to one or more of these departments, and the account structure generally reflects this basis of classification. A broad grouping might be:

| Department Numbers | Kind of Department |
|---|---|
| 10–29 | Marketing |
| 30–79 | Manufacturing |
| 80–89 | Accounting |
| 90–99 | Administration |

Exhibit 8–2

Graham Company

## CHART OF ACCOUNTS

| Acct. No. | Account Title |
|-----------|---------------|
| 100 | Cash |
| 101 | Petty Cash |
| 110 | Notes and Interest Receivable |
| 111 | Accounts Receivable |
| 112 | Allowance for Uncollectible Accounts |
| 120 | Merchandise Inventories |
| 150 | Prepaid Insurance |
| 170 | Land, Buildings, and Equipment |
| 171 | Allowance for Depreciation |
| 200 | Accounts Payable |
| 210 | Salaries and Wages Payable |
| 220 | Payroll Taxes Payable |
| 221 | Other Taxes Payable |
| 230 | Notes and Interest Payable |
| 300 | Capital Stock |
| 310 | Retained Earnings |
| 320 | Dividends Declared |
| 400 | Direct Sales |
| 401 | Direct Sales Returns and Allowances |
| 410 | Dealer Sales |
| 411 | Dealer Sales Returns and Allowances |
| 450 | Interest Income |
| 470 | Other Income |
| 500 | Cost of Goods Sold |
| 510 | Head Office Salaries and Wages |
| 511 | Other Head Office Expenses |
| 520 | Eastern Region Salaries and Wages |
| 521 | Other Eastern Region Expenses |
| 530 | Western Region Salaries and Wages |
| 531 | Other Western Region Expenses |
| 550 | Interest Expense |
| 560 | Income Taxes |

Thus the salary of a man in the marketing research department might be assigned to account 601 (salary expense), department 22 (marketing research); and the full coding would be 601–22. The larger the organization and the more kinds of data desired, the longer and more complicated this account identification will be.

Probably the most important purpose of organizational classification is in providing routine internal control reports. The responsibilities of various people within the business organization require that they be currently informed of the impact of financial events upon those business activities over which they have jurisdiction. This requires classification of costs and revenues by responsibility, and responsibility typically can be expressed in organizational terms.

The Graham Company's chart of accounts, reproduced in Exhibit 8–2, is very simple. Product revenues are divided into only two categories, direct sales and dealer sales, while expenses are divided among only three general organization units (head office, eastern region, and western region). Of course, even though the management of the Graham Company is very close to the day-to-day operations of the business, and thus has less need for the kind of impersonal financial information that stems from the accounting system, the accounts in Exhibit 8–2 are not sufficiently detailed to provide management with essential information. This shortcoming is remedied by subdividing many of the accounts to provide additional detail. For the moment, these additional refinements are ignored in order to concentrate more fully on other aspects of the company's system.

## Multicolumn Journals: Purchases

Once the account structure has been established, the accountant's next task is to decide how each class of transactions is to be read into the accounting system. One of the most important classes of transactions in the Graham Company is the purchase of merchandise, equipment, and supplies. As indicated previously, the first place at which such a transaction would enter the accounting system would be in the journal, or chronological record of transactions. Until now it has been assumed that all transactions, regardless of type, are recorded in only one journal. Thus in chronological sequence might be found a purchase, a sale, a payment, another sale, etc.

A moment's reflection will indicate that even in the smallest companies this procedure would be unnecessarily tedious and expensive. For each transaction at least two account titles would have to be written out in full in the journal. Then each dollar figure would have to be posted to an appropriate ledger account. Thus, every number would have to be recorded twice. If 100 different purchases of merchandise were recorded during a given week, 100 separate entries of the following form would be necessary, identical in all respects except amount and vendor name:

Merchandise Inventories. . . . . . . . . . . . . . . . . . . . . . . . . . . . . . xxx
    Accounts Payable — Vendor X . . . . . . . . . . . . . . . . . . . . . .        xxx

One way to cut down on the amount of clerical work involved would be to add extra columns to the journal. For example, the journal might show the following column headings:

| Date | Explanation | Debit | | | Credit | | |
| | | 120 Merchandise Inventories | Other Debits | | 200 Accounts Payable | Other Credits | |
| | | | Acct. | Amount | | Acct. | Amount |
| | | | | | | | |
| | | | | | | | |
| | | | | | | | |
| | | | | | | | |

This is known as a *multicolumn journal* and has two main advantages over the two-column journal: (1) the merchandise inventory and accounts payable account titles do not have to be written out each time a transaction affects those accounts; and (2) the effort of posting debits to Merchandise Inventories and credits to Accounts Payable may be reduced by posting only the column totals instead of each item. Thus if 15 purchases of merchandise are listed on a single page of the journal, only one number needs to be posted to the Merchandise Inventories account instead of 15.

These advantages are important, but a single multicolumn journal is seldom sufficient except for very small enterprises with relatively few accounts. To reap the benefits from the multicolumn journal, a separate column must be made for each account that is encountered frequently, which typically would require too many columns for efficient use.

### Special Journals: The Purchases Journal

The Graham Company goes one step farther and uses what is known as a *special journal* to record purchases. This journal, generally known as the purchases journal or voucher register, is shown in Exhibit 8–3. Because most purchases are either of merchandise or of supplies for the head or regional offices, special columns have been established for debits to the four accounts designed to receive these costs. Debits to other accounts must be recorded in the two rightmost columns of the journal and posted individually.

For example, office equipment costing $737 was included in the January 3 purchase from the ABC Company (Voucher No. 1002). Because equipment purchases are relatively infrequent in the Graham Company, no separate column is provided for them.

The charge to account No. 170 – Land, Buildings, and Equipment – was therefore recorded in the right-hand pair of columns.

Exhibit 8–3

Graham Company

PURCHASES JOURNAL

| Date | Voucher No. | Name of Supplier | Credit | Debit | | | | | | |
|------|-------------|------------------|--------|-------|---|---|---|---|---|---|
| | | | 200 Accts. Payable | 120 Merch. Inventories | 511 Head Office Expense | 521 Eastern Region Expense | 531 Western Region Expense | Other Accounts | | |
| | | | | | | | | No. | Amt. |
| 1/3 | 1001 | Jones, Inc. | 300 | 300 | | | | | |
| 1/3 | 1002 | ABC Co. | 867 | 130 | | | | 170 | 737 |
| 1/4 | 1003 | Ulm Bros. | 242 | | 141 | 23 | 78 | | |
| | | | | | | | | | |
| | | | Only column totals posted | | | | | Individual amounts posted | |

As the exhibit shows, each purchase is assigned a "voucher number." The Graham Company's *voucher system* requires that a voucher be issued for each purchase of outside goods and services except small cash purchases which are handled by simpler means, as described later in this chapter. The purpose of this voucher is to notify the company's treasurer that the vendor's charges are legitimate, and no payment can be made unless a voucher has been issued. The purpose of this restriction is to provide an opportunity for a member of the controller's staff to answer such questions as: Was the purchase approved by someone authorized to do so? Were the goods received? Have the amounts been transcribed correctly?[1]

The sequence of events in processing a purchase transaction may be summarized briefly:

---

[1] For more information on voucher systems, see Arthur W. Holmes and Wayne S. Overmyer, *Auditing: Principles and Procedures* (7th ed.; Homewood, Ill.: Richard D. Irwin, Inc., 1971), especially chaps. iv and v.

1. An executive (e.g., the warehouse manager) prepares a *requisition* or request for the item.
2. The requisition is *approved* by the appropriate senior executive (for purchase of equipment at the Graham Company, presidential approval is required).
3. The purchasing agent places a *purchase order* with a supplier.
4. The supplier ships the order and sends an *invoice* or bill and a shipping notice or *bill of lading.*
5. Upon arrival, the goods are inspected for quantity and condition. Any shortages or defects are noted on the bill of lading which is then forwarded to the accounting department as a *receiving report.*
6. In the accounting department the invoice and receiving report are matched; a *purchase voucher* is issued, recorded in the *purchases journal,* and filed in the purchase voucher file.

In the case of services which are provided on a regular basis, such as telephone service, the requisition procedure can be bypassed, but the controller still has the obligation to examine the invoices and determine whether the charges are correct.

It should be noted that the form of the journal illustrated in Exhibit 8–3 is designed to accommodate a complete transaction on each line. Journals such as this are commonly prepared on a bookkeeping machine which is essentially a typewriter combined with several adding machine registers used to accumulate column totals. With the aid of carbon paper, individual postings may be made to account cards and to record the amounts owed to individual suppliers simultaneously with production of the journal record. In fact, in modern practice the journal is often more accurately described as a by-product of these other operations.

## Specialization in Data Processing

The above procedure is a good example of what is known as *batch processing.* In batch processing, transactions are normally grouped or sorted out in some fashion before processing so that the sequence of processing is different from the sequence in which the transactions enter the system. For example, the purchase transactions are pulled out of the random flow of transactions and processed as a group. After this kind of initial sorting, the input documents may undergo a second sorting into batches, each batch being homogeneous with respect to some characteristic.

For example, employee attendance cards for the week may be sorted first according to the department to which the employee is assigned so that the cards for all employees in a given department can be processed as a single batch. In other cases, the batching may be more random in nature. Thus, customer orders may be allowed to accumulate until 30 or 40 are on the supervisor's desk, at which point they will be gathered together as a batch. Batching permits a form of control over the data in that some key total may be determined when the batch is made up, such as the total number of hours or total number of dollars. This control then serves at later stages of processing as a partial check against loss or misreading of a document.

At the other extreme is *real-time processing*. It calls for processing each transaction as soon as it occurs and in the same sequence, with no intermediate batching or sorting. Such a system would permit each transaction to be put into some kind of transmitting device as it takes place and fed into a centralized computer which would identify the accounts affected, make the necessary entries, and issue instructions for the printing of any output documents required. The most familiar examples of real-time processing are in stock market transactions reporting, airline reservations accounting, and air defense warning systems; in such systems, delays may occur if the lines of communication to the processor are busy, in which case transactions must wait in line until the communication lines are cleared. For example, when trading is heavy on the stock exchange, the ticker may fall several minutes behind because the speed of the processor is inadequate to handle all of the incoming data.

The major advantage of real-time processing is its ability to keep the master files current. In certain business situations, a delay cannot be tolerated; the files must be kept up-to-date continuously. Real-time processing is the best means of achieving this goal, provided of course that satisfactory equipment is available. For example, an airline reservation system has to be so organized that the availability of passenger space on any flight can be determined at any time. Interrogations of the files may come from one or many locations, and the system must provide answers to the interrogations. Therefore, as soon as a reservation is made, the master file must be corrected so that the next interrogation will not receive a misleading answer.

The main disadvantage of real-time processing, of course, is that more complex and costly equipment is required, equipment that will be at least partially idle most of the time. Because all transactions enter the processing system in a random mix, the central processor must have access to the complete files at all times. This need for rapid access means in effect that the files must be stored within or linked to the central processor in ways that will reduce the search time necessary to locate any given bit of data. Such large-scale, random-access storage is expensive.

Most accounting transactions are currently handled by batching techniques. Bank checks are handled in batches. Payrolls are divided into groups, each group being handled as a separate payroll. Sales slips are also processed in batches. Batching permits a division of labor among the available personnel so that the work load is evenly distributed. The amount of idle time at any processing stage is reduced because the entire system does not have to be scaled to fit the speed of the slowest processing operation. For example, equipment to convert data into a form that is acceptable to electronic computers normally operates at a much slower speed than the computer itself. Similarly, the equipment used to convert the computer output into visible documents is also slower than the computer. Therefore, if these slow operations are performed *off line,* the central computer need be tied up only for computations. Data input can be stored temporarily on magnetic or paper tape and information output can be accumulated on magnetic tape for later printing on off-line printers. While the input and output operations are being performed, the computer is free to process other kinds of data.

### Subsidiary Ledgers

Up to now, Accounts Payable has been assumed to be the one account that is credited when a purchase is made. While this may be true, some kind of supplementary record of the amounts owed to individual suppliers is also generally desirable. This record may take the form of a file of cards, one for each vendor, or a file of unpaid invoices, or perhaps a reel of magnetic tape containing the same kinds of information. Such a supplementary record is known as a *subsidiary ledger* to distinguish it from the *general ledger* which is the one reflected in the chart of accounts in Exhibit 8–2 above.

The main purpose of the subsidiary ledger is to permit the accumulation of a considerable amount of detail on some aspects of the company's operations without unduly expanding the main file of accounts, or general ledger. The physical separation of the supplementary record and the general ledger facilitates posting to the subsidiary accounts. The clerical force can make entries in the accounts payable records, for example, without tying up the general ledger for long periods of time.

Any account that is supported by additional classified data is

*Exhibit 8-4*

Graham Company

GENERAL LEDGER CONTROL ACCOUNTS AND SUBSIDIARY LEDGERS

| *Acct. No.* | *Control Account Title* | *Subsidiary Ledger* |
|---|---|---|
| 110 ......... | Notes and Interest Receivable | Notes Receivable File |
| 111 ......... | Accounts Receivable | Customers Ledger |
| 120 ......... | Merchandise Inventories | Stock Records |
| 150 ......... | Prepaid Insurance | Insurance Policy File |
| 170 ......... | Land, Buildings, and Equipment | Property Records |
| 171 ......... | Allowance for Depreciation | Property Records |
| 200 ......... | Accounts Payable | Purchase Voucher File |
| 210 ......... | Salaries and Wages Payable | Employee Pay Records |
| 220 ......... | Payroll Taxes Payable | Employee Pay Records |
| 221 ......... | Other Taxes Payable | Tax Voucher File |
| 230 ......... | Notes and Interest Payable | Notes Payable File |
| 300 ......... | Capital Stock | Stockholders Register* |

* Maintained by the bank acting as the company's agent for recording transfers of stock ownership and for payment of dividends.

known as a *control account*. The balance in the control account at any time should be the same as the sum of the balances in the related subsidiary accounts. The Graham Company has a number of control accounts in its general ledger. These accounts, together with the associated subsidiary ledger in each case, are shown in Exhibit 8-4. In the course of this chapter several of these subsidiary ledgers will be discussed, but at the moment the only concern is with purchases and thus with the records underlying the Merchandise Inventory and Accounts Payable accounts.

The Graham Company uses a perpetual inventory system to determine the cost of goods sold. The stock records cards show both the quantities on hand and their cost. The items sold each day are identified by code numbers on the sales slips. Both physical quantities and dollar costs are subtracted from the balances shown on the stock cards. The total cost of the items sold each day is recorded by a single entry in the *cost of goods sold* journal. This does not distinguish between different categories of merchandise —if a detailed breakdown of the cost of goods sold becomes necessary, it is obtained by reprocessing the sales slips.

In some instances, the merchandise inventory records do not constitute a subsidiary ledger because they are kept in physical quantities only. This is a minor quibble, however, in that the stock records perform the same general kind of function as a subsidiary ledger except that they do not permit a cross-check on dollar account balances. The physical quantity records are maintained at the warehouse or in the stockroom and are used primarily as a means of keeping track of quantities on hand and on order, thus serving to alert the warehouse or stockroom manager when it is time to reorder specific items of merchandise.

The balance in the Graham Company's Accounts Payable account is supported by the purchase voucher file. Each vendor invoice is trated as a separate payable, and thus the file of unpaid vouchers can serve as the subsidiary ledger supporting the control account, Accounts Payable.

### Cash Disbursements: The Check Register

Once purchases have been duly recorded, the only step remaining is to pay the supplier and record this payment in the accounts. The purchase voucher provides authority for payment, and each day all invoices due for payment that day are withdrawn from the purchase voucher file and delivered to the treasurer. Attached to each voucher is an unsigned *check* that was prepared at the time the purchase voucher was made out and bearing the same identifying number as the voucher. This check is then signed by the treasurer. The check is recorded in the *check register* or *cash disbursements journal*, illustrated in Exhibit 8–5, and then mailed to the supplier along with a copy of the invoice.

Exhibit 8–5

Graham Company

CHECK REGISTER

| Date | Check No. | Payee | Credit | Debit | | | | |
|------|-----------|-------|--------|-------|---|---|---|---|
| | | | 100 Cash | 200 Accts. Payable | 210 Salaries and Wages Payable | Other Accounts | | |
| | | | | | | No. | Amt. |
| 1/3 | 8946 | Ace Stores | 680.03 | 680.03 | | | | |
| 1/3 | 1004 | 1st National Bank | 1400.00 | | | | 220 | 1,400.00 |
| | | | Only column totals posted | | | Individual amounts posted | | |

The check register is very similar in form to the purchases journal, except for differences in column headings. Again special columns are prepared only for those accounts that are affected by large numbers of cash transactions. In many small companies, the check register and its companion, the *cash receipts journal*, may constitute the only books of original entry used in the routine recording of transactions. Accrual entries are made infrequently, perhaps no more often than once a year, if at all. In most business firms of any size, however, other journals will be necessary, and two of these will be examined shortly.

It should be emphasized again that the main purpose of most of the documents involved in the purchase-payment sequence of transactions was not to provide for accounting entries. Instead, they were designed to communicate action information (how much to order, how much to pay, etc.). Their use as sources of input data for the bookkeeping records is a bonus, obtainable at little or no extra cost.

### Processing Payrolls

The Graham Company's system for handling its payrolls is tailored to the fact that a substantial amount of data must be recorded for each transaction. Although a number of alternatives exist, Graham has decided to use *punched card equipment.*

The basic feature of a punched card system is the transfer of data from the original document to a punched card in a form that can be read directly by a data processing machine. Data on the original document are transcribed onto a card by punching a series of holes representing numerals or alphabetic characters. Some of the data are transcribed in the form in which they appear on the original document (dollar amounts, customer name, and so forth) and some are first restated in terms of some code designator (account number, product number, class of customer, and so on). By reading the position of the holes and by identifying the column in which they appear, the processing machines are able to interpret the data correctly.

The card punching machine has a typewriter-like keyboard, but instead of printing letters or numerals on the card it punches holes. A separate vertical space or column must be reserved for each character, and the width of the card determines how many different letters or numbers can be punched, the most common number being 80. The position of the hole or holes punched in any one column indicates the letter or number that has been entered in that column. Once the data have been punched into cards, the original document is no longer of any use except as an evidentiary record of the transaction.

In the Graham Company, a payroll data card is maintained for each employee. This card shows the employee's name, department, rate of pay, number of dependents, and other facts needed for payroll preparation, plus a cumulative record of gross pay and withholdings to date for the current calendar year. At the end of each period, attendance cards or *clock cards* for all hourly employees are collected from the time clocks, showing the number of hours worked during the period. These data are coded and punched into a separate set of cards. All the basic data are now ready for payroll preparation.

The input data described above are now processed by machines. The processing sequence is as follows:

1. Each set of cards is *sorted* alphabetically.
2. The two sets of cards are then *collated* (matched) so that each employee's attendance or performance card is paired with his pay record card.
3. The collated cards are then fed into the processing machine which *computes* automatically gross pay, tax and other withholdings, net pay, and employer's payroll tax liabilities.
4. The computed amounts are then *accumulated* in a series of adding machine registers inside the processor, one for each of the accounts affected. Thus gross pay is accumulated in accounts 510, 520, and 530, while a parallel set of debits is made to accounts 511, 521, and 531 for the employer's share of payroll taxes. The credits are made to accounts 210 and 220 (including both employee and employer payroll tax contributions).

The exact means by which the processor performs the computations depends on the design of the equipment and the way it has been instructed or *programmed* to do the job. Programming a payroll is generally quite simple, in contrast to many business and scientific applications of electronic computers for which highly sophisticated programs are necessary.

Payroll preparation is characterized by a large number and variety of output documents. These may be produced immediately as each set of computations is completed, or the results of the computations may be stored temporarily on magnetic tape and printed later. The Graham Company's equipment is designed for batch processing, in which the input cards for one employee are read in and processed before the next pair of cards is introduced. The output for each employee is printed while the next pair of cards is being read in.

The Graham Company's payroll processing system has three basic kinds of output:

1. A *paycheck* for each employee, complete except for signature, with an attached stub showing gross pay, deductions, and net pay.
2. A new set of *pay record cards* with corrected cumulative amounts.
3. A *payroll journal*, showing all pertinent amounts, one line for each employee. The column totals provide the basis for entries in the ledger accounts. An example of a payroll journal is shown in Exhibit 8–6.

*Exhibit 8–6*

Graham Company

**PAYROLL JOURNAL**

| Date | Name of Employee | Debit | | | | | | Credit | |
|------|------------------|-------|-----|-----|-----|-----|-----|--------|-----|
| | | 510 | 511 | 520 | 521 | 530 | 531 | 210 | 220 |
| 4/26 | Adams, A. P. | 80.00 | 5.30 | | | | | 66.40 | 18.90 |
| 4/26 | Allen, D. G. | | | 100.00 | 6.63 | | | 83.80 | 22.83 |
| 4/26 | Andrews, R. | 120.00 | 7.95 | | | | | 96.50 | 31.45 |
| 4/26 | Arturo, P. X. | | | | | 90.00 | 5.96 | 80.10 | 15.86 |
| 4/26 | Bates, E. K. | | | | | 160.00 | 10.60 | 130.40 | 40.20 |
| 4/26 | · | · | · | · | · | · | · | · | · |
| 4/26 | · | · | · | · | · | · | · | · | · |
| 4/26 | · | · | · | · | · | · | · | · | · |

The completed payroll journal for a given pay period serves as the supporting voucher for all paychecks. All paychecks are numbered sequentially, and the total only is entered in one line of the check register as a debit to Salaries and Wages Payable and a credit to Cash.

## Processing Sales Transactions

Since the Graham Company's procedures for recording sales and cash receipts do not introduce any new concepts, they can be covered quickly. The principal documents associated with sales transactions in this firm are the *sales order* prepared by the sales-man, the *shipping document* prepared by the warehouse, the *invoice,* and the customer's *check.* The copies made of these documents and the disposition of each is depicted, with minor simplification, in Exhibit 8–7. Solid lines represent action com-munications; broken lines information communications. Copy 3 of the sales order goes to the office as a basis for follow-up on the

Exhibit 8–7

Graham Company

SALES DOCUMENT FLOWS

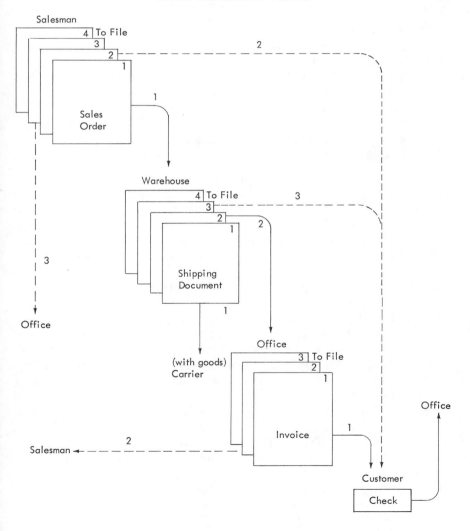

warehouse response to the original. Copy 2 of the invoice is kept by the salesman as evidence of the commission due him on the sale.

The office copies of the sales order and shipping documents together constitute the *sales voucher*, that is, the authority for preparing the invoice and recording the transaction. Since customers often pay more than one invoice with a single check, the sales vouchers and invoice copies are filed by customer. This file is the customers ledger. If an inquiry is received as to the balance of a customer's account, the answer is readily found by summing the totals of the vouchers contained in his folder.

The information given on each sales voucher is transferred to a punched card, thus making available data coded for machine reading. Any or all of the following outputs can then be produced:

1.  Itemized invoices ready for mailing.
2.  Sales by salesmen, and hence statistics for performance analysis; and in conjunction with the pay record cards, the sales payroll.
3.  Sales by inventory classes to reveal trends.
4.  Sales by customer further classified by (*a*) geographical area and (*b*) order size (this information is deemed useful in evaluating and directing sales efforts).

Once a month the sales cards are fed into a tabulating machine which then prints a *sales journal.* The sales journal is very simple, with columns for invoice number, debits to account 112-Accounts Receivable, and credits to accounts 400-Direct Sales and 410-Dealer Sales. The column totals are printed automatically at the end of the card run and are posted from there to the ledger.

The cards are then sorted by salesmen and run through the tabulating machine again. This time, however, only the total sales for each salesman are shown on the printed sheet; the amounts of the individual sales are accumulated inside the tabulating machine but are not printed. In this same tabulator run, the Graham Company's management obtains the third kind of output listed above, the amount of sales in each of the company's six main product lines.

These two card runs are made routinely each month. Sales analyses by customer group, order size, and other characteristics are performed less frequently, but having the data in coded form permits such analyses to be performed quickly and on short notice.

The point of primary interest is that *the same raw data can be classified in a number of different ways in order to extract their total information content.* Note, too, that not all of these analyses need be built into the formal account structure, nor must they be carried out routinely each month.

## Recording Cash Receipts

By far the greatest number of cash receipts in the Graham Company are collections from customers on accounts receivable. Thus, the *cash receipts journal,* which is illustrated in Exhibit 8–8, has only two special columns.

Exhibit 8–8

Graham Company

### CASH RECEIPTS JOURNAL

| Date | Ref. No. | Payer | Debit | Credit | | |
|------|----------|-------|-------|--------|--|--|
| | | | 100 Cash | 111 Accts. Receivable | Other Accounts | |
| | | | | | No. | Amt. |
| 1/1/xx | 12–211 | A. O. Aneen | 550 | 550 | | |
| 1/1/xx | N–27 | Renton's Market | 808 | | 110 | 808 |
| 1/1/xx | 12–212 | T. H. Count | 300 | 300 | | |

## The General Journal

The transactions that occur too infrequently to justify the establishment of a special journal are recorded in the general journal. In the Graham Company, periodic depreciation, property retirements, and other transactions not involving purchases, sales, or the payment or receipt of cash are recorded in the general journal. These constitute a relatively minor proportion of Graham's transactions, and it would actually be more costly to set up special journals than to continue to provide for them in the general journal.

To summarize, the accounting data flows in the Graham Company follow the streams indicated in Exhibit 8–9. Documents of various sorts provide the basic data not only for journalization but also for direct entries to some of the subsidiary ledgers. The general ledger includes a number of control accounts which serve to tie the subsidiary ledgers into the overall account structure and at the same time provide one check on the posting of data from documents to the subsidiary ledger accounts.

*Exhibit 8–9*
## ACCOUNTING RECORDS AND DATA FLOWS

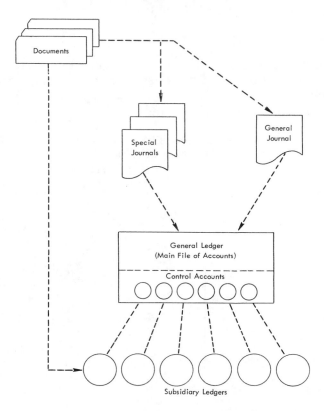

## OTHER DIMENSIONS OF ACCOUNTING DATA PROCESSING SYSTEMS

The procedures described above are essentially means of carrying out the physical task of converting given inputs into desired data or document outputs. The criteria for success are much the same as in any other production process: degree of adherence to scheduled completion dates and cost effectiveness.

A similar set of criteria applies to the data files: speed of access and cost, plus the added consideration of the adaptability of the data to the many different kinds of uses to which they can be put. "Trade-offs" between these criteria are inevitable; and finding the proper balance among cost, speed, and adaptability is no easy matter.

This situation is further complicated by the need for the system to meet other constraints, and brief mention of three of these is necessary before this chapter can be brought to a close:

1. The system must provide for an adequate system of safeguards against loss of assets through fraud or carelessness.
2. The system must be so constructed as to permit an independent verification that transactions have been recorded properly.
3. The system should provide some way of handling small cash disbursement transactions at low cost and minimal delay.

While these three constraints may not be of equal importance, all of them deserve at least brief discussion here.

## Internal Control

One of the main constraints imposed on any data processing system is that it provide reasonable protection against the loss of assets through fraud or carelessness. Each item of equipment purchased, for example, is typically assigned an identifying number. The *property records*, which consist of an inventory of these items, will show such details as the date purchased, original cost, dates and costs of alterations or major overhauls, and where the equipment is located. Part of this is to provide data for financial reporting or managerial decisions, but much of it is designed primarily to make sure that the company can keep track of what it owns.

Similarly, purchase orders, checks, and customer invoice forms are often numbered serially to guard against loss or unauthorized use. Totals shown on cash register tapes are checked against the amount of cash actually received. Internal audits are conducted periodically, primarily to insure that prescribed procedures are being followed, partly to discover procedures that need to be improved, and partly to prevent or detect asset losses.

The procedures illustrated above also contain internal control features, centering primarily on the division of responsibility for initiating and approving transactions. For example, the Graham Company's order clerk prepares a purchase order for the purchase of merchandise and supplies, but he does this only after receiving a purchase requisition signed by someone authorized to initiate purchases. After the goods are received, a different person, the controller, approves payment of the vendor's invoice by signing a voucher. Finally, the actual payment of cash is made by a third person, the treasurer.

This division of labor is occasioned largely by the need for different kinds of specialized skills, but also in part by the need for protecting the firm's assets. The functions of accounting and cash disbursement are divided between the controller and the treasurer primarily for the latter reason. This division is not a matter of distrusting the executives but of following the first principle of internal control, which requires that significant transactions be reviewed by more than one person. Thus, embezzlement becomes more difficult and a means of preventing costly and misleading errors is also provided.

Design of the internal control system is a problem in resource allocation no less than any other financial decision. The amount of *redundancy*, or duplication of paper work, that is built into a system depends on the size of the risk it is designed to insure against. The smaller the risk, the smaller the amount that should be spent to reduce it. Absolute protection is unobtainable in any case, and management has to learn to accept a certain amount of petty theft because it would cost more to prevent it than it would cost to replace the stolen items.

## The Audit Trail

Even in the light of the need for internal checks and balances, some of the procedures that have been described may have seemed wasteful and unnecessarily costly. Many accounting systems do include unnecessarily costly procedures. Much of what seems to be duplication of bookkeeping effort often does have a purpose, however, which is to leave a trail that someone else (the auditor) can retrace if he wishes to verify the legitimacy of the transactions and the accuracy of the classification and recording of the effects of the transactions. The trail is a means of locating numerical errors revealed in summarization and of preserving the raw data if later demands for information require reclassification on some new basis.

In some cases, the chronological record (the journal) may be dispensed with entirely, although so doing poses some problems for the auditor who is concerned with retracing the trail left by individual transactions. Furthermore, in the present state of the art, this kind of direct posting of individual transactions is rarely economical in processing accounting data.

The problem of tracing accounting transactions can be especially difficult in data processing systems that rely heavily on electronic equipment. Here the data are typically stored in a form illegible to an auditor – as magnetized spots on a tape, for example. To reconstruct a series of transactions in such a case is often quite difficult, and the accounting profession has had to devise auditing techniques to cope with this difficulty.

## Petty Cash: Imprest Funds

The final constraint that we shall discuss is of a different order. Processing all cash payment transactions through the stages of purchase voucher and check preparation is seldom feasible. It is convenient to transfer small amounts of cash to *petty cash funds* (technically known as imprest funds) in the hands of supervisory employees, so that small items such as local taxi fare or C.O.D. charges can be paid quickly and with a minimum of red tape. The transfer is recorded initially by a very simple entry in the check register:[2]

| 101 | Petty Cash | 100 | |
|-----|------------|-----|-----|
| 100 | Cash | | 100 |

The fund custodian or cashier then cashes the check and the fund is in operation. As disbursements are made from the fund, the custodian collects receipts from those to whom payments are made. When the cash balance in the fund gets low, the custodian takes these receipts to the accounting department where a purchase voucher is prepared and a check is issued. For example, if the custodian turns in 12 receipts for postage, taxi fare, and supplies totaling $43, the entry in the purchases journal might show the following:

| 511 | Other Head Office Expenses | 43 | |
|-----|----------------------------|-----|-----|
| 200 | Accounts Payable | | 43 |

The entry in the check register to record the issuance of the check to replenish the petty cash fund would be:

| 200 | Accounts Payable | 43 | |
|-----|------------------|-----|-----|
| 100 | Cash | | 43 |

Only one entry appears in the purchase journal instead of 12, a substantial saving in clerical effort. The credit in the check register is to Cash, not to Petty Cash, because the accounting records

---

[2] This entry and most of the others in this and later chapters would of course appear in columnar form in the various special journals, but the general journal form of notation is used in text presentation for clarity and brevity.

recognize no outlays from petty cash; only disbursements from the company's bank accounts give rise to journal entries. Thus, no entry to petty cash is made unless the amount of the fund is increased or decreased.

## SUMMARY

Any accounting system must provide for the orderly and economical preparation of the data and document outputs demanded of the system. Procedures vary widely, depending on what kinds of outputs are desired and what kinds of equipment are available. Although modern electronic equipment has brought the day closer when each transaction can be posted directly to the affected accounts as soon as it occurs, the time-honored techniques of specialization of files and processing channels to carry out the accounting task are still necessary.

Specialized files, known generally as subsidiary ledgers, serve to keep a mass of data in accessible form, physically separated from other portions of the company's files. Specialized processing channels take the form of single-function clerical personnel, recording the transactions in special journals. This facilitates processing and reduces the subsequent labor of recording the effects of transactions in ledger accounts. Some equipment may also be specialized in this way (e.g., a machine that is used solely for preparing customer invoices), but the economies of joint use of the larger data processing machines are normally too great to be ignored.

The system described in this chapter should not be regarded as a model or even as typical, largely because practice varies too much for anything to be typical. The reader should concentrate on the underlying concepts, which are fundamental.

## QUESTIONS AND PROBLEMS

1. Explain the nature and purposes of subsidiary ledgers. Illustrate.

2. What is a control account? Give some common examples.

3. What is a voucher system? What are its main purposes?

4. In preparing a balance sheet for a company, is it necessary to know the balances of individual accounts in the accounts receivable ledger? The accounts payable ledger? Explain.

5. Explain how there may be two debits of $1 each for one credit of $1 without disturbing the fundamental balance of accounts.

6. Discuss the functions of basic documents.

7. What purpose is served by having more than one debit and/or credit column in a journal?

8. The agreement of the balances of a control account and its subsidiary ledger proves the accuracy of the latter. Do you agree? Explain.

9. What is batching and why is it used?

10. Distinguish between batch processing and real-time processing. Why is most accounting done by off-line techniques?

11. Electronic computers may be described in terms of their input speed, number of calculations performed per minute, data storage capacity, and so forth. Improvement in any one of these characteristics is usually obtainable only at higher cost. Therefore, different computers stress different characteristics, depending on the market they are intended to reach. If you were designing an electronic computer solely for use in processing accounting data, what characteristics do you think you would stress? Explain.

12. If you were designing the data processing system of a small typewriter repair shop and wished to have as few journals as feasible, what journals would you probably have? Explain.

13. Describe the procedural steps which might be necessary to make and record the purchase of raw materials in a large manufacturing firm, indicating the nature and probable uses of any written documents that might be employed.

14. You visit a local hardware store to buy a screwdriver. You select the one you want, pay for it, take it in your hand, and leave. You cross the street to the five-and-ten and select a small picture frame and some screws. Here the clerk asks you to give her the merchandise you have selected and the money in payment for it. She rings up the sale and places the goods in a paper bag which she then returns to you with the change, if any. A cash register receipt is in the bag. Why the formality in the latter case? What differences in internal control are indicated?

15. What business documents might attest to the occurrence of the following events?

a) A purchase of supplies on credit.
b) Receipt of cash from a credit customer.
c) Sale of merchandise to a customer on credit.
d) Sale of merchandise to a customer for cash.

16. Late one afternoon the president of Elliot Industries, Inc., learned

of the necessity for making a quick business trip to a city some distance away. He promptly asked the cashier for an advance of $200 for expenses. The cashier always kept enough currency on hand to be able to fill requests of this sort by authorized personnel.

a)  What documents would the executive or the cashier need for this transaction? What entry, if any, would be made in the accounts to record the transfer of cash from the cashier to the executive?

b)  How does the cashier replenish his supply of currency when it runs low? What entry, if any, would be made to record this?

17.  Describe the documents which might support the bookkeeping record of a purchase of:

a)  Office supplies by an office supply company.
b)  Professional legal advice by a truck line.
c)  Production machinery by a manufacturing company.
d)  The services of handbill distributors by a grocery store manager.

*18.  The sales journal of the Bemis Basket Company shows in parallel columns the amount of sales billed to customers and the cost of the particular merchandise sold. The column totals for the month of October were: sales, $50,000; cost of goods sold, $39,000.

a)  To what ledger accounts should amounts be posted from this journal?
b)  Which, if any, of these accounts are likely to be control accounts?

19.  Shown below is a page from a special journal:

| Date | Received from | Debit | | Credit | | | | | |
|---|---|---|---|---|---|---|---|---|---|
| | | Cash | Cash Discounts | Accounts Receivable | | Sales | Miscellaneous | | |
| | | | | No. | Amount | | No. | Amount | |
| | Totals brought forward | 26,605.50 | 285.70 | ✔ | 16,785.20 | 267.35 | ✔ | 9,838.65 | |
| 26 | Seneca Shops | 3,234.00 | 66.00 | 11–2 | 3,300.00 | | | | |
| 28 | City National Bank | 3,000.00 | | | | | 44 | 3,000.00 | |
| 29 | Towle Tool Company | 850.00 | | 11–7 | 850.00 | | | | |
| 30 | Cash sale | 12.40 | | | | 12.40 | | | |
| 31 | Collection of note receivable | 502.31 | | | | | 68 | 2.31 | |
| | | | | | | | 23 | 500.00 | |
| | Total | 34,204.21 | 351.70 | | 20,935.20 | 279.75 | | 13,340.96 | |
| | | (1) | (63) | | (11) | (61) | | ✔ | |

---

* Solutions to problems marked with an asterisk (*) are found in Appendix B.

*a)* What kind of a journal is this?
*b)* What postings are made from each column?
*c)* What control accounts are represented here?

**20.** Shown below is a page from a special journal:

| Date of Invoice | Name | Terms | Inv. No. | Credit | | Debit | | | | | |
|---|---|---|---|---|---|---|---|---|---|---|---|
| | | | | Accounts Payable | | Merchandise Inventory | Expense Ledger | | Miscellaneous | |
| | | | | No. | Amount | | No. | Amount | No. | Amount |
| | Total brought forward | | | ✓ | 23,851.92 | 22,830.52 | ✓ | 713.50 | ✓ | 307.90 |
| 24 | G. E. West Mfg. Co. ... | 2/10, n/60 | 114 | 41–3 | 2,688.15 | 2,688.15 | | | | |
| 28 | Dunne Insurance Co. | Net 30 | 115 | 41–9 | 240.00 | | | | 26 | 240.00 |
| 26 | Hamler Electric Co. ... | 2/10, n/60 | 116 | 41–1 | 1,192.70 | 1,192.70 | | | | |
| 31 | Edison Co. ........... | Net | 117 | 41–7 | 42.10 | | 94 | 42.10 | | |
| | Total................ | | | | 28,014.87 (41) | 26,711.37 (71) | | 755.60 (80) | | 547.90 ✓ |

*a)* What kind of a journal is this?
*b)* What postings are made from each column?
*c)* What control accounts are represented here?

*21. The manager of the Arlington branch store of the Wherewithal Company of America has been given a "petty cash fund" of $300 to pay small bills which are incurred at his store. In March, he spent $215 and mailed vouchers (receipts) for the following payments to the area office for reimbursement:

| | |
|---|---|
| Extra help on three Saturdays ...................... | $116 |
| Miscellaneous drayage and cartage.................. | 32 |
| Rubbish removal .................................... | 26 |
| Taxi fares to bank – daily deposits .................. | 19 |
| Advertising at local charity ball..................... | 10 |
| Night watchman service............................ | 8 |
| Postage............................................ | 4 |
| Total ......................................... | $215 |

*a)* What records must be maintained in the store in connection with this fund?
*b)* By what entry was the fund originally set up on the books by the area office?
*c)* What entry is made by the area office bookkeeper when the vouchers are received from the Arlington store manager?

**22.** The cashier of the Willoughby Company has been custodian of a small petty cash fund ever since the company was first organized. This arrangement proved adequate for some time, but shortly after the company opened its new uptown branch office it became apparent that something would have to be done to cover small cash expenditures at the branch more conveniently.

Accordingly, a new petty cash fund was established and placed in the custody of the receptionist at the uptown branch. She was directed to prepare receipts in duplicate for each payment made. Any cash received at the branch was to be similarly receipted, but was to be remitted directly to the main office. No such funds were to be used for direct replenishment of the branch petty cash fund.

Prepare journal entries to record any of the following events that should be entered in the main office books (if no entry is required, write "no entry"):

  (1)  Fund established by check payable to receptionist, $100.
  (2)  Delivery charge on advertising materials, paid from fund, $3.50.
  (3)  Branch manager reimbursed from fund for theater tickets purchased for entertainment of customer, $17.60.
  (4)  Cash received from a customer for C.O.D. shipment, $43.12; cash collected by branch and forwarded to head office.
  (5)  Branch janitor reimbursed from fund for cost of a new broom, $2.50.
  (6)  Dry cleaner paid from fund for cleaning curtains in branch office, $33.50.
  (7)  Receipts for above expenditures delivered by branch receptionist to head office; check issued to replenish fund.
  (8)  Customer paid from fund, refund for returned merchandise, $27.50.
  (9)  Branch manager's request for a larger fund is granted and a check payable to the receptionist is issued, $50.
(10)  A retiring branch salesman returns to branch receptionist the unused portion of his expense advance, $47.65, plus travel expense statements totaling $102.35 covering the balance of the amount advanced to him; receptionist forwards cash and receipts to main office.
(11)  Postage stamps purchased from fund at branch, $30.
(12)  Fund replenished.

**23.** The Antrax Corporation is a retailer of electrical appliances and parts. It maintains a cashbook (for cash receipts and disbursements), a voucher register, a payroll register, and a general journal. A voucher system similar to the one described in this chapter is in force.

*a*)  Which of the following events would give rise to an entry in the voucher register? What internal evidence would you have for each event (e.g., invoice, purchase order, etc.)?

Sept. 1  Ordered and received television sets from TV Wholesalers, Inc. $2,500
1  Received notice from Begg Realty to pay September store rental    250
2  T. Buran submitted travel expense statement for August......    150
2  Ordered television tubes from ABC Electronics...............    300
6  Received invoice and shipment of refrigerators from Home
   Appliances, Inc.........................................    2,000
6  Received monthly telephone bill from Central Telephone and
   Telegraph Company.......................................    115
8  Received and paid cash for stationery from Pacific Stationers    100
9  Received invoice for washing machines from Williams
   Company; machines have not yet arrived .................    1,500
12  Ordered radio tubes from Electric Parts, Inc..................    175
12  Received invoice covering shipment of television antennas
   from Jones Radio Supply, Inc.; shipment received in good
   condition...............................................    350
14  Received statement from Billett Oil Company, gas and oil for
   delivery truck .........................................    50
15  Ordered and received carbon paper and typewriter ribbons from
   Argus Office Supplies ..................................    60
16  Received invoice from ABC Electronics, covering order of
   September 2.............................................    300
16  Received invoice from Peters Company covering delivery today
   of typewriter to be used in office......................    160
19  Received monthly electricity bill from Union Edison..........    140
21  Received bill for advertising space, Morning News ...........    200
23  Received shipment from ABC Electronics, invoice of
   September 16 ...........................................    300
28  Purchased on account radio parts from Jones Radio Supply;
   shipment received in good condition.....................    220
30  Paid salesmen's salaries for September.....................    3,100

b) Set up a voucher register for the Antrax Corporation and record the
entries indicated in (a) above. Place a check mark opposite each figure to be posted to the general ledger. You should have the following
columns:

   Date
   Vendor
   Voucher Number
   Credit:  Vouchers Payable
   Debits:  Appliances Inventory
           Parts Inventory
           Office Supplies Expense
           Other Debits (two columns: Accounts Title and Amount)

**24.** The Halsey Typewriter Company sells and services typewriters.
Typewriter sales are on terms of net 30 days. Service is done on contract
or on order. Customers are billed monthly for contract services; all other
service is on a cash basis.

The company has two salesmen, one clerk-bookkeeper-typist, and four
repair men. Payroll deductions are made for F.I.C.A. taxes, federal income taxes, state income taxes, Blue Cross premiums, and pension
contributions.

The company makes frequent purchases of typewriters and of repair

supplies. These purchases are recorded in the cash disbursements journal at the time of payment. No recording is made at the time the invoices
or goods are received.

The company maintains a perpetual inventory of its typewriters. The
cost of each typewriter in stock is recorded on a stock card and is transferred to the cost of goods sold at the time of shipment to the customer.
No other inventory accounts are maintained.

Indicate what column headings you think would be necessary for:

a) The sales journal.
b) The payroll register.
c) The cash disbursements journal.
d) The cash receipts journal.

*25. The principal accounting records of the Mercantile Company con-
sist of a general ledger, a customers' ledger, and the following books of
original entry: cash receipts book (CR), cash disbursements book (CD),
voucher register (VR), sales journal (S), and general journal (J).

Record in two-column journal form the transactions described below
as they would appear in the special journals, and, for each entry, indicate
the journal in which it would be made. (These transactions all occurred
during December.)

*Example:*
Transaction: Cash purchase of merchandise, $500.
Entries:

```
VR    Merchandise Inventory .......................... 500
          Vouchers Payable............................        500
CD    Vouchers Payable................................ 500
          Cash........................................        500
```

*Transactions:*

(1)  Sale on account to John Jones, Inc., $1,000. A cash discount of 2
     percent is offered for payment within 10 days.
(2)  Purchase of new delivery truck from the Speedy Motor Company
     for $2,700. Terms: net amount due in 30 days. Estimated life of
     the truck is 1½ years; estimated scrap value, $900.
(3)  Cash sale to the Rainbow Corporation, $750.
(4)  Payment received within discount period from John Jones, Inc.,
     for purchase of transaction (1).
(5)  Payment of $180 made to the *Texas Bugle* for a series of nine ad-
     vertisements in successive Sunday editions starting December 2
     and continuing to January 27. No previous recording has been
     made relative to this transaction.
(6)  One month's depreciation on delivery truck purchased in trans-
     action (2) is recorded.
(7)  Salesmen and office employees are paid weekly. Last payment

was made on Saturday, December 29, for the week ending that date. Employees work a full six-day week. Weekly salaries total $1,500 for salesmen and $1,200 for office personnel. Adjustments for wages and salaries are made prior to closing the books for the year. (Ignore withholdings, etc.)

**26.** Early in June, Morris Slade entered the retail coal business under the name of the Slade Coal Company. The principal accounting records of the company consist of a general ledger, a customers ledger, and the following books of original entry: cash receipts book (CR), cash disbursements book (CD), voucher register (VR), sales journal (S), and general journal (J).

Record in two-column journal form the transactions described below as they would appear in the specialized journals, and for each entry indicate the specialized journal in which it would be made. (See Question 25 for sample entry.)

| Date | Transaction Number | Transaction | Amount |
|------|------|------|------|
| June 10 | 1 | Mr. Slade invested cash................$35,000 | |
| | 2 | Rent was paid for June ................. | 500 |
| 12 | 3 | Coal was bought on account from the Atlantic Coal Company ............... | 3,000 |
| | 4 | Office furniture was purchased for cash... | 2,500 |
| 13 | 5 | Sold coal on account to M. Musgrave..... | 45 |
| 14 | 6 | Bought coal on account from the Devon Coal Company....................... | 3,750 |
| 15 | 7 | Cash sales of coal...................... | 1,500 |
| | 8 | Sales on account to: | |
| | | K. Muran ........................... | 75 |
| | | L. Travers........................... | 100 |
| 16 | 9 | Sold additional coal on account to M. Musgrave....................... | 65 |
| 17 | 10 | Received cash in settlement of account of L. Travers........................... | 100 |
| 17 | 11 | Cash sales ........................... | 3,250 |
| | 12 | Paid clerk's salary ...................... | 150 |
| 19 | 13 | Received 60-day note from M. Musgrave in settlement of account ............... | 110 |
| 20 | 14 | Sold additional coal to K. Muran ......... | 80 |
| 22 | 15 | Paid Atlantic Coal Company ............ | 3,000 |
| 23 | 16 | Sales to A. Burton on account........... | 90 |
| 24 | 17 | Received payment from K. Muran on account.............................. | 60 |
| | 18 | Paid clerk's salary ...................... | 150 |
| 26 | 19 | Sale to S. Atkins on account.............. | 155 |
| 30 | 20 | Paid office expenses.................... | 300 |

**27.** The General Paper Supply Company commenced business on September 1, 19x4. The accountant for the company established the following chart of accounts. Not all of the accounts will be necessary to account for the transactions listed below, but it should not be necessary to open new accounts.

| Code | Account Title | Code | Account Title |
|---|---|---|---|
| 100 .... | Cash | 500 .... | Purchases |
| 110 .... | Marketable Securities | 505 .... | Freight-In |
| 120 .... | Accounts Receivable | 510 .... | Purchases Returns and |
| 121 .... | Notes Receivable | | Allowances |
| 130 .... | Allowance for Bad Debts | 520 .... | Purchases Discounts |
| 200 .... | Inventory | 600 .... | I. Fand, Owner |
| 220 .... | Prepaid Insurance | 700 .... | Sales Revenue |
| 300 .... | Land | 720 .... | Sales Returns and |
| 310 .... | Building | | Allowances |
| 320 .... | Accumulated Deprecia- | 725 .... | Sales Discounts |
| | tion – Building | 730 .... | Interest Income |
| 330 .... | Furniture and Fixtures | 800 .... | Cost of Goods Sold |
| 340 .... | Accumulated Deprecia- | 821 .... | Sales Salaries |
| | tion – Furniture and | 822 .... | Store Supplies Expense |
| | Fixtures | 823 .... | Advertising Expense |
| 350 .... | Equipment | 841 .... | Office Salaries |
| 360 .... | Accumulated Deprecia- | 842 .... | Office Supplies Expense |
| | tion – Equipment | 851 .... | Telephone Expense |
| 400 .... | Accounts Payable | 852 .... | Heat, Light, and Power |
| 410 .... | Notes Payable | 861 .... | Warehouse Salaries |
| 420 .... | Social Security Taxes | 862 .... | Warehouse Supplies |
| | Payable | | Expense |
| 425 .... | Income Taxes Withheld | 870 .... | Delivery Expenses |
| 430 .... | Salaries Payable | 881 .... | Administrative Salaries |
| 450 .... | Mortgage Payable | 890 .... | Interest Expense |

Certain of the transactions for the month follow:

Sept.  1    Mr. Fand, the owner, invested $140,000 cash in the business, as well as land and a building that he had acquired. The land had cost $25,000 and the building $130,000. The building was subject to a $90,000, 5 percent, 20-year mortgage with interest payable quarterly.

       1    Office furniture and fixtures costing $9,400 were acquired from the City Office Supply Company; terms, 1/10, n/30.

       1    Warehouse equipment costing $18,700 was acquired from Steel Shelving Company; terms, 2/10, n/30.

       2    Merchandise costing $19,000 was purchased from Wandthe and Company; terms, 2/10, n/30.

       3    Warehouse supplies costing $650 and office supplies costing $400 were purchased from Merchants Supply Company; terms, n/30.

       4    Sold merchandise to M. Rows for $3,750; terms, 2/10, n/30.

       5    Sold merchandise for cash, $450.

       6    Purchased merchandise from D. Nerwin for $8,750; terms, 1/10, n/30.

       6    Acquired and paid $490 for a two-year insurance policy on the premises and its contents, effective September 1, 19x4.

Sept. 8  Paid delivery charges on merchandise purchased from D. Nerwin, $80.

9  Paid $280 for a mailing advertising the company.

9  Returned merchandise costing $680 to Wandthe and Company.

9  Paid City Office Supply Company.

10  Gave M. Rows a credit of $250 on merchandise returned.

10  Paid Steel Shelving Company.

11  Paid the telephone company $30 for phone installation and $60 for an ad in the yellow pages to cover a six-month period.

12  Sold merchandise to Bowle and Sons for $1,800; terms, 2/10, n/30.

12  Paid Wandthe and Company.

13  Sold merchandise to Krieger Company for $1,250; terms, 2/10, n/30.

15  Prepared semimonthly payrolls and paid amounts due to employees:

| | |
|---|---:|
| Sales salaries | $1,900 |
| Office salaries | 600 |
| Warehouse salaries | 1,200 |
| Deductions: | |
| Federal income tax | 550 |
| Social security taxes | 240 |

16  Paid Merchants Supply Company.

16  Paid D. Nerwin.

16  Received payment from M. Rows with the discount taken.

17  Received payment from Bowle and Sons.

18  Sold merchandise 2/10, n/30 to:

| | |
|---|---:|
| M. Fried | $ 850 |
| W. Topper | 1,970 |

19  Obtained an allowance of $800 on the merchandise purchased from D. Nerwin.

20  Purchased $7,500 in merchandise from D. Nerwin.

22  Cash sales, $2,450.

22  Sold merchandise to M. Bales for $2,150.

23  Purchased a delivery truck for $2,800, paying $800 down and signing a 9 percent, 180-day note for the balance.

26  Received bill for $125 for delivery service from Delivery, Inc.

27  Paid electric bill for first 21 days of month, $36.

30  Prepared semimonthly payrolls and paid amounts due to employees:

| | |
|---|---:|
| Sales salaries | $1,900 |
| Office salaries | 600 |
| Warehouse salaries | 1,200 |
| Administrative salaries | 1,600 |
| Deductions: | |
| Federal income tax | 800 |
| Social security taxes | 340 |

*a*)  Set up the following:

(1)  Two-column general journal.
(2)  Three-column sales journal.
(3)  Seven-column payroll journal.
(4)  One-column purchases journal.
(5)  Four-column cash receipts journal.
(6)  Six-column cash disbursements journal.
(7)  Accounts receivable ledger.
(8)  Accounts payable ledger.
(9)  General ledger.

*b*)  Journalize the above transactions in the appropriate journals and post the figures to the ledgers.
*c*)  Compute the September 30 balances in all ledger accounts.
*d*)  What other entries would have to be made before financial statements for the month could be prepared, and in which journal or journals might they be recorded? Explain.

**28.** The Crandall Hardware Company operates a large retail hardware store. Its special journals have the following column headings:

Sales journal:    Date
                  Accounts Receivable, Dr.
                  Sales, Cr.
Voucher register:    Date
                     Voucher Number
                     Vendor's Name
                     Accounts Payable, Cr.
                     Wages and Salaries Payable, Cr.
                     Payroll Taxes Payable, Cr.
                     Merchandise Inventories, Dr.
                     Wages and Salaries Expense, Dr.
                     Other Accounts, Dr. (Account Title, Amount)
Cash receipts journal:    Date
                          Name of Payer
                          Cash, Dr.
                          Sales, Cr.
                          Accounts Receivable, Cr.
                          Other Accounts, Cr. (Account Title, Amount)
Cash disbursements journal:    Date
                               Check Number
                               Voucher Number
                               Payee
                               Cash, Cr.
                               Purchases Discounts, Cr.
                               Accounts Payable, Dr.
                               Wages and Salaries Payable, Dr.
                               Other Accounts (Account Title, Amount)

On February 1, the accounts receivable and accounts payable sub-sidiary ledgers showed the following balances:

*Accounts Receivable*

| | |
|---|---:|
| Joseph Borman........................... $ | 86 |
| Brown Manufacturing Company.......... | 348 |
| Corson Playschool....................... | 12 |
| Jones Brothers ........................... | 763 |
| King's Service Station ................... | 44 |
| Robert Mason ........................... | 15 |
| Charles Nelson........................... | 50 |
| Frank Peters ........................... | 70 |
| Thompson Enterprises................... | 188 |
| Val-U Supermarket...................... | 25 |
| Total ............................... $ | 1,601 |

*Accounts Payable*

| | |
|---|---:|
| Ajax Hardware Suppliers................. $ | 1,742 |
| Edison Electric Company................ | 108 |
| Franklin Paint Company ................ | 350 |
| Grant Stationers........................ | 45 |
| Harkness Delivery Service............... | 250 |
| Peerless Electric Supply................. | 6,050 |
| Roberts Manufacturing Company........ | 2,200 |
| Sunline Products, Inc.................... | 550 |
| Trabert Distributors .................... | 4,810 |
| Warren Sales Corporation ............... | 1,843 |
| Total ............................... | $17,948 |

Cash sales are journalized daily from cash register tapes. Credit sales are recorded weekly in the sales journal; postings to the accounts receiv-able ledger accounts are made directly from the individual sales slips.

Purchases are recorded at gross price. No cash disbursement is made without an approved voucher. Postings to the accounts payable ledger are made directly from the vouchers, which also provide the information necessary for completion of the voucher register.

All payments are made by check. A single voucher is prepared for each payroll, but a separate check is issued to each employee. A single entry is made in the voucher register to record each payroll, leaving all supporting detail on the payroll work sheets which are filed separately. Separate vouchers are prepared for payment of payroll taxes.

The first voucher issued in February was number 1076; the first check was number 3625.

The following transactions took place during the month of February:

Feb.  1  Purchased merchandise from Cranmore Distributors, $850; terms, 2/10, n/30.

  1  Paid the following vouchers (starred items (*) are subject to 2 percent cash discount):

| Voucher No. | Payee | Amount |
|---|---|---|
| 1038 | Edison Electric Company ............. $ | 108 |
| 1029 | Franklin Paint Company............. | 350* |
| 1030 | Peerless Electric Supply ............. | 3,800* |
| 1033 | Roberts Manufacturing Company .... | 2,200* |
| 1040 | Trabert Distributors................. | 4,810 |

Feb. 1 Cash sales, $1,000.
2 Received payment of amounts due from Joseph Borman and Thompson Enterprises.
2 Cash sales, $1,462.
3 Purchased merchandise from Ajax Hardware Suppliers, $418; terms, n/30.
3 Paid Ajax Hardware Suppliers, $763, Voucher No. 1018.
3 Paid Sunline Products, account balance less 2 percent discount, Voucher No. 1041.
3 Cash sales, $765.
4 Received bill from State Telephone Company, $186.
4 Purchased merchandise from Galbraith Manufacturing Company, $1,800; terms, 3/10, n/30.
4 Cash sales, $1,440.
5 Received payment of amounts due from Brown Manufacturing Company, Corson Playschool, Robert Mason, and Val-U Supermarket.
5 Prepared and paid weekly payroll for employees: gross payroll, $825, less tax withholdings of $225.
5 Purchased merchandise from Corbin Brush Company, $400; terms, 2/10, n/30.
5 Paid amount due to Warren Sales Corporation, Voucher No. 1045.
5 Borrowed $5,000 on 30-day note from First National Bank.
5 Cash sales, $1,341.
6 Cash sales, $3,108.
6 Credit sales for the week: Joseph Borman, $45; Brown Manufacturing Company, $80; Johnson Brothers, $165; Santos & Son, $75.
8 Paid Ajax Hardware Suppliers, $979, Voucher No. 1046.
8 Purchased merchandise from Trabert Distributors, $1,463; terms, n/30.
8 Received payment of amount due from King's Service Station.
8 Cash sales, $814.
9 Paid Internal Revenue Service for January payroll taxes and withholdings, $1,260.
9 Received $40 from Eben Tallman for month's rental of desk space in rear of store.
9 Cash sales, $1,145.
10 Purchased merchandise from Ajax Hardware Suppliers, $5,200; terms, n/30.
10 Paid Peerless Electric Supply, $2,250 less 2 percent cash discount, Voucher No. 1070.
10 Cash sales, $846.
11 Paid Cranmore Distributors (purchase of February 1).
11 Received payment from Frank Peters.
11 Cash sales, $1,221.
12 Weekly payroll, $900, less tax withholdings of $235.

Feb. 12 Purchased office supplies from Grant Stationers, $362.

12 Cash sales, $1,809.

13 Paid Brown & Altman for preparing tax return, $1,650 (treat as current expense).

13 Credit sales for the week: Brown Manufacturing Company, $450; King's Service Station, $10; Robert Mason, $25; Thompson Enterprises, $600; Helen's Beauty Shop, $85; Alvin and Bronson, $475.

13 Cash sales, $1,560.

15 Paid Corbin Brush Company (purchase of February 5).

15 Cash sales, $540.

16 Blizzard; store closed.

17 Received bill from Brown & Son, plumbers, for repair of frozen water pipes, $32.

17 Received $50 from Daniel Green, a clerk in the store, in repayment of loan.

17 Cash sales, $1,111.

18 Paid Grant Stationers and Harkness Delivery Service amounts due at beginning of month, Vouchers Nos. 1071 and 1072.

18 Purchased merchandise from Warren Sales Corporation, $6,040; terms, n/30.

18 Cash sales, $1,200.

19 Weekly payroll, $800, less tax withholdings of $220.

19 Received bill from the Morning News for classified advertising, $80.

19 Cash sales, $1,380.

20 Cash sales, $1,995.

22 Store closed, holiday.

23 Paid State Telephone Company bill of February 4.

23 Cash sales, $840.

24 Increased amount in petty cash fund by drawing check on regular checking account, $50.

24 Cash sales, $1,230.

25 Purchased merchandise from Peerless Electric Supply, $3,700; terms 2/10, n/30.

25 Cash sales, $943.

26 Weekly payroll, $850, less tax withholdings of $230.

26 Monthly payroll, $3,200, less tax withholdings of $600.

26 Paid Morning News bill of February 19.

26 Cash sales, $2,106.

27 Received notification from attorneys that Jones Brothers have just filed bankruptcy papers; no assets are available to satisfy the claims of trade creditors (Crandall Hardware Company uses an Allowance for Bad Debts account).

27 Credit sales for week: Brown Manufacturing Company, $126; Frank Peters, $15; Thompson Enterprises, $145.

27 Cash sales, $1,656.

27 Accrued February interest on note payable, $29.

*a)*  Prepare columnar accounting paper to serve as journals, using the column headings given at the beginning of this problem.

*b)*  Prepare subsidiary accounts receivable and accounts payable ledgers, with a separate account for each vendor and each credit customer, and enter the opening balances (you may save space by putting three or four accounts on each page).

*c)*  Enter each of the above transactions in the appropriate journal and make the necessary postings to the subsidiary accounts receivable and accounts payable ledgers.

*d)*  List the amounts that would be posted directly to the general ledger from each of the special journals at the end of the month.

# 9

## INTRODUCTION TO FINANCIAL STATEMENT ANALYSIS

THE KNOWLEDGE OF ACCOUNTING gained from study of the previous chapters is of interest to managers not as an end in itself but as a necessary step toward using financial statements for decision making. The purpose of the present chapter is to identify some of the basic tools of financial statement analysis, thereby providing essential background information for the materials in the next eight chapters. We must emphasize, however, that no one can analyze financial statements effectively without an adequate understanding of the accounting measurement methods to be discussed in Part II.

### OBJECTIVES OF FINANCIAL STATEMENT ANALYSIS

Financial statement analysis embraces the methods by which management, investors, and others interested in the affairs of a corporation obtain information from financial statements as a basis for the decisions they make in regard to the corporation. Present and prospective stockholders need to decide whether to buy or sell the company's stock and whether to vote their shares for or against the company's management. Creditors are concerned with whether to extend or renew credit. Management decisions which center on the fortunes of the company as a whole, such as dividend and financing decisions, also require the analysis of financial statements.

It should be recognized at the outset that stockholders, creditors, and managers are all interested in the future, not the past.

A shrewd investor, for example, will buy a stock with a dark past but a bright future in preference to one with a brilliant past and dim prospects. Even so, forecasting usually starts with a study of the past and the analysis of financial statements can be of considerable value in arriving at judgments on the following questions of interest to investors: What is the best estimate of a company's future income? What is the uncertainty or variability of future income? What is the ability of a company to sustain losses for a period of time without becoming *insolvent* (unable to pay its debts) in the near future and in the long run?

## ILLUSTRATIVE STATEMENTS

Since a real company's statements would raise questions of measurement and terminology for which we are not yet ready, we shall use the financial statements of a hypothetical firm, the Alpha Company, to illustrate the methods of statement analysis. Exhibit 9–1 presents the Alpha Company's balance sheets as of the end of 19x1 and 19x2. Exhibit 9–2 shows the company's income statement for 19x2.

One feature of these statements needs explanation. Although previous chapters have mentioned only one class of capital stock, the Alpha Company has two — preferred stock and common stock. In many respects they are similar. Both represent ownership equities in the business, and neither preferred nor common dividends are deducted in calculated net income. From the viewpoint of the common stockholder, however, preferred stock is more like debt than stock. Preferred stockholders have a *prior* and a *fixed* claim to dividends and to assets in liquidation. In Alpha's case the preferred dividend is limited to 5 percent of the so-called *par value* of the shares, or 50 cents a share.

The preferred shares are shown on the December 31, 19x2, balance sheet at their par value of $7,000, or $10 a share. The common stock also has a par value, in this case $10,000, or $5 a share. The amounts of assets received by the Alpha Company for shares of its stock, however, exceeded their par value by $12,600. By convention, this amount is usually shown separately from the par value. The dividend rate on common stock is not fixed in advance but decreases and increases with the ebb and flow of the company's fortunes.

## MEASURES OF PROFITABILITY

An investor becomes and remains a stockholder in a company because he believes that dividends and capital gains (increases in

*Exhibit 9–1*

Alpha Company

STATEMENTS OF FINANCIAL POSITION

December 31, 19x1, and 19x2

ASSETS

| | *19x2* | *19x1* |
|---|---|---|
| *Current Assets:* | | |
| Cash.............................................. | $ 2,600 | $ 4,300 |
| Receivables....................................... | 19,800 | 17,100 |
| Inventories....................................... | 35,900 | 28,700 |
| Total Current Assets ........................ | $58,300 | $50,100 |
| *Long-Term Assets:* | | |
| Buildings and equipment........................... | $49,100 | $42,900 |
| Less: Accumulated depreciation.................. | 19,400 | 18,100 |
| Net buildings and equipment ...................... | $29,700 | $24,800 |
| Land................................................. | 1,400 | 1,900 |
| Total Assets............................. | $89,400 | $76,800 |

LIABILITIES AND SHAREHOLDERS' EQUITY

| | | |
|---|---|---|
| *Current Liabilities:* | | |
| Accounts payable ................................. | $ 6,600 | $ 4,800 |
| Notes payable....................................... | 15,500 | 6,200 |
| Federal income taxes............................... | 2,100 | 2,200 |
| Total Current Liabilities...................... | $24,200 | $13,200 |
| Long-term debt....................................... | 11,700 | 17,400 |
| Total Liabilities ......................... | $35,900 | $30,600 |
| *Shareholders' equity:* | | |
| 5% preferred stock, 700 shares..................... | $ 7,000 | $ 7,000 |
| Common stock, par value $5 a share ............... | 10,000 | 9,000 |
| Capital in excess of par value ..................... | 12,600 | 9,900 |
| Retained earnings.................................. | 23,900 | 20,300 |
| Total Shareholders' Equity ................... | $53,500 | $46,200 |
| Total Liabilities and Shareholders' Equity | $89,400 | $76,800 |

*Exhibit 9–2*

Alpha Company

INCOME STATEMENT

For the Year Ended December 31, 19x2

| | | |
|---|---|---|
| Sales revenue........................................ | | $105,200 |
| Expenses: | | |
| Cost of products sold (except depreciation)......... | $57,700 | |
| Depreciation........................................ | 2,500 | |
| Research and development......................... | 5,600 | |
| Selling and administration......................... | 27,400 | 93,200 |
| Income before interest and taxes.................... | | $ 12,000 |
| Interest expense .................................. | | 1,400 |
| Income before taxes .............................. | | $ 10,600 |
| Income taxes ..................................... | | 4,850 |
| Net income ......................................... | | $ 5,750 |
| Dividends on preferred stock....................... | | 350 |
| Income available for common stockholders .......... | | $ 5,400 |
| Dividends on common stock........................ | | 1,800 |
| Current Income Retained in the Business............ | | $ 3,600 |

the price of the stock) will compare favorably with the rate of return he can earn on alternative investments of comparable risk. The most important determinant of the future dividends and capital gains on a share is the corporation's future earnings, and the first source of data for use in forecasting future earnings is the corporation's past earnings record. Three ratios used widely as measures of the company's past earnings record are earnings per share of common stock, return on common equity, and return on total assets.

## Earnings per Common Share

The most widely used measure of financial performance is net after-tax earnings per common share. Dividends to which holders of any preferred stock are entitled must be subtracted from net income to get earnings applicable to the common stock. For the Alpha Company the 19x2 calculation is:

$$\frac{\text{Net Income} - \text{Preferred Dividends}}{\text{No. of Common Shares}} = \frac{\$5,750 - \$350}{2,000}$$

$$= \$2.70 \text{ per share.}$$

Earnings per share figures are used to compare one year's earnings with those of prior years. They are also combined with other figures, such as market price per share, to reveal relationships that the analyst wishes to examine.

The earnings component of the earnings per share figure must be examined carefully. The major questions of interpretation will be discussed in Part II, but one observation can be made now. Many items that used to be reported as extraordinary items, at the bottom of the income statement, must now be included in ordinary income. The total amount of income or loss from these sources is likely to fluctuate more widely than income from other sources. The analyst should be alert to identify the underlying movements in earnings behind these fluctuations.

## Return on Common Equity

The absolute amount of income is an inadequate measure of profitability because it does not indicate how much had to be invested to achieve it. One way to put earnings and investment figures together is to compute the rate of return on common equity, that is, the ratio of net income available to the common shareholders to the *book value* of the common shareholders' equity in the company. In this case the book value of the common equity was the total of capital stock at par value, capital in excess of par value, and retained earnings, adding up to $46,500 at the end of 19x2.[1] The rate of return on common equity therefore was as follows:

$$\frac{\text{Net Income} - \text{Preferred Dividends}}{\text{Common Equity}} = \frac{\$5,750 - \$350}{\$46,500} = 11.6 \text{ percent.}$$

In reaching a judgment as to whether this represents good or bad performance, a number of questions must be answered. For example, how does this figure compare with the return of other firms in the industry and in industry in general? Is this company's rate of return holding steady, going up, or declining? How wide are the year-to-year fluctuations in rate of return?

It will be recalled that the investor's primary interest is in Alpha's earnings and rate of return in the future. From that point of view, the 19x2 figures may be biased. For example, the company's sales force may be engaged in heavy promotional activities on new products. Sales revenues from these activities will not be recognized until some time in the future, but the salesmen's salaries and travel costs show up among the current year's expenses. Similarly, if equipment replacement prices have been rising rapidly, current depreciation charges are likely to be much lower than they will be in the future when the present equipment is replaced. Considerations of this sort will be discussed in Part II.

### Return on Assets and the Leverage Effect

A corporation's return on its common equity is a consequence of two factors: (1) its return on assets, and (2) the extent to which *leverage* is employed by the company. Return on assets is defined as the ratio of earnings before interest to total assets. Leverage is the percentage of total assets that is supplied by creditors and preferred shareholders.[2]

For example, if a company has $100 in assets on which it earns $11 a year before interest on its debts, its before-tax return on assets will be 11 percent. The reason for using earnings before

---

[1] Earnings may be related to the investment at the beginning of the year, the investment at the end of the year, or an average of the two. We have used year-end investment because it is generally the most convenient.

[2] Leverage can also be defined as the ratio of *long-term* debt and preferred stock to the book value of the common stock, or as the ratio of *interest-bearing* debt and preferred stock to common equity. The definition above is appropriate when the comparison is to be made between return on total assets and return on the common shareholders' equity in those assets, as it is here.

interest and dividends as the numerator in this ratio is that the denominator represents all assets, not just those supplied by the shareholders. To be comparable, the earnings figure should measure earnings before distributions either to creditors (interest) or shareholders (dividends).

By using leverage, the company may be able to earn a rate of return on total assets that is less than that achieved by other companies but still achieve a higher return on common equity. Suppose, for example, that the company has obtained 40 percent of its capital ($40) by borrowing at an interest rate of 5 percent ($2 a year). The return on equity will be:

$$\frac{\text{Earnings} - \text{Interest}}{\text{Total Assets} - \text{Debt}} = \frac{\$11 - \$2}{\$100 - \$40} = 15 \text{ percent.}$$

This is *successful* leverage because the 5 percent borrowing rate of interest is less than the overall earnings rate on total capital (11 percent). The common shareholders, in other words, gain the full 11 percent on their own investment plus more than half (11 percent − 5 percent = 6 percent) of the return on the assets financed by creditors.

### After-Tax Return on Assets

Return on equity is almost always an after-tax figure. To be fully comparable, therefore, the return on assets figure should also be stated on an after-tax basis. At first glance, this may seem to be simply a matter of subtracting the year's income taxes from earnings before interest and taxes. Unfortunately, this cannot be done because interest is deductible in computing the income tax on the year's earnings. This amount of the gross earnings is shielded from the tax man's bite. The appropriate after-tax figure is the income that would have been reported if the same amount of capital had been provided by the owners alone. This will provide a true bench mark for use in evaluating the net effect of leverage.

Turning back to the Alpha Company's figures, earnings before interest and taxes were $12,000. Dividing this by the $89,400 total assets at the end of the year gives a before-tax rate of return of 13.4 percent. To convert this to an after-tax basis, the $12,000 should be multiplied by the actual tax rates that would be applied to this amount of income. The outsider seldom has access to this information, but he can compute the ratio of current taxes to income before taxes. In this case the ratio was:

$$\frac{\text{Income Taxes}}{\text{Income before Income Taxes}} = \frac{\$4,850}{\$10,600} = 45.7 \text{ percent.}$$

This ratio will be inaccurate if different amounts of income are taxed at different rates, but the analyst can usually assume that it is not too far from the truth.

Multiplying this rate (45.7 percent) by the Alpha Company's earnings before interest and taxes ($12,000) indicates that the tax bill would have been $5,484 in the absence of debt financing. The after-tax income would then have been $12,000 − $5,484 = $6,516. The after-tax return on assets, therefore, was:

$$\frac{\text{Adjusted After-Tax Income}}{\text{Total Assets}} = \frac{\$6,516}{\$89,400} = 7.3 \text{ percent.}$$

This is the return Alpha would have earned on the common equity if no debt or preferred financing had been employed. The use of debt and preferred stock, in other words, raised Alpha's return on its common equity from 7.3 percent to 11.6 percent. This is shown in the following table:

|  | *Before Tax* | *After Tax* |
|---|---|---|
| Return on assets......................... | 13.4% | 7.3% |
| Return on common equity .............. | 22.0 | 11.6 |

## Profit Margin Ratios

It is often useful to recognize that a corporation's return on assets is a consequence of its asset turnover and its profit margin on sales. The higher the ratio of sales to assets and the higher the ratio of profit to sales, the higher the rate of return on assets. These statements can be stated in the form of the following equation:

$$\text{Return on Assets} = \text{Asset Turnover} \times \text{Profit Margin}$$

$$= \frac{\text{Sales}}{\text{Assets}} \times \frac{\text{Income}}{\text{Sales}}$$

Profit margins, or *percentage-of-sales* ratios, are widely used in profitability analysis, mainly to identify trends or intercompany differences. Probably the most commonly computed profit margin ratio is the ratio of net income to gross revenues. For consistency, the profit figure should be the same one used for return on investment comparisons. In other words, if return on investment is computed on the basis of total assets, then the income figure should be before interest but after taxes, the tax figure being adjusted to eliminate the tax effect of interest deductibility, as described above. On this basis, Alpha's profit margin for 19x2 was:

$$\frac{\text{Adjusted Net Income}}{\text{Sales Revenue}} = \frac{\$6,516}{\$105,200} = 6.2 \text{ percent.}$$

Other profit margin ratios often used by analysts are the ratio of operating expenses to operating revenues (the *operating ratio*), the ratio of the cost of goods sold to gross sales, and the ratio of research and development expense to gross sales.

### Asset Turnover Ratios

The main difficulty with any and all of these profit ratios is that differences in margin on sales do not indicate differences in economic efficiency. Businesses such as grocery chains and meat-packing companies operate with exceptionally narrow margins on sales and rely on a large sales volume to cover operating expenses and yield a satisfactory return on investment. Others, such as high-fashion clothing shops and yacht manufacturers, take the opposite tack and operate with low volume and high markups.

The solution to this problem is to supplement the profit margin ratios with asset turnover ratios. The principal turnover ratio is the ratio of total sales to total assets. Using year-end total assets as the base, this ratio for Alpha in 19x2 was:

$$\frac{\text{Sales Revenue}}{\text{Total Assets}} = \frac{\$105,200}{\$89,400} = 1.18.$$

In other words, $1 of assets was required to support every $1.18 of sales.

Once again, the main use of this kind of ratio is to identify ways in which the company is departing from its own previous operating pattern or from that of its competitors. Turnover and percentage-of-sales ratios must be examined together, in parallel – the significance of a change in one can be appraised only if movements in the other are known.

## SOURCES AND USES OF FUNDS

As we indicated earlier, the manner in which a company obtains the funds used to acquire its assets has a considerable influence on its profitability. We shall see shortly that it also influences financial position, the ability to sustain losses without becoming insolvent. The uses a company makes of its funds – that is, the types of assets it acquires – also have a considerable influence on profitability and financial position. Hence, analysis of the company's sources and uses of funds is an important ingredient of financial statement analysis.

## Analysis of the Funds Structure

To the layman, funds and money are synonymous terms. This is so because funds are means of acquiring assets and paying bills, and it is clear that money is eminently usable for these purposes. Let us go one step farther, however, and ask what are a company's sources and uses of funds. It is clear that creditors and stockholders are sources of funds for a company, and that the various assets, including money in the bank, are uses of funds. Accordingly, the balance sheet as of some date is a statement of the firm's net sources and uses of funds up to that date, and the first kind of analysis of the sources and uses of funds is a study of the *structure* of the firm's assets and of its liabilities and owners' equities.

*Equity Structure.* The order in which the sources of funds are listed in the balance sheet corresponds to two important characteristics: the interest cost of obtaining the funds and the risk they bring with them. Current liabilities are an attractive source of funds because the interest cost of this capital is low. However, since they fall due in a relatively short period, the risk cost is high. They may fall due for payment just when the company finds itself temporarily short of cash. Long-term debt, in contrast, typically carries a higher interest rate but poses a smaller immediate threat of insolvency. Furthermore, the company can ordinarily pick a convenient time to refinance long-term debt before it falls due, thereby minimizing the likelihood that it will fall due during a period of losses and inability to raise funds.

Finally, funds obtained from shareholders through the sale of stock or retention of earnings carry no risk of insolvency. The company has no contractual obligations to make payments on specified dates, even to the preferred shareholders. In return for removing this risk from the corporation, the stockholders expect a higher yield on their investment than that earned by the company's creditors. This desired yield can and should be considered a cost of stockholder capital.

*Equity Structure Ratios.* The relative importance of debt in the equity structure is measured by a number of different ratios, of which we shall consider only four. The first of these, the *debt/equity ratio*, is obtained by dividing the book value of the long-term debt by the book value of the owners' equity. (The term "equity" is usually used by financial analysts to refer to the owners' equity rather than to the total of liabilities and owners' equity. The definition is usually clear from the context, however.) For Alpha at the end of 19x2, this ratio was:

$$\frac{\text{Long-term debt}}{\text{Pfd. Stock} + \text{Common Equity}} = \frac{\$11,700}{\$7,000 + \$46,500} = 21.9 \text{ percent.}$$

This ratio is used as a measure of risk. Because only the near-term debt retirement and interest requirements constitute an immediate danger to the company's solvency, this ratio applies more to long-term than to short-term risks.

A variant of the debt/equity ratio is the ratio of total debt, including short-term as well as long-term debt, to the owners' equity. To distinguish it, let us refer to it as the *total debt ratio.* This is a more inclusive measure of risk than the long-term debt ratio and more quickly responsive to changes in risk. Pressure for additional funds ordinarily can be relieved faster by increasing short-term debt than by any other means.

In 19x2, for example, the Alpha Company increased its short-term debt and decreased its long-term debt. As a result, the total debt ratio remained almost constant, but the *short-term debt ratio* (current liabilities divided by total liabilities plus owners' equity) increased from 17.2 percent at the end of 19x1 to 27.1 percent a year later. Other things being equal, this represented an increase in risk.

A great many factors enter into the determination of the risk associated with a given equity structure ratio. The average level and volatility of the firm's earnings, the size of its liquid asset reserves, the rate of price inflation in the economy as a whole, and the debt's maturity structure all have their effect. Consequently, it is unwise to specify a figure that may be used as an evaluation standard without first examining the firm and its environment. Even more important, different companies can use different methods of asset measurement, even within the same industry, and the analyst must try to identify these differences before comparing equity structure ratios of different companies. These differences are discussed in Part II.

*Asset Structure.* The way in which the firm's funds have been used is also significant. The company must hold current assets if it wishes to obtain orders and satisfy its customers. Up to a point, more receivables and more inventories will produce enough additional revenues to make the additional investment worth while. More cash will enable the company to take advantage of purchase opportunities and save on bank charges. Beyond some point; however, further investment in current assets will not be productive.

Current assets do have the advantage of liquidity, of course. Money in the bank enjoys little or no rate of return, but it is very liquid—that is, it can be taken out of the bank and put to another use at a moment's notice with no sacrifice in value. Plant and equipment, on the other hand, have very little liquidity. The funds invested in these assets are recovered only slowly, as the assets are used in operations. The sale of such assets in a short period of time to obtain liquid funds would typically take place at a substantial loss.

Ratios of cash to total assets, or of liquid assets to total assets can give some indication of asset structure. Both the absolute level of the asset structure ratios and their changes from period to period are significant in this respect. The Alpha Company had 34.8 percent of its assets in long-term assets at the end of 19x2, virtually unchanged from a year earlier. The analyst can compare this figure with those of comparable companies.

### Funds Flow Analysis

Analysis of the balance sheet structure at a given point in time can tell a good deal about the company's management of its sources and uses of funds. Analysis of *changes* in structure may be even more revealing, however; and this is the domain of *funds flow analysis*. By examining the changes in balance sheet items between balance sheet dates, one may determine the sources of the funds obtained and the ways in which these funds were used during this *limited time period*.

Funds flow analysis is of such importance that an entire chapter is devoted to it later in the book (Chapter 17). The basic idea can be seen, however, by examining Exhibit 9–3. This is simply a list of balance sheet changes, taken directly from Exhibit 9–1 by subtracting the figures in one column from those in the other. The rules by which these changes were organized in the statement given in Exhibit 9–3 are simplicity itself:

1. An increase in an asset is a *use* of funds.
2. A decrease in a liability or owners' equity is a *use* of funds.
3. An increase in a liability or owners' equity is a *source* of funds.
4. A decrease in an asset is a *source* of funds.

It is interesting to note that only 38 percent of Alpha's funds requirements were obtained from long-term sources (sale of stock, earnings retention, and sale of land), while 51 percent of the funds were put to long-term uses (debt retirement and investment in plant and equipment).

Exhibit 9–3

Alpha Company

STATEMENT OF SOURCES AND USES OF FUNDS

For the Year Ended December 31, 19x2

Sources of funds:

| | |
|---|---:|
| From decrease in cash | $ 1,700 |
| From decrease in land | 500 |
| From increase in accounts payable | 1,800 |
| From increase in notes payable | 9,300 |
| From increase in common stock and capital in excess of par value | 3,700 |
| From increase in retained earnings | 3,600 |
| Total Sources of Funds | $20,600 |

Uses of funds:

| | |
|---|---:|
| To increase receivables | $ 2,700 |
| To increase inventories | 7,200 |
| To increase building and equipment | 4,900 |
| To decrease income taxes payable | 100 |
| To decrease long-term debt | 5,700 |
| Total Uses of Funds | $20,600 |

Strictly speaking, Exhibit 9–3 is not a flow of funds statement. Instead, it is something simpler, often referred to as a "where got, where gone" statement. For example, land is shown as having produced a $500 funds inflow. In fact, the land may have been sold for more or less than this amount. If it had been sold for, say, $1,100, the $600 gain on the sale would have been included in the $3,600 net increase in retained earnings. If that is the case, the flow of funds from the sale of land is understated in Exhibit 9–3, while the net flow of funds from the year's operating earnings is overstated.

A more sophisticated and informative means of deriving funds flow statements will be taken up in Chapter 17. It should be noted, however, that funds flow analysis complements rather than substitutes for profitability analysis. It is designed to throw light on management's financing and investing activities before they have had a chance to affect earnings significantly.

## MEASURES OF SHORT-TERM DEBT-PAYING ABILITY

Since future earnings are uncertain, a concern of management and investors alike is the company's ability to sustain losses with-

out being forced to liquidate or undergo a financial reorganization—in other words, its ability to remain solvent. Management's
main method of analysis designed to answer this question is its
*cash budget*, summarizing the results of its operating and financial plans for the coming period. Outsiders, too, may attempt to
prepare rough forecasts of the company's cash flows for the
immediate future, but in general they lack the necessary information and must fall back upon analysis of the historical financial statements.

The funds flow statements discussed in the previous section
are probably the most valuable single basis for judging short-
term debt-paying ability, but other techniques are also available.
The remainder of this chapter will be concerned with a number
of ratios derived from financial statement information that are
widely used for this purpose.

## Coverage Ratios

One measure of a company's short-term vulnerability to fluctuations in earnings is the coverage ratio or *times-charges-
earned ratio*. In its simplest form, the coverage ratio is the ratio
of earnings before taxes and interest to annual interest charges.
Although preferred dividend requirements cannot be an immediate cause of insolvency, they can be a source of financial
embarrassment. For this reason, they are usually combined with
the interest charge element in the coverage ratio formula. On
this basis, the Alpha ratio for 19x2 was:

$$\frac{\text{Earnings before Interest and Taxes}}{\text{Interest} + \text{Preferred Dividends}} = \frac{\$12,000}{\$1,750} = 6.8.$$

In other words, the company's earnings could shrink to one sixth
of their 19x2 size and still be adequate to cover the interest and
preferred dividend requirements.[3]

This ratio has one important advantage over all the ratios discussed previously—it is derived entirely from *flow* information.
The funds for interest and dividend payments must come in the
final analysis from the funds generated by the firm's operations.
Most balance sheet resources are ordinarily required to support
day-to-day operations and can be used to meet the company's
pressing obligations only at a sacrifice of business efficiency.

---

[3] Preferred dividends are not deductible from revenues in computing taxable income.
Therefore, the amount entered in the coverage ratio formula ought to be the *pre-tax* amounts
necessary to provide for preferred dividends. This added refinement can be left for more
advanced texts on the grounds that it will be important only if the coverage ratio is very low.

This argument actually can be carried a good deal farther. A better coverage ratio would be the ratio of cash generated by operations, before deducting fixed charges, to the total of *all* of the company's fixed cash obligations during the same period — property rentals and scheduled debt repayments as well as interest and dividends. An argument can even be made for including management salaries and other cash operating expenses that would not shrink automatically in the face of a massive reduction in company sales.

These questions will be examined further in Chapter 17, dealing with funds statement preparation, and Chapter 20, which includes a brief discussion of a technique known as *break-even analysis*. In any case, however, the coverage ratio must be examined in conjunction with some measure of volatility — that is, the amplitude of fluctuations in annual earnings or operating cash flows before taxes and interest. Presumably, the higher the earnings volatility, the higher should be the coverage ratio.

## Current Ratio

The most popular indicator of near-term liquidity is the current ratio, the ratio of current assets to current liabilities. Looking back at Exhibit 9–2 we see that the Alpha Corporation current ratio at the end of 19x2 was:

$$\frac{\text{Current Assets}}{\text{Current Liabilities}} = \frac{\$58,300}{\$24,200} = 2.41.$$

The best guarantee of a short-term loan or trade credit is a short-term excess of operating receipts over operating outlays. However, when a short-term downturn in business conditions takes place, a good current ratio provides a secondary line of defense insofar as current assets can be reduced to meet obligations due to operating losses and a shrinkage of short-term credit. It is likely that a firm with a low current ratio cannot obtain funds by reducing inventory or customer credit without severely impairing its ability to obtain and fill customer orders.

Whether Alpha's current ratio of 2.41 represents an adequate margin of safety depends on the variability of cash flows, operating liquidity of the current assets — that is, the ability of the company to reduce these assets without impairing operating performance — and the extent to which the firm's short-term debt is likely to be presented for payment on short notice. Information on questions such as these may be obtained by analysis of various operating ratios and by other means such as the determination of how inventory is measured on the company's books. Finally, it should be noted that the trend and variability over time is as important for this and other ratios as the most recent figure.

## Quick Ratio

One defect of the current ratio is that it conveys no information on the *composition* of the current assets. Clearly, a dollar of cash or even of accounts receivable is more readily made available to meet obligations than a dollar of most kinds of inventory. A measure designed to overcome this defect is the *acid test* or quick ratio. This is the ratio of cash, short-term marketable securities, and receivables to current liabilities. This ratio for Alpha was as follows at the end of 19x2:

$$\frac{\text{Quick Assets}}{\text{Current Liabilities}} = \frac{\$2,600 + \$19,800}{\$24,200} = 0.93.$$

This represented a sharp decline from the previous year's value of ($4,300 + $17,100) ÷ $13,200 = 1.62, reflecting the large increase in inventory and notes payable. This shift might be regarded as a cause for some concern.

It should be recognized that high current and quick ratios are desirable in that they provide high liquidity and a strong short-term financial position. They are undesirable, however, insofar as they reflect unprofitable uses of funds and reduced utilization of low-cost, short-term credit.

## Receivables Turnover

One final set of ratios remains to be considered here: receivables and inventory turnover ratios. The accounts receivable turnover ratio is the ratio of annual sales to accounts receivable. Based on 19x2 year-end receivables balances, this ratio for Alpha was:

$$\frac{\text{Sales Revenues}}{\text{Receivables}} = \frac{\$105,200}{\$19,800} = 5.3.$$

What this says is that the receivables "turned over" 5.3 times during the year.

A related and perhaps more easily understood statistic is the *collection period*—the number of days' sales in accounts receivable. On the basis of a 360-day year, $105,200 ÷ 360 = $291.60 is the average daily sales. Dividing the accounts receivable balance by this figure produces $19,800 ÷ $291.60 = 68, the number of days' sales in accounts receivable.

These ratios are regarded as indicators of (1) the liquidity of the receivables, (2) the quality of the receivables, and (3) management's credit-granting policies. A low turnover ratio—that is, a long collection period—means that in the normal course of business receivables can be turned into cash only slowly. A collection period that is long relative to the normal credit period in the industry indicates either that the firm is using a liberal credit policy to stimulate sales or that the receivables are of low quality, with many customers failing to pay their bills on time. If Alpha's terms of sale call for payment within 30 days, for example, its collection period would be regarded as quite long.

These two ratios do not give the same results that an aging of receivables would give, of course. If this company has selected its fiscal year in such a way that its receivables are considerably lower at year-end than at other times during the year, the average age of the receivables outstanding may be considerably greater than the collection period. Furthermore, if many sales are cash sales, the actual collection period on credit sales may be considerably greater than the calculation indicates. For these reasons, the emphasis again must be less on the absolute size of the ratio than on trends and intercompany comparisons.

A high turnover of receivables may not always be the most efficient policy for a firm. It may be the consequence of a tight credit policy and a vigorous collection program that unduly restricts the volume of sales. A loosening of credit standards will often increase receivables by a larger percentage than the increase in sales, but the increase in profit may be considerably higher than the company's desired rate of return on the added investment.

### Inventory Turnover

Another ratio similar in purpose to the receivables turnover ratio is the inventory turnover ratio. Inventory and revenue figures are not precisely comparable: the former are on a cost basis, while the latter represent sale prices. The number of days' inventory on hand thus can be computed only if the cost of goods sold is known, in which case the ratio is cost of goods sold per day, divided by inventory. Much the same purpose can be served by sales/inventory ratios, however, and inventory turnover is often computed on this basis. Based on the year-end inventory, the 19x2 inventory turnover ratio for Alpha was:

$$\frac{\text{Sales Revenues}}{\text{Inventories}} = \frac{\$105,200}{\$35,900} = 2.9.$$

A low ratio is indicative of slow-moving inventory, and a ratio that is falling or lower than competitors' or both is a sign of potential danger. On the other hand, a company may deliberately carry large inventories to reduce the loss of sales caused by inadequate stocks and to avail itself of economies of large purchase or production lots. Nevertheless, a falling ratio is presumptive evidence of a decline in liquidity, high carrying costs, and potential future losses from obsolescence.

Inventory turnover ratios are subject to the same defects as receivables turnover ratios. They say little about the quality of the year-end inventory mix, nor do they reflect seasonal variations in sales and inventories. Probably even more important, however, are the effects on these ratios of the inventory measurement rules used by the company. Differences among companies in this respect make the inventory ratios virtually useless for intercompany comparisons without supplementary information from the companies concerned. These measurement problems are the subject of the chapters that follow, particularly Chapter 11.

## SUMMARY

Outside analysts use a company's financial statements in predicting the company's future earnings (profitability analysis) or its short-term debt-paying ability (solvency analysis).

The main index of past earnings performance is return on investment. This may be computed as a return on assets or as a return on the common stockholders' equity. The difference between these two rates is the effect of leverage, the use of capital sources other than the common shareholders. The return on investment figures can also be broken down into asset turnover and profit margin components for a more detailed analysis of trends and intercompany comparisons.

Solvency analysis focuses on comparisons of estimated cash inflows and outflows in the near future. The basic tool of this kind of analysis is the flow of funds statement. This is supplemented by examination of the relationships among various balance sheet groupings.

The validity of both kinds of analysis is conditioned not only by the comparability of past and future but also by the quality of the underlying data. The measurement rules used in preparing company financial statements have great effects on the ratios discussed in this chapter, and these effects will be the focus of the chapters that follow.

## QUESTIONS AND PROBLEMS

1. An executive has to make a recommendation on the amount of the dividend to be declared by his company. How can financial statement analysis assist him?

2. Financial statements are concerned with the past. An individual who is interested in a company wants to forecast, among other things, the future profits of that company. How can financial statement analysis be useful to him?

3. Indicate how you would calculate earnings per common share when an issue of preferred stock is outstanding.

4. How does the earnings per common share differ from the return on common equity?

5. What is leverage? What effect does it have on return on common equity?

6. Company X's profit margin (net income as a percent of sales) is 2 percent, but its return on assets is 14 percent. Explain how this can be true.

7. A company's return on total assets is 4 percent. Its return on common equity is 3 percent. What do these figures indicate?

8. Company A has obtained half of its long-term capital from borrowing; Company B has no long-term debt. How would you reflect these differences in your analysis of the relative profitability of these two companies?

9. How can the financial statements of two companies of different sizes be transformed to permit a test of the hypothesis that the two companies are similar except for size?

10. A company reported net income of $10,000 for 19x1, but its cash balance at the end of 19x1 was $5,000 less than it had been at the beginning of the year. How could this have happened?

11. A company's times-charges-earned ratio declined from 3.2 to 1.2. What conclusions could be drawn from this change?

12. A current ratio of 3.0 and a quick ratio of 1.0 give some information about the structure of the balance sheet. What information do they give?

13. What is meant by the structure of a firm's assets and equities? What purpose is analysis of this structure expected to achieve?

**14.** What purposes are served by a summary of the annual *changes* in the balances of balance sheet accounts? Can these purposes be served equally well by income statements?

**15.** A company has just sold one of its buildings at a price equal to its book value and has used the proceeds from the sale to retire long-term bonds payable. The price paid to retire the bonds was equal to the amount at which they were shown on the balance sheet. Upon selling the building, the company entered into a 20-year lease with the new owner. What effects did this series of transactions have on the following ratios:

*a)* Debt/equity ratio?
*b)* Current ratio?
*c)* Asset turnover ratio?

**16.** The Casey Company has a current ratio of 3.0, a quick ratio of 1.5, a receivables turnover of 6.1, and an inventory turnover of 4.5. How will each of the transactions listed below affect these ratios?

*a)* Purchase of merchandise for cash.
*b)* Purchase of merchandise on credit.
*c)* Sale of a marketable security at cost (i.e., at zero gain or loss).
*d)* Sale of merchandise for cash.

**\*17.** The following data have been taken from the financial statements of a manufacturing company:

| | |
|---|---|
| Total assets .............................. | $100,000 |
| Interest expense........................... | $  2,000 |
| Tax rate..................................... | 45% |
| Return on common equity................... | 7.2% |
| Debt/equity ratio ......................... | 0.25 |

The company has no preferred stock outstanding.

*a)* Calculate the overall rate of profitability (return on assets).
*b)* Did the company use leverage successfully?

**18.** The Doud Company has a return on common equity of 12 percent, based on income after taxes of $12,000. Its debt/equity ratio is 50 percent and the income tax rate is 40 percent. Interest expense is $4,500 a year.

*a)* Calculate the before-tax rate of return on total assets.
*b)* Calculate the after-tax rate of return on total assets. Is this company using leverage successfully?

**19.** A list of the largest merchandising firms in the United States showed the following data for three well-known firms:

---

\* Solutions to problems marked with an asterisk (\*) are found in Appendix B.

|                                   | Company A      | Company B        | Company C        |
| --------------------------------- | -------------- | ---------------- | ---------------- |
| Rank (by sales) among             |                |                  |                  |
| merchandising firms..             | 26             | 11               | 2                |
| Sales ...................         | $627,349,000   | $1,293,765,000   | $5,458,824,000   |
| Assets .................          | 120,363,000    | 274,603,000      | 884,001,000      |
| Net income............            | 11,477,000     | 8,327,000        | 55,897,000       |
| Shareholder's equity....          | 43,554,000     | 163,317,000      | 627,366,000      |

a) Compute the profit margin as a percentage of sales, asset turnover, return on assets, return on equity, and debt/asset ratio for each of these three companies.

b) For return on common equity, Company A ranked first, Company B ranked 46th, and Company C ranked 39th among the merchandising companies on the list. Basing your analysis on the financial statement data alone, prepare an explanation of the difference between the relative sales ranking and the relative return on common equity ranking.

*20. The Barnes Company had net income after taxes of $106.0 million for 19x4, $111.3 million for 19x5, and $109.1 million for 19x6. Preferred dividends were $10.0 million in each year. The shareholders' equity section of the company's balance sheets during this period showed the following:

|                          | 12/31/x3         | 12/31/x4         | 12/31/x5         | 12/31/x6         |
| ------------------------ | ---------------- | ---------------- | ---------------- | ---------------- |
| Preferred stock.......... | $ 170,000,000   | $ 170,000,000    | $ 170,000,000    | $ 170,000,000    |
| Common stock, $1 par...  | 50,000,000       | 50,000,000       | 52,000,000       | 52,000,000       |
| Additional paid-in       |                  |                  |                  |                  |
| capital ...............  | 200,000,000      | 200,000,000      | 238,000,000      | 238,000,000      |
| Retained earnings.......  | 580,000,000      | 626,000,000      | 677,300,000      | 724,400,000      |
| Total.............. | $1,000,000,000   | $1,046,000,000   | $1,137,300,000   | $1,184,400,000   |

a) Compute the earnings per common share in 19x4, 19x5, and 19x6, basing your calculations on the number of shares outstanding at the end of the year.

b) Compute the book value per common share at each balance sheet date.

c) Compute the return on common equity for 19x4, 19x5, and 19x6. In each case, base your calculations on average common equity for the year.

√ 21. Analysis of a company's financial statements reveals the following information for the last three years:

|                          | 19x1   | 19x2   | 19x3   |
| ------------------------ | ------ | ------ | ------ |
| Return on common equity...................... | 8.1%   | 9.7%   | 10.5%  |
| Current ratio.................................. | 2.5:1  | 2.7:1  | 2.6:1  |
| Earnings per share........................... | $1.62  | $2.04  | $2.31  |
| Times charges earned......................... | 10.0   | 4.2    | 3.9    |
| Debt/equity ratio ............................. | 1:5    | 2:3    | 9:11   |

The tax rate was 50 percent in each of these years and 50,000 shares of common stock were outstanding throughout the entire three-year period.

a)  Did the company's basic profitability increase during this period? Support your position with figures developed from the information supplied above.  *yes*

b)  Did the shareowners' risk increase? Cite figures to support your position.  *Time changes earned is one of the measures*

    *∴ TCE ↓ ∴ risk ↑*

*22.  Below are the comparative balance sheets of the George Corporation as of December 31, 19x1, and 19x2:

|  | 19x1 | 19x2 |
|---|---|---|
| **ASSETS** | | |
| Current assets.............................. | $16,000 | $25,000 |
| Buildings and equipment.................. | 36,000 | 44,500 |
| Accumulated depreciation................. | (5,000) | (8,500) |
| Land ....................................... | 3,000 | 5,000 |
| Total ............................. | $50,000 | $66,000 |
| **LIABILITIES AND OWNERS' EQUITY** | | |
| Current liabilities......................... | $ 9,000 | $ 6,000 |
| Long-term debt............................ | 10,000 | 20,000 |
| Capital stock ............................. | 12,000 | 17,000 |
| Retained earnings......................... | 19,000 | 23,000 |
| Total ............................. | $50,000 | $66,000 |

Depreciation for the year was $3,500.

Prepare a statement of balance sheet changes that will describe most clearly the company's sources and uses of funds for 19x2.

23.  The Davis Company's financial statements for June 19x2 are provided below:

### STATEMENTS OF FINANCIAL POSITION

| ASSETS | June 1 | July 1 | LIABILITIES AND OWNERS' EQUITY | June 1 | July 1 |
|---|---|---|---|---|---|
| Cash...................... | $ 2,000 | $ 7,000 | Accounts payable....... | $ 3,000 | $ 3,000 |
| Accounts receivable....... | 3,000 | 3,000 | Capital stock........... | 10,000 | 14,000 |
| Inventory................. | 5,000 | 8,000 | Retained earnings ...... | 3,000 | 5,000 |
| Plant and equipment (net) | 6,000 | 4,000 | | | |
| Total............. | $16,000 | $22,000 | Total........... | $16,000 | $22,000 |

### INCOME STATEMENT
#### For June, 19x2

| | |
|---|---|
| Sales .................................... | $12,000 |
| Cost of goods sold..................... | $ 7,000 |
| Depreciation expense.................. | 2,000 |
| Other expenses........................ | 1,000 |
| Net Income........................... | $ 2,000 |

*a)* Prepare a statement of balance sheet changes for the month that will show, insofar as possible, (1) how much cash was collected during the month and where it came from; and (2) how much cash was spent during the month and for what purposes.

*b)* What was the net effect of the company's sales to its customers on its cash balance? How does this differ from net income?

**24.** Delta Company and Gamma Company sell similar lines of products. The manager of Delta Company has collected the following statistics:

|  | Delta | Gamma |
|---|---|---|
| Sales, 19x3 | $7,000,000 | $5,000,000 |
| Estimated customer defaults, 19x3 | 35,000 | 50,000 |
| Income before interest and taxes, 19x3 | 600,000 | 500,000 |
| Total assets, December 31, 19x3 | 4,800,000 | 4,000,000 |
| Accounts receivable, December 31, 19x3 | 800,000 | 750,000 |

The manager wants the answers to the questions stated below. You are expected to answer the questions if possible. If the information provided is not adequate for a satisfactory answer, you are to state the additional information you need and explain how you would use this information to answer the questions.

*a)* Which company has the more liberal credit policy?
*b)* Which company has the more liquid receivables?
*c)* By how much will Delta's accounts receivable increase during 19x4?
*d)* Which company is managing its accounts receivable more profitably?

**25.** Below are the income statements and balance sheets of two companies. On the basis of the available information, which do you consider to be (1) more liquid? (2) more solvent? (3) more profitable? Explain your conclusions.

### INCOME STATEMENT
### For the Year 19x1

|  | Franklin Company | Morgan Company |
|---|---|---|
| Sales | $8,000,000 | $7,000,000 |
| Cost of goods sold | $6,000,000 | $4,700,000 |
| Selling, general, and administrative expenses | 1,200,000 | 1,900,000 |
| Interest on debt | | 70,000 |
| Income before taxes | $ 800,000 | $ 330,000 |
| Income taxes | 390,000 | 160,000 |
| Net Income | $ 410,000 | $ 170,000 |
| Dividends Declared | $ 100,000 | $ 70,000 |

### STATEMENTS OF FINANCIAL POSITION
### As of December 31, 19x1

| ASSETS | Franklin Company | Morgan Company |
|---|---|---|
| Cash | $ 300,000 | $ 300,000 |
| Accounts receivable | 800,000 | 650,000 |
| Inventory | 1,300,000 | 850,000 |
| Net plant and equipment | 2,100,000 | 1,500,000 |
| Total | $4,500,000 | $3,300,000 |

| LIABILITIES AND OWNERS' EQUITY | | |
|---|---|---|
| Accounts payable | $ 710,000 | $ 400,000 |
| Taxes payable | 390,000 | 160,000 |
| Long-term debt | ......... | 1,400,000 |
| Capital stock | 2,200,000 | 800,000 |
| Retained earnings | 1,200,000 | 540,000 |
| Total | $4,500,000 | $3,300,000 |

26. The Alpha Company (see Exhibits 9–1 and 9–2 in the chapter) reported the following financial statements at the end of 19x3:

### Alpha Company
### STATEMENT OF FINANCIAL POSITION
### December 31, 19x3

#### ASSETS

Current Assets:
| | |
|---|---|
| Cash | $ 3,000 |
| Receivables | 20,000 |
| Inventories | 42,000 |
| Total Current Assets | $65,000 |

Long-Term Assets:
| | |
|---|---|
| Buildings and equipment | $54,000 |
| Less: Accumulated depreciation | 22,100 |
| Net buildings and equipment | $31,900 |
| Land | 1,400 |
| Total Assets | $98,300 |

#### LIABILITIES AND STOCKHOLDERS' EQUITY

Current Liabilities:
| | |
|---|---|
| Accounts payable | $ 8,400 |
| Notes payable | 17,100 |
| Federal income taxes payable | 2,400 |
| Total Current Liabilities | $27,900 |
| Long-term debt | 13,600 |
| Total Liabilities | $41,500 |

Stockholders' equity:
| | |
|---|---|
| 5% preferred stock, 700 shares | 7,000 |
| Common stock, 2,000 shares | 10,000 |
| Capital in excess of par value | 12,600 |
| Retained earnings | 27,200 |
| Total Liabilities and Stockholders' Equity | $98,300 |

Alpha Company
## INCOME STATEMENT
### For the Year Ended December 31, 19x3

| | | |
|---|---|---:|
| Sales revenue...................................... | | $106,700 |
| Expenses: | | |
| Cost of products sold (except depreciation)...... | $58,700 | |
| Depreciation..................................... | 2,700 | |
| Research and development..................... | 5,800 | |
| Selling and administration....................... | 27,900 | 95,100 |
| Income before interest and taxes................. | | $ 11,600 |
| Interest expense ................................. | | 1,500 |
| Income before taxes............................. | | $ 10,100 |
| Income taxes.................................... | | 4,650 |
| Net income ..................................... | | $  5,450 |
| Dividends on preferred stock...................... | | 350 |
| Income available for common stockholders........ | | $  5,100 |
| Dividends on common stock...................... | | 1,800 |
| Current Income Retained in the Business......... | | $  3,300 |

Did Alpha Company earn adequate profits in 19x3? (Hint: Decide which ratios are relevant to the question, then make the needed calculations.) Can Alpha meet its obligations promptly? Is an investment in Alpha safe?

**27.** The following data were taken from the 19x1 financial statements of two companies in the same industry:

| | Company A | Company B |
|---|---:|---:|
| Cash ........................... | $  8,000 | $ 24,000 |
| Accounts receivable ............ | 17,000 | 19,200 |
| Inventories..................... | 27,200 | 29,568 |
| Prepaid expenses................ | 2,000 | 4,000 |
| Property and equipment......... | 100,000 | 220,000 |
| Accumulated depreciation....... | (62,400) | (57,152) |
| Total ................... | $ 91,800 | $239,616 |
| | | |
| Current liabilities............... | $ 20,000 | $ 40,000 |
| Long-term debt – 6%............. | 40,000 | ....... |
| Long-term debt – 9%............. | ....... | 20,000 |
| Stockholders' equity............. | 31,800 | 179,616 |
| Total ................... | $ 91,800 | $239,616 |
| | | |
| Sales........................... | $204,000 | $460,800 |
| Cost of goods sold ............. | (163,200) | (354,816) |
| Other expenses................. | (22,440) | (46,080) |
| Interest........................ | (2,400) | (1,800) |
| Income taxes.................... | (3,990) | (14,526) |
| Net Income ................... | $ 11,970 | $ 43,578 |

a) All sales are on account and there are only minor seasonal variations in sales. Compare the current debt-paying ability of the two firms. To what extent can the inventories be looked upon as a means of paying debts due in 30 days? In 60 days?

b) Compare the profitability of the two firms. What factors account for the difference? (The income tax rate is 25 percent.)

c) Compare the long-term debt-paying ability of the two firms.

28. Below are the comparative balance sheets and income statements of North Printing Company for the years 19x0 to 19x2:

## STATEMENTS OF FINANCIAL POSITION
### For the Years 19x0–x2

|  | December 31, 19x0 | December 31, 19x1 | December 31, 19x2 |
|---|---|---|---|
| ASSETS |  |  |  |
| *Current Assets:* |  |  |  |
| Cash......................... | $ 4,000 | $ 5,000 | $ 2,000 |
| Receivables, net............. | 20,000 | 15,000 | 17,000 |
| Inventories.................. | 18,000 | 25,000 | 30,000 |
| Total Current Assets .... | $42,000 | $45,000 | $49,000 |
| Net property ................. | 13,000 | 18,000 | 18,000 |
| Other assets.................. | 1,000 | 2,000 | 3,000 |
| Total Assets............. | $56,000 | $65,000 | $70,000 |
| LIABILITIES AND SHAREHOLDERS' EQUITY |  |  |  |
| *Current Liabilities:* |  |  |  |
| Accounts payable ........... | $ 5,000 | $ 6,000 | $ 7,000 |
| Notes payable (9%) ......... | 3,000 | 9,000 | 11,000 |
| Other current liabilities ..... | 2,000 | 1,000 | 1,500 |
| Total Current Liabilities... | $10,000 | $16,000 | $19,500 |
| Long-term debt (8%).......... | 8,000 | 10,000 | 9,000 |
| Shareholders' equity .......... | 38,000 | 39,000 | 41,500 |
| Total Liabilities and Shareholders' Equity.... | $56,000 | $65,000 | $70,000 |

## COMPARATIVE INCOME STATEMENTS
### For the Years 19x0–x2

|  | 19x0 |  | 19x1 |  | 19x2 |  |
|---|---|---|---|---|---|---|
| Sales.............. |  | $100,000 |  | $105,000 |  | $120,000 |
| Materials........ | $35,000 |  | $37,000 |  | $43,000 |  |
| Labor ........... | 28,000 |  | 30,000 |  | 35,000 |  |
| Heat, light and power......... | 3,700 |  | 4,000 |  | 4,500 |  |
| Depreciation (10%)......... | 1,300 | 68,000 | 1,500 | 72,500 | 1,500 | 84,000 |
| Gross profit....... |  | $ 32,000 |  | $ 32,500 |  | $ 36,000 |
| Selling expenses. | $17,000 |  | $17,500 |  | $18,000 |  |
| General and administrative expenses...... | 10,500 | $ 27,500 | 11,000 | 28,500 | 12,000 | 30,000 |
| Operating profit... |  | 4,500 |  | 4,000 |  | 6,000 |
| Less interest expense....... |  | 1,000 |  | 1,600 |  | 1,700 |
| Income before taxes............ |  | $ 3,500 |  | $ 2,400 |  | $ 4,300 |
| Federal income taxes............ |  | 1,500 |  | 1,000 |  | 1,900 |
| Net Income ....... |  | $ 2,000 |  | $ 1,400 |  | $ 2,400 |

The following table was prepared by a financial analyst to help him compare various companies in the printing industry with what he considered to be the "norm" for the industry:

| | 19x0 | | 19x1 | | 19x2 | |
|---|---|---|---|---|---|---|
| | Company | Norm | Company | Norm | Company | Norm |
| 1.  Current Assets / Current Liabilities | | 3.2 | | 3.3 | | 3.4 |
| 2.  Inventory / Net Working Capital | | 69.4 | | 75.0 | | 81.0 |
| 3.  Sales / Inventory (at Book) | | 5.6 | | 5.8 | | 6.0 |
| 4. Collection period (days) | | 37.0 | | 35.0 | | 33.0 |
| 5.  Fixed Assets / Owners' Equity | | 32.0 | | 33.1 | | 35.0 |
| 6. Current Liabilities / Owners' Equity | | 27.6 | | 26.9 | | 26.3 |
| 7.  Total Debt / Owners' Equity | | 49.3 | | 49.5 | | 52.0 |
| 8. Current Liabilities / Inventory | | 55.2 | | 53.2 | | 51.0 |
| 9. Sales / Assets | | 1.8 | | 1.9 | | 2.1 |
| 10. Net Income / Sales | | 2.5 | | 2.6 | | 2.8 |
| 11.  Net Income / Owners' Equity | | 6.6 | | 6.8 | | 7.2 |
| 12. Operating Profit / Total Assets | | 7.5 | | 7.8 | | 8.5 |

*a)* Compute the ratios necessary to fill in the blanks in the analyst's table, using end-of-year figures for the required balance sheet items.

*b)* Another analyst comments that of the 12 ratios listed in the table above, only eight are of real value. The other four, he argues, contain little if any information beyond that contained in the ratios numbered 1, 3, 4, 7, 9, 10, 11, and 12. Explain why you do or do not agree with the analyst's conclusion on each of the other four ratios.

*c)* Prepare statements of balance sheet changes for the years 19x1 and 19x2.

*d)* Using whatever data seem pertinent, evaluate the profitability, liquidity, and strength of North Printing Company.

# Part II

# External Financial Reporting

# *10*

# PRESENT VALUE

MANAGEMENT AND INVESTORS ALIKE have a vital stake in events that change the value of a business firm. Many changes in value do not appear in the income statement, however, because they arise from events that the accountant does not measure. For the same reason, the value of the business at any point in time may be very different from the amounts reported in the balance sheet.

Even though the financial statements do not measure value, the accountant does use the economic theory of value to resolve some of the more difficult problems that are encountered in the application of the cost basis of measurement. Value theory is also highly useful in various kinds of management decisions, and provides a reference point against which other accounting measures can be compared. For these reasons, we need to examine this theory before moving to the main subject of Part II, a review of various aspects of corporate financial reporting. In the process, we shall see how this theory might be used to develop a set of value-based financial statements.

## THE MEASUREMENT OF PRESENT VALUE

The word value has been the subject of extensive analysis and debate in philosophy, economics, and other fields of thought. At first glance, it might seem that the monetary value of an asset is simply the price at which it can be sold — market value. For assets such as used equipment and product components, however, management would object that market values are far less than the

245

assets are worth. Assets such as these are acquired for the future benefits they will produce. Because resale markets are imperfect, with few readily identifiable buyers, the benefits from owning or using assets are usually far greater than the amounts that they would bring if sold piecemeal on the market. When this is the case, estimated economic value must be based on estimates of the economic benefits to be derived from asset ownership or use.

### The Nature of Economic Benefits

Economic benefits take the form of net cash inflows from asset ownership or use. A business asset has value because it can be sold to an outsider (bottled soft drinks, for example), used to produce goods that can be sold to an outsider (a bottling machine), or used to reduce the cost of the company's operations (a bookkeeping machine). In each case, the benefit takes the form of greater net cash inflows for the firm.

The economic value, or *present value*, of these anticipated cash inflows is less than their amount, however. For one thing, a dollar now is worth more than a dollar in the future, because a dollar now can be invested to earn interest and grow to more than a dollar. Second, future cash receipts are uncertain, which ordinarily makes them seem less attractive than present amounts which are unclouded by uncertainty. The measurement problem, therefore, is to find a way of converting estimates of future cash flows into their equivalent present values.

### Compound Interest

The mechanism for calculating the present value of future cash flows is provided by the theory of compound interest. To illustrate, if a bank will pay $1,050 one year from now in return for a $1,000 deposit today, it is paying interest at the rate of 5 percent a year. This relationship can be expressed mathematically in the following expression:

$$F_1 = P(1 + r), \tag{1}$$

in which $P$ = the present outlay or deposit in the bank, $r$ = the rate of interest, and $F_1$ = future value. If $P = \$1,000$ and $r = 0.05$, then $F_1 = \$1,050$.

Continuing the example, if the $1,050 is left in the bank for another year, it will build up by the end of two years to a balance of $1,050 + (\$1,050 \times 0.05) = \$1,102.50$. Interest in this second year amounts to $52.50 and is greater than the first year's interest because the bank is now paying interest not only on the original investment but also on the interest earned during the first year.

This form of interest calculation is known as *compounding*. In this case, interest has been compounded *annually*, meaning that interest is added to the bank balance only once a year. It is more likely that interest will be compounded quarterly or even more frequently. The shorter the interest period, the sooner the interest is added to the amount on which interest is earned and the faster the amount will grow. This is how some banks are able to advertise that although they pay 6 percent interest, it is equivalent to an annual yield of 6.27 percent.

The mathematical formula for computing the future value of a present sum two years later is:

$$F_2 = F_1(1 + r) = P(1 + r)(1 + r) = P(1 + r)^2 \qquad (2)$$

In general, it can be shown that if an amount $P$ is put out at interest of $r$ percent a year, compounded annually, at the end of $n$ years it will have grown to:

$$F_n = P(1 + r)^n \qquad (3)$$

## Present Value

Although value can be thought of as the future equivalent of a present cash sum, a more customary and generally more useful practice is to define it as the *present equivalent* or *present value* of anticipated future cash sums. Present value is the amount which, if invested at the specified rate of return, will grow to an amount equal to the anticipated cash amount at the specified future date. In this case, $1,000 is the present value at 5 percent of $1,050 to be received one year in the future. It is the amount that the future cash receipt ($1,050) is worth today to an investor who regards 5 percent as a satisfactory return on his money.

The relationship between present and future values is shown graphically in Exhibit 10–1. Starting with $1,000, the depositor's asset will build at 5 percent to $1,050 in one year, $1,102.50 in two years, and so on, up to $2,653.30 at the end of 20 years. Therefore, $1,000 can be said to be the present value at 5 percent of $1,628.90 to be received 10 years from now or $2,653.30 to be received in 20 years' time, and so on.

The formula for computing present value from known or esti-

Exhibit 10-1

FUTURE VALUES EQUIVALENT TO PRESENT VALUE OF $1,000
(annual compounding at 5 percent a year)

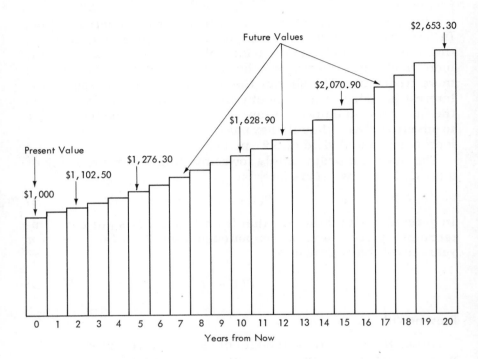

mated future values can be found by turning equation (3) around.
Since $F_n = P(1 + r)^n$, then

$$P = F_n \frac{1}{(1 + r)^n} \tag{4}$$

This shows that the present value of any future sum can be determined by dividing the latter by $(1 + r)^n$ or by multiplying it by
$(1 + r)^{-n}$. If $n$ is two years, $r$ is 5 percent, and the asset is expected
to yield a cash inflow of $1,000 two years from now, then its value
today is:

$$P = \frac{\$1,000}{(1.05)^2} = \frac{\$1,000}{1.1025} = \$907.03.$$

In other words, $907.03 will grow to $1,000 in two years if it is
invested now at 5 percent interest, compounded annually; it is
therefore the present value of that future amount.

## The Value of a Series of Cash Receipts

While some assets derive all of their value from the expectation of a single cash receipt, the value of others is based on not one but a series of future cash receipts. The value of an asset of this kind is the sum of the values of the various cash flows.

For example, suppose that an investor is satisfied with nothing less than an 8 percent return on his investment. A local merchant has accepted a note from one of his customers entitling him to collect $5,000 a year from now and $10,000 at the end of the following year. The merchant is short of cash and wishes to sell the note.

If the investor were satisfied with a zero rate of return, he would be willing to pay $5,000 + $10,000 = $15,000 for this note. Because he demands an 8 percent return, however, he must *discount* each future payment to its present value — that is, deduct from the future cash receipt the amount that represents interest at 8 percent on the purchase price of the note.

Since $1 now is equivalent to $1.08 a year from now, the present value of the first $5,000 can be derived by substituting these figures in equation (4):

$$\text{Present value} = \$5,000 \times \frac{1}{1.08} = \$4,630.$$

Similarly, the present value of $10,000 to be received two years from now can be calculated by dividing $10,000 by $(1.08)^2$, or 1.1664. The results of these calculations are summarized in the following table:

| (1) Years from Now | (2) Cash Receipt | (3) Multiplier | (4) Present Value at 8% (2) × (3) |
|---|---|---|---|
| 1 ............ | $ 5,000 | 1/1.0800 | $ 4,630 |
| 2 ............ | 10,000 | 1/1.1664 | 8,573 |
| Total ...... | | | $13,203 |

The value of this asset to this investor is thus $13,203. He should be willing to buy the note at any figure less than this.

## Interest Tables

This kind of calculation is time-consuming and expensive. Fortunately, the most laborious part — the derivation of $(1 + r)^{-n}$

for all important values of $r$ and $n$ — has already been done by mathematicians. The results of these calculations are available in published *interest tables.* Alternatively, a computer can be programmed to calculate these multipliers quickly and at low cost, and some miniature electronic calculators can be used directly to do the same thing.

Although the remainder of this chapter can be read and understood without the aid of computers or interest tables, something of this sort must be used to solve the problems and exercises at the end of the chapter. To meet this need, we have provided an abbreviated set of interest tables in Appendix A at the end of the book, together with instructions for using them.

## FINANCIAL STATEMENTS BASED ON PRESENT VALUE

Our main reason for studying present value at this point is that the accountant uses present value computations in accounting for a wide variety of items such as pensions and long-term receivables that we shall examine in the chapters that follow. Present value calculations are also used extensively in managerial decision making.

The reason for the widespread use of present value in these applications is that future cash flows and their present values are the relevant data for decision making. Given this, it might be argued that management and investors would be better served if financial statements were based on estimates of present value rather than on historical cost. For example, it will be recalled from Chapter 2 that when Mr. Erskine wanted a bank loan he was disappointed to discover that his balance sheet did not show the value of his dealer franchise and other intangible assets. The same issue from a different point of view arises when stockholders are told that their stock is worthless, even though the book value of the corporation's assets exceeds its liabilities by a large amount.

The accounting profession is very aware of these problems and is vigorously seeking ways of solving them. It has made no move toward substituting present value for cost as the basis for company financial reporting, however. To see why this is so, we need to examine what the accountant would have to do to use the method in company financial reporting.[1]

---

[1] Arguments in support of present value may be found in David Solomons' "Economic and Accounting Concepts of Income," *The Accounting Review,* Vol. 26, no. 3 (July 1961), pp. 374–83. For more extensive coverage, see S. S. Alexander and David Solomons, "Income Measurement in a Dynamic Economy," in W. T. Baxter and S. Davidson, *Studies in Accounting Theory* (Homewood, Ill.: Richard D. Irwin, Inc., 1962), pp. 126–200.

## Valuation of a Going Concern

The use of discounted cash flows in the valuation of a going concern can be illustrated by considering the history of the Precision Instrument Company. The corporation was formed in 19x0 by four young men to market a simple but revolutionary measuring instrument invented by one of its founders.

As a means of conserving its limited capital, the company opened for business in rented quarters equipped with a few thousand dollars worth of equipment that was used primarily for research and development work. Arrangements were made with established manufacturers to build instruments on order to specifications rigidly supervised by one of the young associates. Because of the scientific need filled by the new instrument, this new company was able to report a modest profit after only two years of operation.

These four men proved to be an unusually well-balanced scientific, engineering, and managerial team, and it was not long before they had developed three more instruments that were very well received by both institutional research laboratories and industrial customers. By 19x7, sales had grown to about $1,400,000, and net income amounted to about $114,000 a year.

The company's latest balance sheet, shown in Exhibit 10–2, listed a total owners' equity of $280,000. Annual earnings therefore represented an after-tax rate of return of slightly more than 40 percent of the reported owners' equity. This high return was

*Exhibit 10–2*

Precision Instrument Company

STATEMENT OF FINANCIAL POSITION

December 31, 19x7

ASSETS

*Current Assets:*

| | |
|---|---|
| Cash | $ 25,000 |
| Receivables | 160,000 |
| Inventories | 120,000 |
| Current Assets | $305,000 |
| Equipment | 80,000 |
| Total Assets | $385,000 |

LIABILITIES AND OWNERS' EQUITY

*Current Liabilities:*

| | |
|---|---|
| Taxes payable | $ 15,000 |
| Accounts payable | 90,000 |
| Current Liabilities | $105,000 |
| Owners' equity | 280,000 |
| Total Liabilities and Owners' Equity | $385,000 |

due in part to the use of other firms for manufacturing. The primary factors, however, were the increasing value of the company's patents and the scientific and managerial skill of the company's officers.

At this point the owners had to make a decision. The management of the R. F. Walden Corporation offered to buy the company at what seemed like a good price. The four owners promised to consider the offer, but asked for a few weeks to make up their minds.

### Calculation of Present Value

As the owners saw it, they had established a small but solid position in the industry. They served a portion of the market that their larger competitors were not well equipped to handle and their relationships with their customers were very good. They had no doubt that they would be able to maintain this position, but they felt that the potential for further growth was very small. They drew very good salaries, about what they would continue to receive if they sold out to Walden, so that was not a factor.

To figure out how much their equity in Precision Instruments was worth to them, the four men started by forecasting the company's future cash flows. For example, suppose that they believed that Precision's net income would be approximately $114,000 a year for the next 10 years. Suppose also that equipment replacement expenditures would be approximately equal to the annual depreciation charges and that working capital requirements would not change. If these assumptions were valid, the annual cash flow would equal the annual net income, $114,000.

Finally, suppose that the owners believed that if they did not sell out in 19x8 they could sell their owners' equity in Precision 10 years later for about $400,000. Under these assumptions the anticipated cash flows from continued ownership would be as follows:

| Year | Receipts |
|------|----------|
| 1 to 10 | $114,000 a year |
| 10 | 400,000 |

The next step was to calculate the present value of these cash flows. Precision's owners estimated that 12 percent after taxes was a satisfactory return on investment for the type of business in which Precision was engaged. The question was how much the anticipated cash flows were worth at this rate.

Present value can be calculated quite simply with the aid of figures from Appendix A. Because the cash flows were expected to be constant throughout the 10-year period, Table 4 can be used. The multiplier for 10 equal annual receipts, discounted at the desired earnings rate of 12 percent, is 5.650. The $400,000 figure, in contrast, is a single lump-sum receipt, and Table 3 must be used. The multiplier for a receipt at the end of 10 years is 0.322.

The calculation of present value can now be summarized as follows:

| Year | Receipts | Multiplier | Present Value |
|------|----------|------------|---------------|
| 1 to 10 ...... | $114,000 a year | 5.650 | $644,100 |
| 10 .......... | 400,000 | 0.322 | 128,800 |
| Total...... | | | $772,900 |

In other words, under these assumptions, the owners should have accepted nothing less than $772,900 for their equity in Precision Instrument.

These calculations reflected a forecast that Precision would continue to generate cash flows for 10 years only. In fact, the four owners felt that cash would continue to flow in at the rate of $114,000 a year indefinitely if the operation was managed adequately. Present value in this case can be calculated very simply, by dividing annual net cash receipts by the desired rate of return:

$$\frac{\$114,000}{0.12} = \$950,000$$

On this basis, the owners estimated that the value of their equity in Precision Instrument Company was $950,000.

This process is known as the *capitalization of earnings*. Its basis is that if $950,000 is paid for an infinitely long series of payments of $114,000 each, the rate of return on the investment will be 12 percent:

$$\frac{\$114,000}{\$950,000} = 12 \text{ percent.}$$

It should be emphasized that although this is called a capitalization of *earnings* formula, it must in fact be applied to forecasts of *cash flows*, as in the example above. *Use of net income to represent cash flow is acceptable only if it can reasonably be assumed that the two figures will be approximately the same.*

## Goodwill

Not surprisingly, the owners' equity shown in Exhibit 10–2 was a good deal less than its indicated $950,000 value to its owners. One possible explanation for this difference is that the historical cost of the inventories or equipment was less than it would have cost the company to replace them. In this case, however, both Walden's management and Precision's owners agreed that the amounts shown were reasonably close to their current replacement cost.

The real reason here was that the historical balance sheet contained no reference to the firm's *intangible assets* – its patents, copyrights, customer relationships, and management skill and technical knowledge. These intangibles are ordinarily referred to collectively as *goodwill*, the source of earnings in excess of a normal rate of return on the tangible assets. The estimated value of the goodwill of Precision Instrument was $950,000 – $280,000 = $670,000.

## A Balance Sheet Based on Present Value

Strictly speaking, a balance sheet based on present value should list each asset at its present value to the organization as a whole. Since this is seldom feasible, something else must be tried. Exhibit 10–3 illustrates one such possibility. In this exhibit all

*Exhibit 10–3*

Precision Instrument Company

ADJUSTED STATEMENT OF FINANCIAL POSITION
December 31, 19x7

ASSETS

| | | |
|---|---|---:|
| *Current Assets:* | | |
| Cash | $ | 25,000 |
| Receivables | | 160,000 |
| Inventories | | 120,000 |
| Current Assets | $ | 305,000 |
| Equipment | | 80,000 |
| Tangible Assets | $ | 385,000 |
| Goodwill | | 670,000 |
| Total Assets | | $1,055,000 |

LIABILITIES AND OWNERS' EQUITY

| | | |
|---|---|---:|
| *Current Liabilities:* | | |
| Taxes payable | $ | 15,000 |
| Accounts payable | | 90,000 |
| Current Liabilities | $ | 105,000 |
| Owners' equity | | 950,000 |
| Total Liabilities and Owners' Equity | | $1,055,000 |

tangible assets and all liabilities have been reported on the traditional accounting basis. The difference between this measure of *net tangible assets* (tangible assets minus liabilities) and the *going concern value* of the company (the capitalized value of its future cash flows) is imputed to the intangibles, referred to collectively as goodwill.

It is worth repeating that the going concern value underlying this exhibit reflects the same assumptions that the company's owners made in appraising the value of their equity — that is, that Precision's cash flow would amount to $114,000 a year indefinitely and that 12 percent was the appropriate capitalization rate. On this basis, earnings at the normal rate attributable to the tangible assets would be 12 percent of $280,000, or $33,600 a year. Thus, the remaining $80,400 of the annual earnings must be attributable to the earning power of the intangible assets. The present value of this excess earnings stream is the imputed value of the company's goodwill.

### Income Measurement on a Present Value Basis

Each basis of measurement carries with it a related concept of income. The economic concept of income is defined as the amount an individual can spend on consumption or a company can pay in dividends to its owners during a period and be as well off financially at the end as at the start of the period. A company remains as well off if the present value of the owners' equity at the end of the period but before the payment of dividends is equal to its present value at the start. This means that income is the present value of the total assets less liabilities at the end of the period less the corresponding quantity at the start, plus any dividends that have been paid during the period.

To illustrate, suppose that during 19x8 Precision Instrument Company developed a new device which permitted greater automation of a wide variety of chemical processes. New orders increased rapidly in the final quarter of 19x8, and earnings in 19x9 and later years were expected to amount to $144,000. All of this would be paid out to the owners because further growth of the company would not be feasible. Using the same capitalization rate and the same assumptions as in the previous example, the value of the enterprise at the end of 19x8 would be:

$$\frac{\$144,000}{0.12} = \$1,200,000.$$

This represents an increase of $250,000 over the comparable beginning-of-year figure. The shareholders are that much better off as a result of the events of 19x8, and this would be recognized as income in an income statement based on present value. In addition, assume that during 19x8 the owners withdrew $114,000 in addition to their salaries. The total increase in their well-being thus amounted to $364,000. This calculation can be summarized in the following manner:

*Net assets at end of year:*
  Present value of net future payments to owners............. $1,200,000
*Net assets at start of year:*
  Present value of net future payments to owners.............   950,000
Net increase in value ........................................ $  250,000
Add back: Owners' cash withdrawals during the year.........   114,000
Economic Net Income before Imputed Interest ............... $  364,000

Note that income defined in this way includes *all* value changes, whether realized or unrealized. In other words, under the present value basis of measurement, income is not recognized at the time of production or of sale. It is recognized at the time the company recognizes a change in the future receipts the asset will produce.

These figures can be embodied in an income statement, but only with some simplification. Value increases result from a combination of factors—discoveries, changes in expectations, and changes in the desired rate of return. The easiest possibility is to reproduce the conventional income statement, with a balancing figure at the bottom to bring the net income into agreement with the calculated change in value. Exhibit 10–4, for example, shows an income statement for Precision Instrument Company for 19x8. Net income calculated on the usual accounting basis is labeled "realized net income." The remainder of the change in present value was unrealized, and is shown separately on the next line.

*Exhibit 10–4*

Precision Instrument Company
ADJUSTED INCOME STATEMENT
For the Year Ended December 31, 19x8

Sales Revenues.................................... $1,400,000
Cost of goods sold................................   840,000
Gross margin ..................................... $  560,000
Less: Operating expenses........................ $334,000
     Income taxes ............................. 112,000   446,000
Realized net income ............................. $  114,000
Unrealized increase in the present value of
   future cash flows .............................   250,000
Net Value Change ................................ $  364,000

This concept of income is not an easy one to digest and possibly the following situation, which is a perfect analogy, will be helpful. Mr. Johnson bought a share of stock in the Camden Corporation on January 1, 19x3, for $25. On December 31, 19x3, the corporation paid him a $1 dividend and reported that the company earned $2.50 per share. The newspaper that day reported that the price of Camden stock was $31 per share.

On a market value basis, the shareholder has gained $6 a share from the price rise plus $1 of dividend, a total of $7. The price of the share went up because the expectations of purchasers of this stock increased sharply during the year. If Mr. Johnson had sold his stock on December 31, his income would have been reported as $7, under either basis of income measurement. Of this, $6 would have been defined as a gain on the sale and $1 as ordinary income. Only if Mr. Johnson did not sell his stock would the two bases of income measurement differ, because traditional cost-based accounting does not recognize unrealized gains.

### The Case against Present Value

Because present value is generally recognized as directly relevant to managerial and investor decisions, there is no doubt that it would be employed in the accounts if it could be determined with little or no margin of error. To understand why it is not used, therefore, we must consider the problems of accuracy. These are of two kinds:

1. The appropriate discounting rate varies from individual to individual.
2. The cash flow estimates in most cases are not subject to adequate verification.

*Objection: Multiplicity of discounting rates.* The value figures developed above for Precision Instrument Company were heavily dependent on the discount rate used. This can be demonstrated by substituting various interest rates in the capitalization formula:

| Interest Rate | Present Value December 31, 19x7 (Based on $114,000 Annual Cash Flow) | Present Value December 31, 19x8 (Based on $144,000 Annual Cash Flow) | Income for 19x8 (Including $114,000 in Dividends) |
|---|---|---|---|
| 6% .... | $1,900,000 | $2,400,000 | $614,000 |
| 8 ...... | 1,425,000 | 1,800,000 | 489,000 |
| 12 ...... | 950,000 | 1,200,000 | 364,000 |
| 15 ...... | 760,000 | 960,000 | 314,000 |
| 20 ...... | 570,000 | 720,000 | 264,000 |

This would not be a fatal objection if the only problem were the difficulty of estimating the current rate of discount. After all, depreciation estimates are far from accurate in most cases, but the inaccuracy is generally regarded as far less serious than the error that would result from abandonment of the depreciation concept.

The main difficulty with the discount rate is that each investor has his own rate. Although the owners used a 12 percent rate in valuing Precision Instrument, others might have been satisfied with, say, 8 percent and thus would have been willing to pay more than $950,000. This difficulty could be resolved by reporting only the company's cash flow predictions, letting the reader apply his own discount rate. This solution might work, awkward though it may seem, but it is unlikely to be put to the test unless the second objection to present value accounting can be overcome.

*Objection: Subjectivity of cash flow estimates.* The second objection is that the future cash flows of a business are highly uncertain. Two accountants called upon to prepare financial statements for a company could easily come up with radically different figures for the value of the company's assets and its income. Present value financial statements therefore would at best represent no more than the accountant's judgment as to the firm's future prospects. Some accountants have good business judgment and management may consult them, but the ultimate responsibility and decisions are management's. Management will not and cannot surrender these to the accountant. In other words, the accountant has no more competence to estimate cash flows and present values than anyone else with the same degree of participation in management decision making.

From the viewpoint of the outside investor, the situation is even worse. The management of a firm is far better qualified than its public accountants to forecast the firm's future cash flows. With no objective basis for the independent verification of management's forecasts or the defense of his own, the public accountant would be reduced to reporting to stockholders whatever the management told him to report.

## Alternatives to Present Value

Demonstrating that financial statements based on present value are impractical does not necessarily mean that cost-based statements are ideal. The defects of cost-based financial statements will not disappear just because we have decided that we cannot replace them with value-based statements. In fact, if cost-based statements provide information that could lead management or investors to make incorrect decisions, then we might be better off to stop measuring entirely until we have found something better.

We are much more optimistic than this. Despite all their defects, cost-based statements do provide useful data to those who know how to use them. Our main task in the chapters that follow will be to examine the meaning of various cost-based accounting measures. Whenever the figures produced by one method seem likely to be more useful to management than those produced by other methods, we shall say so. If departures from historical cost seem desirable on these grounds, we shall say that, too. In general, however, our purpose is to help the reader interpret the statements that he or she will see, and to suggest ways in which these can be improved.

## SUMMARY

Conventional business financial statements do not pretend to indicate how much the business is worth or how much its value has increased or decreased in the period covered by the statements. Accountants could prepare statements that would present information in this form, but to do so they would have to estimate or verify management's estimates of the company's future cash flows and discount them to their present value.

Statements prepared on this basis would be of limited usefulness, first because forecasts of future cash flows are highly subjective and second because each present or potential owner has his own desired rate of return on investment and this may not coincide with the rate the accountants have used to calculate present value. This is not to say that accountants should ignore value changes entirely, but the direct incorporation of figures based on present value calculations must be limited to elements which permit ready identification of future cash flows and the appropriate discount rate.

## QUESTIONS AND PROBLEMS (Also covering Appendix A)

1. Define "present value." What is its relationship to "future value"?

2. What is "economic value"? How is it determined? By whom?

3. Formulate a rule, using the concept of present value, that you might be willing to follow when making certain kinds of decisions.

4. Explain the relationship between the present value of a single sum and the present value of a series of annual sums.

**5.** Distinguish between tangible and intangible assets.

**6.** What is a "going concern"? What is the main source of the value of a going concern?

**7.** What effect would you expect a sharp rise in corporate bond yields to have on stock market prices, other things being equal? Explain.

**8.** Define the economic concept of income. What are the obstacles to its adoption by accountants for external financial reporting?

**9.** What is the economic definition of goodwill? Under what circumstances would you expect to see goodwill, other than in a nominal $1 amount, listed explicitly on a company's balance sheet?

**10.** Is it possible to define the economic value of a single asset that is part of an integrated group of assets? Illustrate your answer in terms of a pump on an oil pipeline — if the pump breaks down, the entire pipeline ceases to operate. What is the value of the pump? What is the value of the other elements of the pipeline?

**11.** The management of the Gupta Corporation has recently been cited by a national society of industrial engineers for its efficiency in organizing and controlling the company's affairs. The aggregate market value of the company's stock, based on the current market price per share, is $10 million; book value is only $4 million. Management's own forecast of future cash flows, discounted at an interest rate that seems appropriate for a company of its size and class, is $9 million.

The board of directors of the Marshall Company has just made a cash offer of $12 million for the outstanding stock in the Gupta Corporation. What might account for the premium valuation placed by Marshall on the Gupta Corporation?

$$P = 100/(1.1)^6 =$$

**12.** Without using the interest tables, calculate the present value at 10 percent of a single sum of $100 to be received six years from now. Then verify your figure by using the appropriate table in Appendix A.

**13.** The present value of an annuity in arrears of one dollar at 5 percent for five periods is $4.3295.

*a)* Explain what this means.
*b)* Explain how this amount is determined. Do not refer to the interest tables.      $$P = A \sum_{t=1}^{5} \frac{1}{1.05}$$

**14.** Using Table 4 in Appendix A, determine the present value of a series of payments of $100 a year for each of the next 6 years. Assume that the first payment is received one year from now and that the interest rate is 12 percent.

15. Check your answer to question 14 by using Table 3.

16. You are considering the purchase of six non-interest-bearing notes. Three of them have face values of $100 and will come due one each at the end of years 3, 4, and 5. The other three have face values of $150 and come due one each at the end of years 6, 7, and 8. If your interest rate is 15 percent, what will you be willing to pay for these now? (Use Table 3 in Appendix A.)

17. Use Table 4 to solve question 16. You should get the same answer.

✓ 18. Compute the present value of each of the following at 10 percent, using the interest tables in Appendix A:

a)  $100,000 to be received 10 years from now. Interest is compounded annually.
b)  $10,000 to be received at the end of each of the next 10 years. Interest is compounded annually.
c)  $5,000 to be received at the end of each of the next five years, plus $15,000 to be received at the end of each of the five years after that. Interest is compounded annually.
d)  $15,000 to be received at the end of each of the next five years, plus $5,000 to be received at the end of each of the five years after that. Interest is compounded annually.
e)  $5,000 to be received at the end of each of the next 20 six-month periods. Interest is compounded semiannually.

*19. The Future Company has just borrowed $1 million. Interest on this amount will be paid to the lender each year for 10 years. In addition, the $1 million will have to be repaid to the lender at the end of 10 years. How much will the Future Company have to deposit in the bank at the end of each of the next 10 years to enable it to repay the $1 million at the end of the 10 years if the bank compounds interest annually at a rate of 8 percent? An identical amount is to be deposited each year.

*20. Calculate the value on January 1, 1975, of assets that have the following cash flows, with interest at 12 percent:

a)  Outlay:     $35,000 on January 1, 1975.
    Receipt:    $100,000 on January 1, 1985.
b)  Outlays:    $80,000 on January 1, 1975.
                 20,000 on January 1, 1980.
    Receipts:   $10,000 on each January 1, 1976 through 1981.
                 20,000 on each January 1, 1982 through 1991.
c)  Outlays:    $20,000 on each January 1, 1975 through 1985.
    Receipts:   $250,000 on January 1, 1987.

_____

* Solutions to problems marked with an asterisk (*) are found in Appendix B.

*21. You will need $4,000 a year for 5 years, starting exactly 4 years from today. You wish to purchase this annuity by making a series of 7 annual payments of equal size. The first of these payments will be made immediately. Interest will accrue at a rate of 8 percent, compounded annually. Calculate the size of the annual payment.

22. A house can be bought for $21,000, payable in cash immediately. Alternatively, the seller will accept a series of cash payments, starting with $10,000 immediately and then $2,000 at the end of each of the next eight years.

a)  If a buyer can always invest his money at 10 percent, compounded annually, which of these alternatives should he prefer?
b)  Assuming that the seller can invest his money at 8 percent, what is the series of payments worth to him?

23. A man leases a store for three years. He pays rent of $2,000 each year and sublets it to someone else for $3,000 a year, both payable yearly in advance. If he invests the difference at 8 percent, how much will he have gained by the end of the third year?

*24. Mr. Provident is 30 years old. He desires to have at age 50 a savings fund of $100,000. He expects to earn 6 percent compounded annually on what he saves. How much must he set aside out of his earnings at the end of each year for the 20 years to accumulate his $100,000?

25. You have three assets for which you forecast the following cash flows:

| Years from Now | Asset A | Asset B | Asset C |
|---|---|---|---|
| 1 ......... | +$1,000 | | |
| 2 ......... | + 1,000 | | |
| 3 ......... | + 1,000 | +$1,700 | |
| 4 ......... | + 1,000 | + 1,700 | |
| 5 ......... | + 1,000 | + 1,700 | +$2,000 |
| 6 ......... | | | + 2,000 |
| 7 ......... | | | + 2,000 |

Each of these assets is being managed by one of your firm's trainees. You have asked them to calculate the values of these assets, assuming that money is worth 10 percent. They have given you the following figures:

Asset A:   present value today, $3,791.
Asset B:   present value 3 years from now, $4,650.
Asset C:   future value 7 years from now, $6,620.

Which of these assets is the most valuable? Which is the least valuable? Show your calculations.

**26.** You can buy industrial bonds now at a yield of 9 percent. You have just been offered the opportunity to invest $10,000 in bonded whiskey. The whiskey will be removed from bond and sold gradually, beginning 3 years from now. Meanwhile, you will have to pay warehousing fees. The anticipated cash flows will be as follows:

| Years from Now | Cash Flow |
|---|---|
| 1 ...... | −$  300 |
| 2 ...... | −   300 |
| 3 ...... | +  3,000 |
| 4 ...... | +  3,500 |
| 5 ...... | +  3,500 |
| 6 ...... | +  3,500 |
| 7 ...... | +  3,500 |

Should you accept this opportunity? (Ignore income taxes.)

*27. John Hastings has just received a tax-paid inheritance of $100,000. He has decided to use part of the inheritance to purchase an annuity from an insurance company. Under the terms of the annuity contract, the insurance company will pay Mr. Hastings $15,000 a year for 10 years. The first of these payments will be made seven years from now.

In computing the amount to charge for such an annuity, the insurance company uses an interest rate of 6 percent, compounded annually. How much of his inheritance will Mr. Hastings have left to spend after paying for the annuity?

**28.** Thomas Peterson is an investor who expects to earn at least 8 percent a year on his investments. He estimates that an investment in a new mine will bring him $10,000 in cash at the end of each of the next 15 years. At the end of that time, the mine will be worthless.

*a)* How much is the mine worth to Mr. Peterson?
*b)* How much would the mine be worth to Mr. Peterson if it were to produce $10,000 a year for 25 years? For 40 years? For 50 years?
*c)* Prepare a diagram with "values" on the vertical scale and the number of years on the horizontal scale. Enter your answers to (a) and (b) on this diagram. From the diagram, try to estimate how much the mine would be worth if it were to be productive at the present rate for 100 years. What other method or methods could you have used to calculate this figure?

**29.** John Hancock has plans to retire at the age of 60 and wishes to provide an income of $25,000 a year until he is 75 years old. He plans to do his saving for his old age during the 15 years prior to reaching the age of 50, leaving the resulting fund to accumulate for the next 10 years. Assuming that his savings will earn 6 percent annually, how much must he deposit at the beginning of each year starting on his 35th birthday?

**30.** The Carrington Corporation has been in operation for three years. It markets a new kind of plastic foam for sale to industrial customers. The company has reported a net loss each year since it was founded, but sales are now increasing and management expects to report a small net income this year.

To finance the company's growth and broaden its ownership base, the owner-managers have decided to "go public" and have offered to sell shares of the company's common stock at a price of $10 a share. Book value per share is now $4.

You have $25,000 which you wish to invest in a growth situation of this sort, and you are willing to buy this stock if you think that it will yield you an annual return of 12 percent before taxes.

You forecast that the Carrington Corporation will report earnings and pay dividends as follows:

| Years from Now | Earnings per Share | Dividends per Share |
|---|---|---|
| 1 ...... | $0.10 | – |
| 2 ...... | 0.75 | $0.50 |
| 3 ...... | 1.00 | 0.50 |
| 4 ...... | 1.25 | 0.50 |
| 5 ...... | 1.50 | 0.50 |
| 6 ...... | 1.75 | 0.50 |
| 7 ...... | 2.00 | 1.00 |
| 8 ...... | 2.00 | 1.00 |
| 9 ...... | 2.00 | 1.00 |
| 10 ...... | 2.00 | 1.00 |

(For simplicity, you should assume that dividends will be paid once each year, at the end of the year.)

You believe that the market price of this stock 10 years from now will probably be about $16 a share.

What is this stock worth to you? Show the calculations which support your answer. Ignore income taxes.

**31.** Jones owns some property which he has leased to DelBello for $20,000 a year. DelBello no longer wishes to use this property, but the lease still has 10 years to run and he still has 10 more annual payments to make to Jones. The first of these payments is due next week.

Larsen has just offered to sublease the property from DelBello at an annual rental of $60,000, payable at the beginning of each year. DelBello would continue to pay $20,000 a year to Jones.

*a)* What is the value of the lease to DelBello if he considers 10 percent a necessary rate of return on his money?

*b)* DelBello says that he would prefer to transfer the lease to Larsen for an immediate lump-sum payment of $300,000. Larsen would then pay Jones the contract rental of $20,000 a year. Would you advise Larsen to accept DelBello's counterproposal or to press for acceptance of his initial proposal? The cost of money to Larsen is 8 percent. Show your calculations.

32. Mr. William Lazere wished to arrange for the college education of his three children. He estimated that he would need the following amounts:

| | |
|---|---:|
| August 31, 1980 | $ 5,000 |
| August 31, 1981 | 10,000 |
| August 31, 1982 | 15,000 |
| August 31, 1983 | 15,000 |
| August 31, 1984 | 10,000 |
| August 31, 1985 | 5,000 |

On September 1, 1973, he asked the representative of an insurance company to draw up an endowment policy that would provide these amounts. The insurance representative said that his company compounded interest annually at 6 percent.

a) What is the amount of the *annuity* that Mr. Lazere had to pay each September 1 from 1973 to 1984, inclusive, to obtain the funds needed for his children's education? Show your calculations.

b) Recompute your answer to (a) on the basis of a 7 percent interest rate.

33. The Loralee Corporation's sole asset is a 100 percent stock ownership of the New York, Chicago, and Pacific Railway Company. The latter's only asset is 200 miles of mainline railroad track which it has leased on a 99-year lease to the Pennsylvania and Chesapeake Railroad at a semiannual rental of $50,000. This lease still has 25 years to run, and the P. & C. is one of the strongest railway companies in the country.

The book value of the ownership equity in the New York, Chicago, and Pacific on its own books is $1,200,000. The Loralee Corporation carries its investment on its books at an original cost of $900,000. Loralee Corporation stockholders are satisfied with a 12 percent before-tax return on their investment. Loralee stock is now selling at $800,000.

a) What is the value of the Loralee Corporation's goodwill if it is assumed that cash flows after the end of 25 years will be zero? (Interest should be compounded semiannually.)

b) What is the value of the goodwill if it is assumed that the semiannual rental will remain at its present level forever?

c) Should the stockholders keep or sell their Loralee stock? State any assumptions you have made and show all your computations.

*34. William Appersham operates a ferry service across Deepwater Bay. A bridge is now being built across the bay. When it is completed two years from now, Mr. Appersham will close the ferry service and retire to his plantation in the Virgin Islands. He expects the following cash flows from the ferry operation:

| Year | Cash Receipts | Cash Disbursements | Net Cash Receipts |
|------|--------------|--------------------|-------------------|
| 1 . . . . . . . . . | $300,000 | $200,000 | $100,000 |
| 2 . . . . . . . . . | 350,000 | 220,000 | 130,000 |

At the end of each year he will withdraw the year's net cash receipts and invest them in highway bonds where they will earn interest at an annual rate of 6 percent, compounded annually. In addition, at the end of year 2 he will be able to withdraw the $50,000 that he now must maintain as a working cash fund to keep his ferry service going.

The sale value of his ferry boats two years from now will be virtually zero.

*a)* What is the present value of the ferry service to Mr. Appersham now?

*b)* Assuming that all forecasts are correct, what will be the present value of the assets of the ferry service a year from now, before Mr. Appersham withdraws the net cash receipts of the first year's operations?

*c)* Compute the net income of the ferry service for the first year on a present value basis, assuming that all forecasts are correct.

*d)* Compute the ferry service's income for the second year on a present value basis, again assuming that all forecasts are correct.

**35.** The city of Hicksville has decided to sponsor an international exposition promoting the values of rural living. The exposition will operate for a period of four years. The city will provide a site for the exposition in Bucolic Park, rent-free.

Turning to experts, the city has asked the International Corporation for Expositions (ICE) to construct the buildings and to operate the exposition. ICE has prepared the following estimates of operating cash receipts and cash disbursements:

| Year | Receipts | Disbursements |
|------|----------|---------------|
| 1 . . . . . . . . . | $2,000,000 | $1,300,000 |
| 2 . . . . . . . . . | 3,000,000 | 1,500,000 |
| 3 . . . . . . . . . | 2,000,000 | 800,000 |
| 4 . . . . . . . . . | 1,350,000 | 350,000 |

Construction costs, all to be paid at the beginning of year 1, are estimated to be $4,000,000. An additional investment of $300,000 will be necessary at that time to provide a working cash fund; the need for this will continue throughout the four-year period. The exposition buildings will be sold to the city at the end of year 4 for $1,000,000.

ICE has enough confidence in the predictions to participate in the venture if it will earn a return of 10 percent before income taxes. If it decides to do so, it will form a subsidiary, the Hicksville Exposition Corporation. This subsidiary will issue common stock to ICE for $1,000 and will borrow the remaining $4,299,000 from ICE, giving non-interest-bearing notes as evidence of its indebtedness. The subsidiary will repay the notes as rapidly as possible, keeping only a cash balance of $300,000. ICE assumes in all of its calculations that all cash receipts and disbursements take place at the end of the year.

The subsidiary will be liquidated at the end of year 4, and its remaining cash assets will be paid back to ICE at that time.

*a)* Assuming that ICE agrees to undertake this project and that all the forecasts are correct, compute the subsidiary's income for each year if assets are measured by the present value approach. Ignore income taxes.

*b)* If the historical cost approach is used instead of present value, what will be the income for each year? Historical cost depreciation will be the same for each of the four years. Ignore income taxes.

**36.** On January 1, 1973, the Vista Hotel opened its doors. The hotel had just been completed at a cost of $6 million, and it had an expected life of 30 years. The hotel had been built by the Vista Realty Corporation on land acquired on a 30-year, nonrenewable lease at a rental of $75,000 per year. Vista Realty, in turn, leased the hotel on a 30-year lease to the Vista Operating Company, which was to operate the hotel and pay all operating expenses. The annual rental to be paid by Vista Operating to Vista Realty was to be 40 percent of the hotel's revenue with a minimum rental of $400,000 per year.

Realty's management estimated that the hotel would gross an annual revenue of $1,800,000. It was not ordinarily willing to undertake projects of this kind unless the anticipated rate of return on investment was at least 10 percent before income taxes.

In 1973, the Hotel earned revenue of $1,600,000. Toward the end of 1973, the city began building an auditorium and related facilities for conventions, indoor sports, and so forth. The management of Vista Realty believed that this would increase annual hotel revenue to about $2,000,000 a year starting in 1975. The projection for 1974 remained at $1,800,000.

*a)* Assuming that the hotel is the sole asset of Vista Realty and that its entire cost was financed by stockholder investment, present a balance sheet as of January 1, 1973, under (1) the historical cost basis, and (2) the present value basis of measurement.

*b)* Mr. Jones, a wealthy investor, has the opportunity to buy a 10 percent interest in Vista Realty on December 31, 1973, and he asks you to advise him what is the most he should be willing to pay for the stock if he requires a 10 percent return on his investment.

*c)* Present financial statements as of December 31, 1973, under the two bases of measurement. (Ignore income taxes.)

**37.** In June, 1967, Franchise Golf, Inc., was formed and announced that it would put on a golf tournament each year for the next 20 years. The prizes would be: 1st place, $75,000; 2d place, $50,000; and 3d place,

$25,000. Only five players would compete in each tournament and they were to be selected as follows: Franchise Golf, Inc., would sell five franchises. The owner of each franchise would select one player for each tournament. The owner would pay his player an agreed salary. Each year the player's contract would come up for renewal. The player's salary was to be negotiable, but if the owner's maximum offer were less than the player's salary for the previous year, the player would be free to reject the offer and sign up with another owner if he could find one to offer him a higher price. If the offer were equal to or higher than the player's salary for the previous year, however, the player could refuse to renew the contract but could not sign up with another owner for the next two years.

Gene Hogan, a wealthy retired golf professional, believed that he could obtain a golfer for $15,000 a tournament who had as good a chance to win as any other entry. Hogan and three members of the Rolling Hills Golf Club formed the R. H. Corporation and bought a franchise from Franchise Golf, Inc., for $100,000. They contracted with Gary Palmer, a promising young golfer, to play in the first tournament for $15,000, and he won first place in the first playing of the tournament in June, 1968.

By the end of the year, Palmer's victory and his performance in other tournaments established him as one of the top two players in the country, and it appeared likely that he would keep this position for at least five years. The managers of the R. H. Corporation believed that young Palmer would be likely to place either first or second in 60 percent of the tournaments, and place third in another 10 percent. With this in mind, they decided to raise his salary to $20,000 per tournament, a figure that was acceptable to young Palmer.

a) What would have been a fair price for Hogan to pay for a franchise as of January 1, 1968, if he wanted a 10 percent return on his investment?

b) Prepare a balance sheet and income statement for the R. H. Corporation for the year ending December 31, 1968, using historical cost as the basis of measurement.

c) A stockholder who owned a 25 percent interest in R. H. Corporation wanted to sell out on December 31, 1968. Recommend a fair price for his equity.

d) Prepare a balance sheet as of January 1, 1968, and financial statements as of December 31, 1968, for the R. H. Corporation, using present value as a basis of measurement.

# *11*

# INVENTORY COSTING METHODS

THE USE OF HISTORICAL COSTS as a basis of asset measurement and income determination is neither as straightforward nor as free of problems as one might infer from the material in Part I. This chapter presents and evaluates the alternative practices that have been developed to measure the cost of end-of-period inventories and cost of goods sold.

## HISTORICAL COSTING METHODS

In historical costing systems, the total of the cost of goods sold and the cost of the ending inventory must equal the total of the costs of the goods available for sale during the period. In other words:

Begin. Inventory + Goods Acquired = Goods Sold + End. Inventory

Five methods that fit within this framework need to be mentioned:

1. First-in, first-out (Fifo) costing.
2. Last-in, first-out (Lifo) costing.
3. Cost or market, whichever is lower.
4. Specific lot costing.
5. Moving average costing.

We shall discuss only the first three of these. Specific lot costing is used only rarely, whenever each product unit or lot is

269

unique. Moving average costing is widely used, but it is more a method of cost bookkeeping than a separate measurement method. It produces results that are generally close to those produced by Fifo.

For convenience, all of the illustrations will relate to the merchandise inventories of trading companies. The same methods can be applied, with suitable procedural adjustments, to manufacturing firms' inventories of raw material or finished goods, and even to work in process.

### First-in, First-out (Fifo) Costing

The Fifo method assigns the oldest costs in the inventory accounts to the items that are transferred out of the stockroom first; the ending inventory is measured by the cost of the units most recently acquired.

For example, suppose that The Plastics Supply Company started the year 19x4 with an inventory of 100,000 yards of plastic sheeting and purchased 340,000 yards during the year. The company recognized revenues at the time sheeting was shipped to customers, and inventories were measured at historical cost.

The historical costs of the goods available for sale were as follows:

| | | |
|---|---|---|
| The cost of the goods on hand at the beginning of the year: 100,000 yards at $0.20 . . . . . . . . . | | $ 20,000 |
| Plus the cost of the goods purchased: | | |
| First six months: 170,000 yards at $0.25 . . . | $42,500 | |
| Second six months: 170,000 yards at $0.30 . . | 51,000 | 93,500 |
| Equals the cost of the goods available for sale: | | |
| 440,000 yards with a total cost of . . . . . . . . . | | $113,500 |

In other words, a total of $113,500 in costs had to be accounted for.

Suppose further that the company sold 400,000 yards of plastic sheeting during 19x4, leaving 40,000 yards of sheeting on hand at the end of the year. Under Fifo, this inventory would be assigned the cost of the *last* 40,000 units purchased during the year: 40,000 yards × $0.30 = $12,000. The remainder of the costs of the goods available for sale ($113,500 − $12,000 = $101,500) would be the Fifo cost of the 400,000 yards sold during the year. This last figure can also be derived by adding up the cost of the *first* 400,000 units available for sale during the year:

| | Quantity (Yards) | Unit Price | Total Cost |
|---|---|---|---|
| Opening inventory ................. | 100,000 | $0.20 | $ 20,000 |
| Purchases, first half............... | 170,000 | 0.25 | 42,500 |
| Purchases, second half............. | 130,000 | 0.30 | 39,000 |
| Total....................... | 400,000 | | $101,500 |

It should be noted that the costs of the last 40,000 yards purchased are assigned to the ending inventory under Fifo regardless of whether these specific units are the ones in inventory at the end of the year. Comparable statements can be made about the other inventory costing schemes that we shall discuss. The assignment of costs is an accounting question, to be decided in favor of the method with the greatest information value. The physical movement of goods has no bearing on information value and therefore should be ignored.

### Last-In, First-Out (Lifo) Costing

Although we could start our explanation of the Lifo method by computing the Lifo cost of goods sold, it is probably clearer to begin by showing how Lifo inventory cost is determined. Suppose that Plastics Supply Company had decided to adopt the Lifo method as of January 1, 19x1, three years before the year to which our earlier figures related. At that time the company had 20,000 yards of plastic sheeting on hand, listed in the inventory accounts at a cost of 11 cents a yard, $2,200 in all. During 19x1 the firm bought 100,000 yards of sheeting at a price of 15 cents a yard and sold 70,000 yards, ending the year with 50,000 yards in inventory.

Under Lifo, the cost assigned to this ending inventory would consist of the costs shown in the inventory account at the beginning of the year (the *base quantity* of 20,000 yards at 11 cents a yard), plus the cost of 30,000 yards purchased during the year at 15 cents a yard, referred to as the 19x1 *layer* or increment in the inventory:

| | | |
|---|---|---|
| 19x0 base quantity ............... 20,000 yards × $0.11 | $2,200 |
| 19x1 layer....................... 30,000 yards × $0.15 | 4,500 |
| Total ...................... 50,000 yards | $6,700 |

Lifo, in other words, could also be described as a First-in, last-out (Filo) system. Since the costs assigned to the opening inventory are the first costs in, they are always the last to be taken out.

Once the cost of the ending inventory has been identified, it is a simple matter to determine the cost of goods sold:

| | |
|---|---:|
| Opening inventory, January 1, 19x1 | $ 2,200 |
| Purchases during 19x1 | 15,000 |
| Goods available for sale | $17,200 |
| Ending inventory, December 31, 19x1 | 6,700 |
| Cost of Goods Sold | $10,500 |

This is the cost of the last 70,000 units received in inventory, in this case entirely from the purchases made during the year.

Inventories increased again in 19x2, this time by 50,000 yards at a unit cost of 20 cents, for a 19x2 layer of $10,000. The costs of the rest of the year's purchases were charged to the cost of goods sold because they were the most recently acquired units. The Lifo inventory at the end of 19x2, therefore, consisted of the Lifo base quantity costed at 19x0 prices, plus two layers, each costed at the prices prevailing in the year in which the layer was added to inventory:

| | | |
|---|---|---:|
| 19x0 base quantity | 20,000 yards × $0.11 | $ 2,200 |
| 19x1 layer | 30,000 yards × $0.15 | 4,500 |
| 19x2 layer | 50,000 yards × $0.20 | 10,000 |
| Total | 100,000 yards | $16,700 |

During 19x3 Plastics Supply Company purchased and sold exactly 400,000 yards of sheeting. The purchase price was 20 cents a yard. None of these costs was assigned to the end-of-year inventory, however. The Lifo cost of the December 31, 19x3, inventory was exactly the same as the Lifo cost of the beginning inventory ($16,700), because the inventory quantity was the same. The cost of goods sold therefore was 400,000 × $0.20 = $80,000, the cost of the 400,000 yards purchased during the year.

As this shows, adoption of Lifo in 19x1 brought the company into 19x4 with an inventory cost of $16,700, $3,300 less than the $20,000 Fifo would have produced. Sales in 19x4 remained at 400,000 yards, but only 340,000 yards were purchased. This reduced the ending inventory to 40,000 yards, and under Lifo this quantity was measured entirely at the unit cost of the oldest layers in the opening inventory:

| | | |
|---|---|---:|
| Base quantity | 20,000 yards × $0.11 | $2,200 |
| 19x1 layer | 20,000 yards × $0.15 | 3,000 |
| Total inventory | 40,000 yards | $5,200 |

The cost of goods available in this case was the Lifo cost of the opening inventory ($16,700) plus the cost of the year's purchases ($93,500). By deduction, then, the cost of goods sold was $16,700 + $93,500 − $5,200 = $105,000. The same figure can be derived by adding the cost of all current purchases (the last units in) to the cost of 60,000 yards from the *youngest* layers in the opening inventory:

| | | |
|---|---|---|
| 19x4 purchases................ | 340,000 yards | $ 93,500 |
| 19x2 layer..................... | 50,000 yards × $0.20 | 10,000 |
| From the 19x1 layer ........... | 10,000 yards × $0.15 | 1,500 |
| Total Cost of Goods Sold .. | | $105,000 |

The procedure described in the above illustration may be summarized as follows:

1. When the quantity of goods purchased during a year is *equal* to the quantity sold, the purchases are charged against sales and the closing inventory is the same (in price as well as in quantity) as the opening inventory.
2. When the quantity purchased is *greater* than the quantity sold, say by x units, the quantity purchased less the x units is charged against sales and the closing inventory is the opening inventory plus this increment.[1]
3. When the quantity purchased is *less* than the quantity sold, say by y units, sales are charged with the purchases for the year plus the cost of y units taken from inventory. The decremental y units are costed out of inventory on a last-layer-in, first-layer-out basis.

Two aspects of this method deserve emphasis at this point. First, the method does not require the *physical* movement of inventory on a last-in, first-out basis. The method is used only in the *costing* of inventory and goods sold. Second, inventory fluctuations during the year do not affect the end-of-year Lifo inventory calculation. Even if inventories drop to zero during the year, the unit costs in the beginning inventory will carry over to the year-end inventory if inventory quantities have been restored before the end of the year.

This second feature means that Lifo cannot be used as a method of inventory bookkeeping in a perpetual inventory system. If Lifo were used for inventory bookkeeping, it would result in transfers of costs out of the most recent inventory layers whenever the physical inventory quantity fell below the quantity

---

[1] The increment of x units may be costed at the cost of the first purchases, the last purchases, or an average of all purchases during the year. Election from among these options must be made in the year of Lifo adoption, and the procedure elected must be followed consistently thereafter.

on hand at the beginning of the year, even if the inventory was restored to its former levels the very next day. This is inconsistent with the annual basis on which Lifo operates. Some other method therefore must be used for inventory bookkeeping to generate the figures on which interim financial statements are based.[2] When this is done, the accountant must make an end-of-year adjustment to bring the inventory figure to its correct Lifo level.

### Cost or Market, Whichever Is Lower

No matter what costing method is used, the end-of-year inventories are written down whenever an inventory's year-end market value is less than the cost figure shown in the ledger. This is known as the *cost or market rule*. Since Lifo cost is generally far less than current market value, the cost or market rule is generally applied only when inventory cost is measured on a Fifo basis or an approximation to it.

To illustrate how the method works, let us assume that Plastics Supply Company was using Fifo and that the market value of the inventory had dipped suddenly to 15 cents at the end of 19x3, instead of increasing as we have been assuming. Fifo cost, as measured earlier, was 20 cents a yard, or $20,000 in total. The cost or market rule would have required a year-end write-down to 15 cents, a decrease of $5,000. This would have increased the cost of goods sold in 19x3 by $5,000.

## MEASUREMENT AT CURRENT COST

Management has a free choice among the inventory costing methods described above—that is, the accounting profession has not established criteria that would dictate the use of Fifo in one case and Lifo in another. Accordingly, two identical companies can report different net income figures simply because they choose to measure their inventories differently. In fact, individual companies often use different methods for different parts of their inventories.

To examine the effects of these choices on net income and on the reported cost of inventories, we need to introduce a new measurement concept, *current cost*. The current cost of a company's inventories on any date is the amount the company would

---

[2] A *moving average* is often used for this purpose. After each purchase, the costs of units purchased are added to the costs in the inventory account and a new average cost is computed. This unit cost is used to calculate the cost of goods issued until the next purchase is made.

have to spend to replace them at the prices prevailing on that date. The current cost of the goods that are sold is their replacement cost on the date of the sale.

Measurement of both inventories and the cost of goods sold on a current-cost basis is not currently accepted for financial reporting in the United States. We are introducing it here because it gives us a common benchmark against which to evaluate the main inventory costing methods that are in use.

## Current Gross Margins

The spread between the current selling price and the current purchase price of replacement merchandise on any date can be referred to as the *current gross margin.* To illustrate, let us see what happened to Plastics Supply Company during 19x4 and 19x5. Purchase and selling prices were at the levels shown in Exhibit 11–1. No purchases or sales were made between December 29 and December 31 in either year, and the current gross margin remained steady at 10 cents a yard. (A more realistic set of assumptions could be devised, but they would merely complicate the illustration without altering the conclusions.)

*Exhibit 11–1*

Plastics Supply Company

PRICES OF PLASTIC SHEETING

December 29, 19x3 — June 28, 19x6

| Period | Purchase Price | Selling Price | Current Gross Margin |
|---|---|---|---|
| December 29, 19x3–June 28, 19x4 | $0.25 | $0.35 | $0.10 |
| June 29, 19x4–December 28, 19x4 | 0.30 | 0.40 | 0.10 |
| December 29, 19x4–June 28, 19x5 | 0.40 | 0.50 | 0.10 |
| June 29, 19x5–December 28, 19x5 | 0.35 | 0.45 | 0.10 |
| December 29, 19x5–June 28, 19x6 | 0.30 | 0.40 | 0.10 |

The relationship between the current gross margin and the firm's operating expenses measures its current operating effectiveness. For example, the operations of the Plastics Supply Company consist of buying sheeting from manufacturers and selling it to consumers. If the company could buy and sell sheeting simultaneously, thereby eliminating the need to carry inventory, and if it also chose not to carry any inventory, the current gross margin would be its sole source of income. Since serving its customers is the company's main business purpose, then the current gross margin must indicate the effectiveness of the company's current operating expenditures.

## Holding Gains and Losses

Few businesses are able to operate without inventory. Firms that carry inventories are likely to have holding gains and losses as well as operating income. A holding gain or loss occurs every time the replacement cost of an item in inventory changes. For each such change, the holding gain or loss can be calculated by multiplying the change per unit by the number of units on hand at the time of the change. The total holding gain or loss for the period is then the sum of these gains and losses.

To continue our illustration, the yardage purchased, sold, and on hand during 19x4 and 19x5 was as follows:

| Period | Purchases | Sales | Ending Inventory |
|---|---|---|---|
| January 1, 19x4–June 28, 19x4 ...... | 170,000 | 200,000 | 70,000 |
| July 1, 19x4–December 28, 19x4 ..... | 170,000 | 200,000 | 40,000 |
| January 1, 19x5–June 28, 19x5 ...... | 230,000 | 200,000 | 70,000 |
| July 1, 19x5–December 28, 19x5 ..... | 230,000 | 200,000 | 100,000 |

The price changes listed in Exhibit 11–1 above always occurred on June 29 or December 29. Since no purchases or sales took place between then and the end of the month, the quantities subject to the holding gain or loss were the quantities on hand at the end of each six-month period. The holding gains and losses on these quantities are shown in Exhibit 11–2.

As this shows, holding gains took place during 19x4 as prices

### Exhibit 11–2

#### Plastics Supply Company

### CALCULATION OF HOLDING GAINS AND LOSSES

| (1) Date of Price Change | (2) Yards in Inventory at Time of Price Change | (3) Amount of Price Change | (4) Holding Gain or (Loss) (2) − (3) |
|---|---|---|---|
| June 29, 19x4 .......... | 70,000 | +$0.05 | $3,500 |
| December 29, 19x4 ..... | 40,000 | + 0.10 | 4,000 |
| June 29, 19x5 .......... | 70,000 | − 0.05 | (3,500) |
| December 29, 19x5 ..... | 100,000 | − 0.05 | (5,000) |
| Total ............. | | | $(1,000) |

were rising; holding losses arose in 19x5 as prices fell. Although prices didn't fall quite as far as they had risen, a net holding loss of $1,000 took place for the two years as a whole.[3]

## Speculative Gains and Losses

If ordinary business operations did not require holding any inventory, then the only reason for holding it would be the expectation of a rise in price. Holding inventory for this purpose is called speculation, and the holding gains or losses could then be called speculative gains or losses.

Businesses also need to carry inventories to enable them to fill orders that would otherwise go to competitors, to achieve savings by buying or manufacturing in large lots, or to achieve economies from smooth work flows. The amounts of these operating inventories depend on the relative costs and benefits of having inventories, assuming stable purchase prices.

Holding gains and losses on what we have just called operating inventories are strictly a by-product of the firm's business operations. The only speculative gains and losses are those that arise from price changes that take place when the inventory quantities differ from optimal operating levels.

Space is too limited here to permit us to provide enough quantitative information to calculate the speculative holding gains and losses that arose in the Plastics Supply Company in 19x4 and 19x5. Our main purpose in introducing the topic is to point out that most holding gains and losses are *not* the result of speculation. A second purpose is to indicate that a clear conceptual basis exists for measuring speculative gains and losses. Whenever a company deliberately engages in speculation, its accountants have a clear responsibility to calculate speculative gains and losses for management's information.

## Financial Statements Based on Current Cost

If financial statements were to be prepared on a current cost basis, the income statement would be divided into two sections, one representing the results of manufacturing and trading operations, the other reporting the holding gains and losses. Cost of goods sold would be measured at replacement price as of the *date*

---

[3] A thorough examination of the use of current cost in accounting has been undertaken by Lawrence Revsine, *Replacement Cost Accounting* (Englewood Cliffs, N.J.: Prentice-Hall, Inc., 1973). Professor Revsine's definitions of the current cost of goods sold and holding gains and losses in that work (Chapter 3) are the same as ours.

*of each sale,* and inventories would be measured at the replacement price on the *date of the statement.*

The statements would not break the holding gain or loss into its speculative and nonspeculative components. A management that allowed its purchasing agents to speculate would be very interested in this breakdown and would obtain it. The company's auditors have no independent, objective basis for verifying such breakdowns, however, because only management can establish the amount by which the inventory level required for the normal course of business operations differs from the actual inventory.

Exhibit 11–3

Plastics Supply Company

CURRENT COSTING INCOME STATEMENTS

For the Years 19x4 and 19x5

|  | 19x4 | | 19x5 | |
|---|---|---|---|---|
|  | First Half | Second Half | First Half | Second Half |
| Sales revenues ........... | $70,000 | $80,000 | $100,000 | $90,000 |
| Cost of goods sold........ | 50,000 | 60,000 | 80,000 | 70,000 |
| Current gross margin..... | $20,000 | $20,000 | $ 20,000 | $20,000 |
| Holding gain (loss) ....... | 3,500 | 4,000 | (3,500) | (5,000) |
| Net Income.............. | $23,500 | $24,000 | $ 16,500 | $15,000 |

Current costing income statements for the four half-years in the illustration are shown in Exhibit 11–3. (To simplify the exhibit, we have assumed that selling and administrative expenses were zero.) Sales revenues in the first six months, for example, amounted to 200,000 yards at 35 cents a yard, a total of $70,000. The $50,000 current cost of goods sold is the same quantity at 25 cents a yard, the price that prevailed while all of the sales of this six-month period took place. Subtracting this figure from the revenues produces the current gross margin figure on the third line of the exhibit. Adding the holding gain from Exhibit 11–2 produces the net income figure shown on the bottom line.

The main argument for an income statement structured in this way is that operating and holding gains measure two different aspects of the enterprise's performance. A surgeon making $80,000 a year from his professional practice can be very badly off if his investments consistently turn out to be losers, and business firms have the same kind of problem. Poor operating performance may be masked by holding gains during a period of rising prices, and good operating performance may be offset by holding losses during a period of falling prices.

## ANALYSIS OF FIFO COSTING

Current costing is not used for external financial reporting. It is analytically useful, however, because it permits us to estimate how much of the reported income in historical costing systems is the result of inventory holding gains and losses. Specifically, we shall try to answer two questions:

1. Under what circumstances will holding gains and losses on inventories be included in reported net income?
2. How large an element in reported net income are these holding gains and losses likely to be?

In doing this, we shall look first at Fifo costing, then at Fifo cost or market, and finally at Lifo.

### Fifo Financial Statements

Under Fifo, the ending inventory is measured at the actual cost of the most recent purchases which add up to the quantity on hand. The average Fifo cost of the ending inventory therefore typically will be somewhere between the ending purchase price and the average purchase price of the preceding year.

The table in Exhibit 11–4 shows the result of applying Fifo costing to the Plastics Supply Company's inventories of plastic sheeting in 19x4 and 19x5. The company started the year 19x4 with an inventory of 100,000 yards of sheeting. Under Fifo, these

Exhibit 11–4

Plastics Supply Company

FIFO-BASED INCOME STATEMENTS

For 19x4 and 19x5

|  | 19x4 | | 19x5 | |
|---|---|---|---|---|
|  | First Half | Second Half | First Half | Second Half |
| Initial inventory............ | $20,000 | $17,500 | $ 12,000 | $ 28,000 |
| Purchases................... | 42,500 | 51,000 | 92,000 | 80,500 |
| Goods available .......... | $62,500 | $68,500 | $104,000 | $108,500 |
| Ending inventory........... | 17,500 | 12,000 | 28,000 | 35,000 |
| Fifo cost of goods sold..... | $45,000 | $56,500 | $ 76,000 | $ 73,500 |
| Sales revenues ............. | 70,000 | 80,000 | 100,000 | 90,000 |
| Net Income ................ | $25,000 | $23,500 | $ 24,000 | $ 16,500 |

units were assigned the cost of the last 100,000 yards purchased in 19x3, or 20 cents a yard and $20,000 in all. This is the first figure shown in the first column of the exhibit.

Plastics Supply Company purchased 170,000 yards of sheeting during the first half of 19x4 for $42,500 (25 cents a yard) and another 170,000 yards for 51,000 (30 cents a yard) during the second half. The Fifo cost of the ending inventory therefore was $17,500 at the end of the first half year (70,000 yards × $0.25) and $12,000 at the end of the year (40,000 yards × $0.30). Purchases in 19x5 were 230,000 yards in each six-month period, at prices of 40 cents and 35 cents a yard. These prices were used to measure the inventory quantities of 70,000 and 100,000 yards at the middle and end of 19x5, producing the figures shown in the right-hand columns of the exhibit.

### Realized versus Unrealized Holding Gains and Losses

The relationship between Fifo net income and net income on a current costing basis (ignoring income taxes and selling and administrative expenses) is summarized in the following table:

| Period | Current Costing Net Income | Fifo Net Income | Difference |
|--------|---------------------------|-----------------|------------|
| 19x4: | | | |
| First half ........... | $23,500 | $25,000 | $ 1,500 |
| Second half......... | 24,000 | 23,500 | (500) |
| 19x5: | | | |
| First half ........... | 16,500 | 24,000 | 7,500 |
| Second half......... | 15,000 | 16,500 | 1,500 |
| Total ................ | $79,000 | $89,000 | $10,000 |

The differences in the right-hand column all arose because Fifo and current costing recognize inventory holding gains and losses at different times. In the first half of 19x4, for example, the Fifo gross margin included $5,000 in holding gains which current costing would have included in reported income for 19x3. This time lag arose because the Fifo cost of the first 100,000 yards sold in 19x4 was the Fifo cost of the opening inventory, 100,000 yards × $0.20 = $20,000, whereas current cost was 25 cents a yard, or $25,000. In other words, $5,000 of the Fifo gross margin for 19x4 represented holding gains that had taken place during 19x3, while the replacement cost of the inventory rose by 5 cents a yard.

Accountants would say that this $5,000 was *realized* through the sale of plastic sheeting in the first half of 19x4. In contrast, the 70,000 yards of sheeting in the ending inventory carried an *unrealized* holding gain of 5 cents a yard because their Fifo cost was 25 cents, or 5 cents less than their current replacement cost at that time. The realized inventory holding gains and losses — that is, the amounts included in reported income for the year — are often referred to as *inventory profits and losses.*

The inventory profits and losses under Fifo can be summarized as follows:

| Period | (1) Opening Inventory Quantity (Yards) | (2) Difference between Fifo Cost and Current Cost per Yard at Time of Sale | (3) Fifo Inventory Profit or (Loss) (1) × (2) |
|---|---|---|---|
| 19x4: | | | |
| First half ............ | 100,000 | $0.05 | $5,000 |
| Second half ......... | 70,000 | 0.05 | 3,500 |
| 19x5: | | | |
| First half ............ | 40,000 | 0.10 | 4,000 |
| Second half ......... | 70,000 | (0.05) | (3,500) |
| Total................. | | | $9,000 |

Current costing, in contrast, would have reported $7,500 in inventory holding gains and $8,500 in inventory holding losses during these two years, as we saw earlier:

| Period | Fifo Inventory Profit or (Loss) | Current Costing Holding Gain or (Loss) |
|---|---|---|
| 19x4: | | |
| First half ............ | $5,000 | $3,500 |
| Second half ......... | 3,500 | 4,000 |
| 19x5: | | |
| First half ............ | 4,000 | (3,500) |
| Second half ......... | (3,500) | (5,000) |
| Total................. | $9,000 | ($1,000) |

As this shows, Fifo in this instance put the holding gains into reported income one period after they would have been recognized under current costing. The differences were not large in 19x4, but in the first half of 19x5 the Fifo gross margin included $4,000 in holding gains while the company was suffering a holding loss of $3,500 during the period. For the two years as a whole, the Fifo gross margin was $10,000 greater than the current costing gross margin.

In summary, Fifo recognizes holding gains and losses when the accountant says they are realized, whereas current costing recognizes them when they arise. If the unrealized gain or loss at the beginning of a period differs from the unrealized gain or loss at the end of the period, Fifo net income will differ from net income calculated on a current costing basis.

## Evaluation of Fifo

The merit of excluding a holding gain or loss from income solely because it has not been realized has been the subject of considerable debate. An economist would say that the holder of an asset that has increased in value is better off as a result and therefore has had a gain. By the same token, an investor who buys a share of stock for $35 and holds it while its price goes up to $60 probably feels wealthier. He probably would resist calling the $25 increment income, however, partly because he associates income measurement with income taxation and partly because he confuses income with cash flow.

Unrealized inventory holding gains and losses were large enough at Plastics Supply Company in 19x4 and 19x5 to make this a real issue. This is seldom the case, however. The current replacement cost of a firm's year-end inventories typically does not differ materially from their Fifo purchase cost, since the latter is usually based on the prices prevailing during the last few months of the year. Only if prices are changing rapidly during these months or if inventory turnover is extremely slow is the unrealized holding gain or loss likely to be large.

The main shortcoming of the Fifo method is its failure to separate inventory profits and losses from merchandising gains and losses. This is a problem because they represent two distinct sources of income—ordinary trading or manufacturing operations and holding operations. The income streams from these two sources are likely to behave very differently, and lumping them together seriously impairs the informational value of financial statements. Plastics Supply Company's Fifo gross margin, for example, would be more meaningful if it were subdivided as follows:

| Period | Merchandising Income | Inventory Profit/(Loss) | Fifo Gross Margin |
|---|---|---|---|
| 19x4: | | | |
| First half ........... | $20,000 | $5,000 | $25,000 |
| Second half ........ | 20,000 | 3,500 | 23,500 |
| 19x5: | | | |
| First half ........... | 20,000 | 4,000 | 24,000 |
| Second half ........ | 20,000 | (3,500) | 16,500 |
| Total................. | $80,000 | $9,000 | $89,000 |

The importance of this defect depends on the magnitude of holding gains or losses in relation to current cost operating income. The importance increases with the size of the inventory in relation to the cost of goods sold, the variability of purchase prices from period to period, and the narrowness of the current cost margin. In other words, a firm with a low inventory turnover of merchandise that fluctuates significantly in price, and with a narrow margin between purchase and selling price, will have a Fifo gross margin that includes a large percentage of holding gains and losses.

## Evaluating Fifo Cost or Market

Grafting the cost or market rule onto Fifo costing introduces only one new element, the recognition of unrealized holding losses as a determinant of the reported gross margin. In a period of generally falling prices, this may make a substantial difference, but in a rising market it is likely to have no effect.

The main objection to this method is that it produces results that are inconsistent from period to period. Unrealized holding gains are not reported while prices are rising; some holding losses will be reported while prices are falling. Reported income means one thing when prices are going up and another when they are going down.

The argument usually used to support the cost of market rule is that it is conservative. This is ironic, because in the period after a write-down the cost of goods sold will be lower and reported income will be higher. In fact, corporations have sometimes been accused of excessive zeal in initiating write-downs of various kinds of assets in years in which earnings are low anyway. This is known as "taking a bath," and it sets the stage for a more impressive jump in net income when conditions improve.

## ANALYSIS OF LIFO COSTING

Lifo costing systems are designed to exclude inventory holding gains and losses from reported income, but the technique represents a highly opportunistic means for realizing the goal. The consequence is that such gains and losses do get included in income under certain circumstances and in a very distorted way. We need to examine the reasons for this before attempting to evaluate the Lifo method.

### Holding Gains and Losses under Lifo

Exhibit 11–5 presents the Lifo income statements for 19x3, 19x4, and 19x5, using the same format that we used for Fifo in Exhibit 11–4. Because Lifo cost of goods sold is determined annually, only the annual totals are shown here. To facilitate comprehension of the statements, the cost structure of the Lifo inventories is shown the bottom of the exhibit.

In 19x3 the ending inventory quantity was exactly equal to the beginning quantity. This meant that, based on the measurement rules that we described earlier, the Lifo cost of the ending inventory was the same as the Lifo cost of the inventory at the beginning of the year. The cost of goods sold was equal to the total cost of goods purchased during the year.

*Exhibit 11–5*

**Plastics Supply Company**

### INCOME STATEMENTS

|  | *19x3* | *19x4* | *19x5* |
|---|---|---|---|
| Initial inventory . . . . . . . . . . . . . . . . . . | $ 16,700 | $ 16,700 | $  5,200 |
| Add: Purchases . . . . . . . . . . . . . . . . | 80,000 | 93,500 | 172,500 |
| Cost of goods available . . . . . . . . . . | $ 96,700 | $110,200 | $177,700 |
| Less: Ending inventory . . . . . . . . . | 16,700 | 5,200 | 27,700 |
| Lifo cost of goods sold . . . . . . . . . . . | $ 80,000 | $105,000 | $150,000 |
| Sales revenues . . . . . . . . . . . . . . . . . . | 120,000 | 150,000 | 190,000 |
| Net Income . . . . . . . . . . . . . . . . . . . . . | $ 40,000 | $ 45,000 | $ 40,000 |

### COMPOSITION OF LIFO INVENTORY

|  | *December 31, 19x2* | *December 31, 19x3* | *December 31, 19x4* | *December 31, 19x5* |
|---|---|---|---|---|
| Base quantity (11¢) | $ 2,200 | $ 2,200 | $2,200 | $2,200 |
| 19x1 layer (15¢) | 4,500 | 4,500 | 3,000 | 3,000 |
| 19x2 layer (20¢) | 10,000 | 10,000 | – | – |
| 19x5 layer (37.5¢) | – | – | – | 22,500 |
| Total . . . . . . . . | $16,700 | $16,700 | $5,200 | $27,700 |

Under these circumstances, the cost of goods sold in 19x3 was all measured at 19x3 replacement prices. Holding gains or losses would be included in the Lifo gross margin only if inventories fluctuated during the year, with purchases made at one price and sales made at times when replacement prices were different. For example, if goods were bought for 15 cents in January and sold in August when replacement prices were 21 cents, the Lifo gross margin would include a 6-cent holding gain.

Although these intrayear holding gains and losses may be substantial in some firms in some periods, our main concern will be with a different holding gain component of the Lifo gross margin. Since sales for the year 19x4 exceeded purchases by 60,000 yards, the cost of this quantity had to be transferred from the January 1, 19x4, Lifo inventory — starting with the 50,000 yards in the 19x2 layer (the last units in), and ending with 10,000 yards from the 19x1 layer. The costs removed from the inventory account because of these liquidations were as follows:

| | | | |
|---|---|---|---|
| 19x2 layer................. | 50,000 yards × $0.20 | $10,000 | |
| 19x1 layer................. | 10,000 yards × 0.15 | 1,500 | |
| Total................. | | $11,500 | |

The Lifo cost of goods sold, in other words, was a combination of 19x1, 19x2, and 19x4 purchase prices. The difference between the Lifo cost and the replacement cost at the time of sale was a realized holding gain.

To avoid these liquidations, the company would have had to buy an additional 30,000 yards of sheeting in the first half of the year and another 30,000 yards in the second half, at the following cost:

| | | | |
|---|---|---|---|
| 1st 6 months................. | 30,000 yards × $0.25 | $ 7,500 | |
| 2nd 6 months................. | 30,000 yards × 0.30 | 9,000 | |
| Total................. | | $16,500 | |

This amount would have appeared in the cost of goods sold. The difference between this sum and the $11,500 that actually was transferred from the Lifo inventory account was the realized holding gain for the year, reported as part of the Lifo cost margin:

| | |
|---|---|
| Reported cost of units liquidated .................... | $11,500 |
| Replacement cost at time of sale .................... | 16,500 |
| Holding gain included in reported income ..... | $ 5,000 |

In other words, reported income before taxes included $5,000 which would not have been reported if inventories had not been reduced during the year. This is called a *liquidation profit.* It is the realized holding gain on the 60,000 yards of sheeting from the opening inventory. Most of this holding gain actually arose in previous years, but was unrealized until 19x4.

### Effect on Inventory Balances

Inventory balances under Lifo costing typically reflect purchase prices of much earlier periods. When purchase prices have been rising for many years, the Lifo figures may be only a small fraction of their current replacement cost. This will affect the reported rate of return on investment and make comparisons with companies using Fifo very difficult.

In the example, the unrealized holding gain was $8,300 at the beginning of 19x4. This was the difference between current replacement cost at 25 cents and the Lifo inventory cost of $16,700. The Lifo figure, in other words, understated current cost by 33 percent at that time. The liquidation-replenishment cycle in 19x4–19x5 added $11,000 to the inventory account balance, with no increase in the physical inventory quantity over the 19x3 level. Even with this, the Lifo cost of the inventory was still smaller than the end-of-year replacement cost (100,000 yards at 30 cents) because part of the inventory was measured at the low purchase prices of 19x0 and 19x1. Thus an unrealized holding gain amounting to $2,300 was still excluded from the balance sheet and income statement.

### Avoiding Lifo Liquidation Profits

The reason why the use of Lifo is restricted entirely to annual financial reporting should now be clear. If Lifo were to be used for daily bookkeeping, inventory liquidations would be much more frequent. These would deprive Lifo of its major informational and tax advantage.[4] For example, if the inventories of sheeting had declined temporarily to zero during 19x4, Lifo-basis bookkeeping would have transferred the entire base quantity cost to the cost of goods sold at 19x0 prices. The ending inventory

---

[4] Lifo is widely used in the United States because it offers substantial tax advantages and because companies that use it for tax purposes are required to use it for public financial reporting as well. This is probably the most obvious example of the impact of United States tax laws and regulations on accounting measurements for purposes other than taxation. Lifo is not allowed for tax purposes in most countries and is rarely if ever used outside the United States.

would have reflected 19x4 prices only and a holding gain would have been included in reported income and in taxable income as well.

A practice called *dollar value Lifo* has been developed to extend the benefits of Lifo to firms which cannot keep the year-end physical quantity of each item of inventory at the same level year after year. For instance, an automobile manufacturer may carry the same total inventory of spare parts year after year, but the parts inventory for automobiles of any given model year will decline from year to year and eventually reach zero. Treating each part separately would result in the recognition of holding gains and losses as the inventory declined.

It is beyond the scope of this book to do more than indicate the basic nature of dollar value Lifo. Essentially, the method is to estimate the physical change in the total quantity of a large number of different items, treated as a single group. Since different items are measured in different physical units, dollar value Lifo measures the quantity of each of them in dollars, adjusted by index numbers to a common base. Declines in the inventories of some items are largely offset by increases in the inventory quantities of others. Liquidation profits or losses are recognized only if the inventory declines in total.

## Evaluation of Lifo Costing

We are now in a position to evaluate the strengths and weaknesses of Lifo costing. The main case for Lifo is that in most years it produces net income figures that are closer to current cost *operating* income than any other historical costing method. In our example, the current cost operating income was $20,000 every six months, or $40,000 a year. Lifo net income was identical to this, except in 19x4 when an inventory liquidation took place. Since the current cost operating income is the best available index of the product's ability to support the costs of marketing it, this has to be chalked up as an advantage of Lifo costing.

To the extent that Lifo succeeds in making the reported gross margin measure the current gross margin, it does so by excluding holding gains and losses from the income statement. If it is believed that holding gains and losses are also income, their exclusion from the income statement when inventory is constant or rising is a serious defect. It is not universally agreed that holding gains should be included in income, however. One defense of Lifo is that realization through sale is an illusion for a going concern since the continued operation of the business requires the replacement of the merchandise in one form or another. The cash flows identified as holding gains are tied up in maintaining the same level of inventory and cannot be used to pay dividends or buy additional inventory. A holding gain is realized, the defenders of Lifo argue, only when the inventory is liquidated and the cash flow can be used elsewhere. We shall return to this point at the end of this chapter.

One undisputed weakness of Lifo costing is that the exclusion of holding gains and losses from reported income is not achieved consistently every year. Whereas realized holding gains and losses that arise as a result of differential timing of purchases and sales within individual years are a more or less regular feature of Lifo systems, those arising from inventory liquidations are highly erratic. Furthermore, since a long time can elapse between the acquisition of an inventory layer and its liquidation, the holding gain included in income can be very large and unrelated to the holding gain or loss that actually took place during the year. As with Fifo costing, neither the manager nor the outsider is likely to be able to segregate this component of net income.

Another serious limitation of Lifo is the exclusion of holding gains and losses from the inventory. After Lifo has been used for a number of years, the inventory figure on the balance sheet becomes a meaningless conglomeration of layers of the same item measured at prices prevailing in a number of different years, some in the distant past. For some companies, the total may be close to current replacement cost; for others a large gap will arise. The outsider has no way of judging the extent of these unrealized inventory holding gains and losses and no meaning can be attached to the inventory figure. Since the inventory figure is so difficult to interpret, any other quantity dependent on it — the current ratio, for example — is also less useful for either interfirm or interperiod comparisons.

## A COMPROMISE SOLUTION

The implied recommendation in this chapter is to measure both inventories and the cost of goods sold at current cost. Acceptance of this position by the accounting profession in the near future seems unlikely, but a movement in this direction is clearly feasible.

One part of the solution would be to report both the current cost and the historical cost of the ending inventories, if the differences are material. This could be done either with Fifo or with

Lifo, although the only material differences are likely to arise with Lifo. For example, the Lifo cost of the Plastics Supply Company's 40,000-yard inventory on December 31, 19x4, could be shown as follows:

| | |
|---|---:|
| Inventory, at current replacement cost | $16,000 |
| Less: Unrealized holding gains | 10,800 |
| Inventory, at Lifo historical cost | $ 5,200 |

Many companies provide information of this kind for their Lifo inventories, usually in footnotes. The difference between Lifo cost and the figure used for inventory bookkeeping (Fifo or moving average) is identified as a "Lifo reserve." This can generally be interpreted as the unrealized holding gain on the balance sheet date.

Current cost could also be shown on the income statement, even though reported income was based on Fifo or Lifo costing. Using the 19x4 Lifo figures, one possible format would show the following:

| | |
|---|---:|
| Sales revenues | $150,000 |
| Cost of goods sold (at current cost) | 110,000 |
| Current operating margin | $ 40,000 |
| Add: Prior-year holding gains realized in 19x4 | 5,000 |
| Gross margin | $ 45,000 |

This could be accompanied by a footnote, indicating that the actual holding gain for the year was $7,500 (from Exhibit 11–2).

In some cases measurement of current cost may be difficult or expensive. Reasonable approximations are ordinarily feasible at moderate cost, however, and when holding gains and losses are large the effort should be made because the information may be significant to readers of the statements.

## PRICE LEVEL ADJUSTMENTS

Many accountants recognize that the use of historical cost as the basis for financial measurement severely impairs the validity of financial statements in any economy with a fluctuating or rising price level. A comprehensive survey of the alternatives to historical cost measurement is beyond the scope of this text, but a few words on changes in the purchasing power of the dollar and financial statements is desirable. The main argument is that what counts is what a dollar can buy, not the dollar itself. Hence, holding gains and losses that originate in changes in the general purchasing power of the dollar are not real and should not be included in income. For example, suppose that replacement cost rises from $.50 to $.55 cents a yard, while the purchasing power index remains constant. The 5-cent holding gain in this case is real because the company has an asset that can buy 10 percent more other goods and services.

If the index of prices in general has also gone up by 10 percent during this period, however, the monetary gain has been offset by the decline in the size (purchasing power) of the monetary unit. The company is no better off in terms of what a unit of inventory can buy at the end of the year than it was at the start of the year. If the rise in the price level has been more than 10 percent, the holding gain on the unit of inventory is negative in real terms.

A general implementation of this idea would require the restatement of all accounting quantities in units of purchasing power rather than in ordinary monetary units. None of the inventory costing methods that we have discussed in in this chapter does this; all of them are based on the assumption that the size of the monetary unit remains stable. This means that each user of the financial statements must decide for himself whether holding gains and losses, reported and unreported, are real.[5]

## SUMMARY

Without inventory holding gains and losses, all inventory costing methods would be interchangeable. Inventory holding gains and losses are common, however, and are frequently substantial. The choice of inventory method will neither increase nor decrease these holding gains or losses, but it will affect the amounts that are reported in the financial statements.

Lifo tends to exclude a substantial proportion of holding gains and losses from inventory account balances; Fifo ordinarily does not. Both methods, however, include inventory profits and losses as part of the operating margin. Fifo does this systematically, Lifo intermittently. Lifo is more likely than Fifo to exclude hold-

---

[5] For a review of the issues in price level adjustments, see American Institute of Certified Public Accountants, *Reporting the Financial Effects of Price-Level Changes,* Accounting Research Study No. 6 (New York: AICPA, 1963); Accounting Principles Board, *Financial Statements Restated for General Price-Level Changes,* APB Statement No. 3 (New York: AICPA, 1969); and Financial Accounting Standards Board, *Discussion Memorandum: Reporting the Effects of General Price-Level Changes in Financial Statements* (Stamford, Conn.: FASB, 1974).

ing gains and losses from the income statement, but is more erratic. Neither method provides investors with information on unrealized holding gains and losses, and neither segregates realized inventory holding gains and losses from operating profits. The result is to deny investors and management significant information on the company's economic performance.

The adoption of current costing would provide investors and management with more complete and more consistent information on operating and holding gains and losses, but it would mean the abandonment of total historical cost as a measure of the amount of resources available for sale, a step that the accounting profession is not yet ready to accept. Progress can be achieved, however, by reporting both historical cost and current cost in the financial statements, thereby permitting the reader to evaluate management's performance both in ordinary operations and in its decisions on inventory levels.

## QUESTIONS AND PROBLEMS

1. Under what conditions will the choice of inventory costing method have a large impact on net income?

2. How does an inventory holding gain or loss arise? How does it differ from an "inventory profit or loss?"

3. Explain the nature, purpose, and effect of the "cost or market" rule. Does it represent a "conservative" accounting practice?

4. What is meant by the "inventory turnover rate"? How does the magnitude of this rate affect the magnitude of the "inventory profit or loss"?

5. What are the objectives of Lifo? How well do you feel that it meets these objectives?

6. What does the difference between the historical cost margin and the current cost margin mean? Under currently accepted accounting methods, which of these would be reported on the current year's income statement?

7. The Lifo method has been criticized on a number of grounds. List the major objections to the use of this method and indicate how, if at all, the method might be modified to meet any objection that you feel is valid.

8. How does "dollar value Lifo" differ from the basic Lifo method described in this chapter? When would you expect it to be used?

9. A businessman made the following statement: "We bought these goods last year before prices went up. This gives us a competitive edge, and we can continue selling these goods at our old prices until we have to start dipping into the stocks we bought this year. Our competitors are on Lifo and can't do that."

Evaluate this statement. Does the method of inventory costing affect the firm's ability to compete? In setting prices is current cost or historical cost likely to be more useful to management?

10. Companies that use Lifo usually use some other method such as Fifo or a moving average for inventory bookkeeping during the year. The difference between the Lifo cost of the inventory and the amounts shown in the inventory accounts themselves is often referred to as the "Lifo reserve."

If an account were to be set up to show the balance in this reserve, what kind of account would it be and where would it be shown on the balance sheet? What does the word "reserve" mean in this context? Is it a good word to convey the meaning of the account balance?

11. The Mead Corporation listed inventories of $152,442,000 in its 1971 annual report. The following note was included in the report:

*Accounting principles: Inventory* — The inventories are stated at cost, determined principally on the last-in, first-out (Lifo) basis, which is less than market value. The Lifo inventory method results in a conservative inventory valuation during inflationary times. At December 31, 1971, the Lifo reserve was $26,016,000. In 1971, this reserve increased by $5,208,000 which, after taxes, decreased earnings by $.16 per Common Share.

a) What is this "Lifo reserve"? Why did it increase? Why did this increase lead to a decrease in earnings per share?
b) Were the prices paid by the Mead Corporation rising or falling in 1971? In general, how would you expect rising purchase prices to affect the size of the Lifo reserve?

12. The notes to the 1971 financial statements of The Budd Company included the following paragraph:

Effective January 1, 1971 the company changed its method of pricing that portion of its inventories previously stated on the last-in, first-out cost basis (Lifo) to the lower of average cost or market. As a result of this change, net earnings in 1971 were increased by approximately $450,000 (7¢ per share). The use of the Lifo inventory method was discontinued because (a) the Lifo values were not used in determining product selling prices or in measuring divisional operating results and (b) fourth-quarter earnings were distorted since adjustments to the Lifo reserve for the year normally had been provided in that quarter. The financial statements for 1970 have been restated for the resultant increase in 1970 inventories of $2,438,000; the effect on the loss for 1970 was negligible.

a) Why did the company have to make adjustments to the "Lifo reserve" in the fourth quarter of each year? What effect did these adjustments probably have? Why did the company regard this as an argument for dropping Lifo?

b) Why did the $2,438,000 inventory adjustment in 1970 have only a negligible effect on net income for that year? Why did the change increase the 1971 net income by $450,000?

c) Do you think that the company's reasons for switching from Lifo were valid?

**13.** The balance sheet in a company's annual report described the company's inventories as follows:

> Inventories — substantially all stated at cost on "last-in,
> first-out" basis with current replacement cost approxi-
> mately $28,100,000 in excess of stated value.............. $53,334,933

A year earlier, the corresponding inventory figure was $56,047,919, and current replacement cost was approximately $24,200,000 in excess of stated value.

What information about the financial position and operations of the company do the figures on excess of replacement cost over stated value provide?

**14.** A balance sheet included the following item among the current liabilities:

> Provision for replacement of basic Lifo inventories............. $650,000

This account did not appear in the previous year's balance sheet.

The balance in the inventory account at the close of each of the two years was as follows:

> Most recent year.......................... $11,735,039
> Previous year............................ 12,785,001

a) What is the meaning of the "provision" account, and what effect did it have on the reported income for the year?

b) The balance in this account went back to zero at the end of the next year. What happened?

c) Do you think that the company's method was a desirable accounting practice?

**\*15.** The Winchester Coal Company marketed stove, nut, and powder coal. One year's transactions in nut coal were:

---

\* Solutions to problems marked with an asterisk (\*) are found in Appendix B.

| Month | Tons Purchased | Purchase Price per Ton | Tons Sold |
|---|---|---|---|
| January 1, beginning inventory ....... | 1,000 | $41.00 | |
| January............................ | 100 | 41.20 | 300 |
| February........................... | | | 400 |
| March.............................. | | | 300 |
| April............................... | 100 | 41.30 | 100 |
| May................................ | | | 50 |
| June............................... | 200 | 41.50 | |
| July................................ | 200 | 41.50 | |
| August............................. | 300 | 41.55 | 50 |
| September.......................... | 300 | 41.55 | 100 |
| October............................ | 300 | 41.60 | 150 |
| November.......................... | 400 | 41.60 | 250 |
| December.......................... | 200 | 41.70 | 300 |
| Total.......................... | 3,100 | | 2,000 |
| December 31, Ending Inventory ....... | 1,100 | | |

a) What was the cost of the ending inventory on the basis of—
   (1) First-in, first-out?
   (2) Last-in, first-out?
b) What effect did the choice of one of these methods instead of the other have on net income for the year?

*16. The following data are taken from the records of the Briggs Sales Company of East Greenwich, Vermont:

| | Units | Unit Cost | Total Cost |
|---|---|---|---|
| Inventory—March 1.................... | 1,600 | $10 | $16,000 |
| Purchase—March 5 .................. | 800 | 11 | 8,800 |
| Purchase—March 20................. | 500 | 13 | 6,500 |
| Purchase—March 31................. | 1,400 | 12 | 16,800 |

During the month, the following number of units were sold:

| | |
|---|---|
| March 3 ................. | 900 |
| March 10................. | 800 |
| March 23................. | 700 |

The market value of the March 31 inventory was $12 a unit.

What were the March cost of the goods sold and the March 31 inventory figures:

a) Assuming cost to be determined on a first-in, first-out basis?
b) Assuming cost to be determined on an average cost basis?
c) Assuming application of the "cost or market" rule in connection with (a) above?

*17. The Higby Company had 10,000 pounds of product in inventory on January 1, 19x1 at a Fifo cost of $30,000. Management decided to switch to the Lifo method, beginning in 19x1. Purchases and sales for the next eight years were as follows:

| Year | Purchases | Sales (pounds) |
|------|-----------|----------------|
| 19x1 | 60,000 × $3.10 = $186,000 | 55,000 |
| 19x2 | 70,000 × $3.50 = 245,000 | 68,000 |
| 19x3 | 90,000 × $3.75 = 337,500 | 80,000 |
| 19x4 | 70,000 × $3.80 = 266,000 | 72,000 |
| 19x5 | 80,000 × $4.00 = 320,000 | 75,000 |
| 19x6 | 70,000 × $4.25 = 297,500 | 80,000 |
| 19x7 | 100,000 × $4.40 = 440,000 | 85,000 |
| 19x8 | 95,000 × $4.50 = 427,500 | 95,000 |

a)  Calculate the Lifo cost of goods sold for each year and the Lifo cost of the inventory at the end of each year.
b)  Calculate the Fifo cost of goods sold for each year and the Fifo cost of the inventory at the end of each year.
c)  Which of these methods would have included the greater amount of inventory profit in reported income for the 8-year period as a whole? Calculate the amount of the difference.

18. The Weeks Woolen Company has always used the first-in, first-out method of inventory costing. For the calendar years 19x7 and 19x8, its reported net income or loss before deducting income taxes was as follows:

$$1967 \ldots\ldots\ldots \ \$234,690 \text{ profit}$$
$$1968 \ldots\ldots\ldots \ \ 60,140 \text{ loss}$$

Early in 1969, the company's management was considering shifting to a last-in, first-out basis. Investigation revealed that the inventory figures for the three years were or would have been as follows:

|  | Pounds | Fifo Amount | Lifo Amount |
|--|--------|-------------|-------------|
| December 31, 19x6......... | 500,000 | $225,000 | $225,000 |
| December 31, 19x7......... | 475,000 | 403,000 | 210,000 |
| December 31, 19x8......... | 513,000 | 338,000 | 235,000 |

a)  Compute the net income before income taxes that the company would have reported each year if it had adopted the Lifo method of inventory costing as of January 1, 19x7. Would adoption of Lifo as of that date have led to more informative income statements for the two years? Explain your reasoning.
b)  By the beginning of 19x9, management no longer had the option of adopting Lifo as of January 1, 19x7, but it could adopt it as of January 1, 19x8. Write a brief report to management, recommending

for or against adoption of Lifo as of that date, giving your reasons for your recommendation.

19. The Tanlon Corporation determines its cost of goods sold as follows. The units sold during a quarter are measured at the average cost of the inventory on hand at the start of the period. At the end of the quarter, a new average is computed on the basis of the inventory remaining at the end of the quarter. Below are the transactions for 19x1 and 19x2:

| Period | Units Purchased | Units Sold |
|---|---|---|
| Balance January 1, 19x1......... | 10,000 at $0.60 | |
| Quarter I, 19x1 ................. | 6,000 at  0.56 | 9,000 |
| II ..................... | 8,000 at  0.52 | 6,000 |
| III ..................... | 6,000 at  0.52 | 5,000 |
| IV ..................... | 4,000 at  0.48 | 3,000 |
| I, 19x2................. | 4,000 at  0.45 | 4,000 |
| II ..................... | 5,000 at  0.48 | 6,000 |
| III ..................... | 5,000 at  0.50 | 9,000 |
| IV ..................... | 10,000 at  0.54 | 6,000 |

a) Determine the cost of goods sold and the ending inventory for 19x1 and 19x2.
b) Compute the cost of goods sold for each year on a Fifo basis.
c) Compute the cost of goods sold for each year on a "current cost" basis. How much holding loss or gain would be included in ordinary income each year by each of the above methods? (Assume that replacement prices remained constant in each period.)

20. The XYZ Company uses Fifo for inventory bookkeeping in its perpetual inventory system, and Lifo for external financial reporting. The inventory accounts showed the following balances on January 1, 19x1:

Inventories (50,000 units).......... $50,000 dr.
Lifo Inventory Adjustment.........   20,000 cr.

The balance in the Lifo Inventory Adjustment account measured the difference between Lifo and Fifo inventory cost on that date.
Purchases and sales during the year were as follows:

| Quarter | Purchases | Sales |
|---|---|---|
| 1.............. | 50,000 units × $1.10 | 45,000 units |
| 2.............. | 40,000      ×  1.15 | 50,000 |
| 3.............. | 60,000      ×  1.12 | 55,000 |
| 4.............. | 70,000      ×  1.25 | 60,000 |

Annual increments to the Lifo inventory were measured at the prices paid for the first units purchased during the year.

a) Calculate the Fifo cost of goods sold for each quarter and for the year as a whole.
b) Calculate the Lifo cost of goods sold for the year.

c) Set up a T-account to represent the Inventories account, enter the opening balance, record the purchases and cost of goods sold as the company would record them each quarter, and calculate the ending balance in this account.

d) Prepare the entry that should be made to adjust the balance in the Lifo Inventory Adjustment account at the end of the year.

e) Management told the shareholders that inventory losses in the fourth quarter erased most of the net income reported on the interim financial statements for the first three quarters of the year, despite record fourth-quarter sales. Explain what happened.

21. A manufacturer had 30,000 pounds of raw material in inventory on January 1, 19x9. It had the following Lifo cost:

| | | |
|---|---|---|
| Base quantity......... | 15,000 lbs. × $0.10 | $1,500 |
| 19x0 layer ............ | 5,000 lbs. × 0.20 | 1,000 |
| 19x2 layer ............ | 3,000 lbs. × 0.22 | 660 |
| 19x5 layer ............ | 6,000 lbs. × 0.26 | 1,560 |
| 19x7 layer ............ | 1,000 lbs. × 0.28 | 280 |
| Total........... | 30,000 lbs. | $5,000 |

The last 30,000 pounds purchased in 19x8 cost 30 cents a pound.

The following purchases and issues of this raw material were made during 19x9:

Purchases:
| | | |
|---|---|---|
| January 20 .......... | 22,000 lbs. at $0.35......... | $ 7,700 |
| February 16 ......... | 20,000 lbs. at 0.38......... | 7,600 |
| March 12............ | 28,000 lbs. at 0.40......... | 11,200 |
| April 5 ............. | 25,000 lbs. at 0.34......... | 8,500 |
| April 30 ............ | 20,000 lbs. at 0.33......... | 6,600 |
| May 27............. | 27,000 lbs. at 0.32......... | 8,640 |
| June 21 ............ | 30,000 lbs. at 0.37......... | 11,100 |
| July 18............. | 24,000 lbs. at 0.41......... | 9,840 |
| August 14........... | 20,000 lbs. at 0.43......... | 8,600 |
| September 8......... | 25,000 lbs. at 0.40......... | 10,000 |
| October 2 .......... | 33,000 lbs. at 0.38......... | 12,540 |
| November 1 ......... | 28,000 lbs. at 0.39......... | 10,920 |
| December 1 ......... | 31,000 lbs. at 0.36......... | 11,160 |

Issues:
| | |
|---|---|
| January 1–January 20 ............. | 20,000 lbs. |
| January 21–February 16 ........... | 26,000 |
| February 17–March 12 ............ | 21,000 |
| March 13–April 5 ................. | 28,000 |
| April 6–April 30 .................. | 22,000 |
| May 1–May 27 ..................... | 24,000 |
| May 28–June 21 ................... | 22,000 |
| June 22–July 18 ................... | 25,000 |
| July 19–August 14................. | 21,000 |
| August 15–September 8 ........... | 19,000 |
| September 9–October 2 ............ | 20,000 |
| October 3–November 1 ............ | 24,000 |
| November 2–December 1 .......... | 21,000 |
| December 2–December 31 ......... | 19,000 |

Determine the cost of materials used during the year and the cost of the year-ending inventory:

a) By the Lifo method. Increments to the Lifo inventory are measured by cumulating the costs of the first purchases made during the year until the incremental quantity has been reached.

b) By the Fifo method, on the assumption that the company had been on Fifo through 19x8.

c) By the Fifo method coupled with the cost or market rule, assuming the year-end market value to be 37 cents a pound.

19/25    **22.** Investigation shows that the replacement price of the raw material in problem 21 was 30 cents on January 1, 19x9. Purchase prices changed often during the year, the changes timed to fall on a date on which a purchase was made. In other words, the price remained at 30 cents until January 20, when it rose to 35 cents, the price at which the year's first purchase was made. It rose again on February 16 to 38 cents, rose to 40 cents on March 12, fell to 34 cents on April 5, and so on. On December 31, the price rose from 36 to 37 cents a pound.

a) Calculate, on a current cost basis:
   (1) The cost of the January 1, 19x9, inventory.
   (2) The cost of the December 31, 19x9, inventory.
   (3) The cost of materials used during 19x9.
b) Calculate the total holding gain or loss for the year as a whole.
c) Calculate the realized holding gain or loss for the year:
   (1) Under Lifo.
   (2) Under Fifo.
   (3) Under Fifo cost or market.

**23.** The Fine Thread Company uses Lifo and counts its entire inventory in terms of equivalent pounds of cotton. On January 1, 1972, the company had the following inventory:

| | | |
|---|---|---|
| Base quantity................. | 100,000 lbs. at $0.18 | $18,000 |
| 1958 layer.................... | 20,000 lbs. at 0.24 | 4,800 |
| 1966 layer.................... | 30,000 lbs. at 0.30 | 9,000 |
| 1968 layer.................... | 20,000 lbs. at 0.32 | 6,400 |
| Total.................... | 170,000 lbs. | $38,200 |

During 1972 and 1973, the company had the following transactions:

| Period | Purchases | Sales |
|---|---|---|
| Quarter I, 1972......... | 120,000 lbs. at $0.40 | 100,000 lbs. |
| II............. | 60,000 lbs. at 0.42 | 90,000 |
| III............. | 40,000 lbs. at 0.42 | 80,000 |
| IV ............. | 180,000 lbs. at 0.38 | 110,000 |
| I, 1973......... | 110,000 lbs. at 0.38 | 90,000 |
| II............. | 50,000 lbs. at 0.36 | 70,000 |
| III ............. | 20,000 lbs. at 0.36 | 80,000 |
| IV ............. | 130,000 lbs. at 0.35 | 110,000 |

a) Determine the cost of goods sold and year-end inventory for 1972 and for 1973.
b) Compute the cost of goods sold and year-end inventory for each year on a "current cost" basis.

*c)* Show how you might present both Lifo and current cost figures in the company's annual reports for the two years. In what respects, if any, would your method of presentation improve the quality of the information given to the shareholders?

**24.** A company started the year 19x8 with an inventory of 50,000 units of product at the following Lifo cost:

| | | |
|---|---|---|
| Base quantity......... | 30,000 units × $1.00 | $30,000 |
| 19x2 layer ............ | 16,000 units × 1.40 | 22,400 |
| 19x5 layer ............ | 4,000 units × 1.65 | 6,600 |
| Total........... | 50,000 units | $59,000 |

You have the following additional information:

(1) The last 50,000 units purchased in 19x7 cost $2 a unit.
(2) The replacement price was $2 a unit on January 1, rose to $2.50 on March 22, to $2.80 on July 1, and to $3.00 on September 16. It remained at $3.00 to the end of the year.
(3) The following purchases and sales were made during 19x8:

| Period | Units Purchased | Units Sold |
|---|---|---|
| 1/1–3/21 | 60,000 × $2.00 | 45,000 |
| 3/22–6/30 | 70,000 × 2.50 | 65,000 |
| 7/1–9/15 | 50,000 × 2.80 | 65,000 |
| 9/16–12/31 | 40,000 × 3.00 | 60,000 |

(4) The market value of the inventory on December 31, 19x8, was $2.90 a unit.
(5) Reported income for the year, before deducting the cost of goods sold, was $575,000.

*a)* Determine the cost of goods sold, net income (ignoring income taxes), and the cost of the ending inventory:

(1) On a Lifo basis.
(2) As they would have been reported if the company had used Fifo in 19x7 and 19x8.
(3) By the Fifo method, coupled with the cost or market rule.

*b)* Calculate the realized inventory holding gain (inventory profit) under each of the three historical inventory costing bases.
*c)* Calculate the total holding gain or loss for the year as a whole.

*\*25.* The Franklin Steel Warehouse Company adopted Lifo on January 1, 1972, and its 15,000-ton inventory was costed at its Fifo cost of $125 a ton on that date, a total of $1,875,000.

During 1972, the company purchased 100,000 tons at an average price of $130 a ton, and sold 95,000 tons. The last 20,000 tons purchased during December, 1972, cost $135 a ton.

Sales in 1973 amounted to 105,000 tons, but purchases totaled only 90,000 tons at an average cost of $140 a ton. (The last 5,000 tons purchased during 1973 also cost $140 a ton.) The inventory was down to 5,000 tons at the end of 1973 because a steel strike had cut off supplies. The company expected to rebuild its inventories to 15,000 tons as soon as steel became available again in 1974.

The Franklin Steel Warehouse Company measures the annual increments to its Lifo inventory at the average of all purchase prices paid during the year.

a)  Provide the figures necessary to complete the following table, showing inventories and cost of goods sold on both a Fifo and a Lifo basis:

|  | Inventory Cost | | | Cost of Goods Sold | |
|---|---|---|---|---|---|
|  | Fifo | Lifo | | Fifo | Lifo |
| January 1, 1972 | $1,875,000 | $1,875,000 | | | |
|  | | | 1972 | _____ | _____ |
| December 31, 1972 | _____ | _____ | | | |
|  | | | 1973 | _____ | _____ |
| December 31, 1973 | _____ | _____ | | | |

b)  Assuming that 15,000 tons is the normal inventory quantity and that the company intended to rebuild its inventories to this level as soon as possible, what was the effect of the "involuntary liquidation" of inventory on reported profit for 1973? (Remember that the company was on Lifo.)

c)  Assuming that inventories were increased to 15,000 tons by the end of 1974, with 1974 purchases at an average cost of $145 a ton, what was the net effect of the 1973 involuntary liquidation on Lifo inventory cost as of December 31, 1974?

26. The Alpha Company and the Omega Company are both engaged in the smelting and refining of copper. The following inventory data were taken from the annual reports of these two companies for the year ending December 31, 19x8:

|  | December 31, 19x7 | December 31, 19x8 |
|---|---|---|
| Alpha Company inventories (Lifo) .... | $32,825,000 | $26,450,000 |
| Omega Company inventories | | |
| (Fifo, lower of cost or market) ...... | $77,140,000 | $63,750,000 |

The income statements for the two companies for the year ending December 31, 19x8, were as follows:

|  | Alpha | Omega |
|---|---|---|
| Sales ........................... | $95,000,000 | $215,000,000 |
| Cost of goods sold .............. | $74,300,000 | $180,000,000 |
| Depreciation.................... | 3,700,000 | 9,000,000 |
| Other expenses ................. | 9,000,000 | 20,000,000 |
| Total Expenses ............ | $87,000,000 | $209,000,000 |
| Income before taxes ............. | $ 8,000,000 | $  6,000,000 |
| Income taxes ................... | 4,000,000 | 3,000,000 |
| Net Income..................... | $ 4,000,000 | $  3,000,000 |

a) Assuming that the market prices of copper and of unsmelted ores were approximately the same at the end of 19x8 as they were at the end of 19x7, how. would the companies' inventory measurement methods influence your interpretation of the companies' financial statements for the year 19x8?

b) How would your answer to (a) differ if prices in December, 19x8 were lower than in December, 19x7?

**27.** The Carson Company adopted Lifo as of January 1, 1948. It had 40,000 units in inventory on December 31, 1971, with the following Lifo cost:

| | | |
|---|---|---|
| Base quantity......... | 30,000 units × $0.20 | $ 6,000 |
| 1952 layer ........... | 10,000 units ×  0.40 | 4,000 |
| Total........... | | $10,000 |

The company's practice was to cost any annual increments to its Lifo inventories at the prices paid for the first purchases of equivalent quantities during the year.

The company entered into the following purchase and sale transactions:

| | Units Purchased | Units Sold |
|---|---|---|
| **1972:** | | |
| 1st quarter........... | 80,000 at $1.00/unit | 40,000 at $1.20/unit |
| 2d quarter ........... | 80,000 at $1.02/unit | 60,000 at $1.22/unit |
| 3d quarter ........... | 50,000 at $1.04/unit | 75,000 at $1.24/unit |
| 4th quarter .......... | 50,000 at $1.06/unit | 75,000 at $1.26/unit |
| **1973:** | | |
| 1st quarter........... | 90,000 at $1.08/unit | 60,000 at $1.28/unit |
| 2d quarter ........... | 80,000 at $1.06/unit | 70,000 at $1.27/unit |
| 3d quarter ........... | 70,000 at $1.08/unit | 100,000 at $1.29/unit |
| 4th quarter .......... | 60,000 at $1.10/unit | 100,000 at $1.30/unit |
| **1974:** | | |
| 1st quarter........... | 75,000 at $1.12/unit | (Data not available) |

All price changes became effective on the first day of the quarter and the new prices remained constant throughout the quarter. The purchase price at the end of 1971 was $1.00 a unit.

All revenues and expenses were reported in the financial statements at the amounts that were listed on the company's income tax returns. Income was taxed at a 40 percent rate. Expenses other than the cost of goods sold and income taxes were:

| | |
|---|---|
| 1972......... | $51,000 |
| 1973......... | 65,400 |

a) Compute income before taxes and net income for each year on a Lifo basis.

b) Compute income before taxes for each year on a current costing

basis. Show separately the amounts due to holding gains and losses
and the amounts due to merchandising operations. (Ignore income
taxes.)

c) For each year, calculate the realized holding gain or loss before
taxes (inventory profit or loss component of Lifo income before
taxes).

d) The company's management was considering a switch from Lifo to
Fifo in 1973. Net income for 1973 would be reported on a Fifo
basis, and for comparative purposes the December 31, 1972 inventory would be restated on a Fifo basis.

(1) Calculate Fifo net income for 1973.
(2) How would the restatement of the December 31, 1972 inventory be reflected in the 1973 financial statements?
(3) State any arguments that you think are important either for
or against the switch.

28. "We'd be foolish to buy now," the Carthage Company's purchasing agent said. "The price can't be any higher next spring than it is now
and I expect it to be much lower. We can make $7,000 by keeping our
inventory down to 80,000 pounds until the new crop comes in next
year."

"You forget," the company's controller replied, "that if we don't replace these inventories before the end of the year we'll lose our favorable Lifo base. Not only that, but if you aim at an 80,000-pound inventory
you'll be buying in uneconomically small lots. You'll probably have to
pay premiums on rush orders, too."

The Carthage Company is a large wholesale distributor of food products. One of these products is made from citrus fruits. The annual price
is determined largely by the size of the winter crop in Florida. A very
severe winter in 1967–68 caused heavy damage to the Florida citrus
crop. The purchase price went up to $0.32 a pound in January of 1968
and remained at this level throughout the year.

In 1962, the company had adopted the Lifo method of inventory
costing for all of its products, both for tax purposes and for financial
reporting. The balances in the company's inventory accounts on January 1, 1962, became the costs of the Lifo base quantities.

Separate accounts were established at that time for the materials
cost and processing cost and processing cost components of the Lifo
inventories. The company's inventories of its citrus-based product on
January 1, 1962, contained materials with a purchase weight of 100,000
pounds, at an inventory cost of $0.20 a pound, a total of $20,000. Increments to inventories in subsequent years were priced at the prices paid
for the first purchases during the year cumulating to the incremental
quantity.

The following table shows purchases and inventory data for the materials content of this product for the years 1962 through 1968:

| Year | Beginning-of-Year Inventory (Pounds) | Price Paid for First Purchases (per Pound) | Total Cost of Materials Purchased |
|------|------|------|------|
| 1962........ | 100,000 | $0.20 | $ 60,000 |
| 1963........ | 100,000 | 0.22 | 74,000 |
| 1964........ | 110,000 | 0.23 | 92,000 |
| 1965........ | 150,000 | 0.24 | 96,000 |
| 1966........ | 180,000 | 0.30 | 88,000 |
| 1967........ | 130,000 | 0.26 | 112,000 |
| 1968........ | 200,000 | 0.32 · | ? |

Because of the high purchase prices, the purchasing agent in 1968 deliberately bought less citrus fruit than the company was using. As a result, the inventory had dropped to 80,000 pounds by the end of October, 1968, the quantity referred to in the conversation quoted earlier. The purchasing agent's recommendation was to maintain inventories of this product at this level until the new crop was processed in the spring of 1969.

The controller opposed this and recommended that inventories be rebuilt to 200,000 pounds by the end of 1968, at a purchase price of about 32 cents a pound. He estimated that if this were not done, the lower inventory levels would increase purchasing and handling costs by $2,000 in 1968 and $400 in 1969.

Both executives were agreed that an inventory of 200,000 pounds of this product represented an optimum inventory level. If his proposal was accepted, the purchasing agent planned to rebuild inventories to this level as soon as the 1969 crop was processed. An average crop in 1969 would lead to a price of about $0.26 a pound.

The income tax in both years was 55 percent of taxable income.

a) Calculate the materials cost of goods sold and the materials cost of the end-of-year inventory of this product for each year, 1962–67.

b) Calculate the inventory holding gain or loss for each year, 1962–68. To do this, you should assume that citrus prices changed each year early in January, when inventories were still at their beginning-of-year levels, and remained constant throughout the year.

c) By how much would 1968 reported income before taxes have been increased or decreased if the purchasing agent's proposal had been accepted?

d) Assuming that all purchases are paid for immediately in cash, would the purchasing agent's proposal or the controller's alternative have led to a larger cash balance after inventories were replenished in 1969? What would have been the amount of the difference? Ignore interest costs.

e) Should the purchasing agent's proposal have been accepted? Would your conclusion be different if the company's inventory had been on Fifo? How, if at all, does the inventory costing method influence decisions of this kind?

# *12*

# DEPRECIATION POLICY

INVENTORIES consist of items that will provide their services all at once, when the individual items are used or sold. Long-life assets, in contrast, are bundles of services available for use in the future. These services will be used or wasted gradually, and service consumption is not directly observable. The depreciation charge is the accountant's effort to measure the proportion of a long-life asset's total lifetime *service potential* that has expired during the period. Similarly, the accumulated depreciation is the accountant's measure of the proportion of the total lifetime service potential that expired prior to the balance sheet date.

The purpose of this chapter is to explore the factors that the accountant might consider in calculating periodic depreciation charges:

1. The length of the asset's life.
2. The time pattern of the asset's usefulness.
3. Mortality distributions of groups of similar assets.
4. Changes in the underlying assumptions.
5. Changes in replacement cost.

Before examining these, however, we need to look briefly at three other approaches to the depreciation calculation.

## DEPRECIATION FOR NONACCOUNTING PURPOSES

Depreciation figures of a sort are required for several purposes other than the measurement of an organization's economic performance. These other depreciation figures should not be confused with depreciation estimates designed for use in the measurement of an entity's economic performance. Three of these are:

1. Depreciation for acquisition, use, and disposal decisions.
2. Depreciation for tax purposes.
3. Accumulation of funds for asset replacement.

### Depreciation for Acquisition, Use, and Disposal Decisions

The relevant measure of depreciation for any decision to acquire, use, or dispose of a long-life asset is the difference between the asset's current cash value and its cash value at the end of the period covered by the decision.

For instance, suppose that a machine costs $100,000 and that the expected future cash flows from its use amount to $12,000 a year for 20 years. The machine's scrap value is expected to be $5,000 at the end of that time. Lifetime depreciation in this case is $95,000, measured by the difference between the initial outlay and the end-of-life salvage value.

This depreciation is highly relevant to the decision to buy this machine, but it should not be expressed as a series of annual sums. Instead, it should be reflected in the analysis by entering one negative number ($100,000) and one positive number ($5,000) in a time table of anticipated cash flows:

| Years from Now | Cash Flow |
|---|---|
| 0 | −$100,000 |
| 1–20 | +    12,000/year |
| 20 | +     5,000 |

Management's concern is whether the present value of the operating cash flows exceeds the difference between the initial outlay and the present value of the end-of-life salvage value. How the accountant spreads the depreciation over the asset's life has no influence on the decision. Such charges neither increase nor decrease the amount of cash that management can spend or distribute in individual periods, and therefore must be ignored.[1]

The same kind of depreciation calculation applies to decisions made after an asset is acquired. If management is thinking of

---

[1] The present values of $12,000 a year for 20 years and of the $5,000 salvage value can be calculated by the methods described in Chapter 10. The capital expenditure decision will be examined further in Chapter 22.

selling an asset, for example, depreciation is measured by the difference between its current cash value and the cash value it will have in the future if it is not sold now, appropriately discounted. The decision is not affected by the machine's book value, based on the depreciation to date, or by the size of the annual depreciation charges during its remaining life.

### Depreciation and Taxes

Depreciation is also an allowable deduction from revenues for income tax determination. Since taxes are levied annually, portions of an asset's lifetime depreciation must be assigned to individual years for tax purposes. The allocation may be far different from the one appropriate for annual financial reporting, however. Although income tax regulations start from an accounting concept of income (and depreciation), they quickly acquire an overlay of adjustments and allowances designed to further specific public objectives.

For example, to encourage the purchase of certain kinds of assets, the government may allow taxpayers to expense the entire cost of any such purchases on the current tax return, even though the assets will be useful for many years. Depreciation measured in this way is not a measure of resource consumption and therefore has no legitimate place in income measurement.

### Depreciation and Asset Replacement

One of management's most important tasks is to see that funds are available when they are needed for the replacement of assets that have outlived their usefulness. Depreciation is expected to reduce the book value of the replaced assets to their salvage value at this time, but it should not be expected to generate the funds that will be necessary to pay for the replacement. This is not always understood.

To illustrate, let us assume that a firm's operating cash receipts exceed operating cash payments by $500,000. This $500,000 is available for capital expenditures and other purposes. The size of the depreciation charge affects only the amount of reported *income*, and not the *cash flow*. If the net cash flow from operations is negative, it provides no funds for replacement no matter how large the depreciation charge may be.

Another possible misunderstanding is very similar. Some have argued that the purpose of depreciation is to deduct from revenues an amount sufficient to recover the original investment (i.e., acquisition cost). Once again, the problem is that cost recovery depends on effective use of the asset rather than on depreciation policy. If the initial investment decision was sound and if assets have been managed effectively, the original cost will be recovered with enough funds left over to provide an adequate return on investment. If these conditions are absent, the original cost may not be recovered in full, no matter how large the depreciation charges are.

Depreciation deductions for tax purposes do affect annual cash flows, of course, because they affect the amount of the annual tax payments. As we have already noted, however, tax depreciation is not what we are talking about. The size of the annual depreciation charge for financial reporting affects the annual cash flow only in an indirect way. Depreciation charges make stockholders and directors aware of capital consumption. This may lead to smaller dividends and a retention of funds in the business. Although this is the effect, it is not the reason for depreciation. Directors may choose to declare dividends in excess of current income or, in the more usual case, to retain and reinvest portions of the funds generated by profitable operations. Depreciation in itself neither generates nor retains funds in the business.

## ECONOMIC LIFE

The first of the determinants of the accountant's depreciation charge is the period of time during which the asset will be useful. This period is known as the asset's economic life. It comes to an end and the asset is retired when either physical deterioration or obsolescence reduces the present value of the asset's future cash flows to less than its liquidation value.

### Physical Deterioration

Physical deterioration arises through asset use, the passage of time, or accidental damage. Its consequence is a decline in the quantity or quality of the asset's output or a rise in its unit cost. The effect of wear and age on output quantity or quality often can be offset or at least reduced by maintenance expenditures. At some point, however, the maintenance outlays needed to accomplish this begin to increase, and eventually they become so large that replacement or retirement becomes preferable to continued operation.

## Obsolescence

In a dynamic economy, obsolescence is frequently more important than wear and age in impairing and eventually terminating the useful lives of plant and equipment.

Obsolescence sometimes results from a revolutionary development such as a sudden shift in market demand. When this happens, the asset's life is likely to come to a sudden end if it is highly specialized and incapable of being converted to other uses.

Evolutionary obsolescence takes place more gradually, through developments that lower the cost or increase the output of the latest available equipment. As this happens, the old asset will have a greater and greater disadvantage in annual cash flows relative to the best available alternative. When this spread gets large enough, replacement will become profitable and the old asset's life will come to an end.

Economic life is more likely to be determined by obsolescence than by wear and tear. Few assets are replaced in kind because they are worn out. Most are either replaced by something better or are retired because they no longer serve a big enough need. This must be taken into consideration in the establishment of the rate and pattern of depreciation charges.

## DEPRECIATION TIME PATTERNS

Once life has been estimated, the next problem is to decide what percentage of the asset's total lifetime service potential is likely to expire each year.

Depreciation in practice is almost always calculated either by straight-line or by diminishing-charge methods. Before we examine these, however, we need to look briefly at two other methods: implicit interest and production-unit depreciation.

### Implicit Interest Depreciation

A depreciation method that is consistent with the economics of the acquisition decision is the implicit interest method. This method produces a constant reported return on reported investment throughout the asset's life, if the cash flows materialize as predicted.

For example, suppose that a new machine costing $36,000 is expected to produce cash receipts of $10,000 a year for 12 years. The company expects to be able to sell the machine for $1,500 at the end of that time. Although in practice end-of-life resale value for most depreciable assets is assumed to be zero, we shall assume a value of $1,500 as a means of bringing all of the determinants of the depreciation charge into the illustration.

These cash flows can be found to be equivalent to an annual rate of return of 26.13 percent over the asset's entire life.[2] A depreciation schedule to produce this rate of return every year, if the cash flows are as predicted, is reproduced in Exhibit 12–1. As

Exhibit 12–1

IMPLICIT INTEREST DEPRECIATION

(Annual Cash Flow, $10,000; Life, 12 Years; Salvage, $1,500)

| (1) Year | (2) Book Value, Beginning of Year | (3) Income For Year (2) x 26.13% | (4) Depreciation for Year $10,000 − (3) |
|---|---|---|---|
| 1 | $36,000 | $9,407 | $ 593 |
| 2 | 35,407 | 9,252 | 748 |
| 3 | 34,659 | 9,056 | 944 |
| 4 | 33,715 | 8,810 | 1,190 |
| 5 | 32,525 | 8,499 | 1,501 |
| 6 | 31,024 | 8,107 | 1,893 |
| 7 | 29,131 | 7,612 | 2,388 |
| 8 | 26,743 | 6,988 | 3,012 |
| 9 | 23,731 | 6,201 | 3,799 |
| 10 | 19,932 | 5,208 | 4,792 |
| 11 | 15,140 | 3,956 | 6,044 |
| 12 | 9,096 | 2,377 | 7,623 |
| 13 | 1,473 | — | — |
| Total | | | $34,527* |

* The $27 difference from total depreciable cost ($36,000 − $1,500) is due to rounding errors.

this shows, earnings for the first year must be $9,407 if the asset is to earn 26.13 percent on the initial investment of $36,000. ($9,407 ÷ $36,000 = 26.13%.) This leaves only $593 of the $10,000 cash flow to cover amortization of the asset's cost.

The book value at the start of the second year therefore is $36,000 − $593 = $35,407 (column 2, line 2). A 26.13 percent return on this amount would be $9,252 (column 3), leaving $748 of the $10,000 cash flow for depreciation. Repeating this process

[2] This is the rate of discount at which the present value of the anticipated future savings plus the present value of the end-of-life salvage is equal to the initial outlay of $36,000. The techniques employed to make this calculation were described in Chapter 10 and will be explained further in Chapter 22.

for all 12 years produces the figures shown in column 4 of the exhibit.

This method is virtually unused in external financial reporting. One possible reason is that a cash flow forecast is not always made or given to the accountant. This is a weak argument, however, because every depreciation method is based either implicitly or explicitly on cash flow forecasts. The issue cannot be dodged.

Probably more important, depreciation charges that increase as assets get older run counter to the popular presumption that assets are at worst equally productive throughout their lives and at best more productive in their early years than later on. The implicit interest method is more likely than other methods to produce depreciation charges that increase as the assets age, and it is rejected for this reason.

### Production-Unit Depreciation

One method that ignores implicit interest is production-unit depreciation. This method is based on two assumptions: (1) that the asset's life will end as soon as it has yielded a specified number of units of output or hours of use, and (2) that each unit is equally valuable. The depreciation rate is calculated as follows:

$$\text{Depreciation/unit} = \frac{\text{Original Cost} - \text{Estimated Salvage Value}}{\text{Lifetime Production Capacity (Units)}}.$$

The depreciation charge in any year is then equal to the number of units of output (pounds, gallons, or usage hours) multiplied by the unit depreciation rate.

For example, suppose that abrasion of certain high-cost moving parts is expected to limit the life of the new machine to 20,000 hours, after which it will have a $1,500 salvage value. The rate reflecting these assumptions is:

$$\frac{\$36,000 - \$1,500}{20,000 \text{ hours}} = \$1.725 \text{ an hour.}$$

If the machine is used for 1,000 hours during the first year, production-unit depreciation for that year will be 1,000 × $1.725 = $1,725.

This method is used most widely in recording *depletion* of such natural resources as mineral deposits, in which useful life ordinarily terminates with the exhaustion of the deposits. For most other assets, life is determined more by obsolescence than by use, and other methods are appropriate.

## Straight-Line Depreciation

In straight-line depreciation, the depreciation charge is the same amount each year, no matter how lightly or heavily the asset is used. If our new machine is expected to last 12 years, with a $1,500 end-of-life resale value, the straight-line annual charge will be:

$$\frac{\$36,000 - \$1,500}{12} = \$2,875.$$

The argument for straight-line depreciation is that it parallels the time pattern of benefits whenever these benefits are expected to remain constant from year to year. If interest were taken into consideration in the calculation of benefits, straight-line depreciation would be appropriate only when the interest-free benefits were heavy in the early years and declined steadily thereafter. Since accepted accounting practice is to ignore the interest element of service benefit, however, straight-line depreciation is sanctioned when pre-interest benefits are expected to remain constant.

## Diminishing-Charge Depreciation Methods

As the term implies, diminishing-charge depreciation methods produce periodic depreciation charges that decline from year to year during the asset's life. Methods of this type are presumed to be appropriate if the benefits are expected to decline as the asset gets older.

The ideal way to implement this idea would be to base each year's depreciation on that year's proportionate share of the estimated total net cash receipts during the asset's lifetime. For example, suppose that savings from the machine during its entire lifetime are expected to total $90,000, with $18,000 coming in the first year and $15,000 in the second. The correct depreciation under these circumstances would be one fifth of the depreciable cost, or $6,900, in the first year, and one sixth, or $5,750, in the second year.

Unfortunately, this solution requires a more precise knowledge of the year-to-year pattern of cash flows than is likely to obtain in practice. For these reasons, declining-charge depreciation is usually derived from some simple formula. The most widely used diminishing-charge formulas in the United States are the *sum-of-the-years' digits* and *double rate, declining balance* formulas.

The depreciation patterns that these formulas produce are to some extent arbitrary, but they may conform more closely than straight-line methods to the expected pattern of cash receipts.

*Sum-of-the-Years' Digits Depreciation.* The first step in the sum-of-the-years' digits method is to number each year of the asset's anticipated life, starting with the number one for the first year, two for the second, and so on. Thus if $n$ represents the asset's life in years, each year from 1 to $n$ can be represented by a digit, 1, 2, 3, . . . ., $n$.

The next step is to add these digits together to get their sum. For example, if $n = 12$, the sum of the digits is $1 + 2 + . . . + 12 = 78$. Next, a depreciation rate is computed for each year by dividing the sum of the digits (78) into the individual digits arranged in reverse order. In this case, the digit 12 is assigned to year 1, the digit 11 to year 2, and so on. The depreciation rates are 12/78 for the first year, 11/78 for the second, and so on. Finally, these rates are multiplied by the depreciable amount (cost less estimated salvage value) to determine the annual depreciation charges.

In the example, total depreciable cost is $36,000 − $1,500 = $34,500. The first year's depreciation is 12/78 x $34,500 = $5,308. This figure is shown in the first line of the second column of Exhibit 12–2. The rest of this column lists the depreciation charges for subsequent years, computed in this way. Book value at the end of 12 years is $1,500, the estimated resale value at that time.

*Exhibit 12–2*

COMPARISON OF DEPRECIATION METHODS

| Year | Sum-of-the-Years' Digits | | Double-Rate, Declining-Balance | | Straight-Line | |
|---|---|---|---|---|---|---|
| | Beginning Book Value | Annual Charge | Beginning Book Value | Annual Charge | Beginning Book Value | Annual Charge |
| 1 ........ | $36,000 | $ 5,308 | $36,000 | $ 6,000 | $36,000 | $ 2,875 |
| 2 ........ | 30,692 | 4,865 | 30,000 | 5,000 | 33,125 | 2,875 |
| 3 ........ | 25,827 | 4,423 | 25,000 | 4,167 | 30,250 | 2,875 |
| 4 ........ | 21,404 | 3,981 | 20,833 | 3,472 | 27,375 | 2,875 |
| 5 ........ | 17,423 | 3,538 | 17,361 | 2,894 | 24,500 | 2,875 |
| 6 ........ | 13,885 | 3,096 | 14,467 | 2,411 | 21,625 | 2,875 |
| 7 ........ | 10,789 | 2,654 | 12,056 | 2,009 | 18,750 | 2,875 |
| 8 ........ | 8,135 | 2,211 | 10,047 | 1,709 | 15,875 | 2,875 |
| 9 ........ | 5,924 | 1,769 | 8,338 | 1,709 | 13,000 | 2,875 |
| 10 ........ | 4,155 | 1,327 | 6,629 | 1,709 | 10,125 | 2,875 |
| 11 ........ | 2,828 | 885 | 4,920 | 1,709 | 7,250 | 2,875 |
| 12 ........ | 1,943 | 443 | 3,211 | 1,709 | 4,375 | 2,875 |
| 13 ........ | 1,500 | − | 1,502 | − | 1,500 | − |
| Total | | $34,500 | | $34,498 | | $34,500 |

*Double-Rate, Declining-Balance Depreciation.* Double-rate, declining-balance depreciation is calculated by multiplying a fixed rate by the asset's book value at the beginning of each year. Since book value declines each year, the depreciation charge also declines.

The depreciation rate specified in this method is twice the reciprocal of the asset's expected life, with no explicit recognition of the anticipated end-of-life salvage value. For our machine with a life of 12 years, the rate is $2 \times 1/12 = 16 \ 2/3$ percent. The depreciation charges determined by this method are shown in the fourth column of Exhibit 13–2. The charge is $0.167 \times \$36,000 = \$6,000$ for the first year, $0.167 \times (\$36,000 - \$6,000) = \$5,000$ the second year, and so on.

Notice that the annual depreciation charge stabilizes at \$1,709 in the eighth year. This is necessary if the depreciation charges are to reduce the machine's book value to \$1,500 at the end of 12 years.[3] Unless modified in this way, declining-charge depreciation for the seventh year would be only $0.167 \times \$10,047 = \$1,674$. This is less than one-fifth of the amount still to be depreciated ($\$10,047 - \$1,500 = \$8,547$), and use of the declining charge for the final five years would leave a final book value far in excess of the anticipated salvage value. To avoid this, the practice is to switch to straight-line depreciation in the year that the declining balance charge falls below the average remaining depreciable amount. This took place in the eighth year.

Both sum-of-the-years' digits and double-rate, declining-balance depreciation methods will produce depreciation charges that are greater than straight-line depreciation in the earlier years of an asset's life and smaller in the later years. (Figures for the straight-line method are shown for comparison in the right-hand column of Exhibit 12–2.) Book values under either of the diminishing-charge methods are lower in all years than book values under straight-line depreciation.

## Pragmatic Considerations

For accuracy in income measurement, management should use the depreciation formula that most closely approximates the anticipated pattern of benefits from the ownership and use of the asset. Unfortunately, the independent public accountant cannot

---

[3] In the absence of strong opposing evidence, business firms tend to estimate zero salvage value for this purpose. In this case, the depreciation charge for each of the last five years would be $\$10,047 \div 5 = \$2,009$.

really enforce this kind of accounting standard. Solid evidence to support or refute management's choice of a depreciation pattern is almost never available, and in the absence of such evidence management is free to use any method it chooses.

This being the case, management's choice is likely to be based either on convenience or on the effect on reported income. The cheapest and most convenient solution is to base depreciation for public reporting on the method used for income tax purposes. Pragmatic considerations support the use of a declining charge method for tax purposes, since taxable income and taxes paid are lower as long as the firm's depreciable assets are growing. Convenience, therefore, would seem to dictate the use of a declining charge method for external financial reporting as well.

In this situation, however, convenience is likely to be less important than the effect on reported income. Since straight-line depreciation in a growing company is smaller than declining-charge depreciation, use of the latter for external reporting will depress reported income. If management wishes to show a larger net income figure on its annual report without losing its tax advantages, it will use straight-line depreciation for public reporting and declining-charge depreciation for tax purposes. Some of the issues that this raises will be examined in Chapter 14.

In this connection, it is interesting to note that a number of companies changed their depreciation method during the business recession of the early 1970s. Most of these changes substituted straight-line depreciation for declining-charge methods and the effect was to increase reported income.[4] Providing more operational criteria for the selection of depreciation methods is one of the accounting profession's most pressing tasks.

## GROUP DEPRECIATION

The statement that the expected life of an asset, say a truck, is six years means that the *average* truck will last six years. Some trucks will, in fact, be retired in their first year, and some will remain in use 10 years or longer. This is the *normal* expectation. It may, therefore, be considered incorrect to assign a life of six years to *each* truck and to recognize a gain or loss on retirement for any individual truck that has a life of more or less than six years.

On this reasoning, and for other reasons to be noted shortly, many companies use *group depreciation* for many of their assets

---

[4] Charles W. Lamden and Dale L. Gerboth, "Depreciation: The Incantation and the Reality," *PMM&Co. World*, Autumn, 1972, pp. 6–13.

instead of the *item depreciation* that has been implicit in all the previous discussion. Under group depreciation, all items with generally similar average life expectancies are grouped together in a single asset category. One summary account is established for each group, and the original cost of all assets in the group is charged to this account. Depreciation is charged for the group in total and not item by item, and may be either straight-line or declining-balance. The depreciation rate is based on expected average service life for the group, and this rate is multiplied by the depreciable amount to determine the depreciation charge for the year.

Up to now, nothing has been introduced to distinguish group depreciation from item depreciation. The only really unique feature of the group method is that *each unit retired is assumed to be fully depreciated down to the actual proceeds from the sale of the unit.* Thus, no gain or loss is recorded on any item retired in the normal course of events.

To illustrate, assume that a company purchases 100 identical machines on January 1 at a cost of $1,000 each. On the basis of the company's past experience, these 100 machines are expected to follow the mortality pattern shown in the first two columns of Exhibit 12–3. Although the average life expectancy for these

### Exhibit 12–3
### GROUP METHOD DEPRECIATION FOR A GROUP
### OF 100 IDENTICAL ASSETS COSTING $1,000 EACH

| (1)<br>Years<br>after<br>Acquisition | (2)<br>No. of<br>Items<br>Retired<br>during<br>Year | (3)<br>Average<br>Age<br>of Items<br>Retired<br>during Year | (4)<br>Total Life<br>of Items<br>Retired<br>during Year<br>(2) × (3) | (5)<br>Number of<br>Machines<br>in Use<br>during<br>Year | (6)<br>Group<br>Method<br>Depreciation<br>for Year<br>(5) × $200 |
|---|---|---|---|---|---|
| 1 . . . . . . . . . . | 3 | 1 | 3 | 100 | $ 20,000 |
| 2 . . . . . . . . . . | 9 | 2 | 18 | 97 | 19,400 |
| 3 . . . . . . . . . . | 15 | 3 | 45 | 88 | 17,600 |
| 4 . . . . . . . . . . | 25 | 4 | 100 | 73 | 14,600 |
| 5 . . . . . . . . . . | 14 | 5 | 70 | 48 | 9,600 |
| 6 . . . . . . . . . . | 10 | 6 | 60 | 34 | 6,800 |
| 7 . . . . . . . . . . | 8 | 7 | 56 | 24 | 4,800 |
| 8 . . . . . . . . . . | 6 | 8 | 48 | 16 | 3,200 |
| 9 . . . . . . . . . . | 4 | 9 | 36 | 10 | 2,000 |
| 10 . . . . . . . . . . | 3 | 10 | 30 | 6 | 1,200 |
| 11 . . . . . . . . . . | 2 | 11 | 22 | 3 | 600 |
| 12 . . . . . . . . . . | 1 | 12 | 12 | 1 | 200 |
| Total . . . . . . | 100 | | 500 | 500 | $100,000 |

machines is five years,[5] 34 of them will still be in service at the beginning of the 6th year, and all the machines will not be retired until the end of year 12.

To simplify the calculations, depreciation is assumed to be by the straight-line method, with estimated salvage value of zero. It is also assumed, again for simplicity, that retirements always take place at the end of the year.

The average life expectancy is used as the basis for depreciation charges both in group depreciation and in item depreciation. The straight-line rate for a five-year life is 20 percent, or $200 per machine. Under either method, the first year's depreciation would be 20 percent of $100,000, or $20,000. The difference between the two methods lies in the treatment of the machines retired during the year. Under item depreciation, the accountant would record a $2,400 loss on retirement (original cost of $3,000, less a year's depreciation, 20 percent of $3,000, or $600). Under the group method, in contrast, it is assumed that $3,000 of the first year's depreciation for the group applies to the items retired. In other words, book value is assumed to be equal to the sale value of the property retired, in this case zero. The entry will be:

Allowance for Depreciation ....................... 3,000
    Machines .......................................         3,000

No gain or loss will be recognized as a result of the retirements because *they are entirely expected.*

If the actual mortality experience is as shown in column 2 of Exhibit 12–3 and if salvage value at retirement is always zero, group depreciation charges will be as shown in column 6. These figures are obtained by multiplying the original cost of the machines still in service at the beginning of the year by 20 percent (or by multiplying the number of active machines by $200, which amounts to the same thing).

Notice that group depreciation charges are made as long as the assets are in service, provided that the original mortality estimates were correct. Under item depreciation, in contrast, charges are made only for the first five years, as in Exhibit 12–4. Depreciation charges (column 5 of this exhibit) are the same for these five years as under group depreciation. In addition, however, a retirement loss is recognized on each machine retired during this

---

[5] The calculation of average service life is summarized in column (4). The three machines retired during the first year are assumed to have "lived" approximately one year each, or three years in total. The entire group of 100 machines is expected to live a total of 500 machine-years, an average of 5 years per machine. This is the actuarially determined expected average service life of all the assets in this group.

*Exhibit 12–4*

### DEPRECIATION CHARGES AND RETIREMENT LOSSES
### UNDER ITEM METHOD OF DEPRECIATION

| (1) Year | (2) Number of Items Retired during Year | (3) End-of-Year Book Value per Machine | (4) Loss on Retirement (2) × (3) | (5) Depreciation (from Exhibit 12–3) | (6) Total Charges (4) + (5) |
|---|---|---|---|---|---|
| 1 . . . . . . . | 3 | $800 | $ 2,400 | $20,000 | $ 22,400 |
| 2 . . . . . . . | 9 | 600 | 5,400 | 19,400 | 24,800 |
| 3 . . . . . . . | 15 | 400 | 6,000 | 17,600 | 23,600 |
| 4 . . . . . . . | 25 | 200 | 5,000 | 14,600 | 19,600 |
| 5 . . . . . . . | 14 | 0 | 0 | 9,600 | 9,600 |
| Total . | 66 | | $18,800 | $81,200 | $100,000 |

period. Because salvage value is zero, the retirement loss is the book value of the machines retired. At the end of 5 years, the assets are fully depreciated, even though 34 of them are still in service.

The year-by-year differences in charges against revenues are pictured in Exhibit 12–5. During the first four years, the depreciation and retirement losses under item depreciation are substantially greater than those under the group method. The two meth-

*Exhibit 12–5*

### ITEM VERSUS GROUP DEPRECIATION:
### ANNUAL DIFFERENCES IN REVENUE DEDUCTIONS
(Depreciation plus Retirement Losses)

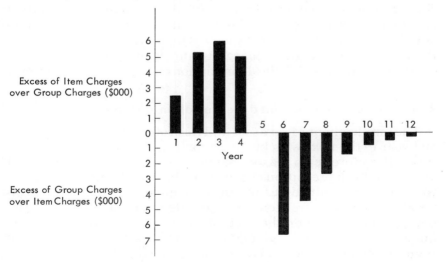

ods produce the same net results in the fifth year, but thereafter group depreciation charges continue whereas item depreciation charges are zero. The details will differ with different assumptions as to the mortality pattern, but this is representative of the general result.

The figures will be different if salvage values are present, of course, but the approach is the same. Suppose, for example, that the depreciation rate of 20 percent was based on a four-year estimated life and $200 salvage value per machine. Suppose further that the three machines retired in the first year are sold for a total price of $350. Unless the evidence is strong that this represents an abnormally high mortality rate, group depreciation will recognize no gain or loss on the retirements. The entry will be:

```
Cash..............................................    350
Allowance for Depreciation ......................  2,650
     Machines ....................................         3,000
```

Salvage on these three machines is below expectations, but this might be offset by above-average recoveries in the future. The depreciation rate will not be changed until more evidence is accumulated that the original forecasts were wrong.

## DEPRECIATION ADJUSTMENTS

The depreciation charge in each year of an asset's life is determined by the cost and estimated life at time of acquisition and by the depreciation method in force at the time of acquisition. This complete predetermination of the periodic depreciation charge is departed from on the basis of subsequent information only in exceptional circumstances. Why is that so if accuracy in the periodic depreciation charge is important, and what are the conditions under which the depreciation charges will be changed?

### Rationale for Predetermined Depreciation Charges

The employment of an asset and its profitability fluctuate from one year to the next with business conditions and other factors. It might therefore seem reasonable to believe that in the interest of accuracy the depreciation charge in each year should depart from the figure determined at the time of acquisition. At one time corporations had the freedom to adjust depreciation charges from one year to the next on the basis of current conditions. The consequence was that the depreciation charge was raised in years of high profits before depreciation and reduced in bad years.

High profits are usually associated with operations at a high percentage of capacity and vice versa. Raising the depreciation charge when profits are high and vice versa might therefore seem reasonable if usage is the primary determinant of depreciation. However, for most assets obsolescence is a more important cause of depreciation than wear and tear. When business is good the threat of obsolescence recedes into the future; when an asset is idle because there are few or no opportunities for its profitable use, the likelihood that it will be retired or abandoned soon increases. Furthermore, it is extremely difficult for the accountant to determine objectively how much the depreciation charge for a year should be reduced due to lower use and how much it should be increased due to higher obsolescence. A flexible depreciation schedule therefore would give management a great deal of latitude in setting the depreciation charge. This latitude might even be great enough to permit management to adjust reported income to any level it wishes to present in its annual report.

To avoid this, accountants have concluded that the periodic charging of depreciation is an area in which the informational content of financial statements is better served by objectivity than by accuracy. The predetermination of depreciation charges at the time of acquisition undoubtedly results in measurement errors. Attempting to reduce these errors by allowing management to vary the depreciation charge at will opens the financial statements to manipulation by management, and this is considered even more damaging to the usefulness of the statements.

## Write-Downs of Assets

The accountant is not completely inflexible in adhering to the predetermined schedule of depreciation charges over an asset's life. He will make such changes if they are supported by evidence that is highly convincing.

This happens very infrequently, but revisions are sometimes made when it becomes inescapably clear that the economic value of the asset's remaining service potential or profitability has fallen materially below its book value, to such an extent that future cyclical fluctuations in business conditions are unlikely to reverse this development. A write-down of the asset is appropriate to recognize both the decline in the asset and the decline in the owners' equity. An entry to accomplish this would be:

Write-down of Fixed Assets.......................... xxx  
    Accumulated Depreciation .......................     xxx

A write-down of this kind would be deducted from revenues on the current period's income statement. After this was done, depreciation for subsequent periods would be recomputed so as to amortize the remaining depreciable cost over the remaining life.

## Change in Depreciation Method

Another occasion for adjustment is a decision that the wrong depreciation method has been used. After an asset or group of assets has been in service for a full year or more, the owner may decide that the original choice of a depreciation method was incorrect. When a change is made from one method to another, the beginning-of-year balance in the Accumulated Depreciation account must be restated at the level it would have reached if the new method had been used from the outset.

For example, suppose that Stengel Electric selected the sum-of-the-years'-digits method to calculate depreciation on the McGraw machine. At the end of four years, accumulated depreciation amounted to $18,577 (see Exhibit 12–2). During the fifth year, management decided that straight-line depreciation would have been more appropriate for this asset and the public accountant agreed. The annual depreciation charge on a straight-line basis would have been $2,875, adding up to $11,500 for the first four years. To effect the change in method, therefore, the accountant would have to reduce the beginning balance in the Accumulated Depreciation account by $7,077. The entry would be:

Accumulated Depreciation . . . . . . . . . . . . . . . . . . . . . . . . 7,077
    Change in Depreciation Method . . . . . . . . . . . . . . . .       7,077

The Change in Depreciation Method account is a temporary owners' equity account. If the straight-line method had been used from the beginning, prior years' income before taxes would have been $7,077 greater than the total amount reported. The credit to this account is to restore this amount to the owners' equity. At one time the adjustment would have been credited directly to Retained Earnings, as a correction to prior years' income figures which were reflected incorrectly in the retained earnings balance at the beginning of the year. To provide greater visibility for the effects of these changes, however, the accounting profession now insists that they be shown on the income statement, after any extraordinary items but before the net income figure.

As we shall see in more detail in Chapter 14, reported income tax expense is based on the revenues and expenses shown on the income statement rather than the figures on the income tax return. Revision of past depreciation expense therefore requires retroactive revision of past income tax expense. This means that the adjustment to retained earnings must reflect both the retroactive change in depreciation charges and the retroactive change in income tax expense. In this case, the after-tax adjustment, based on an assumed tax rate of 55 percent, would have been $3,185. In other words, the balance in Retained Earnings would have been $3,185 greater if straight-line depreciation had been used from the outset.[6]

### Revision of Life Estimates

When evidence is found that a life estimate is seriously wrong, a change in the depreciation rate is necessary. Errors of this sort are inevitable, and discoveries of such errors are likely to occur frequently. The accounting profession has taken the position that repeated adjustments of reported income to reflect changes in accounting estimates would be more confusing than informative. As a result, the accepted practice is to spread the remaining depreciable amount over the revised estimate of remaining life, with no retroactive correction.[7]

For example, suppose that an asset's book value is $150,000 and that the remaining life estimate has been shortened from five years to three, with no salvage value. Under straight-line depreciation, the annual depreciation charge would be raised from $30,000 to $50,000 a year. The accumulated depreciation from prior years would not be changed to reflect the new estimate.

A related issue is how to account for major overhauls that extend an asset's total economic life. This is really a question of whether to capitalize the cost of the overhaul, and we shall deal with it when we consider questions of this sort in the next chapter.

## DEPRECIATION BASED ON CURRENT COST

The ownership of fixed assets gives rise to the same kind of holding gains and losses as ownership of inventories. Furthermore, depreciation based on historical cost introduces a portion of these holding gains and losses into reported income without labeling them as holding gains and losses.

Conversion of the fixed assets to a current cost basis is ordinarily more difficult than current costing of inventories. Many

---

[6] For a more complete statement of this adjustment, see American Institute of Certified Public Accountants, *APB Accounting Principles: Current Text* (New York: Commerce Clearing House, Inc. 1972), Sec. 1051.22.

[7] *APB Accounting Principles*, Sec. 1051.31.

fixed assets are unique (a particular plot of land, a particular building, a special-purpose machine), while others are no longer included in the manufacturer's catalog. In both cases, specific replacement prices are not readily available. Instead, index numbers representing changes in the replacement prices of broad categories of assets (industrial equipment, office buildings, and so forth) must be used to approximate current cost.

For example, suppose that the price index for industrial machinery was 120 at the time the machine in our earlier example was bought and rose by six points every six months thereafter. To simplify the arithmetic, let us assume that historical cost depreciation was $3,000 a year, based on a 12-year life, straight-line depreciation, and zero salvage value. Since the average index number for the first year was 126, current cost depreciation was $126/120 \times \$3,000 = \$3,150$. In other words, $150 of the reported income for the year really represented a holding gain on this machine, not part of the operating margin.

To compute the current cost of the machine at the end of the year, both the original cost and the accumulated depreciation must be restated. With the year-end index six points higher than the average, at 132, the conversion of the original cost would be $132/120 \times \$36,000 = \$39,600$. The $3,000 accumulated depreciation would be converted in the same way: $132/120 \times \$3,000 = \$3,300$. Book value, in other words, would be $\$39,600 - \$3,300 = \$36,300$. This contrasts with the historical cost book value of $\$36,000 - \$3,000 = \$33,000$. The $3,300 difference between these two book value figures was the unrealized holding gain for the year.

The arguments for current costing here are the same as those summarized in our discussion of inventory costing in Chapter 11. As time goes by, the price paid for an asset is less and less likely to be an adequate measure of the current cost of equivalent services. The income statement becomes a mixture of revenues measured in terms of the current value of assets received in exchange for the company's goods and services, expenses measured in terms of the current prices of goods and services used, and other expenses measured in terms of prices that prevailed in various periods in the past.

Furthermore, the historical cost margin provides a poorer basis for forecasting future income than the current cost margin. As assets are replaced, historical cost depreciation will rise. An investor who bases his share purchase decision on an assumption that current income margins will continue is likely to be disappointed.

Further discussion would be inappropriate here, but it is worth mentioning that current costing of fixed assets has been used in a number of countries that have experienced extreme rates of inflation. In these cases, unrealized holding gains have been excluded from reported income on the grounds that they are unreal, the result of the erosion of the purchasing power of money. Fairly crude index numbers have been used in most of these cases, easy to administer and politically acceptable. Probably the most careful and painstaking application to public financial reporting has been made by several large Dutch companies, notably the huge Philips group, but this has had little impact on practice in the United States.[8]

## SUMMARY

Reporting annual depreciation charges and the book value of depreciated assets serves no purpose unless these figures affect decisions. The accounting model presumes that income and asset figures will influence investors' decisions to buy or sell shares in the company and a wide variety of managerial decisions as well.

For these purposes the accountant must estimate the amount of each asset's service potential that is consumed during each period and the amount that remains at the end of the period. Because patterns of depreciation are difficult to identify, the accountant has generally used some simple formula as an approximation. The most widely used formulas are straight-line (uniform annual amounts) and declining-charge methods (smaller amounts in each succeeding year).

Many authorities believe that these formulas should be applied to estimates of current replacement cost each year rather than to original cost. This would eliminate holding gains from the reported operating margin, thereby making operating income a better indicator of the economic viability of the company's operations. Although this has been done in a number of countries, in the United States historical cost always sets an upper limit on the amount of depreciation to be charged during an asset's lifetime.

Depreciation charges calculated on a group basis are likely to reflect the expiration of service potentials better than individual

---

[8] The Philips method has been described by A. Goudeket, "An Application of Replacement Value Theory," *The Journal of Accountancy*, July 1960, pp. 37–47. The limited United States experience is described in American Institute of Certified Public Accountants, *Reporting the Financial Effects of Price-Level Changes*, Accounting Research Study No. 6 (New York: AICPA, 1963).

item depreciation. Forecasting errors occur even when this is done, however, and the accountant must be prepared to revise depreciation rates whenever substantial evidence is found that the pattern of service potential consumption differs from the forecasted pattern.

## QUESTIONS AND PROBLEMS

1. Why is the depreciation expense for any one year more difficult to calculate than insurance expense? Can depreciation be measured by factual observation?

2. What is meant by "service potential?" Why is it important in discussions of depreciation policy?

3. Is depreciation purely a concept related to public financial reporting or does it have managerial significance as well?

4. To what extent, if at all, is the objective of depreciation to provide funds for the replacement of depreciating plant and equipment?

5. What are the causes of depreciation? To what extent can they be controlled by management?

6. What is meant by the "economic life" of a depreciating asset? When does it come to an end?

7. Should the depreciation shown on the firm's published income statement always be identical to that shown on its income tax return?

8. In concept, the size of an asset's estimated end-of-life salvage value should influence the depreciation schedule for the asset. In practice, depreciation schedules are often drawn on the assumption that salvage value will be zero. What effects will this assumption have on the company's financial statements?

9. Company X depreciates its equipment on a straight-line basis, while Company Y uses a declining-charge method. Are the depreciation charges of these two companies necessarily noncomparable?

10. What kind of evidence would the public accountant need if he wished to dispute management's choice of a depreciation method? Is this evidence likely to be readily available?

11. The Pilot Company has just purchased a piece of equipment. This equipment is expected to produce approximately the same number of units of product each year until it is retired, and the company sees no

reason why the prices of the products sold will either increase or decrease during the machine's lifetime. Operating and repair costs per year are expected to increase each year, however, and economic life is expected to come to an end seven years from now when the cost savings from a new machine will be adequate to justify replacement.

What method would you use to calculate annual depreciation charges on this machine? State your reasons.

**12.** How does group depreciation differ from item depreciation? Under what circumstances would group depreciation be preferable to item depreciation?

**13.** State the argument for basing depreciation on current replacement cost rather than original cost. If current cost depreciation is used, is it likely that the lifetime total of these charges will equal the asset's replacement cost at the time of replacement?

**14.** Depreciation methods that led to an earlier amortization of cost used to find support from corporate executives as a partial means of adjusting the income statement for the effects of inflation. This argument was not heard in the inflation of the early 1970s; instead, many corporations shifted from diminshing-charge depreciation methods to straight-line methods for external financial reporting.

*a)* To what extent, if any, does diminishing-charge depreciation provide an adjustment for inflation?
*b)* What might account for the apparent change of opinion in the early 1970s?

**15.** The controller of Miller Enterprises, Inc., proposes that in view of rising prices of equipment, depreciation charges should be based on replacement cost. He suggests the use of the following journal entry:

```
Depreciation .................................................. X
    Allowance for Depreciation ...............................     Y
    Reserve for Replacement...................................     Z
```

where X is the depreciation charge based on replacement cost and Y is the regular depreciation charge based on acquisition cost.

*a)* What is the effect of the proposed method on reported profit during and after a period of rising equipment prices?
*b)* Where would the Reserve for Replacement appear on the company's statements? How would you interpret it?

**16.** A company purchased a large piece of equipment 15 years ago at a cost of $300,000. At that time it was estimated that the economic life of the equipment would be 20 years and that its ultimate scrap value would be $30,000.

Assuming that the company uses straight-line depreciation, study the following events and state whether each one necessitates a revision of the original depreciation rate, with reasons for your answer.

a) Due to recent price increases, the present replacement cost of the same type of equipment is $500,000.
b) For the same reason as in (a), end-of-life scrap value is now estimated at $50,000.
c) The company could sell the equipment now at a sale price of $100,000.
d) At the end of the last year, a major breakdown impaired the efficiency of this equipment. After a thorough overhaul, the equipment now has a productive capacity of 9,000 units per month instead of the initial capacity of 10,000 units per month. The company still expects to use the equipment for 5 more years, retiring it when it is 20 years old.

*17. T. Best, Inc., has been amortizing the cost of a machine for three years by the sum-of-the-years'-digits method. The machine cost $16,500, had an estimated life of 10 years, and a zero estimated salvage value. In the fourth year, Mr. Best decided that straight-line depreciation would have been more appropriate for this machine and asked the accountant to make the necessary adjustments.

a) Establish the original sum-of-the-years'-digits depreciation schedule for the first three years.
b) Calculate the amount of any adjustment that you think should have been made as of the beginning of the fourth year. (Ignore income taxes.) How would this adjustment be shown on the financial statements for the fourth year?

18. F. Coons, Inc., bought a large dump truck for $10,450. This truck was delivered on January 2, 19x1, and was placed in service immediately. Mr. Coons's past experience led him to believe that the costs of maintaining and operating the truck would rise as it grew older, and he decided to depreciate it by the sum-of-the-years'-digits method, based on a 6-year life and a $1,000 estimated end-of-life salvage value.

a) Prepare a depreciation schedule for this truck.
b) Recompute depreciation by the double-rate, declining-balance method.
c) Do the reasons advanced by Mr. Coons justify the use of sum-of-the-years'-digits depreciation?

19. A large machine costing $44,000 was placed in service on January 2, 19x1. Depreciation was calculated by the sum-of-the-years'-digits method, with an estimated life of 12 years and an estimated end-of-life salvage value of $5,000.

In the fourth year, management decided that depreciation should

---

* Solutions to problems marked with an asterisk (*) are found in Appendix B.

have been calculated on a straight-line basis, and the accountants made the adjustment that was necessary to reflect this change.

In the ninth year, it became clear that technological change in the machinery industry was progressing more slowly than had been originally anticipated and that therefore the machine would probably remain in service for 15 years instead of 12. The end-of-life salvage value was revised downward to $4,000. The accountants made the necessary adjustments to reflect this additional information.

The machine was sold for $2,000 at the end of the fifteenth year.

a) Calculate depreciation for each of the first three years.
b) Determine and describe the adjustment, if any, to be made in the fourth year to reflect the change in the depreciation method.
c) Calculate depreciation for each year from the fourth through the eighth year.
d) Determine and describe the adjustment, if any, to be made in the ninth year to reflect the changes in the estimates.
e) Calculate depreciation for each year from the ninth through the fifteenth year.
f) Prepare a journal entry to record the retirement and sale of the machine at the end of the fifteenth year.

**20.** A company has just bought a new electric typewriter for $500. The manufacturer of the typewriter will provide service on this typewriter for 8 years at an annual cost of $40. With this service contract, the typewriter will be inoperative, awaiting service, for approximately 5 days each year.

After 8 years, the manufacturer will provide service only on a time-and-parts basis. This arrangement is likely to be so expensive that the company will sell the typewriter at the end of 8 years. In the past, used electric typewriters have been sold to employees for about 20 percent of their original cost.

a) Which depreciation method would you recommend for this typewriter? Give your reasons. *straight-line*
b) Calculate the annual depreciation charge for each of the next 8 years. *$50/yr.*

**21.** On January 1, 19x1, the Lubberdink Company purchased a machine for $56,910. The machine was expected to produce cash savings at the rate of $15,000 a year for a period of five years and to have a salvage value of $5,000 at the end of that time.

a) Compare annual depreciation by the straight-line method. For each year, compute the ratio of the machine's earnings after depreciation to its book value as of January 1 of that year.
b) Recompute annual depreciation by the implicit interest method such that the annual rate of return on the machine's January 1 book value is 12 percent each year.
c) Is the rate of 12 percent an appropriate one to use in this case?

Could the implicit interest method have been applied with a rate such as 15 percent? Support your conclusion with appropriate calculations.

*22. A company has been using an annual depreciation rate of 20 percent of original cost for a certain type of office equipment. Now, after several years of experience, a study of actual equipment mortality rates indicates that the rate should have been based on a life of six years and an end-of-life resale value of 16 percent of original cost. The original cost of the equipment now on hand was $200,000, and its age is two years. Straight-line depreciation by the item method has been used.

a) If the company had known at the outset what it knows now, how much more or less would it have charged as depreciation in the past two years?
b) What adjustment, if any, should be made in the accounts at this time?
c) Calculate depreciation on this equipment for each of the next four years.

23. The Prometheus Bindery installed a new binding machine at the beginning of January, 19x1, to take the place of an old machine which had become obsolete. The old machine was sold to a salvage firm for $2,000 cash. Its original cost was $19,000, and depreciation of $12,000 had been accumulated prior to the retirement date.

The new machine was to be depreciated by the double-rate, declining-balance method. The following data were available at the time it was installed:

| | |
|---|---|
| Invoice price | $32,000 |
| Installation cost | 1,600 |
| Cash discount | 600 |
| Estimated end-of-life scrap value | 3,100 |
| Estimated economic life | 15 years |

At the beginning of the year 19x2, while the plant was temporarily closed for stock taking, a conveyor attachment was built onto the machine at a total cost of $2,900. After the books had been closed and the statements prepared for the year 19x1, the management decided, on the basis of the plant engineer's recommendation, that the depreciation on this machine should have been computed (and should be computed in the future) on a *production basis,* using a *machine-hour rate.* The following additional data were available as of January 1, 19x2:

| | |
|---|---|
| Estimated total life of machine from date of installation, January 1, 19x1 | 30,000 machine-hours |
| Production time for the year 19x1 | 3,000    "    " |
| New estimated scrap value of machine, including the conveyor | $ 3,200 |

*a*) Prepare journal entries to record the retirement of the old machine and the installation of the new machine on January 1, 19x1.

*b*) Compute the depreciation on the new machine for the year 19x1.

*c*) Prepare journal entries to record:
   (1) The installation of the conveyor in January, 19x2.
   (2) The correction of the accounts when the machine-hour rate of depreciation was established on January 1, 19x2. Indicate clearly how your adjustments would affect the financial statements for 19x2.

*d*) Compute the depreciation charge for 19x2. The machine operated 2,700 machine-hours during the year.

*24. The Votrun Corporation bought several pieces of equipment in 19x0 at a total price of $100,000. The estimated average service life of this equipment was 10 years, with an expected average salvage value of 10 percent of original cost. Acquisitions and retirements each year were assumed to take place on January 1. The following pieces of equipment were retired during the first three years.

| Year | Original Cost of Equipment Retired | Actual Salvage Recovered |
|---|---|---|
| 19x0.................. | $    0 | $    0 |
| 19x1.................. | 5,000 | 1,000 |
| 19x2.................. | 10,000 | 3,000 |

Give the entries to record depreciation and retirements for each of the three years:

*a*) Using group method, straight-line depreciation.

*b*) Using group method, double-rate, declining-balance depreciation.

25. In 19x1, Company Alpha bought 10 identical machines at a price of $10,000 each. These were thereafter depreciated on a *group basis* at a straight-line rate of 10 percent a year. In 19x4, four other machines of this same type were acquired at a price of $12,000 each, and were thereafter included in the same group with the other 10 for depreciation purposes. At the end of 19x8, two of the original machines were sold for $2,000 each. For convenience in computing depreciation, all purchases were assumed to take place as of the beginning of the year.

*a*) Compute the depreciation charge for the year 19x2.

*b*) Compute the depreciation charge for the year 19x5.

*c*) Prepare a journal entry to record the retirement and sale of two machines in 19x8.

*d*) Compute the depreciation charge for the year 19x9.

26. The Acme Company owns a large quantity of pumps and pumping equipment in various company locations. Although this equipment includes many different kinds and sizes of items, they are all expected to have approximately the same average service life, 10 years. End-of-life salvage value is assumed to be negligible. All equipment in this category is depreciated on a group basis, using a single group to include all items.

On December 31, 19x1, the balances in the property accounts were:

Pumping equipment...................................... $150,000
Allowance for depreciation – pumping equipment......... (75,000)

Acquisitions and retirements subsequent to this date were as follows (for ease of computation, assume that all acquisitions and retirements took place on January 1):

| Year | Acquisitions at Cost | Retirements | |
|---|---|---|---|
| | | Original Cost | Net Salvage |
| 19x2................. | $10,000 | $10,000 | $1,000 |
| 19x3................. | 25,000 | 15,000 | 3,000 |
| 19x4................. | ..... | 10,000 | .... |
| 19x5................. | 20,000 | 8,000 | 1,000 |
| 19x6................. | 25,000 | 30,000 | 4,000 |
| 19x7................. | 35,000 | 20,000 | Insurance |
| 19x8................. | 20,000 | 45,000 | 2,000 |

All retirements were of equipment on hand on December 31, 19x1, except for the 19x7 retirement. In 19x7, equipment that was purchased in 19x5 for $20,000 was completely destroyed by fire. The insurance recovery on the equipment destroyed in 19x7 amounted to $12,000.

a)  Prepare journal entries to record acquisitions and retirements, compute straight-line depreciation for each year, and compute the December 31, 19x8, balances in the two property accounts.

b)  Do this again on the assumption that the Acme Company depreciates each item separately rather than as part of a group, again at a 10 percent rate. Assume for simplicity that each item in the December 31, 19x1, property records was five years old (i.e., that accumulated depreciation was one half of original cost for each item as well as for the group as a whole). Also assume that each year's acquisition consisted of a single item.

c)  Which of these two methods gives (1) a more representative picture of annual income during the period, and (2) a more representative balance sheet as of December 31, 19x8? State your reasons.

27.† Faced with a substantial increase in the replacement cost of its

---

† This problem and the next are based on a situation that most students will regard as ancient history. The problems that U.S. Steel's practices were designed to solve are still present, however, and no recent examples of comparable practices by well-known United States companies are available.

plant and equipment, the United States Steel Corporation attempted to reflect current replacement costs in its depreciation charges for 1947. The method failed to gain wide support within the accounting profession and United States Steel returned to the historical cost basis in 1948. The following notes were appended to the company's financial statements for 1947, 1948, and 1949:

*1947 Annual Report:* "Wear and exhaustion of facilities of $114,045,483 includes $87,745,483 based on original cost of such facilities and $26,300,000 added to cover replacement cost. The added amount is 30 percent of provisions based on original cost, and is a step toward stating wear and exhaustion in an amount which will recover in current dollars of diminished buying power the same purchasing power as the original expenditure. Because it is necessary to recover the purchasing power of sums originally invested in tools so that they may be replaced as they wear out, this added amount is carried as a reserve for replacement of properties. The 30 percent was determined partly through experienced cost increases and partly through study of construction cost index numbers. Although it is materially less than the experienced cost increase in replacing worn out facilities, it was deemed appropriate in view of the newness of the application of this principle to the costing of wear and exhaustion."

*1948 Annual Report:* "A method of accelerated depreciation on cost was adopted in 1948 . . . and was made retroactive to January 1, 1947. Wear and exhaustion of facilities in 1948 includes accelerated depreciation of $55,335,444 including a deficiency of $2,675,094 in the amount of $26,300,000 reported in 1947 as depreciation added to cover replacement cost. Such accelerated depreciation is not presently deductible for federal income tax purposes.

"The accelerated depreciation is applicable to the cost of post-war facilities in the first few years of their lives, when the economic usefulness is greatest. The amount thereof is related to the excess of current operating rate over U.S. Steel's long-term peacetime average rate of 70 percent of capacity. The annual accelerated amount is 10 percent of the cost of facilities in the year in which the expenditures are made and 10 percent in the succeeding year, except that this amount is reduced ratably as the operating rate may drop, no acceleration being made at 70 percent or lower operations. The accelerated depreciation is in addition to the normal depreciation on such facilities but the total depreciation over their expected lives will not exceed the cost of the facilities."

*1949 Annual Report:* "Wear and exhaustion of facilities includes accelerated depreciation of $22,045,743 in 1949 and $55,335,444 in 1948. Such accelerated depreciation is not presently deductible for federal income tax purposes.

"The accelerated depreciation is applicable to the cost of post-war facilities in the first few years of their lives, when the economic usefulness is greatest. The amount thereof is related to the excess of current operating rate over U.S. Steel's long-term peace-time average rate of about 70 percent of capacity. The annual accelerated amount is 10 percent in the succeeding year, except that this amount is reduced ratably as the operating rate may drop, no acceleration being made at 70 percent or lower operations. The accelerated depreciation is in addition to the normal depreciation on such facilities, but the total depreciation over their expected lives will not exceed the cost of the facilities."

The following comment appeared in the corporation's quarterly report for the *fourth quarter* of 1949:

"Because of strikes, United States Steel's production of steel ingots and castings during the fourth quarter of 1949 averaged only 46.6 percent of rated capacity. The operating rate for the entire year of 1949 averaged 82.5 percent of rated capacity. It will be recalled that the corporation's operating rate during the first half of 1949 averaged slightly in excess of 100 percent of rated capacity.

"Shipments of steel products by United States Steel in the fourth quarter of 1949 amounted to 2,662,209 net tons, as compared with shipments of 4,781,000 net tons in the third quarter. Shipments for the year 1949 amounted to 18,211,893 net tons, compared with 20,655,491 net tons in 1948.

"Income of the corporation for the fourth quarter of 1949, before declaration of dividends, was reported on January 31, 1950, as amounting to $32,735,397. Income for the year 1949 was then reported as $165,958,806, or a return of 7.2 percent on sales, as compared with income for 1948 of $129,627,845, or a return of 5.2 percent on sales, all before declaration of dividends.

"The income for the fourth quarter would have been $6,700,000 but for certain adjustments in accounts because of the steel strike. These adjustments resulting from the effect of the strike on the 1949 operating rate and on inventories, increased the income for the fourth quarter by $26,000,000."

a) Would you have supported U.S. Steel in its attempt to introduce the new depreciation method in 1947?
b) Was the new depreciation policy adopted in 1948 designed to meet the same objectives as the policy adopted in 1947 and abandoned in the following year? Explain your reasoning.
c) Contrast the 1948 depreciation method with diminishing-charge methods. Do both of these kinds of methods follow from the same accounting principle or are they fundamentally different?
d) If you had been one of the company's accountants in 1948, would you have favored or opposed the new method? Explain.
e) Explain how the steel strike in the fourth quarter of 1949 led to an increase in the company's fourth-quarter earnings. Should this be possible?

**28.** The 1961 Annual Report of the United States Steel Corporation included the following comment:

> "The $326.8 million of property expenditures compares with recorded wear and exhaustion of $210.5 million for the year. This latter amount was inadequate to recover the buying power originally expended for facilities used up during the year. The resulting deficiency is primarily due to inflation in the cost of new facilities while depreciation under existing tax laws continues to be based on the original cost of facilities purchased many years ago."

The following note appeared among the notes to the financial statements in this report:

> "For a number of years, U.S. Steel has followed the policy of reflecting accelerated depreciation on the cost of new facilities in the first few years of their lives when the economic usefulness is greatest. As permitted under the Internal Revenue Code the declining balance method of depreciation is being applied to the cost of certain facilities; and the cost of certain other facilities is covered by Certificates of Necessity under the Defense Production Act of 1950 and is being written off at the rate of 20 percent per year. The effect thereof is to charge to income a greater portion of their cost in the earlier years of life and, therefore, follows the principle of accelerated depreciation.
> 
> "The amount included in wear and exhaustion for the cost of facilities not covered by the declining balance method of depreciation or Certificates of Necessity is for the most part related to U.S. Steel's rate of operations."

*a)* In what respects did U.S. Steel's depreciation policy change between 1948 and 1961 (see Problem 27)?

*b)* Comment on the impact of the tax law on the company's depreciation policy for public reporting to stockholders.

**29.**‡ The Alexander Cargo Service was started in 1957 to carry freight from a coastal seaport in the United States to several inland locations. By the beginning of 1966, the company had three small cargo vessels capable of operating in the small river which flowed into the port.

A fourth ship was purchased for $110,000 and placed in service on July 1, 1966. The public accountant who prepared the company's annual tax returns ascertained that a life of 20 years had been accepted by the income tax authorities for similar vessels in the past. For tax purposes, depreciation could only be by the straight-line method, but no estimated salvage value had to be entered into the tax depreciation calculations. Mr. Alexander could not agree that the estimated life of this new

---

‡ Abstracted from an original case, copyright 1967 by l'Institute pour l'Etude des Méthodes de Direction de l'Entreprise (IMEDE), Lausanne, Switzerland. Published by permission.

vessel would be as long as 20 years. He had seen so many changes in the transportation pattern in his area just since he started in business that he felt that a 10-year life would be much more likely. From experience that he had had in buying and selling second-hand ships, he also concluded that he could sell the ship for at least $10,000 at the end of 10 years even if economic conditions did not permit its use for containerized service locally after that time.

By the time the ship went into service on July 1, 1966, it was clear to Mr. Alexander that his original estimates were sound, at least for the first few years of the new ship's life. Contracts had been signed with several shippers. Bookings for space on the new vessel continued near capacity throughout the first six months of its operation. Mr. Alexander felt that he might gradually lose some of this business from year to year as the pattern of local cargo operation changed, but he saw no reason why he could not continue to operate the vessel for at least 10 years before the volume of business declined so far that he would find it necessary to take the new vessel out of service and sell it.

Sales revenues of the Alexander Cargo Service amounted to $1,000,000 in 1966, and were expected to reach $1,200,000 in 1967. Net income, before taxes and before deducting depreciation on the new ship amounted to $50,000 in 1966 and was expected to total $100,000 in 1967. The book value of all assets other than this new vessel totaled $250,000 and was expected to remain constant at this level. The income tax rate was 40 percent of taxable income.

The company had in the past sometimes used the tax basis for capitalizing and depreciating costs when this seemed to fit the facts of the case. At other times it felt justified in using some basis other than the tax basis for the financial statements that it issued to its shareholders and to its bank creditors and which its management also used.

For its published statements, the Alexander Cargo Service used only straight-line depreciation or the double-rate, declining-balance method.

a)   What depreciation method should have been used for this new ship in the company's financial reports? Explain your reasoning.

b)   Using this method, calculate depreciation for 1966. (Only one-half year's depreciation should be charged for the year.)

c)   How important was the decision called for in (a)? Support your answer by giving figures from the problem.

30.   Upon its formation on January 1, the Nuovo Company bought inventories at a cost of $2,000 and equipment at a cost of $4,000. The balance sheet at that point was as follows:

| ASSETS | | LIABILITIES AND OWNERS' EQUITY | |
|---|---|---|---|
| Cash | $1,000 | Liabilities | $1,500 |
| Inventory | 2,000 | Capital stock | 5,500 |
| Equipment | 4,000 | Retained earnings | 0 |
| Total | $7,000 | Total | $7,000 |

On that date, of course, the figures for inventory and equipment represented not only original cost but current cost as well. (The Nuovo Company operated in a country which had no income taxes. Its monetary unit was the dollar.)

The income statement for the first year of operations was computed both on a conventional historical cost basis and on a replacement cost basis, using *average* replacement costs for the year. This produced the following figures:

|  | Historical Cost Basis | Replacement Cost Basis |
|---|---|---|
| Sales | $6,000 | $6,000 |
| Cost of goods sold | $4,100 | $4,400 |
| Depreciation | 600 | 612 |
| Other expenses | 900 | 900 |
| Net Income | $ 400 | $ 88 |

The year-end balance sheet was also stated on an historical cost basis and on a replacement cost basis, using *year-end* replacement prices to restate Inventory and Equipment account balances. The figures were:

|  | Historical Cost Basis | | Replacement Cost Basis | |
|---|---|---|---|---|
| ASSETS |  |  |  |  |
| Cash |  | $2,100 |  | $2,100 |
| Inventory |  | 2,300 |  | 2,400 |
| Equipment | $4,000 |  | $4,160 |  |
| Less: Allowance for depreciation | 600 |  | 624 |  |
| Equipment, net |  | 3,400 |  | 3,536 |
| Total Assets |  | $7,800 |  | $8,036 |
| LIABILITIES AND OWNERS' EQUITY |  |  |  |  |
| Liabilities |  | $1,900 |  | $1,900 |
| Common stock |  | 5,500 |  | 5,500 |
| Retained earnings |  | 400 |  | 88 |
| Accumulated holding gains |  | ... |  | 548 |
| Total Liabilities and Owners' Equity |  | $7,800 |  | $8,036 |

The "accumulated holding gains" figure in the right-hand column was obtained as a residual by subtracting the sum of the liabilities, capital stock, and retained earnings from the adjusted asset total.

Further investigation revealed that the general price level on December 31 had reached 110 percent of the January 1 level. The average for the year was 105 percent of the January 1 figure.

After examining these figures, the company's purchasing agent commented that although operating income on a replacement cost basis was not satisfactory, the holding gains experienced during the period were very gratifying. The marketing vice president, on the other hand, rejected the replacement cost figures, saying that he had done his job selling the company's products at a good margin over their cost. No bookkeeper was going to take that away from him.

The treasurer took a different tack. As he put it, the holding gain wasn't a real gain because the purchasing power of the dollar had fallen during the year. Working quickly on the back of an envelope, he produced the following calculation:

(1) Assets, January 1 .......................................... $7,000
(2) Liabilities, January 1 ...................................... 1,500
(3) Net assets, January 1 ([1] − [2]) ........................... $5,500
(4) Purchasing power index, December 31 ...................... 110%
(5) Adjusted net assets, January 1, at end-of-year
    prices ([3] × [4]) .......................................... $6,050
(6) Adjusted net assets, December 31 (from balance sheet) ...... 5,900
(7) Loss in Purchasing Power during the Year ([5] − [6]) ........ $ 150

a) Whose side would you take in this argument? Prepare a short statement that you might use to try to convince the others that you were right?

b) If accounting reports had been stated in units of stable purchasing power, would this company have reported a profit or a loss on its ordinary operations (exclusive of holding gains and losses)? Explain.

c) What changes in management policies would you recommend for the future if events during the next several years seem likely to follow the pattern set this year?

d) What is the explanation of the gap between the treasurer's income figure and income on a replacement cost basis? Do you agree with the treasurer's method of computing a purchasing power loss?

31. Since 1954, the annual reports of the Indiana Telephone Company have included adjustments for price level changes. The 1966 report showed conventional statements and adjusted statements in separate columns. The excerpts below have been condensed from this report (all figures except earnings per common share are in thousands of dollars):

## INCOME STATEMENT

| | Column A Historical Cost | | Column B Historical Cost Restated for Changes in Purchasing Power of the Dollar | |
|---|---|---|---|---|
| | 1966 | 1965 | 1966 | 1965 |
| Operating revenues.............. | $6,254 | $5,593 | $6,254 | $5,593 |
| Operating expenses: | | | | |
| Depreciation: | | | | |
| To cover historical cost....... | $1,039 | $ 926 | $1,039 | $ 926 |
| To recover cost of inflation ... | − | − | 194 | 191 |
| Total Depreciation........ | $1,039 | $ 926 | $1,233 | $1,117 |
| Other operating expenses....... | 4,094 | 3,765 | 4,094 | 3,765 |
| Total Operating Expenses.............. | $5,133 | $4,691 | $5,327 | $4,882 |
| Operating income ............... | $1,121 | $ 902 | $ 927 | $ 711 |
| Income deductions (interest, etc.) . | 363 | 264 | 363 | 264 |
| Net Income..................... | $ 758 | $ 638 | $ 564 | $ 447 |
| Earnings per Common Share..... | $3.13 | $2.67 | $2.26 | $1.79 |

## STATEMENT OF ASSETS
### December 31, 1966

|  | Column A<br>Historical<br>Cost | Column B<br>Historical<br>Cost Restated |
|---|---|---|
| Telephone plant, at original cost............ | $21,909 | $25,473 |
| Less: Accumulated depreciation.......... | 6,051 | 7,549 |
|  | $15,858 | $17,924 |
| Working capital ........................... | 490 | 490 |
| Other assets............................... | 713 | 712 |
| Total Investment.................... | $17,061 | $19,126 |

## COMMON SHAREHOLDERS' INTEREST
### December 31, 1966

|  | Column A<br>Historical<br>Cost | Column B<br>Historical<br>Cost Restated |
|---|---|---|
| Effect of inflation to date:<br>Applicable to earnings since<br>January 1, 1954 ...................... | $ .... | $1,792 |
| Applicable to future earnings............. | .... | 2,066 |
| Retained earnings........................ | 2,217 | 425 |
| Other elements of shareholders' interest.... | 3,162 | 3,162 |
| Total Common Shareholders' Interest... | $5,379 | $7,445 |

*Note 1 to Financial Statements:*

In the accompanying financial statements, costs measured by the dollars disbursed at the time of the expenditure are shown in Column A— Historical Cost. In Column B—Historical Cost Restated for Change in Purchasing Power of Dollar, these dollars of cost have been restated in terms of the price level at December 31, 1965, and 1966, as measured by the Gross National Product Implicit Price Deflator, to recognize the inflation experienced to the date of these statements. The effect of inflation on these dollars of cost has been redetermined each year since 1954 in order to recognize the constantly changing price levels.

Since 1954, the corporation has presented such supplemental financial statements recognizing the effect of the change in the purchasing power of the dollar on the cost of telephone plant and on depreciation expense in the annual report to shareholders in the same basic manner. This accounting has the approval of Arthur Andersen & Co., the corporation's independent public accountants, as set forth in their opinion included herewith.

Dollars are a means of expressing purchasing power at the time of their use. Conversion or restatement of dollars of differing purchasing power to the purchasing power of the dollar at the date of conversion results in all the dollars being treated as mathematical likes for the purpose of significant data. The resulting financial statements recognize the change in price levels between the periods of expenditure of funds and the periods of use of property. Accordingly, the earnings, results of operations, assets, and other data available for use by management and other readers of financial statements provide important information and comparisons not otherwise available.

No one would attempt to add, subtract, multiply, or divide marks, dollars, and pounds. The failure to change the title of the monetary unit may be partially responsible for this violation of mathematical principle. This is important for it conceals the fact that mathematical unlikes are being used and therefore unfortunate results are produced by generally accepted accounting methods. This should help explain why we are talking about income and expenses in terms of current dollars.

*Auditor's Opinion (Final Paragraph):*

In our opinion, however, the accompanying financial statements shown under Column B more fairly present the financial position of the corporation and the results of its operations since appropriate recognition has been given to variations in the purchasing power of the dollar, as explained in [the notes] to the financial statements.

a)   Are these statements expressed in units of common purchasing power? How do they differ, if at all, from "current cost" statements?
b)   How much "extra" depreciation did Indiana Telephone Company charge against revenues during the period 1954–66 inclusive?
c)   What does the amount of $2,066,000 "applicable to future earnings" represent? Why is it included in the "Common Shareholders' Interest?" Do you think it should be reported in some other section of the balance sheet instead of in the shareholders' equity?
d)   Do you agree with the auditors that the column B figures "more fairly" present the company's financial situation? Explain your reasoning. Would you suggest any changes in the company's methods of income measurement?

# 13

# CAPITALIZATION POLICY

ALL COSTS ARE INCURRED to obtain something. This something may be a physical object, a property right, or a service. The purpose of expenditures for each and all of these is to create income, either by producing revenues in excess of the cost (revenue-producing expenditures) or by reducing other costs (cost-saving expenditures). Finally, the expenditure may be designed to increase income in the current period, in some single future period, or in a number of periods.

These distinctions are reflected in the definitions of asset and expense:

1. The cost of any resource that has been consumed in obtaining the *current* period's revenues is an *expense.*
2. The cost of any resource that will be used to obtain revenues or reduce operating costs in *future* accounting periods is the cost of an *asset.*

These definitions are not always easy to apply in practice, and the accountant has to exercise his judgment. Our purpose in this chapter is to examine the factors that affect capitalization decisions on the following three kinds of expenditures:

1. Ancillary expenditures made in connection with the acquisition of long-lived tangible assets.
2. Expenditures for intangible assets.
3. Expenditures in which outlay costs must be approximated.

## CAPITALIZING ANCILLARY EXPENDITURES: BASIC PRINCIPLES

An expenditure to acquire an asset is often accompanied by one or more ancillary expenditures, more or less related to the acquisition. The accountant has to decide whether to capitalize these costs, and under what headings.

### Identifying Capitalizable Costs

Before deciding to acquire an asset, management should estimate all of the costs that must be incurred before the asset can be put to its intended productive use. A decision to go ahead therefore implies that the benefits are great enough to justify all of the expenditures, both direct and indirect. Since they enter into the acquisition decision, *all outlays necessary to render an asset suitable for its intended use should be capitalized.*

For example, the Camden Company decided to install a conveyer system to transport materials, work in process, and finished products between work stations in its two-story plant. The following outlays were direct consequences of this decision:

1. Price of conveyor components ................................. $26,500
2. Freight charges on conveyor components ...................... 800
3. Installation of conveyor ........................................ 3,600
4. Compensation for injuries to an employee of the contractor engaged for conveyor installation ............................ 10,000
5. Alterations to building to accommodate conveyor .............. 4,200
6. Payments to factory employees during period of shutdown for conveyor installation:
    a) For rearranging machines ................................ 1,600
    b) For idle time ............................................. 1,200
7. Training of one employee in conveyor maintenance ........... 300

Except for the $10,000 payment resulting from failure of the contractor to carry compensation insurance, all costs actually incurred, including that of employee idle time, were approximately as had been anticipated in planning the project. In other words, the cost estimate made in deciding whether the outlay would be profitable included all the items but 4 above.

When the base rule is applied to these basic facts, it is clear that every one of these items except the compensation for uninsured injuries (item 4) is an "outlay necessary to render the asset suitable for its intended use," and hence is properly capitalized.

Item 4 is a different matter. Had ordinary caution been exercised, the Camden Company would have either engaged an insured contractor or itself secured the requisite coverage at a nominal charge. In either case, the insurance premium would have been part of the reasonably necessary cost of the asset and therefore capitalizable. Any cost in excess of this amount is clearly wasted and should not be capitalized. Instead, it should be recognized as a loss, charged against revenues of the period in which it occurred.

### Separate Capitalization

Deciding to capitalize these costs is only part of the capitalization decision. A second issue must be resolved: whether to recognize a single asset or more than one in recording the costs arising out of a related set of transactions. Answers to this question are based on the application of two criteria:

1. Do the objects acquired have different life expectancies?
2. Do the objects acquired have different perceived identities?

An affirmative answer to *either* of these questions is a sufficient reason for separate capitalization. For example, few accountants would include item 7, training costs, as part of the cost of the conveyor even if the life expectancies of the conveyor and the training were identical; the reason is that training and conveyors are perceived to be in different asset categories. By the same token, the movable treads on the conveyor might be classified separately if their life expectancy is shorter than that of the conveyor frame and motor, even though few would perceive these as two separate kinds of assets.

Finally, if the alterations to the building are expected to produce benefits after the conveyor's life has come to an end, the expenditures of $4,200 for this purpose should be capitalized separately from those for the conveyor, perhaps as additions to the cost of the building itself.

### Maintenance versus Replacement

The results of the application of these two criteria are often likely to seem arbitrary. For example, although most people would regard an entire airplane as a single asset, an airline might capitalize the costs of the airframe, engines, and interior fittings in three separate asset categories.

The issue here is whether subsequent expenditures are to be treated as maintenance or as replacement costs. Replacement of an entire asset requires removal of that asset from the accounts and the capitalization of the cost of the replacement. The cost of replacing a *part* of an asset, however, is usually treated as a maintenance cost unless it is expected to increase the asset's service potential materially.

The definition, in other words, depends on what has been chosen as the unit of account. For example, if the conveyor is the unit of account and if its estimated useful life is based on the assumption that the treads will be replaced periodically, then later expenditures on replacement treads will be treated as maintenance costs. If the treads are capitalized separately, then the costs of the original treads must be removed from the account when they are replaced and the cost of the replacement treads will be capitalized in their place. If the unit of account is made small enough, even a routine lubrication can be treated as a replacement and no room will be left for the concept of maintenance.

Separate capitalization is likely to have a slight smoothing effect on year-to-year movements in operating costs. For example, suppose that the conveyor is expected to last for 20 years, with treads costing $8,000 to be replaced every five years. If the cost of the first set of treads is capitalized as part of the cost of the conveyor, it will be depreciated over 20 years, at an average of $400 a year. Depreciation and maintenance cost therefore will be $400 in all years except years 6, 11, and 16, when replacements take place. In those three years, the depreciation and maintenance cost will total $8,400. If the treads are capitalized separately, however, they will be depreciated over 5 years, at $1,600 a year. The replacements would also be capitalized and depreciated at these same amounts, thereby smoothing the annual cost.

### Maintenance versus Betterments

Items 5 and 6a present a different set of conceptual problems. On the one hand, they were made necessary by the installation of the conveyor and therefore should be considered as part of its cost. From a different point of view, however, it can be argued that these costs were incurred not "to render the asset suitable" in the sense of our rule but *to preserve the previously existing suitability* of other assets under changed operating conditions. This latter rationale leads to the conclusion that the items in question are in the nature of current (though possibly extraordinary) maintenance costs rather than additions to the cost of the assets to which they relate.

The problem, in other words, is to distinguish between *betterments*, connoting some form of progressive change, and *maintenance*, meaning the prevention or retardation of retrogressive change. Whereas costs of the former are subject to capitalization, those of the latter are properly chargeable to current operations.

A unique conceptual solution to this problem exists, although application of this solution requires the exercise of judgment by the accountant. The *total productive capacity* of a plant asset, or any complex of assets, is a joint function of the output per unit of time and the length of time over which satisfactory output is achieved (economic life), both of which factors are in turn more or less dependent upon the level of maintenance provided. At the time of acquisition, therefore, there is an *expected life-time capacity* reflecting an *intended maintenance policy*. This fact provides a basis for the following rules governing the treatment of subsequent outlays: (1) any cost incurred *to obtain the service initially expected is a maintenance cost;* and (2) any cost *incurred to increase lifetime productive capacity by raising the output rate or by extending the economic life or by reducing operating cost is a capitalizable betterment.*

Application of these rules is most difficult in cases like the Camden Company's conveyor installation. In this case, several physically different assets were readily identifiable. Costs necessary to acquire one of these (the conveyor) were expended to effect physical changes in others (the building and the other machinery). This physical identifiability has nothing to do with the issue, however. The rearrangement and building alteration costs were costs of the conveyor system. If the other assets had given up their income-producing potential more rapidly than was originally anticipated, due to the lack of adequate conveyor facilities, then part of the cost of those assets should have been written off currently as a loss, *regardless of whether the conveyor system was purchased.* If the other assets could have achieved their anticipated productive life without the conveyor, no such write-off would have been necessary. In either case, items 5 and 6a should be capitalized either separately or as part of the cost of the conveyor, depending on their estimated useful lives.

## Major Overhauls

A very similar set of questions arises in connection with expenditures made to effect major overhauls of existing facilities.

If the overhaul is made to restore to the facilities the service potential that was anticipated when the depreciation schedule was originally established, the cost of the overhaul is a maintenance cost. If the overhaul extends an asset's remaining lifetime service potential beyond the amount originally anticipated, however, the cost of achieving any such extension should be capitalized and the depreciation schedule recalculated.

Eighteen years ago, for example, the Puhlan Waite Railway purchased a group of freight cars and began depreciating their cost by the item method at a straight-line rate of 5 percent a year. Ten of these cars were still in service until a few months ago, when they were reconditioned at a cost of $62,000. Their combined book value prior to reconditioning was:

| | |
|---|---|
| Original cost | $100,000 |
| Less: Accumulated depreciation | 90,000 |
| Undepreciated Cost | $ 10,000 |

The original depreciation rate in this case was based on an assumed life of 20 years, with zero salvage value. The reconditioning is expected to extend the life to 10 years from the date of the reconditioning. Salvage value is expected to be negligible at the end of that time.

It should be clear from this description that this expenditure should be capitalized because it was made to obtain a future benefit that was not reflected in the original depreciation rate. One possibility would be to charge the $62,000 to the Freight Cars account without any further adjustment. This would be appropriate if the purpose of the expenditure was to provide the cars with characteristics they had never possessed. In this instance, however, the reconditioning consisted mainly of *replacing* various component parts. The original cost of these parts, therefore, should be removed from the Freight Cars account (and from the allowance for depreciation), to be replaced by the cost of reconditioning the cars.

In practice, the accountant usually cannot identify clearly the original cost of replaced parts. His solution is to charge the expenditure to the accumulated depreciation account:

| | | |
|---|---|---|
| Allowance for Depreciation — Freight Cars | 62,000 | |
| Accounts Payable, etc. | | 62,000 |

This increases the book value of the asset by $62,000 without including both the original cost and the replacement cost in the Freight Cars account. The overhaul is thus seen as a partial restoration of the service potential that expired in previous years, and the $72,000 book value is depreciated over the 10-year remaining life.

## CAPITALIZING ANCILLARY EXPENDITURES: PRAGMATIC CRITERIA

In practice, the facts are often less clear-cut than a textbook description may make them appear. Consequently, the company's accountants have a good deal of latitude in applying the general measurement principle stated above. In exercising his judgment on these questions, he is influenced by a number of pragmatic considerations, most of which generally lead to an earlier recognition of expense than the basic principle would suggest.

### Bookkeeping Convenience

Among the least impressive but by no means least important of such influences is that of bookkeeping convenience. Although the Camden Company did in fact isolate the cost of equipment rearrangement by its own work force, the firm's accounting system might have been so organized that this portion of factory payroll costs could not be readily distinguished. This is often the case when equipment installation, remodeling, and the like are accomplished by regular employees. Under these conditions, management may understandably adopt the view that it is more interested in making money than in measuring precisely how much money it has made. Where the cost to be isolated is relatively small and the cost of isolating it relatively large, this argument is quite persuasive.

A similar argument is often used to justify expensing the cost of hand tools and other high volume, low unit cost items that should be useful for more than one year. The total cost of these items may run into millions of dollars a year in large corporations, but they are expensed to avoid the cost of maintaining detailed property records for them.

### Tax Advantage

A more compelling and entirely rational cause for expensing costs which might otherwise be capitalized is the tax advantage to be gained thereby. So long as a firm has current taxable income, increasing the amount of current expense will have the effect of reducing current tax payments. Transferring cost to expense currently rather than deferring it to future periods generally will inflate future taxable income, but this fact is a deterrent only when an increase in the tax rate is expected.[1] The dollar surely saved this year is unquestionably worth more than the dollar that may be saved in some future year.

Since taxable income is not necessarily the same as reported income, a cost may be capitalized for public reporting while being expensed for tax purposes. However, the taxpayer has a very understandable tendency to buttress the case for current tax deductibility of borderline items by expensing them for both purposes. Thus, tax matters do undoubtedly exert an influence on accounting policy.

### Conservatism

When a legitimate question exists as to whether a cost ought to be capitalized or expensed and the decision will have no impact on tax treatment, the general tendency is to expense the cost on the grounds that it is the conservative thing to do.

For example, as we pointed out earlier, the employee training cost shown as item 7 in the example above was incurred to obtain a future benefit. Although the trained employees can leave the company whenever they wish, taking their skill with them, the initial training cost is like the priming of a pump—once the water is flowing, very little effort is required to keep it flowing. An argument could be made, in other words, for depreciating the initial training cost over the expected useful life of the conveyor system. Most practicing accountants would invoke the notion of conservatism, however, and charge the entire cost to expense, either immediately or over some short future period.

The major consequences of conservatism are (1) the understatement of assets and owners' equity, (2) the understatement of current income, and (3) the overstatement of future income, other things being equal. Probably the main reason for the widespread support of conservatism in the face of these obvious defects is psychological. Large fluctuations in earnings create great expectations on the part of the stockholders one year and bitter disappointment the next. Application of the idea of conservatism tends to limit this. In good years earnings are reduced, and in bad years earnings are raised, since large expenditures that benefit future years and may be expensed currently tend to be made in years when income is otherwise high.

---

[1] In some instances, the tax effect is magnified by the practice of levying local property taxes on the basis of stated book values. Under such conditions, higher asset totals may result in both higher income taxes and higher property taxes.

Conservatism in accounting may also have some impact on the management. Conservative accounting practice may lead management to believe that its assets and income are smaller than they actually are, and as a consequence management may pay smaller dividends, undertake fewer investments, or both. Insofar as this strengthens the financial position of the company and reduces the likelihood of ruin at some future date, some may consider it more than worth the forgone profit and growth opportunities. On the other hand, excessive conservatism may cause the decline of a firm through stagnation.

Understatement of assets and income may also cause a stockholder to make incorrect decisions, either because he believes the firm is less profitable than it in fact is or because he overcompensates for the downward bias he knows is in the data. More recently it has been noted that asset understatement may depress stock prices and make it easier for a "raider" to gain voting control of the company.[2]

### Income Control

All four of the factors that we have just discussed introduce a bias toward expensing expenditures that might on theoretical grounds be capitalized. The fifth factor, income control, can work in either direction.

Management has a substantial interest in controlling the net income figure. Net income, expressed as earnings per share, is widely regarded as a primary index of corporate and management success. If earnings per share exceed the amounts predicted by stock market analysts, the market price of the shares is likely to rise; if the earnings per share figure is disappointing, market price will fall.

Given this, management has powerful incentives to influence the net income figure by varying its capitalization policy from year to year, changes that are very difficult for outsiders to identify. In some years the incentive is to increase reported income; in others, when the market's expectations are low, heavy writeoffs that reduce reported income may seem desirable.

This is not to suggest that income manipulation is rampant, or even that management has a great deal of leeway in most years. Still, to the extent that expenditures fall in the grey area between

---

[2] One study identified a number of instances in which this was true, but it was unable to find a measureable relationship between asset understatement and the likelihood of a takeover bid. See Russell A. Taussig and Samuel L. Hayes, III, "Cash Take-Overs and Accounting Valuations," *The Accounting Review*, January 1968, pp. 68–74.

obvious capitalization and obvious expensing, the objective of income control may exert an influence on practice.

## Consistency and Disclosure

Probably the most serious problem posed by the application of these pragmatic criteria is that they give management a great deal of power to affect reported income. To limit management's ability to use this power in ways that might distort net income, the accounting profession requires the firm to be *consistent* from year to year in its treatment of specific types of cost. If changes are made, the firm must give full *disclosure* of any change in practice from one year to the next. For example, once a firm decides to expense employee training costs, it must do so consistently, year in and year out, regardless of current conditions. This requirement is based on the proposition that a bias consistently followed impairs the usefulness of information less seriously than a bias that depends on what management wants the stockholders to believe.

As one might imagine, consistency is not an unmixed blessing. For example, partly because the amount is not *material* (i.e., not large enough to be significant), a company may decide to expense the cost of alterations to equipment and find this accounting practice to be satisfactory for a number of years. Sooner or later, however, it may come to a year in which the cost is large because of a large-scale plant modernization effort. Under these circumstances, the firm's accountants may well insist that this cost should be capitalized and amortized over the expected remaining life of the equipment. This departure from consistent reporting is justified by the materiality of the amount. The corporation, however, must disclose in its published financial statements the departure from previous practice and its quantitative implications.

Enforcing year-to-year consistency in the capitalization of ancillary expenditures is extremely difficult. Simple changes in the bookkeeping routine can lead to substantial changes in the percentage of ancillary expenditures that will be capitalized, even though the stated capitalization policy remains unchanged. The independent public accountant is alert to this possibility, but these changes are often difficult to detect.

## INTANGIBLE ASSETS

Perhaps the most important reason for expensing items that might in theory be capitalized is neither convenience nor tax deferral nor conservatism, but the difficulty of identifying the cost with specific foreseeable future benefits. This difficulty is most pronounced in connection with the so-called "intangible" assets such as those which arise from sales promotion and research and development expenditures. To illustrate the problems of accounting for intangibles, we shall discuss three of these situations:

1. Purchases of specific intangibles.
2. Sales promotion expenditures.
3. Research and development expenditures.

## Purchases of Specific Intangibles

Patents, franchises, copyrights, and trademarks are sometimes acquired by purchase. Purchases of this kind present no unique problems and the purchase prices are fully capitalized.

Amortization of these costs may also be a simple matter, if clear bases can be found for estimating the anticipated life and productivity patterns. Publishers, for example, can predict the useful life of most textbooks quite accurately and can even predict what proportion of textbook revenues will materialize each year.

Other intangibles are more difficult to identify with specific benefits. A trademark, for example, may live forever or may fade away gradually. When these uncertainties are great, some accountants maintain that the entire cost of the intangible should be charged to expense immediately. Others go to the opposite extreme and oppose any amortization at all whenever the benefits to be derived from the intangible seem likely to continue perpetually.

The methods used in practice represent a compromise between these two viewpoints. When benefit periods and patterns can be predicted well enough, the costs of purchased intangibles are amortized on the basis of these predictions. When no such basis can be found, the cost is amortized over a period not to exceed forty years. The argument for setting an upper limit of this sort is that all intangibles lose their value at some time, meaning that their cost should be deducted from the revenues of the years in which the assets are expected to be productive.[3]

---

[3] This treatment was prescribed by the Accounting Principles Board of the American Institute of Certified Public Accountants, "Opinion No. 17, Intangible Assets," *Journal of Accountancy,* October 1970, pp. 85–89.

## Sales Promotion Expenditures

Most intangibles are probably created by internal expenditures rather than by external purchases. Perhaps the commonest example of this is the development of customer goodwill through sales promotional activities.

Although the bulk of a firm's promotional activity is ordinarily intended to produce current sales, a significant portion is designed to enhance the general reputation of the firm and its products. Costs in this latter category, plus numerous others less easily identified but likewise aimed at building goodwill, are at least partially applicable to *future* revenues. Nevertheless, it is universal practice to expense all selling and promotional costs as incurred.[4]

This practice occasionally leads to glaring inconsistencies. A trademark acquired from another firm will appear in the purchaser's accounts at a substantial figure, based on its purchase cost, while equally important brand names developed internally over time are not carried on the books at all.

The main reason for treating internally created intangibles in this way is that the current and probable future effects of sales promotion and other similar expenditures are very difficult to separate. While the salesman confidently expects that some of today's efforts will produce subsequent orders, he has no clear idea as to when these will materialize. Even if current efforts are directed specifically to the future with every prospect of beneficial results, it may be impossible to establish the periods in which benefits will be realized. Consequently, it will be impossible to establish a valid basis for systematic cost amortization.

Although this approach will often understate the firm's assets, it may not distort the annual expense totals. Sales promotion costs tend to be relatively stable from year to year, either constant or gradually growing, and consistent expensing probably yields significant errors in reported income only in periods in which expenditure rates change abruptly.

## Research and Development Expenditures

The case for capitalizing research and development costs is stronger than it was for sales promotion. *All* of the intended bene-

---

[4] This treatment was made mandatory by the Accounting Principles Board in its Opinion No. 17, *op. cit.*

fits are future benefits; therefore, expensing will lead to a greater distortion of reported income than will expensing of sales promotion outlays, most of which have current as well as future benefits.

A second argument for capitalization is that expensing research and development expenditures may encourage managers to short-change the future to meet short-term income objectives. Although a stable rate of expenditure is often essential to the success of these programs, management ordinarily can increase current net income by cutting back on research and development costs that would, otherwise be expensed immediately, in full. If the costs are capitalized, on the other hand, research cutbacks will have little effect on current net income. This may shield the function to some extent from the impact of short-term business recessions.

The major objection to capitalizing research and development is that at the time an expenditure is made, management is generally uncertain as to what future periods, if any, will be benefited. It is quite possible that the knowledge obtained on any particular project will prove worthless to the firm. The concept of conservatism therefore argues that all outlays be expensed at the time they are made. On these grounds, despite the clear evidence that a firm undertakes research and development because the benefits from the work *in the aggregate* are expected to justify the costs, research and development costs are generally expensed immediately.

One possible procedure for capitalizing research and development cost is to capitalize the total outlay each period, regardless of the nature of the work done or the apparent probability of future success, and then charge the cost against revenues over an arbitrary period of time, say the following 10 years. The validity of any such life assignment is admittedly open to question, but it is likely that any reasonable rule with respect to life will produce better results than treating the entire outlay as an expense of the current period.

Accounting for research and development expenditures for internal management use should be guided by entirely different considerations. Management needs to keep track of the costs of each project, regardless of the period in which the expenditure is made. These costs can be compared with the rate of progress of the research to assist management in judging whether to keep on with the project. Also, after the project is completed, an analysis of its costs and benefits can be useful in the evaluation of subsequent research proposals.

## ACQUISITION COST APPROXIMATIONS

Even if the measurement criteria described above are clearly understood and fully accepted, measurement of the acquisition cost of an asset is not always simple. Three problems deserve brief comment here:

1. Allocation of joint acquisition cost.
2. Noncash acquisitions.
3. Purchase in advance of use.

### Allocation of Joint Acquisition Cost

Two or more assets are sometimes acquired at a single purchase price, known as their *joint cost*. The method usually used for joint cost allocation is the *relative market value* method. This presumes that the anticipated values of the individual assets to the purchaser, and therefore the amounts that he was willing to pay for the various assets, were proportional to the prices they would have commanded if purchased separately. For example, if an independent appraiser says that comparable land could have been bought on the market for $1 million and a comparable building would have cost $4 million, then 20 percent of the total purchase price will be assigned to the land and 80 percent to the building.

This method should not be applied when a group of assets is acquired to obtain one of them. For example, a company may buy an old loft building together with the land on which it is located, intending to raze the building and erect a new one. In this case, the entire purchase price clearly relates to the land. The building is unwanted by the purchaser, and thus any portion of the joint acquisition cost that reflects the capitalization of the future earning power of the building in its former use is really part of the cost of the land. It is for this reason that land acquisition costs in urban slum clearance or redevelopment projects are often almost prohibitively high.

Joint cost problems are encountered in a wide variety of situations, and the accountant must learn to recognize them. One particularly difficult kind of joint cost problem arises when one company buys a package including intangible as well as tangible assets. In Chapter 10 we saw that the value of a company's "goodwill" is the difference between the separate values of the tangible assets and the combined value of the whole. When a company buys goodwill as part of a joint purchase, the cost of the goodwill is the difference between the total package price and the total of the price that the company would have paid to obtain the tangible assets. These figures ordinarily can be approximated by independent appraisers.

## Noncash Acquisitions

Companies sometimes pay for assets with shares of their own stock or with nonmonetary assets, such as securities of other companies. In these cases acquisition cost has to be estimated.

When an asset is acquired in exchange for cash, the amount of cash paid is a perfect measure of the value of the resources sacrificed — that is, the acquisition cost. Similarly, when nonmonetary assets are used to pay for newly acquired assets, their market value is a good measure of the amount of resources sacrificed to effect the purchase. When good evidence of the market value of the assets given up is available, therefore, the accountant should use this figure to measure acquisition cost. If this kind of evidence is not available, then the market value of the assets being acquired should be used to measure acquisition cost. Presumably the seller will not accept anything less than the market value of the assets he is giving up. If neither of these figures is available, an outside independent appraiser should be called in to establish the values of the resources exchanged.

Market value in these cases is clearly superior to the book value of the assets given up as a measure of acquisition cost. Book values get out of date very rapidly and may be far from the current sacrifice made to acquire the new assets. Market price of the goods given up can be taken as the measure of current sacrifice if it can be assumed that the buying company could get this much from some other source.

One apparent exception to this rule arises in connection with exchanges of assets for others that are substantially similar. A good example is the trading of old delivery trucks for new ones. The trade-in allowance in such cases may very well not represent the market value of the old trucks, and market value may be very difficult to establish. To relieve the accountant of the need to establish market value in such cases, the Accounting Principles Board issued an opinion requiring that the cost of the new asset be measured by the undepreciated cost of the asset given up in the exchange, plus any other consideration given to the seller.[5] This can lead to a substantial misstatement of the amount of

---

[5] *Opinion No. 29* (New York: AICPA, 1973), Paragraph 21.

resources sacrificed to obtain the new asset, but that will have to be accepted until better methods of establishing market value in such situations can be identified.

The use of market values to record exchanges of nonmonetary assets is very likely to lead to the recognition of gains or losses. An exchange is a combination of a purchase transaction and a sale. Whenever book value differs from the proceeds from a sale, a gain or a loss is said to occur.

A somewhat similar problem arises when an asset is paid for with shares of the firm's own capital stock. Once again the accountant must make an effort to establish the cost of these assets. Except for a special class of acquisitions that we shall discuss in Chapter 16, the accountant measures cost by the current market value of the stock issued or of the assets acquired, whichever is more clearly evident. In the absence of such evidence, an outside appraisal must be sought.

## Purchase in Advance of Use

Land, plant, or inventory may sometimes be acquired well in advance of its intended use. Under such conditions, the purchaser will presumably anticipate in his offering price any *carrying charges* (storage, property taxes, etc.) likely to be incurred prior to employment of the asset. That is, the purchaser believes that he would have a higher total cost if he were to defer the purchase until he is ready to use the asset. Consequently, carrying charges during the expected holding period are necessary costs of acquisition and should be included in the cost of the asset.

These costs are often expensed for reasons such as conservatism or lack of materiality, but in some situations the case for capitalization is too strong to be ignored. For example, property taxes incurred during the construction period are often added to the cost of buildings if the construction period is long. Similarly, outlays for fire protection and taxes on stands of growing timber are commonly capitalized as acquisition costs of the new growth. In a sense, these situations are similar to manufacturing in that the costs incurred are necessary to the increase in the value of the asset. On the other hand, if the carrying costs are greater than the value increment, they should not be capitalized in full but should be recognized at least in part as losses of the current period. Such losses are occasioned by unexpected delays in construction. This treatment is similar to that afforded to the injury compensation payment (item 4) in the Camden Company illustration, and it is justified by the same line of reasoning.

## SUMMARY

The use of historical cost as the basis of asset measurement at the time of acquisition raises a number of difficult questions. Some of these are questions of fact—e.g., was a particular expenditure necessary to obtain the services of the asset? Others result from uncertainty—e.g., will the expenditure lead to a commensurate future benefit? Still others are definitional—e.g., did the expenditure increase the firm's total productive capacity or merely prevent it from deteriorating? All are alike, however, in that they require the exercise of accounting judgment.

Lacking precise answers to these questions, the accountant needs a conceptual framework on which to build a capitalization policy. The basic concept calls for capitalization of all costs that are incurred in anticipation of a benefit or benefits after the end of the current accounting period. An apparent exception is maintenance cost, but here the future benefit is one that was already assumed in the decision to capitalize the costs of the asset to which the maintenance is applied.

Rigid application of this concept is unlikely, partly due to demands that capitalization policy be conservative, clerically convenient, and tax-sensitive. For expenditures that are designed to create intangibles, the situation is even worse, in that the anticipated future benefits are so uncertain. The result is that accountants typically expense far more costs than a strict application of the basic concept would permit.

The balance sheets that reflect these departures from an ideal capitalization policy are likely to understate the historical cost of the firm's assets. Because the company must follow its policy consistently, year after year, the effects on the income statement will be much weaker than the balance sheet effects, as long as total expenditures in borderline categories are relatively constant from year to year. Even if such expenditures fluctuate, however, or rise or fall along a trend line, consistency will lead to financial statements that are more reliable than those that would result if management were free to change its asset measurement practices at will, depending on its needs of the moment.

## QUESTIONS AND PROBLEMS

1. List and explain the reasons why in borderline cases a business firm may prefer to treat acquisition costs as expenses rather than assets.

2. Discuss the importance of consistency in differentiating between asset and expense.

3. Explain the distinction between "maintenance" and "betterments" and discuss the forms which the latter may take.

4. Discuss the relationship between maintenance policy and the productive capacity of plant assets.

5. What is meant by the "unit of account" for purposes of cost capitalization? Explain how selection of the unit of account bears upon the accounting distinction between "maintenance" and "replacement."

6. State briefly the various circumstances under which appraisal valuations of assets might logically be entered in a company's accounts.

7. A student recently insisted that the only important requirement for a capitalization policy is consistency—in other words, the details of the policy are unimportant so long as it is applied consistently from year to year. Can you identify any possible adverse effects of allowing management to choose its own capitalization policy and apply it consistently? If so, are they likely to be important?

8. After a long study, the Ace Hauling Company decided that substantial savings could be obtained by replacing its present fleet of three trucks with two larger vehicles. This would necessitate enlarging the door openings in the company's garage, purchasing new overhead doors, and strengthening the garage floor to permit it to support the heavier trucks. Should costs of these items be capitalized or expensed? If you decide to capitalize any of these costs, indicate whether you would capitalize it as part of the cost of the trucks or of the garage or of some other asset. Give your reasons.

9. The Coyle Construction Company paid $21,000 for a house and lot. The house was then torn down at an additional cost of $500 so that Coyle could begin to construct a gasoline service station on the site. At the time of the acquisition, an appraisal of the property placed the value of the land at $18,000 and the value of the house at $9,000.

What asset(s) did the company acquire? Calculate the cost of each asset that you have identified.

10. Sussex Sign Company bought a new truck for $3,800, less a trade-in allowance of $350 for its old truck, and detailed one of its employees to letter the company's name and address on the sides. The worker was paid $5 an hour plus payroll taxes of 10 percent. He worked four hours on the job.

The company took out a year's liability and collision insurance on the new truck at a cost of $487. To provide adequate protection against theft, it had a new overhead door installed in the garage at a cost of $240.

The company's old truck had cost $2,500 when new and had accumulated depreciation of $2,400. Before accepting the dealer's trade-in offer, Sussex tried to sell the old truck to someone else, but the best offer he could get was $200.

a) What was the acquisition cost of the new truck? Was any other asset acquired?

b) What amount would be recorded in the ledger as the cost of the new truck?

**11.** A stockholder in an oil company has noted that the company's annual report lists the following items among its assets:

Leasing and exploration costs ................. $28,984,826
Incomplete construction ...................... 62,812,187

The stockholder says, "From what I know of the oil business, exploration costs are the expenses of a bunch of geologists and prospectors who ride around in the mountains on burros looking for signs of oil. Is that what they call an asset? And how about incomplete construction? That represents costs of items not yet productive, some of which may be partly drilled wells. Lots of wells which are drilled prove to be dry holes. These dry holes will actually be liabilities, it seems to me."

Explain to the stockholder the probable reasons for the company's treatment of these items. Do you agree with the treatment? Explain.

**\*12.** As a result of a new building ordinance, the Marble Movie Palace was forced to spend $8,000 to install additional fire escapes on the building that it occupied and to rearrange the seats in the auditorium at a cost of $2,000. The building was leased from a local realty group, and the lease still had 10 years to run.

What effect should each of these expenditures have on the end-of-year balance sheet and on the income statement for the year? Assume that the expenditures were made just prior to the end of the year.

**\*13.** In 1942 the Experimental Company bought 21,600 shares of Respirator, Inc., common stock at a price of $15 a share. On January 1, 1967, this stock was given to Ordway, Inc., in exchange for an office building. The appraised value of the building on that date was $2 million, while the stock was being traded on the market at a price of $105 a share.

The Experimental Company capitalized the new asset (building) at the original cost of the old asset (stock). Do you agree with this treatment? What further information, if any, would you like to have before reaching a final decision on this question?

**\*14.** Six heavy stamping machines were purchased on account by an automobile manufacturer in Detroit at a price of $16,250 each. When they arrived at their destination, the purchaser paid freight charges of

---

* Solutions to problems marked with an asterisk (*) are found in Appendix B.

$4,200 and handling fees of $1,200. Four employees, each earning $6 an hour, worked three 40-hour weeks setting up and testing the machines. Special wiring and other materials applicable to the new machines cost $600.

How much of these costs should be capitalized as costs of these machines?

15. How would you classify (asset or expense) each of the following costs at the time of its incurrence? Give reasons.

a) An outlay of $60,000 by a manufacturer of earth-moving equipment for research aimed at the elimination of certain undesirable operating characteristics in a standard model power shovel. Successful results are achieved in the same accounting period in which the research is authorized.

b) The costs to a chemical company of operating a research laboratory, the primary functions of which are the development of new products and the improvement of processes for the manufacture of established products. Costs average about $300,000 a year.

c) A grant of $200,000 to an engineering school by an airplane manufacturer for basic research in light plane design. All results of such research are to be generally disseminated.

d) Outlays of $1,000,000 incurred by an automotive company in retooling its plant to manufacture a new model passenger car.

e) Expenditures of $25,000 by a mail-order company for preparing and printing a new catalog for the coming year.

f) Expenditures of $30,000 for "institutional" advertising by a manufacturer of optical instruments. These costs are incurred during a year in which the company's entire output is going to the armed services, and are made solely for the purpose of keeping the company's name before the public in contemplation of future civilian sales.

g) Expenditures of $800,000 by a large oil company for exploration of a new territory. These costs include test borings and so forth. The results indicate that development of the area would not be commercially feasible.

16. The Park Wells Company has just purchased all the assets of the Crawford Corporation, giving in exchange government bonds which were purchased two years ago for $1 million. The market price of these bonds was $970,000 on the day when Park Wells purchased the Crawford assets.

On the date of the purchase by Park Wells, Crawford's books showed current assets of $300,000 and plant and equipment with a book value of $200,000. No other assets were listed on the Crawford Corporation's books.

An appraiser hired by Park Wells estimated that the replacement cost of the current assets on the purchase date was $350,000. The replacement cost of the plant and equipment, less an allowance for depreciation, was $400,000.

*a)*  Should the Park Wells Company have recognized $1,000,000, $970,000, or some other figure as the total cost of the Crawford assets?

*b)*  How should this total amount have been allocated among the various assets acquired? Prepare a journal entry reflecting your allocation and give your reasons for your choice.

**17.** In order to obtain a new factory site, the Mosk Manufacturing Company purchased a 12-acre tract of wasteland, paying $13,000 to the former owners. Expenses for searching titles and for drawing and recording deeds amounted to $300. Grading cost $2,800. As only six acres were required for its own factory, it considered two offers for six acres: (1) $12,000 for the north half, and (2) $8,000 for the south half. It accepted the offer of $8,000 for the south half and received a certified check in payment.

*a)*  At what amount should the remaining land be carried on the next balance sheet?

*b)*  What gain or loss, if any, should be reported on the income statement for the current period?

**\*18.** In January, 1959, Abercrombie Mills, Inc., placed in service a new paper machine costing $50,000. Its estimated useful life was 20 years.

In December, 1962, certain improvements were added to this machine at a cost of $6,000. Twelve years later, in the fall of 1974, the machine was thoroughly overhauled and rebuilt at a cost of $12,000. It was estimated that the overhaul would extend the machine's useful life by five years, or until the end of 1983. Depreciation charges for 1974 were unaffected by the overhaul.

*a)*  Show the journal entry required to record the improvements added in December, 1962.

*b)*  Compute depreciation for 1963 on a straight-line basis.

*c)*  Show the journal entry required to record the overhauling of the machine in the fall of 1974.

*d)*  Compute depreciation for 1975 on a straight-line basis.

**19.** The Caldbec Stationery Store has just purchased a photocopying machine and a manual typewriter. The photocopying machine will be used to print copies of documents, manuscripts, and other items for Caldbec customers. The typewriter has been placed on sale in the store. The following data relate to these two acquisitions:

|  | Copier | Typewriter |
|---|---|---|
| Invoice price ......................... | $5,000 | $100 |
| Discount taken ....................... | 2% | 2% |
| Freight cost .......................... | $  200 | $  4 |
| Insurance in transit .................. | 20 | 1 |
| Cost of installation and testing: |  |  |
| Materials............................ | 175 | xxx |
| Labor of company employees ......... | 250 | xxx |
| Bill from electrician for power |  |  |
| connections ...................... | 75 | xxx |

a) Ignoring depreciation, at what amount does accounting theory require the copying machine to be shown on the company's year-end balance sheet?

b) Assuming that the typewriter is still unsold at the end of the year, at what amount does accounting theory require it to be shown on the company's year-end balance sheet? (Note: The cost to replace the item at the end of the year is higher than its original cost.)

c) Are the underlying principles the same in each case or different? Explain briefly.

d) In accounting practice, at what amounts might you expect these assets to be shown? Explain your reasons for any differences between these amounts and those given in answer to parts (a) and (b) above.

20. A machine has cost $21,000 and is expected to be useful for 12 years, with no end-of-life salvage.

A major component of this machine is a heavy-duty air compressor that must be replaced every four years. Replacement compressors cost $6,000 each.

a) Determine for each of the next 12 years the effect on net income of capitalizing the compressor and the other components of the machine in separate accounts instead of in one single account.

b) Which of these two alternatives do you prefer? Give your reasons.

21. In January 19x1 a storekeeper purchased a used delivery truck for $1,000. Before putting the vehicle into service, $140 was spent for painting and decorating the body, and $260 for a complete engine overhaul. Four new tires were bought for $100. The storekeeper expected to keep the truck in service for three years, at the end of which time he anticipated it would have a trade-in value of $300.

Gasoline, oil, and similar items were charged to expense as procured. In January 19x2 a new battery ($20) and miscellaneous repairs ($90) were purchased. Straight-line depreciation was used.

Four new tires were bought for $110 in January 19x3 and the body was repainted at a cost of $175. Miscellaneous repairs were made at a cost of $150.

A new truck costing $3,400 was bought in January 19x4. The trade-in allowance on the old vehicle was $430.

*a*) Which of the outlays made in 19x1 should be capitalized?
*b*) Which of the outlays made in 19x2 and 19x3 should be capitalized?
*c*) Calculate depreciation on a straight-line basis for each year, 19x1 through 19x3. (A full year's depreciation should be taken in each year.)  $(1500 - 300) \div 3 = 400$
*d*) Indicate how the replacement of the old truck by a new one would be accounted for in 19x4.

**22.** A barge with an estimated life of 20 years and no end-of-life salvage value was bought in January 19x1 for $200,000. It proved too small to be profitable, and five years later was lengthened at a cost of $30,000, paid in cash.

At the end of 15 years the barge was thoroughly overhauled and reconditioned at a cost of $40,000, paid in cash. This action was expected to extend the life of the barge to 10 years from the date of the reconditioning (i.e., to 25 years from the original acquisition date.)

Early in its 22nd year the barge was lost in a storm, and $15,000 insurance was collected. Depreciation was by the straight-line method.

*a*) Determine the correct balance in the Barge and Accumulated Depreciation accounts at the end of five years.
*b*) Prepare a journal entry to record the cost of lengthening the barge.
*c*) Calculate depreciation for the sixth year.
*d*) Prepare a journal entry to record the cost of reconditioning the barge.
*e*) Calculate depreciation for the 16th year.
*f*) Determine the correct balance in the Barge and Accumulated Depreciation accounts at the end of 21 years.
*g*) Prepare a journal entry to record the loss of the barge and the collection of the insurance.

**23.** The general ledger of Enter-tane, Inc., a corporation engaged in the development and production of television programs for commercial sponsorship, contains the following accounts before amortization at the end of the current year:

| *Account* | *Balance (Debit)* |
|---|---|
| Sealing Wax and Kings | $51,000 |
| The Messenger | 36,000 |
| The Desperado | 17,500 |
| Shin Bone | 8,000 |
| Studio Rearrangement | 5,000 |

An examination of contracts and records has revealed the following information:

(1) The balances in the first two accounts represent the total cost of completed programs that were televised during the accounting period just ended. Under the terms of an existing contract, Sealing Wax and Kings will be rerun during the next accounting

period at a fee equal to 50 percent of the fee for the first televising of the program. The contract for the first run produced
$300,000 of revenue. The contract with the sponsor of The Mes-
senger provides that he may at his option rerun the program
during the next season at a fee of 75 percent of the fee on the
first televising of the program.

(2)    The balance in The Desperado account is the cost of a new program which has just been completed and is being considered
by several companies for commercial sponsorship.

(3)    The balance in the Shin Bone account represents the cost of a
partially completed program for a projected series that has been
abandoned.

(4)    The balance of the Studio Rearrangement account consists of
payments made to a firm of engineers which prepared a report
recommending a more efficient utilization of existing studio
space and equipment.

*a)*    State the general principle or principles by which accountants guide
themselves in deciding how much of the balances in the first four
accounts should be shown as assets on the company's year-end balance sheet.

*b)*    Applying this principle or principles, how would you report each of
these first four accounts in the year-end financial statements? Explain.

*c)*    In what way, if at all, does the Studio Rearrangement account differ
from the first four? How would you report this account in the company's financial statements for the period?

**24.** Asobat, Inc., commenced its business operations at the beginning
of year 1. At that time its accountants decided, with the approval of
management and the company's independent auditors, to expense immediately the costs of all small tools and other long-life items which cost
less than $50 apiece. The company's purchases of these items during
the first 11 years of operations, together with its reported net income,
were as follows:

| Year | Purchases | Net Income (Loss) Before Taxes |
|------|-----------|-------------------------------|
| 1 | $20,000 | $(21,000) |
| 2 | 2,000 | 400 |
| 3 | 0 | 5,400 |
| 4 | 6,000 | 6,600 |
| 5 | 4,000 | 6,600 |
| 6 | 10,400 | 1,800 |
| 7 | 11,200 | 4,200 |
| 8 | 5,600 | 16,600 |
| 9 | 4,400 | 21,800 |
| 10 | 7,680 | 20,920 |
| 11 | 11,280 | 21,720 |

Having noticed how large these purchases have been in comparison with net income, you asked an assistant to look into the matter. The assistant's inquiry has turned up the following additional information:

(1) Purchases seem to have been amply justified by legitimate operating needs.

(2) 20 percent of the items purchased were discarded after four years' use, another 60 percent were discarded after five years' use, and the remaining 20 percent were disposed of at the end of six years.

(3) The scrap value of the discarded items was negligible.

(4) The company's new computer could be used to calculate annual depreciation charges on these items at a very low cost.

a) Calculate straight-line depreciation, year by year, on the items purchased in the first 11 years of Asobat's existence. Use the group method of depreciation and assume that all purchases were made at the beginning of the year and all retirements took place at the end of the year, after the annual depreciation charge was calculated.

b) Restate income before taxes for each of these years as it would have been reported if these expenditures had been capitalized and depreciated on the basis described in (a).

c) What conclusions, if any, about the firm's capitalization policy do these calculations seem to point to?

**25.** The Beckman Company late in 19x1 requested bids from several equipment manufacturers on the construction of a unique piece of special-purpose equipment to be used in the Beckman factory to replace an outmoded piece of equipment then in use. Several bids were received, the lowest in the amount of $55,000. The management of the Beckman Company felt that this was excessive. Instead, the machine was manufactured in the company's own machine shop which was then operating at substantially less than full capacity.

The machine was built during the early months of 19x2 and was placed in service on July 1, 19x2. The machine was capitalized at $55,000, comprising the following elements:

| | |
|---|---:|
| Raw materials used in construction of new machine | $ 8,000 |
| Direct labor used in construction of new machine | 20,000 |
| Amount paid to Ace Machinery Service Company for installation of new machine | 1,000 |
| Cost of dismantling old machine | 800 |
| Cost of direct labor for trial runs | 1,500 |
| Cost of materials for trial runs | 500 |
| Costs of special tooling for use in operating the machine | 6,000 |
| Savings in construction costs | 17,700 |
| Less: Cash proceeds from sale of old machine | (500) |
| Total Cost of Machine | $55,000 |

The following additional information is available:

(1) Factory costs other than labor and materials averaged 80 percent of direct labor cost. This percentage was used to assign these

other costs to products made in the factory for sale to outside customers.

(2) Freight charges on the materials used in construction of the machine amounted to $250. This amount was debited to the Freight-In account.

(3) Cash discounts on the materials used in construction amounted to $50. This amount was credited to Purchases Discounts.

(4) The replaced equipment had an original cost of $25,000 and accumulated depreciation of $21,000 at the time it was dismantled and sold.

(5) The new machine had an anticipated useful life of 15 years; the special tooling would be useful for 3 years.

(6) Savings in construction costs were computed on the basis of the difference between the lowest outside bid and the net costs charged to the job during construction. These savings were credited to the account, Gain on Construction of Equipment.

(7) Products produced during the trial runs were scrapped; scrap value was negligible.

*a)* At what amount should the new machine have been capitalized in the equipment account on July 1, 19x2? Show the details.

*b)* Explain how you would have accounted for each of the cost elements in the above list that you would not have capitalized as part of the cost of this piece of equipment.

**26.** The Realty Corporation owns a large number of buildings which it rents to commercial and residential tenants. In January, 19x1, it bought a building for conversion into quarters suitable for use by a foreign legation. The building was in an advanced state of disrepair, but was structurally sound except for the top (fourth) floor. This floor had been vacated two years earlier on the order of a city building inspector.

The purchase price of this property was $80,000 for the building and $90,000 for the land. Extensive remodeling and interior decorating was begun immediately to adapt the building to its intended use. The following outlays were made during the period January through June, 19x1:

| | | |
|---|---|---:|
| (1) | Interior painting and decorating | $ 40,000 |
| (2) | Structural alterations including replacement of plumbing fixtures at a cost of $12,000, and landscaping at $8,000 .... | 62,000 |
| (3) | Replacement and renewal of electric wiring............... | 10,000 |
| (4) | Removal of fourth story................................... | 50,000 |
| (5) | Payment of hospital and medical expenses of passerby injured by falling brick..................................... | 2,000 |
| (6) | Architect's fees, building permits, etc. ..................... | 16,000 |
| | Total............................................... | $180,000 |

In addition, property taxes accrued for the period January 1 through June 30 amounted to $3,000.

Late in June, the company was notified that it was being sued for $45,000 for the personal injuries and mental anguish suffered by the passerby who was hit by the falling brick (item 5 above). The suit was scheduled for trial in February 19x2. At the time the remodeling work was done, the Realty Corporation had elected to be its own insurer in matters pertaining to public liability, and therefore it was not insured either for the medical expenses or the amount of any payment that might result from the lawsuit. The premium that an insurance company would have charged for liability coverage during the period of remodeling was $1,250.

The building was ready for occupancy on July 1, 19x1, and a 10-year lease, running from July 1, 19x1, was signed with a foreign government.

Indicate how these facts should have been reflected in the company's accounts as of July 1, 19x1. How much should have been capitalized and under what account titles? How much should have been charged to expense for the first half of 19x1? Give your reasons for your treatment of each item.

# 14

# LIABILITIES

A COMPANY'S CAPITAL STRUCTURE has great significance to management and to outsiders alike. As we saw in Chapter 9, the amount and composition of the liabilities can have a great influence on the profitability of the shareholder's investment and on the risks associated with the enterprise. This chapter will examine the problems encountered in measuring various kinds of liabilities and will discuss their managerial implications.

## LONG-TERM BORROWING

Most large corporations in the United States obtain large quantities of quasi-permanent capital from long-term lenders. As we saw in Chapter 9, debt financing permits the shareholders to benefit from the *leverage* effect of using low-cost funds to finance high-yield operations. It also allows the firm to grow larger than it could if it had to rely on shareholder capital alone.

### Bonds and Bond Values

When a corporation or other entity wishes to borrow from a large number of lenders, it is not feasible to negotiate a separate loan contract with each. Under these circumstances, a single loan contract is signed by the borrower and a representative of the lenders. The contract is known as an *indenture* and the lender's representative is the *trustee*. Each lender is given one or more certificates, called *bonds*, representing his share of the overall loan contract.

Each bond specifies the amounts to be paid the owner of the bond and the times at which the payments are to be made. The final payment, the amount to be paid on the maturity date (the date on which the contract expires if all its provisions have been met), is called the *maturity value* or *face value* of the bond. Interim interest payments are customarily made semiannually, but they are normally expressed as an annual percentage of the face value. This percentage is called the *coupon rate* or *face rate* of interest. Thus a $1,000, 6 percent, 20-year bond represents an agreement to pay $1,000 at the end of 20 years plus $30 (one half of 6 percent of $1,000) at the end of each half-year for 20 years.

The value of this bond to an investor depends on the *yield to maturity* that he could earn on other bonds of comparable risk that are now available on the market. Yield to maturity is the rate of interest the investor can earn if he purchases a bond at a given price, holds it until the maturity date, and then collects the face value from the lender.

For example, suppose that other comparable bonds now yield 7 percent if held to maturity. If the investor buys this 6 percent bond, he becomes entitled to two things: (1) a stream of 40 semi-annual payments of $30 each; and (2) a payment of $1,000 40 periods hence. The present value of these cash flows can be determined by multiplying them by discount factors taken from Tables 3 and 4 in Appendix A. The factors are taken from the 3½ percent columns of the two tables (half of the 7 percent annual rate). The calculation is:

| Period | Amount | Discount Factor | Present Value |
|--------|--------|-----------------|---------------|
| 1 to 40 ......... | $30/period | 21.3551 | $640.65 |
| 40 ............. | $1,000 | 0.2526 | 252.60 |
| Total..... | | | $893.25 |

The value of this 6 percent bond today is thus $893.25 to an investor whose comparable alternative is a bond yielding 7 percent interest, compounded semiannually.[1] The $106.75 difference between this amount and the $1,000 maturity value serves to bring the yield on the bond up from 6 percent to 7 percent.

---

[1] Semiannual compounding is usually used to calculate bond yields. This is convenient because interest on bonds is typically paid semiannually. The payment interval does not necessarily govern the compounding interval, however, and both lenders and borrowers may use monthly, daily, or even continuous compounding if greater accuracy calls for it.

The Use of Bond Value Tables

If investors had to go through the previous calculations every time they considered buying or selling a bond, much time would be wasted unnecessarily. To avoid this, special tables have been prepared for the financial community, based on the kind of calculations just illustrated. A partial set of such tables is included in Appendix A (Tables 5 through 14). The present value of a 20-year, 6 percent bond in a market in which the prevailing yield is 7 percent may be found in Table 9 (the table for a coupon rate of 6 percent) by locating the column for bonds with 20 years to maturity and the row for the 7 percent yield rate. The figure is 89.32, which means that the market price will be $893.20 for each $1,000 of face value. Except for an insignificant rounding error, this is the same figure we obtained using Tables 3 and 4.

The value of the bond will approach face value as it gets closer to maturity, other things being equal. For example, if the 6 percent bond is still outstanding five years later (15 years before maturity), and the market yield rate is still 7 percent at that time, Table 9 indicates that the bond will have a value of $908. If interest rates fall in the meanwhile, however, so that newly issued bonds of comparable risk are being sold to yield 5 percent, then the value of this 6 percent bond with 15 years to go to maturity will have climbed to $1,104.70. This figure is derived from the 110.47 factor listed in the 15-year column, 5 percent row of Table 9.

Conversely, given the market price of the bond, its yield to maturity can be determined and compared with the rate of return obtained elsewhere. For example, if the bond has 10 years to maturity and is selling for $1,015, its yield is 5.8 percent. This can be determined from the 10-year column of Table 9.

Measuring the Initial Liability

The issuing corporation of course views the bonds from the other side. For example, suppose that late in 1972 the Reading Company decided to issue $1 million of 7½ percent, 20-year debenture bonds. By the time the bonds were issued on January 1, 1973, the going market rate of interest had gone up to 8 percent. Therefore, the bonds had to be sold at a *discount* (i.e., the sale price or proceeds was less than face value). The total amount received from the sale was $950,500. The purchasers needed the $49,500 discount from face value to compensate them for accepting annual interest payments of $75,000 (coupon rate times face value) instead of $80,000 (market rate times face value) for the life of the bonds. If the coupon rate had exceeded the market rate, on the other hand, the investor would have been willing to pay a *premium* for the right to the higher annual interest payments.

The general rule in accounting for liabilities and owners' equities is to record for each source of funds *the amount that the investor has invested in the corporation*. Accordingly, the company's accountants first thought of recording the issue of the bonds on the Reading Company's books as follows:

Cash........................................... 950,500
    Bonds Payable ............................            950,500

Although this entry would have been correct, the controller decided to conform to the more usual practice of recording the face value of the bonds and the discount or premium in two separate accounts, as follows:

Cash ....................................... 950,500
Discount on Bonds ......................... 49,500
    Bonds Payable .........................            1,000,000

Some consider this treatment more informative, and in any event it produces the same balance sheet measurement as the first method. The bond and discount would have appeared on a January 1, 1973, balance sheet as:

Bonds payable (face value) ........................... $1,000,000
    Less: Discount on bonds .........................        49,500
Bonds Payable (Book Value) ........................ $  950,500

### Periodic Interest Expense

If the Reading Company's bonds were to remain outstanding until the January 1, 1993, maturity date, the bondholders would receive the $1 million face value plus $1,500,000 in coupon interest payments ($37,500 every 6 months for 20 years). The difference between this lifetime total of $2,500,000 and the $950,500 proceeds of the issue ($1,549,500) represents the price paid by the corporation for the use of the bondholders' money, or *interest expense*. The $49,500 discount is just as much a component of interest expense as the semiannual payment – after all, the company's alternative was to sell the bonds at a higher coupon rate and higher semiannual payments – and the problem is to decide how much of the $1,549,500 interest to charge to expense each period.

The preferred method of doing this is known as the *effective interest* method. This method amortizes bond discount (or premium) so that the ratio of each period's interest expense to the beginning-of-period liability is constant throughout the life of the bond issue. This ratio is the yield to maturity or *effective interest rate*.[2]

In our illustration, the Reading Company obtained $950,500 in return for a promise to pay $37,500 every six months for 20 years, plus $1 million at the end of that time. This produced an effective interest rate of 8.0 percent. (In the 20-year column of Table 12 of Appendix A, we find that a price of $95.05 for each $100 in face value provides a yield to maturity of exactly 8.0 percent.)

Since the interest cost to the company was at an annual rate of 8 percent, it is reasonable that the company should compute interest expense for each six-month period by multiplying half of this rate, or 4 percent, by the amount of the liability at the beginning of the period. The first six months' interest expense, therefore, was 0.04 × $950,500 = $38,020. The interest *payment* at the end of the first six months amounted to only $37,500, however. Interest expense, in other words, was $520 more than the amount paid. This means that the amount invested in the company by the bondholders increased during the period. They agreed to receive in cash less than the full 4 percent to which they were entitled as a result of the condition of the bond market at the time they made their initial investment. The amount of their investment, or *principal*, thus became $951,020 ($950,500 + $520), or approximately $95.10 for each $100 of face value. This is the figure given in Table 12 of Appendix A for a 7½ percent coupon rate, an 8 percent yield rate, and 19½ years to maturity.

The entry to record interest expense for the first six months was as follows:

```
Interest Expense ..............................  38,020
    Cash .......................................          37,500
    Discount on Bonds ..........................            520
```

The credit to Discount on Bonds recorded the increase in the company's liability to its bondholders.

The interest cost during the second six-month period was 4 percent of the amount actually at work during that period — the principal at the beginning of that specific period, $951,020. Interest

---

[2] The Accounting Principles Board made this method mandatory in 1971. See American Institute of Certified Public Accountants, *APB Accounting Principles: Current Text* (New York: Commerce Clearing House, 1972), Section 4111.14.

expense was thus $38,041, which requires amortization of $541 of the bond discount. Interest expense was slightly greater during the second six months than during the first because more money was at work and the liability was greater during the second period. The interest *rate* charged to expense was the same, however.

Interest expense and bond discount amortization were calculated in similar fashion for the other 38 six-month periods. These calculations were summarized in a table, a portion of which is shown in Exhibit 14–1. Notice that, except for slight rounding errors, the liability figures shown in column (2) for January 1, 1983, January 1, 1988, and July 1, 1992 are the same as those computed from Table 12 of Appendix A.

Exhibit 14–1

**LIABILITY AND INTEREST EXPENSE**
(7½ Percent, 20-Year, $1,000,000 Bond Yielding 8 Percent)

| (1) Six-Month Period Beginning on | (2) Beginning Liability (from col. 6, line above) | (3) Interest Expense (2) × .04 | (4) Interest Payment | (5) Amortization of Bond Discount (3) − (4) | (6) Ending Liability (2) + (5) |
|---|---|---|---|---|---|
| Jan. 1, 1973 . . . . . | $950,500 | $38,020 | $37,500 | $   520 | $   951,020 |
| July 1, 1973 . . . . . | 951,020* | 38,041 | 37,500 | 541 | 951,561 |
| Jan. 1, 1974 . . . . . | 951,561 | 38,062 | 37,500 | 562 | 952,123 |
| July 1, 1974 . . . . . | 952,123 | 38,085 | 37,500 | 585 | 952,708 |
| Jan. 1, 1975 . . . . . | 952,708 | 38,108 | 37,500 | 608 | 953,316 |
| July 1, 1975 . . . . . | 953,316 | 38,133 | 37,500 | 633 | 953,949 |
| Jan. 1, 1976 . . . . . | 953,949 | 38,158 | 37,500 | 658 | 954,607 |
| July 1, 1976 . . . . . | 954,607 | 38,184 | 37,500 | 684 | 955,291 |
| Jan. 1, 1977 . . . . . | 955,291 | 38,212 | 37,500 | 712 | 956,003 |
| July 1, 1977 . . . . . | 956,003 | 38,240 | 37,500 | 740 | 956,743 |
| Jan. 1, 1978 . . . . . | 956,743* | 38,270 | 37,500 | 770 | 957,513 |
| — | — | — | — | — | — |
| Jan. 1, 1983 . . . . . | 966,000* | 38,640 | 37,500 | 1,140 | 967,140 |
| — | — | — | — | — | — |
| Jan. 1, 1988 . . . . . | 979,700* | 39,188 | 37,500 | 1,688 | 981,388 |
| — | — | — | — | — | — |
| July 1, 1992 . . . . . | 997,596* | 39,904 | 37,500 | 2,404 | 1,000,000 |

\* This figure can be checked by consulting Table 12, Appendix A.

## Amortization of Bond Premium

The same method is appropriate whenever bonds are sold for more than their face value—that is, at a premium. For example, if the Reading Company had sold its bonds for $1,053,400 to yield 7 percent (see 20-year column, 7.0 row of Table 12), interest expense for the first six months would have been:

$$\$1,053,400 \times 7\% \times \tfrac{1}{2} = \$36,869.$$

This shows that the interest *earned* by the bondholders would have been $631 *less* than the amount paid to them. This means that $631 of the $37,500 interest payment would have been a partial repayment of the amount originally borrowed, thereby reducing the company's liability.

### Retirement of Long-Term Debt

When the corporation buys its bonds back from the bond-holders, the bonds are said to be *retired*. Bonds are sometimes retired at maturity, but other arrangements are also common. For one thing, bond issues are often very large, and it may be more convenient to retire them gradually rather than all at once. Furthermore, a company may not need all of the borrowed funds continuously until the maturity date or may have an opportunity to obtain substitute financing on more favorable terms prior to that date. For these reasons, most bond issues provide the issuing corporation with opportunities for early retirement.

One possibility is to let the bonds be *convertible* into shares of common stock. Such issues are often more properly regarded as indirect means of selling stock than as borrowing transactions, and in some cases the entire issue has been converted within a few years of the date of issue. Convertible bonds will be discussed in the next chapter.

Another possibility is to provide for gradual retirement by making the issue subject to *serial redemption* — that is, by staggering the due dates of the component securities. Thus an issue of $100 million of serial bonds may provide for $10 million to mature each year for 10 years, the first maturity coming 10 years after the date of original issue. Serial bonds are usually offered at a range of prices, set to provide higher yields for the longer maturities. Each separate series is treated as a separate issue, using the accounting method described earlier.

Another device for orderly debt retirement is the *sinking fund*. Each year the corporation sets aside a certain amount of cash for the sinking fund, and this is then used to purchase company bonds. Bond indentures often provide that the corporation or the trustees of the sinking fund have the right to require the holders of some bonds to sell their bonds back to the corporation or to the trustees prior to the maturity date. Such bonds are said to be *callable* for sinking fund purposes. If the market price of the bonds is less than the price at which the bonds can be called (their *call price*), the corporation or trustees will ordinarily buy bonds on the market. Otherwise, enough bonds will be called at the call price to use up the funds available. The call price is either equal to or slightly higher than the maturity value of the bonds.

For example, suppose that because of a general tightening of the bond market, the market yield on the Reading Company's 7½ percent bonds is forced up to 9 percent so that the market price of the bonds on January 1, 1978, is $87.78. (This price can be verified from the 15-year column, 9 percent row of Table 12 in Appendix A.) It might seem profitable to buy bonds at this price. A purchase of $100,000 bonds at $87,780 would lead to a reported gain of $7,894, computed as follows:

| | |
|---|---:|
| Book Value (from Exhibit 14–1) ....................... | $95,674 |
| Purchase price......................................... | 87,780 |
| Gain on Retirement.................................... | $ 7,894 |

The entry to record this purchase would be as follows:

| | | |
|---|---:|---:|
| Bonds Payable ............................... | 100,000 | |
| Discount on Bonds ........................ | | 4,326 |
| Cash ....................................... | | 87,780 |
| Gain on Bond Retirement ................. | | 7,894 |

This gain might be more apparent than real, however. If the Reading Company had need of funds, it would have to obtain them at a cost of at least 9 percent, the current rate of bond interest. In such a case, the gain on retirement would disappear entirely.

Market prices, it should be emphasized, have no effect on the company's accounts unless the firm engages in some market transaction. The company continues to amortize bond discount (or bond premium) on the basis of the original yield rate, as in Exhibit 14–1, on the grounds that this represents the cost of the financing.

## Bond Refunding

For most large corporations, debt is a more or less permanent component of the capital structure. Far from wishing to reduce its indebtedness, the corporation seeks to maintain or increase it. When one bond issue matures, it is succeeded by another. Replacing one bond issue with another is known as *refunding*, and callability permits the corporation to refund prior to maturity if conditions seem right. The borrowing corporation can take advantage of declines in money rates by calling the old higher yield bonds, replacing them with bonds at the new lower rates.

To protect the bondholder, the bond contract usually specifies that an amount greater than the face value of the bond will be paid in the event of premature retirement. This *call price* normally varies with the age of the debt, approaching the face value at maturity or at some earlier date.

To illustrate, suppose that borrowing conditions improve considerably in 1982 and that late in the year an insurance company offers the Reading Company a $1,070,000 loan at 6 percent interest for 10 years. The proceeds would be used to pay off the 7½ percent bond issue at its call price of $107 for each $100 of face value. This refunding would have two effects: (1) a reduction in the interest payments each year, from $75,000 to 6 percent of $1,070,000 = $64,200, a saving of $10,800 a year for 10 years; and (2) a $70,000 increase in the face value to be paid off at the end of 10 years.

Refunding in this case would be profitable unless even greater savings could be obtained by waiting for the interest rate to fall still farther a year or so later. It would be profitable because the present value of $10,800 a year for 10 years (the benefit) is greater than the present value of $70,000 at the end of that time (the cost of obtaining the benefit).

The refunding would present a substantially less favorable picture on the company's financial statements for 1982, however. The book value of the old bond issue on December 31, 1982, would be $966,000, as shown in Exhibit 14–1. This is $104,000 less than the $1,070,000 call price. This $104,000 would be reported as a loss on the income statement for 1982. This is analogous to the loss on the retirement and replacement of a machine that has been made prematurely obsolete by an unexpected technological development.

## INTERPERIOD INCOME TAX ALLOCATIONS

Taxable income, as we have indicated before, may differ substantially from the figures shown in financial statements that are prepared for outside investors. The question is how these differences should be reflected in the company's financial statements.

### Timing Differences

Differences between taxable income and pre-tax income for financial reporting arise in most cases because of differences in timing the recognition of revenues and expenses. For example, Evans Products, Inc., accrues its liabilities for product warranty service at the time merchandise is sold. Warranty expense for income tax purposes, however, must be based on the expenditures actually made under the terms of the warranty. Warranty expense, in other words, is recognized earlier for financial reporting than for income taxation.

The accepted treatment in such cases is to calculate income tax expense on the basis of the financial reporting figures. If this is greater than the income tax shown on the current tax return, a liability is recognized; if it is smaller, an asset is recognized. This process is known as *interperiod income tax allocation.*

For example, suppose that Evans Products started selling a line of products in 19x1 with a one-year repair warranty. Sales of these products in 19x1 totaled $1 million, with an estimated warranty expense of $50,000. Only $20,000 of warranty-related expenditures were actually made in 19x1, however, leaving a $30,000 balance in the liability account:

Liability under Product Warranty

| Expenditures 20,000 | Accruals 50,000 |
|---|---|
| | Bal. 30,000 |

This $30,000 was subject to current income taxation in 19x1. The tax rate in that year was 40 percent, and the company's current tax liability—the amount it actually had to pay in taxes—was $12,000 greater than it would have been if the full warranty expense had been allowed as a tax deduction. The accountant set this up as a long-term *prepayment.* The tax shown on the current income tax return for 19x1 was $70,000 and the entry to record income taxes for the year was:

| Income Tax Expense | 58,000 | |
|---|---|---|
| Deferred Income Taxes | 12,000 | |
| Income Taxes Payable | | 70,000 |

Although situations of this kind are common, most growing companies actually accrue a smaller current tax liability than the amounts they recognize as income tax expense. Before examining an example of this sort, however, let us see what happens when (*a*) the account has a debit balance, and (*b*) the income tax expense exceeds the amount of taxes currently due. In 19x2 the amount accrued for warranty expense totaled $65,000, but the amounts expended totaled $75,000. This meant that taxable income was $10,000 *less* than pre-tax reported income. At a 40 percent tax rate, $4,000 was transferred from the Deferred Income Taxes account. The tax return for 19x2 showed a tax of $80,000, and the entry was:

| | | |
|---|---:|---:|
| Income Tax Expense | 84,000 | |
| Deferred Income Taxes | | 4,000 |
| Income Taxes Payable | | 80,000 |

Income tax expense for the year was $4,000 greater than the tax return showed because warranty expense was $10,000 less than the amount allowed for tax purposes.

## Depreciation Differences

Although the deferred income tax in the preceding example appeared as an asset, most of the differences run in the opposite direction. Most companies therefore report deferred tax *liabilities* in their financial statements.

Many companies use straight-line depreciation for financial reporting but diminishing-charge depreciation for tax purposes. They do this because it reduces taxable income in the early years of asset life, thereby reducing current tax payments. In other words, the company's cash flows come in earlier than they would if it used straight-line depreciation for tax purposes. These cash flows can be invested productively to increase the present value of the firm.

To illustrate, let us assume that a corporation that has been using straight-line depreciation has income before depreciation and taxes of $100,000 a year. Its depreciable property has an original cost of $300,000 and an expected life of 10 years. The company buys new equipment at a cost of $30,000, replacing old equipment with the same original cost and life. In other words, if it continues to use straight-line depreciation, its depreciation charge for the year will remain at $30,000, and its net income will be as follows:

| | |
|---|---:|
| Income before depreciation | $100,000 |
| Depreciation expense | 30,000 |
| Income before tax | $ 70,000 |
| Income tax | 28,000 |
| Net Income | $ 42,000 |

(To simplify the calculation, the income tax rate is once again assumed to be 40 percent. The actual rate is likely to be higher.)

If the company adopts the double-rate, declining-balance method for tax purposes, however, depreciation on this new equipment becomes 2 × 10% × $30,000 = $6,000, as opposed to the $3,000 straight-line figure.[3] The depreciation charge for tax purposes is thus raised to $33,000, and the income tax currently payable is reduced to $26,800.

This company now has a choice. It can report depreciation on its published income statement on either a straight-line or a declining-balance basis, depending on which method seems to represent more faithfully the decline in the assets' service potential. If decline in service potential is best approximated by declining-balance depreciation, the solution is simple: report depreciation on a declining-balance basis; report tax expense as the amount called for by the tax return for the year, as follows:

| | |
|---|---:|
| Income before depreciation | $100,000 |
| Depreciation expense | 33,000 |
| Income before tax | $ 67,000 |
| Income tax | 26,800 |
| Net Income | $ 40,200 |

A problem arises only when the decline in service potential is best measured by some depreciation method other than the method used on the current year's income tax return. For example, if straight-line depreciation represents the service decline, then reported depreciation for the year should be $30,000 and income before taxes should be $70,000. The normal income tax on this amount of income is $28,000, and this is the amount that should be reported on the income statement as current tax expense. Although only $26,800 need to be paid now, because of the liberal features of the tax law, the remaining $1,200 presumably will have to be paid in some future year when declining-balance depreciation falls below the straight-line rate. In this view, the tax has been *deferred*, not avoided.

The reported income calculations under these various alternatives are summarized in Exhibit 14–2. Notice that the net income figures shown in columns (1) and (4) are identical. This reflects the view that if straight-line depreciation is the correct depreciation, it should be used in computing the year's tax expense, no matter when the taxes are payable. The payment date is not relevant to the determination of any other expense and thus should not enter into the calculation of tax expense.

---

[3] Tax depreciation on the other $270,000 in old assets remains on a straight-line basis. Conversion to declining-balance tax depreciation is not possible for these assets.

Exhibit 14–2

### EFFECTS OF DECLINING-CHARGE DEPRECIATION ON AFTER-TAX REPORTED INCOME

|  | (1) Straight-Line Depreciation Used for Tax and Reporting | (2) Declining-Balance Depreciation Used for Tax and Reporting | (3) Reported Tax Is the Amount Currently Due | (4) Reported Tax Includes Deferred Tax |
|---|---|---|---|---|
|  |  |  | Declining-Balance Depreciation Used for Tax; Straight-Line Used for Reporting | |
| Income before depreciation ... | $100,000 | $100,000 | $100,000 | $100,000 |
| Reported depreciation ......... | 30,000 | 33,000 | 30,000 | 30,000 |
| Income before tax............. | $ 70,000 | $ 67,000 | $ 70,000 | $ 70,000 |
| Income tax.................... | 28,000 | 26,800 | 26,800 | 28,000 |
| Net Income .................. | $ 42,000 | $ 40,200 | $ 43,200 | $ 42,000 |

The entry to record the income tax expense for the year under these assumptions is:

| Income Tax Expense ........................... 28,000 | |
|---|---|
| Accrued Taxes Payable...................... | 26,800 |
| Liability for Deferred Income Tax ........... | 1,200 |

If in some future year the normalized tax expense is, say, $40,000, and the amount currently due is, say, $40,500, the entry for that year will be:

| Income Tax Expense ........................... 40,000 | |
|---|---|
| Liability for Deferred Income Tax ............... 500 | |
| Accrued Taxes Payable...................... | 40,500 |

Notice that the deferred taxes are not discounted — that is, they are listed at their face value rather than at their present value. The only justification for this is that the tax prepayment or deferral is in effect an interest-free loan. The amount of the tax is unchanged; only the timing is affected. If this interpretation is accepted, then the appropriate discount rate is zero and present value is equal to the face value of the deferred tax.

### Arguments against Tax Allocation

The case for the allocation of income taxes to the periods in which the related pre-tax income is reported is that it is these revenues and expenses which create the tax liability. When the tax liability is to be paid is a matter for Congress to decide, but how much is to be paid depends on the profitability of the firm's operations and the tax rate that is in force. If Congress decides to collect taxes early, this should not be allowed to obscure the company's underlying profitability. Similarly, if Congress decides to collect taxes late, this should not be allowed to inflate current income figures, thereby possibly misleading the investor.

Not everyone buys this argument. Many financial analysts refuse to treat deferred income tax liabilities as part of the creditors' equities. Their argument is that these liabilities may never have to be paid and if paid, the amounts may be different from the amounts accrued. The liability will never decrease as long as the cumulative differences in tax timing do not decrease. The liability will never be paid in its entirety until that uncertain and distant future date when the corporation is liquidated. Because corporations are rarely liquidated, accrual of this liability is likely to be misleading.

The first part of this argument could be applied to almost any liability however. Accounts payable, for example, are likely to grow as long as the company is growing and will never fall to zero until the company is liquidated. While it is true that the effective tax rate may change in the future, thereby increasing or decreasing the actual tax payment to be made, other liability figures are also based on estimates. Nonrecognition of deferred income taxes would be valid only if many other kinds of liabilities were also excluded from the balance sheet.[4]

## The Investment Credit

The tax laws of many countries provide for complete forgiveness of a portion of income taxes if the taxpayer satisfies specific requirements. A typical provision of this sort is the so-called *investment credit*, which has been available to taxpayers in the United States at various times since it was first introduced in 1962. This permits the taxpayer to subtract from his current income taxes an amount equal to 7 percent of current outlays for certain depreciable assets, subject to certain maximum limitations.

For example, assume that the Trilby Company's equipment purchases for the year amounted to $1 million. Before reflecting the investment credit, its income statement was as follows:

---

[4] This agrees with the position taken by the Accounting Principles Board. See American Institute of Certified Public Accountants, *APB Accounting Principles: Current Text* (New York: Commerce Clearing House, 1972), Section 4091.

| | | |
|---|---:|---:|
| Sales.................................... | | $6,180,000 |
| Less: Cost of sales .................... | $4,206,500 | |
| Other expenses................... | 1,386,000 | 5,592,500 |
| Income before taxes.................... | | $ 587,500 |
| Income taxes........................... | | 235,000 |
| Net Income ........................... | | $ 352,500 |

In this case, the tax credit was 7 percent of $1 million, or $70,000, and the net current income tax liability was thus reduced to $165,000. The company had no liability for the future repayment of this tax reduction.

The accounting question is whether the entire tax credit should flow through into the current income statement or be spread over the estimated life of the depreciable assets acquired. In the *flow-through* method, income tax expense is reduced by the full amount of the investment credit and no deferred tax liability is recognized. In the example above, the company's net income would be increased from $352,500 to $422,500, an increase of almost 20 percent.

Under the so-called *deferral* method, in contrast, the amount would be spread over the useful life of the property. Assuming a 10-year life and straight-line depreciation in the financial statements, only $7,000 of the tax credit would flow into the Trilby Company's income statement for the year; the remaining $63,000 would be listed on the balance sheet and liquidated over the next nine years.

The case for the flow-through method is that the investment credit is simply a tax reduction that leaves income before taxes unchanged, and therefore income after taxes in the current period should be reduced by the full amount of the tax credit. Advocates of the deferral method, on the other hand, argue that the tax credit is conditional on the purchase of equipment, and that therefore it represents a reduction in the cost of the equipment. It is also argued that deferral is required to avoid an abnormal increase in after-tax income. The Accounting Principles Board ruled in favor of deferring the tax credit, but its position was undermined when the Securities and Exchange Commission agreed to accept either method.[5]

The main difficulty with the deferral method is in classifying the deferred tax credit on the balance sheet. Since the deferral method is predicated on the assumption that the credit represents

---

[5] *APB Accounting Principles: Current Text*, Section 4094.

a reduction in the assets' cost, it should be classified as contra to the balance in the asset account. Similarly, in calculating depreciation expense each year, a portion of the investment credit should be offset against the depreciation charges that are based on the purchase price of the equipment.

Most companies report the investment credit either as a liability or as a "deferred credit," listed in the limbo between the liabilities and the owners' equity. This is a way of dodging the issue. It cannot be owners' equity, because this would imply that it reflects a benefit already earned, an assumption that is totally inconsistent with the logic of the deferral method. It can be regarded as a liability, but only if it is assumed to compensate the company for incurring higher operating costs in the future than it would have incurred if it had not purchased the equipment in the first place. The difficulty of verifying this assumption lends further support to our case for listing the deferred investment credit as a reduction of asset cost.

## LIABILITY UNDER PENSION PLANS

One of the more complex questions in the recognition and measurement of liabilities has arisen in connection with the employee pension plans which have been widely adopted during the last two decades. The nonaccounting as well as the accounting issues in these plans are quite complex, and in order to focus attention on the questions of interest, the nonaccounting issues will to the extent possible be passed over.

### Attributes of Pension Plans

The number of variations in pension plans is virtually limitless, but the most important variations come in a few key elements. First, the plan may be *fully vesting, partially vesting,* or *nonvesting.* Under a fully vesting plan, the employee's rights to retirement benefits accrue periodically and cannot be revoked or withdrawn by the employer. If the employee's rights are not vested, however, he loses all his retirement credits under the plan if he leaves the company prior to retirement. Between these two extremes are a host of intermediate arrangements.

Second, the plan may be *funded* or *nonfunded.* In a fully funded plan, enough cash has been set aside to meet the expected future costs of all retirement benefits earned to date, assuming that these segregated funds are invested at the rates of interest assumed or specified in the plan. In a nonfunded plan, the employee relies on the future solvency of his employer; no cash is set aside until actual payments have to be made.

In some plans, retirement benefits are based on the employee's wages or salary during the period immediately prior to retirement; in others, the amounts depend on his actual salary since the inception of the plan or the beginning of his employment. Some plans are partially contributory; others provide that the employer will bear all costs. There are unilateral plans and negotiated plans, cancelable and noncancelable plans, plans tied to social security benefits and plans covering dependents as well as the employees themselves. In short, as stated above, so many variations exist that the discussion could quickly become lost in a sea of detail without covering more than a fraction of the possibilities.

## Accounting Issues

To illustrate the accounting problems raised by the existence of pension plans, assume that the Genesee Corporation adopted a pension plan for the first time on January 1, 1964. Under this plan, the company enters into a *contract* with each *new* employee. This contract requires the company, when the employee retires at age 65, to deposit with an insurance company an amount equal to 5 percent of the employee's wages from date of employment until retirement, compounded annually at 4 percent interest. This money will be used by the insurance company to provide the employee with a pension.[6]

At the time it hires the new employee, Genesee has no pension liability to him. At the end of his first year of employment, the company's liability amounts to 5 percent of the employee's wages for the year. (Because interest is compounded annually under this agreement, the year-end liability includes no accrued interest at the end of the first year.) At the end of $1, 2, 3, \ldots, n$ years, the company has a liability arising from the employment contract

---

[6] Two very common options are (*a*) annuity payments for a fixed number of years, and (*b*) annuity payments for life. In the latter case, the insurance company must consult actuarial tables to find the remaining life expectancy of the retiring employee. For example, if the employee is expected to live for 13 years after retirement, the company's lump sum payment to the insurance company on the retirement date is $18,000, and the insurance company accrues interest at 4 percent, the annual payment to the pensioner will be approximately $1,800 (derived from Table 4 of Appendix A), assuming one payment a year rather than the more usual monthly sums. Under this type of option, if the pensioner lives longer than 13 years, the insurance company will lose; if he dies earlier, the insurance company will gain. Most such options, incidentally, provide for some death benefit for death prior to a specified age, but this is obtained only by accepting a somewhat lower annuity.

equal to 5 percent of the employee's wages for the 1, 2, 3, . . . $n$ years plus interest on these amounts compounded at 4 percent.

Although this plan is not funded, each year Genesee should credit a pension liability account by an amount equal to 5 percent of the wage payroll for the year, plus 4 percent interest on amounts accrued previously. The entry is:

```
Pension Expense ......................................  xxx
    Liability for Pensions..............................       xxx
```

When payment is made to the insurance company at the time of the employee's retirement, the insurance company takes over the obligation and the entry is:

```
Liability for Pensions.................................  xxx
    Cash ..............................................       xxx
```

The discussion thus far has been limited to pension accruals for employees hired after the adoption of the pension plan on January 1, 1964. The company also entered into pension contracts with all employees in active service on that date. These contracts provided that the amount to be paid to the insurance company at retirement would equal 5 percent of wages, compounded annually at 4 percent, from the *date of employment,* not from the date of the contracts. Thus, on January 1, 1964, Genesee has a substantial *liability for past service benefits* that had never been reflected in the company's financial statements.

The main accounting issue with respect to pension plans is whether the liability for past service benefits should be recognized immediately or gradually over time. On the one hand, the liability comes into existence at the time the pension plan is adopted. On the other hand, the company assumed this obligation in the expectation that future production costs would be reduced through lower employee turnover, greater company loyalty, and so forth.

The position of the Accounting Principles Board of the American Institute of Certified Public Accountants is ambivalent. In an opinion issued in 1966, it stated that "the entire cost of benefit payments ultimately to be made should be charged against income subsequent to the adoption or amendment of a plan and that no portion of such cost should be charged directly against retained earnings."[7] Unfortunately, the Board could not agree on a common definition of the "benefit payments ultimately to be made." It authorized companies either to accrue the liability for

---

[7] *Opinion No. 8, Accounting for the Cost of Pension Plans* (New York: AICPA, 1966).

prior service benefits over a 10-year period, or to make no such accruals at all, apparently on the rather curious grounds that these payments will never be made as long as the company remains a going concern.

We remain convinced, however, that no matter what method is used for expense recognition, the balance sheet should reflect the present value of the company's pension commitments, determined actuarially without distinguishing between vested and nonvested rights. Perhaps the best way to accomplish this is to show on the balance sheet the full amount of the estimated liability, with a contra account deduction showing that portion that has not yet been charged to expense. This position is taken with the knowledge that few plans are based on contracts with individual employees and that if the company is sold or liquidated or if it runs into financial difficulties, many of these pension rights will vanish or be severely curtailed. Nevertheless, the company has a moral obligation to honor the commitments, and in the going concern the presumption is that these obligations will indeed be honored.[8]

## LEASES IN LESSEES' FINANCIAL STATEMENTS

Prior to World War II, leasing was limited for the most part to residential property and to space in general-purpose commercial buildings for offices, retailing, and light manufacturing. Furthermore, these leases were short term, a lease that ran for five years or more being quite rare. Accordingly, the signing of a lease was looked on by the accountant as an *agreement* to buy the *use* of property. No transaction was recognized as a consequence of this event. The use of the property, the payment of rent, or the prepayment of rent were the events which gave rise to the recognition of a transaction.

### Leasing Agreements

Since the end of World War II, the *sale-leaseback* and other types of leasing arrangements have become increasingly popular as a means of acquiring the use of land, buildings, and equipment by chain stores, department stores, and companies in many other industries. The essential characteristics of this type of leasing arrangement are provided by the following illustration. To serve

---

[8] For a broader discussion of these matters, see Ernest L. Hicks, *Accounting for the Cost of Pension Plans*, Accounting Research Study No. 8 (New York: AICPA, 1965).

its southeastern market, the Trevett Company has decided to build a new manufacturing plant in a small town about 50 miles from Atlanta, Georgia. The cost of the land and buildings is $1 million, and it is estimated that the facility will be used for 30 to 40 years. The company does not have the liquid assets needed to finance the investment. Its financial position is strong but a firm of investment bankers has advised Trevett against trying to float a bond issue until additional ownership capital has been obtained. Trevett's present owners are unwilling to increase their commitment in the firm and are equally unwilling to endanger their operating control by broadening the ownership base to include new outside owners.

With the conventional avenues to new financing thus closed off, Trevett has explored the feasibility of financing by means of leasing and has decided to enter into a sale-leaseback agreement with the Globe-Wide Insurance Company. This agreement provides that Trevett will have the plant built to its own specifications, after which the insurance company will buy the land and building at Trevett's cost ($1 million) and lease it back to Trevett on a 30-year lease. Trevett will pay Globe-Wide $94,778 at the beginning of each year for 30 years and will also pay property taxes, insurance, maintenance, and all other operating costs. All that Globe-Wide will do each year is collect the rent. At the end of the initial 30-year lease term, Trevett can either vacate the property or buy it by meeting the best offer received by Globe-Wide at that time.

A sale-leaseback of this type differs from a purchase financed by borrowing in that the lease entitles Trevett to the use of the property for a specified period of time, but it does not convey any title to the rights to any residual values at the end of the lease period. If conventional debt financing had been available at an effective interest rate of 8 percent, and if the estimated market value of the property at the end of 30 years is $300,000, the two alternatives might be described as follows:

1. Purchase: Pay $80,000 a year for 30 years and $1 million at the end of the 30 years.
2. Sale-Leaseback: Pay $94,778 a year for 30 years and about $300,000 at the end of the 30 years if the continued use of the property is desired.

In other words, the choice of lease financing requires Trevett to pay $14,778 more each year than if it had borrowed the money in a more conventional manner. If it leases, however, it will have to pay out $700,000 less 30 years from now.

The effective cost of each of these methods of financing can be calculated from an analysis of the anticipated cash flows. In this case, the cost of conventional borrowing is 8 percent before taxes and 4 percent after taxes at a 50 percent tax rate. The cost of lease financing is 10 percent before taxes and more than $5\frac{1}{4}$ percent after taxes.[9]

The popularity of leasing stems from its adaptability to a wide variety of specific circumstances and its availability when conventional borrowing is either not feasible or impossible. In addition, leasing is often a considerably cheaper source of funds than additional ownership investment, when used within limits. Leasing, therefore, affords the stockholder the same kind of leverage that was described earlier in the case of long-term bonds.

## Accounting for Leases

The concern here is not with the desirability of lease financing, difficult though it is to keep away from that topic. The main interest is in the representation of the lease on the company's published financial statements. If the plant were financed by conventional borrowing, the Trevett balance sheet would report an increase in fixed assets and in long-term debt. Investors considering the purchase of the company's stock would note the greater risk caused by the increased leverage. Furthermore, they would also include the $1 million cost of the plant in its asset base in calculating return on investment. By contrast, under the sale-leaseback arrangement no recognized accounting transaction takes place and the corporation's balance sheet is unaffected by the acquisition of the plant. In short, Trevett's debt/equity ratio and return on investment ratio both appear to be materially stronger under the sale-leaseback arrangement.

The word "appear" is used advisedly, because the lease involves no less of a debt burden than the long-term borrowing. If anything, the burden is heavier because the fixed annual payments include the amortization of the principal as well as the interest on the loan. Given this, a strong argument can be made for showing the lessee's rights to use the property and the corresponding liability for future rental payments in both the asset and liability sections of the company's balance sheets.

Balance sheet recognition of this sort is known as *lease capitalization*. Leases can be capitalized in much the same manner

---

[9] At these rates the present value of the future cash flows under leasing is $1 million. The method of deriving these rates will be discussed in Chapter 22.

as any other liability, at the present value of the future obligatory payments under the lease, discounted at a rate equal to the cost of the specific lease. This is the principle implicit in the effective interest method of amortizing bond premium and discount described earlier in this chapter, and is consistent with our method of handling other liabilities.[10] By the time this book appears in print, both the S.E.C. and the accounting profession are likely to require disclosure of the capitalized value of lease payments.

## SUMMARY

In this chapter, consideration has turned from the *forms* capital takes once it has been injected into the enterprise to an examination of some of the problems encountered in accounting for the funds invested by the company's creditors. In the first part of the chapter we outlined a consistent procedure whereby any long-term liability can be capitalized, and illustrated the application of this method to the liability associated with long-term bonds.

We followed this with a discussion of interperiod tax allocation, a practice that is made necessary by differences between the tax and accounting bases for reporting revenues and expenses, gains and losses. Although these allocations occasionally lead to the recognition of assets, in most cases taxes are deferred and a liability is shown on the balance sheet.

The remainder of the chapter was given over to a discussion of the liabilities arising out of company pension plans and leasing arrangements.

## QUESTIONS AND PROBLEMS

1. What kinds of events give rise to liabilities? What events reduce or extinguish liabilities?

2. Why are future interest payments under a long-term liability not shown as separate liabilities on the balance sheet?

3. Explain the difference between the coupon rate and the yield to maturity on a bond. Under what conditions will the two rates be equal?

4. What is the nature and purpose of a call premium on a bond?

---

[10] For further discussion of the merits and mechanics of lease capitalization, see John H. Myers, *Reporting of Leases in Financial Statements*, Accounting Research Study No. 4 (New York: AICPA, 1962); and Gordon Shillinglaw, "Long-Term Leases," in Morton Backer (ed.), *Modern Accounting Theory* (Englewood Cliffs: Printice-Hall, Inc., 1966), chap. 17.

**5.** Justify the use of the effective interest method of amortizing discount or premium on bonds.

**6.** How does a "liability for deferred income tax" arise? Should it be shown on the company's balance sheet?

**7.** An argument against the recognition of deferred income taxes is that in a going concern these may never have to be paid. What response would you make to this argument?

**8.** Under what circumstances would you expect to find deferred income taxes listed in the asset section of a firm's balance sheet? Would they be listed among the current assets or in a non-current category?

**9.** With respect to pension liabilities, how is the problem of funding different from the problems of measuring corporate income?

**10.** What are the similarities between a five-year lease and a five-year bond? What are the differences? Do you think the differences are great enough to warrant the exclusion of leases from the lessee's balance sheet?

**11.** An 8½ percent bond due 12 years from now is selling to yield 8¼ percent.

*a)* What does this statement mean?
*b)* Is the selling price greater than, equal to, or less than the face value? Explain.

*\*12.* How much would you pay for a 10-year bond that has a face value of $100 and a coupon rate of 8 percent if you want a yield of 7 percent and interest is paid and compounded semiannually? (Do not use bond yield tables except to check the accuracy of your answer.)

**13.** What is the maximum price you would pay for a $1,000, 5 percent bond maturing eight years hence if you required an annual return of at least 8 percent on your investment? Coupon payments are made and interest is compounded twice a year. (Do not use the bond yield tables except to check your answer.)

**14.** The Bell Company borrows $100,000 with the understanding that it will pay the interest and principal on the loan in five equal annual payments, the first payment to be a year from the date the money is borrowed.

*a)* If the interest rate is 8 percent, what will be the amount of each annual payment?

---

\* Solutions to problems marked with an asterisk (\*) are found in Appendix B.

*b)* Present a schedule showing the interest and the principal components of each of the five payments, assuming an 8 percent interest rate.

*c)* Prepare journal entries to record the loan and the payment at the end of the first year.

*15. A deed of trust provides that all income from the trust fund shall be paid to the beneficiary during her lifetime, but that the principal shall be held intact and paid to a remainderman on the death of the beneficiary. The trustee buys for $1,034.70 a $1,000, 8 percent bond maturing in ten years.

*a)* Assuming that the bond is held to maturity, how much should the trustee pay to the beneficiary over the 10-year period?

*b)* What is the yield on this bond?

16. Howell Company borrows $2 million. It will repay the loan, with interest, by making 10 annual payments of $311,638 each. The payments are to be in arrears.

*a)* What is the interest rate on the loan? (Assume annual compounding.)

*b)* What is interest expense for the first year? Prepare a journal entry to record the accrual of the first year's interest and the payment to the lender.

*c)* What is Howell's liability at the end of the first year, after making the first payment?

*d)* What is interest expense for the second year?

*17. The Mountain Electric Company sells a million-dollar issue of 8 percent bonds on a 9 percent basis.

*a)* What does this mean?

*b)* The price is $1,092,000 or $908,000. Which, and why?

*c)* What is the term of this issue?

*d)* Calculate interest expense for the first six months. What entry should be made to record the accrual of interest and the payment of the first semi-annual coupon?

*e)* What entry should be made at the second coupon payment?

*f)* How should this bond issue be shown on the balance sheet one year after it is issued and all interest for the year has been paid?

18. At the time of issue, an insurance company purchases $400,000 (face value) of 5 percent, 30-year municipal bonds at a price to yield 5.3 percent. Ten years later, it sells $100,000 (face value) of these bonds for $83,340.

*a)* What is the insurance company's total interest income on these bonds for the first year of ownership? (Interest is paid and compounded semiannually.)

b) What is the gain or loss on the sale 10 years after purchase? What might have happened to cause this?

c) Using the effective interest method, calculate the amount at which the insurance company would report this asset at the end of 10 years, after the receipt of interest for the year and the sale of a portion of the bonds.

d) Do you agree that the figure you derived in answer to (c) is the best measure of this asset? Give your reasons. If you would prefer a different figure, indicate what it would be or how you would derive it.

19. Robert Peters purchased for $1,020 a 20-year, 6½ percent bond issued by the Jasper Corporation. Attached to this bond was a warrant, entitling its owner to purchase 10 shares of Jasper Corporation common stock at a price of $40 a share at any time during the next 10 years. The market price of Jasper Corporation common stock at the time of purchase of the bond was $30. The market yield to maturity on bonds of comparable quality was 6.8 percent at that time.

a) How much of the $1,020 purchase price of the bond was actually a payment for the warrant?

b) Assuming that Mr. Peters expects a 20 percent return before taxes on any speculative investment and that he exercises the warrant five years after he purchased the bond, what is the lowest market price of the common stock at that time that would justify the price he paid for the warrant? (Assume semiannual compounding.)

20. A company uses the same depreciation method for tax and financial reporting purposes. In 19x1 it purchased facilities with a 10-year estimated life, entitling it to a $35,000 investment credit. Its income before taxes and before reflecting the investment credit was $370,000. The income tax rate was 40 percent. The company had 100,000 shares of stock outstanding in 19x1.

a) Calculate the net income and the change, if any, in the balance in the Deferred Income Taxes account in 19x1, on a flow-through basis.

b) Make the same computations, using the deferral method of accounting for the investment credit.

c) Is the difference between your answers to (a) and (b) large enough to be regarded as significant?

*21. The Winston Corporation's income before depreciation and taxes in 19x3 was $6,200,000. Its depreciation for tax purposes was $1,250,000, and the depreciation for financial statement purposes was $850,000. Derive the corporation's income after taxes, assuming a 50 percent tax rate, and present the journal entries that account for the year's depreciation and accrual of the income tax liability for the year.

**22.** The Pelican Corporation has purchased a machine for $10,298, delivered and installed. The service life of the machine is estimated to be 6 years, at the end of which time it is estimated that the machine can be disposed of for $1,100. The machine is put into service on the first day of the fiscal year. It is the firm's only depreciable asset.

The firm uses the straight-line method in its financial statements, and the sum-of-the-years' digits method for income tax purposes. It has no other differences between the amounts shown on the income tax return for the year and the amounts shown on the income statement.

Reported net income before taxes on income is $6,000 for the first year in which the machine is used. The amount of income taxes currently due as a result of the firm's operations for that year is $2,452.50. The income tax rate is 50 percent.

*a)* Calculate the amount of income before deductions for depreciation and income taxes were taken.
*b)* Calculate the net income (after income taxes) that the company will report for the year.
*c)* What is the amount of deferred income taxes for the year?
*d)* Assuming that this is the firm's only asset and that the tax rate does not change, calculate the balance in the deferred income taxes account at the end of each year of the asset's life.

**23.** The Lambert Corporation purchased a mill on January 1, 19x0, at a cost of $10,000,000. A portion of this expenditure was for elements that made the company eligible for an investment credit of $400,000. In addition, the company was allowed to depreciate the full cost of the mill for tax purposes at a straight-line rate of 20 percent of original cost each year for five years.

Management estimated that the mill would be useful for 20 years, with negligible end-of-life salvage value, and that straight-line depreciation would be appropriate for public financial reporting. The mill was the Lambert Corporation's only depreciable asset, and the company's income before depreciation and income taxes was $3,000,000 each year. The income tax rate was 40 percent and the investment credit was to be accounted for by the deferral method.

*a)* Derive the corporation's net income in 19x3 and 19x9, as reported to the stockholders.
*b)* State the balance in the Provision for Deferred Income Taxes at the close of 19x0, 19x2, 19x6, and 19x9.

**24.** A company started business on January 1, 19x1 with the purchase of 20 delivery trucks costing $3,600 each. A full year's depreciation was taken on these trucks in 19x1.

Depreciation for financial reporting purposes was by the straight-line method. Depreciation for tax purposes was by the sum-of-the-years' digits method. The estimated life for tax purposes was 8 years; the estimated life for financial reporting was 10 years. A zero salvage value was assumed for both purposes. Item depreciation was used for each truck.

Two trucks were sold for $2,500 each on December 31, 19x2. A full year's depreciation on these trucks was recorded in the company's accounts before the sale was recorded.

The income tax rate was 40 percent both in 19x1 and in 19x2. This rate was applicable both to ordinary income and to gains and losses on the sale of trucks.

Income before depreciation, taxes, and gains and losses on the sale of trucks amounted to $40,000 each year.

a) Calculate the amount of depreciation that was shown on the income statement for 19x1. *(This has nothing to do with income taxes!)*
b) Calculate net income (after taxes) for 19x1.
c) Calculate the amount of the deferred tax liability that was shown on the company's balance sheet at December 31, 19x1. Did recognition of this liability have an effect that shareholders would have regarded as significant?"
d) Calculate the balance in the deferred income tax account on December 31, 19x2, before the sale of the two trucks was recorded.
e) Calculate the effect of the sale of the trucks on the balance in the deferred income tax account.

**25.** A firm needs an additional machine and determines that it can acquire the use of a particular machine in two ways:

(1) It can buy the machine for $92,442, paying $10,000 in cash on the date of purchase and promising to pay the remainder and 8 percent interest in 14 equal payments of $10,000 a year, starting one year after the date of purchase. Depreciation would be by the straight-line method over the machine's anticipated useful life of 15 years, with no estimated salvage value.

(2) It can lease the machine for 10 years, paying rent of $10,000 at the beginning of each year. The machine is expected to have a market value of $43,121 at the end of the 10 years. The lease contains no purchase or renewal options, and if the firm wanted to continue using the machine after the end of 10 years, it would have to negotiate a new lease.

a) Would the balance sheet at the date of acquisition be any different if the asset were purchased rather than leased? If so, how?
b) Calculate income before taxes for the first year under each of these two methods, assuming that income before taxes, interest, and depreciation or rent on this machine is $50,000.

*26. Company X has leased a truck from Tuck Lessors, Inc. for $2,000 a year, payable at the beginning of each year for 5 years. Company X is responsible for all taxes, insurance, and maintenance on this truck, and the lease is to be accounted for as a means of borrowing money at 12 percent.

a) Show how this lease would be reflected on a balance sheet prepared immediately after it was signed and the first payment was made.
b) Compute the amount of expense that would be reported on the income statement for the first year of the lease, assuming that depreciation was straight-line with zero salvage value.
c) Compute the book value of the asset and of the liability at the beginning of the second year, immediately after the second lease payment.

27. On January 1, 19x0, the Dan Realty Company purchased a supermarket building from Nabor Stores, Inc., at a price of $762,800. Dan Realty immediately leased the store back to Nabor Stores at an annual rental of $100,000, payable in advance on January 1 of each year. The lease term was 15 years, which was also the building's expected useful life. Its expected end-of-life salvage value was zero.

a) Assuming that Nabor Stores treated the lease as an ordinary rental:
  (1) Show how, if at all, this lease would be reflected on a balance sheet prepared immediately after the lease was signed and the first payment was made.
  (2) Compute the amount of expense that would be reported on the income statement for each of the first two years of the lease.
b) Assuming that Nabor Stores treated the signing of the lease as a simultaneous *purchase* of the store and *borrowing* of the purchase price:
  (1) Show how this lease would be reflected on a balance sheet prepared immediately after the lease was signed and the first payment was made.
  (2) Compute the amount of expense that would be reported on the income statement for each of the first two years of the lease, assuming that depreciation was straight-line with zero salvage value.
  (3) Compute the book value of the asset and of the liability at the end of each of the first two years.
c) Comment on any differences between your answers to (a) and (b). How did they arise? Could they have been eliminated?

28. A note to the 1972 financial statements of Kennecott Copper Corporation read in part:

The total pension provisions for 1972 and 1971 were $12,229,000 and $9,257,000, respectively. Unfunded past service liabilities as of December 31, 1972, were $100,500,000, including $34,900,000 representing the actuarially computed value of unfunded vested benefits.

Another note included the following sentence:

The company's pension costs, as actuarially determined, are funded as incurred and include normal costs, interest on unfunded past service costs and, with respect to certain plans, amortization of past service costs over a twenty-five to thirty-year period.

The company's balance sheets made no reference to pension liabilities. The reported shareowners' equity was $1,203,783,131 at the end of 1972; total assets were $1,845,840,271. Net income for the year was $47,423,933.

*a)*   What is the meaning of the statement that pension costs are funded as incurred?

*b)*   Should Kennecott have recognized on its balance sheet its unfunded past service liabilities? What impact would immediate recognition of the full liability have had on the financial statements?

**29.** A company has an unfunded pension plan. When an employee retires, the company gives him or her an annuity policy purchased from an insurance company, the amount depending on the employee's years of service and earnings prior to retirement. Prior to 19x1, pension expense was measured by the amounts paid for annuity policies.

This practice was changed in 19x1. Prior service costs (the present value of future benefits earned prior to 19x1) were to be amortized by charges to expense in equal amounts over a 10-year period. At that time prior service costs amounted to $1,000,000.

Pension expense for 19x1 and later years also was to consist of the present value of the future benefits attributable to the current year's payrolls, plus interest at 6 percent of the beginning-of-year pension liability (including prior service costs). The company's actuaries calculated that the future benefits attributable to 19x1 payrolls were equivalent to annual pension payments of $20,000 a year for 20 years, starting on January 1, 19x2.

Annuities costing $102,963 were purchased and turned over to retiring employees during the year.

*a)*   Calculate pension expense for 19x1.

*b)*   At what amount did the company's balance sheet list the pension liability at the end of 19x1? What was the total liability at that date?

*c)*   Suppose that at the last moment the company's actuaries decided that the appropriate interest rate was 7 percent instead of 6 percent. Would you expect this to increase or decrease the size of the reported pension liability at December 31, 19x1, other assumptions remaining the same? Would it increase or decrease the reported pension expense for 19x1?

**30.** On July 1, 1962, the Vulcan Forge Company sold a $1,000,000 issue of 6 percent, 20-year bonds to an insurance company at a price of $94.45. Interest was payable semiannually, on June 30 and December 31.

The company paid interest regularly for 10 years. In 1972, the need for additional capital prompted Vulcan's management to try to borrow another million dollars. The insurance company refused to renegotiate the loan, but Vulcan found a pension trust that was willing to take a $2,000,000 issue of 8 percent, 20-year bonds at a price of $95.23. Vulcan accepted this offer and used part of the proceeds to retire the 1962 bonds on June 30, 1972 at their call price of 102.

*a)* Indicate how the original bond issue should have been shown on the balance sheet dated July 1, 1962.
*b)* Calculate interest expense for the six months that ended on December 31, 1962. Prepare a journal entry to record the accrual of interest expense and the payment of the December 31, 1962, coupon.
*c)* Indicate how the bond issue would have been shown on the balance sheet dated December 31, 1962, after the December 31, 1962, interest payment.
*d)* Calculate the book value of the original issue at June 30, 1972, after payment of the interest coupon.
*e)* Prepare a journal entry to record the accrual of interest expense and the payment of the June 30, 1972, coupon.
*f)* Prepare a journal entry to record the issuance of the 8 percent bonds in 1972.
*g)* Calculate the gain or loss, if any, from the retirement of the 6 percent bonds. Prepare a journal entry to record the retirement of these bonds.
*h)* Calculate interest expense for the six-month period ended December 31, 1972, and prepare a journal entry to record the accrual of interest for the period and the payment of the December 31, 1972, coupon.

**31.** The 1967 annual report of Uniroyal, Inc., included the following note:

> The company and certain subsidiaries have retirement plans covering the great majority of their employees. Most plans provide for payment to independent trustees of amounts computed by independent actuaries, sufficient to provide for current service costs and the amortization of prior service costs over periods ranging from 24 to 40 years.
>
> In 1967, the total cost before reduction for income taxes of the retirement plans, including health and life insurance, was $30,080,000, of which $28,716,000 was charged to operations and $1,364,000 was applied to the Reserve for Retirement Allowances.
>
> The Reserve for Retirement Allowances was provided from income prior to the adoption of funding; the charges thereto repre-

sent a portion of the funded cost relating to past service cost. At December 31, 1967, the reserve included $3,362,000 which will be used in future years to absorb a portion of the costs relating to past service. The remainder, $2,644,000, covers certain employees ineligible under funded plans.

The actuarially computed value of vested benefits for all plans as of December 31, 1966, adjusted for the substantial increase in retirement benefits granted during the year 1967, exceeded the total of the pension fund and balance sheet accruals by approximately $275,000,000. The 1967 benefit increases were granted to nearly all active and retired employees in the United States.

The 1972 annual report disclosed that the cost of pension plans in 1972 was $47,837,000, while the actuarially computed value of vested benefits under the plans covering domestic employees exceeded the pension fund and balance sheet accruals by $395,000,000.

The following summary financial statistics have been taken from the company's annual reports for these two years:

|  | 1967 | 1972 |
|---|---|---|
| Net income | $    32,978,000 | $    46,654,000 |
| Total assets, end of year | 1,014,517,000 | 1,483,686,000 |
| Stockholders' equity, end of year | 439,042,000 | 579,633,000 |

a)  Explain in your own words the company's methods of accounting for and reporting its retirement allowances in 1967.

b)  Comment on the increase in the excess of the value of vested benefits over the pension fund and balance sheet accruals. How did this probably arise? How, if at all, should it have been recognized in the financial statements?

c)  Should the full actuarially computed value of vested benefits have been recognized in the statements of financial position? How would recognition of this amount in 1967 have affected the financial statements for that year? How might it have affected the company itself?

# 15

# THE SHAREOWNERS' EQUITY

THE OWNERS' EQUITY is at the base of the firm's capital structure. Previous chapters focused on changes in owners' equity resulting from current earnings and the declaration of dividends. In this chapter we shall examine four other topics:

1. Capital stock and shareowners' rights.
2. Issues of additional shares of stock.
3. Structural changes in the owners' equity.
4. Issues of convertible securities.

As we shall see, most of the dividing lines between the various portions of the owners' equity are left over from conditions that existed in the distant past, and no longer have any great significance. They need to be understood, however, and in the process of explaining them we shall try to discuss a number of important current issues.

## CAPITAL STOCK AND SHAREOWNERS' RIGHTS

In the United States, each state has a general incorporation law. Anyone meeting the requirements of this law is entitled to draw up a set of *articles of incorporation* and receive a corporate charter from the state. The owners of the corporation then receive shares of capital stock in exchange for the resources they contribute to the corporation. These shares of stock are evidence that their owners have ownership rights in the corporation. By selling his shares, a stockholder transfers these rights to the purchaser; the assets of the corporation remain undisturbed.

## Shareowners' Rights

The rights enjoyed by the shareowners are very different from those of the creditors. Under most circumstances, the creditor's only right is to receive specified quantities of money, goods, or services on or before specified dates in the future. In contrast, the owner has a wide range of *managerial rights* — rights to employ the company's assets as he pleases, subject to restrictions imposed by law or by his contracts with his employees, creditors, and others — plus residual *financial rights* in the net assets of the firm.

The owners of large corporations seldom exercise their managerial rights directly. The top executives of most large corporations are professional managers, appointed by the shareowners' representatives on the board of directors. The shareowners meet once a year to elect the directors for the next year, to choose the auditors, and to vote on other important matters. Shareowners who cannot attend the annual meeting in person can sign a proxy form, authorizing someone else to attend and vote in their place. In most cases, proxies are solicited and voted by the corporation's management.

The powers, duties, and responsibilities of the directors and the relationships between the shareowners and the board are specified in the corporation's by-laws. These can be changed from time to time by vote of the shareowners. In addition to appointing the officers of the corporation, the board also establishes the basic policies by which the firm's management is guided, approves the firm's operating and financing plans, declares dividends, and reviews the performance of the firm's top management. The board, in turn, is fully answerable to the shareowners, who can bring actions to recover damages they have suffered as a result of any failure of the board to observe the requirements imposed upon it by law or by the by-laws.

The owner's financial rights are subordinate to those of the corporation's creditors. If the company is liquidated, the creditors' claims must be satisfied first; the shareowner is entitled only to any residual that may remain after the creditors have been paid off.[1] If the company is successful, however, the value of the shareowner's investment can climb dramatically, while

---

[1] Outright liquidation of the assets of a large corporation to satisfy the demands of creditors is extremely rare. Instead, the assets are transferred by agreement to a new or reorganized corporation under a reorganization plan in which both owners and creditors share in the reorganization loss. The owners' share of this loss is greater than that of the creditors.

the creditor will have to be satisfied with the amounts specified in his agreement with the corporation. This means that in any given company the shareowner assumes a greater risk than a creditor with an identical investment in the company, but has an opportunity for a far greater reward.

## Common Stock

When a corporation has only one class of capital stock, it is usually referred to as common stock. In such cases, each share of common stock represents a proportionate share of all of the ownership rights in the corporation.

The articles of incorporation specify the number of shares of common stock that the corporation is authorized to issue and the *par value* of each share. In some cases, the articles will specify that the shares are *no-par* shares, in which case either the articles or the directors will designate a portion of the issue price as the *stated value* of the stock.

Par value had its origin in the concept of legal capital. Since the owners are not personally liable for the corporation's debts, the corporation's creditors can count on recovering the amounts due them only if the corporation has enough assets to cover their claims. The amount designated as the legal capital establishes a minimum limit on the owners' equity. The owners cannot withdraw funds if this would reduce the owners' equity to less than the legal capital. In concept, this provides a cushion or margin of protection for the creditors. Since the assets' cash value is likely to be less than their book value in case of forced liquidation, the presence of a certain amount of legal capital would appear to give the creditor a greater degree of assurance that his claims will be met if the firm is forced into bankruptcy. If the directors declare dividends or take other actions that impair the legal capital directly, they are liable for any damages suffered by the creditors as a result.

Par value still measures the legal capital in some jurisdictions, but not in all. The United States alone has more than 50 separate incorporation laws, and they are not at all uniform. In any event, the economic significance of par or stated value today is minimal. The issue price of shares of common stock in the United States is frequently a large multiple of the par or stated value; par value then is a very small percentage of the total liabilities. The creditor's protection comes from the size of the cash flow stream rather than from the designation of part of the owners' equity as legal capital.

The spread between the issue price and par or stated value is reported on the balance sheet under some heading such as Additional Paid-In Capital or Capital in Excess of Par Value. The entry to record the issue of 100,000 shares of $1 par common stock in exchange for $1,000,000 in cash would be as follows:

```
Cash ...................................... 1,000,000
    Common Stock ..........................            100,000
    Additional Paid-In Capital..............            900,000
```

Additional paid-in capital used to be referred to as capital surplus or paid-in surplus, but this terminology is gradually falling into disuse. The word surplus may convey the misleading impression that the corporation has surplus liquid funds that might safely be withdrawn for use elsewhere. The balances in the owners' equity accounts have no necessary connection with the amount of liquid funds on hand, much less with the amount that can be distributed to the shareholders or made available to the creditors.

For most corporations, the number of shares issued is smaller than the number of shares authorized in the articles of incorporation. The availability of a large number of authorized but unissued shares makes it possible for the corporation to use stock to acquire other companies, raise additional capital, or reward key personnel without amending the articles of incorporation. When the number of unissued shares gets low, the shareholders are usually asked to approve an amendment to the articles of incorporation increasing the number of authorized shares. In any event, the amount shown on the statement of financial position as common stock does not include the par value of authorized but unissued shares.

### Preferred Stock

Some corporations have one or more classes of capital stock in addition to the common stock. These are usually called preferred or preference stock. The rights of each class of shares are specified in the articles of incorporation and by-laws, but each share of a given class has the same rights as any other share of that class. Thus an owner of 1,000 shares of $5 preferred stock has twice as many votes as a holder of 500 shares of the $5 preferred, receives twice as much dividend money, and so forth.

The characteristics of preferred stock vary widely from issue to issue, but they usually entitle the holder to a fixed dividend that must be paid before any dividends can be paid on the common stock. They also have precedence over common stock in any liquidation of assets, up to a specified maximum amount per share.

The dividend priority is usually *cumulative*, meaning that no distribution can be made to the common shareholders until all current and back dividends have been paid on the preferred. In most cases, shares of preferred stock are also *callable* at a specified price. This means that the company has the right to repurchase the stock if certain conditions are met, even if the owners of the stock do not wish to sell it.

A preferred stock differs from a bond in that the stockholders have no legal right to insist on payment of their dividends on specified dates. Furthermore, the stock has no maturity date. A corporation may omit or pass the dividend on the preferred indefinitely without being declared insolvent, although some preferred stocks provide for the transfer of corporate control to the preferred shareholders when the dividends have fallen a specified amount in arrears.

Many preferred stocks issued in recent years have been *convertible* into a predetermined number of shares of common stock. The sale of preferred stock and bonds with the conversion privilege or with detachable options to buy common stock is sometimes an indirect way of selling common stock. The interesting features of such securities and the accounting problems they raise will be discussed later in this chapter.

## ADDITIONAL ISSUES OF CAPITAL STOCK

The initial source of corporate financing is the sale or issuance of capital stock. Without an adequate base of ownership capital, the corporation would be unable to obtain debt financing and would even experience difficulties in obtaining short-term trade credit.

Much of the ownership capital needed to finance corporate growth is supplied by the reinvestment of funds generated by operations. This source is often inadequate to support the desired rate of growth, however, and in that case the board of directors may decide to sell additional shares of common stock to obtain the needed cash.

### Registration Requirements

Large corporations wishing to take this route must register each new issue with the Securities and Exchange Commission and make a detailed prospectus available to any potential purchaser of the shares. The task of the S.E.C. is to insure that the information provided in the registration statement is complete and accurate. S.E.C. approval of a registration statement does not constitute or even imply an endorsement of the shares as a sound investment vehicle.

## Dilution of the Equity

The existing shareowners' motive in approving the issuance of additional shares is to participate in the fruits of the growth that the proceeds of the new issue will make possible. Their main concern is to insure that this will not result in an undue dilution of their equity. Shares of stock issued to different individuals or at different times have identical rights, no matter how much or how little the original shareowner paid for his stock. For this reason, the owners are understandably anxious to make sure that others are not allowed to purchase shares from the corporation at prices that will lower the value of their holdings.

Some dilution of the equity occurs whenever shares are issued at a price lower than the price of the outstanding shares. For example, suppose the XYZ Corporation has 100,000 shares of common stock outstanding with a market value of $50 a share. If the company sells an additional 100,000 shares at $40 a share, a reasonable expectation is that all of the shares will trade at $45 a share. If this happens, the market value of the old shareowners' holdings will fall from $5 million to $4.5 million; the new shareowners will pay $4 million for stock worth $4.5 million. This transfer of part of the equity of the old shareholders to the new shareholders dilutes the equity of the former.

No board of directors would dare approve this kind of dilutive transaction if the same shares could be sold to other investors at or near the current $50 market price. Dilution of the equity can take place in less transparent ways, however. For example, Space Age Corporation was organized in 19x1 and was authorized to issue 200,000 shares of common stock with no par value. The stated value of the stock was $10 a share. Some 10,000 shares were issued initially: 8,000 in exchange for a patent and 2,000 for the services of an entrepreneur who organized the corporation and would serve as its president. Shortly thereafter another 40,000 shares were sold to the public for cash at a price of $25 a share.

In this case, all of the shares were assumed to have been issued at a price of $25 a share. The journal entry to record all of these issues was:

| | | |
|---|---|---|
| Cash ....................................... | 1,000,000 | |
| Patent...................................... | 200,000 | |
| Organization Costs ......................... | 50,000 | |
| Common Stock .......................... | | 500,000 |
| Additional Paid-In Capital............... | | 750,000 |

This entry was based on the assumption that the assets received in exchange for each of the first 10,000 shares were worth the same amount as the assets received for each of the next 40,000 shares. This is presumed to be true whenever transactions are at *arm's length* — that is, whenever buyer and seller are independent of each other. In this case, however, at least one of the figures is suspect because the entrepreneur probably decided how many shares to issue to himself in exchange for his organizational activities. It is clear that if the patent and organizational activities were worth less than the amounts stated, the equity of the other shareholders was diluted. To protect the other shareholders against dilution of their equity from transactions of this sort, the accountant should identify transactions that are not at arm's length, obtain an independent appraisal of the assets acquired, and value them accordingly.

The term "dilution of the equity" is sometimes used in a different way. When a company's stock is selling at a price less than its book value per share, the sale of additional shares at the market price reduces the book value per share. Since the sale of additional shares may well be in the best interest of the existing shareowners, it is probably undesirable to say that such a sale dilutes their equity. Strictly speaking, however, the book value of the equity has been diluted.

With the benefit of hindsight it is easy to discover other cases of dilution. For example, the market value of the Space Age stock might rise to $100 a share within a few years due to the extraordinary value of the patent. Hindsight tells us that the inventor should have received more than 16 percent of the company's stock in exchange for the patent. In judging the fairness of a transaction, however, hindsight is not available.

### Dilution of Earnings

Dilution of earnings is a term even more widely used than dilution of the equity. The funds obtained from the sale of additional shares are unlikely to generate earnings during the first year or two that are large enough to keep earnings per share unchanged. If the shares are issued to retire debt, for example, interest expense will fall and total net income will rise. The percentage increase in the number of shares outstanding will probably be larger than the percentage increase in net income, however, and earnings per share will fall. This reduction in earnings per share is referred to as dilution of the earnings due to the stock issue. Again, this does not mean that the stock issue is unwise; it may be fully justified as a means of reducing risk or increasing future earnings.

## CAPITALIZATION OF RETAINED EARNINGS

Corporations often restructure their owners' equity in ways other than by issuing additional shares of capital stock. In this section we shall see how stock dividends and stock splits are used. The next two sections will deal with the structural changes accompanying appropriations of retained earnings and treasury stock transactions.

### Stock Dividends

Space Age Corporation had been extraordinarily successful during its early years of operation, and the balance in retained earnings had reached $715,000 by the end of 19x6. The demand for funds to finance the company's growth was equally strong, however, and consequently no cash dividends were declared after the second year. Noting the large retained earnings balance, several stockholders were exerting pressure on the board to declare a dividend. Unfortunately, dividends are paid with cash, not with retained earnings, and Space Age was chronically short of cash. Each year the company had invested its available funds in operating assets, and at the end of 19x6 it had only $50,000 in the bank. Since $50,000 was barely adequate to meet the day-to-day operating needs for cash, the company had no money to pay dividends.

In this situation, to give partial satisfaction to the stockholders' demands and to advise them that the funds generated by profitable operations had in large measure been *permanently* reinvested in the company, the directors decided to declare a 10 percent *stock dividend*. A stock dividend consists of the distribution of additional shares of stock to the existing stockholders in proportion to their holdings. With 55,000 shares outstanding, the Space Age 10 percent dividend consisted of 5,500 shares, 1 for every 10 outstanding.

This transaction was treated as if the corporation had declared a cash dividend equal to the market value of the 5,500 shares and the stockholders had simultaneously purchased the 5,500 shares at their market price.[2] Because the market price of the stock at the time of the stock dividend was $60, the journal entry was:

Retained Earnings ........................... 330,000
    Common Stock........................... 55,000
    Additional Paid-In Capital................ 275,000

The "dividend" reduced retained earnings, and the "stock sale" increased the paid-in capital by the market value of the number of shares. The owners' equity accounts before and after the stock dividend appear in Exhibit 15–1.

Exhibit 15–1

Space Age Corporation
SHAREHOLDERS' EQUITY
December 31, 19x6

| | Before Stock Dividend | | After Stock Dividend | |
|---|---|---|---|---|
| | Total | per Share | Total | per Share |
| Common stock – stated value... | $ 550,000 | $10.00 | $ 605,000 | $10.00 |
| Additional paid-in capital ...... | 935,000 | 17.00 | 1,210,000 | 20.00 |
| Retained earnings.............. | 715,000 | 13.00 | 385,000 | 6.36 |
| Total Shareholders' Equity. | $2,200,000 | $40.00 | $2,200,000 | $36.36 |

It should be evident that the stock dividend may properly be called a paper transaction. After the dividend, each stockholder had 11 shares which conveyed the same rights as the 10 shares he had owned previously. The total owners' equity was unaffected by the stock dividend; it was merely divided into a larger number of shares, each one representing a smaller portion of the company than formerly. After the dividend, 11 shares had the same $400 book value (11 × $36.36) that the owner's 10 shares had had before.

Although the stock dividend does not give the stockholder any new asset, the market in the stock may be slightly more active than formerly because of the increase in the number of shares outstanding. Many companies also follow the practice of paying the same cash dividend per share after the stock dividend that they had been paying previously. Furthermore, the market often interprets the declaration of a stock dividend as evidence of man-

---

[2] Measuring the stock dividend at the market value of the shares is logically inconsistent. The stock dividend itself does not increase the total market value of the company's stock. The main reason for measuring the additional shares at amounts greater than par value or other legal minimum is probably that this permits the capitalization of a larger portion of the retained earnings with a given increment in the number of shares outstanding.

agement's faith in the continued growth of the company. The combined effect of these and other factors often is to increase the total market value of the company's stock. In other words, although 11 shares should sell for what 10 shares would have brought previously (10 × $60 = $600), in fact they may sell for more (e.g., 11 × $56 = $616). This effect will not persist, however, if the expected growth does not materialize.

## Stock Splits

A stock split is akin to a stock dividend in that each stockholder is given additional shares in proportion to the number he owns. The par or stated value is usually reduced to accompany a stock split, but the main difference is in the number of shares distributed. When an increase of more than about 20 or 25 percent in the number of shares outstanding is to be achieved, the mechanism of the stock split is usually employed.[3]

Stock splits are used to bring the price of the company's shares down to a level that the market will find attractive. When corporate growth is financed by the reinvestment of large portions of the funds generated by profitable operations, stock prices are likely to rise. To prevent this, the corporation will probably split its stock from time to time, thereby making it more marketable.

For example, the market price of Space Age Corporation had risen to $90 by the end of 19x9, and the board of directors decided to declare a 2 for 1 stock split and to reduce the stated value of the stock from $10 to $5. The journal entry that gave effect to this transaction was:

Common Stock (Stated Value $10) ............ 605,000
    Common Stock (Stated Value $5)...........     605,000

Only the common stock account was affected by this transaction, and no transfers occurred between the various ownership accounts, as shown in Exhibit 15–2.

A few months after the stock split, the new shares were selling for $49, something more than half the price of the stock prior to the split. The reduction in the stock's price range may have been partly responsible for this increase in market value, although a larger share of the responsibility was probably attributable to circulation of rumors that the company was about to begin paying dividends.

---

[3] This is the dividing line prescribed by the American Institute of Certified Public Accountants, *APB Accounting Principles: Current Text* (New York: Commerce Clearing House, Inc., 1972), Sec. 5561.15.

Exhibit 15–2

Space Age Corporation

SHAREHOLDERS' EQUITY

December 31, 19x9

|  | Before Stock Split | | After Stock Split | |
| --- | --- | --- | --- | --- |
|  | Total | per Share | Total | per Share |
| Common stock – stated value... | $ 605,000 | $10 | $ 605,000 | $ 5 |
| Additional paid-in capital ...... | 1,210,000 | 20 | 1,210,000 | 10 |
| Retained Earnings ............. | 1,089,000 | 18 | 1,089,000 | 9 |
| Total Shareholders' Equity . | $2,904,000 | $48 | $2,904,000 | $24 |

Our need to discuss both stock dividends and stock splits in a very short space for the sake of concise illustration should not be allowed to obscure the basic importance of cash dividends. Dividends and the prospect of dividends in the near future are usually necessary to a sustained growth in market prices, and stockholders' demands for dividends usually cannot be long ignored.

## RESERVES AND APPROPRIATIONS

One way to inform stockholders that large portions of the funds generated by profitable operations have been more or less permanently reinvested is to declare stock dividends. Another way is to identify part of the balance in retained earnings as an appropriation for some specific purpose or purposes. The practice of appropriating retained earnings is now rarely encountered. The line between appropriated earnings and liabilities is sometimes very fuzzy, however, and earnings appropriations may actually appear on the balance sheet under the guise of liabilities or even as deductions from asset balances. To understand these distinctions, we need to review the earnings appropriation process.

### Appropriations of Retained Earnings

The clearest kind of earnings appropriation is an appropriation to call shareholders' attention to an event or events that prevent the distribution of dividends. For example, the directors of Space Age Corporation decided to appropriate $200,000 for debt retirement. The entry was:

Retained Earnings ........................... 200,000
    Earnings Appropriated for Debt Retirement        200,000

This reduced the balance in Retained Earnings and created a

$200,000 credit balance in a new account, Earnings Appropriated for Debt Retirement.

An action of this kind serves simply as a memorandum to stockholders that one reason dividends will not be declared is that the company needs to accumulate funds for debt retirement. It does not indicate that a corresponding amount of cash is being held in readiness for this or any other purpose – this can be revealed only by an analysis of the company's cash balances.

Balances in earnings appropriations accounts are subdivisions of retained earnings. They are created by debits to the Retained Earnings account; when their purpose has been served, the balances in the appropriations accounts can be transferred back to Retained Earnings or left intact. In other words, when Space Age Corporation uses its cash to retire the debt, only the cash and liability accounts are affected; the balance in the appropriation account remains until the board of directors decides to reclassify it as part of the unappropriated retained earnings.

Whether this practice constitutes an effective means of disclosure is debatable. If the intent is permanent retention of funds in the business, it can be argued that capitalization, as by a stock dividend, is preferable. Furthermore, if *any* portions of retained earnings are appropriated in this manner, then perhaps the *entire* amount ought to be appropriated, to indicate all of the reasons for increasing the owners' equity by retaining funds in the business. Otherwise, the stockholder may get the impression that an amount of cash equal to the unappropriated balance represents idle funds, available for dividend distribution.

### Contingency Reserves

One of the most widely used kinds of earnings appropriations in the past was the so-called reserve for contingencies. A reserve for contingencies is a subdivision of the owners' equity to call attention to the *possibility* that a present condition or commitment will lead to a future event that will reduce the firm's assets or increase its liabilities.

For example, suppose that most of a company's facilities are located in an area that is subject to the possibility of earthquakes. Management has decided that outside insurance against earthquake damage is too expensive. Instead, it has decided to show in its financial statements that its investment in plant, equipment and inventories is subject to the risk of loss due to earthquakes.

At one time the firm would have accomplished this through

periodic charges against revenues, in the form shown below:

<pre>
Earthquake Damage Expense ......................... xxx
        Reserve for Contingencies ........................    xxx
</pre>

If an earthquake did occur, the cost of any damage was charged directly to the reserve by entries like the following:

<pre>
Reserve for Contingencies ........................... xxx
        Various Assets.....................................    xxx
</pre>

The difficulty with this practice is that the company has no objective basis on which to estimate the annual cost of earthquake damage. The size of the reserve may be far too large or far too small, but the company's public accountants cannot prove it. Furthermore, charges against the reserve are not readily identifiable, and may go unnoticed by unsophisticated readers of the financial statements.

For these reasons, the accounting profession has taken the position that losses of this kind should not be shown on the income statement until the accountant has adequate evidence to establish the probable amount of the loss. Contingency reserves can be created only by transfers from retained earnings; losses are charged against revenues when they become measurable and are not charged against the reserves. Any such reserve remains part of retained earnings and should be labeled as such.[4]

## Other Types of "Reserves"

The term "reserve" is very imprecise. For one thing, it may imply that it measures the amount of liquid resources that the firm keeps on hand for use in times of need. This is highly unlikely to be true.

A second problem is that this term may be used in the titles of three distinct types of accounts: appropriations of retained earnings, discussed above; contra-assets or *valuation reserves*, such as the reserves (allowances) for depreciation and uncollectible accounts; and *liability reserves*, such as the reserve (provision) for income taxes. All three are based on estimates and all have credit balances—otherwise, they have nothing in common.

To avoid confusion on both of these counts, the term reserve should be avoided. The major difficulty runs deeper than a mere confusion of terminology, however. Many companies show reserves in their annual reports without describing them clearly.

---

[4] *APB Accounting Principles*, Sec. 5513.

They are often shown at the end of the liabilities, with no information to indicate whether they represent liabilities — that is, the present value of future cash outlays which past events have obligated the company to make — or appropriations of retained earnings. Use of a separate category implies that these items somehow are neither liabilities nor owners' equities, which is merely a way of dodging the issue.

In short, if management has an objective basis for anticipating an event and for deciding how much of any resultant losses should be charged against the current year's revenues, then the reserve is either a liability or a contra-asset. Otherwise, it is an appropriation of retained earnings and should be classified as part of the owners' equity.

## Hidden Reserves

The term reserve is also used in another connection. Any difference between the economic value of an asset or liability and the amount at which that asset or liability is carried on the balance sheet is called a *hidden reserve.*

A hidden reserve will arise if an asset has been measured at a lower figure than is warranted by the strict application of accounting principles. The use of generally accepted accounting principles does not eliminate hidden reserves, however. For example, a company which has spent large sums on advertising and other activities to establish the value of a trademark but which has charged all of these expenditures to expense is very likely to have a hidden reserve. Similarly, if straight-line depreciation is the closest approximation to the pattern of the decline in the service potential of plant and equipment but the company uses declining-balance depreciation on its published financial statements, a hidden reserve will arise. A good financial analyst will try to identify hidden reserves, no matter what their source, but this is seldom easy.

## TREASURY STOCK

Corporations from time to time have occasion to repurchase shares of their own stock. Such repurchased shares are called treasury stock.

## Objectives of Treasury Stock Purchases

Share repurchase may have a number of objectives. Some reacquired shares may be used for distribution to executives in bonus or stock option plans. Others may be used for distribution to shareholders as stock dividends, to employees in stock purchase plans, or to the company's pension funds for long-term investment. Share repurchase may also be viewed as a more profitable use of the company's funds than the available alternatives. If the company has more cash than it can invest profitably internally, stock repurchase may prevent a dilution in earnings per share, particularly when market prices seem unjustifiably low.[5]

The negative aspects of these transactions should not be overlooked, however. For one thing, the purchase and sale of treasury stock in any volume can generate short-term movements in the price of the stock which might be interpreted as the use of the corporation's funds by "insiders" to influence the price of the stock to their advantage. Similar objections can be raised to the use of the corporation's funds to purchase stock to prevent voting control from being concentrated in unfriendly hands. Furthermore, the purchase of treasury shares might weaken the company's financial position and thereby impair the rights of the company's creditors, employees, and remaining stockholders.

### Reporting Treasury Stock at Cost

The customary method of accounting for treasury stock is to carry it in a separate account, measured at the price paid to acquire it. This is the cost method, used by most companies to record temporary reacquisitions of common shares. Under this method, the cost of treasury shares is shown on the balance sheet as a negative element of owners' equity.

For example, if Space Age Corporation were to repurchase for $46,000 a total of 1,000 shares of its common stock after the stock split on December 31, 19x9, the revised December 31, 19x9, balance sheet would show the following:

| | |
|---|---|
| Common stock—stated value........................ | $ 605,000 |
| Additional paid-in capital ........................... | 1,210,000 |
| Earnings retained in the business................... | 1,089,000 |
| Total......................................... | $2,904,000 |
| Less: Treasury stock (at cost) ...................... | (46,000) |
| Total Shareholders' Equity.................... | $2,858,000 |

Treasury stock is not an asset, although it is sometimes re-

---

[5] This last objective was strongly supported by Charles D. Ellis, "Repurchase Stock to Revitalize Equity," *Harvard Business Review*, July–August, 1965, pp. 119–28. A lively exchange of views on the wisdom and propriety of share repurchases was presented in the same issue under the heading, "Letters from the Thoughtful Businessman," pp. 30–40, 178.

ported as one. Shares of stock represent portions of the owners' equity in the firm. When the shares are repurchased, the assets are reduced and so is the owners' equity. To treat treasury stock as an asset would imply that the company has ownership rights in itself, and this is not true. Treasury shares cannot be voted, nor do they participate in cash dividends or carry any other perquisites of ownership. The purchase of treasury shares represents a partial and perhaps temporary liquidation of the enterprise and represents a reduction in both total assets and total owners' equities. Thus, the amount paid for the stock should be deducted from the shareholders' equity. It should not be included among the assets.

Resale of treasury stock at prices different from their acquisition cost is not reported as a gain or loss on the company's income statement. The company cannot make or lose money by buying and selling a portion of itself, although the equity of the surviving shareholders can be increased or decreased by such actions. Instead, the difference should be carried to the Additional Paid-In Capital account to show that the amounts received from shareholders have increased or decreased. If the stock is resold at a price less than its acquisition cost, however, any excess of (a) the difference between the proceeds from resale and the acquisition cost of the stock over (b) the credit balance in the Additional Paid-In Capital account should be charged to retained earnings. The purchase and sale of the treasury stock in this case constitute a permanent liquidation of part of the assets contributed by profitable operations in previous years.

## CONVERTIBLE SECURITIES AND STOCK PURCHASE OPTIONS

Corporations often issue shares of common stock to their executives in connection with established stock option plans or to holders of the company's convertible bonds and preferred stock. The implications of any such conversion or purchase options should be clearly understood. We shall look briefly at three of these: convertible preferred stock, stock options, and executive performance shares.

### Convertible Preferred Stock

The purchaser of convertible preferred stock obtains a more or less assured dividend plus an opportunity to participate in any growth in the company's earnings by converting his preferred shares into common shares when the common dividend and market price have risen above the fixed preferred dividend and the preferred price.

For example, in 19x1 a corporation issued 1,000 shares of convertible preferred stock at an issue price of $100 a share. The annual dividend on the preferred was $5, and each share was convertible into 5 shares of common stock at the discretion of the holder.

Earnings per common share amounted to $1.50 in 19x1, with an annual cash dividend of 75 cents a share. The market price of the common shares at that time was $18 a share. Given these figures, the preferred stockholder had no incentive to exercise his conversion option. By converting a share of preferred into 5 shares of common, he would have lost $1.25 in dividends and $10 in market value:

| | | |
|---|---|---|
| Preferred share | $5.00 | $100 |
| 5 common shares | 3.75 | 90 |
| Difference | $1.25 | $ 10 |

This does not mean that the conversion option was valueless, however. If earnings and dividends on the common stock continued to rise in the years ahead, the market price of the common would probably rise, too. If that happened, conversion could become very desirable. Suppose, for example, that the cash dividend on the common rose to $1.60 a share in 19x6 and that the market price of a common share at that time was $40. Conversion of the preferred shares at that time would give the preferred shareholder $8 in dividends instead of $5, and the market value of his investment would be $200 (5 shares at $40 each). In other words, the conversion privilege clearly has value if the price of the common is expected to rise.[6]

Issuing convertible securities also involves a cost to the common shareholders. To retire the 1,000 shares of preferred in 19x6, the company had to issue 5,000 shares of common, worth about $200,000. If the preferred had been callable at $100, however, the company could have retired the entire issue with the payment of $100,000 in cash. This $100,000 could have been obtained by issuing only 2,500 shares at $40 a share. The conversion privilege, in other words, carries with it a potential dilution of the common equity.

In recognition of this potential dilution, corporations do not give this conversion privilege for nothing. Without it, the pre-

---

[6] For more on the economics of convertible securities, see E. F. Brigham, "An Analysis of Convertible Debentures," *Journal of Finance*, January 1966, pp. 35–54.

ferred would have carried a higher dividend rate, say $9 a share if that was the going market rate on this kind of security at the time. The buyer of the convertible, in other words, exchanged a reasonably certain $4 in additional dividends for a larger but uncertain expected increase in the value of the preferred. This $4 difference accrued to the benefit of the common shareholder so long as the conversion feature remained unexercised.

The accounting issue in all this is whether, in calculating earnings per common share, the deduction of the $5 preferred dividend from net income is adequate. Because the probabilities and timing of future conversions are highly uncertain, the accounting profession does not try to record the amount by which the true cost of the preferred exceeds the amount paid in dividends in any year. The profession has nonetheless been troubled by the overstatement of common earnings that results from showing only the dividend as the portion of net income attributable to the preferred. To deal with this problem, in calculating earnings per share, corporations are required to treat convertible securities as equivalent to common stock if the percentage yield at the time of issuance is less than two-thirds of the prime rate applicable to banks' loans to their lowest risk customers. The figure for earnings per share calculated on this basis is known as *primary* earnings per share.[7]

For example, suppose that when the $5 convertible preferred was issued, the prime rate was more than 7½ percent. 20,000 shares of common and 1,000 shares of convertible preferred were outstanding in 19x5 and the earnings of the company before deducting the preferred dividends were $65,000. Ignoring the potential dilution, earnings per common share would be calculated as follows:

| | |
|---|---:|
| Net income | $65,000 |
| Less: Dividends on preferred stock | |
| (1,000 shares at $5) | 5,000 |
| Income Available to Common Stock | $60,000 |
| Divided by: Number of common shares | 20,000 |
| Earnings per Common Share | $3.00 |

The conversion of all of the preferred, however, would raise the number of common shares outstanding to 25,000. Dividing this into $65,000 results in a primary earnings per share of $2.60.

---

[7] This dividing line is highly arbitrary, and was adopted by the Accounting Principles Board as a means of achieving uniformity of treatment in this calculation. American Institute of Certified Public Accountants, *APB Accounting Principles: Current Text* (New York: Commerce Clearing House, Inc., 1972), Section 2011.33.

Some companies also have convertible securities that do not qualify as common stock equivalents on the basis of the test described above. If the $5 preferred had been issued when the prime rate was 6 percent, for example, primary earnings per share would have been $3. In such cases, the financial statements must include a second figure, labeled *fully diluted* earnings per share, calculated by the method described above. (The actual calculations are likely to be much more complex than this simple illustration would imply, but these complexities can be ignored here.)

### Stock Options

Options to purchase corporate stock are often issued for various reasons. One purpose may be to reduce annual interest payments. For example, suppose the interest rate at which a company can borrow is 8½ percent and the price of the stock is $45 a share. Wishing to keep interest payments low, the company has decided to market a new issue of bonds with a coupon rate of only 6½ percent. Each $1,000 bond will have detachable options to buy 20 shares of common stock at a price of $50 a share.

The company's investment bankers are confident that potential bond buyers will assign a high enough value to these options to be willing to buy the bonds at their face value, even though the coupon rate is 2 percent lower than the going market rate. This will not only reduce annual interest payments, but may give the company a way of raising additional equity capital at a later date. If all twenty of the options are exercised, the corporation will receive $1,000 in cash. This will be enough to retire the bonds or to expand the scope of the company's operations.

Stock options have also won wide acceptance as a form of executive compensation. In most option plans, key executives are given options to buy specified numbers of shares at a fixed price, usually the market price at the time the options are granted. If market price goes up in the future, the executive can exercise some or all of his options and participate in the gain.

The argument for executive stock options is that they provide executives with a strong inducement to perform effectively so that the price of the company's stock will rise. In other words, the executive gets nothing unless the stockholders also benefit.

When detachable stock options are used, the company must divide the proceeds of the issue between the bonds and the options. For example, a 20-year, 6½ percent, $1,000 bond sold in a 8½ percent market should sell at a price of $809.20. If the proceeds from each bond amount to $1,000, then the buyer must be paying $190.80 for the options. This amount should be shown as part of the shareholders' equity and the liability should be listed at its face value less a $190.80 discount, to be amortized by the methods described in the preceding chapter.[8]

Because the company receives no direct payment when stock options are granted to employees, no changes in the owners' equity can be recognized. The potential dilution must be recognized in the financial statements, however. This is accomplished by disclosing such information as the number of options outstanding and the option price, and by calculating earnings per share on the assumption that all outstanding options have been exercised in full. We shall leave the details of these calculations to more advanced texts.

### Performance Shares

The stock market collapse of the early 1970s destroyed the value of most executive stock options outstanding at that time. New options granted during that period did little better. In an attempt to give top management an incentive to improve the company's financial performance while conserving the company's cash, a number of firms began to offer free shares of stock to executives whose performance met or exceeded preestablished goals.

The market value of these so-called performance shares is treated as an expense of the period in which the shares are distributed, on the grounds that the executives have paid for them by contributing to higher operating margins than would otherwise have been achieved. The proceeds are credited to the stock and premium accounts, in the same manner as any other issue of shares. Performance shares have an even greater potential dilution effect than stock options because the option price is in effect zero. This should be reflected in the fully diluted earnings per share.

### SUMMARY

Most of the problems of accounting for the common stock equity arise in connection with the reinvestment of funds that have been generated by profitable operations. This may be em-

---

[8] *APB Accounting Principles*, Sec. 5516.14.

phasized by declaration of a stock dividend or, occasionally, by earmarking of retained earnings to indicate some specific purpose or purposes of reinvestment. If the investment of funds is successful, stock splits will be necessary to keep the market price of the stock within a range appropriate for trading. If internal investment opportunities fall off, however, purchases of treasury stock may be made to provide a partial distribution of funds previously invested by the shareholders and increase the yield for those who continue to keep their funds invested in the company.

The accounting for these events is relatively simple, and in general requires only the shuffling of numbers from account to account in the owners' equity section. A more complex set of problems has arisen in connection with the existence of corporate commitments to issue shares of stock at fixed prices. Convertible securities, executive stock option plans, and performance share plans all create potential dilutions of the stockholders' equity. These must be disclosed and their effects measured.

## QUESTIONS AND PROBLEMS

1. What does the owners' equity in a company represent? What rights do the owners have?

2. Explain the meaning of "6 percent, cumulative, convertible, callable, $100 par value preferred stock."

3. What advantages and disadvantages do the cumulative, callable, and convertible features of preferred stock confer on the company's management? On the preferred stockholders?

4. What is meant by dilution of the stockholders' equity? Give an example.

5. "Stock options provide a means of compensating the company's officers without cost to the other stockholders." Discuss.

6. How may a corporate stockholder benefit from the retention of corporate earnings as opposed to their distribution in the form of cash dividends?

7. Distinguish between a stock dividend and a stock split. Do they serve the same purpose or do they have different objectives?

8. What is the purpose of appropriations of retained earnings? Should

direct charges against the balances in the appropriation accounts be permitted?

9. Distinguish between a "contingency reserve" and a "liability reserve." Which of these contains cash?

10. What arguments can you advance for giving corporations the right to acquire treasury stock by open-market purchases? Is this practice subject to any dangers?

11. Should the company report a gain or loss on the purchase and sale of treasury stock? Should it report a gain or loss on the purchase and retirement of shares of its own stock? Explain.

12. Distinguish between ordinary and extraordinary earnings. What is the main alternative to showing extraordinary earnings on the income statement for the year? Which alternative do you prefer, and why?

*13. Company A's board of directors declared a stock dividend of one share of common stock for each 20 shares outstanding. Prior to the stock dividend, 20,000 shares were outstanding with a par value of $10 a share. The company's accountants decided to capitalize the stock dividend at $30 a share. Present the required journal entries.

*14. On January 4, Company B repurchases 100 shares of its $5 par common stock at a price of $30 a share. The shares are held as treasury stock. On March 18, it resells these shares at a price of $40 a share. Present entries for both dates.

*15. Company C's board of directors votes to appropriate $1,000,000 of earnings to provide for future debt retirement. At the same time it votes to transfer $800,000 in cash to the sinking fund for bond retirement. Present the related entries.

*16. Beehive Industries secures permission to issue 3,000,000 no-par shares at a stated value of $5. The stock is placed on the market at $7.50 a share, and 400,000 shares are sold at that price.
Show the entry that you would make on the books of the company.

*17. The Myrex Preparations Company appropriated $10,000 of retained earnings for the contingency of an expected lawsuit arising out of the harm suffered by one of its customers through the use of its product. The suit was settled for $11,500 in the year following the appropriation. Indicate the pertinent journal entries in the two years.

---

* Solutions to problems marked with an asterisk (*) are found in Appendix B.

18. On January 8, 19x0, the Alpine Company started operations by issuing 100,000 shares of common stock, $10 par, at a price of $15 a share. Retained earnings of the company as of December 31, 19x3, totaled $2,000,000.

a) Prepare a journal entry to record the issuance of the stock.
b) What was the book value per share of common stock as of December 31, 19x3?

19. On January 2, 19x4, the Alpine Company (see Problem 18) repurchased 1,000 shares of its stock at the market price of $28 a share. This stock was held as treasury stock.

a) How should this treasury stock have been listed on the company's June 30, 19x4, balance sheet?
b) Did the purchase of this treasury stock increase, decrease, or leave unchanged the book value per share of stock issued and outstanding?
c) Should a gain or loss be shown in the 19x4 income statement as a result of the repurchase of the stock? Why?

20. On July 1, 19x4, the Alpine Company (see Problem 19) resold its treasury stock at a price of $34 a share.

a) Prepare a journal entry recording the sale.
b) Should a gain or loss be shown on the 19x4 income statement as a result of the resale of the stock? Why?

21. A balance sheet showed the following owners' equity section on December 31:

Stockholders' investment:
$5 par value common stock (5,559,500 shares issued)...... $27,797,500
Other paid-in capital...................................... 10,960,500
Income invested in the business .......................... 55,389,500
Cost of shares held by the company (9,500 shares)......... (153,500)
    Total Stockholders' Investment ....................... $93,994,000

The market price of the stock on December 31 was $25 per share.

a) What was the book value per share of common stock issued and outstanding at the end of the year?
b) Give three alternative explanations as to how the "Other paid-in capital" might have been accumulated. (One phrase or sentence for each will be adequate.)
c) If the corporation decided to cancel and retire the 9,500 "shares held by the company," what journal entry should be made? Explain your choice.

22. Assume that the corporation in Problem 21 declared a 10 percent stock dividend on December 31.

*a)* What journal entry would the corporation make?
*b)* What would be the new book value per share?
*c)* What would be the new book value (on the corporation's books) of the shares owned by an investor who had owned 10 shares of stock prior to the stock dividend?

23. Assume that *instead of* a stock dividend, the corporation in Problem 21 declared a 2-for-1 stock split (two new shares for each old one), and changed the par value to $3 per share.

*a)* What journal entry would the corporation make?
*b)* What would be the new book value per share?
*c)* What would be the new book value (on the corporation's books) of the shares owned by an investor who had owned 10 shares of stock prior to the stock split?

24. The following balance sheet items were taken from an annual report of the Multnomah Corporation:

| | |
|---|---:|
| Reserve for federal income taxes | $  120,000 |
| Reserve to reduce inventory values to market | 40,000 |
| Reserve for possible losses on foreign investments | 1,000,000 |
| Reserve for depreciation on plant | 875,000 |
| Reserve for expansion of plant | 500,000 |
| Reserve for employees' pensions | 329,000 |
| Common stock issued | 2,000,000 |
| Bonds | 1,500,000 |
| Treasury stock (at par) | 100,000 |
| Sinking fund for retirement of bonds | 800,000 |
| Goodwill | 50,000 |
| Retained earnings | 1,400,000 |

*a)* Describe the probable nature of each of the items above which are captioned "Reserve." Your description should include reference to the following points:
    (1) The probable origin of the reserve (i.e., whether it arose out of an accounting entry debiting expense or one debiting retained earnings).
    (2) The purpose and function of the reserve.
    (3) Whether the reserve is essentially a deduction-from-asset contra account, a liability, or retained earnings.
*b)* Prepare a schedule of the corporation's *owners' equity.*

*25. The Denver Corporation in 19x1 had a net income of $312,000. It had 100,000 shares of common stock outstanding and 10,000 shares of $5 convertible preferred stock. Each share of preferred was convertible into two shares of common.

*a)* Calculate primary earnings per common share, ignoring the convertibility of the preferred stock.
*b)* Calculate the fully diluted earnings per common share.

**26.** The Massena Corporation in 19x1 had a net income of $4,416,000, after taxes. It had 1,000,000 shares of common stock outstanding and 100,000 shares of $6 convertible preferred. Each share of preferred was convertible into 1.5 shares of common stock.

The company also had $5,000,000 in 5 percent bonds payable, convertible into common shares at a ratio of 16 shares of common for every $1,000 in bonds. The effective tax rate in 19x1 was 40 percent.

a) Calculate primary earnings per common share, ignoring the convertibility of the bonds and the preferred stock.
b) Calculate the fully diluted earnings per common share.

**27.** A company needs approximately $1,000,000 in new capital for long-term investment. Management is undecided whether to obtain the needed funds from the sale of bonds or from the sale of additional shares of common stock. Given the following information, prepare an analysis to show the earnings per share under each method of financing.

(1) Number of shares of stock now outstanding: 300,000.
(2) Current annual earnings after taxes: $1,200,000 ($4 per share).
(3) Anticipated increase in earnings (before interest and income taxes) from investment of additional capital: $400,000.
(4) The proposed bond issue would consist of 20-year, 8 percent bonds with a face value of $1,000,000, to be sold to an insurance company at their face value.
(5) The proposed stock issue would consist of 40,000 shares of common stock, to be sold at a price of $25 a share.
(6) The effective income tax rate is 40 percent.

*28. The Randolph Corporation is planning to expand its manufacturing plant and requires $5,000,000 of new long-term capital for this purpose. It is anticipated that the proposed expansion will increase annual net income before interest and taxes to $2,500,000 from its present level of $1,500,000. It appears feasible to raise these funds by sale of either 8 percent, 20-year bonds or additional capital stock. The company now has no long-term debt outstanding, the stock is selling at $8 a share, and 1 million shares of stock are now outstanding. The income tax rate is 45 percent.

a) Analyze the effect of the proposed expansion in terms of earnings per share:
(1) Assuming borrowing.
(2) Assuming stock sale at the current market price.
b) What other factors should be considered in reaching a decision?

**29.** On December 31, 19x5, the stockholders' equity section of the Broadmoor Corporation was as follows:

```
Common stock, 400,000 shares, par value $1................. $  400,000
Additional paid-in capital ...................................   3,000,000
Retained earnings .........................................   2,700,000
            Total..............................................  $6,100,000
```

The following events took place during 19x6, in the sequence given:
  (1)  A cash dividend of 50 cents a share was declared.
  (2)  A stock dividend of 5 percent was declared and issued; the stock was capitalized at the market price of $40 a share.
  (3)  5,000 shares of stock were repurchased to be held as treasury stock; the cost was $42 a share.
  (4)  3,000 shares of treasury stock were sold at $45 a share.
  (5)  A contingency reserve of $400,000 was set up for possible future losses on overseas investments.
  (6)  40,000 new shares of stock were issued at a price of $48 a share.
  (7)  The stock was split 2 for 1 without changing the par value. The treasury shares participated in the split.
  (8)  Net income for 19x6 was $900,000.

*a*)  Enter the opening balances and record the above transactions in appropriate T-accounts.
*b*)  Prepare the owners' equity section of the corporation's balance sheet on December 31, 19x6.
*c*)  How many shares were issued as of December 31, 19x6?
*d*)  How many shares were outstanding as of December 31, 19x6?
*e*)  What was the book value per share on December 31, 19x6?

**30.**  The shareholders' equity section of the Corky Company's balance sheet showed the following amounts on January 1:

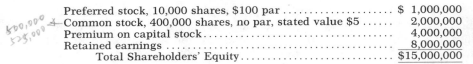

```
Preferred stock, 10,000 shares, $100 par ....................  $  1,000,000
Common stock, 400,000 shares, no par, stated value $5 ......     2,000,000
Premium on capital stock.....................................     4,000,000
Retained earnings .........................................     8,000,000
        Total Shareholders' Equity............................  $15,000,000
```

The following transactions affecting the shareholders' equity took place during the year:

Jan. 1    Sale of common stock, 100,000 shares at $12 a share — proceeds received in cash.
Jan. 20   Declaration and payment of cash dividend: common stock, $0.25 a share; preferred stock, $1.50 a share.
Mar. 20   Declaration and distribution of stock dividend, one common share for each 20 common shares outstanding — to be capitalized at the stock's current market price of $18.
Apr. 20   Declaration and payment of cash dividends: $0.25 a share on common stock; $1.50 a share on preferred stock.
Apr. 28   Purchase of 2,000 shares of the company's common stock for cash, $20 per share.

| | |
|---|---|
| June 1 | Repurchase and retirement of preferred stock by cash payment of $110 a share. The stock thus reacquired was canceled, not held as treasury stock. |
| July 20 | Declaration and payment of cash dividends on common stock outstanding, $0.25 a share. |
| Aug. 15 | Appropriation by the board of directors of $5,000,000 of retained earnings for plant expansion. |
| Oct. 20 | Declaration and payment of cash dividends on common stock outstanding, $0.50 a share. |
| Nov. 15 | Sale of treasury stock, 2,000 shares at $22 a share. |
| Dec. 1 | Stock split 2 for 1; new stated value $2.50 a share. |

*a)* Prepare journal entries to record each of the above transactions.
*b)* Present the owners' equity section of the balance sheet as it would appear on December 31 after all of the above transactions were recorded. Net income for the year was $1,000,000.

**31.** On February 12, 19x1, the Burgoyne Corporation issued 100,000 shares of $3.50, no-par, convertible preferred stock at an issue price of $55 a share. All shares were paid for in cash. These shares were convertible into common stock (par value, $5 a share) at a rate of 2½ shares of common stock for each share of preferred. The preferred stock was issued when the banks' prime rate of interest was 5 percent, and it was not regarded as equivalent to common stock in the calculation of primary earnings per share.

The company's earnings increased sharply during the next two years, and during the second quarter of 19x3 all shares of preferred were converted into common shares. If the conversion had not taken place, the company's primary earnings per share for 19x3 would have amounted to $2. Other data were as follows:

| | February 12, 19x1 | Second Quarter, 19x3 |
|---|---|---|
| Market prices: | | |
| Burgoyne common stock | $ 20 | $ 40 |
| Burgoyne $3.50 preferred stock | 55 | 110 |
| Index of common stock prices | 100 | 109 |
| Book value per Burgoyne common share (before conversion of preferred) | 28 | 32 |

*a)* What was the effect of the conversion on book values and primary earnings per common share? One million common shares were outstanding prior to the conversion. What was the effect of the conversion on fully-diluted earnings per share?
*b)* Did the conversion of the preferred shares into common stock lead to a dilution of the common shareholders' equity? Explain your reasoning.
*c)* Prepare journal entries to record the issuance and conversion of the preferred stock.

32. The Speed Corporation had been expanding rapidly to take advantage of growth opportunities, and in March, 19x1, it approached the Apex Insurance Company for a $2,000,000 loan. Apex replied that Speed's operations were too risky for an insurance company's portfolio, but suggested other possible sources of funds. The Apex representative thought that Speed should be able to borrow the amount it needed at an interest rate of about 9 percent.

Speed's management then asked a wealthy investor to provide the money. He was not interested in a straight loan, but offered to lend the $2,000,000 for 10 years at 7 percent if Speed would give him the option to buy 40,000 shares of Speed common stock at $20 a share. The option was to expire five years from the date of the loan.

Speed agreed and the loan was made. Speed's common stock was then selling at a market price of $16 a share. In February, 19x6, when Speed stock was selling at $42 a share, the investor exercised the warrants and purchased the 40,000 shares.

a) Did use of the detachable stock warrants reduce the cost of borrowing?

b) How should the loan have been recorded in Speed's accounts? Explain any calculations that you had to make.

c) How did exercise of the warrants affect the company's liabilities and owners' equities?

d) Did the exercise of the warrants constitute dilution of the equity?

e) What information would you have provided in the 19x1 financial statements? Why would it have been desirable to provide this information? What harm would failure to disclose this information have done?

33. The stockholders of Topper Corporation voted approval of an executive stock option plan at the annual stockholders' meeting on May 14, 19x0. The vote authorized the board of directors to grant purchase options to key executives up to a maximum of 30,000 shares of the company's previously unissued stock.

The first options were granted on September 10, 19x0. Various executives were given rights to purchase a total of 12,000 shares at $22 a share, the market price of the stock at the close of trading on that date. These options would lapse if they were not exercised within two years.

On June 1, 19x2, officers were given three-year options to buy an additional 15,000 shares at $28 a share, the market price on that date.

Options on 8,000 shares at $22 a share were exercised in November, 19x3. The company's stock was then selling at $36 a share.

In 19x4 the stockholders approved the addition of another 20,000 shares to the stock option plan. In September of that year three-year options were granted on 6,000 shares at $43 a share, the market price at that time.

Options on 4,000 shares at $22 a share and 3,000 shares at $28 a share were exercised in 19x4. The stock was selling at $40 a share at the time.

*a)* Prepare a footnote to be appended to the 19x0 financial statements, giving adequate disclosure of the stock option plan. The company's fiscal year ends on December 31 each year.

*b)* Prepare a footnote on the stock option plan for the 19x4 financial statements. Explain your reasons for disclosing each item that you have included in your footnote. Why is it important to disclose this information?

*c)* Did the exercise of the options in 19x3 and 19x4 constitute dilution of the equity? Explain.

*d)* What was the effect of all the above transactions on the stockholders' equity in Topper Corporation?

# *16*

# CORPORATE INVESTMENTS
# IN SECURITIES

THREE BASIC TYPES of investments in securities, each with its own accounting problems, are frequently encountered on corporate balance sheets: (1) temporary investments of funds that are temporarily in excess of current requirements; (2) noncontrolling ownership interests in other corporations; and (3) controlling ownership interests in other companies.

The purpose of this chapter is to examine the various kinds of intercorporate investments by nonfinancial corporations and to study some of the accounting problems such investments create. The chapter will then close with a brief discussion of one of the most controversial current issues: how much detail relating to the operations of individual company product lines or other activities the corporation should be required to disclose.

## MARKETABLE SECURITIES

Cash temporarily in excess of current operating needs is often invested in government securities, high-grade commercial paper such as the promissory notes of other business firms, and similar credit instruments. Investments of this type are commonly carried in an account titled Marketable Securities. The primary consideration in selecting securities for this purpose is the safety and liquidity of the amount invested. The principal should be readily convertible back into cash without substantial loss; the return on the investment is secondary. Accordingly, the term *marketable securities* is ordinarily restricted to those that can be sold on short notice at relatively stable market prices.

The only accounting issue with respect to marketable securities is whether they should be carried on the balance sheet at cost or at market value. We have argued before that holding gains and losses should be recognized when they occur if adequate supporting evidence can be found. The organization's wealth has changed, and both management and investors should be informed of this fact. This would call for measuring marketable securities at their market value.

The accounting profession has not accepted this point of view, preferring to wait until the securities are sold before recognizing holding gains. The most common practice is to carry the securities at cost, showing their market value parenthetically. This should be regarded as minimum disclosure.

## MINORITY STOCK INTERESTS IN OTHER CORPORATIONS

Apart from marketable securities, the securities held by a corporation are typically the common stocks of other corporations. The objective in acquiring such stocks may be either to produce income for the shareholders or to control the other company, which also has an income objective. In either case, the stock is not purchased and sold in response to short-term changes in cash position.

Except for financial institutions such as mutual funds, investment companies, and insurance companies, most companies' purchases of shares of stock in other companies are for the purpose of obtaining managerial control. A block of stock that is a *minority interest* in another corporation—less than 50 percent of its stock—may be acquired as a step in the direction of obtaining a majority or all of the stock. In the interim, the minority interest may provide a voice in the management or even effective control over its affairs.

The purchase by one company of shares of stock in another is always recorded at cost. For example, suppose that the National Company buys 30,000 shares of the Local Company's common stock (a minority interest). The price paid is $30 a share, and the purchase is recorded as follows:

Investment in Local Stock .................... 900,000
    Cash ....................................... 900,000

## Recognizing Income: Dividend Basis

The simplest method of recognizing income on these shares is to recognize as income only National's portion of the dividends declared by Local during the period. For example, if Local earns $3.25 a share and declares a dividend of $1.50 a share, National's 30,000 shares will be entitled to $45,000 in dividends. The entry on National's books will be:

Dividends Receivable (or Cash)................. 45,000
    Revenue from Investments .................        45,000

The argument for this treatment is that only the dividends declared by Local are subject to National's control. If Local declares no dividends, it will provide National with no funds to finance dividends to its shareholders or other corporate activities. If income is viewed as a measure of the amount of funds generated for internal investment or external distribution, then only Local's dividends should be included.

## Recognizing Income: Equity Basis

The policy of recognizing only dividends received as income has been criticized on the grounds that the shareholders benefit from the accumulation of retained earnings over time. Evidence shows a very high correlation in the long run between increases in a corporation's retained earnings and increases in its shares' market value, earnings, and dividends.[1] It is true that the company holding the stock does not have amounts equal to its share of Local's earnings available in cash for the payment of dividends to its stockholders, but this is not relevant. Income derived from products sold on account or exchanged for notes is not available in cash either and yet it is reported as current income without hesitation. The owning company's share of the other company's earnings retention represents no less an investment of corporate funds than the purchase of additional securities or plant and equipment. In all cases, the underlying justification is that the investment will produce future earnings at a satisfactory rate.

According to this reasoning, a corporation should treat as income the *earnings* on the stock it owns and not merely the dividends declared. Applying this reasoning to National's investment in Local requires the following entry:

---

[1] For example, see Myron J. Gordon, *The Investment, Financing, and Valuation of the Corporation* (Homewood, Ill.: Richard D. Irwin, Inc., 1962).

Dividends Receivable (or Cash)................. 45,000
Investment in Local Stock...................... 52,500
    Revenue from Investments.................           97,500

In other words, National's equity in the earnings retained by the Local Company (30,000 shares at $1.75 a share) is added to the balance in National's investment account. The balance in this account at any date thus equals cost at the date of acquisition plus the subsequent retained earnings on the shares owned. This can be interpreted as the amount paid for the company's equity in the shares held, which is wholly consistent with the cost basis of measurement.

The accounting profession in the United States now requires the application of this method to virtually all nonmajority-owned investments (50 percent or less) by nonfinancial corporations in which the investment is large enough to give the owner an influential voice. Just how large this is is a matter of judgment, but the Accounting Principles Board suggests that ownership of 20 percent or more of the voting stock will ordinarily give the owner enough influence to require the use of the equity method.[2] A survey of the 1971 financial statements of major United States corporations with investments of this type revealed that about two-thirds of these companies used a version of the equity method to account for these investments.[3]

### Recognizing Income: Market Value Basis

Still a third alternative might be considered: measuring investment income by the amount of dividends plus or minus the change in the market value of the securities. In other words, unrealized holding gains and losses would be recognized as current income.

This method is applied in the United States to the investments of mutual funds, but not to those of industrial corporations. One reason is that the industrial corporation's investment purpose is long-term growth, not market appreciation; another is that quoted prices do not necessarily indicate the amounts at which large holdings of securities actually could be sold. Market prices are also highly volatile in many cases, thus making market value calculations more difficult.

---

[2] American Institute of Certified Public Accountants, *APB Accounting Principles: Current Text* (New York: Commerce Clearing House, Inc., 1972), Sec. 5131.17.

[3] AICPA, *Accounting Trends and Techniques, 1972* (26th ed.; New York: AICPA, 1972), p. 96.

## CONTROLLING STOCK INTEREST IN OTHER CORPORATIONS

When a company owns more than 50 percent of the stock in another company, it has a controlling interest in the other company.[4] The former is commonly referred to as the *parent* company, and the controlled company is referred to as its *subsidiary*.

Some companies obtain subsidiaries by buying the shares of corporations that have been operating under other ownership. Investments of this kind are called acquisitions and reflect management's view that this is the most effective way to expand and diversify the firm's operations.

Other subsidiaries are created out of whole cloth by the parent to carry on certain kinds of operations or operations in specific geographical areas. A single company may have real estate subsidiaries, leasing subsidiaries, finance company subsidiaries, foreign subsidiaries, and many more. The reasons for separate incorporation are legal in nature and therefore are generally not our concern. What is important to us is how investments in subsidiaries, whether acquired or created, should be measured and reported.

### Reasons for Consolidated Statements

A parent that merely showed one figure for its investment in a subsidiary and one figure for the income on the investment would not be providing adequate information on its assets and operations. Within very broad limits, the parent company's management can use the resources of one legal entity to finance the requirements of another, and often it can allocate the given total earnings arbitrarily among them. Thus it is the *total* assets and total earnings of the parent and subsidiaries *combined* that are significant.

A parent company report showing the investment in the subsidiary and the income from it as single figures would be like a company report showing only a total asset figure and a net income figure. In fact, a parent company which is solely a *holding company*, with no direct operations of its own, would present such a report if it reported on a parent-only basis. Its only assets would be its investment in subsidiaries, and its income statement

---

[4] Although control often can be exercised with less than a majority ownership, this chapter will identify as subsidiaries only those companies in which the parent owns more than 50 percent of the voting power.

would show merely the subsidiaries' net income figures or the amount of dividends received from them.

To meet the informational needs of investors in the parent company and others, financial statements can be drawn up to present the combined assets, equities, and operating results of the group of related corporations. Known as *consolidated statements*, their objective is to reproduce the results that would have been achieved had all transactions been recorded in a single set of accounts. For example, the consolidated balance sheet will show the cash balances of the parent and its consolidated subsidiaries as a single figure, representing the sum of the cash balances of the individual companies in the consolidation. Similarly, the sales revenue figure on the consolidated income statement will show the combined sales revenues of all the consolidated companies rather than those of the parent company only.

The argument for preparing consolidated statements is that it is the entire group of companies that the investor is placing his trust in, not just the parent. The various corporations are separate *legal entities*, but common control serves to merge them into a single *economic entity*. For this economic entity, it is argued, consolidated statements portray overall performance and status more accurately than separate statements for the parent and each subsidiary. Even the minority stockholders in the various subsidiaries need consolidated statements in addition to the unconsolidated statements of their companies alone. In the final analysis, the strength of the subsidiary depends largely on the strength of the consolidated group and on the competence of the parent company management. The main interest in the consolidated statements, however, comes from investors and potential investors in the parent.

## Consolidation Policy

The consolidated financial statements of nonfinancial corporations in the United States often exclude the accounts of some of its wholly owned subsidiaries from the consolidation. These non-consolidated subsidiaries fall largely into two categories: (*a*) customer finance companies, and (*b*) foreign subsidiaries.

The financial subsidiaries are usually excluded on the ground that their operations are so different from those of the parent that to include them would produce distorted statements. For example, the General Motors Acceptance Corporation (GMAC) was organized to finance consumer purchases of General Motors cars and other products. Like banks and independent finance companies, the common equity in this subsidiary finances a very small percentage of its total assets. GMAC assets are almost exclusively the notes of the purchasers of General Motors products, and GMAC finances this extension of credit predominantly by borrowing. Since the financial structure of a financial subsidiary is so different from its parent's, consolidation would seriously alter the picture presented by the consolidated statements. Common practice, therefore, is to report the financial subsidiary's statements separately in the corporation's annual report.

Most companies with foreign operations now consolidate the results of operations and the resources of their foreign subsidiaries with those of the parent for external financial reporting. About 40 percent of the corporations covered by a recent survey, however, excluded one or more of their foreign subsidiaries from the consolidated group.[5] The main rationale for excluding these is that the subsidiaries' operations are highly regulated, expropriation is a near possibility, or the repatriation of dividends is severely restricted or prohibited.

The exclusion of foreign subsidiaries from the consolidation should be justified by the circumstances of each individual case. A general policy of excluding all foreign subsidiaries may produce misleading financial statements. Corporations with rapidly growing foreign subsidiaries will allow a large fraction of the foreign earnings to remain abroad, while other corporations may be drawing dividends in excess of earnings from their foreign subsidiaries. Hence the dividend is a very poor basis on which to report earnings of most foreign subsidiaries.

## THE CONSOLIDATED BALANCE SHEET

The issues and techniques in the development of consolidated financial statements are among the most complicated and difficult in the whole field of accounting, and we shall not attempt to cover them in detail. To read consolidated statements with an adequate degree of comprehension, however, some study of the commonly encountered practices is necessary. This section will deal with the balance sheet and the next section with the income statement.

### The Consolidation Process

To consolidate the accounts of parent and subsidiary, the accountant must cancel out the effects of transactions between

---

[5] *Accounting Trends and Techniques,* 1972, op. cit., p. 31.

members of the group. For example, the parent company carries its investment in each subsidiary's common stock in an asset account. The accountant cannot show both the investment and the subsidiary's assets in a consolidated statement, however, because this would count the same set of resources twice. The balance in the parent's investment account is its surrogate for the net assets of the subsidiary.

To show how the accountant avoids this kind of double counting, let us assume that Parent Corporation has just purchased 100 percent of the common stock of Subsidiary Corporation (10,000 shares) at a total price of $400,000. Subsidiary has assets with a book value of $500,000 and liabilities of $100,000. Its owners' equity is thus $400,000, or $40 a share. In other words, the book value of Parent's equity (10,000 shares at $40 per share) is just equal to its cost ($400,000).

Consolidation in this case would be very simple. Subsidiary's $500,000 assets and $100,000 in liabilities would be substituted on the consolidated balance sheet for the $400,000 balance in the parent's investment account.

Similarly, the consolidated statement cannot show both the owners' equity in the subsidiary and the owners' equity in the parent. The consolidated statement shows only the equity of outside investors.

The accountant uses a formal work sheet to consolidate the accounts of parent and subsidiaries. No entries are made in the ledger accounts of either parent or subsidiary. One work sheet format lists the accounts of parent and subsidiaries in parallel columns, with all like items (e.g., cash in bank) on a single line, followed by two columns for "eliminations." The amounts entered in the elimination columns are those amounts which should not appear on the consolidated statements. The elimination is performed by crediting the accounts having any unwanted debit balances and debiting accounts with redundant credit balances.

Exhibit 16–1 illustrates this format. Because the consolidated balance sheet should show neither the balance shown in Parent's investments account nor Subsidiary's shareholders' equity account balances, these amounts must be "eliminated" in the consolidation. The eliminating entry in this exhibit can also be expressed in conventional journal form:

(1)

| | | |
|---|---|---|
| Common Stock (Subsidiary) ................. | 50,000 | |
| Additional Paid-In Capital (Subsidiary)........ | 100,000 | |
| Retained Earnings (Subsidiary) .............. | 250,000 | |
|     Investment in Subsidiary (Parent) ........ | | 400,000 |

*Exhibit 16–1*

Parent Corporation and Subsidiary

CONDENSED CONSOLIDATED BALANCE SHEET WORK SHEET

| | Parent | Subsidiary | Eliminations | | Consolidated |
| | | | Debits | Credits | |
|---|---|---|---|---|---|
| ASSETS | | | | | |
| Investment in | | | | | |
| Subsidiary............ | $ 400,000 | – | | (1)$400,000 | – |
| Other assets............ | 5,000,000 | $500,000 | | | $5,500,000 |
| Total ............. | $5,400,000 | $500,000 | | | $5,500,000 |
| | | | | | |
| LIABILITIES AND | | | | | |
| OWNERS' EQUITY | | | | | |
| Liabilities .............. | $1,000,000 | $100,000 | | | $1,100,000 |
| Shareholders' equity: | | | | | |
| Common stock ....... | 1,200,000 | 50,000 | (1)$ 50,000 | | 1,200,000 |
| Additional paid-in | | | | | |
| capital ............. | 800,000 | 100,000 | (1) 100,000 | | 800,000 |
| Retained earnings .... | 2,400,000 | 250,000 | (1) 250,000 | | 2,400,000 |
| Total ............. | $5,400,000 | $500,000 | | | $5,500,000 |

The net result is to produce a balance sheet representing the combined assets, liabilities, and owners' equities of the economic entity – the resources of the integrated operation under the common control of the owners of the parent company. In this case the total operating assets amount to $5,500,000, not $5,400,000 as indicated by the balances in the parent company accounts alone.

Notice that this entry completely eliminates the subsidiary's retained earnings. The consolidated retained earnings at the date of acquisition would be $2,400,000 – that is, the retained earnings of Parent Corporation only. In other words, the intent is that the retained earnings figure shown on the consolidated balance sheet should represent the earnings accruing to the parent company's shareholders from operations under their control. By purchasing Subsidiary's stock, Parent bought a share of the earnings retained prior to the acquisition, but in no sense did Parent or its shareholders *earn* this amount. Thus consolidated retained earnings represents the retained earnings of the parent company plus the parent's share of any earnings retained by the subsidiary *after* the date of acquisition.

### Minority Interests

The foregoing procedure would have to be modified if Parent had purchased less than a 100 percent ownership interest in Subsidiary. For example, if Parent had bought only 8,000 shares (an 80 percent interest) for $320,000, its balance sheet immediately after the acquisition would have been as follows:

| | | |
|---|---|---|
| Investment in Subsidiary | | $ 320,000 |
| Other assets | | 5,080,000 |
| Total Assets | | $5,400,000 |
| | | |
| Liabilities | | $1,000,000 |
| Shareholders' equity: | | |
| Common stock | $1,200,000 | |
| Additional paid-in capital | 800,000 | |
| Retained earnings | 2,400,000 | 4,400,000 |
| Total Liabilities and Shareholders' Equity. | | $5,400,000 |

Parent's total assets are the same as in Exhibit 16–1, but its investment in Subsidiary is smaller, leaving more in other asset categories.

In this situation, the equity of the owners of the 2,000 shares not bought by Parent (the *minority* shareholders) would have been $80,000—that is, 20 percent of the total owners' equity in Subsidiary, corresponding to their holding of 20 percent of Subsidiary's shares.

When the assets, liabilities, and owners' equities of the two companies are consolidated, this amount must be treated as one of the equities in the consolidated assets.

The consolidation process under these circumstances is illustrated in Exhibit 16–2. First, Parent's investment is offset against its 80 percent equity in Subsidiary:

### Exhibit 16–2

### Parent Corporation and Subsidiary

### CONDENSED CONSOLIDATED BALANCE SHEET WORK SHEET

| | Parent | Subsidiary | Eliminations Debits | Eliminations Credits | Consolidated |
|---|---|---|---|---|---|
| **ASSETS** | | | | | |
| Investment in | | | | | |
| Subsidiary | $ 320,000 | — | | (1a)$320,000 | — |
| Other assets | 5,080,000 | $500,000 | | | $5,580,000 |
| Total | $5,400,000 | $500,000 | | | $5,580,000 |
| | | | | | |
| **LIABILITIES AND OWNERS' EQUITY** | | | | | |
| Liabilities | $1,000,000 | $100,000 | | | $1,100,000 |
| Shareholders' equity: | | | | | |
| Common stock | 1,200,000 | 50,000 | (1a)$  40,000 (1b)    10,000 | | 1,200,000 |
| Additional paid-in capital | 800,000 | 100,000 | (1a)    80,000 (1b)    20,000 | | 800,000 |
| Retained earnings | 2,400,000 | 250,000 | (1a) 200,000 (1b)    50,000 | | 2,400,000 |
| Minority interest | — | — | | (1b)  80,000 | 80,000 |
| Total | $5,400,000 | $500,000 | | | $5,580,000 |

(1a)

| | | |
|---|---|---|
| Common Stock............................... | 40,000 | |
| Additional Paid-In Capital ................... | 80,000 | |
| Retained Earnings .......................... | 200,000 | |
|     Investment in Subsidiary ................. | | 320,000 |

The assets, liabilities, and owners' equity could be consolidated at this point without further adjustment, but it is customary to represent the equity of the minority shareholders by a single figure instead of by three figures corresponding to their share of the balances in Subsidiary's three owners' equity accounts. This transfer is made by entry (1b):

(1b)

| | | |
|---|---|---|
| Common Stock ................................. | 10,000 | |
| Additional Paid-In Capital ..................... | 20,000 | |
| Retained Earnings.............................. | 50,000 | |
|     Minority Interest .......................... | | 80,000 |

The consolidated balance sheet then would show the figures in the right-hand column of Exhibit 16–2.

Notice that the consolidated list of assets and liabilities includes *all* of the assets and liabilities of Subsidiary, not merely amounts representing Parent's ownership percentage. It does so because Parent's ownership percentage is big enough to give it control over all of Subsidiary's net assets.

### Consolidation Goodwill

An additional complication is introduced whenever the parent company pays more or less than the book value per share for the common stock of its subsidiary. For example, suppose that Parent Corporation paid $55 a share for 8,000 shares of Subsidiary Corporation. This was $15 a share greater than the book value of these shares on Subsidiary's books at the date of acquisition.

Why might Parent have been willing to pay this premium price? One possible reason is that Subsidiary's accounting practices (e.g., Lifo) may have resulted in an understatement of the current replacement cost of certain tangible assets. Second, Subsidiary's intangible assets, reflected in the earning power of the company as a whole, may have justified a higher price than the tangible assets themselves would have commanded. Finally, Subsidiary's earning power as an integrated unit in Parent's empire may have been in excess of its independent earning power, thus justifying a premium price.

Regardless of the cause, Parent paid $440,000 for its 8,000

shares of Subsidiary's stock, and this was $120,000 more than the book value of the equity acquired (8,000 shares × $15 a share). If the accountants had been able to find objective evidence that specific tangible assets were understated on Subsidiary's books, they could have written these assets up to an appropriate level. Otherwise, the excess of cost over the book value of the underlying equity would be treated as an amount paid for Subsidiary's intangible assets. The traditional name for this amount is *consolidation goodwill*, although modern practice leans toward some title such as "investment in subsidiary in excess of equity in tangible assets."

Notice that Parent would record the investment in Subsidiary on its own books at the full cost of $440,000. In the consolidated balance sheet, this would be replaced by the following items:

Assets:
| | | |
|---|---:|---:|
| Tangible assets | | $500,000 |
| Consolidation goodwill | | 120,000 |
| Total Assets | | $620,000 |
| Liabilities and minority interest: | | |
| Liabilities | $100,000 | |
| Minority interest | 80,000 | |
| Total Liabilities and Minority Interest | | $180,000 |

Parent's investment and its equity in Subsidiary can be eliminated on the work sheet by the following entry:

(1a)
| | | |
|---|---:|---:|
| Consolidation Goodwill | 120,000 | |
| Common Stock (Subsidiary) | 40,000 | |
| Additional Paid-In Capital (Subsidiary) | 80,000 | |
| Retained Earnings (Subsidiary) | 200,000 | |
| Investment in Subsidiary | | 440,000 |

The premium purchase price does not affect the calculation of minority interest, which remained at $80,000. Entry (1b) described above is the appropriate work sheet entry.

### Intercompany Receivables and Payables

Prior to the acquisition of stock, Parent had lent $60,000 to Subsidiary. This amount was included among Parent's assets and among Subsidiary's liabilities. The consolidated group as a whole, however, had neither asset nor liability in this amount. The group had no claim on any party outside the group, nor did it have any obligation to make payments to anyone outside the group.

To avoid double counting, in other words, this $60,000 must be subtracted from both the assets and the liabilities. The eliminating entry in this case would be as follows:

(2)

Liabilities (Subsidiary) .......................... 60,000
　　Other Assets (Parent) ...................... 　　　　60,000

The final consolidation work sheet would take the form illustrated in Exhibit 16–3. This work sheet differs from the one in Exhibit 16–2 in two ways. First, the price paid exceeded the book value of the equity acquired, resulting in the recognition of consolidation goodwill. Second, $60,000 has been eliminated from consolidated assets and liabilities to cancel the intercompany loan.

*Exhibit 16–3*

Parent Corporation and Subsidiary

CONDENSED CONSOLIDATED BALANCE SHEET WORK SHEET

| | Parent | Subsidiary | Eliminations | | Consolidated |
| --- | --- | --- | --- | --- | --- |
| | | | *Debits* | *Credits* | |
| ASSETS | | | | | |
| Investment in Subsidiary............ | $ 440,000 | – | | (1a)$440,000 | – |
| Other assets............. | 4,960,000 | $500,000 | | (2)　 60,000 | $5,400,000 |
| Consolidation goodwill .. | – | – | (1a)$120,000 | | 120,000 |
| Total............. | $5,400,000 | $500,000 | | | $5,520,000 |
| LIABILITIES AND OWNERS' EQUITY | | | | | |
| Liabilities............... | $1,000,000 | $100,000 | (2)　 60,000 | | $1,040,000 |
| Shareholders' equity: | | | | | |
| Common stock........ | 1,200,000 | 50,000 | (1a)　 40,000 (1b)　 10,000 | | 1,200,000 |
| Additional paid-in capital ............. | 800,000 | 100,000 | (1a)　 80,000 (1b)　 20,000 | | 800,000 |
| Retained earnings..... | 2,400,000 | 250,000 | (1a) 200,000 (1b)　 50,000 | | 2,400,000 |
| Minority interest........ | – | – | | (1b)　 80,000 | 80,000 |
| Total.............. | $5,400,000 | $500,000 | | | $5,520,000 |

## Negative Goodwill

A corporation's equity in a controlled subsidiary may have been purchased, of course, at a price per share *less than* the book value of the subsidiary's stock. Sometimes this means that the stock was obtained at a bargain price, far less than its true worth, but in general the implication must be that the subsidiary's assets were worth less than their book value. Thus, they should be written down to the value indicated by the purchase price.

Whenever sufficient supporting evidence exists, specific assets should be written down. More often, however, the depressed price of the stock is due to the poor earning power of the subsidiary as a whole rather than to any one asset or group of assets. By analogy with the earlier discussion, this is *negative goodwill*, indicating that the value of the tangible assets is less than their total cost.

This is now handled by deducting the negative goodwill from the calculated cost of the noncurrent assets. If the cost assigned to the noncurrent assets is less than the amount of the negative goodwill, the difference is shown as a "deferred credit" to be amortized over a period not to exceed 40 years.[6] "Deferred credits" are typically shown on the balance sheet either as liabilities or in a separate category between the liabilities and the owners' equity. In this case, however, it would seem more logical to show the unamortized negative goodwill, if any, as a deduction from the consolidated asset total.

## THE CONSOLIDATED INCOME STATEMENT

Income statement consolidation is based on the same principles. The income statement for the parent company alone may have a separate legal significance, but as long as the earnings of the subsidiaries are subject to the parent's control it is the total controlled earnings that parent company investors are interested in.

Exhibit 16–4 shows the separate income statements of Parent Corporation and its subsidiary, Subsidiary Corporation, for the

*Exhibit 16–4*

Parent Corporation and Subsidiary Corporation

STATEMENTS OF INCOME AND DIVIDENDS FOR THE YEAR

| | | *Parent* | | *Subsidiary* |
|---|---|---|---|---|
| Revenue from sales................ | | $7,500,000 | | $700,000 |
| Revenue from dividends .......... | | 28,000 | | – |
| Total Revenue ................ | | $7,528,000 | | $700,000 |
| Cost of goods sold................ | $4,700,000 | | $500,000 | |
| Other expenses .................. | 1,900,000 | | 150,000 | |
| Total Expense ............... | | 6,600,000 | | 650,000 |
| Net income ...................... | | $  928,000 | | $ 50,000 |
| Dividends declared .............. | | 500,000 | | 35,000 |
| Net Addition to Retained Earnings | | $  428,000 | | $ 15,000 |

---

[6] *APB Accounting Principles: Current Text,* Sec. 1091.91.

year following the acquisition. This exhibit will be the basis for our discussion of four items:

1. Intercorporate dividends.
2. Amortization of consolidation goodwill.
3. Minority interests in consolidated net income.
4. Intercompany sales.

### Intercorporate Dividends

The $28,000 shown on Parent's statement as revenue from investments represents dividends received from Subsidiary. To avoid double counting, this amount must be eliminated in the consolidation.[7] In the absence of any other adjustments, therefore, consolidated net income would be as follows:

| | |
|---|---:|
| Parent Corporation income ........................... | $928,000 |
| Subsidiary Corporation income ....................... | 50,000 |
|    Less: Parent Corporation's share in Subsidiary | |
|       Corporation's dividends........................ | (28,000) |
| Consolidated Income before Minority Interest.......... | $950,000 |

### Amortization of Consolidation Goodwill

The price Parent paid for its share of Subsidiary's stock exceeded the book value of the underlying equity by $120,000. Although it can be argued that with proper care Parent can maintain the economic value of Subsidiary's goodwill indefinitely, accepted practice in the United States is to amortize purchased goodwill systematically over a period not to exceed 40 years. The reasoning is that the factors that created the goodwill will disappear gradually, perhaps to be replaced by others, perhaps not. Since the original goodwill will dissipate gradually, its cost should be amortized gradually.

Parent decided on a 20-year amortization period, leading to an amortization of $6,000 a year. Thus in consolidation $6,000 had to be deducted from revenues for the year and from the balance sheet figure for goodwill. This reduced the consolidated net income figure to $944,000.

----

[7] If Parent Corporation took up its full equity in Subsidiary's earnings as its revenue from investments, then the amount shown on its income statement would be 80 percent of $50,000, or $40,000. In that case, this is the amount that would have to be eliminated in the consolidation.

## Minority Interest in Consolidated Net Income

Not all of the consolidated net income was assignable to the equity of Parent's shareholders. The minority shareholders had a 20 percent share in Subsidiary's net income, or $10,000. The net income applicable to Parent's shareholders was thus $944,000 less $10,000, or $934,000. This is reflected in Exhibit 16–5.

*Exhibit 16–5*

Parent Corporation and Subsidiary

CONSOLIDATED INCOME STATEMENT FOR THE YEAR

| | | |
|---|---:|---:|
| Revenue from sales . . . . . . . . . . . . . . . . . . . . . . . . . . . . . | | $8,200,000 |
| Less: Cost of goods sold . . . . . . . . . . . . . . . . . . . . . . . | $5,200,000 | |
| Amortization of goodwill . . . . . . . . . . . . . . . . | 6,000 | |
| Other expenses . . . . . . . . . . . . . . . . . . . . . . . . | 2,050,000 | |
| Total Expenses. . . . . . . . . . . . . . . . . . . . . | | 7,256,000 |
| Income before minority interest . . . . . . . . . . . . . . . . | | $ 944,000 |
| Less: Equity of minority shareholders in net income of Subsidiary. . . . . . . . . . . . . . . . . | | 10,000 |
| Net Income . . . . . . . . . . . . . . . . . . . . . . . . . . . . . . . . . | | $ 934,000 |
| Dividends declared. . . . . . . . . . . . . . . . . . . . . . . . . . . . . | | 500,000 |
| Net Addition to Retained Earnings . . . . . . . . . . . . . | | $ 434,000 |

The minority interest in the consolidated net assets at the end of the year was $83,000, calculated as follows:

| | |
|---|---:|
| Minority interest, beginning of year (Exhibit 16–3) . . . . . . | $80,000 |
| Add: Equity of minority shareholders in net income of Subsidiary . . . . . . . . . . . . . . . . . . . . . . . . . . . . . . . . . | 10,000 |
| Less: Dividends paid by Subsidiary to minority shareholders . . . . . . . . . . . . . . . . . . . . . . . . . . . . . . . . . . | (7,000) |
| Minority interest, end of year . . . . . . . . . . . . . . . . . . . . . . . | $83,000 |

The consolidated retained earnings at the end of the year was $434,000 plus the balance at the beginning of the year, or $2,834,000. This is Parent's own retained earnings, plus its equity in the earnings of Subsidiary *since the date of the acquisition.*

### Intercompany Sales

Exhibit 16–5 reflects the assumption that neither company bought any goods or services from the other during the year. Thus all sales were to customers outside the consolidated entity, and consolidated sales revenue, cost of goods sold, and other expenses could be determined simply by adding together the figures for the two companies, without elimination of any kind.

This is not always the case. The prime motive in the acquisition of another company quite often is not merely ownership but a full or partial integration of the operations of the two companies. For instance, a shoe manufacturer may acquire a chain of shoe stores to assure a market for his products. The manufacturer's trial balance, therefore, will have sales and receivables that correspond to purchases and payables in the accounts of the chain. When the two legal entities are consolidated, these *inter-company* transactions become *intrafirm transfers.* Adding the total sales and cost of goods sold of the two companies to obtain the consolidated sales and cost of goods sold would be like treating every transfer of merchandise from one department to another within a company as a sale and purchase.[8] No matter how many sales the two companies make to each other, the parent company stockholders gain nothing unless sales are made to outsiders as well. In other words, to avoid double counting, all intrafirm sales and purchases, like intrafirm receivables and payables, must be netted out.

For example, assume that a parent company sold merchandise costing $700,000 to its wholly owned subsidiary for $1,000,000. The subsidiary then sold this merchandise to outside customers for $1,200,000. The total gross margin on these sales was $500,000 ($1,200,000 less $700,000), $300,000 on the parent's books and $200,000 on the subsidiary's. The consolidated net income figure was not overstated. Total sales, however, amounted to only $1,200,000, not the $2,200,000 that would be obtained by adding the companies' sales figures together without adjustment. Similarly, the cost of goods sold was only $700,000, not $1,700,000. In this situation, an eliminating entry is required to eliminate the overstatement in both accounts:

Sales ..................................... 1,000,000
    Cost of Goods Sold.....................           1,000,000

A more difficult problem is posed by the shoe manufacturer's inventory on the chain's shelves. The manufacturer sold the shoes to the chain and recorded a gross margin on his own books.

---

[8] Many companies do in fact treat internal transfers as sales for the purpose of measuring the profit performance of each of the various divisions or departments of the company. In preparing company-wide financial statements, however, these internal sales must be canceled out, using techniques identical to those used in preparing consolidated statements for two or more corporations.

If the stores and the plant were part of a single corporation, however, the corporation as a whole would recognize no profit on this transaction. The shoes would be transferred to the stores at cost, and the combined manufacturing and retailing profit would be earned by the company only when the stores sold the shoes to consumers.

The interposition of a corporate frontier between these two units makes no fundamental difference in the situation. Any intrafirm profit on inventories of goods must be eliminated in consolidation. For example, if the entire $1,000,000 transfer discussed earlier remained in the subsidiary's inventory at year end, the eliminating entries would be:

```
Sales (Parent)............................. 1,000,000
    Cost of Goods Sold (Parent) .............          700,000
    Inventory (Subsidiary)...................          300,000
```

This reduces the inventory to cost and eliminates the $300,000 parent gross margin from consolidated income. If only part of the inventory had been resold, then the eliminating entry would have been somewhere between this one and the one discussed above.

## ACQUISITIONS BY EXCHANGE OF STOCK

The method described above to account for Parent's acquisition of Subsidiary's stock is known as the *purchase method* of accounting for a combination of businesses. It was appropriate because Parent purchased the stock in exchange for cash.

The purchase method is also used when assets other than cash are given in exchange for the subsidiary's stock. A more significant question is whether it should be used in accounting for the many mergers in which a company exchanges shares of its own stock for shares of the stock of another company, undoubtedly the dominant means of effecting mergers today.

### Application of the Purchase Method

If the exchange of stock is regarded as a purchase, the accountant has to determine the cost of the stock acquired. The procedure is the same as in the acquisition of a minority interest in another company. In general, cost is measured by the market value of the stock issued by the parent company. The excess of this amount over the parent company's share of the book value of the subsidiary's net assets indicates that either the market value of the subsidiary's tangible assets is greater than their depreciated cost or the subsidiary has substantial intangible assets that the parent is willing to pay for.

The appropriate procedure is to obtain an appraisal of the fair values of the tangible assets and to use these figures to measure the tangibles in consolidated financial reporting. The excess of the fair value of the stock exchanged over the appraised value of the net tangibles acquired is shown as goodwill, to be amortized as described earlier.

For example, instead of paying cash for its 80 percent interest in Subsidiary Corporation, Parent issued 10,000 new shares of its own $10 par common stock, which then had a market value of $44 a share. The acquisition was recorded on Parent's books as follows:

| | | |
|---|---|---|
| Investment in Subsidiary .................... 440,000 | | |
| Common Stock............................ | 100,000 | |
| Additional Paid-In Capital ............... | 340,000 | |

Parent's balance sheet immediately after the acquisition showed the following:

| | |
|---|---|
| Investment in Subsidiary Corporation........................ | $  440,000 |
| Other assets ............................................... | 5,400,000 |
| Total...................................................... | $5,840,000 |
| Liabilities................................................. | $1,000,000 |
| Shareholders' equity: | |
| Common stock............................................ | 1,300,000 |
| Additional paid-in capital ................................ | 1,140,000 |
| Retained earnings ....................................... | 2,400,000 |
| Total...................................................... | $5,840,000 |

An appraisal made at this time indicated that the book value of Subsidiary's tangible assets was a reasonable measure of their fair value. The book value of Parent's 80 percent equity in Subsidiary's tangible assets therefore was 80 percent of $400,000, or $320,000. The issuance of stock worth $440,000 implied that Subsidiary's intangible assets were worth $120,000 to Parent. This amount had to be shown on the consolidated balance sheet as goodwill. The consolidation process is illustrated in Exhibit 16–6.

Parent then started amortizing the goodwill by charges to expense amounting to $6,000 a year, as illustrated in Exhibit 16–5 above.

*Exhibit 16–6*

Parent Corporation and Subsidiary

CONDENSED CONSOLIDATED BALANCE SHEET WORK SHEET

| | Parent | Subsidiary | Eliminations | | Consolidated |
|---|---|---|---|---|---|
| | | | Debits | Credits | |
| Investment in subsidiary. | $ 440,000 | – | | (1a)$440,000 | – |
| Goodwill................ | – | – | (1a)$120,000 | | $ 120,000 |
| Other assets............. | 5,400,000 | $500,000 | | | 5,900,000 |
| Total ............. | $5,840,000 | $500,000 | | | $6,020,000 |
| Liabilities .............. | $1,000,000 | $100,000 | | | $1,100,000 |
| Shareholders' equity: | | | | | |
| Common stock ........ | 1,300,000 | 50,000 | (1a)   40,000 | | 1,300,000 |
| | | | (1b)   10,000 | | |
| Additional paid-in | | | | | |
| capital ............. | 1,140,000 | 100,000 | (1a)   80,000 | | 1,140,000 |
| | | | (1b)   20,000 | | |
| Retained earnings..... | 2,400,000 | 250,000 | (1a) 200,000 | | 2,400,000 |
| | | | (1b)   50,000 | | |
| Total ............. | $5,840,000 | $500,000 | | | $6,020,000 |

## Pooling of Interests

The amortization of goodwill under the purchase method reduces reported income. The impact is even greater because
amortization of goodwill is not recognized as an expense for tax
purposes. This means that the *full* amount of the amortization is
a deduction from net income. If earnings are not exceptionally
high otherwise, the amortization may convert an apparently
favorable financial record into a picture embarrassing to management.

This provides a substantial incentive for the merging corporations to structure the exchange of stock so that the transaction
can be regarded as a *pooling of interests.* In a pooling of interests, it is assumed that the operations of the combining corporations are continued in the joint enterprise. The recorded costs of
the assets of the constituent companies prior to the pooling remain the basis for measurement in the consolidated statements.
No additional goodwill is recognized.

To illustrate this method, let us assume that all of the shares
of Subsidiary's stock were exchanged for 10,000 shares of
Parent's stock. The accounting assumption underlying the pooling method is that both companies pool their assets, their liabilities, their paid-in capital, and their retained earnings. This means
that the paid-in capital of both companies constitutes the paid-in
capital of the pooled group; consolidated retained earnings is the

sum of the retained earnings of the combined companies. Because Subsidiary's paid-in capital amounted to $150,000, this was the amount to be added to Parent's paid-in capital in consolidation. With Parent's stock at a par value of $10 a share, Subsidiary's paid-in capital was added to Parent's as follows:

Common stock....................................... $100,000
Additional paid-in capital............................. 50,000

The full $250,000 balance in Subsidiary's retained earnings account was included in the consolidated retained earnings at the time of acquisition.

In other words, the assets, liabilities, and owners' equity of the two companies were added together as follows:

|  | Parent | Subsidiary | Consolidated |
|---|---|---|---|
| Assets ......................... | $5,400,000 | $500,000 | $5,900,000 |
| Liabilities ...................... | $1,000,000 | $100,000 | $1,100,000 |
| Shareholders' equity: |  |  |  |
| Common stock ................ | 1,200,000 | 100,000 | 1,300,000 |
| Additional paid-in capital....... | 800,000 | 50,000 | 850,000 |
| Retained earnings............. | 2,400,000 | 250,000 | 2,650,000 |
| Total .................... | $5,400,000 | $500,000 | $5,900,000 |

The total paid-in capital was $2,150,000, just equal to the combined paid-in capital of the two companies prior to the pooling ($2,000,000 + $150,000). Similarly, the combined retained earnings was the sum of the retained earnings of the constituent companies. The distribution of Subsidiary's paid-in capital between Parent's common stock and additional paid-in capital is governed by the number and par value of Parent's shares issued in the pooling.

The pooling of interests method must be used whenever the acquisition satisfies the conditions specified by the Accounting Principles Board. These specifications are highly technical, but in essence they require that the acquisition be of an independent, going concern, that substantially all of its stock (at least 90 percent) be obtained in exchange for full voting stock of the acquiring corporation, and that the acquiring corporation expects to continue the operation and activities of the acquired corporation.[9] All other acquisitions must be treated as purchases.

---

[9] APB Accounting Principles: Current Text, op. cit., Sec. 1091.45.

# FINANCIAL REPORTING BY CONGLOMERATE COMPANIES

The merits of consolidated financial statements have become so widely recognized in the United States that advocates of reporting on a parent-company-only basis are hard to find.[10] Controversy now focuses on whether, *in addition to* consolidated statements, the so-called "conglomerate" corporation should be required to provide separate financial statements for each of the company's major lines of business.

## Nature of the Conglomerate Company

A conglomerate corporation is diversified into a number of product lines which are relatively unrelated with respect to manufacturing facilities and marketing organization. The conglomerate is a recent phenomenon. Until the 1950s, mergers and acquisitions involved firms in related fields of business. For example, a shoe manufacturer might acquire another shoe manufacturer, a chain of retail shoe stores, or a leather tanner. The motive for the acquisition would be the higher profits from large-scale operations, the reduction in competition, or vertical integration. The acquisition of a firm in an unrelated line of business was frowned upon because it offered none of the above advantages and it presented difficult and costly problems of management.

Diversification can be a profitable mode of growth, however, and many firms have taken this route to growth. As a result, individual firms may be engaged in such diverse businesses as ocean shipping, industrial chemicals, electronic equipment, and consumer food products.

## Arguments for More Detailed Disclosure

The basic argument for separate financial statements for each of the major product lines or divisions of a conglomerate corporation is that investors need such information to evaluate the past properly and forecast the future. For instance, a given net income figure combines the results of profitable and unprofitable lines of business. If these are developing at different rates, the outsider will be hard-pressed to identify the component trends on which forecasts of the future need to be based.

---

[10] Not so in Western Europe, where only a minority of companies issue financial statements on a fully consolidated basis.

A second argument is that diversification has specific benefits as well as costs, and that to evaluate the company's management the investor is entitled to know something about the company's efforts to diversify. As one writer suggests, "It is . . . fair to assume that investors would want to measure both flexibility achieved and its cost in terms of profits forgone in order to avoid undervaluation of their investment."[11]

## Difficulties in Product-Line Reporting

Product-line reporting is opposed by some on the grounds that it would disclose information of benefit to competitors, or that disclosure of high rates of profit in certain activities would lead to regulatory pressures from the government, wage pressures from labor unions, or price pressures from customers. Most opposition, however, centers on measurement difficulties, and these must either be solved or circumvented before product-line reporting can become widespread.

Two kinds of measurement difficulties should be noted: (1) difficulties in finding an adequate classification of industries or product lines for which separate reports must be issued; and (2) difficulties in measuring assets, liabilities, and income for individual product lines. On the first of these, Mautz could find no single classification of industries or activities that could be used as a reporting basis by all diversified companies.[12] After examining the defects of industry classification schemes used by the United States government and by individual companies, he concluded that the classification scheme must be flexible and adaptable to the specific circumstances of each diversified company.

The main problem is that no matter how the company's activities are classified, some financial data are going to be extremely difficult to identify on a divisional basis. If two divisions share a common manufacturing facility or sales organization, allocations of assets and of expenses must be made to obtain separate financial statements. If one division sells part of its output to another, similar allocation problems arise. At the very least, the divisions of a conglomerate have a common top management. As will be seen in Part III, company managements are able to solve these

---

[11] Leopold Schachner, "Corporate Diversification and Financial Reporting," *The Journal of Accountancy*, April 1967, pp. 43–50.

[12] Robert K. Mautz, "Bases for More Detailed Reporting by Diversified Companies," *Financial Executive*, November 1967, pp. 52–60.

allocation problems for internal reporting and management control purposes. However, using such allocations in published financial statements poses problems of objectivity and verifiability that public and corporate accountants have not resolved to their complete satisfaction.[13]

Many companies now publish partial breakdowns of their financial statements on a product-line basis, without apparent damage to their competitive position.[14] Financial statements filed with the SEC now must include segment sales and income information, and this requirement is likely to be extended to the statements issued to shareholders and others.

## SUMMARY

Nonfinancial corporations often hold government and commercial securities as a means of earning a return on temporarily idle funds. Securities held for this purpose ordinarily earn relatively low yields but are highly liquid. Called "marketable securities," they are usually listed among the current assets on a cost basis.

The securities held for longer-term investment are mostly common stocks of other corporations. The primary motive is to produce income, and short-term marketability is seldom a consideration. When such investments constitute a majority of the voting power in the other corporation, the holder is referred to as a parent company. Its financial statements will ordinarily represent the consolidated results and position of parent and subsidiary combined. This means, for example, that instead of an "investments" figure on the balance sheet, the assets and liabilities of the subsidiary will be merged with those of the parent.

Some companies are now supplementing their consolidated financial statements by publishing information on the results of individual segments of the business, using geographical, industry, or customer-group breakdowns, as appropriate. This form of disclosure poses a number of measurement problems, but enough attention is being given to it to justify a prediction that some form of segment reporting is likely to become the general rule in the United States within a fairly short period of time.

---

[13] For a discussion of these problems, see Alfred Rappaport and Eugene M. Lerner, *Segment Reporting for Managers and Investors* (New York: National Association of Accountants, 1972), Chapter 3.

[14] Rappaport and Lerner, Chapter 4, and American Institute of Certified Public Accountants, *Accounting Trends and Techniques, 1972* (New York: A.I.C.P.A., 1972), pp. 26–28.

## QUESTIONS AND PROBLEMS

1. What is a consolidated financial statement, why is it used, and what is it intended to reveal?

2. List and explain the reasons for the more common adjustments required in the preparation of consolidated financial statements.

3. Explain the probable nature and origin of balance sheet items captioned "consolidation goodwill" or "negative goodwill."

4. How do "inventory profits on intercompany sales" arise and how are they treated in the preparation of consolidated financial statements?

5. What is a "minority interest"? How does it arise? In what part of the balance sheet does it appear?

6. How do "marketable securities" differ from "investments"? To what extent should the accounting treatment of these two items differ?

7. What is the rationale of the "pooling of interests" concept in financial statement consolidation?

8. If conglomerate companies are required to disclose separately the results of individual divisions or activities, should they also be required to prepare and publish consolidated statements? Would these two requirements be consistent with each other?

9. Company P has just acquired all of the assets of Company Q by an exchange of stock. Company Q has achieved a notable rate of growth in recent years, both in sales and in earnings, and its stock has been selling at market prices considerably in excess of its book value. The financial statements of Company P are footnoted to indicate that this acquisition was treated as a pooling of interests.

In what ways would next year's reported net income and the end-of-year balance sheet have differed if the acquisition had been treated as a purchase rather than as a pooling of interests?

10. The board of directors of a U.S. corporation is often self-perpetuating in that the voting stockholders typically elect to the board the slate of candidates proposed by the board. Often the board offers in nomination no one who is not already a member of the board. Under these circumstances a small group of owners is able to control a corporation with total shareholdings of only a tiny fraction of the shares outstanding.

a) Company A owns 25 percent of the stock of Company B and its representatives constitute a majority of the board of Company B. Should consolidated financial statements be prepared for these two companies? Give reasons.

b)   How, if at all, would your answer differ if Company A owned 51 percent of the stock of Company B? 75 percent? 99 percent?

11.  The Merton Company paid $16,000 to its wholly owned subsidiary for certain equipment. This equipment had been carried on the subsidiary's books at its original cost of $31,000, less accumulated depreciation of $17,000.

a)   At what amount would the Merton Company show this equipment on its own unconsolidated balance sheet? At what amount would it be shown on the consolidated balance sheet?

b)   Show in journal form the eliminating entries, if any, that would be required to prepare consolidated financial statements immediately after this transaction.

12.  On December 31, 19x1, the Pilot Company paid $92,000 in cash for an 80 percent interest in the Essex Company. The Essex balance sheet on that date showed the following balances in the shareholders' equity accounts:

| | |
|---|---:|
| Common stock | $ 40,000 |
| Additional paid-in capital | 20,000 |
| Retained earnings | 50,000 |
| Total | $110,000 |

a)   What was the amount of the consolidation goodwill on the date of the purchase?

b)   What was the amount of the minority interest on this date?

13.  On December 31, 19x5, the Ajax Company purchased 8,000 shares of the common stock of the Achilles Company from John and Alfred Achilles, the majority shareholders. The purchase price was $11 a share, paid in cash. These shares constituted 80 percent of the Achilles Company's outstanding common stock. The Achilles Company balance sheet on that date showed the following balances in its stockholders' equity accounts:

| | |
|---|---:|
| Common stock | $ 60,000 |
| Additional paid-in capital | 10,000 |
| Retained earnings | 50,000 |
| Total | $120,000 |

The Achilles Company had only one asset, the patent rights to a hair-coloring compound, listed on the December 31, 19x5, balance sheet at $120,000. The company had no liabilities on that date.

a)   Show how the assets and owners' equity of the Achilles Company would appear on the Ajax Company's consolidated balance sheet on January 1, 19x6, immediately after the purchase.

*b)* What alternative accounting treatments did you consider? Give your reasons in favor of the treatment you selected.

**14.** The Homer Company purchased 8,000 shares of the common stock of the Cicero Corporation on December 31, 19x3. The purchase price was $12 a share, paid in cash. These shares constituted 80 percent of the Cicero Corporation's outstanding common stock. Cicero's balance sheet on that date showed the following balances in its shareholders' equity accounts:

| | |
|---|---|
| Common stock | $ 60,000 |
| Additional paid-in capital | 25,000 |
| Retained earnings | 35,000 |
| Total | $120,000 |

In 19x4 the Cicero Corporation had net income of $30,000 and paid $20,000 in dividends to its stockholders. The Homer Company's net income for the year amounted to $50,000, including dividends from Cicero. Neither company included any intercompany profit in the inventory it reported at the end of the year.

*a)* What was the amount of the consolidated net income for 19x4, after providing for minority interests?
*b)* At what amount would minority interest be shown on the December 31, 19x4, consolidated balance sheet?
*c)* How much of Cicero's retained earnings would be shown in consolidated retained earnings as of December 31, 19x4?

*15.* Among the assets on the December 31, 19x4, balance sheet of the Wolfe Corporation was the following:

Investment in Lamb Company:
   1,000 shares at $90, bought January 1, 19x4 ......... $90,000

The stockholders' equity section of the balance sheet of the Lamb Company on the same date was as follows:

| | | |
|---|---|---|
| Capital stock, 1,000 shares | | $100,000 |
| Deficit, January 1, 19x4 | $20,000 | |
| Less: Operating profit 19x4 | 15,000 | |
| Deficit, December 31, 19x4 | | (5,000) |
| Total Stockholders' Equity | | $ 95,000 |

*a)* Indicate how the above information would be reflected on a December 31, 19x4, consolidated balance sheet.
*b)* Show in journal form the entry to eliminate the intercompany investment that would be shown on a consolidated work sheet for 19x4.

*16.* Company X purchased an 80 percent interest in Company Y on January 1, 19x2. The price was $80,000, paid in cash, and the purchase was recorded in the Investments account of Company X.

---

* Solutions to problems marked with an asterisk (*) are found in Appendix B.

The directors of Company Y declared cash dividends in the amount of $10,000 during 19x2.

When Company X received its share of Company Y's dividends, it debited Cash and credited Dividend Income. Company X's unconsolidated reported earnings for 19x2 amounted to $55,000, including dividend income. No other transactions between Company X and Company Y took place during the year.

Company X declared cash dividends of $30,000 during 19x2.

The stockholders' equity sections of the beginning and ending balance sheets of the two corporations showed the following:

|  | Company X | | Company Y | |
| --- | --- | --- | --- | --- |
|  | 1/1/62 | 12/31/62 | 1/1/62 | 12/31/62 |
| Common stock................. | $100,000 | $100,000 | $ 30,000 | $ 30,000 |
| Premium on common stock ..... | 20,000 | 20,000 | 10,000 | 10,000 |
| Retained earnings ............. | 375,000 | 400,000 | 60,000 | 65,000 |
| Total...................... | $495,000 | $520,000 | $100,000 | $105,000 |

a) What was consolidated net income for 19x2?
b) Show the stockholders' equity section of the consolidated balance sheet as of December 31, 19x2.

17. Company A and Company B were two completely independent companies. Neither had invested in the other; neither had ever bought goods or services from the other. These two companies merged with each other at the beginning of this year. Immediately before the merger, their balance sheets showed the following:

|  | Company A | Company B |
| --- | --- | --- |
| Cash........................................ | $290 | $ 30 |
| Other current assets ........................ | 90 | 60 |
| Property and equipment (net)................ | 120 | 60 |
| Total.................................. | $500 | $150 |
| Liabilities.................................. | $100 | $ 50 |
| Common stock............................. | 200 | 60 |
| Retained earnings .......................... | 200 | 40 |
| Total.................................. | $500 | $150 |

The amounts shown for common stock were the full amount of paid-in capital, not the par value of the shares.

a) Assume that Company A purchased the net assets of Company B ($100) for $160 cash and operated B as one of its divisions. The difference of $60 arose because B's property and equipment was appraised at $120. What would A's balance sheet show immediately after this purchase?
b) Assume that Company A purchased all of the outstanding common stock of Company B for $160 cash and operated B as a subsidiary (thereby preserving B as a separate legal entity). The appraised value of the property and equipment was equal to its book value.

What would A's consolidated balance sheet show immediately after the acquisition?

c) Assume that Company A acquired all of the outstanding stock of Company B, issuing in exchange its own stock with a market value of $160 (par $40). The merger of the two companies is treated as a pooling of interests. After the acquisition, what would appear on A's consolidated balance sheet?

d) For the year preceding the merger, net income was $50 for Company A and $11 for Company B (after depreciation of $6). Assuming the same operating revenues and expenses for the year after merger except as they may be affected by the accounting method, what net income would be reported under each of the three circumstances described above? (Where appropriate, assume that company policy calls for consolidation goodwill to be written off on a straight-line basis over a 5-year period.)

e) Compare the results under the three sets of circumstances. Which is most attractive to a management that is interested in putting its best foot forward?

*18. Two companies had the following balance sheets on December 31, 19x1:

|  | Company X | Company Y |
|---|---|---|
| Current assets | $ 5,500 | $1,000 |
| Plant and equipment, net | 7,000 | 1,700 |
| Total | $12,500 | $2,700 |
|  |  |  |
| Current liabilities | $ 2,500 | $ 500 |
| Common stock ($5 par) | 2,000 | 250 |
| Additional paid-in capital | 3,000 | 750 |
| Retained earnings | 5,000 | 1,200 |
| Total | $12,500 | $2,700 |

These balance sheets included $200 that Company Y owed Company X for goods purchased during 19x1 and sold by Company Y to its customers.

These two companies merged on January 1, 19x2, Company X issuing 100 shares of its common stock in exchange for all of the common shares of Company Y. The fair value of a share of Company X's stock at that time was $30.

In 19x2, Company X reported unconsolidated net income of $1,000, including $100 in cash dividends from Company Y. Company X paid $400 in cash dividends to its shareholders. Company Y reported unconsolidated net income of $180. No intercompany sales were made during the year and the $200 beginning-of-year debt was paid by Company Y during the year.

a) Prepare a consolidated balance sheet immediately after the merger.
b) Prepare a consolidated income statement for the year 19x2.

*c*) Prepare the owners' equity section of the consolidated balance sheet at December 31, 19x2.

**19.** Company P owns 80 percent of the shares of Company S. It carries these shares on its balance sheet at acquisition cost—that is, the price it paid to the previous owners of the shares when it acquired them. This cost was $100,000, and at that time the balance sheet of Company S showed assets of $300,000 and liabilities of $200,000. Company S at that time had 10,000 shares outstanding with a par value of $1 each.

During 19x4, Company P sold half of its output to Company S at a total price of $100,000. The cost of the goods to Company P was $70,000. One fifth of the goods were in Company S's inventory on December 31, 19x4. The two companies' books showed the following totals for 19x4:

|  | Company P | Company S |
|---|---|---|
| Sales | $240,000 | $500,000 |
| Cost of goods sold | 140,000 | 300,000 |

*a*) Did Company P pay for goodwill? If so, was it positive or negative goodwill? How much, if anything, did Company P pay for this goodwill? Show your computations and give *one sentence* to explain your answer.
*b*) Compute consolidated sales and consolidated cost of goods sold for 19x4. Show your calculations.

**20.** On November 30, 19x3, the Fair Deal Corporation exchanged 10,000 shares of its $5 par common stock for a 100 percent ownership in Strate & Shute, Inc. At that time, Fair Deal stock was selling at a market price of $40 per share; Strate & Shute was a family-owned corporation, and there was no market in its shares. The acquisition was treated as a pooling of interests.

Balance sheets drawn up for the two corporations as of November 30, 19x3, just before the acquisition transaction was consummated showed the following (in summary form):

| ASSETS | Fair Deal | Strate & Shute |
|---|---|---|
| Assets | $1,000,000 | $250,000 |

| OWNERS' EQUITY | | |
|---|---|---|
| Common Stock | $ 200,000 | $100,000 |
| Premium on Common Stock | 300,000 | 70,000 |
| Retained Earnings | 500,000 | 80,000 |
| Total Owners' Equity | $1,000,000 | $250,000 |

Earnings for the two companies for 19x3 were:

|  | Fair Deal | Strate & Shute |
|---|---|---|
| January 1–November 30 | $120,000 | $40,000 |
| December 1–December 31 | 20,000 | 5,000 |
| Total | $140,000 | $45,000 |

There were no intercompany sales during the year. No dividends were declared by either company during the year. A set of consolidated financial statements was prepared at the end of 19x3.

a) At what amounts would goodwill and retained earnings appear on the consolidated balance sheet at December 31, 19x3?
b) Calculate consolidated net income for the year. (Consolidation goodwill, if any, is to be amortized in equal amounts for 20 years.)
c) How would your answers to (a) and (b) have differed if the Strate and Shute stock had been acquired in exchange for $394,000 in cash?

21. Below are the balance sheets of the Single and Multiple Product Corporations as of December 31, 19x3:

|  | Single | Multiple |
|---|---|---|
| Assets | $156,000 | $3,400,000 |
| Liabilities | $ 50,000 | $ 650,000 |
| Capital stock, 32,000 shares | 32,000 | |
| Capital stock, 800,000 shares | | 800,000 |
| Capital contributed in excess of par value | 17,000 | 600,000 |
| Retained earnings | 57,000 | 1,350,000 |
| Total | $156,000 | $3,400,000 |

At the start of 19x4 Multiple paid $190,000 in cash for the 32,000 shares of Single. The two companies' income statements for 19x4 prior to consolidation showed the following:

|  | Single | Multiple |
|---|---|---|
| Sales | $800,000 | $10,000,000 |
| Expenses | 700,000 | 8,700,000 |
| Operating income | $100,000 | $ 1,300,000 |
| Dividend received | | 40,000 |
| Income before Taxes | $100,000 | $ 1,340,000 |

a) Would the merger have been accounted for as a purchase or as a pooling of interests? Why?
b) Prepare a consolidated balance sheet at the beginning of 19x4.
c) Present a consolidated income statement. Consolidation goodwill, if any, was to be amortized equally over seven years. Income was taxed at a rate of 50 percent.
d) How, if at all, would your answers to the questions above have differed if the shares of Single had been obtained in exchange for 20,000 shares of Multiple's stock, valued at $9.50 a share?

*22. Prepare a consolidated income statement and balance sheet from the following data relating to the Sumner Corporation and its subsidiary, the Acme Company:

## BALANCE SHEETS
### As of December 31, 19x1

|  | Sumner Corporation | Acme Company |
|---|---|---|
| **ASSETS** | | |
| Cash | $ 3,450 | $ 2,400 |
| Accounts receivable | 6,500 | 4,250 |
| Inventory | 7,100 | 6,500 |
| Investments | 21,000 | – |
| Fixed assets (at net book value) | 15,500 | 14,850 |
| Total | $53,550 | $28,000 |
| **LIABILITIES AND OWNERS' EQUITY** | | |
| Accounts payable | $ 5,200 | $ 1,700 |
| Capital stock (par value $1 per share) | 35,000 | 20,000 |
| Retained earnings | 13,350 | 6,300 |
| Total | $53,550 | $28,000 |

### Income Statements for the Year 19x1

|  | Sumner Corporation | Acme Company |
|---|---|---|
| Sales | $60,000 | $30,000 |
| Cost of goods sold | 48,000 | 19,800 |
| Gross margin | $12,000 | $10,200 |
| General expenses | 3,400 | 6,900 |
| Operating income | $ 8,600 | $ 3,300 |
| Other income | 750 | – |
| Net income | $ 9,350 | $ 3,300 |
| Dividends paid | 5,000 | 1,000 |
| Retained earnings for the year | $ 4,350 | $ 2,300 |
| Retained earnings, December 31, 19x0 | 9,000 | 4,000 |
| Retained earnings, December 31, 19x1 | $13,350 | $ 6,300 |

NOTES:

(1)  Of the total sales of the Sumner Corporation, $10,000 were to the Acme Company. The cost to Sumner of the merchandise sold to Acme was $8,000.

(2)  The "other income" of $750 recorded by the Sumner Corporation represented dividends received from the Acme Company.

(3)  The investments owned by the Sumner Corporation consisted of 15,000 shares in the Acme Company purchased on December 31, 19x0.

(4)  Of the inventory on hand in the Acme Company at December 31, 19x1, $1,000 represented materials purchased from the Sumner Corporation. The cost of the merchandise to Sumner was $800.

(5)  As of December 31, 19x1, the Sumner Corporation had $700 accounts receivable from the Acme Company.

**23.** The Sutton Company is a wholly owned subsidiary of the Porter Company. The assets, liabilities, and stockholders' equities reported by these two companies as of December 31, 19x9, were as follows:

|                                           | Porter Company | Sutton Company |
|-------------------------------------------|----------------|----------------|
| Cash.......................................... | $ 250,000 | $ 130,000 |
| Marketable securities ......................... | 400,000 | 150,000 |
| Accounts receivable – customers ............... | 1,250,000 | 540,000 |
| Allowance for doubtful accounts .............. | (25,000) | (10,000) |
| Accounts receivable – subsidiary .............. | 100,000 | |
| Inventories.................................... | 1,100,000 | 600,000 |
| Stock of Sutton Company (at cost) ............ | 150,000 | |
| Advances to subsidiary........................ | 420,000 | |
| Plant, property, and equipment (net) .......... | 1,525,000 | 710,000 |
| Total.................................. | $5,170,000 | $2,120,000 |
| Accounts payable – trade ...................... | $ 575,000 | $ 185,000 |
| Accounts payable – parent..................... | | 90,000 |
| Accrued liabilities............................ | 350,000 | 100,000 |
| Taxes payable................................ | 525,000 | 275,000 |
| Advances from parent ........................ | | 420,000 |
| Capital stock................................. | 1,000,000 | 140,000 |
| Retained earnings, 1/1/x9 ..................... | 2,420,000 | 835,000 |
| Net income, 19x9 ............................ | 650,000 | 250,000 |
| Dividends declared, 19x9...................... | (300,000) | (175,000) |
| Treasury stock ............................... | (50,000) | |
| Total.................................. | $5,170,000 | $2,120,000 |

The two companies' income statements for 19x9 showed the following figures:

|                                           | Porter Company | Sutton Company |
|-------------------------------------------|----------------|----------------|
| Net sales ..................................... | $10,000,000 | $4,600,000 |
| Other income ................................ | 250,000 | 20,000 |
| Cost of goods sold............................ | (6,700,000) | (3,210,000) |
| Selling, general, and administrative expenses.. | (2,400,000) | (900,000) |
| Income taxes for the year.................... | (500,000) | (260,000) |
| Net Income................................... | $ 650,000 | $ 250,000 |

Further information:

(1) Porter purchased the Sutton stock in 19x1 for $150,000 in cash. As shown on Sutton's books, the book value of Porter's equity at that time was $120,000.

(2) Merchandise in transit from the Porter Company to the Sutton Company on December 31, 19x9, was recorded by Porter as a sale transaction, billed at $10,000. This transaction had not yet been recorded by Sutton.

(3) Sales by Porter to Sutton in 19x9 totaled $1,700,000, including the transaction described in item (2) above. Sutton made no sales to Porter during the year.

(4) Porter's billings for merchandise shipped by Porter to Sutton during the year but not sold by Sutton prior to December 31, 19x9, included an intercompany profit of $20,000.

a) Prepare a consolidated balance sheet as of December 31, 19x9.
b) Prepare a consolidated income statement for the year 19x9.

**24.** Late in 1967 the Glarus Corporation, a manufacturer of grinding wheels and other abrasive products, accepted an offer of $3 million for the assets of its plastics division. Introduced as the first step in a diversification program some 10 years earlier, the plastics division had never reported a profit and management finally decided to sell.

Opportunities for successful expansion in abrasive products seemed unattractive in 1967, and Glarus invested the proceeds from the sale of the plastics division temporarily in short-term government securities.

In January 1968, Mr. Theodore Grumek, the company's treasurer, saw an opportunity to invest these funds profitably in the stock of the Urban Corporation, a manufacturer of office copying machines. He sold the short-term government securities for $3 million and used the proceeds to buy 100,000 shares of Urban stock from their former owners. This represented a 10 percent ownership interest in Urban. The book value per common share on Urban's books was $18 a share at that time.

Urban's earnings for 1968 amounted to $3 per common share; cash dividends of $1.20 a share were distributed to Urban's shareholders during the year.

*a*) As a stockholder in the Glarus Corporation, how much of the Urban Corporation's earnings for 1968 would you want Glarus Corporation to include in its reported net income for the year? Write a letter to the management, giving your reasons for your recommendation. (You may assume that income taxes would be totally unaffected by the choice. You may also assume that all of Urban's income and dividends took place after the date of Glarus's acquisition of the stock.)

*b*) Should Glarus prepare consolidated financial statements, including the Urban Corporation in the consolidated group?

*c*) Indicate the amount at which Glarus would report its investment in Urban on its December 31, 1968, balance sheet if it used the equity basis of measurement.

**25.** Reichhold Chemicals, Inc., changed its method of reporting its investments in nonconsolidated foreign affiliates in 1971 to conform to the APB opinion effective that year. Its method prior to 1971 was described as follows:

> Investments in foreign associated companies are carried at the corporation's equity therein based on underlying book values reflected on the latest available audited or unaudited balance sheets, foreign currency being converted at year-end rates of exchange. Changes in equity in the investment in each company are accounted for through the account "Excess of equity over cost of investments in foreign associated companies," except that changes in equity in the subsidiary when below cost are accounted for in the income statement.
>
> As investments are sold, the difference between proceeds and average cost (equity in subsidiary when below cost) is credited or charged to income.

The company's 1970 annual report contained the following summary of its investments in its nonconsolidated affiliates, reflecting the method in use up to that time:

|  | Cost | Equity |
|---|---|---|
| Investments in foreign affiliates, December 31, 1970: | | |
| Listed securities | $ 746,949 | $1,649,836 |
| Unlisted securities | 1,199,286 | 1,615,487 |
| Total | $1,946,235 | $3,265,323 |

The 1970 income statement showed an extraordinary gain on the sale of foreign investments of $1,000,894 (after provision for income taxes of $402,885). A supporting schedule showed the following changes in the "excess of equity over cost" account:

| | |
|---|---|
| Balance, January 1, 1970 | $1,654,379 |
| Add:   Increase in equity in investments | 223,215 |
| Deduct:   Portion applicable to investments sold | (588,506) |
| Balance, December 31, 1970 | $1,289,088 |

The company's financial statements for 1971 were based on the full application of the equity method to its investments in affiliated Canadian and Caribbean companies, and the cost method for its other foreign investments. The investments were listed as follows:

|  | 1971 | 1970 |
|---|---|---|
| Carried at equity (Reichhold Chemicals (Canada) Ltd., 32% owned, and Reichhold Chemicals del Caribe, Inc., 25% owned) | $1,733,993 | $1,568,835 |
| Others, carried at cost | 1,190,869 | 1,280,352 |
| Total | $2,924,862 | $2,849,187 |

The effect of the change in accounting method was described in the 1972 statement as follows:

> Commencing in 1971, the corporation adopted the equity method of accounting for its investments in certain foreign associated companies. The retroactive application of this method increased (decreased) previously reported net income as follows: 1968, ($7,327); 1969, $88,785, ($.01 a share); 1970, $58,433 ($.01 a share), and net income for 1971 increased by $165,158 ($.03 a share). The cumulative effect on years prior to 1968 was an increase in retained earnings of $733,061 and the elimination of the stockholders' equity account, "Excess of equity over cost of investments in foreign associated companies," $1,135,665. The related dividends, which have been credited to "Investments in foreign associated companies," were as follows: 1968, $28,060; 1969, $34,675; 1970, $35,729; 1971, $37,040.

The following amounts were included in income during these three years:

|  | 1972 | 1971 | 1970 |
|---|---|---|---|
| Royalties and sales of technical assistance to foreign associated companies............................ | $331,127 | $435,727 | $625,704 |
| Dividends from foreign associated companies................. | 131,412 | 21,345 | 125,815 |
| Equity in income of foreign associated companies................. | 323,347 | 166,741 | 30,148 |

Net income for 1970 as originally reported amounted to $3,178,625, or $.47 a share. Restated net income for the year was $3,237,058, or $.48 a share.

a)  To what extent did the 1971 change in accounting policy increase the quality of the information available to the company's shareholders and others?

b)  Recognizing that prior to 1971 the company could choose among several alternative measurement methods, would you have preferred the company to use a method different from the one it did use in those years? Give your reasons.

**26.** The Radio Corporation of America manufactures and sells a wide variety of products and services, including the following:

Radio and television receivers.
Tape recorders and phonographs.
Phonograph records and tapes.
Broadcasting (National Broadcasting Company).
Publishing (Random House).
Vehicle and equipment renting (Hertz).
Frozen prepared foods (Banquet Foods).
Commerical real estate.
Electronic components.
International communications.
Defense products.
Space research.

The company's 1970 annual report included the following information on segment profitability (in millions of dollars):

|  | Revenues | | Net Income | |
|---|---|---|---|---|
|  | 1970 | 1969 | 1970 | 1969 |
| Home products, computer systems, and other commercial products and services ........................ | $1,567.0 | $1,651.3 | $26.7 | $ 89.5 |
| Broadcasting, communications, publishing, and education........... | 748.9 | 757.3 | 46.1 | 51.5 |
| Vehicle renting and related services............................ | 563.2 | 510.7 | 15.6 | 15.4 |
| Space, defense, and other government business ............... | 446.5 | 490.6 | 3.3 | 3.4 |
| Total........................... | $3,325.6 | $3,409.9 | $91.7 | $159.8 |

The following statements were included in other parts of the annual report:

> RCA computer operations remained in a loss position during 1970, although revenue derived from sales and leasing of computer equipment was higher than in the prior year. The 1970 result was attributable in part to heavy continuing expenses in marketing, engineering, and systems programming areas, none of which have been deferred. However, these expenses and additional investments in facilities provide the basis for further growth in the computer business. New orders booked for future computer shipments again were higher in 1970 than in prior years. . . .
>
> RCA's most significant growth area in the seventies is expected to be in information processing. The first year of the new decade provided a promising beginning. The domestic computer industry as a whole experienced the largest decline in shipments in its history in 1970. Yet, domestic bookings of RCA systems were 15 percent higher than in 1969, while shipments rose by more than 50 percent. We attracted three times as many new accounts as in 1969. Our share of the market, based on estimated industry shipments, nearly doubled.

During 1971 the company announced that it was discontinuing the manufacture and sale of general purpose computers. The annual report for that year showed the following revenue and income figures for the discontinued computer business (in millions of dollars):

|  | 1971 | 1970 |
|---|---|---|
| Revenues | $182.0 | $266.0 |
| Loss | (34.5) | (16.0) |

The 1971 financial statements filed with the S.E.C. showed the following losses for the four previous years (in millions of dollars):

| | |
|---|---|
| 1969 | $10.8 |
| 1968 | 13.6 |
| 1967 | 15.3 |
| 1966 | 12.9 |

In addition to the operating loss for the year, RCA recognized an extraordinary loss of $490 million in 1971, less $240 million in tax credits. Charges against the $490 million provision totaled more than $306 million in 1971 and $41 million in 1972, leaving $11.8 million as a deduction from assets and $131.4 million as a liability at the end of 1972.

RCA reported the following revenues and income for its continuing operations, excluding the discontinued computer business, in its 1971 annual report (in millions of dollars):

| | Revenues | | Net Income | |
|---|---|---|---|---|
| | 1971 | 1970 | 1971 | 1970 |
| Home products and other commercial products and services ................. | $1,771 | $1,604 | $ 75.5 | $ 41.0 |
| Broadcasting, communication, publishing, and education ............. | 754 | 753 | 38.0 | 47.4 |
| Vehicle renting and related services..... | 597 | 563 | 10.1 | 15.6 |
| Space, defense, and other government business.................. | 423 | 420 | 5.0 | 3.4 |
| Total ........................... | $3,535 | $3,340 | $128.6 | $107.4 |

The vehicle assets and long-term debt of the Hertz Corporation were shown separately on the company's balance sheet and in the notes to the financial statements. Information on other individual RCA businesses was provided in qualitative or relative terms only.

*a)* Comment on RCA's method of reporting on its computer operations in 1970. What arguments could have been advanced in 1970 and earlier for disclosing the losses being incurred in this line of business? What counterarguments could have been made?

*b)* As an RCA stockholder, would you support a proposal to require the company to disclose separately the financial results of its various major activities? Would you change in any way the company's present approach to reporting the activities of its various divisions and subsidiaries? Write a letter to the board of directors stating and supporting your views on these questions.

*c)* As a member of the company's board of directors, what action would you take in response to a request by a number of stockholders to include in future annual reports separate income statements and balance sheets for Hertz, Random House, National Broadcasting Company, RCA Communications, and other major company subdivisions? Explain your reasons.

# *17*

## CASH FLOWS AND STATEMENTS OF CHANGES IN FINANCIAL POSITION

THE ABILITY OF THE FIRM to generate income is not necessarily correlated with its ability to generate funds to finance its operations. How management obtains funds and how it uses these funds are matters of great concern, both to outside investors and to management itself.

The accountant can prepare two kinds of financial statements to throw light on these questions: cash flow statements and statements of changes in financial position. Although we introduced cash flow statements in Chapter 4 and a rudimentary kind of statement of changes in financial position in Chapter 9, much had to be left unsaid. Our purpose in this chapter is to see what statements of cash flows and statements of changes in financial position are intended to show and how they relate to each other and to the income statement and statement of financial position.

### CASH FLOWS VERSUS FUNDS FLOWS

Cash flow statements summarize the movements of cash into and out of the organization. Statements of changes in financial position summarize the movements of all financial resources, not just cash.

#### Statement of Personal Cash Flows

To illustrate this distinction, let us examine a simple personal example. John Prout is a junior executive in a large corporation.

His salary last year was $24,000 and he received $2,000 in dividends and interest on his investments. He paid $18,000 for day-to-day living expenses, $7,000 for income taxes, and ended the year owing $500 for items he had bought on various credit cards during November and December. He had owed nothing for credit card purchases at the beginning of the year.

Mr. Prout bought a house for $60,000 at the end of December, paying $20,000 in cash and borrowing the remaining $40,000 from a mortgage institution. He received an inheritance of $15,000 from the estate of a great-uncle who had died during the previous year, and bought a new sports car with part of the proceeds, paying $7,000 in cash at the time of delivery. Finally, he discovered that he had paid the government $1,300 too much in income taxes during the year, thereby entitling him to a $1,300 refund sometime within the next few months. He had $12,000 in his bank account at the beginning of the year and $1,000 at the end.

The cash flows in these transactions are all summarized in Exhibit 17–1. Cash receipts totaled $41,000, but cash disbursements amounted to $52,000, thereby bringing the cash balance down by $11,000.

*Exhibit 17–1*

John Prout

SUMMARY OF CASH RECEIPTS AND DISBURSEMENTS

For Last Year

| | | |
|---|---|---|
| *Cash receipts:* | | |
| Cash received from earnings: | | |
| Salary | $24,000 | |
| Interest and dividends | 2,000 | $26,000 |
| Cash received from inheritance | | 15,000 |
| Total cash receipts | | $41,000 |
| *Cash disbursements:* | | |
| For living expenses | $18,000 | |
| For income taxes | 7,000 | |
| For new house | 20,000 | |
| For new car | 7,000 | |
| Total cash disbursements | | 52,000 |
| Net decrease in bank balance | | $11,000 |

## Statement of Changes in Financial Position

The statement of changes in financial position in Exhibit 17–2 is very similar in structure, but is much more comprehensive. It shows all of the flows of financial resources arising out of the transactions above, not just the flows of cash. In this case, only

Exhibit 17–2

John Prout

STATEMENT OF CHANGES IN FINANCIAL POSITION

For Last Year

*Inflows of financial resources:*
Funds from current operations:

| | | |
|---|---:|---:|
| Salary | $24,000 | |
| Interest and dividends | 2,000 | $26,000 |
| Inheritance | | 15,000 |
| Mortgage loan | | 40,000 |
| Total inflows of financial resources | | $81,000 |
| *Uses of financial resources:* | | |
| For living expenses | $18,500 | |
| For income taxes | 5,700 | |
| To buy a new house | 60,000 | |
| To buy a new car | 7,000 | |
| Total uses of financial resources | | 91,200 |
| Net Decrease in Working Capital | | $10,200 |

three differences between resource flows and cash flows appeared. First, the full purchase price of the house is shown as a use of financial resources, and the mortgage loan is shown as a source. Second, the figure for living expenses in Exhibit 17–2 is $500 greater than the corresponding figure in Exhibit 17–1. Third, the income tax figure in Exhibit 17–2 is $1,300 less than the taxes paid.

Perhaps the best way to explain these differences is to point out that the statement of changes in financial position is often regarded as a summary of inflows and outflows of the firm's working capital. In fact, the statement is sometimes called a statement of changes in working capital. Consistent with this, the figure labeled "funds from current operations" measures the effects of Mr. Prout's income-producing activities on his working capital. (In this context, "funds" is a synonym for working capital, and it is convenient if not wholly accurate to refer to statements of this kind as *funds statements.*)

The $40,000 mortgage loan differs from the other inflows of funds in that it had no direct effect on Mr. Prout's working capital. We can rationalize including it by regarding the mortgage transaction as a two-stage process: (1) an inflow of working capital through borrowing, and (2) an outflow of working capital to acquire the house. This is not a bad assumption. Mr. Prout's borrowing power is a valuable resource and is far from unlimited. By borrowing to buy a house, he used some of this resource, thereby reducing his ability to borrow later for other purposes. A statement of changes in financial position that overlooked this fact would be far from complete and much less useful. The greater value of the more comprehensive statement easily justifies treating the mortgage transaction as a simultaneous inflow and outflow of funds (working capital).

This should also explain why the figure for living expenses in Exhibit 17–2 is greater than the one in the cash flow statement. Although Mr. Prout paid $18,000 in cash for food, transportation, insurance, and other living expenses, he used $18,500 of his working capital for this purpose. The $500 in credit purchases placed him in a poorer current financial position than he had been before. The issuers of credit cards ordinarily limit the amount of credit the card holder can use. Unused credit is a financial resource and purchases that reduce this quantity certainly qualify as a use of current financial resources, or funds.

In summary, Mr. Prout was able to finance all of his purchases during the year only by reducing his working capital by $10,200. A review of Mr. Prout's current assets and current liabilities confirms this figure:

|  | Beginning of Year | End of Year | Increase (Decrease) |
|---|---|---|---|
| Cash............................... | $12,000 | $1,000 | $(11,000) |
| Accounts receivable................. | – | 1,300 | 1,300 |
| Current assets ................... | $12,000 | $2,300 | $( 9,700) |
| Accounts payable .................. | – | 500 | 500 |
| Working Capital ................. | $12,000 | $1,800 | $(10,200) |

The $10,200 decrease in working capital appears in Exhibit 17–2 as a balancing item at the bottom, but it could just as well have been classified as a source of some of the funds that Mr. Prout used to finance his purchases.

## USES OF CASH FLOW AND FUNDS FLOW DATA

This simple example cannot be extended much further, but it should be sufficient to demonstrate the usefulness of these kinds of statements.

### Uses of Cash Flow Data

Probably the most obvious use of an historical cash flow statement is to throw some light on why the cash balance increased or decreased during the period. Exhibit 17–1 is wholly adequate for this purpose. It shows that Mr. Prout's receipts from his salary, interest, and dividends paid his living expenses and taxes for the year. His cash problem arose because his purchases of house and car required far more cash than his modest inheritance provided.

Mr. Prout's banker might also use this statement if Mr. Prout were to apply for a loan. He might think, for example, that the $7,000 outlay for a sports car in a year in which Mr. Prout bought a new house was evidence of a certain lack of financial discretion.

Neither Mr. Prout nor his banker would find this historical statement adequate, however. The main question is not what Mr. Prout did last year but what he will do or should do this year. By projecting a similar statement for this year, Mr. Prout can see whether he is likely to have enough funds to pay for all the things he would like to do. He might wish to buy shares of his employer's common stock, for example, or take an expensive summer vacation. A projected funds statement might show him that he could do these things only if another relative died or if he sold investments that he had made to provide for his children's education.

A banker considering a short-term loan to Mr. Prout can use the same kind of statement to see whether Mr. Prout is likely to be able to repay the loan when it comes due. Only if the margin of receipts over disbursements is expected to be big enough *during the term of the loan* to repay the loan plus interest with something to spare will the banker grant the loan.

## Uses of Financial Resource Flow Data

The cash flow statement is useful in connection with short-term decisions. For uses with a longer focus, however, it has two major defects. First, it often excludes significant financial events, such as the mortgage loan that Mr. Prout took out last year. If Mr. Prout had exchanged some of his investments for a parcel of real estate, neither the acquisition of the real estate nor the transfer of the investments would have appeared on the cash flow statement. Anyone interested in analyzing how Mr. Prout has increased the amount of resources at his command and what form these increases have taken will find the cash flow statement inadequate.

Second, receipts and disbursements of cash do not measure the financial effects of current operations. Mr. Prout, for example, actually paid $1,300 more in taxes than he should have. This $1,300 would not have been very useful if Mr. Prout had needed it to pay off a short-term loan, but it would have been available to pay off a two-year note.

## Funds Statements of Business Firms

The funds statements of business firms can be used in just the same way as the statement in this simple personal illustration. The outside investor's interest in the flow of funds stems from his need to appraise a company's performance in using the funds that he has invested or might invest in the future. He is interested in the current funds-generating capacity of the normal operations of the business, and in the company's financing policy as indicated by the methods of financing it has used in the recent past. He wants to know what current and long-term drains on the funds are likely to occur and he needs information on how management has used liquid funds in the past.

Management imposes a different set of demands on the funds analysis. Funds statements enter into the evaluation of alternative financing plans and into long-range forecasts of the need for and availability of funds. Frequently they are tied into the long-term capital expenditure plan by indicating the estimated amount of funds available for this purpose. These are primarily forward projections rather than historical statements, but the historical analysis is used as a point of reference.

Financial analysts who focus on long-term investments in stocks and bonds prefer to work with funds statements rather than cash flow statements. This is because their interest is focused more on fundamental relationships than on short-term variations in liquidity. For example, they want to know how much was spent to acquire plant and equipment, not necessarily whether payment was made immediately in cash.

To understand these points more clearly, we must now move on to a more complete illustration, covering the financial activities of a business firm. In passing, however, we should emphasize that the reasons for preparing statements of changes in financial position are so compelling that one of these statements must accompany the income statement and statement of financial position whenever audited financial statements are prepared for external use.[1]

## THE STATEMENT OF CHANGES IN FINANCIAL POSITION

The statement of changes in financial position, like the income statement, summarizes the effects of events occurring during a specified period of time, such as one year. But whereas the

---

[1] American Institute of Certified Public Accountants, *APB Accounting Principles: Current Text* (New York: Commerce Clearing House, Inc., 1972), Sec. 2021.07.

income statement accounts for one portion of the change in *owners' equity* between two successive balance sheet dates, the funds statement attempts to summarize all of the balance sheet changes arising from the flow of resources into and out of the firm during the period.

### First Approximation: Balance Sheet Changes

The first step in funds statement preparation is to tabulate the changes in individual balance sheet items that have occurred between two successive balance sheet dates. For example, the balance sheets of Peabody, Inc., on January 1 and December 31, 19x1, are shown in Exhibit 17–3.

Exhibit 17–3

Peabody, Inc.

COMPARATIVE STATEMENTS OF FINANCIAL POSITION

January 1 and December 31, 19x1

|  | January 1 | December 31 | Increase (Decrease) |
|---|---|---|---|
| *Current assets:* |  |  |  |
| Cash...................................... | $ 30,000 | $ 14,000 |  |
| Accounts receivable............... | 70,000 | 85,000 |  |
| Inventories......................... | 90,000 | 95,000 |  |
| Total current assets........... | $190,000 | $194,000 |  |
| *Current liabilities:* |  |  |  |
| Accounts payable ................. | $ 79,000 | $ 69,000 |  |
| Salaries payable.................. | 1,000 | 1,000 |  |
| Income taxes payable ............ | 10,000 | 12,000 |  |
| Total current liabilities........ | $ 90,000 | $ 82,000 |  |
| Working capital .................... | $100,000 | $112,000 | $ 12,000 |
| Plant and equipment, net .......... | 200,000 | 235,000 | 35,000 |
| Total....................... | $300,000 | $347,000 | $ 47,000 |
| | | | |
| *Long-term liabilities:* |  |  |  |
| Bonds payable.................... | $ 90,000 | $ 80,000 | $(10,000) |
| Deferred taxes ................... | 15,000 | 20,000 | 5,000 |
| *Shareowners' equity:* |  |  |  |
| Common stock ................... | 100,000 | 150,000 | 50,000 |
| Retained earnings................ | 95,000 | 97,000 | 2,000 |
| Total....................... | $300,000 | $347,000 | $ 47,000 |

To facilitate the analysis, current assets and current liabilities are grouped at the top of the statement. Details of changes in individual current assets and current liabilities do not enter into the calculation of the figures on the funds statement. For this reason they have been omitted entirely from this exhibit.

The changes shown in the right-hand column are the basic raw materials from which funds statements are prepared. We could begin, for example, by listing three uses of funds:

| | |
|---|---|
| Increase in working capital .................. | $12,000 |
| Increase in plant and equipment ............. | 35,000 |
| Decrease in bonds payable .................. | 10,000 |
| Total.................................. | $57,000 |

The major source of funds to finance these activities apparently was the issuance of additional shares of common stock ($50,000), supplemented by modest increases in the deferred tax liability and in retained earnings.

## Additional Information: Changes in Owners' Equity

A statement based solely on these balance sheet changes would be a "where got, where gone" statement, discussed in Chapter 9. A statement of this kind does not really say very much about the sources and uses of resources, however. Most of the changes were net changes, the result of offsetting the increases originating in some transactions against the decreases coming from others. In many cases the individual increases and decreases that are hidden in the overall total may be highly significant.

Some of the information needed to explain the changes in the right-hand column of Exhibit 17–3 can be found in the statement of changes in retained earnings:

| | | |
|---|---|---|
| Retained earnings, January 1 .................. | | $ 95,000 |
| Add:  Net income ............................ | | 39,000 |
| | | $134,000 |
| Less:  Cash dividends ........................ | $17,000 | |
| Stock dividends........................ | 20,000 | 37,000 |
| Retained Earnings, December 31............... | | $ 97,000 |

In addition, a footnote to the financial statements reveals that the company issued new shares of its common stock during the year for $30,000 in cash.

With this information, the $52,000 change in owners' equity can be restated as follows:

| | |
|---|---|
| Sources of funds: | |
| Net income ................................ | $39,000 |
| Sale of stock .............................. | 30,000 |
| Total..................................... | $69,000 |
| Uses of funds: | |
| Cash dividends ............................ | 17,000 |
| Net Change in Owners' Equity............... | $52,000 |

Notice that this summary makes no mention of the stock dividend. The stock dividend merely represented a transfer from one owners' equity account to another; no resources flowed into or out of the firm as a result.

## Funds Provided by Operations

Although we listed net income as a source of funds in the table above, it is likely to be a very poor measure of the amount of funds generated by current revenue-producing operations. The relationship between net income and the amount of funds provided by operations is illustrated in a simple way in Exhibit 17–4. This exhibit shows how Peabody's income statement for the year

*Exhibit 17–4*

Peabody, Inc.

**INCOME STATEMENT**

For the Year Ended December 31, 19x1

| | | | |
|---|---|---:|---:|
| Sales revenue........................................... | | | $400,000 |
| Less: | Cost of goods sold............................... | $240,000 | |
| | Selling and administrative salaries .............. | 56,000 | |
| | Sundry selling and administrative expenses ...... | 20,500 | |
| | Interest........................................ | 7,000 | |
| | Income taxes – current portion................... | 21,000 | 344,500 |
| Funds provided by operations ........................... | | | $ 55,500 |
| Less: | Depreciation.................................... | $ 11,000 | |
| | Income taxes – deferred portion.................. | 5,000 | |
| | Loss on sale of equipment ...................... | 1,000 | (17,000) |
| Add: | Gain on debt retirement......................... | | 500 |
| Net Income............................................. | | | $ 39,000 |

might have been drawn up if expenses, gains, and losses not representing expenditures or receipts of current funds had been separated from other income statement items. The amount of funds provided by operations is calculated by subtracting the amount of "funds-consuming" expenses – that is, those requiring increases in current liabilities or decreases in current assets – from current revenues, as in the upper portion of Exhibit 17–4.

## Cash Flow from Operations

"Funds provided by operations" is sometimes referred to in the financial press and even in some finance textbooks as the firm's cash flow, but it is worth reemphasizing at this point that this is a misnomer. Current revenues are treated as inflows of funds, even if they are not currently realized in cash; current expenses are treated as operating outflows of funds if they represent expenditures of current assets or creation of current liabilities.

Funds flow differs from cash flow mainly to the extent that inventories, current receivables, and current payables change during the period. Peabody's revenues, for example, totaled $400,000 but its receivables were $15,000 greater at year end than on January 1 – collections from customers thus amounting to only $385,000. Similarly, the current portion of income tax expense was $21,000, but only $19,000 of this was actually paid out in cash during the year – the balance in accrued income taxes having gone up by $2,000.

Salary and interest payments during the year were equal to salary and interest expense because no changes in the liabilities for these items were reported. Payments for merchandise and other goods and services used in operations differed from the amounts shown as expense, however. First, we know from Exhibit 17–3 that inventories increased by $5,000. Thus purchases must have exceeded the cost of goods sold by this amount, bringing the total up to $245,000. Next we find that current accounts payable went down by $10,000, indicating that cash payments exceeded the cost of purchased goods and services by that amount. Total cash payments therefore amounted to $245,000 + $20,500 + $10,000 = $275,500, or $15,000 more than the total of the cost of goods sold and the sundry selling and administrative expenses. The cash flow from operations can now be calculated as follows:

| | |
|---|---:|
| Funds provided by operations | $55,500 |
| Add:  Increase in current income taxes payable | 2,000 |
| Less:  Increase in current receivables | (15,000) |
| Increase in inventories | ( 5,000) |
| Decrease in current accounts payable | (10,000) |
| Cash Flow from Operations | $27,500 |

### Reconciling Net Income with Funds Provided by Operations

Until now we have not mentioned the four items that appeared on the income statement but did not measure current inflows or outflows of working capital. These were depreciation, the deferred portion of income tax expense for the year, the loss on the sale of equipment, and the gain on debt retirement. Although these need not be listed on a funds statement at all, most such statements start with net income on the first line, to help the reader identify the sources of the difference between net income and funds provided by operations.

In other words, the analyst starts with net income as his *first approximation* to the amount of funds provided by operations. He then has to *add back* such items as depreciation, the deferred portion of current income taxes, losses and other amortizations of long-life assets, and *subtract* such items as nonoperating gains. Peabody's statement for 19x1 would show the following:

| | |
|---|---:|
| Net income .......................................... | $39,000 |
| Add: Depreciation .................................... | 11,000 |
| Deferred portion of current income tax expense ... | 5,000 |
| Loss on sale of equipment ........................ | 1,000 |
| Subtract: Gain on debt retirement ..................... | (500) |
| Funds Provided by Operations ........................ | $55,500 |

Depreciation, income tax deferrals, and losses have to be added back because they do not measure current outflows of funds. They are not appropriate deductions from revenues in the calculation of the amount of funds provided by operations. Gains, on the other hand, may measure cash inflows, but it is better to report them as part of the cash flows arising from the transactions which led to the recognition of the gain. We shall consider this point at greater length later in this section.

### Purchases and Sales of Fixed Assets

Once the amount of funds provided by operations has been calculated, the other elements of the funds statement can be put together. Some of these can be found by examining the transactions affecting the plant and equipment accounts during the year. In Exhibit 17–3 we saw that net plant and equipment increased from $200,000 to $235,000 during the year. If depreciation had been the only item affecting this set of accounts, however, the net balance would have *decreased* by $11,000. To achieve the net increase of $35,000, gross increases in the account must have amounted to $46,000:

Plant and Equipment

| | | | |
|---|---:|---|---:|
| Bal. 1/1 | 200,000 | Depreciation for the year | 11,000 |
| ??? | 46,000 | | |
| Bal. 12/31 235,000 | | | |

Without further information, the likeliest explanation of this

$46,000 change is that it represented purchases of plant and equipment during the year. Fortunately, most company statements provide supplementary information on property changes, so even this figure can be checked. For example, Peabody's annual report included the figures shown in Exhibit 17–5. The figure for additions to gross plant and equipment shows that equipment purchased during the year amounted to $50,000. From the retirements line we learn that property with an original cost of $30,000 and a net book value of $4,000 was retired during the year.

Exhibit 17–5

Peabody, Inc.

### STATEMENT OF PLANT AND EQUIPMENT ·CHANGES
#### For the Year Ended December 31, 19x1

|  | Original Cost | Accumulated Depreciation | Net Plant and Equipment |
|---|---|---|---|
| Balance, January 1 ........... | $290,000 | $90,000 | $200,000 |
| Additions ..................... | 50,000 | 11,000 | 39,000 |
| Retirements ................. | (30,000) | (26,000) | (4,000) |
| Balance, December 31 ........ | $310,000 | $75,000 | $235,000 |

If no further information on these retirements is provided in the financial statements, the $4,000 can be assumed to approximate the proceeds from the sale of these assets. In this case, however, we know that Peabody's income statement listed a $1,000 loss on the sale of equipment. This means that the equipment must have been sold for $1,000 less than its book value— that is, for $3,000—and two items have to be reflected in the funds statement: the $3,000 proceeds from the sale of equipment and the $1,000 loss on that sale. The $3,000 is clearly a nonoperating source of funds; the $1,000 loss, as we saw earlier, has to be included in the calculation of the amount of funds provided by operations.

A similar treatment would have to be afforded such items as a write-off of a portion of goodwill against current revenues. *Any deduction from revenues which did not represent a current outflow of funds must be added back to net income in order to get a correct statement of the amount of funds provided by operations.*

The original $35,000 increase in the balance in the Plant and Equipment account can now be replaced on the funds statement by the following four items:

|                                                                                      | Sources  | Uses      |
|--------------------------------------------------------------------------------------|----------|-----------|
| Used to acquire plant and equipment..................                                |          | $50,000   |
| Obtained from sale of plant and equipment ...........                                | $ 3,000  |           |
| Added to net income in calculating the amount of funds provided by operations:       |          |           |
| Depreciation .......................................                                 | 11,000   |           |
| Loss on sale of equipment.........................                                   | 1,000    |           |

## Depreciation Is Not a Source of Funds!

The mechanics of adding depreciation back to net income on the funds statement may lead to the hasty conclusion that depreciation is a source of funds. It must be emphasized most strongly that this is not the case. Funds, if any, come from operations. If no sales are made, then no funds are derived from operations no matter how big the annual depreciation charge.

Similarly, although losses must be added back to net income to get a correct measure of the funds provided by operations, these losses are not sources of funds. Depreciation and losses allowed in the computation of taxable income do affect the amount of taxes currently payable, but even here the funds flow is reflected in the tax figure and not in the write-off or amortization of the cost.

## Retirement of Long-Term Debt

Returning to Exhibit 17–3, we find that the amount of bonds payable outstanding declined by $10,000. Without further information, we would enter this in the funds statement as a use of funds. From the income statement, however, we know that the company realized a $500 gain on debt retirement. Thus the bonds must have been repurchased at a cost of $9,500, and instead of one entry in the funds statement we have two:

| | |
|---|---|
| Funds used to retire debt........................................ | $ 9,500 |
| Amount to be subtracted from net income in computing funds provided by operations ........................................ | 500 |
| Total..................................................... | $10,000 |

## Adjustments to Retained Earnings

Adjustments representing corrections of figures for prior years are sometimes charged or credited directly to retained earnings. When this is the case, they should not be added back to or subtracted from net income in the calculation of funds provided by operations but should be treated independently.

For example, suppose that a tax refund is received in 19x1 because the company overpaid its taxes in a previous year. The amount was $700, and the credit was made directly to the Retained Earnings account. This doesn't have to be subtracted from net income because it was never included in net income in the first place. A separate $700 item should be shown on the funds statement as a source of funds.

Or, suppose that a bookkeeping error in calculating depreciation in a prior year was corrected in 19x1 by charging $600 directly against the Retained Earnings account. This doesn't have to be added back to net income because it was not deducted from revenue. In this case, no funds flow occurred and this transaction should not be recorded on the funds statement at all.

### Format of the Statement

The statement of changes in financial position for Peabody, Inc., is shown in Exhibit 17–6. Notice how much more informative this is than a "where got, where gone" summary of simple balance sheet changes. This statement identifies flows of resources, not just changes in account balances. More detail has been inserted to account for every balance sheet change except the change in working capital.

This statement is in what is called a balanced format—that is, total sources and total uses of funds are identical in amount.

Exhibit 17–6

Peabody, Inc.

STATEMENT OF CHANGES IN FINANCIAL POSITION
For the Year Ended December 31, 19x1

Sources of funds:
From operations:
Net income ............................................... $39,000
Add: Depreciation.......................................... 11,000
Deferred portion of income tax expense................. 5,000
Loss on sale of equipment ............................. 1,000
Total.................................................. $56,000
Less: Gain on debt retirement............................. 500
Funds provided by operations ............................ $55,500
From sale of common stock................................. 30,000
From sale of plant and equipment.......................... 3,000
Total Sources of Funds.................................... $88,500

Uses of funds:
To purchase plant and equipment........................... $50,000
To pay cash dividends...................................... 17,000
To retire debt............................................ 9,500
To increase working capital............................... 12,000
Total Uses of Funds....................................... $88,500

Another way of presenting the same information would be to treat the change in working capital as a residual—that is, show total sources of $88,500 but total uses of only $76,500, leaving the $12,000 change in working capital to be derived by subtracting the second of these figures from the first.

The issue is of no great moment, but we prefer the balanced format because the residual format focuses attention unduly on the change in working capital, which may be the least important figure in the statement. The purpose of the funds statement is not to explain the change in working capital, but to show how management obtained resources during the period and how it used them.

## The Extended Funds Statement

Fluctuations in individual current assets and current liabilities are part of the normal course of events, and the increases or decreases that take place in any year are not very significant. When the composition of working capital changes drastically, however, the change in each current asset and each current liability may become very important.

One way to report these changes is to supplement the funds statement with a schedule of changes in current assets and current liabilities. The schedule for Peabody, Inc., is shown in Exhibit 17–7.

Another way to present this same information is to insert these account changes in the funds statement itself. Exhibit 17–8, for example, shows how Peabody's statement would look if this were

Exhibit 17–7

Peabody, Inc.

SCHEDULE OF CHANGES IN CURRENT ASSETS AND CURRENT LIABILITIES

For the Year Ended December 31, 19x1

|  | January 1 | December 31 | Increase (Decrease) |
|---|---|---|---|
| Current assets: |  |  |  |
| Cash......................... | $ 30,000 | $ 14,000 | $(16,000) |
| Accounts receivable............ | 70,000 | 85,000 | 15,000 |
| Inventories.................... | 90,000 | 95,000 | 5,000 |
| Total...................... | $190,000 | $194,000 | $ 4,000 |
| Current liabilities: |  |  |  |
| Accounts payable ............. | $ 79,000 | $ 69,000 | $(10,000) |
| Salaries payable .............. | 1,000 | 1,000 | – |
| Income taxes payable.......... | 10,000 | 12,000 | 2,000 |
| Total...................... | $ 90,000 | $ 82,000 | $ (8,000) |
| Working Capital ............... | $100,000 | $112,000 | $ 12,000 |

done. It differs from the statement in Exhibit 17–6 only in that five changes in individual current assets and current liabilities have been substituted for one figure representing the net change in working capital.

Exhibit 17–8

Peabody, Inc.

EXTENDED STATEMENT OF CHANGES IN FINANCIAL POSITION
For the Year Ended December 31, 19x1

Sources of funds:

| | |
|---|---|
| Operations....................................... | $ 55,500 |
| Sale of equipment............................... | 3,000 |
| Sale of common stock............................ | 30,000 |
| Increase in current income taxes payable......... | 2,000 |
| Decrease in cash balance........................ | 16,000 |
| Total Sources.............................. | $106,500 |

Uses of funds:

| | |
|---|---|
| Purchase of plant and equipment................. | $ 50,000 |
| Cash dividends................................... | 17,000 |
| Debt retirement................................. | 9,500 |
| Increase in accounts receivable.................. | 15,000 |
| Increase inventories ............................ | 5,000 |
| Reduce accounts payable ........................ | 10,000 |
| Total Uses................................. | $106,500 |

This is sometimes referred to as "defining funds as cash," but the result is very different from a statement of cash flows. Funds provided by operations still shows how operations have affected working capital, not how they have affected cash. (The operating cash flow in our example was $27,500, as we saw earlier.) The logic behind this is that changes in receivables, inventories, and payables are to some extent the result of separate managerial decisions, not just of the current level of revenues. As such they should be shown separately, not merged with the funds flow into a single figure.[2]

## PREPARING THE FUNDS STATEMENT

The analysis in the previous section was conducted informally, more or less on the back of an envelope. In simple situations this procedure is adequate, but in the more common practical case some kind of organized approach is generally necessary to keep

---

[2] Another problem is that it is seldom feasible to classify all cash disbursements between amounts paid to suppliers of goods and services for current use and payments to vendors of plant and equipment. Even without this difficulty, however, we would continue to prefer the treatment recommended here.

the analysis under control; that is (1) to prevent errors, and (2) to discover information that might otherwise go unnoticed.

## The Work Sheet Method

All formal methods of statement preparation start with a list of balance sheet changes between two dates. These are shown in T-account form in Exhibit 17–9, based on the account balances listed in Exhibit 17–3. Our objective will be to reproduce the journal entries that together produced these balance sheet changes. (The three blank T-accounts at the bottom of the exhibit are analytical accounts, inserted explicitly for use in statement preparation.)

*Exhibit 17–9*

Peabody, Inc.

**T-ACCOUNT WORK SHEET FOR FUNDS STATEMENT PREPARATION**

For the Year Ended December 31, 19x1

| Working Capital | | Bonds Payable | |
|---|---|---|---|
| Net change  12,000 | | Net change  10,000 | |

| Plant and Equipment | | Deferred Income Taxes | |
|---|---|---|---|
| Net change  20,000 | | | Net change    5,000 |

| Accumulated Depreciation | | Common Stock | |
|---|---|---|---|
| Net change  15,000 | | | Net change  50,000 |

| Funds Provided by Operations | | Retained Earnings | |
|---|---|---|---|
| | | | Net change    2,000 |

| Other Sources of Funds | | Uses of Funds | |
|---|---|---|---|
| | | | |

## Reconstructing Transactions

The first account to be examined is the Common Stock account. This showed an increase of $50,000 during the year. Of this amount, $30,000 represented the proceeds from the sale of new shares of stock to outside investors. The entry that would have been made to record this is:

Cash............................................. 30,000
  Common Stock ............................        30,000

Since cash is a component of working capital and the sale of stock produced an inflow of cash, the sale of stock was a source of funds. Therefore we can restate this entry as follows on the work sheet:

(1)

Other Sources of Funds......................... 30,000
  Common Stock ............................        30,000

This can be translated into a general rule: each work sheet entry should be identical to the entry that was made to record the transaction on the company's books, with one slight change: whenever a transaction embodies a funds flow or a correction of a funds flow item in another transaction, one of the three analytical accounts—Funds Provided by Operations, Other Sources of Funds, or Uses of Funds—is debited or credited instead of the working capital account that was actually affected.

The remaining $20,000 increase in the Common Stock account resulted from a stock dividend issued during the year. The entry to record this is:

(2)

Retained Earnings............................. 20,000
  Common Stock ............................        20,000

This transaction had no effect on funds flows and therefore requires no entry in any of the funds change accounts on the work sheet. It was simply a paper transaction, transferring figures from one owners' equity account to another.

The Common Stock T-account on the work sheet now shows the following:

Common Stock

| | Net change | 50,000 |
|---|---|---|
| | (1) | 30,000 |
| | (2) | 20,000 |

Since the total of the amounts "below the line" just equals the net change in this account balance, and since no further information is available, it is safe to assume that the change in this account has been completely explained. We can move on to another account.

The next account that we shall examine is Retained Earnings. One entry in this account has already been made (entry 2); another can be made to reflect the $39,000 net income for the year:

(3)

Funds Provided by Operations .................. 39,000
    Retained Earnings.........................                39,000

This reflects a fact that should be totally familiar by now: although the determinants of net income are recorded in owners' equity accounts, net income arises because more net assets were earned during the year than were consumed in the process. The debit to Funds Provided by Operations in entry (3) identifies this increase in net assets.

Another change in the Retained Earnings account reflected the declaration of cash dividends for the year. This was clearly a use of funds and can be entered in the work sheet by means of the following entry:

(4)

Retained Earnings............................. 17,000
    Uses of Funds ............................             17,000

The Retained Earnings account on the work sheet now shows the following:

Retained Earnings

|  |  | Net change | 2,000 |
|---|---|---|---|
| (2) Stock dividend | 20,000 | (3) Net income | 39,000 |
| (4) Cash dividend | 17,000 |  |  |

The three changes recorded in this account fully explain the net change in the account balance, and thus we can once again pass on to the analysis of another account.

It will be recalled that the $10,000 reduction in bonds payable was accomplished by repurchasing bonds at a price of $9,500. The entry to record this was:

Bonds Payable................................... 10,000
    Cash.......................................              9,500
    Gain on Debt Retirement ....................               500

The $9,500 outlay of cash was definitely a use of funds, and the work sheet entry is to debit Bonds Payable and credit Uses of Funds. The appropriate treatment of the $500 gain, on the other hand, is to subtract it from the net income figure in computing the amount of funds provided by operations. Because the net income figure was debited in entry (2) to the Funds Provided by Operations work sheet account, the $500 gain should be credited to that account. The composite work sheet entry is:

(5)

```
Bonds Payable.................................... 10,000
    Uses of Funds ...............................         9,500
    Funds Provided by Operations ...............          500
```

This leaves only the fixed asset accounts to be analyzed. The next work sheet entry records the purchase of plant and equipment during the year:

(6)

```
Plant and Equipment........................... 50,000
    Uses of Funds..............................          50,000
```

The next entry records depreciation:

(7)

```
Funds Provided by Operations.................. 11,000
    Accumulated Depreciation...................          11,000
```

(Remember again that the depreciation amount is placed in the Funds Provided by Operations account as an adjustment to net income—it is not a source of funds in its own right.)

Finally, the entry that was made to record the retirement and sale of equipment during the year was:

```
Cash ..........................................  3,000
Loss on Sale of Equipment .....................  1,000
Accumulated Depreciation....................... 26,000
    Plant and Equipment.......................          30,000
```

On the funds statement work sheet this would appear as:

(8)

```
Other Sources of Funds.........................  3,000
Funds Provided by Operations ..................  1,000
Accumulated Depreciation....................... 26,000
    Plant and Equipment.......................          30,000
```

With these three entries, we have accounted for all of the changes in the plant and equipment accounts.

This leaves only two balance sheet changes to be accounted for. The first of these, the $5,000 increase in the balance in the Deferred Income Income Taxes account, was produced by non-funds charges against revenues and must be added back to net income. The work sheet entry is:

(9)

```
Funds Provided by Operations .................. 5,000
    Deferred Income Taxes .....................          5,000
```

The final item to be entered on the work sheet is the change in working capital. Because this figure is not to be subjected to further analysis, it can be accounted for by a single entry:

(10)

Working Capital .............................. 12,000
Uses of Funds .............................. 12,000

In other words, resources amounting to $12,000 were used to increase working capital during the year.

### The Completed Work Sheet

This completes the analysis. The work sheet now appears as in Exhibit 17–10. Notice that for each of the original accounts the sum of the entries below the line is equal to the net change in the account balance shown in the upper part of the account. The other three accounts contain all the items that will go into the funds statement itself. The funds statement in Exhibit 17–6 is simply a formal presentation of the amounts shown in these three analytical accounts.

### SUMMARY

The objective of the income statement is to summarize the economic productivity of the firm's resources during the period. Cash flow statements summarize the receipts and disbursements of cash, and are intended to measure the firm's ability to meet its short-term needs for cash. Statements of changes in financial position, in contrast, are designed to show how the firm obtained and used financial resources during the period. The relationships between the structure of the resources provided and the amounts devoted to such uses as dividends, property additions, and debt retirement are important pieces of information for the evaluation of the firm's financial management, and for future planning by management.

Statements of changes in financial position (funds statements) are more widely used than cash flow statements in analyses of corporations' fundamental financial strengths and weaknesses. The reason is that the cash flow from operations in one period can be increased by delaying payments to creditors until the beginning of the next period, but the underlying funds flow is not affected. Similarly, a purchase of equipment on credit may be a highly significant transaction, but it does not appear in a cash flow statement.

The point is not that cash flow statements are inferior to funds statements, but that they are different. Failure to recognize this simple distinction is responsible for two widely believed fallacies. First, the term cash flow is often used to describe the amount of working capital provided by operations. As we have just seen, this is clearly incorrect. Second, many casual readers of financial

Exhibit 17–10

Peabody, Inc.

COMPLETED FUNDS STATEMENT WORK SHEET

For the Year Ended December 31, 19x1

### Working Capital

| | |
|---|---|
| Net change  12,000 | |
| (10)         12,000 | |

### Bonds Payable

| | |
|---|---|
| Net change  10,000 | |
| (5)          10,000 | |

### Plant and Equipment

| | |
|---|---|
| Net change  20,000 | |
| (6)          50,000 | (8)         30,000 |

### Deferred Income Taxes

| | |
|---|---|
| | Net change    5,000 |
| | (9)           5,000 |

### Accumulated Depreciation

| | |
|---|---|
| Net change  15,000 | |
| (8)          26,000 | (7)         11,000 |

### Common Stock

| | |
|---|---|
| | Net change  50,000 |
| | (1)         30,000 |
| | (2)         20,000 |

### Funds Provided by Operations

| | |
|---|---|
| (3) Income       39,000 | (5) Gain on |
| (7) Depre-       | debt re- |
| ciation   11,000 | tirement        500 |
| (8) Loss on      | |
| sale of          | |
| equip-           | |
| ment       1,000 | |
| (9) Deferred     | |
| income           | |
| taxes      5,000 | |

### Retained Earnings

| | |
|---|---|
| | Net change    2,000 |
| (2)        20,000 | (3)         39,000 |
| (4)        17,000 | |

### Uses of Funds

| | |
|---|---|
| (4) Divi- | |
| dends     17,000 | |
| (5) Debt | |
| retire- | |
| ment       9,500 | |
| (6) Equip- | |
| ment | |
| pur- | |
| chases    50,000 | |
| (10) In- | |
| crease | |
| work- | |
| ing | |
| capital   12,000 | |

### Other Sources of Funds

| | |
|---|---|
| (1) Sale of | |
| stock      30,000 | |
| (8) Sale of | |
| equip- | |
| ment        3,000 | |

statements assume that cash flow can be calculated by adding depreciation to net income. This does not always equal the amount of *funds* provided by operations, and it almost certainly does not measure cash flow.

This chapter has tried to explain what funds flows are and has presented a simple method that can be used to develop funds statements from income statement and balance sheet information. The method itself is less important, however, than the relationships between the funds statement and the other financial statements with which it is coupled.

## QUESTIONS AND PROBLEMS

1. Explain the nature and functions of a funds statement.

2. Describe and explain some of the important differences between revenues and expenses, on the one hand, and sources and uses of funds, on the other.

3. How significant was the difference between cash flow from operations and funds provided by operations at Peabody, Inc., during 19x1? How did this difference arise?

4. "You can't pay your creditors with 'funds.' The only sensible solution, therefore, is to use cash as your definition of funds." For what purpose or purposes does the author of this comment probably use funds statements? Explain.

5. Why may it be reasonable to assume that there has been no gain or loss on the retirement of capital assets in the absence of statement evidence to the contrary?

6. The following comment appeared in an annual report: "Funds provided by depreciation were adequate to finance only 50 percent of our purchases of plant and equipment during the year. Earnings for the year were inadequate to finance the balance and so your company was forced to resort to borrowing." In what sense were funds provided by depreciation?

7. Explain the effect of each of the following on the company's working capital:

*a*) Receipt of dividends from a consolidated subsidiary.
*b*) Write-off of an uncollectible account against the allowance provided.
*c*) A stock split.
*d*) A stock dividend.
*e*) Purchase of treasury stock.

*f)* Write-off of goodwill.
*g)* Sale of machinery subject to group depreciation.

**8.** Why does the accountant include the exchange of capital stock for land in the funds statement, even though working capital is neither increased nor decreased by the transaction?

**9.** A newspaper headline some years ago read: "Company Borrows $200 Million to Pay Income Taxes." Explain the company's action in the face of the fact that taxes are levied only on income and income typically provides funds.

**10.** The Tanker Corporation has financed the acquisition of a fleet of tankers which cost $10,000,000 by means of a 10-year, 9% bond issue. The bonds are to be retired by lot at the rate of 10 percent a year. The president of the company asks why depreciation must be charged on the tankers, which have an expected life of 15 years, in view of the provision for retiring the debt. The company uses the sum-of-digits method to charge depreciation.

Write a memo to the president which explains the interrelation of the operating and financial consequences of the tanker acquisition.

**11.** Below are certain account balances from the Placque Corporation's financial statements:

BALANCE SHEET

|  | 19x3 | 19x2 |
|---|---|---|
| Plant and equipment | $8,900 | $8,500 |
| Allowance for depreciation | 3,600 | 3,300 |

INCOME STATEMENT

|  |  |
|---|---|
| Depreciation expense | $ 900 |
| Loss on retirements | 400 |

A note to the statement reports that property with an original cost of $1,300 and accumulated depreciation of $600 was sold during 19x3 for $300.

*a)* List the transactions that affected the plant and equipment and allowance for depreciation accounts during the year.
*b)* Indicate how, if at all, each of these would be shown on a statement of changes in financial position.

*12.** A stockholder of the Revolving Dollar Company is alarmed when he finds from the company reports that bank deposits have remained about the same in spite of profits of $16,211,410 during the year and dividends of only $3,000,000. The facts appear as follows in the annual report:

---

* Solutions to problems marked with an asterisk (*) are found in Appendix B.

| ASSETS | December 31 This Year | December 31 Last Year |
|---|---|---|
| Cash | $ 2,271,876 | $ 2,309,929 |
| Marketable securities | 4,000,000 | 3,200,000 |
| Accounts receivable | 6,161,539 | 8,376,036 |
| Inventories | 22,769,013 | 16,670,371 |
| Equipment, land, fixtures, etc. (net) | 26,725,711 | 22,286,333 |
| Total Assets | $61,928,139 | $52,842,669 |

| LIABILITIES | | |
|---|---|---|
| Accounts, notes, and taxes payable | $ 5,324,072 | $ 9,450,012 |
| Bonds outstanding | None | None |
| Net Assets | $56,604,067 | $43,392,657 |

Depreciation for the year amounted to $5,447,120; no capital assets were sold or scrapped.

Explain to the stockholder how all of the year's dollars were spent.

13. In May, 19x2, an investor was studying the desirability of purchasing shares of Marshall Company common stock. The relationship between earnings and market price seemed reasonable and growth prospects seemed good, both for the company and for its industry. A friend suggested that the investor study the company's funds flows before deciding whether to buy the stock, and pointed out the following comparative funds statement in the company's 19x1 annual report:

| | 19x1 | 19x0 |
|---|---|---|
| Sources: | | |
| Operations: | | |
| Net income | $ 3,500,000 | $3,000,000 |
| Depreciation | 2,300,000 | 2,000,000 |
| Total from operations | $ 5,800,000 | $5,000,000 |
| Sale of 9% debentures | ...... | 2,500,000 |
| Sale of 9% convertible preferred | 1,500,000 | ...... |
| Other sources (net) | 100,000 | 200,000 |
| Total Sources of Funds | $ 7,400,000 | $7,700,000 |
| | | |
| Uses: | | |
| Plant additions | $ 4,900,000 | $5,500,000 |
| Dividends | 2,000,000 | 2,000,000 |
| Purchase of stock in Franklin Company | 2,200,000 | ...... |
| Total Uses of Funds | $ 9,100,000 | $7,500,000 |
| Increase (Decrease) in Working Capital | $(1,700,000) | $ 200,000 |

On February 15, 19x2, the board of directors voted the regular quarterly cash dividend of $500,000. On April 1, 19x2, the president of the Marshall Company announced plans to sell several buildings to the Federal Leasing Company and lease them back on long-term leases. Plans to double production capacity in the next five years were announced at the same time. An announcement on the method of financing to be used was to be made shortly.

In what way, if any, would this information have helped the investor to make his decision? Would he have been more likely or less likely to buy the stock as a result of an informed analysis of this information? Support your opinion with figures drawn from the problem.

14. The Arkville Transit Company operates a network of bus lines in a small city. Last year it reported a small operating loss, and earnings are unlikely to improve in the near future. The following income statement for last year is likely to be typical of those to be prepared for the next few years:

| | | |
|---|---|---|
| Fares and other revenues | | $1,000,000 |
| Expenses: | | |
| Salaries and wages | $650,000 | |
| Fuel and lubricants | 170,000 | |
| Depreciation | 100,000 | |
| Tires and batteries | 20,000 | |
| Repair parts | 30,000 | |
| Other expenses | 40,000 | |
| Total Expenses | | 1,010,000 |
| Net Income (Loss) | | $ (10,000) |

The company's balance sheet showed the following amounts at the beginning and end of last year:

| | Beginning of Year | End of Year |
|---|---|---|
| ASSETS | | |
| Current assets: | | |
| Cash | $ 100,000 | $ 90,000 |
| Receivables | 150,000 | 140,000 |
| Inventories | 50,000 | 60,000 |
| Total current | $ 300,000 | $ 290,000 |
| Plant and equipment (net) | 940,000 | 920,000 |
| Total Assets | $1,240,000 | $1,210,000 |
| LIABILITIES AND STOCKHOLDERS' EQUITY | | |
| Current liabilities | $ 70,000 | $ 150,000 |
| Bonds payable | 100,000 | ...... |
| Common stock | 260,000 | 260,000 |
| Retained earnings | 810,000 | 800,000 |
| Total Liabilities and Stockholders' Equity | $1,240,000 | $1,210,000 |

Mr. John Bergson recently bought an 80 percent interest in this company for $200,000. When shown the income statement above, he replied, "Good! That's just what I'd hoped for."

Mr. Bergson is a professional investor, not given to letting sentiment or emotion affect his investment decisions. Furthermore, he has little time to devote to active participation in the management of the companies he invests in.

a) How did he probably justify his decision to invest in the Arkville Transit Company?

b) What plans does he probably have for his investment in Arkville Transit? How do these plans differ from the actions of the previous owners? Do you think that he is likely to achieve his objectives? Support your answers with figures from the problem.

*15. From the following data, prepare a statement of changes in financial position. All balance sheet figures are in thousands of dollars.

### Condensed Comparative Balance Sheets

|  | Last Year | This Year |
|---|---|---|
| Current assets | $56,746 | $ 77,091 |
| Investments in associated companies, at cost | ...... | 1,005 |
| Property, plant, and equipment, at cost | 31,414 | 49,096 |
| Allowances for depreciation | (13,237) | (18,421) |
| Total | $74,923 | $108,771 |
|  |  |  |
| Current liabilities | $42,536 | $ 48,898 |
| Payable to General Tile and Rubber Co. | ...... | 7,000 |
| Total Liabilities | $42,536 | $ 55,898 |
| Preferred stock | 1,347 | 1,123 |
| Common stock, at par ($1 per share) | 4,317 | 4,492 |
| Additional paid-in capital | 7,179 | 19,551 |
| Retained earnings | 19,544 | 27,707 |
| Total | $74,923 | $108,771 |

Additional information:
(1)  Sale of common stock during the year, 175,000 shares.
(2)  Net income for the year, $8,203,000.
(3)  Preferred dividends paid, $40,000.
(4)  Depreciation and amortization for the year, $5,501,000.
(5)  Property, plant and equipment acquired during the year, $18,082,000.

16. You have the following information about the financial affairs of the XYZ Company:

Information from the balance sheet:

|  | Beginning of Year | End of Year |
|---|---|---|
| Current assets | $10 | $11 |
| Plant and equipment, original cost | 20 | 24 |
| Plant and equipment, accumulated depreciation | 8 | 9 |
| Current liabilities | 5 | 7 |
| Common stock (including premiums on common stock) | 6 | 9 |
| Retained earnings | 11 | 10 |

Information from income statement:

Net income, $6
Depreciation, $4
Gain on retirement and sale of plant and equipment, $5

Other information:

Cash dividends declared to holders of shares of common stock, $4
Stock dividends, capitalized at $3
Original cost of plant and equipment retired and sold during the year, $7

Prepare a statement of changes in financial position.

**17.** The Sandwich Company's balance sheets for 19x3 showed the following:

|  | December 31, 19x2 Debit | December 31, 19x2 Credit | December 31, 19x3 Debit | December 31, 19x3 Credit |
|---|---|---|---|---|
| Current assets. | $400 |  | $460 |  |
| Investments | 100 |  | 60 |  |
| Plant and equipment (net) | 330 |  | 380 |  |
| Unamortized bond discount | 5 |  | . . . |  |
| Current liabilities | | $200 |  | $290 |
| Bonds payable | | 100 |  | . . . |
| Reserve for contingencies | | . . . |  | 40 |
| Common stock | | 200 |  | 220 |
| Additional paid-in capital | | 50 |  | 60 |
| Retained earnings | | 285 |  | 290 |
| Total | $835 | $835 | $900 | $900 |

The Retained Earnings account for the year 19x3 showed the following transactions:

**Retained Earnings**

| | | | |
|---|---|---|---|
| Stock dividend | 30 | Net income | 130 |
| Cash dividend | 60 | Income tax refund | 5 |
| Appropriation for contingencies | 40 | | |

Bonds payable were retired on January 1, 19x3. Investments with a book value of $40 were sold during the year for $57.

The declaration of a 10 percent stock dividend was recorded by transferring $20 to the Common Stock account and $10 to Additional Paid-In Capital.

Land and equipment that had a book value of $112 was sold for $127. Expenditures for additions to plant and equipment amounted to $208 during the year. Depreciation recorded for the year was $46.

Prepare a statement of changes in financial position.

*18. The following information was taken from an annual report (all figures are in thousands of dollars):

## Balance Sheet

|  | August 31 This Year | | August 31 Last Year | |
|---|---|---|---|---|
| Current Assets: | | | | |
| Cash................................ | | $   883 | | $    954 |
| U.S. government securities........... | | 1,222 | | 1,704 |
| Accounts receivable.................. | $1,504 | | $1,553 | |
| Allowance for uncollectible accounts. | 119 | 1,385 | 115 | 1,438 |
| Inventories......................... | | 1,946 | | 2,651 |
| Prepaid expenses.................... | | 170 | | 88 |
| Total Current Assets ........... | | $5,606 | | $ 6,835 |
| Long-Life Assets (at Cost): | | | | |
| Land................................ | | 295 | | 295 |
| Building, machinery, and equipment. | $6,610 | | $5,998 | |
| Allowances for depreciation.......... | 2,685 | 3,925 | 2,410 | 3,588 |
| Total Assets.................... | | $9,826 | | $10,718 |
| | | | | |
| Current Liabilities: | | | | |
| Accounts payable ................... | | $   505 | | $    609 |
| Accrued taxes....................... | | 556 | | $    896 |
| Total Current Liabilities........ | | $1,061 | | $ 1,505 |
| Mortgage bonds payable............... | | 1,000 | | 1,500 |
| Total Liabilities ............... | | $2,061 | | $ 3,005 |
| Stockholders' Equity: | | | | |
| Capital stock........................ | | 7,000 | | 7,000 |
| Retained earnings................... | | 765 | | 713 |
| Total Liabilities and Stock-holders' Equity.............. | | $9,826 | | $10,718 |

## Schedule of Changes in Plant Asset Accounts

|  | August 31 Last Year | Increase | Decrease | August 31 This Year |
|---|---|---|---|---|
| Cost....................... | $5,998 | $894 (additions) | $282* | $6,610 |
| Allowance for depreciation | 2,410 | 350 (depreciation) | 75* | 2,685 |
| Balance................... | $3,588 | | | $3,925 |

* Sale of equipment.

## STATEMENT OF INCOME AND RETAINED EARNINGS
### For the Year Ended August 31, This Year

| | | |
|---|---|---|
| Net sales............................................. | | $13,380 |
| Less: Cost of goods sold ............................... | $10,880 | |
| Selling and administrative expenses.............. | 1,623 | |
| Loss on sale of equipment....................... | 100 | |
| Income taxes.................................... | 367 | |
| Total deductions*............................ | | 12,970 |
| Net income........................................... | | $    410 |
| Retained earnings, beginning of year.................. | | 713 |
| | | $  1,123 |
| Less: Dividends declared.............................. | $   300 | |
| Settlement of prior years' taxes ................. | 58 | 358 |
| Retained Earnings, End of Year...................... | | $    765 |

* Includes depreciation, $350 thousands.

Prepare an extended statement of changes in financial position.

19. The Traydown Corporation's financial position went from bad to worse during 19x8, although net reported income showed a satisfactory increase over that of prior years. Despite the company's negotiation of a $100,000 bank loan early in 19x8, the cash balance decreased to a dangerous point by the end of the year. The balance sheets showed the following:

Traydown Corporation

**COMPARATIVE BALANCE SHEET**

(thousands of dollars)

| ASSETS | December 31, 19x7 | December 31, 19x8 |
|---|---|---|
| Current Assets: | | |
| Cash...................................... | $ 50 | $ 30 |
| Receivables.............................. | 200 | 220 |
| Inventories............................... | 150 | 200 |
| Total Current Assets................. | $400 | $450 |
| Buildings and fixtures..................... | $300 | $280 |
| Less: Allowance for depreciation......... | (90) | (70) |
| Net Buildings and Fixtures .......... | $210 | $210 |
| Total Assets....................... | $610 | $660 |
| | | |
| LIABILITIES AND STOCKHOLDERS' EQUITY | | |
| Current Liabilities: | | |
| Accounts and wages payable............. | $200 | $180 |
| Bank loan payable ...................... | 50 | 150 |
| Total Current Liabilities............. | $250 | $330 |
| Mortgage payable......................... | 70 | 55 |
| Deferred income taxes.................... | 20 | 23 |
| Unfunded pension liability................. | 10 | 12 |
| Total Liabilities..................... | $350 | $420 |
| Stockholders' Equity: | | |
| Common stock (par)..................... | $140 | $130 |
| Retained earnings....................... | 120 | 110 |
| Total Stockholders' Equity ........... | $260 | $240 |
| Total Liabilities and Stockholders' Equity .......................... | $610 | $660 |

NOTES (All figures are in thousands of dollars):
(1) Net income for 19x8 was $30.
(2) Total sales were approximately the same in 19x8 as in 19x7.
(3) A building with an original cost of $50 and accumulated depreciation of $30 was sold for $56, cash.
(4) Depreciation for the year was $10.
(5) Cash dividends paid were $24.
(6) One stockholder sold his common stock back to the company for $26, cash. The par value of this stock was $10, and the remaining $16 of the repurchase price was charged to retained earnings.

a) Prepare an extended statement of changes in financial position.
b) Prepare a brief report, addressed to the loan officer of the company's bank, commenting on any items in your statement that you think would help him reach a decision on renewing or increasing the size of his loan to the company. He has a forecasted statement of cash

flows for 19x9, but feels that the 19x8 funds statement can provide information that the forecast does not provide.

c) Would an ordinary statement of changes in financial position, without details on changes in individual current assets and current liabilities, have been just as good or better in this case? Explain your answer.

**20.** A company's annual report showed the following balance sheets for the beginning and end of its most recent fiscal year:

| | | Beginning | End | Change |
|---|---|---|---|---|
| Current Assets: | | | | |
| Cash......................................... | | $ 10 | $ 20 | +$10 |
| Accounts receivable................... | | 30 | 51 | + 21 |
| Inventory............................. | | 50 | 45 | − 5 |
| Total current assets ............... | | $ 90 | $116 | +$26 |
| Investments in other corporations ....... | | 80 | 50 | − 30 |
| Fixed assets............................ | $220 | $228 | +$8 | |
| Less: Accumulated depreciation........ | 120 | 124 | + 4 | |
| Fixed assets, net .................... | | 100 | 104 | + 4 |
| Total Assets.................... | | $270 | $270 | − |
| Current Liabilities: | | | | |
| Accounts payable..................... | | $ 40 | $ 35 | −$ 5 |
| Dividends payable.................... | | − | 2 | + 2 |
| Total current liabilities........... | | $ 40 | $ 37 | −$ 3 |
| Bonds payable........................ | | 40 | − | − 40 |
| Deferred income taxes ................. | | 20 | 23 | + 3 |
| Total liabilities.................. | | $100 | $ 60 | −$40 |
| Shareowners' equity: | | | | |
| Common stock (par)................... | $ 25 | $ 30 | +$ 5 | |
| Additional paid-in capital............. | 65 | 90 | + 25 | |
| Retained earnings.................... | 80 | 90 | + 10 | |
| Total shareowners' equity ....... | | 170 | 210 | + 40 |
| Total Liabilities and Share- owners' Equity ............. | | $270 | $270 | − |

You have the following additional information:
(1)  Net income for the year, $30.
(2)  Cash dividends declared during the year, $8.
(3)  Stock dividends declared during the year (par value $2), $12.
(4)  Depreciation on fixed assets for the year, $18.
(5)  Purchases of fixed assets during the year:
    For cash, $21.
    In exchange for stock (par value $3), $18.
(6)  Cash proceeds from sale of fixed assets during the year, $2.
(7)  Cash proceeds from sale of investments during the year, $42; no investments were purchased during the year and all investments are shown on the balance sheet at cost.
(8)  All accounts payable were to vendors of merchandise bought for resale.

a) Prepare an extended statement of changes in financial position.

b) Prepare a statement of cash flows with three sections: (1) net cash flow from operations, (2) other cash receipts, and (3) other cash disbursements.

c) The year in question was a year of severe inflation. Judging from the funds statement and from information in the problem, do you think that the actions taken by the management of this company were appropriate in an inflationary situation?

**21.** The net changes in the balance sheet accounts of X Company for the year 19x0 are shown below:

| | Debit | Credit |
|---|---|---|
| Investments.......................... | | $25,000 |
| Land............................... | $ 3,200 | |
| Buildings........................... | 35,000 | |
| Machinery.......................... | 6,000 | |
| Office equipment..................... | | 1,500 |
| Allowance for depreciation: | | |
|    Buildings......................... | | 2,000 |
|    Machinery......................... | | 900 |
|    Office equipment.................. | 600 | |
| Discount on bonds................... | 2,000 | |
| Bonds payable...................... | | 40,000 |
| Capital stock – preferred............. | 10,000 | |
| Capital stock – common ............. | | 12,400 |
| Premium on common stock.......... | | 5,600 |
| Retained earnings................... | | 6,800 |
| Working capital .................... | 37,400 | |
| Total...................... | $94,200 | $94,200 |

Additional information:

(1) Cash dividends of $18,000 were declared December 15, 19x0, payable January 15, 19x1. A 2 percent stock dividend on the common stock was issued March 31, 19x0, when the market value was $12.50 per share.

(2) The investments were sold for $27,500.

(3) A building which cost $45,000 and had a depreciated basis of $40,500 was sold for $50,000.

(4) The following entry was made to record an exchange of an old machine for a new one:

| | | |
|---|---|---|
| Machinery...................................... | 13,000 | |
| Allowance for depreciation – Machinery ......... | 5,000 | |
|    Machinery..................................... | | 7,000 |
|    Cash ........................................ | | 11,000 |

(5) A fully depreciated office machine which cost $1,500 was written off.

(6) Preferred stock of $10,000 par value was redeemed for $10,200.

(7) The company sold 1,000 shares of its common stock (par value $10) on June 15, 19x0, for $15 a share. There were 13,240 shares outstanding on December 31, 19x0.

Prepare a statement of changes in financial position for the year 19x0.
(AICPA Adapted)

**22.** The Apex Company's financial statement for 19x2 showed the following (all figures are in thousands of dollars):

### Balance Sheets

| | December 31, 19x2 | December 31, 19x1 |
|---|---|---|
| **ASSETS** | | |
| *Current Assets:* | | |
| Cash | $ 2,133 | $ 2,250 |
| Accounts receivable, net | 1,382 | 1,064 |
| Inventories | 1,179 | 936 |
| Total Current Assets | $ 4,694 | $ 4,250 |
| *Long-Term Assets:* | | |
| Land | 273 | 198 |
| Buildings, machinery, and equipment | 6,700 | 6,750 |
| Less: Allowance for depreciation | (2,270) | (2,000) |
| Investments in subsidiaries | 3,018 | 3,002 |
| Goodwill | 90 | 100 |
| Total Assets | $12,505 | $12,300 |
| **LIABILITIES AND SHAREOWNERS' EQUITY** | | |
| *Current Liabilities:* | | |
| Accounts payable | $ 1,080 | $ 2,350 |
| Taxes payable | 550 | 650 |
| Dividends payable | 350 | .... |
| Total Current Liabilities | $ 1,980 | $ 3,000 |
| *Long-Term Liabilities:* | | |
| Bonds payable | 1,000 | .... |
| Bond premium | 72 | .... |
| Provision for pensions | 150 | 150 |
| Provision for deferred income taxes | 110 | 90 |
| Total Liabilities | $ 3,312 | $ 3,240 |
| *Shareowners' Equity:* | | |
| Common stock, at par | 1,510 | 1,500 |
| Premium on common stock | 2,000 | 1,910 |
| Appropriation for contingencies | 400 | 300 |
| Retained earnings | 5,283 | 5,350 |
| Total Liabilities and Shareowners' Equity | $12,505 | $12,300 |

### Income Statement
#### For the Year Ended December 31, 19x2

| | | |
|---|---|---|
| Sales | | $ 9,880 |
| Income from unconsolidated subsidiaries | | 206 |
| Gain on sale of land | | 15 |
| Total | | $10,101 |
| Less: Cost of goods sold | $7,414 | |
| Selling and administrative expenses | 1,843 | |
| Amortization of goodwill | 10 | |
| Interest expense | 97 | |
| Income taxes | 354 | |
| Total expenses | | 9,718 |
| Net Income | | $   383 |

Notes to financial statements:
(1) All the company's subsidiaries were located in the United States.

Income on investments in unconsolidated subsidiaries was recognized on an equity basis.

(2)   Expenses for the year included depreciation in the amount of $496 thousands. The Apex Company used the group depreciation method on almost all of its depreciable assets.

(3)   The only dividend declared during the year on Apex common stock was the cash dividend declared during December and payable on January 20, 19x3.

(4)   Buildings, equipment, and machinery purchased in 19x2 cost $246 thousands.

(5)   The Apex Company issued stock during the year in exchange for land. No other common stock transactions occurred during the year.

(6)   Bonds were issued on January 2, 19x2, with a 10% coupon rate.

a)   Prepare a statement of changes in financial position for the year, showing the change in working capital as a single figure.

b)   For what purpose, if any, would you prefer to use an extended statement, including changes in individual current assets and current liabilities?

23. The Mastik Company was incorporated in 1962 by two young electronics engineers, Frank Orsini and Robert Newman, to manufacture and market a new electronic relay that they had developed. The initial share capital consisted of 10,000 shares, divided equally between the two founders. Each of the men paid the company $10,000 in cash for his shares. An additional block of 2,000 shares was issued in 1964 to a friend of the two men. The issue price of these shares was $5 a share.

The company's first product was highly successful, and in 1964 operations were transferred to a larger building which the company leased for five years. Purchase of additional equipment at that time was financed by a five-year loan from an equipment finance company. This same company also granted loans for equipment purchased in subsequent years.

Mastik's sales continued to grow at a rapid rate as new products and services were introduced. Net income grew even faster, as shown in the following table:

| | 1965 | 1966 | 1967 |
|---|---|---|---|
| Sales | $194,000 | $318,000 | $390,000 |
| Expenses: | | | |
| Wages and salaries | $ 87,000 | $178,000 | $191,000 |
| Materials and supplies | 58,000 | 75,000 | 94,000 |
| Rent | 12,000 | 12,000 | 12,000 |
| Depreciation | 5,000 | 7,000 | 8,000 |
| Other operating expenses (including interest) | 20,000 | 22,000 | 31,000 |
| Income taxes | 4,000 | 8,000 | 18,000 |
| Total Expenses | $186,000 | $302,000 | $354,000 |
| Net Income | $   8,000 | $ 16,000 | $ 36,000 |

In March, 1968, however, Mastik's commercial bank notified management that the company's bank balance had fallen to less than the minimum required by the bank. The bank was unwilling to extend additional credit unless the company was able to broaden its ownership base and attract more stockholder capital. The company's balance sheets for the previous four years were as follows:

| | 1964 | 1965 | 1966 | 1967 |
|---|---|---|---|---|
| ASSETS | | | | |
| Current Assets: | | | | |
| Cash............................. | $18,000 | $ 21,000 | $ 15,000 | $ 8,000 |
| Accounts receivable................ | 20,000 | 29,000 | 48,000 | 74,000 |
| Inventories ........................ | 11,000 | 15,000 | 30,000 | 55,000 |
| Prepayments...................... | 2,000 | 3,000 | 4,000 | 5,000 |
| Total Current Assets........... | $51,000 | $ 68,000 | $ 97,000 | $142,000 |
| Long-Term Assets: | | | | |
| Machinery and equipment ......... | $50,000 | $ 60,000 | $ 65,000 | $ 82,000 |
| Less: Accumulated depreciation.. | (6,000) | (11,000) | (18,000) | (26,000) |
| Net Long-Term Assets ......... | $44,000 | $ 49,000 | $ 47,000 | $ 56,000 |
| Total Assets.................. | $95,000 | $117,000 | $144,000 | $198,000 |
| LIABILITIES AND STOCKHOLDERS' EQUITY | | | | |
| Current Liabilities: | | | | |
| Accounts payable.................. | $ 3,000 | $ 6,000 | $ 10,000 | $ 14,000 |
| Wages and taxes payable .......... | 4,000 | 5,000 | 9,000 | 20,000 |
| Notes payable to bank ............. | 2,000 | 7,000 | 12,000 | 20,000 |
| Total Current Liabilities ....... | $ 9,000 | $ 18,000 | $ 31,000 | $ 54,000 |
| Equipment loan payable ............. | 30,000 | 35,000 | 30,000 | 25,000 |
| Notes payable to stockholders........ | 4,000 | 4,000 | 7,000 | 12,000 |
| Total Liabilities.............. | $43,000 | $ 57,000 | $ 68,000 | $ 91,000 |
| Stockholders' Equity: | | | | |
| Common stock..................... | $30,000 | $ 30,000 | $ 30,000 | $ 30,000 |
| Retained earnings ................. | 22,000 | 30,000 | 46,000 | 77,000 |
| Total Stockholders' Equity ..... | $52,000 | $ 60,000 | $ 76,000 | $107,000 |
| Total Liabilities and Stock-holders' Equity............ | $95,000 | $117,000 | $144,000 | $198,000 |

Mr. Orsini and Mr. Newman were stunned by this news. They did not understand how they had gotten into such a difficult position, since they had never reported a loss, even in their first year of operations, their customers were all good credit risks, and finished goods were always shipped soon after completion.

Prepare a report for Mr. Orsini and Mr. Newman explaining to them what had happened.

# Part III

# Accounting Data for Management Planning and Control

# 18

# BUDGETARY PLANNING

MANAGEMENT'S NEEDS for financial information are far from satisfied by the financial information provided to shareholders and the general public. These needs arise largely in connnection with management's efforts to plan and control the organization's activities.

Management exercises control over its operations (1) by selecting the course of action it wishes to follow (*planning* or *decision making*); (2) by issuing instructions and seeing that they are carried out (*direction* and *supervision*); and (3) adjusting its methods or its plans on the basis of analyses of the results achieved (*responsive control*).

The purpose of this chapter is to examine the nature of the planning process and to see what kinds of accounting data this requires. In later chapters we shall see how these data are provided and how they are used in planning. Our final chapters will then examine the kinds of internal reporting system that accountants use to keep management informed on the results of its actions so that it can exercise responsive control.

## THE PLANNING PROCESS

Control always begins at the planning stage. No other technique controls the firm's destiny as planning does, and the difference between effective and ineffective planning can be so great as to overshadow the effect of all other control techniques combined.

Planning is the process of deciding on a course of action, of finding and choosing among the alternatives available. It takes three forms: (1) *policy formulation* – establishment of the major ground rules that determine the basic direction and shape of the enterprise, the limits within which management is free to exercise its discretion; (2) *decision making* – the choice among alternative solutions to specific operating or financial problems within the prescribed policy limits; and (3) *periodic planning* – the preparation of comprehensive operating and financial plans for specific intervals of time.

Exhibit 18–1 represents an attempt to diagram the relationships among these three types of planning. In general, the progression moves from the top of the chart toward the bottom – policies and strategic plans tend to act as tight or loose constraints on the shorter-term processes. This is not wholly rigid, however, in that policies are always subject to review as conditions change or more information becomes available; long-range strategies are also modified for the same reason.

Exhibit 18–1
MANAGEMENT PLANNING PROCESSES

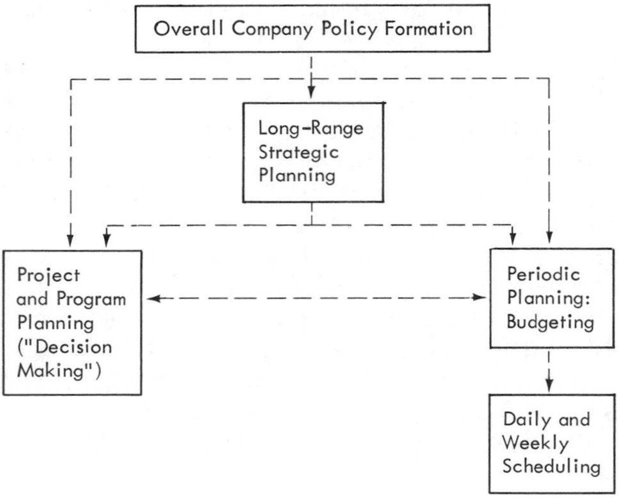

The relationships between project and program planning and periodic planning are more complex. For example, the establishment of a marketing program ordinarily takes place as part of the periodic planning process. Similarly, a decision to promote one product more actively than another may be made in the process of periodic planning. Both of these kinds of decisions may also be made later, however, when changing conditions give evidence that this part of the periodic plan can no longer be carried out effectively or can be improved upon.

*Scheduling*, shown at the bottom of the chart, is really part of periodic planning. It is the process of determining in detail what needs to be done to carry out the planned program, establishing timetables for the performance of these tasks, and seeing to it that men, materials, facilities, and funds are available in the necessary quantities at the necessary times and places to carry out the plan.

## ANNUAL BUDGETING

Periodic planning has both short-term and long-term dimensions. The long-range plan summarizes management's vision of the company's future during the next three to five years, sometimes even longer. Short-term planning, or *budgeting*, typically deals with the next year only, and the annual budget is the first year's segment of the long-range plan. In this introductory survey, we shall limit ourselves to a discussion of the short-term component of budgetary planning.

### Nature of the Budget

The annual budget is the quantitative expression of management's immediate objectives and its plans for operating and financing the organization during the year. This definition can be applied to any kind of organization—a school, a symphony orchestra, an industrial corporation, or even a government department fighting for a share of the tax dollar.

One way to describe the budget is to list its component parts, as in Exhibit 18–2. The left-hand column of this exhibit lists the major physical elements that the management of a manufacturing company must deal with. These are translated in the next two columns into monetary terms as budgeted operating costs, revenues, and expenses. Finally, these cost and profit budgets are brought together with planned capital expenditures and plans for financing the entire package to form the finance budgets shown at the right.

The budget also has an organizational dimension. Each unit has its own portion of the overall plan, and bringing organizational units together may be even more difficult than coordinating production and sales in the aggregate. At low organization

*Exhibit 18–2*
### BUDGET COMPONENTS

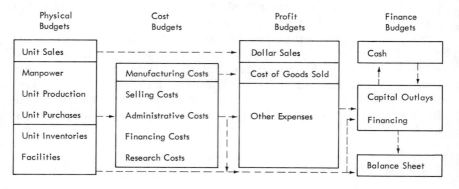

| Physical Budgets | Cost Budgets | Profit Budgets | Finance Budgets |
|---|---|---|---|

levels, the department head is likely to deal with only a few of the budget components shown in Exhibit 18–2. At higher levels, however, the plan is likely to include the same components as the budget of the organization as a whole.

## Purposes of Budgeting

The annual budgetary planning process has at least four major objectives:

1.  To force management to reexamine its objectives, its methods, and its costs.
2.  To encourage executives to quantify their plans and to test them against objective standards of desirability and feasibility.
3.  To give management a chance to anticipate environmental changes, thereby increasing its ability to shape the organization's future.
4.  To develop a formal statement of ends and means that can serve both as a continuing reminder for the guidance of day-to-day management and as a bench mark against which to measure actual performance.

The first three of these are advantages of the process of budgeting; the fourth can be realized only if the budget documents are continually and constructively used.

In none of this has any mention been made of the use of budgets as *limits*. Some of the figures embodied in the budget may indeed be used in this way—for example, budgeted advertising expenditures may be the maximum amount that the advertising manager can spend—but budgeting is in its essence a planning process, not a limiting process. The budgeting procedure should allow for changes in the amount or pattern of the budgeted expenditures as conditions change or as management gains more knowledge of its resources and opportunities.

## The Budgeting Process

Comprehensive budgetary planning ordinarily begins with the distribution to all executives of a set of forecasts and assumptions as to the future state of the economy and its probable impact on the company's business. This may be drawn up with the aid of the company's own planning staff or acquired from outside economic analysts.

Next, the head of each division or department collects the factual information necessary for an informed analysis of past performance and future possibilities. He solicits suggestions and proposals from his subordinates. After an analysis of all of this information, he arrives at what he conceives to be the best course of action with respect to the operations under his control.

These tentative plans are then submitted to higher management for review and consolidation. The reviewing authority may be either the next level in the management chain or a central planning staff or budget department. A proposed plan needs to be examined from three points of view: (1) is it *realistic;* (2) is it *consistent* with company objectives and plans of other parts of the organization; and (3) is it *feasible* in the light of the company's financial, marketing, and production capacities?

This process is more iterative than the above description is likely to imply. That is, tentative budgets are proposed, discussed, and revised again and again as they move upward toward final approval. The process is one of progressive dialogue; and executive seldom receives a budget proposal from a subordinate without having discussed vital aspects of it ahead of time. Through vertical and horizontal communication within the management group, these plans are adjusted and readjusted until they become a set of integrated and realizable objectives consistent with overall company policies.

## Participative Budgeting

This discussion presumes that budgets for each organization unit are established jointly by the manager of that unit and his

or her immediate superior. The purpose of this multilevel participation is partly to increase the motivational impact of the resulting plan. Participation, the argument runs, will lead the subordinate executive to accept the plan more readily and to commit
himself more wholeheartedly to its achievement.

Although behavioral scientists are not entirely agreed on the
implications of the various empirical studies that have been
made, one interpretation is that if participation in profit planning
is to affect performance, it must succeed in increasing the executive's sense of identification with a larger group which accepts
profit generation as a desirable goal.[1] Executives of many companies believe that it does just that.

One point that is often misunderstood in this connection is the
role of higher management. Some people have interpreted participation to mean a complete abdication of responsibility by
managers at higher levels in the organization. This is certainly
not the intent. For one thing, one manager's plan is an integral
part of his superior's plan, so that the latter cannot abdicate responsibility even if he wants to. Secondly, participation is likely
to further company goals only if some leadership force steers it
in that direction.

From this brief description, one point should have emerged
clearly. Budgeting is not simply a matter of forecasting what the
future has to offer. It is a highly creative process, in which executives at all levels are expected to evaluate and compare different
possible courses of action, selecting those which seem most likely
to meet company goals.

## The Role of Accounting Management

As the foregoing would imply, the development of operating
plans is a responsibility of line management. The task of pulling
together all the elements of a profit plan, however, ordinarily falls
to the lot of the budget director or controller.

The budget director or controller is also responsible for designing and securing support for the procedural aspects of periodic
planning, mainly the questions of what is to be budgeted, when,
and by whom. This is ordinarily done by the budget staff, working
closely with operating executives. The final installation is likely

---

[1] Selwyn Becker and David Green, Jr., "Budgeting and Employee Behavior," *The Journal
of Business*, October 1962, pp. 392–402; and George J. Benston, "The Role of the Firm's
Accounting System for Motivation," *The Accounting Review*, April 1963, pp. 347–54.

to be summarized in a budget manual, spelling out deadlines for various budget components, assigning responsibilities for budget preparation, prescribing forms, and describing the overall budget pattern.

Even if budget components have been reviewed carefully and critically all the way up the line within a given segment of the organization, the corporate controller or budget director often has the authority to subject the proposals to his own tests of feasibility and profitability. He is always free to seek clarification or question whether other alternatives have been investigated, and in some cases he even has the power to ask individual managers to revise their programs. It must be emphasized, however, that in taking any action of this sort *the controller is acting as the agent of line management* and is applying tests that line executives would apply.

## PREPARING THE ANNUAL BUDGET

The development of a formal budgetary plan requires a careful examination of the interrelationships among its various components. Although the complexity of this process cannot be conveyed effectively in a few pages, a very simple example may at least identify the problems. Since a manufacturing illustration would be too complex for our purposes at this point, let us see how the management of a small publishing house, Darwin Books, Inc., developed its annual budget for·19x1.

### The Organization

Activities at Darwin Books fall broadly into three major categories: manuscript procurement, production, and sales. "Production," in this case, consists mainly of editing manuscripts, preparing them for typesetting, proofreading, and designing book covers and dust jackets. All printing and binding of books is done on contract by outside printers.

The company has two main product lines—textbooks for college and university use and textbooks for secondary schools—and this provides the basis for the company's organization chart, portions of which are shown in Exhibit 18–3. The vice president in charge of each of the textbook divisions is responsible for both manuscript procurement and sales. Each has a force of field representatives, organized into four regional groups, each headed by a regional manager with the title of field editor. The financial

Exhibit 18–3

Darwin Books, Inc.

**PARTIAL ORGANIZATION CHART**

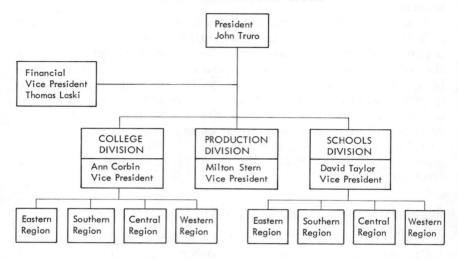

vice president is in charge of all financial activities, including the coordination of the annual budget.

### The Marketing Plan

Darwin's fiscal year begins on July 1 each year. Early in March 19x1, John Truro, the company's president, asked each textbook division manager to submit a tentative marketing plan, showing the size and composition of the field organization, the promotional pattern to be followed, and the anticipated revenues and expenses.

Ann Corbin, the manager of the college division, started by preparing an up-to-date list of the book titles that were then available or were scheduled for production in time for use during the next fiscal year. She gave copies of this list to each of her field editors and asked each of them to spell out in detail a promotional program for the coming year, estimate its cost, and predict the resulting sales volume. Dave Taylor, the schools division manager, followed a similar procedure.

Both division managers reviewed the projected sales and the underlying marketing plans with their field editors. Miss Corbin, for example, compared the proposed expense/sales ratio for each region with the 19x0 ratio and with the ratios in other regions.

She compared the proposed increase in selling expense in each region with the projected increase in sales volume. She prompted her western region field editor to hire an additional field representative to work actively in locating new manuscripts for textbooks in the natural sciences, and her comments and suggestions led to various changes in all of the regional plans.

At one point she turned down a proposal of the southern region field editor to expand his field staff to increase the number of contacts with junior colleges in the area. Darwin Books had few titles that were appropriate for use in the junior college market. She felt that any promotional effort in this market should be concentrated on a few departments in a few of the larger junior colleges. This would not require any increases in the size of the field sales force.

After working with the field editors, the two division managers presented the following tentative sales and expense budgets to Tom Laski, the financial vice president:

|  | College Division | Schools Division |
|---|---|---|
| Sales revenues | $4,200,000 | $2,700,000 |
| Less: returns | 150,000 | 50,000 |
| Net sales | $4,050,000 | $2,650,000 |
| | | |
| Marketing expenses: | | |
| Division office salaries | $ 100,000 | $ 85,000 |
| Field salaries | 400,000 | 300,000 |
| Travel and entertainment | 200,000 | 120,000 |
| Advertising | 50,000 | 50,000 |
| Other | 70,000 | 60,000 |
| Total Marketing Expenses | $ 820,000 | $ 615,000 |

Mr. Laski questioned Dave Taylor, the schools division manager, on the slow growth in sales in his division and the high ratio of marketing expenses to sales. Mr. Taylor blamed both of these on the lack of any large-volume titles in the list. Darwin Books was a relative newcomer in the schools market, with a line of innovative texts, but none of these had broken through with many sales to the large school districts which accounted for the bulk of textbook purchases. Mr. Laski remarked that Mr. Truro would want to discuss the schools division's future with Mr. Taylor at the final budget review session in June.

## The Production Plan

At this point Mr. Laski asked the textbook division managers to meet in his office with Milt Stern, the production manager. The textbook division managers gave Mr. Stern their proposed schedule for new books and new editions and their estimates of sales for each title in the active list. They reviewed inventory figures and identified titles that should be allowed to go out of print as soon as present stocks were exhausted.

Mr. Stern complained that the manuscript preparation schedules were too heavily concentrated in the autumn months. Many of his copy editors were part-time employees, but some things had to be done by full-time personnel and they simply could not handle the projected peak load. Darwin Books had solved this problem occasionally in the past by delaying the publication dates for several books, but this time it seemed more profitable to authorize an increase in the size of Mr. Stern's full-time staff.

### The Profit Plan and Cash Budget

After his meeting with the division vice presidents, Mr. Laski assembled the available data into a tentative profit plan for the coming year. This tentative plan is summarized in Exhibit 18–4.

### Exhibit 18–4
#### Darwin Books, Inc.
#### TENTATIVE PROFIT PLAN
#### For the Year Ending June 30, 19x2

|  | College Division | Schools Division | Total |
|---|---|---|---|
| Net sales | $4,050,000 | $2,650,000 | $6,700,000 |
| Divisional expenses: |  |  |  |
| Printing and binding | $2,400,000 | $1,700,000 | $4,200,000 |
| Copy editing | 100,000 | 80,000 | 180,000 |
| Advertising and selling | 650,000 | 470,000 | 1,120,000 |
| Authors' royalties | 500,000 | 250,000 | 750,000 |
| Administration | 70,000 | 65,000 | 135,000 |
| Total divisional expenses | $3,720,000 | $2,565,000 | $6,285,000 |
| Divisional profit | $ 330,000 | $ 85,000 | $ 415,000 |
| General administrative expenses |  |  | 300,000 |
| Income before income taxes |  |  | $ 115,000 |
| Income taxes |  |  | 50,000 |
| Net Income |  |  | $ 65,000 |

He also assembled proposals for such items as dividends and purchases of furniture and equipment, and prepared the following tentative cash budget for the coming year:

Cash receipts:

| | | |
|---|---:|---:|
| Customers............................. | | $6,500,000 |
| Other sources ......................... | | 100,000 |
| Total cash receipts ................. | | $6,600,000 |
| Cash disbursements: | | |
| Salaries............................. | $1,350,000 | |
| Printing............................. | 4,500,000 | |
| Other suppliers........................ | 210,000 | |
| Authors' royalties...................... | 700,000 | |
| Taxes ................................ | 50,000 | |
| Dividends............................. | 40,000 | |
| Furniture and equipment purchases..... | 60,000 | |
| Total cash disbursements ........... | | 6,910,000 |
| Cash Deficit............................. | | $   310,000 |

As this shows, anticipated cash receipts were $310,000 less than anticipated disbursements. This left management with several options to investigate, mainly the following:

1. Reduce existing cash balances.
2. Defer payments to suppliers.
3. Press customers for prompter payment.
4. Curtail discretionary spending plans.
5. Borrow.
6. Revise marketing plans.
7. Reduce dividends.

Although the choices here are top management's responsibility, the financial executive is usually expected to analyze the alternatives and make recommendations. In practice, he is likely to work closely with top line management, so that the final budget already reflects the consensus of top management's views before it is presented to the Board for approval.

The main problem at this point is to find adequate criteria to guide management's choices among these alternatives. In this case, management felt that any reduction in the dividend would have had an unacceptable effect on the market price of the company's stock. This alternative therefore was regarded as a last resort.

Unless the company's collection efforts have been lax, faster collections from customers ordinarily can be achieved only at the cost of lost sales, usually a very costly effect. Slower payments to suppliers may weaken the company's credit rating and increase purchasing costs. In this case, however, Mr. Laski felt that payments to the company's printers could be cut back by $100,000 without adverse effects.

Ordinarily the cheapest way of covering a cash deficit is to reduce the company's bank balances or liquidate any holdings of short-term marketable securities. In this case Mr. Laski's analysis indicated that reduction of the cash balance would jeopardize the company's ability to meet its payrolls and other obligations on time, and Darwin Books had no marketable securities to liquidate. Fortunately, its credit rating was very good, however, and Mr. Laski was able to get a commitment for a $200,000 line of credit from a local bank, at 8 percent interest. By deferring $15,000 in equipment purchases, the anticipated deficit would be covered. These changes can be summarized as follows:

| | |
|---|---:|
| Borrowing | $200,000 |
| Less: after-tax interest on borrowing | 4,000 |
| Net cash from borrowing | $196,000 |
| Reduction in payments to printers | 100,000 |
| Deferral of equipment purchases | 15,000 |
| Net Cash Effect | $311,000 |

Both the tentative profit plan and the tentative cash budget were modified to reflect these changes. The Board of Directors reviewed and approved the revised plans, but indicated their dissatisfaction with the profit level being achieved. Mr. Truro was asked to work with his division managers on ways to improve profit performance, with particular attention to the schools division. A full-fledged review of the schools division was scheduled for an autumn Board meeting.

### Budgeting as a Decision-Making Process

This brief discussion should make it quite clear that budgeting is a creative, decision-oriented process. It may also be the most important single phase in the management control process, in that much of what the organization will do is settled at this time.

Budget approval is top management's signal that the methods selected and the ends to be achieved are acceptable. When management receives a proposed profit plan, it can either (1) accept it, (2) send it back for revision, or (3) take steps to terminate the operation. In practice, some question is almost always raised about the adequacy of the plan, thus ruling out immediate acceptance. Termination, on the other hand, is unlikely to be ordered unless such a decision has been considered before and deferred to give the division manager an opportunity to come up with a viable alternative.

The result is a response pattern like that schematized in Ex-

Exhibit 18–5
SYSTEM RESPONSES TO PROPOSED PROFIT PLAN

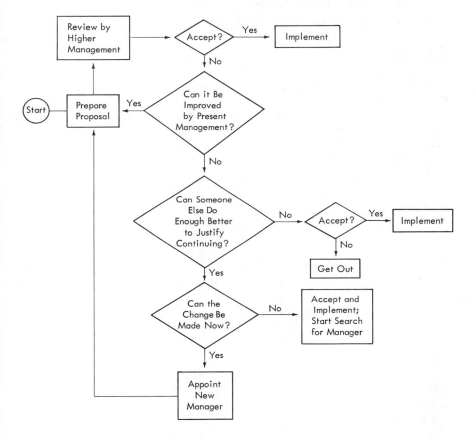

hibit 18–5. Initial rejection ordinarily starts the process over again, as lower management seeks ways to improve the anticipated results. This is shown by the arrows looping back into the block at the upper left-hand corner of the exhibit.

It should be emphasized here that acceptance of a plan implies a commitment to recognize this as satisfactory short-term performance. If Darwin's top management is not convinced that the planned profit represents satisfactory performance in the circumstances, then it should send the plan back for another effort. Budget approval is an extremely important decision. It represents a commitment to the operation for the current period on the terms reflected in the budget. If current performance is unsatisfactory and top management feels that the fault is the manager's, it can seek a new manager. If the ailment is persistent, however, the same issue will arise in the next planning period, and the next, and the next, until management either is able to turn the operation around or gives up and gets out.

## SUMMARY

Periodic planning, or budgeting, is not simply a matter of forecasting what the future has to offer. It is a highly creative process, in which executives at all levels are expected to evaluate and compare different possible courses of action, selecting those which seem more likely to meet company goals. Budgeting, in other words, is a form of decision making.

In this chapter we have tried to convey a feeling for the complexity and dynamism of the budgeting process without getting bogged down in complex numerical examples. In our illustration, budget preparation was initiated by top management, but the major effort took place at the divisional level as the division managers developed their marketing plans and translated them into production requirements and profit estimates. These plans were reviewed, revised, and consolidated before being presented to top management for final approval. They came together eventually in a profit plan and cash budget that were both feasible and acceptable to top management.

As this would imply, budgeting is a responsibility of line management; the controller or other financial executive administers the system and provides useful advice and assistance. When finally completed, the short-term plan, usually one year in length, becomes a managerial commitment and a bench mark against which future performance can be measured. We shall return in the final chapter of this book to examine this final aspect of budgeting.

The data requirements of a budgetary planning system are substantial. The planner needs data on the costs of doing various things, and on the profit margins obtainable from the organization's various products and services. Even more important, he needs data that will help him forecast the *responses* of costs, revenues, and cash flows to various kinds of managerial actions. Not all of these data can be supplied by even the most advanced accounting system, but many of them can be. Our purpose in the next few chapters will be to outline some of the kinds of information the accountant can supply and to indicate how this information can and should be used.

## QUESTIONS AND PROBLEMS

1. Distinguish between planning and responsive control. In what sense are they both control processes?

2. Budgeting has been referred to as an iterative process. What does this imply?

3. Do business budgets and personal budgets serve the same purposes? In what respects are they similar? In what respects do they differ?

4. State the case for participative budgeting. What price should a manager at an intermediate managerial level expect to pay for the right to participate in budget setting?

5. Would you expect the controller to have the authority to reject a budget proposal that is made by one of the company's middle managers? If so, on what grounds could he base his decision? If not, explain why not.

6. In what sense is budgeting a decision making process? How, if at all, does it differ from other forms of business decision making?

7. As an executive charged with the responsibility for reviewing budget proposals, what kinds of data would you want the proponents to supply?

8. What kinds of actions can management take if it finds a budget proposal unsatisfactory? For each of these possible actions, indicate the circumstances under which you think it would be appropriate.

9. How does the problem of reviewing a sales manager's sales and expense budget differ from the task of reviewing the factory manager's proposed budget for the acquisition of factory equipment?

10. If you were preparing a sales and expense budget for a group of products you were responsible for, what kinds of data would you expect the company's accounting system to provide?

11. Hammersmith, Ltd., has three regional factories, each of which manufactures all of the company's products. The sales force is also organized geographically, in 10 regional divisions, and each salesman has a geographic territory in which he is the company's sole representative.

In the past, the annual budgeting process started with the development of tentative sales and marketing plans by the regional sales managers. These were then used to estimate the requirements for production and for administrative support. After review and revision, the final budget was structured along organizational lines.

Hammersmith's management became convinced in the early 1970s that this approach was preventing the development of coherent, aggressive marketing plans for individual products. Four product managers were appointed, each one responsible for setting objectives and developing marketing programs for one of the company's four main product groups. The regional manufacturing and sales organizations remained in being; the product managers were planners and coordinators without direct line authority over factory or sales personnel.

In line with this change, top management decided that all future budgets would be drawn up on a product line basis. Each product manager would draw up a proposed marketing and production plan for his line, working closely with the head office sales and production staffs.

What problems do you foresee in the new system? How would you try to anticipate them and minimize their importance?

**12.** The management of the Cranmore Manufacturing Company at the beginning of 19x1 anticipated (1) a decrease in sales as compared with 19x0 because of production time lost in converting to new products, and (2) a considerably smaller profit margin due to higher material and labor costs. The controller was asked to prepare a cash budget based on estimated 19x1 sales of $2,400,000 (a decrease of $300,000) and, in particular, to forecast the cash position at the close of 19x1.

The treasurer's forecast of certain balance sheet and other items was as follows:

| | |
|---|---|
| Accounts receivable (net)............................ | $ 35,000 decrease |
| Accounts payable.................................... | 20,000 decrease |
| Inventories.......................................... | 17,000 increase |
| Additions to plant (gross)........................... | 125,000 |
| Additions to retained earnings appropriated for contingencies........................................ | 25,000 |
| Net income for 19x1 (after depreciation and before income taxes)...................................... | 95,000 |
| Depreciation expense, 19x1.......................... | 48,000 |
| Income taxes for 19x1 (payable in 19x2).............. | 45,000 |
| Dividend payments (at 19x0 rates).................... | 30,000 |

The cash balance on January 1, 19x1, was $54,000, and the accrued tax liability on that date, arising from 19x0 taxable income, amounted to $93,000. The company had no bank loans outstanding.

a) Assuming that any balance sheet items not listed above would be unchanged, prepare a schedule of forecasted cash receipts and cash disbursements for 19x1 and determine the expected cash balance as of December 31, 19x1.

b) What action would you expect management to take when it sees the cash flow estimates for the year?

13. A consulting firm has a professional staff of 10, giving it a capacity to provide 1,500 hours of consulting service in an average month. Commitments to and from the company's present clients will require the firm to provide them with approximately 1,000 hours of service in each of the next six months, yielding revenues of approximately $40,000 a month and project-related expenses of $10,000 a month. Salaries of the professional staff amount to $25,000 a month; rent and other office expenses average $8,000 a month.

The firm's president would like to submit bids for four additional consulting projects to be completed during the next six months. He has been working closely on each of these with the prospective clients and is quite convinced that his firm will be given the assignments if he can promise completion within the six-month period. His estimates for these four projects are as follows:

|  | Project A | Project B | Project C | Project D |
|---|---|---|---|---|
| Hours per month ................. | 125 | 250 | 375 | 450 |
| Consulting fees to be charged to the client each month .......... | $5,000 | $6,000 | $16,500 | $22,500 |
| Unreimbursed project expenses per month (other than salaries of professional staff, rent, and other office expenses)........... | $ 100 | $ 500 | $ 7,500 | $ 9,000 |

a)  What should the firm do? Show your calculations.
b)  What criterion or criteria did you use in reaching your conclusions?
c)  What other kinds of information about these projects would you, as the budget officer, find useful and perhaps essential in the development of a budget for the next six months?

14. You have just been appointed budget director of a manufacturing company, responsible for reviewing and coordinating the budget proposals submitted by the company's operating executives. On your first day on the job you are given the following summaries of budget proposals for each of the company's three products (all dollar figures are in thousands):

|  | Product A | Product B | Product C |
|---|---|---|---|
| Sales revenues........................ | $6,000 | $3,000 | $1,000 |
| Expenses: |  |  |  |
| Manufacturing cost of the goods sold . | $3,000 | $1,800 | $ 700 |
| Salesmen's salaries .................. | 800 | 300 | 100 |
| Travel and entertainment............ | 1,200 | 400 | 120 |
| Advertising ......................... | 500 | 100 | 60 |
| Total product expenses.......... | $5,500 | $2,600 | $ 980 |
| Product Profit Margin................. | $ 500 | $ 400 | $ 20 |
| Total hours required in the factory finishing department................ | 2,000 | 3,200 | 500 |

All three products are manufactured in the same factory and are sold by the same salesmen. Within the factory, each product has its own production line. The finishing operation on each product must be performed on highly sophisticated equipment, however, and this equipment is so expensive that separate installations for each product line would be uneconomical. For this reason the factory has only one finishing department, which performs the finishing operations on all of the company's products.

The finishing department has a total practical capacity of 5,000 hours a year. Finishing work can also be performed by independent local firms at a cost of $100 an hour.

*a)* Outline the approach that you would use in reviewing these budget proposals. What criterion or criteria would you use in ranking them?

*b)* Using only the information provided above, what course of action would you recommend? State your reasons.

*c)* You have comparable data on each product line for several recent years. What additional data would you like to obtain either from these records or from other sources before making the recommendation called for in part (b)?

**15.** The president of Ethelred, Inc., has a commitment from his bank for a loan of $100,000, if he needs it during the coming year. No other outside source of cash will be available to him during the year.

Ethelred provides bookkeeping services to local business firms and other organizations and has been growing rapidly in recent years. Its experience has been that accounts receivable increase as its sales volume increases. A $10 increase in annual sales volume will require a $1 increase in accounts receivable.

If the company continues its present operations, maintaining its sales force at current levels, total sales volume will increase next year by $100,000 and reported income will be:

| | |
|---|---:|
| Sales................................................... | $1,100,000 |
| Expenses (including $10,000 depreciation).................... | 980,000 |
| Net Income................................................ | $ 120,000 |

The company's present facilities will be adequate to handle this sales volume, requiring expenditures of only $12,000 for routine replacement of furniture and equipment.

The company's president would like to add another salesman to contact a new group of potential customers. Additional data processing equipment would have to be rented to handle any business the new salesman brought in. These changes would increase Ethelred's annual operating expenses by the following amounts:

| | |
|---|---|
| Salesman's salary and expenses ...... | $22,000 |
| Equipment rental.................... | 30,000 |
| Other expenses ..................... | 60,000 + 10% of added sales |

The president believes that the additional sales volume from this market would amount to $50,000 in the first year, but it might amount to nothing at all. If the operation proved successful, revenues in later years would be substantially higher.

Ethelred's shareholders have received cash dividends of $50,000 in each of the last three years, and the board of directors has tentatively decided to increase the dividend next year to $60,000 if the cash flow is adequate. It also wishes to contribute $20,000 to the local art museum as a community service.

a)   Are these proposals feasible? Prepare a tentative profit plan and a tentative cash budget to support your answer. You may assume that all expenses other than depreciation and all equipment expenditures must be accompanied by immediate cash payments.

b)   What action should the president take?

*16.   The Darnell Company is organized in three divisions, each with a division manager, a small office staff, and its own sales force. The various divisions sell different kinds of products and deal with different groups of customers.

The company's budget director has received the following proposals and estimates for next year from the division managers:

|  | Division A | Division B | Division C |
|---|---|---|---|
| Divisional marketing costs amounting to. | $  150 | $  500 | $  300 |
| Will produce revenues of . . . . . . . . . . . . . . . | 1,000 | 3,000 | 2,100 |
| And cost of goods sold of . . . . . . . . . . . . . . . | 650 | 1,650 | 1,260 |
| Administrative expenses to support these activities will total . . . . . . . . . . . . . . . . . . . . | 150 | 300 | 200 |
| Accounts receivable will increase by . . . . . | 10 | 200 | 50 |
| Inventories will exceed this year's ending balances by . . . . . . . . . . . . . . . . . . . . . . . . . . . | 50 | 100 | 50 |
| Accounts payable will increase by . . . . . . . . | 15 | 50 | 80 |

The expenses of the company's central management are tentatively budgeted at $400 for the year, to be paid in cash. Cash purchases of equipment amounting to $130 and cash dividends of $350 are also proposed. Of the equipment purchases, $60 is to replace existing equipment and $70 is for expansion. The expansion proposals, which management has approved in principle, will have no effect on next year's income statement.

Depreciation is included in the administrative expense figures above as follows: central management, $10; Division A, $5; Division B, $15; Division C, $20.

a)   Prepare a tentative profit plan and cash budget for next year, on the assumption that all of these proposals are approved.

b)   The company will start next year with a cash balance of $290 and

---

* Solutions to problems marked with an asterisk (*) are provided in Appendix B.

an unused line of bank credit of $100. The minimum cash balance is
5 percent of sales. Is the tentative plan feasible?

17.  Noting substantial increases in the proposed levels of marketing
and administrative costs over those of the current year, the Darnell Company's budget director asked the company's three division managers for
additional information to be used in reviewing the divisional budget
proposals summarized in problem 16. He could not tell how much of the
increases were due to changes in prices and how much resulted from
changes in the amount or structure of marketing effort.

To supplement the forecasted results for the proposed marketing
plans, the budget director asked each division manager for estimates of
the following:

1.  This year's results.
2.  The results to be expected next year if this year's marketing pro-
    gram were to be continued unchanged.
3.  The results to be expected next year if marketing and administra-
    tive expenses were to be kept at this year's levels (an "austerity
    budget"):

With the help of personnel from the central market research and controller's departments, the division managers supplied the following additional data:

|  | Division A | Division B | Division C |
|---|---|---|---|
| Expected results this year from this year's program: | | | |
| Sales................................. | $800 | $2,000 | $2,000 |
| Cost of goods sold..................... | 496 | 1,200 | 1,200 |
| Marketing expenses.................... | 120 | 380 | 280 |
| Administrative expenses .............. | 110 | 200 | 190 |
| Accounts receivable, year end......... | 40 | 350 | 330 |
| Inventories, year end.................. | 195 | 320 | 360 |
| Accounts payable, year end............ | 60 | 120 | 550 |
| Expected results next year if this year's program were to be repeated: | | | |
| Sales................................. | 840 | 2,400 | 2,000 |
| Cost of goods sold..................... | 546 | 1,392 | 1,260 |
| Marketing expenses.................... | 125 | 400 | 300 |
| Administrative expenses .............. | 120 | 220 | 200 |
| Accounts receivable, year end......... | 42 | 400 | 330 |
| Inventories, year end.................. | 215 | 368 | 360 |
| Accounts payable, year end............ | 64 | 141 | 550 |
| Expected results under austerity budget: | | | |
| Sales................................. | 820 | 2,100 | 1,900 |
| Cost of goods sold..................... | 533 | 1,218 | 1,197 |
| Marketing expenses.................... | 120 | 380 | 280 |
| Administrative expenses .............. | 110 | 200 | 190 |
| Accounts receivable, year end......... | 41 | 360 | 314 |
| Inventories, year end.................. | 205 | 324 | 332 |
| Accounts payable, year end............ | 62 | 124 | 517 |

Central administrative expenses for the current year are expected to total $380, cash purchases of equipment will amount to $120, and cash dividends of $300 will be paid.

*a)* Calculate expected net income for the current year.

*b)* Prepare a profit plan on the assumption that current marketing programs will be continued next year. (Central administrative expenses would be at their proposed level, $400.)

*c)* Prepare an austerity budget profit plan on the assumption that marketing and administrative expenses next year are held to this year's level. (Under an austerity budget, central administrative expenses would amount to $395.)

*d)* Assuming that these estimates are sound, and basing your recommendations solely on the figures given in these two problems, what action should Darnell's management take on the budget proposals?

**18.** "This budget is a big nuisance," said Mr. Hiram Baumgartner, president of Colleyford, Inc., the United States subsidiary of a large European manufacturer of electrical and electronic products. "I have to spend most of my time on it for the better part of a month, and I don't know how many man-hours my controller puts in on it. As far as I'm concerned, it's just another report that I have to make to headquarters."

Colleyford operated one small electronics factory in upstate New York, but otherwise imported all of its needs from parent company factories in Europe and Japan. It operated primarily in the northeastern United States and on the West Coast, and had fairly large product distribution warehouses in New York and San Francisco.

For budgeting purposes, Colleyford used the parent company's product classification scheme. It marketed products in six of the parent's product categories:

1. Lighting products.
2. Electronic tubes and transistors.
3. Components for computers and industrial communications equipment.
4. Radios, television receivers, and phonographs.
5. Industrial equipment and parts.
6. Service and repair.

Some products were marketed through wholesalers, while others were sold directly to industrial consumers by the company's own salesmen. Colleyford had a sales force of approximately 40 men. Although some of these men tended to concentrate on one or two product groups, all of them handled all of the company's lines.

Mr. Baumgartner was allowed to manufacture any product that his plant was equipped to produce. The types and amounts of this production were included in the budget that he submitted to headquarters each November. The parent company headquarters then informed him which factories would supply his remaining requirements. The prices charged for these intergroup transfers were established by the head office in advance of budget preparation.

Two or three staff executives from the parent company's headquarters ordinarily spent a week or so at the Colleyford offices while the budget was being prepared, and were also in frequent communication by telephone. They offered their advice and suggestions, and raised questions about parts of the budget proposal as it was in process. Mr. Baumgartner usually presented his budget to the parent company in person at the end of November; and the final budget received from headquarters in December was ordinarily almost identical to the one submitted by Mr. Baumgartner.

a) What benefits might Mr. Baumgartner reap from the company's system of budgetary planning? Comment on possible reasons for his attitude toward the budget and offer suggestions as to what might be done to give him a more favorable view of the budgetary process.

b) Discuss the problems of data classification in Colleyford, Inc. What kinds of data should the profit plan include, and how should these data be subdivided and classified?

# 19

## PRODUCT COSTING: JOB ORDER PRODUCTION

SOME OF THE MOST IMPORTANT information employed in planning a firm's operations consists of data on the costs of the various products or services that the firm produces. The purpose of this chapter is to describe how the accountant approaches the task of measuring the costs of manufacturing individual products. Since the methods used for product costing are generally similar to those used to measure the costs of service work, this discussion is applicable to the latter as well as to the former.

### TYPES OF COSTING SYSTEMS

The methods used to measure product unit cost depend heavily on the nature of the manufacturing process and are subject to wide variation. Basically, these methods fall into two broad categories: *process costing* and *job order costing.*

*Process costing* is applicable when the production process turns out a single kind of product for long periods of time at a stretch (cement, flour, etc.). In this case, product cost per unit can be computed easily from the formula:

$$\text{Average Unit Cost} = \frac{\text{Total Production Costs for the Period}}{\text{Total Units of Product Manufactured}}.$$

*Job order costing,* in contrast, is used when the production facilities produce many different kinds of products simultaneously or in rapid succession (job printing, furniture manufacture, etc.). In this case, costs must be assigned to each batch or job lot of products so that a separate unit cost figure may be calculated for each.

The simple job order costing system described in the next few pages should be viewed as an unsophisticated introduction to a much more complex subject. Later chapters will indicate how this system can be adapted to meet some of management's needs more satisfactorily.

## A JOB ORDER COSTING SYSTEM

The Pyle Company is a manufacturer of men's work clothes. These clothes are manufactured in batches, and each batch is assigned a production order or job order number. The accounting problem is to measure the costs of manufacturing each batch. Unit cost on any job order is then determined by dividing the total cost of the job by the number of units produced.

For product unit costing purposes, factory costs are divided into three classes in job order costing:

1. Direct materials.
2. Direct labor.
3. Factory overhead.

### Direct versus Overhead Costs

The costs that are traced directly to individual jobs are known as the direct costs of those jobs. For example, when a production order is issued in the Pyle Company, a quantity of cloth is transferred from the storeroom to the cutting room. These are *direct materials* in that their cost can be traced to this specific job order and to none other. *Indirect materials* or *supplies*, on the other hand, are issued for general factory use and not for the specific benefit of any one job.

Similarly, *direct labor* cost is any labor cost that is clearly traceable to one particular job. *Indirect labor* is labor expended on tasks such as machine repair, lubrication, cleaning, or anything else not related directly to a specific production order.

Indirect materials and indirect labor are examples of *overhead costs*. The Pyle Company has many such costs, costs of operating the factory that are not readily traceable to individual job orders. Other examples include the salaries of clerical and supervisory personnel in the factory, depreciation on factory buildings and equipment, taxes on factory buildings, and so forth.

Although most costs classified as overhead *cannot* be traced to individual job orders, two other groups of costs are commonly placed in this category for different reasons. For some, the reason is that tracing the cost to the job would cost more than the added accuracy would be worth. For example, the Pyle Company would find it possible but not economical to measure the amount of thread or buttons consumed on each production order. The costs of these items are therefore classified as overhead costs.

Finally, some costs are treated as overhead because it would be *unsound* to treat them as direct costs. For instance, factory employees are generally paid more than their regular wage rate for hours that they work in excess of some specified amount. When this happens, the difference between the regular wage rate and the special rate (the *overtime premium*), multiplied by the number of overtime hours, should be classified as overhead. The costs of overtime premiums are the result of the total volume of factory work, not the pure result of any one job. The fact that one job happens to be scheduled for overtime hours and another for the regular working day should not affect the direct costs of those two jobs.

### Factory Overhead: The Burden Rate

Since factory overhead represents costs incurred to obtain the production of a period, it would seem reasonable that these costs should be included as part of the cost of the products produced. Doing this poses a problem, however, since the overhead assignable to a job cannot be measured in the same way as the direct costs. The only way overhead costs can be included in product cost is to assign them to jobs on the basis of some average rate. An average of this kind is known as a *burden rate* or *overhead costing rate.*

For example, suppose that the overhead costs for a given period total $118,400. To state this as an average, we must divide it by some measure of the total volume of production activity, such as the total number of units of products produced during the period:

$$\text{Burden Rate} = \frac{\text{Overhead Cost}}{\text{Production Volume}}$$

Units of product output are not usually a very good measure, however, because different products vary so widely in size and complexity. Instead, a measure of production *input* is usually chosen, such as machine-hours or direct labor cost. The choice should depend on which measure of volume best summarizes the factors determining the amount of overhead costs that must be incurred.

Suppose that overhead costs correlate better with the number of direct labor hours than with any other index of volume, and that the volume of activity during the period amounts to 37,000 direct labor hours. With overhead costs of $118,400, the after-the-fact burden rate is:

$$\text{Burden rate} = \frac{\text{Overhead Cost}}{\text{Direct Labor Hours}} = \frac{\$118,400}{37,000} = \$3.20 \text{ an hour.}$$

If this rate were used in product costing, each job would be charged $3.20 for every direct labor hour used on that job.

### Predetermined Burden Rates

Although burden rates representing actual average costs are often used in costing government contracts, *predetermined* rates are more common elsewhere. One reason for this is that the actual overhead cost and actual volume of activity are not known until the end of the period. It would be very inconvenient for the Pyle Company to wait until the end of the period to apply factory overhead because all of the work of costing the job order cost sheets would have to be done at the same time. The bookkeepers' work load would be very uneven or else reports would be considerably delayed.

After-the-fact burden rates can also be attacked on the grounds that the information they provide is less useful than that provided by predetermined rates, but discussion of this point will have to be deferred to a later chapter.

A predetermined burden rate is based on *estimates* of overhead cost and production volume—that is, the rate is not the average overhead cost of each individual period, but the average cost in a "normal" or typical period:

$$\text{Burden rate} = \frac{\text{Estimated overhead costs in a normal month}}{\text{Estimated total volume in a normal month}}$$

These estimates are made before the beginning of the period, usually the company's fiscal year, and the resulting rates are generally used without change throughout the period, no matter what the actual cost experience is.

The Pyle Company's factory was designed to operate most efficiently at a volume of 40,000 direct labor hours a month. In 19x1 management estimated that if this volume were achieved, factory overhead would average $120,000 a month. The burden rate for the year therefore was set at $3 an hour:

$$\text{Burden rate} = \frac{\$120,000}{40,000} = \$3 \text{ an hour.}$$

Using this rate, the accountant would assign $30 in factory over-head cost to a job requiring 10 direct labor hours.

### Collecting Job Order Costs

The costs assigned to individual job orders can be accumulated in various ways, depending on the structure of the data processing system. The Pyle Company uses the form illustrated in Exhibit 19–1, known as a *job cost sheet*. This includes space in which to record the costs of direct materials and direct labor as they are used on the job, as well as a section at the right in which the amount of overhead applicable to the job can be entered.

Data on direct materials costs are taken from *materials requisition* forms. Production foremen must submit these forms to the storeroom in exchange for materials and supplies to be used in production. Each requisition shows the items required and the quantities of each. For direct materials, the requisition

*Exhibit 19–1*

Pyle Company

**JOB ORDER COST SHEET**

JOB COST SHEET

For _____   Job No. _____
Item _____   Start _____
Stock No. _____   Quantity _____   Finish _____

| DIRECT LABOR | | | MATERIALS | | COST SUMMARY | |
|---|---|---|---|---|---|---|
| Card No. | Hours | Amount | Req. No. | Amount | Labor | $ |
| | | $ | | $ | Materials | $ |
| | | | | | Overhead | $ |
| | | | | | Total | $ |
| | | | | | Unit Cost | $ |

shows the job order number, while for indirect materials it shows the department number and an account number indicating how the materials were used (e.g., lubricating materials, cleaning supplies, packing materials, etc.).

The labor counterpart of the materials requisition is the *time ticket*. When a worker begins work on a particular job, the job number is entered on a time ticket which is then stamped with the date and hour. At the end of the day or of the work to be done, or at the time the worker is taken off the job, whichever comes first, the time ticket is again stamped with the time. (For indirect labor the time ticket identifies the department in which the work was done, together with a number denoting the kind of work.) The hours shown on the time tickets are then multiplied by the appropriate hourly rates to derive the amounts to be charged to individual jobs or overhead accounts.

Overhead costs are also entered on the job cost sheet, in this case in the lower right-hand corner. These entries are usually made when the job is completed, by applying predetermined burden rates to the number of activity units used on the job. Thus if activity is measured in direct labor hours, the amount charged to a job will be determined by multiplying the burden rate by the number of direct labor hours used on that job. This amount is often referred to as the *overhead applied* or *overhead absorbed*, to distinguish it from the various overhead costs actually incurred in the factory during the period.

## THE FLOW OF FACTORY COSTS

When we discussed the flow of manufacturing costs through the ledger accounts in Chapter 4, we made no mention of job cost sheets or of the use of burden rates to assign overhead costs to individual jobs. To see how these new elements fit into the development of income statements and balance sheets, let us see how the Pyle Company recorded manufacturing costs in its accounts during 19x1.

### Inventory Accounts

The Pyle Company started 19x1 with the following inventory account balances:

| | |
|---|---:|
| Materials and supplies | $ 98,000 |
| Work in process | 137,000 |
| Finished Goods | 161,000 |

Each of these asset accounts was backed up by a detailed sub-sidiary ledger or file — Materials and Supplies by the stores ledger, showing quantities and costs of each kind of item in the factory materials storeroom, Finished Goods by the finished goods ledger, showing quantities and costs of all products ready for sale, and Work in Process by the file of job order cost sheets for jobs started but not yet finished. The beginning-of-year balance in the Work in Process account, for example, was the sum of the balances in the job cost sheets for the jobs that were in process at that time.

### Direct Materials Costs

The costs of materials purchased during the year amounted to $181,000, and were debited to the Materials and Supplies inventory account:

(1)

| | | |
|---|---|---|
| Materials and Supplies...................... | 181,000 | |
|     Accounts Payable ........................ | | 181,000 |

The costs of direct materials *issued* — that is, transferred from materials and supplies inventory for use on specific job orders — totaled $170,000 in 19x1. The transfer is accounted for in sum-mary with the following entry:

| | | |
|---|---|---|
| Work in Process.............................. | 170,000 | |
|     Materials and Supplies................... | | 170,000 |

The debit to Work in Process summarizes entries in the materials cost columns of the job order cost sheets relating to the jobs for which direct materials were issued during the year. Similarly, the credit to Materials and Supplies summarizes the credits to the individual ledger cards for the various kinds of materials and supplies issued.

### Direct Labor Costs

The Pyle Company's direct labor costs for 19x1 amounted to $185,000. The entries to record these can be summarized suc-cinctly:

(3)

| | | |
|---|---|---|
| Work in Process.............................. | 185,000 | |
|     Accrued Payroll ......................... | | 185,000 |

The debits to inventory served to recognize the creation of an asset; the credits to Accrued Payroll identified the company's liability to pay factory employees for their work on job orders. Once again, the debits to Work in Process were accompanied by similar entries on the individual job cost sheets.

### Actual Factory Overhead Costs

The Pyle Company's factory overhead costs in 19x1 fell into four categories: indirect materials, indirect labor, depreciation, and miscellaneous. Although the Pyle Company used a number of accounts to record these costs, for clarity's sake we shall use only a single summary account, Factory Overhead, to represent them all.

The costs of materials issued for indirect use during the year totaled $21,000. The entries to record these issues can be summarized as follows:

(4)

| | | |
|---|---|---|
| Factory Overhead ............................. | 21,000 | |
| Materials and Supplies ..................... | | 21,000 |

This entry can be regarded as a transfer of costs from one asset account to another. Since factory overhead costs are part of the costs of producing assets (inventories), the Factory Overhead account can be thought of as an asset account. It plays this role only temporarily, however, because the assets themselves are represented by the balances in inventory accounts. Indirect materials costs and other overhead costs enter the inventory accounts through application of burden rates. When this happens, the Factory Overhead account ceases to function as an asset account. We shall return in a moment to explain how this is done.

Indirect labor in the Pyle Company consists of the time spent by factory supervisors, janitors, maintenance men, and so forth. The costs of indirect labor in 19x1 amounted to $54,000, recorded as follows:

(5)

| | | |
|---|---|---|
| Factory Overhead ............................. | 54,000 | |
| Accrued Payroll ............................. | | 54,000 |

Depreciation on factory equipment amounted to $13,000 during the year, and the various other services used in the factory during the year cost $38,000. These costs were charged to factory overhead by means of the following entries:

(6)

| | | |
|---|---|---|
| Factory Overhead ............................. | 13,000 | |
| Accumulated Depreciation ................. | | 13,000 |

(7)

Factory Overhead ............................. 38,000
    Accounts Payable .........................         38,000

## Factory Overhead Absorption

The process of assigning factory overhead costs to individual job orders is commonly called the *application* or *absorption* of overhead. The amount of overhead absorbed in any period is obtained by multiplying the burden rate by the production volume for the period. The Pyle Company, for example, used a predetermined burden rate of $3 a direct labor hour to assign overhead costs to jobs in process during 19x1. Direct labor during the year amounted to 39,000 hours. The total amount absorbed by production in 19x1 — that is, the amount assigned to job orders for work done — therefore amounted to 39,000 × $3 = $117,000.

The Pyle Company's system, in other words, identified $117,000 as the overhead cost of creating new inventory assets during the year. This being the case, the Pyle Company debited this amount to the Work in Process account, just as it debited the cost of direct materials and direct labor.

At this point we must bring the Factory Overhead account back into the picture. It will be recalled that we referred to this account earlier as a temporary asset account. Following the same line of reasoning, the absorption of overhead can be regarded as a transfer of costs from a temporary to a permanent asset account, Work in Process. A summary entry in this case would be:

(8)

Work in Process.............................. 117,000
    Factory Overhead ........................         117,000

This puts us in a position to reclassify the Factory Overhead account as a clearing account that the overhead costs pass through on their way to the job cost sheets and Work in Process account. At the end of the year, the Pyle Company's Factory Overhead account showed the following:

The costs enter at the left and leave in a slightly different guise at the right. The account itself is simply a mechanism to facilitate this movement.

## Overhead Over- or Underabsorbed

The total amount of factory overhead absorbed in this illustration was $9,000 less than the actual factory overhead costs for the year. This should come as no surprise, since it would be most unlikely that the conditions reflected in the predetermined burden rate — that is, normal costs at normal volume — would prevail in any particular short period of time.

The difference between actual and absorbed factory overhead is known as the factory overhead cost *variance* or the over- or underabsorbed overhead. In the illustration, the Pyle Company incurred $9,000 in overhead costs that were not absorbed by the year's production. This amount would be referred to as *underabsorbed.* If the amount absorbed had exceeded the total overhead cost for the period, the excess would have been labeled *overabsorbed.*

The Pyle Company made the following entry to transfer the $9,000 balance from the Factory Overhead account at the end of 19x1:

(9)

| | | |
|---|---|---|
| Underabsorbed Production Costs................... 9,000 | | |
|     Factory Overhead.............................. | | 9,000 |

The credit to Factory Overhead reduced the balance in this account to zero, so that it was ready to receive the record of the next year's transactions. The debit to Underabsorbed Production Costs kept this amount in suspense, to be dealt with later. We shall return in the next section to see how it should be treated for external financial reporting.

## Cost of Goods Finished

The figures on the job cost sheets are used by management in the various purposes for which it requires product cost information. They also provide the accountant with the information he needs to record the completion of individual job orders and the sale of the goods produced.

To continue our example, the Pyle Company completed work during 19x1 on a large number of job orders. The costs accumulated on the job order cost sheets for these jobs totaled $504,000.

A summary entry to record the progression of these jobs from uncompleted to completed status would be as follows:

(10)

| | | |
|---|---|---|
| Finished Goods.............................. | 504,000 | |
| Work in Process.......................... | | 504,000 |

This entry is identical in form to the one that we introduced in Chapter 4; the only difference is that we now know where the accountant obtained the data on which the entry was based.

## Cost of Goods Sold

The final step in the flow of factory costs through the accounts is timed to coincide with the recognition of revenue. Costs from the job cost sheets are transferred to the finished goods ledger cards when the goods are finished; when revenues are recognized, these costs are transferred to the income statement as the cost of goods are sold.

The Pyle Company, for example, recognizes revenue when it ships goods to its customers. At that time the unit costs of the goods shipped are taken from the finished goods ledger and multiplied by the number of units shipped. The resulting entries serve to transfer the cost of the goods from the inventory account to Cost of Goods Sold. The entries to record the cost of the goods sold by the Pyle Company in 19x1 can be summarized as follows:

(11)

| | | |
|---|---|---|
| Cost of Goods Sold .......................... | 437,000 | |
| Finished Goods.......................... | | 437,000 |

## Manufacturing Cost Summary

The Pyle Company's factory costs for the year have been summarized in Exhibit 19–2. Actual costs for the year totaled $481,000, as shown on the "total factory cost" line in the statement. Subtracting the $9,000 in underabsorbed factory overhead gives us the $472,000 actually assigned to job orders during the year. With changes in the work in process and finished goods inventories, the cost of goods sold amounted to $437,000, as shown on the bottom line of the exhibit.

Exhibit 19–3 summarizes all of the year's manufacturing cost transactions in T-account form. Costs enter the Work in Process account from three sources, corresponding to the three elements of product cost in job order production – direct materials, direct labor, and factory overhead. Positive balances remain in the

*Exhibit 19–2*

Pyle Company

STATEMENT OF THE COST OF GOODS MANUFACTURED AND SOLD
(for the year ended December 31, 19x1)

| | | |
|---|---:|---:|
| Direct materials | | $170,000 |
| Direct labor | | 185,000 |
| Factory overhead: | | |
| Indirect materials | $21,000 | |
| Indirect labor | 54,000 | |
| Depreciation | 13,000 | |
| Miscellaneous | 38,000 | 126,000 |
| Total factory cost | | $481,000 |
| Less: underabsorbed overhead | | 9,000 |
| Total cost assigned to production | | $472,000 |
| Add: Work in process, January 1 | | 137,000 |
| Less: Work in process, December 31 | | (105,000) |
| Cost of goods finished | | $504,000 |
| Add: Finished goods inventory, January 1 | | 161,000 |
| Less: Finished goods inventory, December 31 | | (228,000) |
| Cost of Goods Sold | | $437,000 |

*Exhibit 19–3*

Pyle Company

MANUFACTURING COST FLOWS
For the Year Ended December 31, 19x1

**Materials and Supplies**

| Bal. 1/1 | 98,000 | (2) | 170,000 |
| (1) | 181,000 | (4) | 21,000 |
| | 279,000 | | 191,000 |
| Bal. 12/31 | 88,000 | | |

**Work in Process**

| Bal. 1/1 | 137,000 | (10) | 504,000 |
| (2) | 170,000 | | |
| (3) | 185,000 | | |
| (8) | 117,000 | | |
| | 609,000 | | |
| Bal. 12/31 | 105,000 | | |

**Factory Overhead**

| (4) | 21,000 | (8) | 117,000 |
| (5) | 54,000 | (9) | 9,000 |
| (6) | 13,000 | | 126,000 |
| (7) | 38,000 | | |
| | 126,000 | | |

**Finished Goods**

| Bal. 1/1 | 161,000 | (11) | 437,000 |
| (10) | 504,000 | | |
| | 665,000 | | |
| Bal. 12/31 | 228,000 | | |

**Underabsorbed Production Costs**

| (9) | 9,000 | | |

**Cost of Goods Sold**

| (11) | 437,000 | | |

three inventory accounts and two income statement accounts at the end of the period, ready to be used in the preparation of the periodic financial statements. (The Accrued Payroll, Accounts Payable, and Accumulated Depreciation accounts are not reproduced in this exhibit because the balances in these accounts are not used in the preparation of manufacturing cost statements, which is the focus of this section.)

## EXTERNAL REPORTING OF UNDER- OR OVERABSORBED OVERHEAD

The amount of any under- or overabsorbed overhead cost will appear in full on cost reports that are prepared for management's use, as we shall illustrate later in chapters 24 and 25. For external reporting, however, three alternatives might be considered:

1. Report the under- or overabsorption in full as a loss or gain on the income statement for the period in which it arises.
2. Carry any such amounts to the balance sheet for the end of the period, to be added to or offset against similar amounts arising in preceding or succeeding periods.
3. Divide the under- or overabsorption in any period between the income statement and balance sheet in direct proportion to the distribution of the overhead absorbed during the period.

The third possibility in this list implies that the amount of overhead cost assigned to any product should be based on the actual overhead costs during a period and not on the predetermined burden rate. In the illustration, the $9,000 underabsorbed overhead was 7.7 percent of the $117,000 in overhead costs actually assigned to production during the period. If half of the $117,000 was included in the cost of goods sold for the period and half remained in the inventory accounts at the end of the period, then $4,500 would be added to the cost of goods sold and half would be included in the reported inventory figure on the end-of-period balance sheet.

This method reflects an assumption that the resources sacrificed by the company to obtain a unit of production are better measured by actual average costs than by predetermined average costs. This view has many supporters, particularly in the measurement of the costs applicable to government contracts and in calculating taxable income. We remain unconvinced, however. Does a bottle of cola produced in a summer month cost less than one produced in a winter month when volume is lower and costs cannot be spread over as wide a base? Does a ton of steel cost more if produced in a year of low volume than if produced in a year of high volume? Does a ton of steel produced in a period of numerous plant breakdowns and labor unrest cost more than a ton produced in a period of normal efficiency?

Many accountants and managers have decided that the answer is no to all of these questions. They argue that inventory should be measured at costs reflecting (1) a relatively long-term average level of output, and (2) a reasonably attainable level of production efficiency — that is, at *normal cost.* The cost of producing a unit of product does not rise because it was produced in a month or year output is low or when the plant is inefficient. The consequence is that by comparison with the actual burden rate for a period, a predetermined rate based on normal conditions is the *preferred* basis for inventory costing and cost of goods sold determination — not a poor substitute adopted for reasons of convenience.

Under the above reasoning, over- or underabsorbed overhead is a gain or loss due to volume or operating efficiency or inefficiency. If the firm's business is highly seasonal in character, the over- or underabsorbed overhead may be carried forward from one month to the next, the second of the alternatives listed above. While this is sometimes appropriate for interim reporting, seasonal factors presumably work themselves out in the course of a full year, and the net under- or overabsorbed overhead should be carried in full to the annual income statement for the year in which it arises.

While there is little disagreement on the soundness of carrying underabsorbed overhead (not due to seasonal fluctuations in output) to the income statement, many accountants are reluctant to treat overabsorbed overhead in the same way. The principle of conservatism makes them reluctant to show a gain on production.

## SUMMARY

In manufacturing organizations, a key component of the financial information system is the set of procedures used to estimate the unit cost of manufactured products. When products are manufactured in batches or job lots, product cost is often measured by job order costing. In systems of this sort, three categories of factory costs are recognized — direct materials, direct labor, and factory overhead. Direct materials and direct labor costs are traced specifically to individual job orders; factory overhead is assigned to jobs by means of burden rates.

Most burden rates are predetermined; once the amount of materials, labor, or machine time used on a job is known, the overhead cost of the job can be calculated, even if actual overhead costs are still unknown at that time. These predetermined burden rates represent average factory overhead under specified conditions, and reflect the notion that variations in production volume or efficiency lead immediately to gains and losses, but do not affect product cost. In other words, they affect the cost of *production*, but not the cost of individual *products*. If this position is accepted, then the difference between total factory overhead in a given period and the amount absorbed by products — the overhead under- or overabsorbed — should be taken in full to the income statement for the period in which the under- or overabsorption took place.

## QUESTIONS AND PROBLEMS

1. For what purposes is it necessary or desirable to calculate manufacturing cost per unit of product?

2. What is the difference between a job cost system and a process cost system?

3. What basic documents are used by the Pyle Company in connection with its manufacturing operations, and what is the purpose of each?

4. Discuss the functions of the job cost sheet and explain its relation to the inventory accounts.

5. Why is the burden rate usually related to such measures of manufacturing *input* as direct labor hours rather than to some direct measure of output?

6. "The accuracy of manufacturing cost per unit of product is increased by basing the overhead portion on a predetermined burden rate rather than on the average actual overhead cost for the period." Discuss.

7. Distinguish between direct and indirect labor.

8. What is meant by overhead cost absorption? In what sense are costs "absorbed?" Does the absorption of cost guarantee the firm a profit?

9. How should factory overhead cost variances be accounted for in external financial reporting?

10. Would the methods of job order costing be useful in nonmanu-

facturing organizations such as advertising agencies and consulting firms? Is job order costing likely to be feasible in financial organizations, such as banks?

*11. The Basic Foundry prepares metal castings for specific orders, using a job order cost system. During the month of January, job No. 103 calling for 10,000 machine parts was started and completed. Information about this order is summarized as follows:

    (1)   Material requisitioned: 21,000 pounds at $0.66 a pound.
    (2)   Labor hours expended: 2,000 at $4.15 an hour.
    (3)   Manufacturing overhead charged to production: $4.00 a direct labor hour.
    (4)   Unused material returned to storeroom: 800 pounds.
    (5)   Castings completed: 9,800.

*a)*   Find the unit cost of production, accurate to the nearest cent.
*b)*   Prepare journal entries to record these transactions.

12. The Cobbett Woodworking Company manufactures chairs and other pieces of wooden furniture. Production is on a job order basis. The factory burden rate is $2 per direct labor dollar. The following data relate to job No. 876, an order for 200 wooden footstools:

    (1)   Lumber issued from storeroom: $351.
    (2)   Direct labor: 30 hours at $6 an hour plus 9 hours of overtime at $9 an hour.
    (3)   Footstools completed: 195 (5 footstools were rejected in final inspection, broken up and burned).
    (4)   Footstools sold on credit to Ye Olde Roadside Store: 10.

*a)*   Prepare a simple job cost sheet, enter the appropriate cost figures, and compute unit cost.
*b)*   Prepare journal entries to record these transactions.

*13. The burden rate is $2 per direct labor hour and a job order costing system is in use.
    Inventory balances on December 1 were:

| | |
|---|---:|
| Materials | $10,000 |
| Work in process | 15,000 |
| Finished goods | 20,000 |

During December, the following data were recorded:

| | |
|---|---:|
| Materials purchased | $16,000 |
| Direct materials issued | 18,000 |
| Direct labor, 10,000 hours | 47,000 |
| Manufacturing overhead (actual) | 17,000 |
| Cost of goods finished | 80,000 |

On December 31, finished goods costing $23,000 were still on hand.

---

* Solutions to problems marked with an asterisk (*) are found in Appendix B.

*a*)  Prepare entries, in two-column journal form, to record the transactions of the month.
*b*)  What was the cost of goods sold for the month?
*c*)  What was the over- or underabsorbed overhead for the month?
*d*)  What was the December 31 balance in the Work in Process account?

14.  The Bates Company has been using a relatively small percentage of its capacity for the past year and this situation is likely to persist. You have the following data:

(1)  Estimated factory overhead cost at normal volume (10,000 direct labor hours a month), $40,000.
(2)  Estimated factory overhead cost at estimated actual volume (8,000 direct labor hours a month), $36,000.
(3)  Actual factory overhead cost at actual volume for April (7,500 direct labor hours), $37,000.

*a*)  Calculate a predetermined burden rate on the basis of normal volume.
*b*)  Calculate the amount of overhead under- or overabsorbed during April.
*c*)  Would the amount of overhead under- or overabsorbed have been increased or reduced if the burden rate had been based on estimated actual volume? Would you have preferred this alternative? Explain.

15.  A department has four direct production workers. They work an 8-hour day plus occasional overtime. The pay for overtime hours is 150 percent of the regular time rate.

Three jobs (Nos. 125, 127, and 129) were in process when the employees reported for work on the morning of July 6. Operations were begun during the day on four new jobs (Nos. 126, 128, 130, and 131). Work was completed on jobs 125, 126, 127, and 130. The following time tickets were filed for the day's work:

| Employee | Hourly Wage Rate | Job. No. | Hours |
|---|---|---|---|
| Abt, J. . . . . . . . . . . | $4.00 | 127 | 1 |
|  |  | 126 | 5 |
|  |  | Lubrication | 1 |
|  |  | 128 | 1 |
| Davis, P. . . . . . . . | 6.00 | 125 | 1 |
|  |  | 127 | 2 |
|  |  | 130 | 2 |
|  |  | Training | 3 |
|  |  | Clean-up | 1 |
| Rogers, L. . . . . . . | 5.00 | 128 | 4 |
|  |  | Sweeping | 1 |
|  |  | 130 | 3 |
|  |  | 128 | 2 |
| Thomas, G. . . . . . | 7.00 | 129 | 1 |
|  |  | Maintenance | 2 |
|  |  | 129 | 1 |
|  |  | 131 | 4 |
|  |  | 130 | 2 |

These time tickets are listed in the sequence in which the work was performed.

Prior labor costs on jobs in process at the beginning of the day were as follows: Job 125, $28; Job 127, $73; Job 129, $48. Completed jobs were transferred to the finished goods storeroom.

a) Calculate the total direct labor cost for the day. How much should be entered on each of the job order cost sheets? How much would you classify as overhead cost?

b) Indicate any alternative(s) that you considered and rejected in answering part (a) and give your reasons for your choice(s).

c) Calculate the direct labor cost of the goods finished.

d) Calculate the direct labor cost of the work in process at the end of the day.

16. The Oxford Company has a single Work in Process account, plus a Manufacturing Overhead account to accumulate actual factory overhead costs. A burden rate of $1.90 per machine-hour is used to charge factory overhead to individual job orders. The January 1 balance in Work in Process was $17,460 (including direct labor, direct materials, and applied factory overhead at $1.90 per machine-hour). The following data relate to operations during January:

(1) Materials and supplies purchased: $3,500.
(2) Materials and supplies issued:
    For specific job orders, $8,000.
    For general factory use, $700.
(3) Machine-hours: 10,000.
(4) Direct labor:
    On specific job orders, 6,000 hours at $5.50.
    On other factory activities, 1,000 hours at $5.20.
(5) Factory supervision: $4,000.
(6) Other factory costs: $7,800.
(7) Goods completed:
    Direct materials, $7,400.
    Direct labor, $32,000.
    Machine-hours, 9,000.

a) Prepare a manufacturing cost summary for the month, using the following format: actual costs for the month, plus or minus over- or underabsorbed overhead equals costs charged to product accounts; add the beginning balance in Work in Process and distribute the total between ending work in process and the cost of goods finished.

b) Set up appropriate T-accounts, enter the opening balances, if any, and post your analyses of the transactions described above.

17. On November 30, a fire destroyed the plant and factory offices of the Swadburg Company. You are called upon to assist in the preparation of the insurance claim as to inventory costs at November 30. Information you obtain is as follows:

(1) From the balance sheet at November 1 you find the beginning inventories: materials, $5,000; work in process, $15,000; finished goods, $27,500.

(2) The factory burden rate in use during November was $0.80 per dollar of direct material cost.

(3) Total sales for the month amounted to $60,000. The gross profit margin constituted 25 percent of selling price.

(4) Purchases of materials during November amounted to $30,000.

(5) The payroll records show wages accrued during November as $25,000, of which $3,000 was for indirect labor.

(6) The charges to factory overhead accounts totaled $18,000. Of this, $2,000 was for indirect materials and $3,000 was for indirect labor.

(7) The cost of goods completed during November was $52,000.

(8) Underabsorbed overhead amounted to $400. This amount was not deducted in the computation of the gross profit margin [item (3) above].

a) Calculate the amount of cost that had been assigned to the inventories of raw materials, work in process, and finished goods that were on hand at the time of the fire on November 30.

b) The Swadburg Company's management has claimed that a portion of the underabsorbed overhead should be assigned to the inventory, thereby increasing the amount due from the insurance company. The insurance company has denied this claim and you have been called upon to arbitrate the dispute. What answer would you give? What arguments would you advance to support it?

*18. The DEF Company manufactures metal parts to be sold to manufacturers of production machinery. The cost of materials requisitioned for specific job lots is charged to Work in Process. The straight-time wage costs (not including overtime premiums) of all labor traceable to specific job lots is charged to Work in Process. All other costs, including overtime premiums, are charged to a Manufacturing Overhead Cost Summary account. Manufacturing overhead costs are applied to jobs in process at a constant burden rate of $10 per direct labor hour.

During December, the following events were recorded by the DEF Company:

(1) Materials purchased: $50,000.

(2) Materials issued to production:
    Direct materials, $35,000.
    Indirect materials, $12,000.

(3) Direct labor hours: 4,000 (the straight-time wage rate is $5 an hour).

(4) Overtime hours included in direct labor hours: 200 (a premium of $2.50 an hour is paid for overtime labor).

(5) All other manufacturing overhead: $30,000.

(6)  Content of jobs completed and transferred to finished goods inventory:

Materials cost ...................... $32,000
Direct labor hours .................  3,600

*a)*  Prepare journal entries to record the foregoing events.
*b)*  Compute the amount of over- or underabsorbed overhead.
*c)*  Assume that an additional 200 hours of direct labor time at overtime rates occurred during December but were not included in the figures given above. By how much would this change the amount of over- or underabsorbed overhead?

19.  The Sandrex Company uses a job order cost accounting system. Direct labor costs are charged daily to Work in Process and credited to Accrued Wages Payable on the basis of time tickets. Direct materials costs are charged to Work in Process and credited to Materials Inventory. Factory overhead costs are charged initially to a Factory Overhead account. Overhead costs are charged to the Work in Process account by means of a predetermined burden rate of $2 per direct labor hour. The costs of goods finished are transferred from Work in Process to a Finished Goods account at the time each job is completed. A perpetual inventory system is used for both materials and finished goods.

Following are some of the events that took place in 19x1:

(1)  Goods manufactured in 19x0 at a cost of $8,000 were sold on credit for $14,000. The job cost sheets for these goods showed a total of $2,000 for materials, $3,000 for direct labor, and $3,000 for overhead.

(2)  Factory overhead was charged to a job on which 480 direct labor hours were recorded during 19x1. The job was still unfinished at the end of the year.

(3)  It was discovered prior to the end of 19x1 that an error in analyzing a batch of time cards resulted in treating 500 hours of direct labor at $5 an hour as indirect labor (i.e., the charge was made to Factory Overhead). The job on which this labor was used was finished but not sold in 19x1.

(4)  Materials costing $5,000 and supplies costing $500 were issued from the factory storeroom. Of the materials, $1,000 was for use in constructing new display cases in the company's salesrooms. The display cases were completed and placed in use during 19x1. The remaining materials were issued to the factory for specific job orders which were still in process at the end of 19x1. Of the supplies, $100 was for the immediate use of the sales office and the remainder was for general factory use.

(5)  Prior to the end of 19x1, it was discovered that $1,000 of direct materials had been charged to the wrong job. At the time this error was discovered, both jobs had been completed but not yet sold.

(6)  Prior to the end of the year, it was discovered that an error had been made in adding up the direct labor hours on a certain job

order which had been completed and the products sold during 19x1. The dollar amount of direct labor was added correctly, but the hours were overstated by 100.

(7) At the end of 19x1, factory wages earned but still unpaid amounted to $3,000 for direct labor and $1,000 for indirect labor. Employer's payroll taxes on these wages were 9 percent. This company treats all payroll taxes as overhead.

a) Indicate how discovery of these facts would affect the cost assigned to the work in process inventory at the end of the year, the cost of the finished goods inventory, or the cost of goods sold. Each event should be regarded as independent of the others.

b) Prepare journal entries to record these events. If no entry is required, explain why.

**20.** The Broxbo Manufacturing Company uses a job order cost system. On July 1, Work in Process had a balance of $2,700, made up as follows:

| Job No. | Materials | Labor | Overhead |
|---|---|---|---|
| 101.............. | $ 620 | $640 | $340 |
| 102.............. | 730 | 250 | 120 |
| Total ........ | $1,350 | $890 | $460 |

Finished Goods on this same date had a balance of $4,000, representing the cost of job No. 100.

During July, material cost, labor cost, and labor hours were:

| Job. No. | Material Cost | Labor Cost | Labor Hours |
|---|---|---|---|
| 101 .............. | $ 100 | $ 860 | 200 |
| 102 .............. | 200 | 1,900 | 300 |
| 103 .............. | 1,500 | 780 | 150 |
| 104 .............. | 2,000 | 820 | 200 |
| 105 .............. | 3,000 | 245 | 50 |
| Total......... | $6,800 | $4,605 | 900 |

In a normal month, the factory is expected to operate at a volume of 1,000 labor hours, and factory overhead is expected to amount to $3,000. Actual factory overhead cost for July was $2,950.

Job Nos. 101, 102, and 103 were completed during July and were placed in the finished goods storeroom.

Job Nos. 100, 101, and 102 were delivered to customers during July at a billed price of $15,000.

a) Enter the above information on job order cost sheets.
b) What was the total gross margin on job Nos. 100, 101, and 102?
c) What was the amount of the over- or underabsorbed overhead for the month?
d) Prepare summary journal entries to record the above information. Make the simplifying assumption that all factory labor and overhead

costs were paid in cash. All materials came from the materials inventory.

e) For what purposes might management wish to use the information summarized in your answers to (a), (b), and (c) above? Is this information well suited to these purposes?

**21.** The Nesbitt Company uses a Lifo basis for costing its finished goods inventories; materials and parts are costed on a Fifo basis; and work in process is inventoried on the basis of the cost of specific job lots. Annual increments to finished goods inventories are assumed for Lifo purposes to be from the first job lots completed during the year.

One of the company's products is the Model G Hand Stapler, and on January 1, 1973, the Lifo costs of finished units of this product in inventory were:

| | No. of Dozen | Cost per Dozen | Inventory Cost |
|---|---|---|---|
| Base quantity .................. | 1,000 | $25.20 | $25,200 |
| 1962 layer .................... | 100 | 28.80 | 2,880 |
| 1966 layer .................... | 150 | 31.20 | 4,680 |
| Total...................... | 1,250 | | $32,760 |

A burden rate of $2 per direct labor hour was used throughout the factory in 1973. No Model G staplers were in process on January 1, 1973.

The following transactions relating to production and sale of Model G Hand Staplers took place during 1973:

(1) Shipped 250 dozen to customers during January.
(2) Manufactured 1,000 dozen on job No. 2246 during February: direct materials, $9,800; direct labor, 6,000 hours at $4.20 an hour.
(3) Shipped 1,500 dozen to customers during March, April, May, and June.
(4) Manufactured 1,200 dozen on job No. 2873 during July: direct materials, $12,100; direct labor, 7,100 hours at $4.30 an hour.
(5) Shipped 900 dozen to customers during August, September, October, and November.
(6) Started job No. 3045 on November 21, but delays in receiving materials prevented completion of this job in 1973. This job order consisted of 1,000 dozen, with accumulated costs to December 31 of: direct materials, $10,200; direct labor, 5,900 hours at $4.30 an hour.

a) Compute the total cost of Model G Hand Staplers sold in 1973 and the cost of staplers in process and in finished goods inventory on December 31, 1973.

b) The company wishes to keep perpetual inventory records on its finished goods. What problems would be encountered and how would you solve them?

*c*) What additional problems would be raised if materials inventories were costed on a Lifo basis?

**22.** The Subway Car Company manufactures railway and subway cars to customer orders. Revenues are recognized at the time finished products are shipped to customers. A predetermined burden rate of $3.30 per direct labor hour is used in the company's factory.

On March 1, $120,000 in materials and supplies were on hand. The company maintains no inventory of finished goods, but it had three jobs in process in its factory on March 1:

| Job. No. | No. of Cars | Costs Accumulated in Prior Months |
|----------|-------------|-----------------------------------|
| 6456 ............ | 1 | $ 43,000 |
| 6457 ............ | 4 | 134,000 |
| 6459 ............ | 3 | 27,000 |

The following transactions affecting manufacturing costs occurred during the month of March:

(1) A new job order, No. 6460, was placed in production.
(2) Materials, supplies, and parts in the amount of $97,000 were purchased on account.
(3) Materials, supplies, and parts were issued to production departments, as follows:

| | |
|---|---|
| Job No. 6456................................ | $ 2,000 |
| Job No. 6457................................ | 21,000 |
| Job No. 6459................................ | 35,000 |
| Job No. 6460................................ | 5,000 |
| General factory use ........................ | 18,000 |

(4) Labor time tickets showed the following totals:

| | | |
|---|---|---|
| Job No. 6456.................. | 1,200 hours, | $ 5,000 |
| Job No. 6457.................. | 8,000 hours, | 40,000 |
| Job No. 6459.................. | 10,000 hours, | 46,000 |
| Job No. 6460.................. | 800 hours, | 6,000 |
| Indirect labor ................ | 3,000 hours, | 12,400 |

(5) Factory depreciation for the month, $10,000.
(6) Other factory operating costs amounted to $35,000 (credit Accounts Payable).
(7) Job No. 6456 was finished and shipped to the customer on March 18.
(8) Two cars in job No. 6457 were finished and shipped to the customer on March 28. The remaining two cars in the job were one-half completed on March 31.

*a*) Record the above information in appropriately titled T-accounts. Direct labor and direct materials costs are charged directly to a single Work in Process account. When incurred, all manufacturing overhead costs are charged to a Manufacturing Overhead account. Factory overhead absorbed is credited to this account.

b)  Prepare a schedule showing March 31 balances in the Work in Process and Manufacturing Overhead accounts.

**23.** The Lasill Company manufactures several types of pumps, partly to order and partly for stock. In both cases, work is done on the basis of production orders, and costs are recorded by job. The company's balance sheet as of August 31, 19x4, and its transactions for the month of September 19x4, are shown below.

The Lasill Company

**STATEMENT OF FINANCIAL POSITION**

August 31, 19x4

ASSETS

*Current Assets:*

| | | |
|---|---:|---:|
| Cash ........................................... | $ 23,280 | |
| Accounts receivable ........................... | 31,070 | |
| Materials and supplies......................... | 15,120 | |
| Work in process................................ | 8,300 | |
| Finished goods ................................ | 6,730 | $ 84,500 |

*Long-Life Assets:*

| | | |
|---|---:|---:|
| Machinery and equipment....................... | $248,600 | |
| Less: Allowance for depreciation .............. | 83,200 | 165,400 |
| Total ...................................... | | $249,900 |

LIABILITIES AND SHAREHOLDERS' EQUITY

*Current Liabilities:*

| | | |
|---|---:|---:|
| Accounts payable............................... | $ 27,650 | |
| Accrued wages and salaries .................... | 1,830 | $ 29,480 |

*Shareholders' Equity*

| | | |
|---|---:|---:|
| Common stock.................................. | $150,000 | |
| Retained earnings ............................. | 70,420 | 220,420 |
| Total ...................................... | | $249,900 |

Transactions during September:

| | | | | |
|---|---|---|---:|---:|
| (1) | Purchased: Materials and supplies............. | | $28,310 | |
| | Machine......................... | | 21,000 | $ 49,310 |
| (2) | Issued materials and supplies: | | | |
| | Direct materials – job No. 17................. | | $ 2,530 | |
| | No. 18................. | | 7,120 | |
| | No. 19................. | | 6,690 | |
| | Indirect materials............................ | | 4,060 | 20,400 |
| (3) | Accrued wages and salaries: | | | |
| | Direct labor – job No. 16, 1,200 hrs. .......... | | $ 6,440 | |
| | No. 17, 3,600 hrs. .......... | | 17,370 | |
| | No. 18, 5,600 hrs. .......... | | 30,580 | |
| | No. 19,   800 hrs. .......... | | 4,000 | |
| | Indirect labor and supervision ............... | | 9,420 | |
| | Office salaries (administration and sales) .... | | 14,590 | 82,400 |
| (4) | Depreciation on equipment: Plant.............. | | $ 2,040 | |
| | Office ............. | | 120 | 2,160 |
| (5) | Other manufacturing costs: | | | |
| | Power, light, and heat........................ | | $ 3,830 | |
| | Repairs ...................................... | | 1,160 | |
| | Sundry........................................ | | 790 | 5,780 |

| | | |
|---|---|---:|
| (6) | Other administrative and sales expenses....... | 2,770 |
| (7) | Jobs finished during month: Nos. 16–18 | |
| (8) | Sales during month: job No. 15 (balance) ...... $ 8,350 | |
| | No. 16 (all)............  21,300 | |
| | No. 17 (all)............  30,300 | |
| | No. 18 | |
| | (20 out of 50 pumps) ...  28,400 | 88,350 |
| (9) | Received payments from customers on account . | 87,800 |
| (10) | Paid: Accounts payable ...................... $43,690 | |
| | Wages ................................  80,850 | 124,540 |
| (11) | Received loan from bank on September 30 | |
| | (90-day note)................................ | 30,000 |

Additional information:

(1) Payroll deductions and taxes are omitted for purposes of simplification.

(2) All costs incurred other than payrolls and depreciation are in the first instance credited to Accounts Payable.

(3) Manufacturing Overhead is charged to jobs at the rate of $2 per direct labor hour.

(4) The opening balance of Finished Goods represents part of job order No. 15; that of Work in Process, Job No. 16 (Materials, $4,500; Direct Labor, $2,600; Overhead, $1,200).

*a)* Enter the above transactions in T-accounts and job order cost sheets. (Use a single T-account for all factory overhead costs.)

*b)* Prepare financial statements for the month. Over- or underabsorbed overhead is to be entered as a special item on the income statement.

**24.** Dan Roman is a contractor specializing in small house remodeling jobs. Most of his employees are specialists who work for other contractors as well, so that the size of his payroll rises and falls with fluctuations in the amount of work to be done. Higher wage rates are paid to the more highly skilled workers, but the average wage rate in the construction industry in Mr. Roman's area is about $7 an hour.

Mr. Roman recently installed a job order costing system and now has the following labor cost data:

| Job Number | Estimated | | Actual | |
|---|---|---|---|---|
| | Labor Hours | Labor Cost | Labor Hours | Labor Cost |
| 47 ......... | 600 | $4,200 | 650 | $4,900 |
| 48 ......... | 400 | 2,800 | 380 | 3,050 |
| 50 ......... | 900 | 6,300 | 1,000 | 8,200 |
| 51 ......... | 200 | 1,400 | 210 | 1,450 |
| 52 ......... | 500 | 3,500 | 460 | 3,450 |
| 54 ......... | 700 | 4,900 | 750 | 5,200 |
| 55 ......... | 800 | 5,600 | 820 | 7,000 |

During the period covered by these figures, Mr. Roman submitted bids on 18 jobs. Other contractors underbid him on 11 of these; he was the low bidder on the seven jobs shown above. Mr. Roman's profit margin was considerably lower than that of most of his competitors during this period.

a)  What advice can you give Mr. Roman on the basis of these figures? Do they help explain his low profit margin? Is there anything he can do about it?

b)  What further data would you probably find in Mr. Roman's job cost sheets that would throw further light on these questions?

c)  Would charging overhead costs to individual job orders provide Mr. Roman with useful information?

25. Aylesbury, Inc., uses a job order costing system in its factory. It manufactures eight different products, in batches. The production process is a long one, and several jobs are likely to be in process at a time.

During 19x1 the company used a predetermined burden rate of $5 a direct labor hour. Its actual overhead cost for the year amounted to $308,000, and 60,000 direct labor hours were recorded.

Eighteen job orders were completed during the year, and the job order cost sheets for these jobs showed the following data for direct labor and direct materials:

| Date Completed | Job No. | Product | Units | Direct Materials | Direct Labor Hours | Direct Labor Cost |
|---|---|---|---|---|---|---|
| Jan.   8 | X034 | A | 1,000 | $ 7,100 | 3,000 | $ 12,000 |
| 30 | X036 | G | 200 | 3,000 | 2,000 | 9,000 |
| Feb. 15 | X101 | A | 800 | 5,800 | 2,500 | 10,200 |
| Mar.   6 | X103 | B | 500 | 2,500 | 5,000 | 25,000 |
| 24 | X035 | H | 700 | 6,300 | 8,200 | 42,000 |
| Apr. 18 | X104 | C | 100 | 4,000 | 800 | 3,900 |
| May   3 | X105 | A | 1,500 | 10,950 | 4,400 | 18,700 |
| 27 | X102 | D | 300 | 1,500 | 1,200 | 6,000 |
| June   6 | X107 | F | 400 | 800 | 300 | 1,800 |
| July   2 | X110 | G | 200 | 3,300 | 1,900 | 9,500 |
| Aug. 26 | X109 | E | 500 | 5,200 | 600 | 3,300 |
| Sep.   5 | X111 | A | 2,000 | 14,600 | 6,100 | 25,000 |
| 18 | X106 | B | 600 | 3,600 | 5,700 | 30,000 |
| 30 | X112 | H | 700 | 6,440 | 8,400 | 43,400 |
| Oct. 22 | X108 | C | 100 | 4,200 | 750 | 3,700 |
| Nov.   4 | X115 | D | 300 | 1,500 | 1,300 | 6,600 |
| 30 | X114 | A | 1,000 | 7,400 | 3,100 | 13,000 |
| Dec. 14 | X118 | G | 200 | 3,600 | 2,100 | 10,500 |
| Total | | | | $91,790 | 57,350 | $273,600 |

a)  What was the total of the amounts charged to the finished goods inventory accounts during the year?

b)  For what purposes might the figures from the job cost sheets be useful? Illustrate your answer with figures based on the data supplied above.

c)  What further information on direct materials and direct labor costs would you like to have for these purposes? What further information on factory overhead would be useful?

# 20

## INCREMENTAL COSTS
## FOR MANAGEMENT DECISIONS

THE ULTIMATE TEST OF A COSTING SYSTEM is its ability to meet management's needs for cost information at a reasonable cost. It is evident that costing systems based on the principles outlined in Chapter 19 serve the general informational purposes for which financial statements are used. The data produced by these systems require considerable qualification and interpretation for use in price, production, and other operating decisions, however. The purpose of this chapter is to establish the general characteristics of data appropriate for management decisions, with particular reference to operating costs.

### THE INCREMENTAL APPROACH

All decisions are choices among the alternatives that are perceived to be available. The accountant's task, therefore, is to provide information on each alternative that will help management decide which one is likely to be the best for the company.

#### Limitations of Accounting Data

The cost data generated by a firm's accounts cannot be used directly in decision making for a number of reasons.[1] First, the cost data in the accounts are a record of what has taken place,

---

[1] One possible exception to this rule is in connection with decisions on personnel. A manager's ability to control costs is partially indicated by the costs actually recorded. See Chapters 23–24.

while decision making requires future costs. Accounting data therefore are useful only insofar as they can be used to predict future costs. When cost data from the accounts are used in decision making without modification, the implicit assumption is that future costs will be the same as past costs. More often, information from sources other than the accounts can be used to adjust historical costs to provide better forecasts of the costs associated with particular decisions.

Second, management's primary interest is in the effect of its decisions on the present value of the future cash flows that they will lead to. This means that the costs and benefits attached to each alternative should be measured by the cash receipts and disbursements that they are expected to generate, discounted to their present values. Most accounting figures, in contrast, are designed to meet the needs of financial reporting — that is, they measure the revenues, operating costs, expenses, and net income of a given time period. These are likely to differ substantially from the cash receipts and disbursements of that period.

To illustrate, in deciding whether to acquire a machine, management should match costs and benefits by converting the estimated future cash flows into their present value and comparing that present value with the current outlay. Once the machine has been acquired, however, the accountant converts the current outlay into a periodic depreciation charge to include it in the operating cost of each period for financial reporting purposes. This contrast between the accounting and decision making treatments of time will be examined more thoroughly in Chapter 22.

### Incremental versus Average Cost

The most important difference between cost data for decisions and job cost data of the kind described in Chapter 19 lies in the difference between incremental and average cost. *Incremental cost* is the difference between the total cost of operating the company if a specified alternative is selected and total cost under another alternative that has been selected as the basis for comparison. By definition, the relevant cost data for decisions are incremental costs — they measure the effect of the decision on costs. The accountant's product costs, on the other hand, are average costs and may be poor approximations of incremental cost.

For example, Exhibit 20–1 summarizes the costs incurred last year by the Apollo Trucking Company in carrying freight between Chicago and Cleveland, the two cities that the company serves.

*Exhibit 20–1*

Apollo Trucking Company

COSTS OF CARRYING FREIGHT BETWEEN CHICAGO
AND CLEVELAND

| Cost Element | Actual Cost, Last Year | | Incremental Cost | |
| --- | --- | --- | --- | --- |
| | Total | Per Trip | Loaded | Empty |
| Labor..................... | $168,000 | $112 | $112 | $112 |
| Fuel....................... | 90,000 | 60 | 65 | 40 |
| Maintenance and repairs .. | 22,500 | 15 | 11 | 8 |
| Depreciation............... | 12,000 | 8 | – | – |
| Taxes and insurance....... | 6,000 | 4 | – | – |
| Administration ............ | 16,500 | 11 | – | – |
| Total ............... | $315,000 | $210 | $188 | $160 |

The first column shows the total costs of operating the company during the year. The company's trucks made 1,500 one-way trips between these two cities last year, and the figures in the second column were obtained by dividing total cost by 1,500.

The average cost of $210 may be a useful approximation to incremental cost under certain circumstances. For example, it may be a fairly good basis for estimating the incremental cost of doubling the size of the company and doubling the number of trips each year. For other comparisons, however, it is likely to be wide of the mark. The incremental cost figures in the two right-hand columns are based on a comparison of operating the trucks the company now has and leaving them idle.

To begin with, the estimated incremental cost of the first cost element, labor cost, is equal to last year's average cost, $112, and is the same whether the truck is loaded or empty. Fuel costs, however, are expected to amount to $65 whenever a truck is fully loaded but only $40 when it makes the run empty.

Continuing down the list, we find that the average cost of truck maintenance and repairs last year was $15 a trip. Some of these costs will be necessary even if a truck stands unused all year 'round. Use of the truck adds to these standby costs: as the table shows, the company's maintenance and repair costs increase by $11 on the average for each fully loaded trip and by $8 for each empty trip. These are incremental costs of truck usage.

Depreciation, taxes and insurance, and administrative expenses for the year are independent of the number of trips made, given the number of trucks in the fleet. The consequence is that the incremental cost per trip for these cost categories is zero, up to the present capacity of the fleet.

Summing up the various incremental costs, we find that the cost of a trip from one city to another is not the $210 full cost but $188 if the truck is loaded and $160 if the truck is empty.

## Uncertainty and Expected Values

A truck cannot make a one-way trip from one city to the other: it must make a round trip. If freight is carried both ways, the incremental cost of a round trip is $188 + $188 = $376. If the backhaul is empty, the cost of a round trip is $188 + $160 = $348. Finally, the incremental cost of carrying freight on a trip that would otherwise be an empty backhaul is $188 − $160 = $28.

These are the cost figures that management should use whenever it knows with certainty which of these three situations it faces. For example, if the decision is whether to accept a shipment in Cleveland and management knows that it has a return load waiting in Chicago, the incremental cost is $188. If it knows that it has no return load waiting in Chicago and that the truck will have to return empty to Cleveland, the incremental cost is $348. Finally, if a truck is now in Cleveland, ready to head back to Chicago empty, the incremental cost of taking a Chicago-bound shipment is $28.

In many decision situations, however, Apollo's management is uncertain whether a load of freight will be available for the backhaul. In these situations, management uses a decision technique known as *expected value analysis*. This requires the assignment of probabilities to the various possible situations that may exist, and the use of these probabilities to weight the costs that will prevail in these situations.

To illustrate, suppose that Apollo has been offered a one-year contract to haul freight from Chicago to Cleveland. The contract will require it to carry at least two and at most four loads of freight per week. The management has decided that when a Chicago truck is dispatched to carry a load, the incremental cost is the cost of a fully loaded trip to Cleveland plus the cost of an empty backhaul. When a Cleveland truck is available in Chicago to carry a backhaul, the cost of the trip is the incremental cost of a loaded trip over the cost of an empty backhaul, or $28. Management has also estimated that when a load has to be shipped from Chicago to Cleveland, a Cleveland truck will be available for a backhaul 30 percent of the time and a Chicago truck will have to be dispatched for that purpose 70 percent of the time.

This rather complicated set of assumptions is summarized in

the following table, together with the calculation of the "expected value" of the incremental cost:

|  | (1)<br>Cost<br>per<br>Trip | (2)<br>Percentage<br>of Total<br>Trips | (3)<br>Weighted<br>Cost per Trip<br>(1) × (2) |
|---|---|---|---|
| Chicago-based truck: cost of full load plus empty backhaul ...... | $348 | 70% | $243.60 |
| Cleveland-based truck: added cost of loaded backhaul ($188 − $160) ................. | 28 | 30 | 8.40 |
| Expected Value of Haulage Cost per Trip ....................... |  |  | $252.00 |

This shows that 70 percent of the trips will have an incremental cost of $348, while 30 percent will have an incremental cost of only $28. On the average, therefore, the incremental cost will be somewhere between these two figures, in this case $252.

(Notice that if the reverse probabilities hold in Cleveland, the expected value of the cost of carrying a load from there to Chicago is 0.3 × $348 + 0.7 × $28 = $124. The sum of the expected values of the costs each way ($252 + $124 = $376) is just equal to the cost of a round trip for a loaded truck.)

## COST-VOLUME RELATIONSHIPS

More often than not a management decision problem involves an increase or decrease in the output of a product. Consequently, the variation in costs with variations in volume is of particular concern to management. For this reason costs are classified as either variable, semivariable, or fixed in relation to output.

### Variable and Fixed Costs

The firm's operating capacity in any period of time is determined by the size and structure of its physical plant, the number and effectiveness of its managers, and the amount of funds available to it. None of these factors can be changed quickly; most of them can be assumed to remain constant in the near term.

The costs of providing and supporting an organization's operating capacity are its *fixed costs* or *capacity costs*. A cost is a fixed cost if its total is not affected by small changes in operating volume. Conversely, any cost that must be increased or decreased in total to handle small increases or decreases in operating volume is a *variable cost.*

Direct labor and direct materials costs are typically regarded as proportionally variable with volume. Although this may not always be precisely true, we shall not quarrel with this assumption. Our discussion of fixed costs, therefore, will deal specifically with overhead costs, particularly factory overhead costs.

### Cost-Volume Diagrams

Figure 1 in Exhibit 20–2 represents the behavior of a cost element that is proportionally variable with volume. Each dot stands for the cost and volume recorded in one particular month in the past. The line drawn through the dots indicates the cost of the indirect materials that this firm might be expected to use at each level of activity if future conditions are like those of the past.

The line fitted to the observations in Figure 1 is described by the equation:

$$C = bV$$

in which $C$ = total cost per month
$V$ = the volume of activity, measured by direct labor hours
$b$ = the rate of variable cost per direct labor hour.

In this case, average variable cost is constant (and equal to $b$) per unit of output throughout the entire volume range.

In contrast, the horizontal line in Figure 2 represents the relationship between total depreciation cost and the volume of activity. The line of relationship is given by the formula:

$$C = a$$

in which $a$ represents total depreciation cost per month.

Depreciation may vary from one period to the next because of changes in the amount of equipment subject to depreciation, but the depreciation charge is not dependent on the rate of capacity utilization. Within the limits of factory capacity, the total depreciation cost does not vary as a result of output changes, and the cost per unit of output falls as the rate of output per period increases. At any output [V], the average cost is $a/V$.

*Exhibit 20–2*

## COST-VOLUME RELATIONSHIPS

Figure 1.    Proportionally Variable Cost

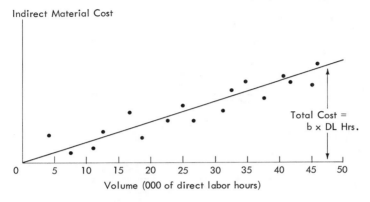

Figure 2.    Fixed Cost

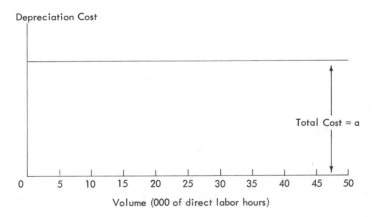

## Semivariable and Stepped Costs

Not all cost elements can be described as totally fixed or proportionally variable. Many other relationships are possible, and two of these are worth mentioning here.

Some costs are partly fixed and partly variable. Figure 1 in Exhibit 20–3 pictures the cost-volume relationship of one of these

*Exhibit 20–3*
COST-VOLUME RELATIONSHIPS

Figure 1.   Semivariable Cost

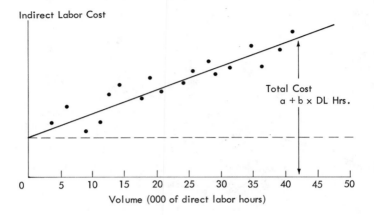

Figure 2.   Stepped Cost

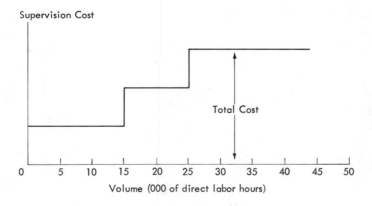

elements. In this case, indirect labor cost falls as volume falls toward zero, but it does not fall proportionately with the change in volume. This kind of cost can be described by an equation which combines the elements included in the other two equations cited earlier:

$$C = a + bV,$$

in which both $a$ and $b$ are positive. Dividing both sides by $V$, we get:

$$\text{Average cost} = C/V = a/V + b.$$

As output $(V)$ increases, $a/V$ decreases and so does average overhead cost per unit $(C/V)$. A cost like this can also be regarded as consisting of two parts: one for the fixed component of the cost $(a)$ and one for the variable component $(bV)$.

Other cost elements may behave in the manner represented in Figure 2 of Exhibit 20–3. As this shows, costs rise in a step-like fashion. The basic supervisory staff can handle all levels of volume up to 15,000 direct labor hours a month. For sustained operations above this level, additional supervisory personnel must be employed and total cost jumps up. Average cost falls as volume expands as long as the increase is not big enough to move supervisory costs to the next level. The average rises at this point and then begins to fall again as volume continues to expand while total cost remains constant.

Stepped costs such as these are generally classified as fixed costs on the grounds that volume generally moves within fairly narrow ranges in the short run. Substantial volume changes require careful planning and conscious decisions to move to higher or lower plateaus.

## Choosing an Index of Volume

The reader may have noted that in the previous discussion direct labor hours was used as the measure of output. For a single-product firm or department, the number of units of product manufactured would be a better measure of output. For a multiproduct department, however, some common denominator of the products must be used as the output measure because the various products are so dissimilar that raw physical unit totals are meaningless. Direct labor hours is one of the most common of these substitute measures. If it is the one selected, the variable cost per unit of a product is the variable cost per direct labor hour multiplied by the number of direct labor hours required to manufacture a unit of the product.

The size of the deviations of the observed data from the line of relationship (the *regression line*) drawn through them can be used in selecting the measure of output. Indirect materials cost in the example could have been plotted against the number of units of product output, the number of pounds of materials processed, the number of machine-hours used, or the number of direct labor hours worked. In each case a regression line could have been drawn through the observations. The closer the observations to the line, the higher the *correlation* between the actual cost at an output level and the cost predicted by the line. The best measure of volume is the one that gives the highest correlation.

For example, if overhead cost varies more closely with direct labor than with the weight of the factory's output, then two products that weigh the same but require different amounts of direct labor will lead to different amounts of overhead cost. In such a case, a cost-volume formula based on direct labor will be a better device for cost forecasting than a formula based on product weight.

In practice, a factory is likely to use more than one volume index. Whereas the number of direct labor hours is likely to be the best index in some departments, machine-hours, materials quantity, or direct labor cost will be better in others. Some departments may even apply one index to some cost elements and a different index to others. Machine-hours are used when machine activity is the predominant feature of the operation. Direct labor hours are preferred when overhead apparently varies with labor usage but is independent of differences in wage rates. Direct labor cost is a superior measure only when overhead costs are higher on jobs involving skilled labor, or are much influenced by changes in wage rates. When no one of these bases appears to be more accurate than any other, the one involving the least bookkeeping is preferred.

## COST CONCEPTS IN INCREMENTAL ANALYSIS

The simplicity of incremental analysis in principle is matched only by its difficulty in application. To deal with the problems of application, a number of cost concepts have been developed. Some of these represent little more than terminology; others represent attributes of costs that must be understood by anyone charged with the task of estimating the incremental costs associated with a decision alternative.

### Cost Variability and Incremental Costs

Our interest in cost variability arises mainly because the only incremental costs for many decisions are the wholly variable costs and the variable components of semivariable cost elements. This is not always true, however. For many other decisions, some or all of the fixed costs are incremental.

The reason for this apparent contradiction in terms is not hard to find. Fixed costs remain constant only so long as capacity is unchanged. Whenever a decision is large in scope or has a long time horizon, at least two of the alternatives will differ in total capacity. This means that some of the fixed costs are likely to differ between alternatives—that is, fixed costs will be incremental costs.

For example, suppose that Apollo has seven trucks, all licensed, insured, and in good operating condition. The costs of licensing and insuring the trucks are fixed costs, in that they will be the same in total whether the trucks operate 50,000 miles this year or 100,000 miles.

In deciding whether to accept a particular shipment, requiring the movement of a truck from Cleveland to Chicago and back, Apollo's management should ignore the costs of licensing and insuring the truck. These costs are *sunk costs* with respect to this decision, in that they will not be affected by this decision.

Suppose, however, that traffic on the Chicago-Cleveland route has declined to such an extent that management is considering the possibility of placing one of the company's trucks in storage for the rest of the year. If this is done, the insurance company will refund the insurance premiums already paid on this truck for the remainder of the year, but the state government will not refund any portion of the license fee. For this decision, therefore, the license fee is a sunk cost but the insurance premium is an incremental cost.

Taking this even further, if business conditions fail to improve by the end of the year, management may be willing to consider obtaining licenses for only six of its trucks next year, leaving the seventh truck in storage. To analyze its alternatives at that point, management should regard the annual license fee as an incremental cost because it will have to be paid if the truck is kept in operation and can be avoided if the truck is kept on blocks in the garage.

Extension of this idea to other situations is the basis for the familiar statement that in the long run all costs are variable. Given a long enough period, the firm can expand its total capacity by making additional expenditures for facilities or reduce its expenditures, thereby reducing its capacity.

For example, suppose that one of the company's trucks has become so costly to operate that management must either replace it or operate the route with only six trucks. In this case, the cost of a replacement truck is an incremental cost of operating a seven-truck fleet instead of a six-truck fleet. We shall return in Chapter 22 to see how expenditures for trucks and other long-lived property should be treated in incremental analysis, but for the moment it is enough to say that they constitute incremental costs if one of the alternatives under consideration requires capacity-maintaining or capacity-expanding expenditures for property and another does not.

### Cash Flow versus Accounting Cost

We stated at the outset that accounting costs may be so different from the cash outflows arising from a decision that management cannot use them in decision making. This deserves particular emphasis in connection with depreciation charges. The depreciation figures in the accounts are allocations of expenditures made in the past. These expenditures are not affected by decisions to use or not use the equipment now.

For example, suppose that one of Apollo's trucks is being depreciated at a rate of $2,000 a year, while each of the others has an annual depreciation charge of $3,000. If management is trying to decide which truck to use on a particular run or which truck to place in storage, this difference in the depreciation charge is irrelevant. Management cannot save $1,000 by using the truck with the $2,000 depreciation, leaving one of the others idle instead.

### Opportunity Costs

Much of the preceding discussion reflected the application of the concept of opportunity cost. For example, David Johnson bought an apple for 10 cents before entering a stadium to see a football game. No apples are on sale inside the stadium, and another spectator has just offered Mr. Johnson 25 cents for the apple. His decision problem, in other words, is whether to eat the apple or to sell it for 25 cents.

If Mr. Johnson had an accounting system, it would probably indicate that the cost of eating the apple would be 10 cents, the historical cost of the apple. This figure is irrelevant, however, because the replacement of the apple is not possible at that price. Mr. Johnson's opportunity cost is the 25 cents that he can get by selling it, not the 10 cents he paid for it earlier.

In general, opportunity cost is what must be sacrificed to obtain the use of a specific resource for a specific use. If a resource cannot be replaced, its opportunity cost is the net cash flow from the best alternative use. If Mr. Johnson has no desire to eat the apple inside the stadium, and if he has no use for it at home, the opportunity cost of selling it is zero.

There is no conflict between the opportunity cost and incremental cost concepts. The term opportunity cost merely calls our attention to the need to recognize forgone receipts as the relevant costs under some circumstances.

## Management Policy Costs

Many fixed costs, such as supervisory costs, are necessitated by the nature of the work to be done. Others, however, are fixed because management's *policy* is not to change the cost in response to a change in output. For example, sometime in the past management may have decided to employ four industrial engineers to study work methods. Although the management may at any time decide to raise or lower the number of industrial engineers, its present policy is to have four, no matter what the current level of output. Accordingly, these costs may be considered as *management policy* costs or *discretionary* costs.

Management policy costs are established by management as part of its overall operating plan for the period. Many of them are incurred to obtain future sales — e.g., some kinds of advertising, research, and product development. Others are incurred to maintain a current position or to facilitate current managerial activity — e.g., legal services, market research, etc. They are fixed costs, however, in that they do not necessarily change in response to changes in volume.

## APPLYING THE INCREMENTAL PRINCIPLE

In applying the incremental principle it is first necessary to identify the relevant alternative courses of action and then to establish the incremental costs associated with each alternative. No general rules can be set forth which guarantee a correct application in every situation; competence can come only with experience. A start in this direction can be obtained, however, by considering two illustrative problems: (1) pricing additional business; and (2) discontinuing a product. Examination of these problems will also show that all of the relevant considerations cannot always be quantified, so that the data themselves do not determine what the decision should be.

## Pricing Additional Business

Most business firms do most of their business with a group of fairly regular customers who buy the products and services that are the firm's regular stock in trade. Opportunities sometimes arise, however, to fill special orders for products that are not part of the regular line. This presents an interesting analytical problem.

An opportunity of this sort came to the management of the Van Horn Company, a manufacturer of lawn mowers. The purchasing agent of the Wilde Company, which operated a chain of automotive and hardware stores, asked Van Horn's sales manager whether Van Horn would be interested in manufacturing 2,000 power mowers to be sold by Wilde under its own brand name, Wilcut. Van Horn could have this order at a price of $48 a unit. Production capacity was easily adequate to handle this order.

The Wilcut mower would be very similar to one of Van Horn's regular mowers and the company's controller prepared the following estimate of unit cost, based on the company's usual full-cost accounting methods:

Manufacturing cost:
| | |
|---|---:|
| Direct materials | $25.80 |
| Direct labor | 7.00 |
| Overhead | 9.35 |
| Total | $42.15 |
| Selling expense | 1.45 |
| Administrative expense | 2.90 |
| Total Cost | $46.50 |

This was only $1.50 less than the estimated price, a margin that the controller regarded as inadequate.

The production manager was eager to have this order accepted. He objected in particular to the $9.35 figure for factory overhead, which was based entirely on the burden rates in use in the factory at that time. He pointed out that the increase in factory overhead would be far less than $9.35 a unit because many of the fixed costs would be unaffected by the decision. He also felt, but could not prove, that the expanded output would lead to improved manufacturing methods and lower costs on *all* of the company's mowers.

With the aid of one of his assistants, the factory controller, the production manager prepared an alternative profit estimate, which were based in part on estimates of cost variability as shown:

|  | Per Unit | Total |
|---|---|---|
| Incremental variable cost: | | |
| Direct materials .................................. | $25.80 | $51,600 |
| Direct labor........................................ | 7.00 | 14,000 |
| Factory overhead ................................ | 5.00 | 10,000 |
| Administration..................................... | .20 | 400 |
| Incremental variable cost....................... | $38.00 | $76,000 |
| Incremental fixed factory overhead ................. | | 2,000 |
| Total incremental cost ........................ | | $78,000 |
| Incremental sales revenues ........................ | $48.00 | 96,000 |
| Incremental Profit ............................ | | $18,000 |

In this analysis, the production manager accepted the original estimates of direct labor and direct materials costs as fully incremental costs because they represented employee salaries and materials purchase costs that would not be incurred if the proposal were rejected.

The variable portion of factory overhead also seemed likely to be fully incremental, and these he estimated at $5 a unit. Fixed factory overhead was mostly sunk, however, and the production manager excluded that portion of the burden rate from the analysis. Instead, he had the factory controller identify any overhead cost elements that might be affected by acceptance of the order. The only increment here seemed to be a slight increase in supervisory costs, adding up to about $2,000 for the contract as a whole. Fixed costs, in other words, can be incremental, but not necessarily in the proportions implied by the regular full-cost burden rate.

The selling and administrative expense figures in the original estimates, like the $9.35 in factory overhead, were based on average cost/revenue ratios for the company as a whole. The production manager saw no reason why selling costs should be affected in any way by acceptance of this order, but he did obtain an estimate from the company's controller that clerical expenses in the accounting department would probably go up by about 20 cents a unit. This increment was also included in the estimates summarized above.

Collection of figures such as these does not necessarily settle the managerial problem. In this case, the sales manager sided with the production manager on the grounds that Van Horn had been losing market share in recent years by not participating in the rapidly growing portion of total mower sales handled by mail-order houses and other large retail distributors. He thought that this initial order would give the company valuable experience in dealing in this market and might lay the groundwork for a substantial penetration of this market in the future.

The president, on the other hand, was afraid that the company's regular customers, mostly small independent dealers, would regard this as unfair to them and might shift to competitors' lines. For his part, the controller suggested that the low price might lead competitors to retaliate by price-cutting on models that competed directly with Van Horn's own branded models. He also worried that if the sales manager were encouraged to cut the price on this occasion he would want to do so again on other occasions, and that this would undermine the company's entire pricing structure.

How this argument was resolved is unimportant here, but it does illustrate two things. First, a purely quantitative analysis is unlikely to resolve the issues in decision-making situations involving major policy questions. Second, the arguments summarized above represent the typical range of managerial reactions to the use of incremental cost data. How the issues are resolved in any case will depend on management's considered judgment on the validity of the arguments raised in this illustration.

### Dropping an Unprofitable Product

Van Horn's management also faced another problem at the same time. One of its regular products, the Estate power mower, was selling at a price that was $4.10 less than the average cost assigned to that product. Van Horn's president asked the controller to prepare an estimate of the financial impact of withdrawing the Estate mower from the line.

The controller's first step was to ask the sales manager whether withdrawal of the Estate mower would affect the company's sales of any of its other mowers. The sales manager reported that if this item were dropped, many buyers would switch to the company's Suburban mower, a slightly cheaper model with many of the same features as the Estate mower. He estimated that sales of the Suburban would increase by about 3,000 units a year. None of the company's other models would be affected.

The controller's next step was to prepare estimates of the variable cost of manufacturing and selling these two mowers. His estimates were as follows:

|  | Estate | Suburban |
|---|---|---|
| Variable factory costs: | | |
| Direct materials .......................... | $32.00 | $27.50 |
| Direct labor............................... | 12.00 | 7.50 |
| Overhead.................................. | 6.00 | 5.00 |
| Total ................................. | $50.00 | $40.00 |
| Variable selling cost ........................ | 3.50 | 3.00 |
| Variable administrative cost ................. | .20 | .20 |
| Total Variable Cost .................... | $53.70 | $43.20 |

Variable selling costs in this table represented the commissions which the company's salesmen received on all sales of the regular lines of mowers.

Finally, the controller tried to estimate how dropping the Estate mowers would affect the fixed factory overhead. This effect was not measured by the burden rate, but had to be estimated from an item-by-item analysis of overhead costs. After careful study, the production manager reported that $27,000 of his overhead costs, which were fixed as long as *any* Estate mowers were manufactured, could be eliminated if *none* were produced. Expansion of production of an additional 3,000 Suburban mowers a year would not lead to any increases in fixed overhead.

The analysis of this proposal is summarized in Exhibit 20–4. Looking at columns (1) and (2) alone, we see that the Estate mower contributed $54,500 toward the company's general overhead costs and profits, after paying for the $27,000 in fixed factory overhead that could be eliminated if the product were abandoned. Because the Suburban mower could fill in part of the gap in the product line that withdrawal of the Estate mower would create, however, the estimated incremental loss from dropping

Exhibit 20–4

Van Horn Company

INCREMENTAL CASH FLOWS FROM ESTATE MOWERS

|  | (1) Estate Mower | (2) Estate Mower | (3) Suburban Mower | (4) Suburban Mower | (5) Incremental Profit |
|---|---|---|---|---|---|
|  | Per Unit | Total | Per Unit | Total | (2) − (4) |
| Incremental revenues ............ | $70.00 | $350,000 | $60.00 | $180,000 | $170,000 |
| Incremental variable cost ........ | 53.70 | 268,500 | 43.20 | 129,600 | 138,900 |
| Variable profit................. | $16.30 | $ 81,500 | $16.80 | $ 50,400 | $ 31,100 |
| Incremental fixed factory overhead .................... |  | 27,000 |  | – | 27,000 |
| Incremental Profit............. |  | $ 54,500 |  | $ 50,400 | $ 4,100 |

the Estate mower was only $4,100, or about 1 percent of sales revenues from this line.

This analysis shows that the Estate mower was not a dead loss, as the original full-cost estimate had implied, but neither was it a great contributor to profit, as the figures in column (2) seemed to indicate. It was of borderline importance and management probably should have looked at it very carefully to see whether its profitability could be improved or whether management's efforts should be expended in other directions.

## BREAK-EVEN CHARTS

The relationships among costs, volume, and profit are often described graphically by *break-even charts* or *profit graphs*, and these too can best be explained with the aid of an example.

### The Basic Chart

The profit graph is simply a diagram showing the amount of profit to be expected at various sales volumes under specified operating conditions. The profit graph developed by Seaton Chemicals, Inc., for its new X-250 plastic is typical. The new product has been brought to the point of being commercially useful, and a study has been undertaken to determine whether it would be profitable to put it on the market at the present time. The sales department reports that X-250 is closest in physical characteristics to Thor, a product of another chemical company, currently selling at $1.30 per pound. It is further estimated that the annual sales of Thor are about five million pounds.

On the basis of data obtained in part from the engineering department, a cost analyst on the controller's staff has estimated the costs of producing and selling X-250, as follows:

| Item | Total Fixed Cost | Variable Cost per Pound |
|---|---|---|
| Direct material | $    — | $0.34 |
| Direct labor | — | 0.27 |
| Manufacturing overhead | 800,000 | 0.21 |
| Selling and administrative costs | 400,000 | 0.08 |
| Total | $1,200,000 | $0.90 |

The proposed plant would cost $5 million, and its capacity would be 10 million pounds.

This information may be stated mathematically as follows. If

X-250 is sold at \$1.30 a pound, then total revenue, $R$, at a level of output, $V$, is

$$R = \$1.30V.$$

The total cost, $C$, at an output of $V$ is

$$C = \$1,200,000 + \$0.90V.$$

The firm will *break even* at the output at which $R = C$. This is found by equating the above two expressions and solving for $V$:

$$1.30V = 1,200,000 + 0.90V$$
$$V = 3,000,000 \text{ pounds.}$$

This analysis appears in graph form in Exhibit 20–5, where output is on the horizontal axis and revenue or cost on the vertical axis. The utility of this device as a means for *presenting* the relevant information is apparent. Here are seen at a glance the fixed costs at zero output, the break-even volume, and the spread between total revenue and total cost at any level of output above or below the break-even point.

*Exhibit 20–5*

Seaton Chemicals, Inc.

**BREAK-EVEN ANALYSIS — PRODUCT X-250**

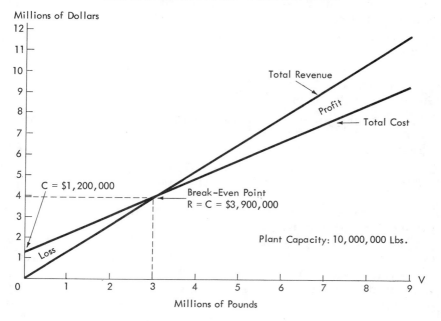

## Using the Chart

As this chart shows, the indicated break-even volume for the X-250 at a price of $1.30 a pound is about 3 million pounds a year, or 60 percent of the present market for the competitor's Thor. At lower volumes the total cost line is higher than the total revenue line, signaling an expected operating loss. At higher volumes, total revenue would exceed total cost and a profit would be recorded.

The company is not in business to break even, however. It wishes to earn a return on investment of at least 20 percent before taxes. Description of the method used to compute return on investment must be deferred to Chapter 22, but the break-even chart can be used to give a rough idea of the product's ability to meet a return on investment test. In this case, the controller estimates that total investment in plant and working capital would be approximately as follows:

$$\text{Investment } (I) = \$6,500,000 + 0.12R.$$

A 20 percent return ($r$) on this investment would be:

$$rI = 0.20 \times \$6,500,000 + 0.20 \times 0.12R$$
$$= \$1,300,000 + 0.024R.$$

This can be regarded as an added amount that must be covered before the product can "break even" in a real sense. In other words, if the investment is to be profitable, then revenue must equal or exceed the total cost plus the required return on investment:

$$R \geq C + rI.$$

Substituting the formulas above in this equation gives:

$$\$1.30V = \$1,200,000 + \$0.90V + \$1,300,000 + 0.024 \times \$1.30V.$$

This reduces to:

$$\$0.3688V = \$2,500,000$$
$$V = 6,779,000 \text{ pounds.}$$

That is, Seaton Chemicals would have to sell more of this new product than the market is now buying from its competitor.

This analysis is presented graphically in Exhibit 20–6. The required return on investment is added to the cost figures to get a new "total requirements" line. The adjusted break-even point is the volume at which this line and the total revenue line intersect. At volumes greater than this, profit is in excess of the required amount; at lower volumes it is less than the amount required.

Exhibit 20–6

Seaton Chemicals, Inc.

### PROFIT REQUIRED TO PRODUCE 20 PERCENT
### RETURN ON INVESTMENT FROM PRODUCT X-250

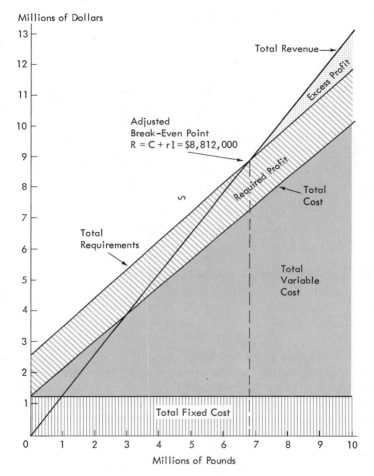

In this case, management concludes that a volume of 6,779,000 pounds a year is too far out of reach to justify introducing product X-250. Consequently, the sales manager is asked to investigate cheaper products for which X-250 might be a substitute, and to estimate the increase in volume that might be obtained by reducing the price to $1.15 a pound. At the same time, the chief engineer is requested to explore the possibility of moving to a smaller plant with lower fixed costs and little or no increase in variable unit costs. Decision as to whether the item should be sold at a lower price, produced in a smaller plant, or kept in the laboratory for a few more years is deferred until further information can be obtained.

### Problems in Break-Even Chart Construction

By the addition of other revenue and cost lines, the break-even chart can be used to diagram the anticipated results of alternative pricing policies or production methods. It can also be used for rough profit forecasting in multiproduct situations.

To illustrate the multiproduct break-even chart, let us assume (1) that the same plant could be used to produce both X-250 and another new chemical, Y-78; (2) that total fixed costs would be, as before, $1,200,000 a year; and (3) that the estimated volume, revenue, and variable cost data for the two products are as follows:

| Item | Sales Volume | Per Unit Price | Per Unit Variable Cost | Total Revenue | Total Variable Cost |
|---|---|---|---|---|---|
| X-250 ....... | 2,000,000 lbs. | $1.30 | $0.90 | $2,600,000 | $1,800,000 |
| Y-78......... | 3,000,000 lbs. | 1.80 | 1.50 | 5,400,000 | 4,500,000 |
| Total .... | | | | $8,000,000 | $6,300,000 |

The $6,300,000 total variable cost is 78.75 percent of the $8 million total revenue for the stated sales volumes. Therefore, as sales volume varies in total *with the product mix unchanged,* cost will increase or decrease by $0.7875 per dollar of sales revenue. This information is presented graphically in Exhibit 20–7. Output is measured on the horizontal axis by sales revenue,[2] and the total cost line is $C = \$1,200,000 + \$0.7875V$. The total revenue line is $R = V$, and the break-even point is found to be at a sales volume of $5,647,059 [i.e., where $C = \$1,200,000 + 0.7875 \times \$5,647,059 = \$5,647,059$].

Break-even charts may be used to describe a wide variety of situations, but care must always be taken to bear in mind the assumptions on which such charts are based. In the present case, the conditions under which the plant will earn the indicated profit at any given level of volume are (1) that the costs and prices for

---

[2] Sales revenue is ordinarily used because physical output measures for the various products are not easily added together.

*Exhibit 20–7*

## BREAK-EVEN CHART FOR TWO PRODUCTS

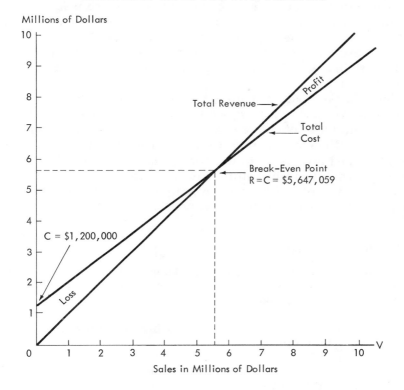

Millions of Dollars

Sales in Millions of Dollars

each product are as estimated, and (2) that the mix in which the two products sell is in the ratio of two pounds of X-250 to three pounds of Y-78.

## SUMMARY

The basic approach to quantitative analysis for management decisions is to estimate the incremental cash flows, the *differences* between the anticipated results of a proposed course of action and the anticipated results of the action the company would take if the proposal were rejected.

This *incremental analysis* is a simple and powerful concept, but one which is by no means easily applied in all cases. In simple situations, for example, a product's variable cost may be a good estimate of the cost of increasing product output, but revenue effects may be extremely difficult to forecast. In other cases, many fixed costs will also be affected, particularly if large amounts of business are affected by the decision.

Although the future is uncertain, it is sometimes possible to estimate the probability of each possible future outcome of a decision and get the expected value of the payoff. In other situations, these uncertainties are more intractable and have to be dealt with in a qualitative way, after the incremental calculations have been made.

This chapter has indicated how costs can be classified into fixed and variable costs to make them more readily usable in decision making. We have examined a number of cost concepts, such as sunk costs and opportunity costs, to obtain a richer understanding of how costs are used in decision making. Finally, we have shown how profit-volume analysis and profit-volume charts can be used to reveal how a company's cost structure influences its profitability when volume is uncertain.

## QUESTIONS AND PROBLEMS

1. What is meant by the "incremental approach" to decision making? Define the terms *incremental cost* and *incremental profit*. Are they the same as *variable cost* and *variable profit*?

2. What problems are encountered in using conventionally developed accounting data in decision making?

3. "We've already spent $100,000 to make this product a success and we can't let that kind of money be wasted. We have to keep on until we succeed." Would you be inclined to agree with this statement? To what extent is the $100,000 relevant to the decision to persist in the effort to market the new product?

4. What are the advantages of using a break-even chart in the analysis of business problems?

5. What are the special situations under which you would consider it sound to sell a product at a price less than its full cost?

6. What is a management policy cost? Is it likely to be variable or fixed?

7. How would you decide how to measure the volume of activity for cost analysis? What criterion would you apply?

8. Of what significance is the break-even point? Inasmuch as the firm is not in business to break even, how would you use break-even information in decision making?

9. Why should decisions be based on cash flows instead of on accounting cost or net income?

10. "We sell everything below cost, and the only way we can manage to make a profit is because our volume is so big." Can this statement be true?

*11. The Robin Company manufactures a single product for which the price is $6.20. The variable cost per unit is $4.50, and the annual fixed cost is $38,000. What sales volume is needed to break even? To earn a 20 percent return on an investment of $160,000?

*12. The Rise Company makes bumper jacks, and last year it sold 50,000 at a price of $3 and produced them at an average cost of $2.25. The sales manager states that at a price of $2.50 he could sell 75,000 units. The plant manager estimates that 75,000 could be produced at a cost of $2 each. What are the incremental revenue, the incremental cost, and the incremental profit on reducing the price to $2.50 each?

13. The Walter Company management believes that the company should earn a 20 percent return on investment before taxes at a sales volume equal to 80 percent of capacity. The company's annual capacity is 150,000 units, and the annual fixed costs are $180,000. The variable cost per unit is $8.50, and the investment is $1,300,000.

Assuming that the required sales volume can be achieved, at what unit price will the company realize its return on investment objective?

*14. The Cranby Company sells a single product for which the following data are available:

Current selling price . . . . . . . . . . . . . . . . . . . . .    $4.90 a unit
Expected sales volume . . . . . . . . . . . . . . . . . .    200,000 units
Expected fixed costs . . . . . . . . . . . . . . . . . . . .    $1.60 a unit
Expected variable costs . . . . . . . . . . . . . . . . .    $2.20 a unit

The company is contemplating an increase in the selling price of its product to $5.40 a unit.

a) What would be the new break-even point?
b) How many units would have to be sold at the new price to produce a 10 percent increase in total profit before taxes?

15. The Meredith Machine Company entered into a contract to manufacture for a foreign concern certain specially designed chemical processing equipment. When the equipment was completed and in the testing stage, currency controls which nullified all import contracts were instituted by the government to which the purchaser was subject. The manufacturing costs incurred by the Meredith Company up to that time

---

* Solutions to problems marked with an asterisk (*) are found in Appendix B.

were slightly over $700,000. The scrap value of the equipment was estimated to be approximately $80,000.

No purchaser could be found for the equipment in its existing form, but one company was interested if certain major modifications were made. This company offered $500,000; the estimated cost of modification to fit the revised specifications was $200,000.

What course of action should the Meredith Company follow? To what extent is the decision affected by the amount of manufacturing cost that has already been incurred?

16. A sales representative of the Morgan Machinery Company has submitted an offer to the Bragan Products Company to supply Bragan with its requirements of a metal casting at a price of 42 cents each. This metal casting is identical to the X52 casting that the Bragan Products Company now manufactures and uses in several of its products. The following estimate of the cost of making X52 castings has been prepared by the cost accounting department:

| | |
|---|---:|
| Material | $0.18 |
| Labor | 0.09 |
| Supplies | 0.06 |
| Other variable costs | 0.07 |
| Depreciation on casting equipment | 0.03 |
| Other fixed costs, including space charges, general factory supervision, etc. | 0.05 |
| Total Manufacturing Cost per Unit | $0.48 |

Prepare a short report analyzing the desirability of accepting the Morgan proposal.

*17. A company uses 100,000 pounds of material X every month. A supplier has offered to supply the company's requirements of this material for the next year at a fixed price of $.80 a pound. The current market price is $.75, but if the facilities of one of this material's principal foreign suppliers are expropriated by the foreign government, total output will fall and the world price is likely to go to $.90 a pound.

In management's judgment, there is about a 40 percent chance that the supplier will be nationalized during the next year. Would you advise management to accept the proposed contract?

18. Product A can be manufactured either on machine X or on machine Y. If machine X is used, direct labor cost will be $200 to set up the machine and $1 a unit to run it. If machine Y is used, direct labor cost will be $100 for set-up plus $1.50 a unit.

Factory overhead cost averages 100 percent of direct labor cost, and can be predicted from the formula:

Total factory overhead = $10,000 a month + 0.5 × direct labor cost.

The cost of direct materials is $1.80 a unit.

Total factory fixed cost would continue to average $10,000 a month even if manufacture of product A were to be discontinued.

The demand for product A is strong, and management usually schedules it for production on machine X, with an average lot size of 500 units. When machine X is fully loaded with other products, however, machine Y is used for product A, with an average lot size of 200 units. Management estimates that 20 percent of the company's output of product A will be produced on machine Y. This percentage is not affected by variations in the sales of product A.

*a*) What unit cost figure would you use in deciding whether to produce and sell product A during the coming year? Explain your calculations.

*b*) Should this same figure be used to measure inventories for public financial reporting? Should unit cost for this purpose differ, depending on which machine is used? Explain.

19. Brown manufactured a single product known as a "hyperflange," and sold it to industrial and commercial users. Brown's total volume was 100,000 hyperflanges a month.

Smith was one of Brown's best customers. Every month Brown sold 10,000 hyperflanges to Smith, at a price of $5 each. Last week, however, Smith gave Brown a chance to increase the size of the monthly shipment to 15,000 units, *provided* that Brown would quote a price of $4 on each of the additional 5,000 units. The price of the first 10,000 units would not change. Smith argued that this would be extra business for Brown, meaning that he need charge no overhead against these additional units. In this case, a $4 price should be adequate.

Brown disagreed. He estimated that he would lose 46 cents a unit at a price of $4, because average unit cost would be $4.46:

|  | At 100,000 units a month | At 105,000 units a month |
|---|---|---|
| Direct labor and materials .............. | $3.00 | $3.00 |
| Other factory costs...................... | 1.00 | .97 |
| Selling and administrative costs ........ | .50 | .49 |
| Average Total Cost................ | $4.50 | $4.46 |

What unit cost figure should Brown use in deciding whether to take on the added business? Show your calculations.

20. A printing firm is considering an offer to print a new monthly magazine for an organization of professional social workers. The organization is not wealthy, and it cannot pay more than 50 cents a copy to have its new magazine printed, or $5,000 a month. The printing firm would like to help out, but only if it could recover its costs, plus a margin of 5 percent of cost to allow for contingencies. If the contingencies did not materialize, the firm would make a small profit.

The costs of direct labor, paper stock, and ink would be completely variable. Printing the magazine would bring the monthly volume in the print shop from 8,000 direct labor hours to 8,500 direct labor hours a month, and average overhead costs would drop from $2 an hour at 8,000 hours to $1.95 an hour at 8,500 hours. Management has drawn up the following profit estimate:

| | | |
|---|---|---|
| Revenue per hour ..................... | | $10.00 |
| Costs per hour: | | |
| Direct labor ......................... | $6.00 | |
| Paper stock and ink ................. | 2.50 | |
| Printing overhead ................... | 1.95 | 10.45 |
| Profit/(Loss) per Hour ................ | | $ (0.45) |

The print shop manager says that print shop overhead is a sunk cost and should be ignored. Since the anticipated margin over direct costs amounts to $1.50, he thinks the job should be taken on.

Prepare an analysis and make a recommendation. If your analysis indicates that the proposal should be rejected, prepare a response to be made to the social workers' representative.

21. The following data represent the departmental direct labor hours and indirect labor cost for a factory department for the past 12 months:

| Direct Labor Hours | Indirect Labor Cost |
|---|---|
| 14,400 ................. | $5,520 |
| 10,650 ................. | 4,140 |
| 14,100 ................. | 5,640 |
| 15,000 ................. | 6,600 |
| 13,650 ................. | 4,680 |
| 13,050 ................. | 5,100 |
| 13,350 ................. | 4,860 |
| 13,500 ................. | 4,740 |
| 13,500 ................. | 5,460 |
| 14,250 ................. | 4,800 |
| 13,200 ................. | 4,140 |
| 13,350 ................. | 4,800 |

a) Plot these data on a sheet of graph paper and draw a straight-line regression line which seems to fit the observations most closely.
b) Derive the mathematical equation that describes this line.
c) What difficulties do you foresee in trying to determine cost-volume relationships by this method? Would you use the method, despite these difficulties?

22. During 19x1, the Arapahoe Company sold 300,000 units of product and made a profit after taxes of $60,000. The variable profit per unit before taxes was $1 and the selling price was $2.50. Fixed costs were $200,000, and the income tax rate was 40 percent.

For 19x2, variable costs went up $0.10 a unit, fixed costs went up $22,000, and income taxes increased to a rate of 50 percent.

a) What was the break-even sales volume for 19x1, in dollars?
b) What will be the break-even sales dollars for 19x2 if the selling price is not changed?
c) How many units will have to be sold to make a profit after taxes of $60,000 for 19x2 if the selling price is not changed?

*d*)  By how much will the selling price have to be increased if the break-even point, in units, is to be the same in 19x2 as in 19x1?

*e*)  At what selling price would the company continue to make $60,000 net income after taxes on sales of 300,000 units?

**23.** The Davis Company produces two products and anticipates, with no changes in prices or programs from the previous year, the following relationships for costs, prices, and volume:

|  | Product A | Product B |
|---|---|---|
| Revenues........................ | $3.00 a unit | $5.00 a unit |
| Variable costs ................. | $1.50 a unit | $2.00 a unit |
| Fixed costs .................... | $45,000 | $60,000 |
| Common fixed costs ............ | $50,000 | |
| Volume........................ | 60,000 units | 40,000 units |

Several changes are being contemplated by management. You are asked to show — arithmetically and graphically — the effect on the break-even point and the effect on anticipated profits of each of the proposed changes. You should consider each proposal independently of the others.

(1)  An outlay of $20,000 for advertising which would result in anticipated volume of 50,000 units of A and 50,000 units of B. The individual who proposes this move states that "B is the high margin product — this is what we want."

(2)  A change in production methods which would increase the annual outlay for common fixed costs by $10,000 but would reduce the variable costs of product A by $0.10 a unit and the variable costs of product B by $0.15 a unit. This change would also expand the capacity of production of A from 70,000 units to 80,000 units, but the sales would not be expected to increase.

(3)  A reduction of the price of B to $4.75 which would increase the volume of B to 45,000 units. This would require a $5,000 increase in B's fixed costs. Sales volume of A would be unaffected.

(4)  An increase in wage rates for the direct labor is being considered; this increase would raise the variable costs of A by $0.10 a unit and of B by $0.15 a unit.

**24.** A company has four large presses of approximately the same capacity. Each was run at close to its full capacity during 19x8. Each machine is depreciated separately; a declining-charge method is used. Data for each press are:

|  | No. 1 | No. 2 | No. 3 | No. 4 |
|---|---|---|---|---|
| Date acquired .......... | 1/1/x0 | 1/1/x4 | 1/1/x6 | 1/1/x7 |
| Cost.................... | $100,000 | $120,000 | $145,000 | $175,000 |
| Operating costs — 19x8: |  |  |  |  |
| Labor ............... | $ 11,000 | $ 10,500 | $ 10,000 | $  9,500 |
| Maintenance ......... | 3,800 | 2,400 | 2,000 | 1,000 |
| Repairs.............. | 600 | 1,200 | 800 | 500 |
| Depreciation ........ | 3,500 | 5,400 | 7,800 | 10,800 |
| Total ............ | $ 18,900 | $ 19,500 | $ 20,600 | $ 21,800 |

It is expected that activity in 19x9 will be substantially less than in 19x8. As a result, one machine is to be put on a standby basis. It has been proposed that No. 4 should be that machine on the grounds that it has the highest operating cost. A standby machine would require neither maintenance nor repairs.

Do you agree with this proposal? Explain, citing figures from the problem.

**25.** The manager of the university print shop is trying to decide whether to meet the prices and delivery-time performance of local commercial printing shops on small printing jobs. The commercial shops quote prices that are 10 percent lower than the university shop's schedule and also offer faster delivery at no extra charge. Until now, university departments have been required to use the university shop for this sort of work, but a mounting volume of complaints has led the university controller to authorize the use of off-campus shops. The university shop will continue to do large-volume jobs and confidential work, such as examinations and research reports. The university shop would require the same amount of equipment it now has, even if it were to let small jobs go outside.

At its present operating volume of 2,000 labor hours per month, the operating costs of the university print shop are:

Paper stock ............................ Varies with nature of work
Labor ................................. $4 per labor hour
Other processing costs ................. $3 per labor hour

All labor is regarded as wholly variable with volume; other processing costs include $4,000 of fixed costs, the remainder being wholly and proportionally variable with volume, volume being measured in terms of labor hours.

Approximately 600 labor hours per month are now being spent on the work affected by the decision. Materials cost on this work is approximately $3,000 a month, and the amount now being charged by the university shop to other university departments for this work is $7,500 a month.

The shop manager is convinced that he will lose the work unless he meets both the competitive price and the competitive delivery time. To permit faster deliveries, an additional 80 hours of labor a month would be required in excess of the 600 labor hours now devoted to this work. Fixed costs would not be affected by this choice between these two alternatives.

Which alternative should the manager choose? Show your calculations.

**26.** Company X manufactures and sells more than 200 products to industrial customers. Management is now reviewing one of these, product T. Although this product seemed highly promising when it was introduced two years ago, competitive developments have cut into its market, and the marketing manager says that no one at all will be buying it three years from now. He wonders whether the company should discontinue manufacturing and selling the product right now or keep it in the line for one, two, or three years. You have been given the following estimates:

| | This Year | Next Year | Year After Next |
|---|---|---|---|
| Sales ......................... | $1,000,000 | $ 600,000 | $ 200,000 |
| Costs: | | | |
| Variable factory ............. | $  500,000 | $ 300,000 | $ 100,000 |
| Fixed factory ............... | 250,000 | 150,000 | 50,000 |
| Development ................ | 200,000 | 200,000 | 200,000 |
| Direct selling ............... | 150,000 | 120,000 | 60,000 |
| Total costs.............. | $1,100,000 | $ 770,000 | $ 410,000 |
| Product Margin............... | $ (100,000) | $(170,000) | $(210,000) |

Further investigation reveals that:

(1) The charges for fixed factory costs in the table shown above are based on predetermined burden rates. When production of this product is discontinued, $70,000 in fixed factory overheads will be eliminated each year.

(2) The company spent $1,000,000 to develop this product. This amount is being amortized over a 5-year period at $200,000 a year, and $600,000 remains unamortized today.

(3) Direct selling costs are all traceable to this product, and consist of items such as salesmen's salaries and travel expenses.

(4) Investment in working capital to support this product is negligible.

Prepare an analysis and recommend a course of action for management to take.

*27. The XYZ Company, a large textile manufacturing concern producing a number of types of textile products, sold most of its output to jobbers, manufacturers, and other purchasers of large quantities. During a period of slack business, when the plant was not operating at full capacity, the sales manager brought in two possible jobs, either of which in addition to the company's regular orders would keep the plant operating at capacity for about six weeks. Since it was not possible to accept both orders, the president asked for cost estimates on each of the jobs.

One of the two orders was from an institutional buyer for 27,000 dozen 63-inch by 108-inch sheets. The other was from a furniture manufacturer for 900,000 yards of gray goods to be used for linings. The proposed prices were $7.5095 net per dozen for the sheets and $0.225 per yard for the gray goods. Cost estimates were as follows:

Estimated Cost of Order
For 27,000 Dozen 63-Inch by 108-Inch Sheets

*Cost per Dozen*

Labor (including $0.2505 fixed labor costs) ............... $2.5045
Manufacturing overhead (including $1.0142 fixed costs)...    1.6904
Process material ........................................    0.4092
Raw material ...........................................    2.8240
Freight ................................................    0.0895
  Total Factory Cost.....................................  $7.5176
Selling and administrative expense
 (5.6% of total factory cost)* ...........................    0.4210
  Total Cost ............................................  $7.9386
Selling price..........................................    7.5095
  Loss per dozen.......................................  $0.4291
                 × 27,000 dozen
  Total Loss ..........................................  $11,586
* Assigned by type of product on basis of past experience.

Estimated Cost of Order
For 900,000 Yards of Gray Goods

*Cost per Yard*

Labor (including $0.0067 fixed labor costs) ............... $0.0681
Manufacturing overhead (including $0.0232 fixed costs)...    0.0386
Process material .......................................    0.0018
Raw material ...........................................    0.1131
  Total Factory Cost.....................................  $0.2216
Selling and administrative expense
 (6.3% of total factory cost)* ...........................    0.0140
  Total Cost ...........................................  $0.2356
Selling price..........................................    0.2250
  Loss per yard........................................  $0.0106
                ×900,000 yards
  Total Loss ..........................................  $ 9,540
* Assigned by type of product on basis of past experience.

Which order, if either, would you advise the company to accept? Why?

**28.** The Mazzini Company manufactures a number of products, three of which can be described as follows:

|  | Rinsol | Sudsit | Sansgrit |
|---|---|---|---|
| Price per case ..................... | $7.60 | $12.00 | $15.00 |
| Cost per case: |  |  |  |
|  Direct materials ................. | $3.00 | $ 3.50 | $ 6.00 |
|  Direct labor...................... | 1.00 | 1.00 | 1.50 |
|  Factory overhead ................ | 2.00 | 2.00 | 3.00 |
|  Administration ................... | .38 | .60 | .75 |
|   Total cost.................... | $6.38 | $ 7.10 | $11.25 |
| Marketing profit per case ......... | $1.22 | $ 4.90 | $ 3.75 |
| Total marketing costs.............. | $400,000 | $4,000,000 | $800,000 |
| Number of cases sold.............. | 400,000 | 1,000,000 | 200,000 |

You have the following additional information:

(1) Factory overhead is assigned to products by means of a burden rate of 200 percent of direct labor cost.

(2)  The variable portion of factory overhead cost amounts to 60 percent of direct labor cost.

(3)  Fixed factory overhead costs will remain constant for all feasible production volumes of these three products. If production of any one of them were to be discontinued entirely, however, the company could reduce its fixed factory overhead by $200,000.

(4)  Administrative costs are assigned to products at amounts equal to 5 percent of sales. Investigation shows that the variable portion of this amounts to 30 cents a case.

(5)  The marketing costs are all fixed. Discontinuation of any product would reduce the amounts shown by 75 percent.

*a)*  Using the company's methods of cost assignment, calculate net income before taxes for each of these three products.

*b)*  Judging solely from the information provided above, would you recommend that any of these three products be discontinued? Show your calculations.

*c)*  You are told further that sale of a case of Rinsol causes the company to lose the sale of three-tenths of a case of Sudsit. Sale of a case of Sansgrit, however, increases sales of Sudsit by one-tenth of a case. No other interproduct relationships can be identified. What recommendation would you make now? Show your calculations.

**29.** The Albegata Company produces four products, Alpha, Beta, Gamma, and Delta. Its income statement for the past year showed the following (in thousands of dollars):

|  | *Alpha* | *Beta* | *Gamma* | *Delta* | *Total* |
|---|---|---|---|---|---|
| Units sold ..................... | 400 | 300 | 200 | 2,000 | – |
| Sales revenues ............... | $4,000 | $3,000 | $2,000 | $1,000 | $10,000 |
| Cost of goods sold: |  |  |  |  |  |
|   Direct material.............. | $1,500 | $1,000 | $ 500 | $ 500 | $ 3,500 |
|   Direct labor ................. | 1,000 | 1,000 | 300 | 200 | 2,500 |
|   Factory overhead absorbed .. | 400 | 400 | 120 | 80 | 1,000 |
|     Total ................... | $2,900 | $2,400 | $ 920 | $ 780 | $ 7,000 |
| Gross margin................. | $1,100 | $ 600 | $1,080 | $ 220 | $ 3,000 |
| Selling expenses: |  |  |  |  |  |
|   Sales commissions .......... | $ 120 | $ 90 | $ 60 | $ 30 | $ 300 |
|   Traceable fixed costs ........ | 200 | 60 | 60 | 60 | 380 |
|   Common fixed costs ........ | 480 | 360 | 240 | 120 | 1,200 |
| Administrative expenses: |  |  |  |  |  |
|   Order processing ............ | 30 | 50 | 20 | 20 | 120 |
|   General administration...... | 320 | 240 | 160 | 80 | 800 |
|     Total operating expense . | $1,150 | $ 800 | $ 540 | $ 310 | $ 2,800 |
| Net Income (Loss) Before Tax. | $ (50) | $ (200) | $ 540 | $ (90) | $ 200 |

It is believed that no external force in the foreseeable future will alter the picture. At the board of directors' meeting, it is decided that something must be done in view of the low overall profit rate (2 percent on sales) and the net loss on all except one product line.

Upon your request, the following additional information is furnished by the company:

(1)  Sales commissions are paid to the company's salesmen at the rate of 3 percent of sales.

(2)  Order processing costs are assigned to products on the basis of the amount of time spent by office employees in recording orders, preparing invoices, and recording the amounts collected from customers. Order processing costs increase in steps, but the steps are narrow enough to justify classifying these costs as variable.

(3)  Analysis of factory overhead and fixed operating expenses:

| | Alpha | Beta | Gamma | Delta |
|---|---|---|---|---|
| Factory overhead: | | | | |
| Variable (with direct labor cost) .. | $150 | $200 | $100 | $ 60 |
| Fixed, but escapable if the line is shut down...................... | 150 | 100 | 10 | 10 |
| Fixed and inescapable if the line is shut down ................... | 100 | 100 | 10 | 10 |
| Traceable selling expense: | | | | |
| Fixed, escapable only by shutdown...................... | 180 | 60 | 50 | 60 |
| Fixed, inescapable by shutdown .. | 20 | – | 10 | – |
| Common fixed selling expense: | | | | |
| Escapable by shutdown........... | 200 | 210 | 200 | 110 |
| Inescapable by shutdown......... | 280 | 150 | 40 | 10 |
| General administrative expense: | | | | |
| Fixed, escapable only by shutdown...................... | 20 | 40 | 10 | 50 |
| Fixed, inescapable by shutdown .. | 300 | 200 | 150 | 30 |

(4)  Products Beta and Alpha share the same equipment, and this is now fully utilized. A unit of Alpha requires the same number of machine hours as a unit of Beta. For competitive reasons, the selling price of neither product can be increased. The marketing manager has no doubt that he could get enough additional orders of either of these products to utilize the equipment fully if protion of the other were to be discontinued, with no change in any marketing costs except sales commissions.

(5)  Product Delta is looked on as a loss leader, since it is feared that sales of Gamma would fall by as much as 20 percent if Delta were dropped from the company's line. Alpha and Beta, on the other hand, are sold to other types of buyers, and their sales would not be affected.

*a)*  Give recommendations when only the additional information in (1), (2), and (3) is known. (All recommendations must be supported by computations showing estimated improvement in profits.)

*b)*  Give recommendations when only the additional information in (1), (2), (3), and (4) is known.

*c)*  Give recommendations when all of the above information is known.

# 21

# REFINEMENTS IN OVERHEAD COSTING

COSTING SYSTEMS ORDINARILY must be considerably more detailed than the Pyle Company's system described in Chapter 19. Some of the additional detail is necessary to provide cost information that can be used in the preparation of estimates of incremental costs; the rest is required to help management control its operating costs.

The purpose of this chapter is to examine some of the refinements in overhead costing that are often used to produce better information for managerial planning. Specifically, we shall deal with three main topics: (1) the departmentalization of costs and the development of departmental burden rates; (2) the development of burden rates based on variable factory overhead costs only; and (3) the relevance of data on fixed factory overheads to catalog pricing decisions.

## DEPARTMENTALIZATION OF COSTS

In preparing budgets and in developing cost estimates for other purposes, management needs to know more about the structure of its factory overhead costs than the burden rate can reveal. To provide for this, the accountant almost always classifies overhead costs in two ways—by organization unit and by descriptive element.

### Organizational Classification

From an accounting viewpoint, the factory can be regarded as a group of interrelated *cost centers*, each relatively homogeneous

in structure and activity. A cost center may be an entire department or part of one. For example, if a factory department en-
compasses both machine-paced and manual operations, the
accountant may well break the department into two separate cost
centers for accounting purposes, each with its own set of accounts.

### Descriptive Classification

For management purposes, the data in each account should be
*homogeneous*. This means that all of the costs assigned to a particular account should exhibit similar patterns of response to the
various determinants of cost behavior.

To provide data of greater homogeneity, each cost center's
costs are typically classified by "natural elements" such as
salaries, supplies, power costs, and so on. This gives the chart of
accounts its second dimension: when a cost is incurred, it must
be classified both by cost center and by the nature of the goods or
services consumed.

Even with this two-way classification, the data contained in
any one account are unlikely to be completely homogeneous. For
one thing, perfect homogeneity is probably unattainable. Costs
are determined by the interaction of a myriad of forces, most of
them either unknown or imperfectly understood. Since the company's knowledge of cost behavior is imperfect, its ability to
classify costs on a behavioral basis is also limited. Second, more
accounts mean higher clerical and storage costs, slower access
time, and added opportunities for error, and at some point any
further trade-off of cost for homogeneity becomes unprofitable.

As a result, management must compromise. It must try to predict which classifications will prove most useful in the future
and most difficult to apply later if they are not applied to the data
now. On these grounds, it is likely that the cost of the outside
consulting services used by a division would be recorded separately from, say, the costs of manufactured parts that have been
purchased from outside subcontractors. It would be most unusual, however, to use separate office supplies accounts for each
of the company's suppliers of this kind of goods. The determinants of office supplies costs are unlikely to be very different from
supplier to supplier and the chance that separate cost information *might* some day be useful to management is likely to be far
too small to justify the added effort required to record the data
separately.

## Departmental Burden Rates

The departmentalization of costs is often carried one step farther, to the development of a separate burden rate for each cost center or each department. For ease of expression we shall refer to these as departmental burden rates, even though the department may be subdivided into two or more cost centers, each with its own burden rate.

Accountants use departmental burden rates to produce more accurate product costs. Different products take different routes through the factory. Some may require only assembly work where overhead costs are relatively low, while others require extensive work in the machine room, where overhead costs are high. The use of a single, factory-wide burden rate in these circumstances would assign some of the machine room overhead to the products of the assembly department. To avoid this, departmental burden rates are used.

For example, the budgeted average overhead cost in the Lion Corporation's three factory production departments was $6 a direct labor hour in 19x1. Behind this average, however, lay a great deal of diversity. Exhibit 21–1 lists the budgeted overhead costs at normal volume for each of these three departments. It shows average overhead costs of $8 an hour in department A, $4 in department B, and $12 in department C.

To illustrate the significance of these variations, let us suppose that two of the products manufactured in this factory require 5 hours of direct labor for each unit. Product X is produced entirely in department B; product Y is manufactured in department C.

A factory-wide burden rate would assign an overhead cost of

### Exhibit 21–1

Lion Corporation

**BUDGETED MONTHLY FACTORY OVERHEAD COSTS AT NORMAL VOLUME**
For the Year 19x1

| Type of Cost | Department | | | Plant Total |
| --- | --- | --- | --- | --- |
| | A | B | C | |
| Indirect labor.................. | $ 7,000 | $15,000 | $ 6,000 | $28,000 |
| Indirect materials ............. | 3,000 | 8,000 | 2,000 | 13,000 |
| Depreciation.................... | 5,000 | 6,000 | 5,000 | 16,000 |
| Power.......................... | 3,000 | 2,000 | 4,000 | 9,000 |
| Other costs..................... | 14,000 | 9,000 | 7,000 | 30,000 |
| Total ..................... | $32,000 | $40,000 | $24,000 | $96,000 |
| Direct labor hours .............. | 4,000 | 10,000 | 2,000 | 16,000 |
| Burden rate per hour ........... | $8 | $4 | $12 | $6 |

$6 x 5 = $30 to each of these products. Using departmental rates, however, product X would be assigned a cost of $4 x 5 = $20, while the overhead cost of a unit of product Y would be $12 x 5 = $60. This is a substantial difference.

## The Importance of Accuracy

Accuracy is important not for its own sake but for its impact on the user of accounting data. Automobile manufacturers, for example, make exhaustive analyses of the costs of manufacturing component parts. Each automobile model is aimed at a particular segment of the market and its price must fall in a narrow range appropriate to that market. If the estimated manufacturing cost is too high to leave an adequate profit margin in that price range, management must either find ways to reduce costs, move to an outside source of supply, or redesign the automobile. Cost estimates for this purpose should reflect the costs of the specific resources to be used, not some broad factory average.

The importance of accuracy and the relevance of product cost data to decisions of this kind are questions of major consequence that cannot be answered easily. Before going into these questions in greater depth, however, we must examine two other matters: (1) the structural changes that departmentalization of the burden rate imposes on the accounting system; and (2) the use of burden rates that exclude fixed overhead costs.

## INTERDEPARTMENTAL COST ALLOCATIONS

Some of the costs of operating the factory are not specifically traceable to the production departments in which the products are actually manufactured. Depreciation on the factory building is one example; the plant manager's salary is another.

Each of these costs can be traced unequivocably to some cost center. The plant manager's salary, for example, can be traced to the factory's administrative office. This is not enough for product costing, however. These cost centers are *service* centers, not production centers. They do not engage directly in production; instead, they contribute to the plant's output by providing services that facilitate the activities of the producing departments. Hence, before the output of a producing department is charged with overhead costs, the department's burden rate is ordinarily expanded to include a provision for the cost of the services provided to it by the service departments. This process is known as *cost allocation* or *cost redistribution*.

## The Allocation Process

Returning to our illustration, we find that the Lion Corporation's factory had three service departments—factory management, building services, and equipment maintenance—as well as the three production departments. The budgeted monthly costs of these three departments were as follows:

|  | Factory Management | Building Service | Equipment Maintenance |
|---|---|---|---|
| Wages and salaries............. | $4,800 | $1,300 | $8,400 |
| Supplies....................... | 200 | 200 | 500 |
| Depreciation .................. | 50 | 1,200 | 200 |
| Power......................... | ... | 400 | 200 |
| Property taxes................. | ... | 700 | ... |
| Other costs................... | 950 | 200 | 300 |
| Total................... | $6,000 | $4,000 | $9,600 |

The accountant's task was to find a way of allocating these costs among the three production departments so that the allocations would most closely approximate the amount of service department cost attributable to each production department.

Allocations in this case were based on the statistics given in Exhibit 21–2. To begin with, the accountants distributed the expected factory management costs among the three production

### Exhibit 21–2

### Lion Corporation

#### ESTIMATES USED IN DISTRIBUTING ESTIMATED SERVICE DEPARTMENT COSTS FOR BURDEN RATE DETERMINATION

| Department | Number of Employees | Floor Space Occupied (Square Feet) | Number of Equipment Maintenance Labor Hours to Be Used Each Month |
|---|---|---|---|
| Department A..................... | 36 | 24,000 | 450 |
| Department B..................... | 81 | 36,000 | 350 |
| Department C..................... | 18 | 20,000 | 400 |
| Subtotal .................... | 135 | 80,000 | 1,200 |
| Factory management ............. | 4 | 2,000 | ... |
| Building service ................. | 2 | 1,000 | 50 |
| Equipment maintenance.......... | 10 | 3,000 | ... |
| Total.................... | 151 | 86,000 | 1,250 |

departments in proportion to the total number of employees (direct and indirect) in those departments. This produced the following:

| Department | (1) Number of Employees | (2) Fraction of Production Employees | (3) Allocation of Factory Management Cost (2)× $6,000 |
|---|---|---|---|
| Department A............. | 36 | 4/15 | $1,600 |
| Department B............. | 81 | 9/15 | 3,600 |
| Department C............. | 18 | 2/15 | 800 |
| Total................. | 135 | | $6,000 |

The justification for using the number of employees as the allocation basis was that this was judged to be the major determinant of the size of the factory management department.

Next, building services costs were allocated among the producing departments on the basis of relative floor space occupied:

| Department | (1) Floor Space Occupied (Square Feet) | (2) Percent of Floor Space Occupied | (3) Allocation of Building Service Cost (2) × $4,000 |
|---|---|---|---|
| Department A............... | 24,000 | 30% | $1,200 |
| Department B............... | 36,000 | 45 | 1,800 |
| Department C............... | 20,000 | 25 | 1,000 |
| Total................. | 80,000 | 100% | $4,000 |

Once again, the assumption was that the cost of providing building service was closely related to the amount of floor space occupied.

Finally, budgeted equipment maintenance costs were allocated in proportion to each department's estimated consumption of maintenance department services. The maintenance department's budgeted cost amounted to $9,600 a month. Spreading this over the 1,200 hours of maintenance services to be provided to the three producing departments during an average month gave a budgeted cost rate of $8 per maintenance hour. Using this rate, the budgeted allocation was:

| Department | Estimated Number of Maintenance Hours Used | Allocation of Maintenance Service Costs at $8 per Maintenance Hour |
|---|---|---|
| Department A....... | 450 | $3,600 |
| Department B....... | 350 | 2,800 |
| Department C....... | 400 | 3,200 |
| Total.......... | 1,200 | $9,600 |

After all these allocations were made, the estimated costs of the three producing departments were as shown in the last three columns of Exhibit 21–3. The burden rates shown at the bottom of these columns are larger than the burden rates in Exhibit 21–1 because they include provision for all factory costs, not just those that were directly traceable to the production departments. The service departments had no burden rates because no production work was done there.

More complex allocation procedures are likely to be used in

Exhibit 21–3

Lion Corporation

FACTORY OVERHEAD COST ALLOCATION FOR 19x1

| | Factory Management | Building Service | Equipment Maintenance | Producing Department | | |
|---|---|---|---|---|---|---|
| | | | | A | B | C |
| Indirect labor....... | $4,800 | $1,300 | $8,400 | $ 7,000 | $15,000 | $ 6,000 |
| Indirect materials .. | 200 | 200 | 500 | 3,000 | 8,000 | 2,000 |
| Depreciation........ | 50 | 1,200 | 200 | 5,000 | 6,000 | 5,000 |
| Power.............. | ... | 400 | 200 | 3,000 | 2,000 | 4,000 |
| Property taxes...... | ... | 700 | ... | ... | ... | ... |
| Other costs......... | 950 | 200 | 300 | 14,000 | 9,000 | 7,000 |
| Total Traceable. | $6,000 | $4,000 | $9,600 | $32,000 | $40,000 | $24,000 |
| Allocated charges: | | | | | | |
| Factory management........... | (6,000) | ... | ... | 1,600 | 3,600 | 800 |
| Building service.. | ... | (4,000) | ... | 1,200 | 1,800 | 1,000 |
| Equipment maintenance ........ | ... | ... | (9,600) | 3,600 | 2,800 | 3,200 |
| Total Budgeted Cost.......... | ... | ... | ... | $38,400 | $48,200 | $29,000 |
| Direct labor hours .. | | | | 4,000 | 10,000 | 2,000 |
| Burden rate (per direct labor hour.)..... | | | | $9.60 | $4.82 | $14.50 |

practice. The objective in all cases is the same, however—to try to make each production department's burden rate represent the costs attributable to that department's operations.

### Relevance of Allocations to Managerial Decisions

The idea behind interdepartmental cost allocations is to produce burden rates that more accurately represent the factory overhead costs attributable to the operations of individual direct production departments. That is, the amount of service department cost allocated to a production department should measure the amount of cost that would not have been incurred if the factory had never included that production department.

This has both a short-term and a long-term meaning. From a short-term point of view, the allocation to any production center should measure the amount of service department cost that could be avoided if the production center were to keep its existing capacity idle. A long-term allocation should indicate the amount of service department cost that could be avoided if the production center were to be eliminated entirely and the service department's capacity reduced accordingly.

The first of these quantities consists mostly of the short-term variable costs of operating the service center; the longer-term figure includes an allocation of the fixed costs of providing service department capacity. In other words, variable costs should be allocated to the departments requiring current service activity, while service department fixed costs should be allocated to the departments which create the need for capacity.

Valid allocation bases reflecting these concepts are hard to find. The result is that allocations are often at least partly arbitrary, thereby reducing their relevance to managerial decisions. Allocations of plant management salaries among production departments on the basis of the relative amounts of time spent in them, for example, do not measure the amounts by which plant management salaries could be reduced if the various departments were to be eliminated. For most purposes it would be better not to allocate at all than to use an arbitrary allocation base such as this.

## VARIABLE COSTING

It should be clear by now that unit costs produced by the methods described so far will seldom equal incremental costs. They are particularly inappropriate when management's decisions have such a short time horizon and such narrow scope that the only incremental costs are the short-run variable costs of utilizing existing production capacity.

To provide unit costs that are more directly useful in such situations and to introduce more flexibility into the cost files generally, many companies calculate product cost on a *direct costing* or *variable costing* basis. Variable costing is a device to permit the segregation of the variable component of manufacturing costs in product cost records and subsequently in internal profit performance reports. *Under variable costing, unit cost is defined as the average variable cost* of manufacturing the product. Fixed manufacturing costs are excluded from product cost completely.

## Application to Job Order Costing

Variable costing differs from full costing in job order costing only in the treatment of factory overhead. Direct labor and direct materials are typically assumed to be fully variable with volume and therefore are assigned to product units in the manner described in Chapter 19. Factory overhead is then included in product cost by means of burden rates that cover only the variable components of the overhead cost elements.

For example, suppose that an analysis of the overhead costs in the Lion Corporation's department C has provided the following formulas:

|  | Fixed Cost per Month | Variable Cost per Direct Labor Hour |
|---|---|---|
| Indirect labor ........................ | $ 4,000 | $1.00 |
| Indirect materials.................... | 500 | .75 |
| Depreciation ......................... | 5,000 | ... |
| Power................................ | ... | 2.00 |
| Other direct departmental costs...... | 3,500 | 1.75 |
| Allocated costs: |  |  |
|     Factory management .............. | 1,200 | ... |
|     Building services.................. | 1,000 | ... |
|     Equipment maintenance........... | 600 | .10 |
|     Total........................ | $15,800 | $5.60 |

In this case the burden rate would be $5.60 a labor hour. A job order requiring 10 labor hours in this department would be charged $56 (10 hours × $5.60) for variable overhead, and no charge would be made for any portion of the $15,800 in a fixed cost.

Both indirect labor and equipment maintenance costs in this case are semivariable. Indirect labor, for example, has a minimum monthly expenditure of $4,000 plus increments of $1.00 a labor hour in response to the use of the department's facilities. The variable and fixed components cannot be recorded separately because the accountant has no way of labeling a particular indirect labor expenditure as fixed or variable at the time it is made. Fortunately, this is no barrier to variable costing. Since the burden rate is predetermined, the only requirement is that a *rate of variability* can be determined for each cost element.

## Variable Costing for Easier Cost Estimation

The main argument for variable costing is that it provides a clearer, more versatile set of data on which to build estimates of incremental costs. For example, suppose that department C in the Lion Corporation's factory is now using 1,500 direct labor hours a month. Of this, 300 hours are devoted to the manufacture of product Y, with an output of 30 units a month.

The company's management is considering a proposal to market this product in the European Economic Community, with an estimated sales volume of 20 units a month in the first year. This would require about 200 additional direct labor hours a month in department C, an increment clearly within existing capacity limits.

Using the burden rates that we developed earlier, the accountant would come up with either of the following overhead cost estimates:

$$\text{Full costing: 200 hours} \times \$12 \quad = \$2,400$$
$$\text{Variable costing: 200 hours} \times \$5.60 = \$1,120$$

It should be obvious that variable costing gives a more relevant cost estimate if fixed costs are not expected to be affected by the decision on this proposal. But what if the addition of 200 direct labor hours would require increases in fixed costs as well as increases in variable costs? Neither average full cost nor average variable cost measures the increment in this case, but the increase is likely to be estimated more readily from variable costing figures than from unit costs derived on a full costing basis.

To illustrate, suppose that this change would increase the fixed component of indirect labor cost by $1,000 a month. The

estimate of incremental factory overhead cost then would be:
$$\$1,000 + 200 \times \$5.60 = \$2,120.$$
To arrive at the same figure with full cost as the starting point would be much more awkward.

Variable costing also makes it easier to give management a clear view of the effect of changes in volume on the company's profits. Suppose, for example, that product Y has direct materials costs of $80, direct labor costs of $50, and no variable selling and administrative costs at all. It would be sold to a European licensee for $300 a unit, and the licensee would pay all freight, duty, and marketing costs. The *variable profit* from the production and sale of additional units of product Y would be $114 a unit:

| | | |
|---|---|---:|
| Selling price...................................... | | $300 |
| Less variable costs: | | |
| Direct materials................................ | $80 | |
| Direct labor ................................... | 50 | |
| Overhead (10 hours × $5.60)..................... | 56 | 186 |
| Variable Profit.................................. | | $114 |

In evaluating this proposal, management is interested in estimating the sensitivity of profit to variations in sales volume. Using the variable profit figures, it is a simple matter to prepare incremental profit estimates for three different volume levels:

| | *10 units* | *20 units* | *30 units* |
|---|---:|---:|---:|
| Sales ($300)............................. | $3,000 | $6,000 | $9,000 |
| Less: Variable costs ($186)............. | 1,860 | 3,720 | 5,580 |
| Variable profit ($114) ................... | $1,140 | $2,280 | $3,420 |
| Less: incremental fixed cost........... | 1,000 | 1,000 | 1,000 |
| Incremental Profit ..................... | $ 140 | $1,280 | $2,420 |

## Average Cost versus Incremental Cost

These arguments for variable costing should not be misinterpreted. The unit costs produced by job order costing are average costs, no matter whether variable costing or full costing is used. These averages are general-purpose figures, and should not be used as direct measures of incremental cost without careful analysis.

For example, suppose that the $50 estimate for direct labor costs applies only to a total production volume of 30 units a month. Expansion of volume by an additional 20 units would reduce average direct labor cost to $45. An unwary analyst might possibly be trapped into using the new average to calculate incremental cost: $20 \times \$45 = \$900$. In fact, the calculation should be:

Total direct labor cost at 50 units a month: $50 \times \$45 = \$2,250$
Total direct labor cost at 30 units a month: $30 \times \$50 = \underline{\phantom{00}1,500}$
Incremental Direct Labor Cost of 20 Additional Units $\underline{\$\phantom{00}750}$

Incremental direct labor cost, in other words, is expected to average $37.50 for each additional unit.

## THE RELEVANCE OF FIXED COST: CATALOG PRICING DECISIONS

Variable costing has been developed to meet management's needs for data relevant to decisions with a short-term impact. For example, we saw in Chapter 20 how variable cost data might be used in pricing additional business during slack periods. Many decisions have a longer time horizon or a larger scope, however, entailing at least some increments in the fixed costs. For some of these, it has been suggested that average full cost rather than average variable cost should be used to approximate average incremental cost. The idea is that given a large enough change in volume and enough time to adjust to the new situation, total cost will vary in direct proportion to changes in operating volumes and average cost will remain constant. The purpose of this section is to examine the validity of this proposition in the context of a pricing decision.

### Catalog Pricing

Many pricing decisions apply not to a single order but to a substantial number of customer orders or inquiries during a period of many months. For want of a better term, we shall refer to these as catalog pricing decisions.

An economist would say that the best approach to catalog pricing is to estimate the effect of price on volume and the effect of volume on cost, selecting the price that seems likely to produce the greatest spread between total revenue and total cost. For example, suppose that a company estimates the following price-volume relationship:

| Price | Units Sold | Revenue |
|-------|-----------|---------|
| $1.25......... | 10,000 | $12,500 |
| 1.50......... | 8,000 | 12,000 |
| 1.75......... | 6,000 | 10,500 |

Estimated costs, including production, selling, and administrative costs, are as follows:

| Units Sold | Total Cost |
|-----------|-----------|
| 10,000......... | $10,000 |
| 8,000......... | 9,000 |
| 6,000......... | 8,000 |

Putting these two sets of estimates together yields the following profit estimates:

| Price | Units Sold | Revenue | Cost | Profit |
|-------|-----------|---------|------|--------|
| $1.25......... | 10,000 | $12,500 | $10,000 | $2,500 |
| 1.50......... | 8,000 | 12,000 | 9,000 | 3,000 |
| 1.75......... | 6,000 | 10,500 | 8,000 | 2,500 |

The optimal price in this case is $1.50.

Price-volume relationships unfortunately are very difficult to identify or predict. Without this information, management is likely to use cost figures alone, at least to calculate what it considers to be a normal price. The normal price is determined by adding to cost a standard, predetermined percentage mark-up. The actual price charged may differ from the normal price for different items in the product line because of demand and other considerations, but the starting point is cost.

This approach is called cost-based formula pricing. The issue that we shall consider in the next few pages is whether the cost figures underlying formula prices should be defined as full factory cost, variable cost, or some other figure.

### The Case for Full Cost

No business can report a net income if the prices of its products do not cover the costs of developing, manufacturing, and selling them, together with the costs of administering and financing the company. If the price of every product covers its share of the company's costs, with at least a little left over, the company will report a profit. A pricing formula that adds a mark-up to full cost therefore would seem to guarantee profitable operations.

Unfortunately, this is not the case. The flaw in this argument is that it fails to recognize the impact of variations in sales volume. Every product may be selling at a price that covers its assigned share of estimated company overheads at normal volume, but actual volume may be so low that the company reports a net loss overall. At low volumes fixed costs must be spread over a smaller number of units, thereby increasing average fixed cost. If the volume reduction is serious enough, price will be less than average actual cost even though it is greater than average estimated cost. Higher prices to cover the higher unit costs are likely to be self-defeating, in that they may cause an even greater reduction in volume. Cost-plus pricing, in other words, is not a sure road to profitability.

A more reasonable case for using full cost in pricing formulas is that cost-based prices may promote price stability in the industry. Without adequate cost records, the businessman is likely to set prices on the basis of off-the-cuff estimates of labor and materials costs, adding a percentage mark-up to cover overhead costs and produce a profit. This procedure is likely to yield satisfactory profits so long as sales volume is high and market conditions are favorable. Given a business recession or overexpansion in the industry, however, an excess of productive capacity is likely to develop, and additional business at any price in excess of direct costs may be looked on as immediately profitable. Under such conditions, competition has been seen to reduce prices to levels but little above the costs of the most efficient producers in the industry and substantially below those of many other firms.

In this situation, better cost information is looked upon as one of the requirements for restoring a healthy state of industry affairs. Better cost information, in this context, is assumed to require burden rates that cover both variable and fixed factory overhead costs—that is, so-called full-cost systems. In some cases, the formulas include average selling and administrative overheads as well as factory overheads, and may even include implicit interest on the investment in product-related facilities and working capital.

The members of the industry are likely to be persuaded that these new cost collection and allocation methods result in "scientifically" determined product costs and, most important, that selling below the figures thus established is not only underhanded but also unprofitable. If enough companies come around to this point of view, costing systems are likely to become relatively uniform throughout the industry, the resulting data will be widely used in pricing, and emphasis will gradually shift from price to other forms of competition such as quality and service. The full-cost burden rates are given a good deal of credit for this new price stability.

Some accountants are devoted to full cost for more general reasons. Production and sales people often have a tendency to be highly volume conscious, sometimes to the extent of indiscriminately sacrificing price for volume. To counteract this bias, some accountants maintain that the full cost of a product is the only figure which should be admitted for management consideration. These accountants fear that acknowledging to operating people the validity of variable cost as a basis for pricing is to invite their cutting prices to this level in the quest for volume. They argue further that costs which are fixed in the short run have a remarkable tendency to become variable with the passage of time. While a plant manager's salary is not a function of production, it may nevertheless be raised as the scale of plant operations increases.

Another argument for full-cost data is that they may help management identify a price that will not be unduly attractive to potential customers. In other words, cost data may help management forecast what sacrifices competitors are making or would have to make to manufacture a similar product, and thereby provide management with a means of estimating a competitive price level. The fact that the manufacture of a particular product requires large amounts of fixed costs may not be relevant in all pricing situations, but it cannot fail to be relevant in some.

## Flexible Solutions

Not even the most hardened advocate of full cost as a basis for pricing would claim that average full cost is the appropriate basis for all managerial decisions or even for all pricing decisions. Full cost may approximate incremental cost in some cases but may be far wide of the mark in others.

To provide management with a more useful data base for decisions, the accountant can design the system to produce "full cost" figures that represent the average cost required for each particular product, including both variable cost and an allowance for the fixed costs attributable to that product. These figures can be subcoded into fixed and variable components, so that variable cost figures can be used when they seem more relevant.[1]

In designing systems of this sort, the accountant should make an effort to see that the allowance for fixed costs measures what it is supposed to measure. Full cost is supposed to measure all of the resources necessary to manufacture the product — that is, the long-run incremental manufacturing cost. The reason it does not do so in many cases is that some of the fixed costs are highly indivisible — that is, the resources they represent are available in large aggregates only. For example, an operation may require a full team of workers no matter how large or small a volume they are called upon to process. In such cases, even total abandonment of major products may lead to no cost reductions; average full cost will overstate the amount of cost that is really attributable to the presence of specific products in the line.

A similar problem is that the service department costs included in the burden rates are very unlikely to measure the amounts of service department cost that are attributable to the production of the product. The problem again is indivisibility of fixed costs. Some service department costs are likely to be highly indivisible, and production department usage of service department services is also likely to be less than perfectly divisible. For example, a production center that consists of a single large machine may need a fixed amount of maintenance time, even if the machine is not used at all. None of the costs of this time can be said to result from any one specific use of this machine. Full cost burden rates that include allocations of these costs are therefore likely to be poor measures of the incremental factory overhead cost that can be associated with the production and sale of a given product.[2]

## THE COSTS OF JOINT PRODUCTS

Overhead costing is difficult in the first instance because overhead costs are *common costs* — that is, they cannot be traced clearly to any one product but are common to all of the products

---

[1] Variable costing is not used for external financial reporting. Companies that use variable costing to provide information to management must include a portion of the fixed factory overheads in supplementary inventory accounts for use in the preparation of company financial statements.

[2] For more discussion on the basis on which fixed costs should be included in product cost for this purpose, see Gordon Shillinglaw, *Cost Accounting: Analysis and Control* (3rd ed.; Homewood, Ill.: Richard D. Irwin, Inc., 1972), Chapters 9 and 10.

manufactured in a particular set of facilities. Common costs are also encountered in another situation, in which the processing of a single raw material or set of materials yields two or more different products simultaneously. The outputs of such processes are known as *joint products* and their costs are known as *joint costs.*

A full explanation of joint product costing would require more space than we are able to give it here, but the basic problem can be sketched rather quickly. Joint costs can be traced to the joint process but not to the individual products that emerge from it. The labor cost of slaughtering a hog is a cost both of the hams and of the pigskin gloves that eventually emerge from production.

Accountants usually divide joint costs among the joint products in proportion to their relative values. Various methods have been developed to implement this idea, but none of them measures each product's share of the joint cost as the amount that could be saved if that one joint product were not produced. Since *all* joint costs are necessary to produce *each* joint product, the amount of the joint cost specifically incurred to get any one of them is zero.

The costing formulas used by accountants to distribute joint costs provide measures of inventory cost that are adequate for overall financial reporting. They are useless for decision making, however. As an example, suppose a process yields two joint products, A and B. The output of joint product A is worth twice as much as the output of product B. If joint cost amounts to $30,000 a month, then $20,000 will be assigned to product A and $10,000 will go to product B. If the output of product B consists of 1,000 units a month, then its unit cost will be $10.

This figure is quite meaningless if management wishes to decide whether to accept an offer for some of its inventories of product B or whether to subject it to further processing. For these purposes only its present opportunity cost (presumably equal to its current market value) is relevant. In other words, if management decides to process some of its output into a more highly refined form, the true cost of this action is the amount of revenue that the company will forgo by not selling product B as it stands.

Meaningful allocations of joint costs sometimes can be made if the relative proportions of the various outputs can be altered by varying the quality or mix of the joint inputs. Returning to our example, we find that the total yield of product B can be increased from 1,000 to 1,100 units a month by buying raw materials of a higher quality. Output of product A will remain unchanged. If the change increases total joint cost from $30,000 to $30,800, then product B can be said to have an incremental cost of $8 a unit. This $8 figure can be used in the analysis of proposals to use small amounts of product B as component parts of other products and in other similar decisions.

The analysis of joint cost is far more complex than this simple illustration would imply. Our main purpose in introducing it at this point is to indicate that the common cost phenomenon is not limited to factory overhead. In the extreme case, in which the common costs are joint costs, incurred specifically to yield two or more products simultaneously and in fixed proportions, no allocation method will provide usable approximations of incremental product cost.

## SUMMARY

Most accounting systems provide for a two-way classification of costs: by organization unit and by descriptive element. Departmentalization of factory overhead costs is often accompanied by departmentalization of the burden rate — that is, each department or cost center is given its own rate, used for assigning overhead costs to the work done within its borders. This requires the allocation of the costs of service departments to the various direct production departments. Development of meaningful allocation bases is difficult, however, and these cost allocations are often not very useful in the estimation of incremental costs.

To provide more useful data for incremental cost estimation, accountants have developed a system of factory overhead costing known as variable costing or direct costing, in which only variable costs are assigned to products. Although incremental cost with respect to a particular decision may not be equal to either variable cost or full cost, it is easier to move from variable cost to incremental cost than to take full cost figures and convert them into estimates of incremental cost. Furthermore, estimates of short-run variability often can be taken directly from a variable costing data bank, whereas special studies are necessary to obtain these data if full costing is used.

An even more difficult problem arises when the direct materials and direct labor in a given process are the joint costs of two or more products. In such cases incremental costs for individual products are difficult and sometimes impossible to estimate, and the analyst must work directly with estimates of opportunity cost.

## QUESTIONS AND PROBLEMS

**1.** Why are departmental burden rates usually thought to be superior to a single plantwide burden rate?

**2.** "Departmental burden rates give an illusion of accuracy that an understanding of cost behavior and overhead allocation methods would soon serve to dispel." To what extent do you agree or disagree with this statement? Explain.

**3.** What is the distinction between a service center and a production center? Why are the costs of one usually reassigned to the other for inclusion in burden rates?

**4.** What does accuracy mean in product costing? How would you decide whether one system produced costs that were more accurate than those generated by another?

**5.** What is variable costing? How does it differ from full costing?

**6.** In the interests of accuracy, an accountant might prefer to use one index (say, direct labor hours) as a base for the burden rate for variable costs and another (say, machine hours) for the burden rate for fixed factory cost. Would this be advisable?

**7.** Why is the product cost information obtained by allocating joint product costs according to the relative market values of the joint products irrelevant for pricing decisions? Is it relevant for other decisions?

**8.** Why might a company choose to use pricing formulas in which the desired price is obtained by adding a predetermined mark-up to estimated full cost?

**9.** What criterion or criteria would you use in selecting a method of allocating budgeted service center costs to production centers for burden rate determination? Explain how you would apply any of these criteria.

**10.** Suggest bases that might be appropriate for distributing the costs of the following service departments and in each case give the reasons for your choice:
- (1) Plant management.
- (2) Building ownership and maintenance.
- (3) Receiving and storeroom.
- (4) Personnel and payroll.
- (5) Power plant.
- (6) Machinery maintenance.
- (7) Production planning.
- (8) Plant safety and medical care.

11. The Baton Company manufactures precision plastic molded products for the electrical and other industries. On occasion, a batch of products does not come up to standards and is scrapped. The production manager has complained that the present practice of including the cost of the defective material in a job's costs is misleading. He argues that the labor and material cost of defective work should be charged to an overhead account and spread over all jobs through the burden rate. Discuss.

12. A company's power department provides power to four factory departments. Power consumption is measured indirectly by the number of horsepower hours used in each department. Consumption data are shown in the following schedule:

### SCHEDULE OF HORSEPOWER HOURS

|  | Producing Departments | | Service Departments | |
|---|---|---|---|---|
|  | A | B | X | Y |
| Needed at capacity production | 10,000 | 20,000 | 12,000 | 8,000 |
| Used during an average month | 8,000 | 13,000 | 7,000 | 6,000 |

The cost of operating the power department was expected to total $2,000 + $0.20 per horsepower hour.

The company wishes to establish burden rates for the two producing departments, both on a full costing and on a variable costing basis. What dollar amounts of power department costs should be included in the budget of each producing and service department? Give reasons for your answer. Indicate why you either did or did not allocate power department costs to the two service departments.

*13. The Robertson Company has been using a single burden rate for its entire factory. An alternative has been proposed: departmental overhead rates. You are given the following information:

(1) Three products (A, B, C) are produced in three departments (1, 2, 3).

(2) Labor hours required for a unit of each product are:

|  | Department | | | Total |
|---|---|---|---|---|
|  | 1 | 2 | 3 |  |
| Product A | 2 | 1 | 1 | 4 |
| Product B | 0 | 2 | 2 | 4 |
| Product C | 2 | 3 | 3 | 8 |

---

* Solutions to problems marked with an asterisk (*) are found in Appendix B.

(3) Products produced in a normal year: A—40,000 units; B—40,000 units; and C—10,000 units.

(4) Overhead incurred in a normal year: department 1—$400,000; department 2—$300,000; and department 3—$100,000.

Should the company use a plantwide or departmental burden rates? Why? (In either case, the burden rate would be based on direct labor hours.)

*14. Department S has the following estimated monthly cost at its normal volume of 1,400 service hours:

| | |
|---|---|
| Service labor | $4,000 |
| Supervision | 700 |
| Supplies | 300 |
| Depreciation | 1,750 |
| Other costs | 250 |
| Total | $7,000 |

All of these except supervision and depreciation are proportionately variable with volume. Supervision and depreciation are fixed.

Departments 1 and 2 use 200 department S hours and 300 department S hours, respectively, in a typical month. Department 1's production volume is measured in direct labor hours, with a normal volume of 10,000 direct labor hours a month. Department 2's output is measured in pounds of product, with a normal volume of 30,000 pounds a month.

A unit of product X weighs 10 pounds and requires 5 direct labor hours in department 1. How much department S cost should be included in the cost of a unit of product X on a full-cost basis and on a variable-cost basis?

15. A company has three production departments, each with its own full-cost burden rate:

| | |
|---|---|
| Department A | $2 per pound of materials |
| Department B | $3 per machine-hour |
| Department C | $4 per direct labor hour |

You are told that at normal volume variable costs account for 40 percent of the overhead cost in department A, 30 percent of the overhead cost in department B, and 60 percent of the overhead cost in department C.

A job lot of 1,000 units of product X was manufactured in April. This job used 2,000 pounds of materials (in department A), 400 machine-hours in department B, and 200 direct labor hours in department C.

a) Calculate the overhead cost of this job lot on a full-costing basis.
b) Calculate the overhead cost of this job lot on a variable costing basis.
c) What do you do with the costs that are included in (a) but excluded in (b)?

*16. The total cost of processing 100,000 barrels of crude petroleum — including raw material, labor, and overhead — is $828,000. Expected yields and market values of products are as shown below. Compute unit product costs for inventory costing purposes.

| Product | Barrel Yield | Estimated Market Values | |
|---|---|---|---|
| | | Per Barrel | Total |
| Aviation gasoline . . . . . . . . . . . . . | 8,000 | $12.50 | $100,000 |
| Motor gasoline . . . . . . . . . . . . . . . | 42,000 | 10.00 | 420,000 |
| Kerosene . . . . . . . . . . . . . . . . . . . . | 10,000 | 8.80 | 88,000 |
| Distillate fuels . . . . . . . . . . . . . . . | 20,000 | 8.00 | 160,000 |
| Lubricants . . . . . . . . . . . . . . . . . . . | 5,000 | 20.00 | 100,000 |
| Residual fuels . . . . . . . . . . . . . . . | 10,000 | 5.20 | 52,000 |
| Gases and loss . . . . . . . . . . . . . . . | 5,000 | — | — |
| Total . . . . . . . . . . . . . . . . . . | 100,000 | | $920,000 |

17. The Rancid City Meat Packing Company sells 5,000 pounds of low-grade beef scraps a week, at a price of 10 cents a pound. By the company's costing method, the cost of these meat scraps has been calculated to be 9 cents a pound.

Rancid City's marketing vice president has just made a proposal to mix the beef scraps with grain, cook them, and pack the resulting mixture in cans under the private brand of a large regional chain of supermarkets. The mixture would be sold as dog food. One pound of beef scraps would provide the basic raw materials for two cans of dog food, which would be sold to the chain for 14 cents a can. Additional processing costs, including the costs of grain and other processing materials, would amount to $920 a week.

Prepare an analysis of this proposal, indicating whether the company should accept or reject it. Show how you dealt with the beef scraps' unit cost figure of 9 cents a pound.

18. The Fantasi Corporation is engaged in setting the price to be placed on a new product. It is estimated that sales of 10,000 units would give the company approximately the same share of this particular market as it has been able to maintain in the markets for the company's other products. The sales manager believes that he can obtain this share if the price is not more than 10 percent higher than $13.50, the price at which the most closely competitive product is now being sold. No estimates of sales volume at other prices are available.

The company's policy is to establish prices on new products at factory cost plus 40 percent to cover selling and administrative expenses and provide a profit. Factory cost is defined as direct labor and materials plus overhead. The burden rate for the department in which the new product will be processed is $3.46 per direct labor hour. Direct costs will be $2.50 for materials and 1.5 hours of direct labor at $1.80 an hour.

*a*) What price should the company establish?
*b*) Would your answer be affected if competing products were priced at $12.50? If so, quote a new price under these circumstances.
*c*) Would your answer differ if the competitive price were $10? Explain.

*19. The Hubbard Woods Company applies manufacturing overhead costs to all job orders by means of departmental burden rates. Separate burden rates are prepared for each of four production centers: (1) melting and pouring, (2) molding, (3) core making, and (4) cleaning and grinding. Monthly factory overhead costs at normal volume are expected to be as follows:

| | |
|---|---:|
| Indirect labor: | |
|   Melting and pouring...................................... | $1,000 |
|   Molding.................................................. | 300 |
|   Core making ............................................ | 100 |
|   Cleaning and grinding .................................. | 300 |
| Supplies used: | |
|   Melting and pouring..................................... | 50 |
|   Molding................................................. | 50 |
|   Core making ............................................ | 200 |
|   Cleaning and grinding .................................. | 100 |
| Taxes (machinery and equipment, $12; building, $24)....... | 36 |
| Compensation insurance ................................... | 65 |
| Power..................................................... | 50 |
| Heat and light............................................ | 80 |
| Depreciation – building ................................... | 64 |
| Depreciation – machinery and equipment.................... | 60 |
|     Total.............................................. | $2,455 |

You have the following information about the production centers:

| Department | Floor Space (Sq. Ft.) | Cost of Machinery and Equipment | Direct Labor per Month | Compen- sation In- surance* | Power Con- sumption |
|---|---|---|---|---|---|
| Melting and pouring .... | 500 | $2,000 | $ — | $2.00 | 10 |
| Molding................. | 2,000 | 500 | 1,200 | 1.00 | — |
| Core making ........... | 500 | 1,500 | 500 | 1.00 | 10 |
| Cleaning and grinding .. | 1,000 | 2,000 | 1,300 | 1.50 | 30 |
| Total............. | 4,000 | $6,000 | $3,000 | — | 50 |

\* Rate per $100 of payroll.

Prepare a schedule in which you allocate the overhead costs among the four production centers for the purpose of deriving a set of full-cost burden rates.

20. Middleton Enterprises, Inc., owns a baseball park with a seating capacity of 5,000. The fixed costs of operating the ball park are $15,000

a year, and variable costs are $0.10 per spectator per game. These variable costs actually increase in steps, an increase of 500 spectators requiring a $50 increase in costs, but management sees no harm in assuming that each spectator requires a 10-cent increase in cost.

One hundred games are played each year, and the average attendance is 1,000 per game. Therefore fixed costs are $0.15 per spectator per game. The stadium is adequate for all games except a special series of five exhibition games with major league teams. For each of these five games, the estimated demand is as follows:

| If the Price Is— | Then Estimated Attendance Is— |
|---|---|
| $3.00 | 2,000 |
| 2.50 | 6,000 |
| 2.00 | 9,000 |
| 1.75 | 11,000 |
| 1.50 | 16,000 |
| 1.00 | 20,000 |

The company can rent a nearby stadium (25,000 capacity) for a fee of $2,000 for each game plus 10 percent of gross receipts. In addition, the company would still have the variable costs of $0.10 per spectator per game.

Assuming that the price charged will be one of the six alternatives above, present a table that will indicate the admission price that will be most profitable for the company and also whether the larger stadium should be rented. Show all calculations.

**21.** The Franklin Company's factory has a drill press department with six style A, three style B, and two style C machines. These machines have the following characteristics:

| | Machine Style A | Machine Style B | Machine Style C |
|---|---|---|---|
| Cost—each machine | $2,000 | $3,000 | $4,500 |
| Space occupied—each machine (sq. ft.) | 20 | 50 | 60 |
| Horsepower hours per month—each machine | 850 | 1,600 | 3,000 |
| Hourly wage rate, machine operators | $5.50 | $6.60 | $7.80 |
| Operating hours per month at normal volume—each machine | 184 | 160 | 150 |

A machine operator operates only one machine at a time; the number of direct labor hours is therefore equal to the number of machine-hours.

The normal overhead costs of the drill press department for one month are as follows:

| | |
|---|---|
| Depreciation, taxes and insurance—buildings | $ 910 |
| Depreciation, taxes and insurance—machinery | 600 |
| Heat and light | 260 |
| Power | 795 |
| Miscellaneous | 330 |
| Total | $2,895 |

a)   Calculate a full-cost burden rate applicable to all of the machines in this department, expressed as a percentage of direct labor cost.

b)   Allocate the departmental overhead costs among the three machine styles and calculate a separate full-cost burden rate for each machine style, expressed as a rate per machine-hour. (Miscellaneous costs are to be divided equally among the eleven machines in the department.)

c)   Job No. 2051 was run on one of the style C machines and required 15 hours of machine time. Compare the amount of overhead costs that would be assigned to this job under the two different absorption systems implicit in (a) and (b) above. How would you choose between the two?

22.  Department A consists of one large machine. Ten employees, working as a team, are necessary to operate this machine. If the machine is not used, two of these employees (the foremen) remain on the payroll for maintenance and other routine duties.

When the machine is fully manned, it and the crew are idle approximately 10 percent of the time due to unavoidable delays and machine adjustments. While the machine is idle, the foremen perform various necessary duties; the other eight crewmen rest.

At normal volume of 150 machine hours a month, the department has the following costs:

> Payroll:
>
> | | |
> |---|---:|
> | Foremen (2) | $ 2,400 |
> | Crew (8) | 7,500 |
> | Fringe benefits (% of payroll) | 2,970 |
> | Supplies | 1,200 |
> | Depreciation | 630 |
> | Other (all fixed) | 300 |
> | Total | $15,000 |

Ninety percent of the supplies costs at normal volume are variable costs; the remainder are fixed.

a)   Calculate direct labor and overhead costing rates per machine-hour for this department. For the overhead, develop one rate based on full costing and another based on variable costing. Describe and justify your treatment of the foremen's salaries and the cost of idle time of the eight crewmen.

b)   Which of these figures would you regard as establishing a minimum level for product pricing? Explain your reasoning.

23.  During the past year the Atom Chemical Company converted certain raw materials into 500,000 pounds of material A and 1,000,000 gallons of liquid B. The total joint cost of production was $388,000. After separation, material A was processed further and converted into material C at an additional cost of 3 cents a pound. The selling price of material C was 40 cents a pound and that of liquid B 30 cents a gallon.

For inventory measurement, the joint costs were allocated between the joint products in proportion to their values before separate processing. For this purpose, the value of material A was measured by the value of material C less the costs of separate processing.

The inventory on December 31 contained 20,000 pounds of material A, 50,000 gallons of liquid B, and 35,000 pounds of material C.

a) Calculate the unit cost and total cost of the December 31 inventories of these three products.

b) After computing your answer to (a), you discover that the company's inventories of C have been increasing by about 15,000 pounds a year for the past two years because customers have been abandoning the process for which it is an essential raw material. This trend is likely to continue, and price reductions would not be an effective means of increasing the sales volume of material C. Sales volume of B is relatively constant from year to year. The purchasing agent of Molecule, Inc., has just offered to sign a contract to buy 25,000 pounds of A during each of the next three years. The price for the first year would be 26 cents a pound; prices for later years would be negotiated later. Prepare a short statement indicating whether the offer should be accepted. Be sure to indicate how you used the unit cost figure you obtained in (a) above.

24. The Sender Company has four production departments (machine No. 1, machine No. 2, assembly, and painting) and three service departments (storage, maintenance, and office), but uses a plantwide burden rate based on direct labor hours. At normal volume, 125,750 direct labor hours would be used and factory overhead costs would be as follows:

Indirect labor and supervision:
| | |
|---|---|
| Machine No. 1 | $33,000 |
| Machine No. 2 | 22,000 |
| Assembly | 11,000 |
| Painting | 7,000 |
| Storage | 44,000 |
| Maintenance | 32,700 |

Indirect materials and supplies:
| | |
|---|---|
| Machine No. 1 | 2,200 |
| Machine No. 2 | 1,100 |
| Assembly | 3,300 |
| Painting | 3,400 |
| Maintenance | 2,800 |

Other:
| | |
|---|---|
| Rent of factory | 96,000 |
| Depreciation of machinery and equipment | 44,000 |
| Insurance and taxes on machinery and equipment | 2,400 |
| Compensation insurance at $2 per $100 of labor payroll | 19,494 |
| Power | 66,000 |
| Factory office salaries | 52,800 |
| General superintendence | 55,000 |
| Miscellaneous office costs | 21,620 |
| Heat and light | 72,000 |
| Miscellaneous storage charges (insurance, etc.) | 3,686 |

You have the following additional information about the various departments:

| Department | Area (Sq. Ft.) | Cost of Machinery and Equipment | Raw Materials Used | Horsepower Rating | Direct Labor Hours | Direct Labor Payroll | Number of Employees |
|---|---|---|---|---|---|---|---|
| Machine No. 1 ....... | 65,000 | $220,000 | $520,000 | 2,000 | 60,000 | $440,000 | 100 |
| Machine No. 2 ....... | 55,000 | 110,000 | 180,000 | 1,000 | 22,000 | 220,000 | 60 |
| Assembly ..... | 44,000 | 55,000 | | 100 | 30,000 | 110,000 | 30 |
| Painting ...... | 32,000 | 22,000 | 90,000 | 200 | 13,750 | 55,000 | 15 |
| Storage ....... | 22,000 | 11,000 | | | | | 14 |
| Maintenance.. | 11,000 | 16,500 | | | | | 10 |
| Office ......... | 11,000 | 5,500 | | | | | 11 |
| Total.... | 240,000 | $440,000 | $790,000 | 3,300 | 125,750 | $825,000 | 240 |

a)  Calculate a plantwide burden rate on a full-cost basis.

b)  Calculate departmental burden rates based on full costing. For this purpose you will need to distribute some of the general overhead costs among the seven departments and then allocate the costs of the service departments among the four production departments. You should allocate office and general superintendence costs on the basis of direct labor hours, maintenance on the basis of machinery and equipment cost, and storage costs on the basis of materials (direct and indirect) used.

c)  What difference would the use of these departmental burden rates make on a job order requiring 100 direct labor hours in machine No. 1, 200 direct labor hours in machine No. 2, 20 hours in assembly, and 10 hours in painting?

25.† "You just can't do it," said Mr. Erik Berggren, controller of AB Sundqvist. "Our policy has always been to bill our distributors at cost and that doesn't mean variable cost. We just can't afford to sell below cost."

AB Sundqvist is a medium-sized manufacturer of cough medicines, headache pills, and similar products. It has three factories and a large sales force, all in Sweden, and a chain of general agents, one in each country in Western Europe. These general agents buy products from Sundqvist "at cost" and sell them to pharmacies for distribution to the ultimate consumer. The general agents, in addition to the cost price of the products themselves, pay Sundqvist a royalty equal to 5 percent of the amounts they bill their customers for Sundqvist products.

---

† Copyright 1968 by l'Institut pour l'Etude des Méthodes de Direction de l'Entreprise (IMEDE), Lausanne, Switzerland. Reprinted by permission.

Sundqvist had been very fortunate in obtaining large, well-managed, and well-financed companies as its general agents. Its general agent in Britain, Edwards Enterprises, Ltd., was a subsidiary of a large Belgian company engaged in the manufacture and distribution of a wide variety of pharmaceutical and cosmetic products. Although Edwards Enterprises did no manufacturing itself, its parent company had manufacturing plants to supply it with products representing approximately 30 percent of its annual sales volume. Edwards Enterprises regarded itself as a marketing organization and was reluctant to get into manufacturing, although the issue had come up from time to time as the company encountered difficulties in obtaining adequate supplies of a specific kind of product at profitable prices.

Edwards Enterprises, like Sundqvist's other general agents, represented several manufacturers, but did not carry directly competing merchandise. In other words, if it obtained a line of face creams from one manufacturer, it would not handle another line of face creams.

The statement quoted at the beginning of this case was made by Mr. Berggren in the course of a conversation with Mr. Nils Lindstrom, the company's manager for foreign markets. Mr. Lindstrom was anxious to build up sales volume abroad, particularly in view of the recent plant expansion program which for the first time had provided enough capacity to supply all the company's markets. Although some operations were still subcontracted during peak seasons, the company's plant was operating at about 85 percent of its annual capacity.

The Sundqvist Company had just developed a new liquid headache remedy which it had introduced on the Swedish market with considerable initial success. Mr. Frank Keeling, president of Edwards Enterprises, was very interested in marketing this new item in Britain. Although his parent company had a somewhat similar product, Mr. Keeling regarded it as inferior in quality to the Sundqvist product and much more difficult to market. The British public had recently shown a preference for Swedish-made products in this field, at least partly because of an intensive advertising campaign carried out by Edwards Enterprises itself.

Mr. Keeling was anxious to capitalize on this preference by offering the Sundqvist product. He was not happy, however, with the price quoted him by Mr. Lindstrom, a price of 10 Swedish crowns for a case of 12 bottles. "Let's face it," he said, "your direct costs of manufacturing this product are probably about 6 crowns per case. We make approximately the same product in Belgium and your cost can't be very different from ours. This means that you're adding four crowns a case to cover your overhead cost. I think this just isn't warranted here, particularly because you get a royalty of 5 percent on our gross sales volume anyway. We would sell this to retailers at about four times the price we pay you. At 6 crowns a case, our price would be 24 crowns and your royalty alone would be about 1.20 crowns. We'd be willing to pay you a little more than your direct cost, but this is just too much to ask."

The accounting system used by AB Sundqvist was a "direct costing" system. In this system, product cost included only labor and material cost, and was broken down into four categories:

1. The materials required for the manufacture of the product itself.
2. Containers, packages, and packing materials.
3. Direct manufacturing labor.
4. Filling and packaging labor.

The labor charges included a provision for social benefits of 20 percent, which was almost exactly the cost of these benefits to the Sundqvist Company. The salaries of the foremen in the direct production department were not included in direct cost.

For pricing purposes, Mr. Berggren included in product cost an allowance of 175 percent of direct cost to allow for factory, sales, technical, and administrative overhead costs. This was based on the breakdown shown in Exhibit 1. The 175 percent rate was computed as follows:

$$\frac{\text{Overhead Cost}}{\text{Direct Cost of Goods Sold}} = \frac{\text{Kr. }5{,}700{,}000}{\text{Kr. }3{,}260{,}000} = 175 \text{ percent.}$$

### Exhibit 1

### Ab Sundqvist

#### BUDGETED INCOME STATEMENT
(figures in thousands)

| | | |
|---|---:|---:|
| Sales | | Kr. 10,390 |
| Direct cost of goods sold | | 3,260 |
| Direct margin | | Kr. 7,130 |
| Overheads: | | |
| Top management | Kr. 160 | |
| Staff (finance, tax, purchasing) | 230 | |
| Routine clerical | 1,060 | |
| Selling expense—Sweden | 3,080 | |
| Warehousing and shipping | 550 | |
| Export sales expense | 60 | |
| Factory overhead (see Schedule A) | 430 | |
| Research and testing | 130 | |
| Total Overheads | | 5,700 |
| Net Income before Taxes | | Kr. 1,430 |

#### Schedule A: Budgeted Factory Overhead Costs

| | | |
|---|---:|---:|
| Materials control | Kr. | 100 |
| Engineering | | 105 |
| Supervision | | 15 |
| Indirect labor | | 30 |
| Outside services | | 30 |
| Maintenance | | 35 |
| Utilities | | 20 |
| Work clothes | | 15 |
| Other | | 80 |
| Total Factory Overhead Costs | Kr. | 430 |

The company's accounts included no provision for depreciation on plant and equipment. The original cost of the factory buildings amounted to Kr. 1,400,000, while factory equipment had cost Kr. 350,000. As far as the building was concerned, one company official stated that increases in the market value of the land were expected to exceed any depreciation on the building itself and that depreciation was therefore unnecessary. Comparable buildings in Sweden were likely to remain in productive use for 50 years or even longer. The equipment was a different matter. On the average, it was likely to last for 5–7 years, but this was such an uncertain figure that Mr. Berggren was unwilling to reflect it in the accounts.

Mr. Lindstrom persisted in his argument with Mr. Berggren. "After all," he said, "if we can increase our sales, only the variable costs will increase; the fixed costs will remain constant. Besides, it is a fact that we can make money on the royalties we get on the added sales."

Mr. Berggren was unimpressed. "If your sales expand by as much as you hope they will," he said, "we'll have to add another shift in at least one factory and make some additional investments in mixing machinery. If you're really successful, we'll even have to expand one of the plants earlier than we now plan. Your variable cost figures ignore these facts. I'm perfectly willing to work out some figures on the profitability of the added volume that might come from price reductions, but don't try to get me to support your bid to sell the product at direct cost. Cost is cost, and that's all there is to it."

*a)* Would you have supported Mr. Lindstrom or Mr. Berggren? Does it appear that a price equal to direct product cost plus a royalty of 5 percent of the agents' billing price would be profitable or unprofitable for the Sundqvist company?

*b)* What changes in this company's accounting system, if any, would yield data that are more relevant to decisions of this type?

*c)* Would your answer to (*a*) differ in any way if there were a one-time order for a single shipment of a product made to a customer's specifications?

*d)* Would you describe Sundqvist's direct cost system as a variable costing system? How different is it?

*e)* The company's contracts with its general agents call for billing the latter "at cost." Because of the controversy that arose in this case, the company planned to revise its contract forms to provide a more specific definition of cost. What items do you think should be included as "cost"?

# 22

# THE CAPITAL EXPENDITURE
# DECISION

WHEN A DECISION cannot be made on the basis of the cash flows anticipated during a single time period, it is an investment problem. Typical examples are proposals to build, acquire, replace, or expand long-lived productive assets—that is, capital expenditures. Capital expenditure decisions require a slightly different approach from that developed in Chapter 20; the purpose of this chapter is to see why a different approach is needed and how it can be carried out.

## THE PRESENT VALUE APPROACH

An investment outlay may be defined as *an expenditure of cash or its equivalent in one time period or periods in order to obtain a net inflow of cash or its equivalent in some other time period or periods.*

For example, suppose that a company has an opportunity to rearrange the layout of one of its factories at an outlay of $60,000. This will permit the company to save $25,000 a year in the manufacture of a product which it expects to produce for the next three years. The cash flows in this example can be arranged in a *timetable* like the following:

| *Years from Now* | *Cash Inflow* (+) or *Outflow* (−) |
|---|---|
| 0................... | −$60,000 |
| 0 to 1.............. | + 25,000 |
| 1 to 2.............. | + 25,000 |
| 2 to 3.............. | + 25,000 |
| Total........ | +$15,000 |

This is a typical investment problem—a cash outflow is made immediately to get cash inflows in each of the next three periods. The decision cannot be based on the anticipated cash flows for the first period alone or on the undiscounted total of the cash flows.

The most widely recommended method of evaluating proposals to invest the company's scarce capital funds is to calculate for each proposal the present value of the anticipated cash flows, using the technique described in Chapter 10, and accept only those proposals that seem to promise a positive net present value. This kind of analysis consists of three steps:

1.  Estimate the amount and timing of the cash flows that are expected to result from each alternative under consideration.
2.  Compute the present value of each of these cash flow streams.
3.  Select the alternative promising the greatest present value.

The principal argument for present value is that it is sensitive to differences in the *timing* of the cash flows associated with an investment proposal. To illustrate, let us assume that the company can choose among the following three proposals:

| *Years from Now* | *Net Cash Receipts (+) or Cash Outlays (−)* | | |
| --- | --- | --- | --- |
| | *Proposal A* | *Proposal B* | *Proposal C* |
| 0 ............................... | −$13,000 | −$13,000 | −$13,000 |
| 1 ............................... | + 1,000 | + 5,000 | + 9,000 |
| 2 ............................... | + 5,000 | + 5,000 | + 5,000 |
| 3 ............................... | + 9,000 | + 5,000 | + 1,000 |
| Total Cash Flow.............. | +$ 2,000 | +$ 2,000 | +$ 2,000 |

These three proposals have identical lifetime total cash flows, but they are far from equally desirable. Proposal C would ordinarily be regarded as the best proposal because cash is received earlier under this proposal than under either of the others.

This difference appears clearly in present value calculations. Assuming that 8 percent is an appropriate capitalization rate for future cash flows, the present values of these three proposals are:

| Years from Now | Present Values of Cash Flows at 8% | | |
|---|---|---|---|
| | Proposal A | Proposal B | Proposal C |
| 0 .................................... | −$13,000 | −$13,000 | −$13,000 |
| 1 .................................... | + 926 | + 4,630 | + 8,333 |
| 2 .................................... | + 4,286 | + 4,286 | + 4,286 |
| 3 .................................... | + 7,144 | + 3,969 | + 794 |
| Net Present Value............. | −$ 644 | −$ 115 | +$ 413 |

The present values of the future cash receipts from each proposal were obtained by multiplying the cash flows in the table on page 614 by discount factors taken from the 8 percent column of Table 3 in Appendix A.

If net present value is greater than zero, this means that the future cash receipts are more than adequate to provide a return on capital equal to the rate which was used in discounting. In this case, proposals A and B promise a return on capital of less than 8 percent; only proposal C promises a return in excess of 8 percent and is therefore good enough to meet the company's minimum profitability standard.

The present value measure, in other words, permits management to compare proposals that differ in the timing of their cash flows. Present value is the means by which all cash flows of all proposals can be restated at their equivalent values at a common point in time. These proposals can therefore be compared directly with each other.

### The Treatment of Depreciation

Capital expenditure analysis is concerned only with the amounts and timing of cash flows. Depreciation enters into the analysis, but only insofar as it affects cash flows. That is, depreciation is represented by the difference between the initial outlay and the end-of-life salvage value, rather than by a series of annual depreciation charges.

For example, for an investment proposal calling for an outlay of $60,000 now and a residual value of $3,000 in three years' time, the timetable would show the following:

| Time | Cash Flow |
|---|---|
| 0 .......... | −$60,000 |
| 3 .......... | + 3,000 |
| Total ........ | −$57,000 |

Lifetime depreciation is $57,000.

The accountant would spread this $57,000 over the three years for financial reporting. This is valid for that purpose, but it has no bearing on the capital expenditure decision. The cash outflow takes place now, not in annual installments. The timetable must reflect this fact.

### The Treatment of Income Taxes

Although depreciation does not represent a cash flow, income taxes do, and income taxes depend on the amounts of depreciation that are claimed on the company's annual income tax returns. For example, assume that a company has two capital expenditure proposals, each requiring an initial outlay of $60,000 and providing a pretax cash inflow of $25,000 a year for three years. On proposal A, the $60,000 cost may be charged as an expense immediately for tax purposes, while on proposal B the $60,000 cost can only be depreciated at $20,000 a year for three years.

The present value analysis of proposal A on an after-tax basis with a 40 percent tax rate and a 10 percent discount rate is presented in the top panel of Exhibit 22–1. With the purchase price allowed as an expense at the time of purchase, the after-tax initial cash outflow is only $36,000. With no depreciation charged against the subsequent inflows, however, their after-tax amounts are only $15,000 a year. The net present value of the cash flows is $1,302, meaning that the rate of return on the proposal is in excess of 10 percent.

The bottom panel of Exhibit 22–1 summarizes the present value analysis of proposal B, assuming the same tax and discount rates. The after-tax outflow at time zero is now the full $60,000, but, with taxable income in each year reduced by the depreciation charge, the after-tax inflows are raised to $23,000 a year. The net present value of the cash flows on proposal B is −$2,804, meaning that the rate of return is less than 10 percent.

A comparison of the income tax columns shows why the difference in the tax treatment of the asset's cost makes proposal A profitable and proposal B unprofitable. In each case the government nets $6,000 in taxes. With proposal A, however, the company gets $24,000 from the government initially and then pays $10,000 a year. Under proposal B, the company gets nothing initially and then pays $2,000 a year. Since the use of money is worth money, this illustration demonstrates quite dramatically why present value should be used in evaluating investment proposals and why the evaluation must be on an after-tax basis.

## ESTIMATING THE INITIAL OUTLAYS

As stated earlier, it is conceptually unnecessary in capital expenditure analyses to distinguish among different types of cash flows. Only the amounts, their signs (inflow or outflow), and the time they take place need be specified. The complexities encountered in estimating the cash flows make it useful, however, to classify them according to whether they are investment outlays or operating flows. In this section we shall illustrate some of the questions that arise in identifying the initial investment outlays associated with a capital expenditure proposal.

### Outlays for Plant and Equipment

For most proposals, the major outlays are for the acquisition and installation of physical facilities. For example, a proposal to

*Exhibit 22-1*

PRESENT VALUE ANALYSIS OF TWO INVESTMENT PROPOSALS

Proposal A — Cost A Tax-Allowed Expense

| (1) | (2) | (3) | (4) | (5) | (6) | (7) |
|---|---|---|---|---|---|---|
| | | | Income | After-Tax | Present Value | |
| Time | Before-Tax Cash Flow | Taxable Income | Tax 40% of (3) | Cash Flow (2) − (4) | Factor | Amount |
| 0 | −$60,000 | −$60,000 | −$24,000 | −$36,000 | 1.0000 | −$36,000 |
| 1 | + 25,000 | + 25,000 | + 10,000 | + 15,000 | .9091 | + 13,636 |
| 2 | + 25,000 | + 25,000 | + 10,000 | + 15,000 | .8264 | + 12,396 |
| 3 | + 25,000 | + 25,000 | + 10,000 | + 15,000 | .7513 | + 11,270 |
| Total | | | | | | +$ 1,302 |

Proposal B — Cost Subject to Depreciation

| (1) | (2) | (3) | (4) | (5) | (6) | (7) |
|---|---|---|---|---|---|---|
| | | | Income | After-Tax | Present Value | |
| Time | Before-Tax Cash Flow | Taxable Income | Tax 40% of (3) | Cash Flow (2) − (4) | Factor | Amount |
| 0 | −$60,000 | — | — | −$60,000 | 1.0000 | −$60,000 |
| 1 | + 25,000 | +$ 5,000 | +$ 2,000 | + 23,000 | .9091 | + 20,909 |
| 2 | + 25,000 | + 5,000 | + 2,000 | + 23,000 | .8264 | + 19,007 |
| 3 | + 25,000 | + 5,000 | + 2,000 | + 23,000 | .7513 | + 17,280 |
| Total | | | | | | −$ 2,804 |

modernize a factory is expected to require the following outlays before the investment begins to bring in cash receipts:

| | |
|---|---:|
| Equipment.................. | $80,000 |
| Installation.................. | 10,000 |
| Training and test runs....... | 7,000 |
| Total Expenditures...... | $97,000 |

Payment is to be due for all three of these items when the facilities are placed in full company operation. For convenience, this can be designated as the zero date.

### Working Capital

These are not the only outlays required by this proposal. Once the new equipment is in operation, management expects that it will support a larger volume of sales. These will require a $5,000 increase in the company's working capital. The outlay of funds to maintain a higher level of inventory and accounts receivable may not be as apparent as the outlays listed above, but it is no less real.

The build-up of working capital is ordinarily timed differently from the rest of the initial investment outlay, and in some cases it may be stretched out over a number of years. In the present case, it is expected to take place during the first six months after the modernization is completed, and there is little error in adding it to the outlays at the time the investment is made. This is an acceptable way of insuring that this element of the cash flow is not overlooked.

### Opportunity Cost

The proposal also calls for the use of a machine that is already owned by the company but is now idle. This is one of the resources that will be tied up if the proposal is accepted; the question is how, if at all, to represent it in the cash flow timetable.

We have here another application of the opportunity cost concept that we introduced in Chapter 20. Recall that the opportunity cost of an asset is what that asset can bring in its best alternative use. Management estimates that in this case the best alternative to the proposed use of the machine is to sell it for $12,000. Since the machine would bring $12,000 into the company if the modernization program were not carried out, the $12,000 must be regarded as part of the investment outlay. A cash receipt forgone is always equivalent to a cash outlay made.

## After-Tax Outlay

The initial outlay before taxes can now be computed from the above figures:

| | |
|---|---:|
| Equipment. | $ 80,000 |
| Installation | 10,000 |
| Working capital. | 5,000 |
| Training and test runs | 7,000 |
| Presently owned surplus equipment to be used (resale value) ... | 12,000 |
| Gross Outlay. | $114,000 |

Some of these outlays would have an immediate impact on income taxes, and their impact must be reflected in the cash flow estimates, for the reasons cited earlier. The $80,000 purchase price of the new equipment would be subject to a 7 percent "investment credit" of the kind discussed in Chapter 14. Current tax payments would thereby be reduced by $5,600 (7 percent of $80,000).

The installation costs and the working capital investment, on the other hand, are subject to no special tax treatment, and the after-tax cash flows are identical to the before-tax cash flows for these items.

Finally, the $7,000 outlay for training and test runs would be fully deductible from taxable revenues right away. At a 40 percent tax rate, current income taxes would be reduced by $2,800. The after-tax outlay, in other words, would be $7,000 − $2,800 = $4,200.

The fifth item on the list, the standby equipment, has a before-tax opportunity cost of $12,000, its current resale value. The records show that its book value for tax purposes (in technical language, its adjusted basis) is $20,000. If the proposal is rejected, the equipment will be sold, an $8,000 loss will be reported on the income tax return, and the company's taxes will be reduced by $3,200. If the proposal is accepted, on the other hand, the equipment cannot be sold and the company's taxes will be $3,200 more than they would have been had the equipment been sold and the loss declared for tax purposes. This $3,200 increase in taxes is an outlay attributable to the modernization proposal. The after-tax outlay required to retain this surplus equipment therefore is:

| | | |
|---|---|---:|
| (1) | Before-tax cash flow | $12,000 |
| (2) | Book value for tax purposes | 20,000 |
| (3) | Taxable gain or (loss): (1) − (2) | $ (8,000) |
| (4) | Tax or (credit): (3) × 40% | (3,200) |
| (5) | After-tax cash flow: (1) − (4) | $15,200 |

These adjustments are summarized in Exhibit 22–2. In this case the net difference between the before-tax and the after-tax amount is relatively small, less than 5 percent; in other cases it will be much higher.

The assumption that tax payments or receipts take place simultaneously with the before-tax cash flows is a simplification. The time lag before tax payments are due is relatively short, however, and a difference in timing probably should be recognized in the timetable only if the deferral is longer than six months.

Exhibit 22–2

CALCULATION OF AFTER-TAX INVESTMENT OUTLAY

| Item | Outlay before Tax | Tax Effect | Outlay after Tax |
|---|---|---|---|
| Equipment .................... | $ 80,000 | $(5,600) | $ 74,400 |
| Installation .................... | 10,000 | 0 | 10,000 |
| Working capital................ | 5,000 | 0 | 5,000 |
| Training and test runs ......... | 7,000 | (2,800) | 4,200 |
| Surplus equipment used ........ | 12,000 | 3,200 | 15,200 |
| Total .................... | $114,000 | $(5,200) | $108,800 |

## ECONOMIC LIFE

The economic life of any particular asset may be defined as *the time interval that is expected to elapse between the time of acquisition and the time at which the combined forces of obsolescence and deterioration will justify retirement of the asset.* Economic life is the *shortest* of the following three figures:

1. Physical life of the tangible assets.
2. Technological life of the tangible assets.
3. Market life of the assets' output.

Although many assets can be repaired and kept in service almost indefinitely, physical life generally comes to an end when replacing it is cheaper than continuing to repair it. Physical life is seldom the measure of economic life in a rapidly changing economy, however. New processes and new equipment often make existing equipment obsolete long before physical life comes to an end – that is, the spread between the cash flows from operating the asset and the cash flows from operating a new asset may become wide enough to justify replacement even if the old asset's operating costs have not risen at all.

Finally, the product market may change even before this happens, so that the company can no longer sell the asset's output at a profitable price. In other words, if market life is shorter than technological life, it becomes the measure of economic life.

For our illustrative modernization proposal, management estimates that the modernized plant could remain in operation for about 10 years before another major renovation would be required. All calculations therefore will be based on a 10-year life.

## SUBSEQUENT CASH FLOWS

If the initial cash outflows are to be justified, they must generate adequate cash flows in the future. For convenience, these may be divided into three main categories:

1. Operating cash flows.
2. Additional investment outlays.
3. End-of-life salvage values.

Forecasts of all three of these need to be incorporated into the evaluation of each expenditure proposal, and these forecasts should have a sound conceptual foundation. We attempted to provide such a foundation for the investment outlays in the preceding section, leaving operating cash flows and salvage values to be discussed here.

### Operating Cash Flows

The project analyst must forecast the operating flows on a year-by-year basis. For some investments, negative cash flows (net outflows) can be anticipated for the first year or so; for others, the cash inflows will be concentrated in the early years. Because time patterns are usually impossible to predict with any precision, most project analysts use formulistic approximations such as uniform annual amounts or linearly declining amounts, depending on the nature of the benefits to be reaped.

In our example, the main benefit is expected to take the form of reduced operating costs and increased manufacturing capacity. Although the cash costs of operating the plant would undoubtedly rise as the facilities grow older, the difference between the before-tax cash flows associated with the company's current facilities and those incurred in operating the renovated facilities would be relatively constant at $25,000 a year for 10 years.

Realizing these cash flows would also require a $20,000 expenditure to refurbish the plant at the end of year five.

Estimates of operating cash flows should be based strictly on the incremental principle developed in Chapter 20. For example, the project analyst purposely ignored one figure that will appear in the factory cost accounts if the modernization expenditures are made. The company uses a formula to allocate a portion of head office administrative costs to each factory, mainly to permit them to enter into the cost figures submitted to customers for work done on cost-plus contracts. The formula is such that modernization of the plant would increase the amount allocated to the factory, although head office administrative costs in total would not change. The analyst was correct in ignoring the increase; allocated costs should be reflected in the incremental cash flow estimates only to the extent that they represent differences among alternatives in total company cash flows.

### After-Tax Cash Flows

Once the before-tax cash flows have been estimated, they must be adjusted to reflect the effects of income taxation. The income tax effect is estimated by multiplying the applicable tax rate not by the incremental cash flow but by the estimated increment in taxable income. To determine the annual depreciation charges we must first establish the incremental depreciable amount for tax purposes.

The renovation proposal, it will be recalled, calls for before-tax incremental outlays totaling $114,000. Of this amount, $7,000 would be immediately deductible from taxable income, and $5,000 represents working capital which is not depreciable. This leaves two elements of the initial outlay to affect taxes on the incremental operating cash flows:

|  | Before-Tax Cash Flow | Tax Basis | Depreciation Rate for Tax Purposes |
|---|---|---|---|
| New equipment ................ | −$ 90,000 | $ 90,000 | 20% of declining balance |
| Surplus equipment incorporated in the project.......... | − 12,000 | 20,000 | |
| Total equipment required........ | −$102,000 | $110,000 | |

Depreciation on the surplus equipment should be deducted because it will be included on the annual tax returns in this way only if the proposal is accepted. It therefore affects the incremental tax.

Taken together, the new and surplus equipment has a depreciable total (tax basis) of $110,000. The first year's tax depreciation is 20 percent of this, or $22,000. This reduces the tax basis to $88,000, and the tax depreciation for the second year is 20 percent of $88,000, or $17,600.

The depreciation calculations for the entire 10-year period are summarized in Exhibit 22–3. For simplicity, declining-balance depreciation has been used for the full 10 years; in practice, a

Exhibit 22–3

TAX DEPRECIATION ON NEW AND RETAINED FACILITIES

| Year | (1) Tax Basis, Start of Year | (2) Additions | (3) Tax Depreciation 20% × [(1) + (2)] | (4) Tax Basis, End of Year (1) + (2) − (3) |
|---|---|---|---|---|
| 1 | $110,000 | — | $22,000 | $88,000 |
| 2 | 88,000 | — | 17,600 | 70,400 |
| 3 | 70,400 | — | 14,080 | 56,320 |
| 4 | 56,320 | — | 11,264 | 45,056 |
| 5 | 45,056 | — | 9,012 | 36,044 |
| 6 | 36,044 | $20,000 | 11,209 | 44,835 |
| 7 | 44,835 | — | 8,967 | 35,868 |
| 8 | 35,868 | — | 7,174 | 28,694 |
| 9 | 28,694 | — | 5,739 | 22,955 |
| 10 | 22,955 | — | 4,591 | 18,364 |

slightly more complicated schedule is likely to be necessary. We have also assumed that retirements will be zero prior to the end of the ten years and that the additional expenditure at the end of five years is added in full to the tax base. Finally, we have assumed that tax depreciation will be based on the estimated life of the project rather than some other life. These assumptions are not always valid. They make the illustration easier to follow, but they should not be used in a practical application without verification.

Given the before-tax cash flows and the tax depreciation figures, it is a simple matter to calculate taxable income, income tax effects, and after-tax cash flows. Exhibit 22–4 summarizes these calculations for our plant modernization proposal. With the before-tax figures in the left-hand column, the three middle columns are used to compute the income tax effect. The after-tax cash flow is then found by deducting the tax from the before-tax cash flow.

Exhibit 22–4

CALCULATION OF AFTER-TAX OPERATING CASH FLOWS

| Year | (1) Cash Flow before Taxes | (2) Tax Depreciation | (3) Taxable Income (1) − (2) | (4) Income Tax 40% × (3) | (5) Cash Flow after Taxes (1) − (4) |
|---|---|---|---|---|---|
| 1 .......... | $ 25,000 | $ 22,000 | $ 3,000 | $ 1,200 | $ 23,800 |
| 2 .......... | 25,000 | 17,600 | 7,400 | 2,960 | 22,040 |
| 3 .......... | 25,000 | 14,080 | 10,920 | 4,368 | 20,632 |
| 4 .......... | 25,000 | 11,264 | 13,736 | 5,494 | 19,506 |
| 5 .......... | 25,000 | 9,012 | 15,988 | 6,395 | 18,605 |
| 6 .......... | 25,000 | 11,209 | 13,791 | 5,516 | 19,484 |
| 7 .......... | 25,000 | 8,967 | 16,033 | 6,413 | 18,587 |
| 8 .......... | 25,000 | 7,174 | 17,826 | 7,130 | 17,870 |
| 9 .......... | 25,000 | 5,739 | 19,261 | 7,704 | 17,296 |
| 10 .......... | 25,000 | 4,591 | 20,409 | 8,164 | 16,836 |
| Total ..... | $250,000 | $110,636 | $139,364 | $55,744 | $194,256 |

Notice how the declining-charge depreciation has changed the constant annual before-tax cash flow into a stream of gradually declining amounts. This makes this proposal more valuable than if only the straight-line method were available.

### End-of-Life Salvage Value

The final element in the incremental cash flow timetable is end-of-life salvage value. This consists of the after-tax amount realizable from liquidation of the working capital and sale of the facilities, or the internal value of the assets to the company at the end of the project's life, if this is greater than liquidation value.

Suppose that the estimated liquidation value of the working capital 10 years from now is equal to its book value for tax purposes ($5,000), and that the liquidation value of the equipment would be $20,000. From the bottom line of Exhibit 22–3 we find that the book value of the equipment would be $18,364, leaving a taxable gain of $1,636. At a tax rate of 40 percent, the tax would be $654 and the after-tax cash flow would be $5,000 + $20,000 − $654 = $24,346.

### DISCOUNTED CASH FLOW ANALYSIS

All of the cash flows for the modernization proposal are summarized in Exhibit 22–5. If the company requires an after-tax return on investment of 10 percent, the present value of the proposal is $11,104, as shown on the bottom line of the exhibit. This means that, if the estimates are correct, the future operating cash receipts will be large enough to pay back the amounts invested ($108,800 and $20,000) and pay interest on these amounts at an annual rate of 10 percent, with enough left over to increase the company's value by $11,104. Other things being equal, this proposal should be accepted.

Exhibit 22–5

CALCULATION OF PRESENT VALUE

| Years from Now | Investment Cash Flow after Taxes | Operating Cash Flow after Taxes | Total Cash Flow after Taxes | Present Value @ 10% Multiplier* | Amount |
|---|---|---|---|---|---|
| 0......... | −$108,800 | — | −$108,800 | 1.0000 | −$108,800 |
| 1......... | — | +$23,800 | + 23,800 | 0.9091 | + 21,637 |
| 2......... | — | + 22,040 | + 22,040 | 0.8264 | + 18,214 |
| 3......... | — | + 20,632 | + 20,632 | 0.7513 | + 15,501 |
| 4......... | — | + 19,506 | + 19,506 | 0.6830 | + 13,323 |
| 5......... | − 20,000 | + 18,605 | − 1,395 | 0.6209 | − 866 |
| 6......... | — | + 19,484 | + 19,484 | 0.5645 | + 10,999 |
| 7......... | — | + 18,587 | + 18,587 | 0.5132 | + 9,539 |
| 8......... | — | + 17,870 | + 17,870 | 0.4665 | + 8,336 |
| 9......... | — | + 17,296 | + 17,296 | 0.4241 | + 7,335 |
| 10......... | + 24,346 | + 16,863 | + 41,209 | 0.3855 | + 15,886 |
| Total... | | | | | +$ 11,104 |

* From Table 3, Appendix A.

Calculations of this kind are often referred to as *discounted cash flow* (DCF) analysis. The conclusions to be drawn from this analysis are not always as clear-cut as we may have implied, however, and we should at least mention five issues before we move on:

1. Selecting the right bench mark.
2. Choosing the discount rate.
3. Dealing with uncertainty.
4. Recognizing sunk costs.
5. Allowing for interest on investment.

## Selecting the Right Bench Mark

Implicit in the above analysis was the assumption that the alternative to the investment proposal under consideration is continuing to operate as before. This is commonly but not always the relevant bench mark. Another possible bench mark is the alternative of manufacturing the product in another plant that has excess capacity. Still another alternative to improving or expanding a plant is to liquidate it and cease manufacturing the product altogether. In some cases, this will be the relevant alternative.

To illustrate, suppose that the company could liquidate the present plant, equipment, and working capital now for $500,000 after taxes. If the plant were kept open, its annual operating cash flow after taxes would be about $60,000, but routine replacement expenditures would run about $40,000 a year. At the end of 10 years the plant, equipment, and working capital would bring in about $400,000, again after taxes.

These figures are summarized in Exhibit 22–6. As this shows,

### Exhibit 22–6
### PRESENT VALUE OF CONTINUING PRESENT OPERATION

| Years from Now | Cash Flow after Taxes | | | Present Value @ 10% | |
| --- | --- | --- | --- | --- | --- |
| | If Sell Now | If Keep | Difference | Multiplier | Amount |
| 0 .............. | +$500,000 | — | −$500,000 | 1.0000 | −$500,000 |
| 1 to 10.......... | — | +$ 20,000 a year | + 20,000 a year | 6.1446 | + 122,892 |
| 10 .............. | — | + 400,000 | + 400,000 | 0.3855 | + 154,200 |
| Total ........ | | | | | −$222,908 |

the present value of the cash flows from continued operation ($122,892 + $154,200) is less than the current market value of the investment ($500,000). This means that unless something drastic can be done to improve the cash flows, the plant should be closed. This being the case, continued operation is no longer the relevant bench mark. The question now is whether the proposed modernization is good enough to restore this operation to health. If not, the additional expenditure would be wasted. The comparison, in other words, should be between the proposal and the best available alternative, in this case to close down. The calculation is:

Present value if operated in present condition ................. −$222,908
Present value of contribution from renovation................. +    11,104
Net present value ............................................ −$211,804

The renovation proposal is not good enough. Instead of pouring good money after bad, the company should close the plant and reinvest the proceeds elsewhere.

## Choosing the Discount Rate

Under both the internal rate of return and the net present value methods for evaluating a capital expenditure proposal, the analyst must have a figure for the discount rate or rate of return that the company requires as a condition for making the investment. While projecting the net operating cash flows is the most difficult practical task in arriving at a capital expenditure decision, selecting the discount rate is the most difficult theoretical decision.

The rate of return that a firm should require on an investment is a difficult figure to identify because the future is uncertain and investors have aversion to risk. An investor is willing to include in his portfolio of securities government bonds which yield, say, a 6 percent rate of return, because the interest and principal payments on the bonds are free of risk. Investment in common stocks, however, typically carries with it a greater degree of uncertainty and of risk, and the average purchaser of common stocks does so in anticipation of dividends and capital gains that will yield a return considerably in excess of that available from the bonds of the same companies.

To compensate existing shareowners for the risks they bear and to provide an earnings base adequate to induce additional ownership investment in the business, management must try to *make investments that will produce returns equal to or exceeding the minimum rate acceptable to the company's stockholders.* If management fails in this, stockholders will find the value of their stock declining and management will find it extremely difficult to raise additional funds from the sale of stock.

The minimum acceptable rate of return on an investment, often referred to as the *cost of capital,* is the rate that will not depress the price of the company's stock. The cost of capital will vary from company to company, depending on the market's evaluation of the degree of risk. The greater the risk, the less the stockholder will be willing to pay for a dollar of anticipated earnings. Thus, the stock of a metropolitan electric power company would be expected to yield a far smaller return on its market value than the stock of an oil exploration company, and typically the latter requires a considerably higher rate of return on its investments than the former.[1]

---

[1] For further discussion of the subject see F. Modigliani and Merton Miller, "The Cost of Capital, Corporation Finance, and the Theory of Investment," *American Economic Review,* June 1958, pp. 261–97, and M. J. Gordon, *The Investment, Financing and Valuation of the Corporation* (Homewood, Ill.; Richard D. Irwin, Inc., 1962).

## Dealing with Uncertainty

Uncertainty as to the future means that the future cash flow for a period may have two or more possible values. One way to deal with uncertainty is to take each possible cash flow for a period, assign a probability to the amount, and compute the mean or expected value of the cash flow. The expected value of the cash flow is then discounted to its present value.

Unfortunately, the development of a probability distribution for the cash flow in each future period on a long-life investment project requires so much data estimation as to make the task unmanageable or the resultant estimate highly questionable. More commonly, the analyst proceeds directly to a figure that he considers the mean of the possible cash flows for the period.

Managements sometimes find that the expected values of the future cash flows, regardless of how they are arrived at, do not provide adequate information for investment decisions. A management might also want to know what the cash flows would be under pessimistic and optimistic forecasts of the future. Pessimistic figures, for example, might indicate a negative present value of, say, $20,000 for the renovation proposal, whereas optimistic figures might yield a positive present value of $80,000. This is crude in that it ignores the probabilities associated with the various outcomes, but it does give management some feel for the risks associated with estimating errors.

## The Sunk Cost Fallacy

Despite general understanding of the incremental principle, capital expenditure decisions are sometimes influenced by the amounts spent in the past to provide equipment or to develop new products. Suppose, for example, that an automobile company has spent $200 million to design, test, tool, and market a new model. Sales have been disappointing and management is considering discontinuing the model. The first year's operating loss, as shown on the company's internal profit report, was (in millions):

| | | |
|---|---:|---:|
| Sales | | $400 |
| Less: Out-of-pocket operating costs | $380 | |
| Amortization of past tooling and development costs | 80 | 460 |
| Net operating loss | | $ (60) |

One mistake would be to conclude that the company must continue the model because it has not yet recovered its initial investment. The $120 million of the original $200 million development cost that has not yet been charged to expense is irrelevant to the decision. The question is not whether all past costs have been recovered or charged to expense, but rather whether future receipts from sale of the product are likely to cover future outlays with enough left over to justify continued expenditure of management time and continued investment of liquid resources.

A second and perhaps more common mistake is to decide that the new model should not be continued unless its future revenues will cover not only future costs but depreciation of past outlays as well. For example, assume that the company is considering the following profit plan for the next year (in millions):

| | | |
|---|---:|---:|
| Sales......................................................... | | $450 |
| Less: Out-of-pocket operating costs.............................. | $400 | |
| Amortization of past tooling and development costs......... | 60 | 460 |
| Estimated net operating loss....................................... | | $ (10) |

A recommendation based on net profit rather than incremental profit would be to discontinue the model rather than incur a $10 million loss, despite the forecast of a $50 million incremental cash profit.

These are two illustrations of the sunk cost fallacy, the notion that costs not yet recovered are somehow relevant for decision making. The relevant concept in both cases is opportunity cost: what is the present salvage value of the investment, and by how much will that salvage value decline if the investment is not liquidated now?

## Treatment of Interest

Interest on long-term debt is a component of the cost of capital. The discounting process allows for this component, and neither interest nor debt amortization should be deducted explicitly from project cash flows even when the project is financed specifically by a particular issue of long-term debt.

Nonseasonal short-term interest-bearing debt should be classified as long-term debt for this purpose, because it provides part of the long-term capital to finance the project. Interest on seasonal short-term debt, on the other hand, is an explicit cash outlay that is not provided for by the discounting process. It should be deducted in computing annual cash flows. Similarly, interest on any seasonal investment of project funds can be regarded as a cash inflow for the project.

## INTERNAL RATE OF RETURN

Management is used to return-on-investment figures as measures of investment yield. This suggests that the profitability of investment proposals might usefully be expressed as a return-on-investment ratio instead of as net present value.

Unfortunately, a simple ratio of average annual earnings to the average book value of the investment during the project's life is inaccurate because it overlooks the vital element of timing.[2] Instead, many companies use the internal rate of return, defined as that rate of discount at which the sum of the positive present values is equal to the sum of the negative present values. In other words, the internal rate of return is the rate at which the net present value of the cash flows is zero.

The equations for the internal rate of return cannot be solved explicitly. Instead, a cumbersome trial-and-error procedure must be used. Although computer programs are available to take the burden out of this, it may be useful to do it once manually, using a simpler set of cash flows than in the previous illustration.

Suppose that a $48,000 outlay will produce cash flows of $10,000 a year for 10 years, with no end-of-life salvage. The first step in computing the rate of return for this project is to discount all of the cash flows at some rate that seems likely to be close to the true rate. Suppose that we choose 15 percent as this first trial rate. Using the multiplier for 15 percent on the 10-year line in Table 4 of Appendix A (5.019), we find that the present value of the cash inflows exceeds the present value of the initial outlay by $2,190:

$$
\begin{array}{lr}
\text{Outlay: } \$48,000 \times 1.000 \dots\dots\dots\dots\dots & -\$48,000 \\
\text{Receipts: } \$10,000 \times 5.019 \dots\dots\dots\dots\dots & +\ \underline{50,190} \\
\text{Net present value} \dots\dots\dots\dots\dots\dots\dots & +\underline{\$\ \ 2,190}
\end{array}
$$

This indicates that the project earns more than 15 percent on the investment, but it doesn't show how much more. The next step is to try another rate, higher than the first. Discounting at 20 percent, the present value of the cash receipts is $41,920, and this is $6,080 less than the present value of the outlay. This means that the project earns less than 20 percent. The true before-tax rate of return is somewhere in between, approximately

---

[2] An even simpler measure in the *payback period,* the number of years that will elapse before cumulative net cash receipts are just equal to the initial outlay. This measure ignores economic life and reflects the timing of the cash flows only crudely and incompletely.

one quarter of the distance between 15 percent and 20 percent:

$$\text{Internal rate} = 15\% + \frac{\$2,190}{\$2,190 + \$6,080} \times (20\% - 15\%) = 16.3\%$$

## SUMMARY

Capital expenditure proposals need to be tested against company-wide standards of minimum acceptable profitability. These standards are ordinarily related to the cost of capital—the anticipated rate of return that shareholders and other investors demand as the price of providing funds to the company.

The cash flow streams to which profitability tests must be applied should represent the anticipated differential after-tax cash flows associated with the proposal. Four kinds of cash flows can be distinguished: initial investment outlays, subsequent investment outlays, operating receipts and disbursements, and end-of-life salvage value. These differentials should be measured from a bench mark that will be acceptable to the company, and opportunity costs must not be neglected.

Once the incremental cash flows have been estimated, their present value can be determined. Other things being equal, proposals should be accepted if they offer a positive net present value. If two alternative proposals are being compared, the better one is the proposal promising the greater net present value. The cash flow estimates are always uncertain, however, and management may wish to compute cash flows and present values on optimistic and pessimistic bases to provide a broader measure of project risks and opportunities.

## QUESTIONS AND PROBLEMS

1. Define a capital expenditure. Would you classify research and development costs as capital expenditures? Increased inventory requirements?

2. What does a decision to build a new factory have in common with a decision to refund long-term debt at a lower rate of interest?

3. What is the internal rate of return for a proposed capital expenditure? What relationship does it bear to the present value of the proposal?

4. The amounts included in the company's capital budget usually cover only the direct costs of the plant and equipment to be acquired. What should be done to make sure that working capital requirements are not overlooked?

**5.** In what ways does the concept of opportunity cost enter into the evaluation of capital expenditure proposals?

**6.** What is the "sunk cost fallacy"? What can be done about it?

**7.** "Taxes merely take a proportionate share of earnings. Therefore the decision based on a before-tax analysis will be the same as one based on an after-tax analysis." Discuss.

**8.** What reasons might support the continuation of operations of a division for which a low return on investment is reported?

**9.** Most large capital expenditure proposals are approved twice — once when they are included in the annual capital budget and again when the sponsor is ready to commit the first funds to it. Is this duplication of effort desirable? Explain.

**10.** There is no contractual obligation to make interest or dividend payments to the common stockholders. How can common equity capital be said to have a "cost"?

**11.** Which of the following are likely to be "investment problems" and why?
*a)* Asset replacement decisions.
*b)* Rate of output decisions.
*c)* Decisions to advertise special "sales" in local newspapers.
*d)* Decisions to rent or buy equipment.
*e)* Product-discontinuation decisions.

**12.** On April 24 the X Manufacturing Company completed the installation of a new made-to-order packaging machine at a cost of $50,000. On the following morning an equipment salesman offered the president of the X Company, at an installed price of $35,000, a newly developed standard machine guaranteed to do exactly the same job. The expected economic life, eight years, was the same for both pieces of equipment. But whereas the projected annual out-of-pocket operating costs were $14,000 on the first machine, A, they were only $8,000 on the second machine, B. Unfortunately, the company could expect to salvage no more than $20,000 from its recent purchase should it decide to replace immediately.
*a)* Should the X Company seriously consider acquiring the new machine? What factors bear upon the decision?
*b)* With respect to (*a*) above, would it make any difference if the cost of the original machine had been $70,000? Why or why not?

**13.** An engineer with the Zimmerman Brothers Company sent a memorandum to the controller which read in part as follows: "An operation in the stamping department now being performed with hand tools could be mechanized by the purchase of the machine described in the attached folder. The machine costs $40,000 installed, and it would probably have an economic life of 20 years.

"The machine would save $5,500 a year in labor costs at the present volume of activity. Space requirements would be reduced by 3,000 square feet which at the current charge of $0.50 per square foot is another $1,500. Maintenance, repairs, and all other operating costs would remain unchanged. The old hand tools have a zero scrap value.

"The return on investment in equipment is the saving in operating cost less the depreciation on the machine divided by one half of the investment. This is:

$$R = (\$7,000 - \$2,000)/\$20,000 = 25 \text{ percent.}$$

Since the company requires a 20 percent return on investment, this machine should be purchased."

Do you agree with the engineer's analysis? Why?

**14.** Company B is currently considering the possibility of replacing one of its machines with a new one which will yield savings in both labor and material spoilage costs because it is equipped with improved automatic controls. The salvage value of the present machine is considerably less than its book value. If the new machine is purchased, the installation cost will be substantial.

The company is currently in the 50 percent tax bracket and expects to remain there indefinitely. If the new machine is purchased, it will be permissible to depreciate it for tax purchases by either the double-rate, declining-balance method or the sum-of-the-years'-digits method.

a)  How, if at all, may the fact of income taxation influence either the company's decision to acquire the machine or its accounting for the outlays if the machine is acquired? Explain.
b)  How, if at all, does the freedom of election with respect to depreciation bear upon this decision? Explain.

*15. The Arnold Machine Company has been having a neighboring company perform certain operations on a part used in its product at a cost of 50 cents per part. The annual production of this part is expected to average 6,000 pieces.

The Arnold Machine Company can perform this operation itself by bringing into operation two machines: a spare lathe which has a net book value of $2,000, and a new machine which can be purchased at a price of $7,000. The new machine is expected to last seven years. The old machine has a remaining physical life of at least 10 years and could be sold now for approximately $1,500. The final salvage of both ma-

---

* Solutions to problems marked with an asterisk (*) are found in Appendix B.

chines is considered negligible. In performing the operation itself, the Arnold Company will incur out-of-pocket costs for direct labor, power, supplies, etc., of 20 cents per part.

Prepare an analysis (including explanatory comments) which would help to determine whether it is profitable for the Arnold Company to perform these operations itself. The company normally expects to earn a rate of return before taxes of about 15 percent on its invested capital. (Ignore income tax effects.)

16. J. T. Long, owner of the Long Office Building, was recently approached by a buyer for that property. The offer consisted of $200,000 down plus $50,000 at the end of each of the next five years — a total of $450,000.

Mr. Long had bought the land and built the building 15 years earlier. The land had cost $40,000; the building had cost $600,000. Annual depreciation for tax purposes had been charged at a straight-line rate of $20,000 a year.

The appraised value of the land at the time of the offer was $100,000. The remaining useful life of the building at that time seemed to be about 10 years. At the end of that time the land and building probably could be sold to a developer for $150,000. The amount of working capital required to support the operation of this building was negligible and seemed likely to remain so.

Mr. Long expected future income to be about $30,000 a year for the remaining life, calculated as below:

| | | |
|---|---:|---:|
| Yearly revenues from office rental........... | | $79,000 |
| Yearly expenses: | | |
| Taxes .................................. | $ 4,000 | |
| Repairs................................. | 12,000 | |
| Depreciation ........................... | 20,000 | |
| Heat and miscellaneous.................. | 13,000 | 49,000 |
| Total Income...................... | | $30,000 |

The cash flows from ownership of the property each year would become available to Mr. Long at the end of the year. He expected to be able to invest any cash he would receive at 10 percent, compounded annually.

a) Disregarding tax considerations, would you advise Mr. Long to keep or sell the building? Present a brief table showing the figures supporting your recommendation.
b) Would your answer differ if the remaining life of the building were to be 15 years instead of 10?

17. The initial investment outlay is $40,000, of which $30,000 will be capitalized for tax purposes. Before-tax operating cash receipts will be $12,000 a year for five years; these amounts will be received at the end of each year. Estimated end-of-life salvage value is zero.

Straight-line depreciation and a five-year life are to be used for tax purposes. The tax rate is 40 percent. Taxes are paid or tax credits are received immediately, as soon as the taxable or tax-deductible transaction takes place.

*a)* What is the present value of this proposal at an annual interest rate of 8 percent?
*b)* What is the after-tax internal rate of return?
*c)* What would be the internal rate of return if end-of-life salvage were to be $5,000 but annual depreciation for tax purposes continued to be based on zero salvage?
*d)* What would be the rate of return on investment if economic life and tax life were both six years, with zero salvage value?
*e)* What would be the rate of return if economic life and tax life were five years, salvage were zero, and double-rate, declining-balance depreciation were used for tax purposes?
*f)* Prepare a short commentary on the relationships indicated by your answers to the previous parts of this question.

18. The Griffa Machine Company has been purchasing from a neighboring company a part used in one of its products. The purchase price of this part is 95 cents each, and the expected average annual production is 6,000 parts.

The methods department of the Griffa Machine Company has submitted a proposal to manufacture this part in the company's own plant. To do this, the company would have to purchase a new machine at a price of $10,800. It would also use a lathe now owned by the company but not in current use. This lathe has an estimated market value now of $1,000, but its book value is $2,000. Depreciation for tax purposes on the old lathe is at a straight-line rate of $400 a year. The new machine would be depreciated for tax purposes by the sum-of-the-years'-digits method over an eight-year period. Griffa's management believes that both machines would be usable for 10 years if the proposal were accepted, and the final salvage value of both machines is assumed to be negligible.

The incremental costs of operating the two machines, other than depreciation costs, would be as follows:

|  | Unit Cost |
|---|---|
| Direct labor, 0.1 hour at $4 an hour | $0.40 |
| Direct materials | $0.10 |
| Power, supplies, etc. | $0.05 |

All other factory costs would be unaffected by the decision to manufacture this part. The company uses a burden rate of $3 per direct labor hour to absorb factory overhead costs.

Assuming an income tax rate of 50 percent and a minimum acceptable rate of return on investment of 10 percent after taxes, should this proposal be accepted?

*19. Under a new proposal just submitted by the production manager of the Romano Company, the proposed facilities will cost $100,000, half of which will be capitalized for tax purposes. The rest will be expensed immediately. A government investment incentive device known as an investment credit allows the company an immediate tax rebate of 7 percent of the capitalized portion of the outlay. Depreciation charges for subsequent years will be based on the full amount capitalized, however.

The proposal will also require a $10,000 increase in working capital.

Cash operating savings are expected to amount to $20,000 a year. Expected life for tax purposes is eight years, and the double-rate, declining-balance method is used in computing depreciation. The tax rate is 50 percent.

a)  Compute the after-tax initial cash outlay for this proposal.
b)  Compute the after-tax cash saving for each of the first two years of the life of the facilities.

*20. The Walpole Cotton Company is currently considering the installation of weaving equipment with a total cost including freight and installation of $44,000. If this proposal is accepted, this equipment will replace equipment which three years before cost $55,000 and is still in good running order. Because of the greater efficiency of the new equipment, the present equipment now has a resale value of only $5,000. The cost of removing the old equipment and revamping the machine service facilities will be $15,000, of which $5,000 is considered a part of the installation cost and is included in the $44,000 to be capitalized, while the remaining $10,000 is to be charged to expense.

The manufacturing cost tabulation shows a substantial reduction in annual operating cost, as follows:

|  | At Present | After New Installation |
|---|---|---|
| Annual costs: |  |  |
| Labor...................................... | $ 12,500 | $  3,000 |
| Depreciation (10% of cost, straight-line) . | 5,500 | 4,400 |
| Supplies, repairs, and power ............. | 4,000 | 3,400 |
| Taxes, insurance, and miscellaneous..... | 900 | 1,000 |
| Total............................... | $ 22,900 | $ 11,800 |
| Annual Production – Units ................ | 500,000 | 500,000 |

The original life estimate on the present equipment was based on a forecast that a major technical improvement would be introduced in equipment that would become available at the end of 10 years from the date of installation. This major technical improvement has been incorporated in the new equipment now available, 7 years ahead of time. If the equipment is not replaced now, management believes that another 10 years will pass before replacement is justifiable.

The present equipment is being depreciated for tax purposes by the sum-of-the-years'-digits method over a 10-year period. Tax depreciation on the new equipment would be calculated in a similar fashion.

The machines are expected to have only a negligible salvage value at the end of 10 years.

a) If a 16 percent return on investment before taxes is required, would you recommend the expenditure?

b) If a 10 percent return on investment after taxes is required, would you recommend the expenditure? Assume a tax rate of 50 percent.

**21.** The management of the Taunton Cotton Company is considering the acquisition of new spinning machinery, partially to replace certain less efficient equipment and partially to increase total productive capacity. Market surveys indicate that the anticipated increase in productive capacity can be disposed of only by additional sales effort coupled with a price reduction. Pertinent data are as indicated below:

| | |
|---|---:|
| Cost of new equipment, including freight and installation............. | $55,000 |
| Cost of removal of equipment replaced, rearrangement and revamping, etc., to be charged to expense for tax purposes ............. | 25,000 |
| Net book value of equipment replaced (original cost: $40,000)......... | 8,000 |
| Amount to be realized from sale of equipment replaced ................ | 5,000 |

| Annual Processing Costs | Present | | Proposed | |
|---|---|---|---|---|
| | Dollars | Per Lb. | Dollars | Per Lb. |
| Labor................................ | $120,000 | $0.0600 | $135,000 | $0.0540 |
| Supplies, repairs, and power........... | 80,000 | 0.0400 | 93,000 | 0.0372 |
| Taxes, insurance, and miscellaneous... | 20,000 | 0.0100 | 22,000 | 0.0088 |
| Depreciation (10% of cost, straight-line). | 4,000 | 0.0020 | 6,000 | 0.0024 |
| Total......................... | $224,000 | $0.1120 | $256,000 | $0.1024 |

Annual production:
| | |
|---|---:|
| Present...................................................... | 2,000,000 lbs. |
| Proposed .................................................... | 2,500,000 lbs. |

Estimated manufacturing margin (estimated selling price minus estimated material cost):
| | |
|---|---:|
| Present...................................................... | $ 0.150 |
| Proposed (allowing for reduction of ½¢ in selling price)............. | 0.145 |

Estimated additional selling and administrative expenses:
| | |
|---|---:|
| Commissions.................................................. | $ 5,000 |
| Branch office sales expense (including advertising)................. | 11,000 |
| Billing and miscellaneous administrative.......................... | 1,500 |
| Total..................................................... | $17,500 |

Depreciation for tax purposes on present equipment has been by the straight-line method at 10 percent of cost. Tax depreciation on the new equipment would be by the sum-of-the-years'-digits method over a 10-year period. Expected salvage value is zero.

a) Would you recommend this expenditure if a 16 percent return before taxes is required?

b) Would you recommend the expenditure if a 10 percent return after taxes is required? Assume a tax rate of 50 percent.

*22. The expected life of a facility proposal is 10 years, the installed cost will be $50,000, and the expected end-of-life salvage value is zero. The equipment will replace facilities now in use that have a book value of $30,000 and a market value of $10,000. The remaining tax life of the old facilities is eight years.

Double-rate, declining-balance depreciation will be used for tax purposes on the new facilities. No "investment credit" or other tax rebate is available. The present facilities are being depreciated for tax purposes by the straight-line method down to an end-of-life salvage value of zero.

Estimated before-tax, before-depreciation cash savings amount to $20,000 a year. The tax rate is 50 percent, and all savings are assumed to take place at the end of each year.

a) Compute the incremental after-tax present value of this proposal at 10 percent, compounded annually.

b) Compute the incremental after-tax discounted cash-flow rate of return on this proposal.

23. Company Z has contracted to supply a governmental agency with 50,000 units of a product each year for the next five years. A certain component of this product can be either manufactured by Company Z or purchased from the X Corporation, which has indicated a willingness to enter into a subcontract for 50,000 units of the component each year for five years if the price offered is satisfactory. These alternative methods of procurement are regarded as equally dependable.

If Company Z decides to manufacture the component, it expects the following to occur:

(1) A special-purpose machine costing $110,000 will have to be purchased. No other equipment will be required.

(2) For tax purposes, this machine will be assumed to have a 10-year life, but management does not expect the machine to be useful beyond the contract period. Estimated salvage value at the end of five years is $10,000.

(3) Depreciation for tax purposes will be by the double-rate, declining-balance method. The item method of depreciation will be used. There will be no "investment credit."

(4) The manufacturing operation will require 1,000 feet of productive floor space. This space is available in a building owned by Company Z and will not be needed for any other purpose in the foreseeable future. The costs of maintaining this building (including repairs, utilities, taxes, and depreciation) amount to $2 per square foot of productive floor space per year.

(5) Variable manufacturing costs—materials, direct labor, etc.—are estimated to be $0.50 a unit.

(6) Fixed factory costs other than those mentioned in (1) through (4) —e.g., supervision, etc.—are estimated at $20,000 a year.

(7) Income taxes are computed at the rate of 50 percent of taxable income or taxable savings.

(8) The policy of Company Z is to subcontract if and only if the costs saved by manufacturing instead of subcontracting provide less than a 10 percent annual return on investment. For this purpose, return on investment is defined as the relationship between cost saving, after provision for income taxes, and the capital investment that will have to be made to permit Company Z to manufacture the component in its own plant.

What is the maximum price per unit which Company Z should be willing to offer to the X Corporation? Make explicit any assumptions which you believe to be necessary in solving the problem.

**24.** Mr. Adams burst into the office of his supervisor, the works manager, one day to announce that a new machine which had just come out should be bought to replace the one used in the manufacture of product W. To support his argument, he presented the following comparative income statements for product W:

|  | Using the Present Machine | Using the New Machine |
|---|---|---|
| Expenses: |  |  |
| Factory direct materials.................. | $ 50,000 | $ 50,000 |
| Factory direct labor...................... | 40,000 | 30,000 |
| Machinery depreciation.................. | 5,000 | 10,000 |
| Other factory overhead (200% of direct labor).................. | 80,000 | 60,000 |
| Selling and administrative expenses (15% of sales)................. | 30,000 | 30,000 |
| Total...................................... | $205,000 | $180,000 |
| Sales revenues............................ | 200,000 | 200,000 |
| Income (Loss) before taxes................. | $ (5,000) | $ 20,000 |
| Less: Income taxes....................... | (2,500) | 10,000 |
| Net Income (Loss)........................ | $ (2,500) | $ 10,000 |

"The cost of the present machine is a sunk cost," Mr. Adams said. "The new machine will cost us $105,000 and since it will increase our net income by $12,500 a year, it will bring us a good deal more than the 8 percent annual after-tax return on investment that we want."

Upon investigation, you discover the following additional information:

(1) Machine data:

|  | Present Machine | New Machine |
|---|---|---|
| Expected life................................. | Not applicable | 10 years |
| Original cost ................................ | $ 55,000 | $110,000 |
| Tax depreciation to date..................... | 27,000 | 0 |
| Present trade-in value....................... | 10,000 | Not applicable |
| Expected trade-in value after 7 years.......... | 5,000 | 35,000 |
| Expected trade-in value after 10 years......... | 0 | 10,000 |
| Capacity in units per year .................... | 60,000 | 80,000 |
| Expected output (units per year).............. | 50,000 | 50,000 |

(2)  Several products are manufactured in the same factory. Product W is now being assigned 25 percent of the total factory overhead cost other than equipment depreciation. Factory overhead other than equipment depreciation can be predicted from the following formula:

$$\$240,000 + 0.5 \times \text{Direct labor cost.}$$

Installation of the new machine would add $500 a year in electric power costs over and above the amounts indicated by this formula.

(3)  Tax depreciation on the old machine has been calculated on the sum-of-the-years'-digits method, based on a 10-year life and zero salvage. Tax depreciation on the new equipment would follow the same pattern. Gains and losses on the sale of equipment would be taxed at the regular tax rate, and no "investment credit" is available. Depreciation for internal financial reporting is calculated on a straight-line basis.

(4)  If production of product W were discontinued, the present machine could be disposed of. None of the fixed factory overhead costs other than equipment depreciation would be affected by discontinuation of product W, nor would any saving in selling and administrative expenses be made. Working capital of $10,000 would be released for use elsewhere, however.

Present and support a recommendation as to the desirability of continuing the manufacture of product W and purchasing the new machine. Establish the alternatives clearly and indicate the consequences of each.

**25.**  The Caldwell Manufacturing Company is using a special-purpose A-16 machine in the manufacture of a certain product. Because of expected increases in sales volume, additional capacity will have to be acquired. Two possibilities are under review:

A.  Purchase an additional A-16 machine identical to the present one, and operate the two machines; or
B.  Purchase a new high-speed B-32 machine with double the capacity of the present machine and keep the present A-16 machine as standby equipment.

The following information is available:

(1)  Production requirements are expected to average 70,000 units a year.
(2)  All machines are assumed to have a 10-year life from date of installation, with zero salvage value at the end of that time. Sum-of-the-years'-digits depreciation is used for tax purposes.
(3)  The present A-16 machine had a cost of $8,800 four years ago. Its present market value is $4,800.
(4)  The price of the new A-16 machine is $9,900. Unless the B-32

machine is bought now, the present A-16 will have to be replaced six years from now at a cost of $11,000. The market value of this replacement machine will be about $5,000 when it is four years old.

(5) The price of a new B-32 machine is $39,600.
(6) Repair and maintenance costs for an A-16 machine used regularly during the year are $2,800 a year.
(7) Repair and maintenance costs for the B-32 machine and an A-16 machine used for standby purposes would total $4,000 a year.
(8) Comparative variable costs per unit of output are:

|  | A-16 | B-32 |
|---|---|---|
| Materials | $0.136 | $0.208 |
| Supplies | 0.052 | 0.024 |
| Labor | 0.212 | 0.088 |
| Total | $0.400 | $0.320 |

(9) The minimum acceptable rate of return is 8 percent after taxes. Income tax rate is 50 percent.

a) Which alternative would you choose? Show your calculations.
b) Indicate for *each* of the following whether the purchase of the B-32 machine would become more or less desirable. Explain your answer.

(1) New labor contract raises wage rates.
(2) After-tax minimum acceptable rate of return increases.
(3) Demand for product increases, so machine usage is increased to 80,000 units a year.
(4) Materials prices increase.

**26.** Early in 1969, the Nonon Company was considering whether to begin the manufacture and sale of a new product. Information on the new product is summarized below:

(1) Development costs through the end of 1968 were $80,000. Further development costs of $100,000 in 1969 and $200,000 in 1970 would be required.
(2) A manufacturing facility would be built in 1970. The plant would cost $1,200,000 and have a life of 25 years. The equipment would cost $2,000,000 and have an average life of 15 years.
(3) The estimated price and cost data developed on the new product were:

| | |
|---|---|
| Sales price per pound | $ 0.90 |
| Variable manufacturing cost per pound | 0.40 |
| Variable selling and administrative cost per pound | 0.10 |
| Fixed factory cost per year exclusive of depreciation | 225,000 |
| Fixed selling and administrative cost per year | 150,000 |

(4) The sales forecast for the product was:

```
1971 ...................   500,000 lbs.
1972 ................... 1,500,000
1973 ................... 2,000,000
1974 ................... 2,700,000
1975 ................... 3,000,000
```

(5)  The plant had a capacity of 3.5 million pounds, but it could readily be increased if the demand should go above that level. It was expected that sales would continue to grow after 1975 at a modest rate. However, a forecast of sales for the first five years was difficult, and forecasting beyond that year was largely guess work. It was therefore decided to make the analyses on the assumption that sales of 3,000,000 units would be maintained through 1995.

(6)  The company is subject to a 50 percent tax rate and has been quite profitable. It uses double-rate, declining-balance depreciation for book and tax purposes.

(7)  From 1971 to 1975, the expenditures on plant and equipment not included in the above costs were expected to be negligible. From 1976 to 1995, they were expected to be about equal to the depreciation expense which would be maintained at about the 1976 level by these expenditures.

(8)  Introduction of the new product would require additional working capital totaling $700,000, but not all of this would be necessary immediately. The working capital would be built up according to the following schedule (increments would be required as of the *beginning* of each year):

```
1971 ................. $200,000
1972 .................  300,000
1973 .................  150,000
1974 .................   50,000
```

(9)  In 1995, the plant was expected to be worth $300,000, the equipment $1,400,000, and the working capital the amount invested.

(10) The corporation requires a 10 percent return on investment after taxes.

Should the Nonon Company have continued the development of this new product in 1969? (Except for the increments in working capital, all cash flows should be assumed to take place at the *end* of the year.)

27.† Mr. Walter Weber, general manager of Sovad, S.A., looked across his desk at Mr. Karl Huber, the company's sales manager. Mr. Huber had just suggested that Sovad increase its capacity to manufacture automatic timing devices.

"All right," said Mr. Weber, "let's see if the profits from the increased sales will give us a big enough return on investment. As soon as you're

---

† Copyright 1968 by l'Institut pour l'Etude des Méthodes de Direction de l'Entreprise (IMEDE), Lausanne, Switzerland. Reprinted by permission.

ready, give Mr. Berner (the company's controller) your estimates of sales and what you'll need for advertising and sales promotion. He can work with purchasing and manufacturing to get the rest of the data he needs. I'll ask him to give me a recommendation on your proposal sometime next week."

Sovad, S.A. was a manufacturer of industrial controls and precision instruments, with headquarters and manufacturing facilities in Winterthur, Switzerland. Its manufacturing operations in 1967 were conducted entirely in Winterthur, but more than half of its 1967 sales were made in other countries.

First introduced in 1964, the company's automatic timers had been well received by Sovad's customers both at home and abroad. By 1967 Sovad was selling all that it could manufacture. Mr. Huber was convinced that he could expand his sales in Switzerland by large amounts if adequate factory capacity could be provided.

Before coming to Mr. Weber with his suggestion, Mr. Huber had discussed the idea of expansion with Mr. Gluck, the company's director of manufacturing. "Our Winterthur factory is already crowded," Mr. Gluck told him. "The authorities won't give us a building permit to expand it, but I know of some vacant space that we can rent in Zurich for Fr. 50,000 a year. We could put all the timer operations in there." Zurich is only 20 kilometers from Winterthur and Mr. Gluck was confident that he could supervise manufacturing operations in both places without difficulty.

Working with Mr. Gluck, Mr. Huber prepared the preliminary estimates shown in Exhibit 1. As he gave this exhibit to Mr. Berner, Mr. Huber remarked that an eight-month payback period was hard to beat.

### Exhibit 1
#### Zurich Timer Factory
#### PRELIMINARY PROFITABILITY ESTIMATE

| | | |
|---|---:|---:|
| Sales (30,000 units at Fr. 50)..................... | | Fr. 1,500,000 |
| Out of pocket expenses: | | |
| Factory labor and materials (30,000 units at Fr. 28.40)................................. | Fr. 852,000 | |
| Rent ........................................... | 50,000 | |
| Other factory costs (not including depreciation).. | 70,000 | |
| Marketing expenses............................ | 160,000 | |
| Total Expenses.......................... | | 1,132,000 |
| Profit Contribution ............................... | | Fr. 368,000 |
| | | |
| Equipment required: | | |
| New equipment to be purchased ................ | Fr. 250,000 | |
| Old equipment, to be moved from Winterthur .... | 1 | |
| Cost of moving old equipment from Winterthur and installing it at Zurich..................... | 5,000 | |
| Total........................................ | | Fr. 255,000 |

$$\text{Payback Period} = \frac{\text{Fr. 255,000}}{\text{Fr. 368,000}} = 0.69 \text{ Year} = 8.3 \text{ Months.}$$

He hoped that Mr. Berner wouldn't take too long to pass the proposal on to Mr. Weber for approval.

In the course of his examination of these figures, Mr. Berner discovered two things. First, the sales and expense figures given in Exhibit 1 were not expected to be achieved until the third year of the new factory's operation. Second, they represented the *total* sales and expenses of the timers. Since the company was already selling 10,000 timers a year, Mr. Berner did not believe that the profit on these units should be used to justify the opening of the new factory. As he put it, "The data that we need are differential or incremental figures, the differences between having the new factory and not having it." Mr. Huber estimated that he would be able to sell 30,000 timers a year after a two-year introductory period. His detailed estimates of annual sales and marketing expenses are summarized in Exhibit 2.

Mr. Berner knew that these volumes of sales would require sizable investments in working capital which Mr. Huber had omitted from Exhibit 1. On the basis of the company's past experience, he estimated that the *cumulative* balance of working capital required at the beginning of each year would be as follows:

If timers are manufactured in Zurich:
| | |
|---|---:|
| Year 1 | Fr. 700,000 |
| Year 2 | 750,000 |
| Year 3 and after | 800,000 |
| If timers are not manufactured in Zurich | Fr. 300,000 |

Exhibit 2

Zurich Timer Factory

ESTIMATED ANNUAL TIMER SALES

AND MARKETING EXPENSES

| | Annual Sales | | Annual Marketing Costs |
|---|---|---|---|
| | Units | Value | |
| If all timers are manufactured in Zurich: | | | |
| Year 1 | 20,000 | Fr. 1,000,000 | Fr. 260,000 |
| Year 2 | 25,000 | 1,250,000 | 260,000 |
| Year 3 and after | 30,000 | 1,500,000 | 160,000 |
| If timers are not manufactured in | | | |
| Zurich | 10,000 | Fr. 500,000 | Fr. 60,000 |

When questioned about the manufacturing cost estimates in Exhibit 1, Mr. Gluck gave Mr. Berner the figures shown in Exhibit 3. Mr. Gluck explained that if the Zurich factory were opened, all automatic timer production would be shifted to Zurich. If the expansion proposal were to be rejected, however, the cost of producing 10,000 timers a year at Winterthur would be Fr. 31 per unit plus Fr. 20,000 a year. All of these costs could be eliminated if operations were transferred to Zurich.

Mr. Berner also questioned Mr. Gluck about the equipment that would be moved from Winterthur to Zurich. "That is the old test equipment that we are now replacing here in Winterthur," he replied. "It's perfectly adequate for the timers, and it saves us from buying new equipment for the new location. It's fully depreciated on our books, but it's in perfect condition and I see no reason why it wouldn't last for years.

"If we don't open up in Zurich, we'll sell this old equipment locally for about Fr. 10,000. If we keep it, our only cost will be about Fr. 5,000 to get it from Winterthur to Zurich. We can subtract this Fr. 5,000 from

Exhibit 3

Zurich Timer Factory

ESTIMATED FACTORY COSTS

| | Variable Costs per Unit | Fixed Costs per Year | | |
| --- | --- | --- | --- | --- |
| | | Rental | Depreciation | Other |
| Year 1..................... | Fr. 29.60 | Fr. 50,000 | Fr. 25,000 | Fr. 70,000 |
| Year 2..................... | 28.80 | 50,000 | 25,000 | 70,000 |
| Year 3 and after.......... | 28.40 | 50,000 | 25,000 | 70,000 |

the taxable income from our other operations right away, even before we start operating at Zurich."

For purposes of analysis, Mr. Berner and Mr. Huber agreed that the new Zurich plant should be able to operate for at least 10 years and that the company's investment in working capital would be a reasonable measure of the value of the Zurich assets at the end of that time.

In evaluating capital expenditure proposals, Mr. Berner used an income tax rate of 30 percent of ordinary taxable income. Gains on the sale of equipment were also taxed at a 30 percent rate. Depreciation for tax purposes on the new equipment to be purchased for the Zurich plant would be Fr. 50,000 a year for five years.

a) Prepare a timetable of the before-tax cash flows that are relevant to the evaluation of this expansion proposal. Do you agree with Mr. Berner that these should be differential figures?

b) If Sovad required at least a 20 percent return on investment, before income taxes, should Sovad have opened the Zurich factory?

c) How would your analysis differ if you were to use after-tax cash flows and a minimum acceptable rate of return of 14 percent?

# *23*

# THE CONTROL PROCESS: STANDARD COSTING

ONCE MANAGEMENT HAS ESTABLISHED its plans, it needs to keep informed on the organization's successes and failures in implementing these plans. Providing this kind of *feedback information* is a key accounting responsibility. The purpose of this chapter is to explain how management can use feedback information and how the accountant can generate it.

To avoid unnecessary confusion, we shall concentrate here very narrowly, on the problems of developing and using feedback data in the control of factory direct labor and direct materials costs. Before doing so, however, let us look briefly at the management process in which feedback information is used.

## RESPONSIVE CONTROL

Control reporting is tied closely to the concept of responsibility — that is, that results should be reported to those executives who are responsible for achieving them. This concept is reflected in the company's organization chart. Each block in the chart represents a *responsibility center* — an organization unit headed by a single person, *answerable* to higher authority and obligated to perform certain tasks. The responsibility centers of the lowest level are known by different names in different companies, *department* being perhaps the most common.

Information on the absolute level of performance is of little use in responsive control unless it is accompanied by information that will put it in perspective — that is, control reports are always comparative, embodying or facilitating comparisons between observed performance and some reference set.

In most cases this reference information consists of expressed or implied standards of what performance should have been. For example, an outside temperature of 78° F. would be considered cool after several days of intense heat, but would be judged hot on a late fall day.

Standards for use in financial reporting to management are usually expressions of the performance level that management believes ought to be achieved. In the aggregate, these standards are provided by budget figures of the kinds described in Chapter 18. The budget represents the level of performance that management has agreed is both attainable and satisfactory.

In any case, control reports should identify the *deviations* of actual performance from the planned or prior performance that is being used as the reference point. Each manager should be informed of deviations within his own area of responsibility, so that he can investigate the causes and take whatever action seems most appropriate. The subdivision of managerial accounting that deals with these matters is known as *responsibility accounting*.

This emphasis on deviations is part of what is known as *management by exception*. The underlying notion is that as long as actual performance in a given area is close to planned performance, management can assume that operations in this area are under control. It can therefore feel secure in directing its attention elsewhere. Substantial deviations from plan, on the other hand, signal the presence of unplanned conditions that should be investigated if the costs of investigation are not too high.

If the investigation indicates that the deviations are the result of environmental conditions different from those on which the plan was predicated, then the remedy is to revise the plan. Replanning is also appropriate if the actual performance was better than the plan, and if the causes of this were internal. If internal causes led to poor performance, however, the appropriate response is to take actions that will remove the causes. Replanning is an *adaptive* response; remedial effort is a *corrective* response.

## A STANDARD COSTING SYSTEM FOR DIRECT LABOR AND MATERIALS

The management of the Landau Company, a small manufacturer of industrial equipment, has made sure that managers at all levels receive feedback information on a regular basis. The information provided to each manager is tailored to that manager's specific needs.

## The Need for Information

The company's factory manager needs and receives a good deal of information, some of it daily, some weekly, some monthly, and some only when he asks for it. He needs information on direct labor and direct materials costs in the factory's two production departments, machining and assembly, for one purpose only— to give him a measure of how effectively the department foremen have controlled these costs. If a foreman's performance appears to be good, the factory manager makes a point of praising him. If costs seem to have got out of control, he asks the foreman for an explanation and a plan to bring them back into line.

The foremen themselves do not need accounting reports to tell them when control efforts are needed—they are close enough to their own operations to identify problems as they arise and respond to them. They need the reports only as a kind of score card, to reinforce their motivation to control costs and to indicate how successful their efforts have been.

## Standard Product Costs

To provide this information, the company's accountants have installed a simple form of standard costing system. To do this, they have developed a file of standard costs for each product the firm manufactures.

Exhibit 23–1 presents the Landau Company's standard cost sheet for one of its products, No. 6948. The first column lists all the items of direct material and all the direct labor operations required in the manufacture of the product. The next three columns contain the standard quantity of material required per 1,000 units of the product, the standard price per unit of the material item, and the standard cost of the standard material quantity. The next three columns contain the analogous information for direct labor.

The development of a standard cost sheet for each product is facilitated by the prior development of standard cost files for materials and labor. The materials cost file contains the standard price for each item of direct material purchased by the company, and the labor cost file contains the standard wage rate for each class of labor. The standard materials prices and wage rates are set by the Landau Company prior to the start of each year, and

*Exhibit 23–1*
## A STANDARD COST SHEET

| Department | Machining | | | Quantity | 1,000 | |
|---|---|---|---|---|---|---|
| Description | Door Front No. 6948 | | | | | |
| Standard Cost | $457.00 | | | Standard Cost per Unit | $0.457 | |

| Operation or Item | Materials | | | Labor | | |
|---|---|---|---|---|---|---|
| | Quantity | Price | Total | Hours | Rate | Total |
| Steel Sheet | 3,600 | $0.08 | $288.00 | | | |
| Cut | | | | 4.8 | $3.50 | $ 16.80 |
| Drill | | | | 16.0 | 3.75 | 60.00 |
| Stamp | | | | 7.3 | 4.00 | 29.20 |
| Finish | | | | 18.0 | 3.50 | 63.00 |
| Total | | | $288.00 | | | $169.00 |

they represent the expected materials prices and wage rates that will prevail for the coming year.

The other ingredient underlying standard product costs is a statement of the quantities of materials and labor that are necessary to the manufacture of individual products. The *bill of materials* for each product lists the kinds of materials to be used, together with an estimate of the quantity of each that should be necessary in the manufacture of a standard-sized batch of the product. ("Materials" in this context includes component parts that are obtained either from stock or from outside vendors.)

The *operations routing sheet* provides the same kind of information for direct labor. It lists the operations to be performed in the manufacture of the product, the classes of labor to be used, and the amount of labor time that should be necessary to perform each operation.

## Quantity Variances

Standard product costs can be used in a number of ways. Our interest centers on their use in feedback reporting, however, particularly in the development and reporting of *quantity variances* in direct labor and direct materials costs. A quantity variance is a difference between a standard quantity of labor or materials and the quantity actually used, both multiplied by the standard price or rate.

For example, suppose that 3 pounds of material are required per unit of output and that the standard cost per pound of material is $0.50, so that the standard material cost per unit of output is $1.50. Assume also that the department received 3,600 pounds of material, delivered 1,100 units of finished product, and had no material in process either at the start or at the end of the period. The materials quantity variance would be determined as follows:

Standard quantity:       1,100 units × 3 pounds × $0.50 = $1,650
Actual quantity:                   3,600 pounds × $0.50 =  1,800
    Materials Quantity Variance:    300 pounds × $0.50 = $  (150)

In this case the departments used 300 pounds more than the standard quantity, or $150 at the standard price of 50 cents a pound. This is by definition an *unfavorable* variance; if the standard quantity exceeds the actual quantity used, the variance is said to be *favorable*.

## Price Variances

Because both quantities in this calculation were multiplied by the same price, the variance can be ascribed to quantity differences only. The prices actually paid for materials and labor are seldom exactly equal to standard prices, however, and differences of this kind give rise to price variances. A price variance is the difference between the standard price and the price actually paid to acquire a resource. Labor price variances are known as *labor rate variances*.

Price variances should be reported to those who make purchasing or personnel compensation decisions. Since they typically do not result from the actions or decisions of production department foremen, they should not be reported to them or attributed to their operations. Price variances may or may not be controllable by anyone in the organization, but it is essential in any case to keep them separate from the quantity variances.

## Determining the Quantity Variance

Because the Landau Company's management does not use its standard costing system to identify specific control problems for its foremen, it does not need to accumulate and report quantity variances in great detail. Variances are calculated monthly, in total for each department. Actual quantities of labor and materials used are classified by department only; no job order cost sheets are used.

To see how these variances are determined, let us examine the materials cost figures for Landau's machining department for the month of September, 19x1. The jobs completed by this department during the month had a total standard materials cost of $57,250. This was not a perfect measure of the standard materials cost of the work actually done, however, because the department had a number of jobs in process both at the beginning and at the end of the month. The standard materials cost of the ending work in process was $24,000, as opposed to $23,240 on September 1. This $760 increase in the standard materials cost of the department's inventory represented work done during the month, and the standard cost of the work done can be calculated as follows:

| | |
|---|---:|
| Jobs finished, at standard materials cost | $57,250 |
| Jobs in process, end-of-month, at standard materials cost | 24,000 |
| Total | $81,250 |
| Less: jobs in process, beginning-of-month, at standard materials cost | 23,240 |
| Standard Materials Cost of Work Done | $58,010 |

To measure the departmental materials quantity variance for the month, we must compare this standard cost with the cost of the quantity of materials actually used. In this case the materials issued to the machining department during September had a total standard cost of $53,200. Since the standard materials quantities and the actual quantities used were both measured at standard materials prices, the differences between these two totals measured the quantity variance only:

| | |
|---|---:|
| Standard quantities at standard prices | $58,010 |
| Actual quantities at standard prices | 53,200 |
| Materials Quantity Variance | $ 4,810 |

In this case the department used less material than the standards called for, leading to a substantial favorable quantity variance.

## ACCOUNTS FOR STANDARD COSTING

Although standard cost variances can be generated outside the ledger accounts, through calculations like those we have just illustrated, it is usually more economical or more convenient to tie them into the regular factory cost records.

## The Basic Structure

The mechanism by which this is accomplished begins with the departmentalization of costs. Exhibit 23-2 shows the balances in the Landau Company's factory inventory accounts on September 1, 19x1. Each inventory in this list is measured at standard cost, and each department has its own work in process accounts, one for materials and the other for labor. Separate work in process accounts are used for labor and materials costs to facilitate the isolation of the quantity variances. (Overhead costs are ignored in this illustration, and will be considered in Chapter 24.)

Exhibit 23-2

Landau Company

FACTORY INVENTORY ACCOUNT BALANCES
September 1, 19x1

| | |
|---|---:|
| Raw material | $ 32,800 |
| Material in process—machining | 23,240 |
| Labor in process—machining | 8,500 |
| Material in process—assembly | 31,300 |
| Labor in process—assembly | 10,100 |
| Finished goods | 51,000 |
| Total | $156,940 |

Most factories have many departments rather than just two, but the accounts required to implement a standard costing system for fifty production departments present no conceptual problems beyond those to be encountered in two. No useful purpose would be served by burdening this illustration with additional departments.

The Landau Company's standard costing system is one of the simplest and least expensive. Known as a *basic plan* system, it has five main features:

1. Materials price variances are segregated at the time of purchase and do not enter the inventory accounts.
2. Each department is charged with the actual quantities of all of the direct labor and direct materials that it uses, multiplied by standard wage rates or standard materials prices.
3. Each department is credited with the standard cost of all of the products it completes during each month.
4. Usage variances are measured at the end of each month in the form of departmental totals; they are not measured for individual job orders or individual operations.

5. All work in process inventory account balances are restated at standard cost at the end of each month.

## Purchases of Materials

When material is purchased, the goods acquired are charged by the Landau Company to the Raw Material account at standard cost. To accomplish this, each item on the vendor's invoice is re-priced at its standard cost, obtained from the standard cost file mentioned earlier. Of course, the supplier must be paid the actual cost or invoice prices of the material, and the difference is charged to a *material price variance* account.

During September the actual cost of the material purchased by the Landau Company was $63,800, while the same material priced at standard was $60,250. A summary entry covering all these purchases would be:

(1)

| | | |
|---|---|---|
| Raw Material..................................... | 60,250 | |
| Material Price Variance ....................... | 3,550 | |
| Accounts Payable .......................... | | 63,800 |

The balance in this variance account is to be interpreted in the same way as under- or overabsorbed overhead. A debit balance is unfavorable in that the actual cost is greater than the standard cost, while a credit variance is favorable because the goods were acquired at less than standard cost.

## Issues of Materials

When material is requisitioned by one of the manufacturing departments, the *standard* cost of that material is credited to the Raw Material account and charged to the department's Material in Process account. The entries that were made to record the direct materials issued during the month of September can be summarized as follows:

(2)

| | | |
|---|---|---|
| Material in Process—Machining ................. | 53,200 | |
| Material in Process—Assembly ................. | 15,800 | |
| Raw Material............................... | | 69,000 |

Notice that no reference is made here to entries on job cost sheets. Although standard cost systems can be designed to provide for this added feature, the basic plan used by the Landau Company makes no such provision. Instead, the *department* is the basic unit to which actual costs are assigned. Furthermore, when all materials inventories are priced at standard prices, the materials ledger can be kept in physical quantities only – dollar amounts can be computed at any time by multiplying the quantities on hand by their standard prices.

### Accounting for Labor Costs

Direct labor costs, like direct materials costs, are charged to departments and not to jobs. Each department is charged with the direct labor hours it uses, multiplied by the standard wage rates for each class of labor employed. On this basis, an entry summarizing the actual direct labor hours used in the Landau Company's two departments during September would be:

(3)

| | | |
|---|---|---|
| Labor in Process – Machining.................... | 21,400 | |
| Labor in Process – Assembly .................... | 20,000 | |
| Accrued Labor............................. | | 41,400 |

The Accrued Labor account is a temporary clearing account. The credit balance in this account after entry (3) was made was a first approximation to the liability arising from the use of direct labor during the month. The company's actual liability, however, was for the actual wages earned by the employees, not the standard rate of pay. This was determined when the payrolls for the period were prepared, reflecting the actual hours worked and the actual wage rate for each employee. The payrolls for September can be summarized in the following entry:

(4)

| | | |
|---|---|---|
| Accrued Labor.................................. | 39,220 | |
| Wages Payable ............................ | | 39,220 |

The credit to Wages Payable records the correct amount of the company's wage liability. If actual and standard wage rates have been identical, the debit to Accrued Labor will return the balance in this account to zero. If actual rates have differed from standard, however, the account balance will represent the labor rate variance. This can be seen by looking at a schematic representation of this account:

Accrued Labor

| Actual hours × <br> actual wage rates | Actual hours × <br> standard wage rates |
|---|---|

Since the same number of hours appears on both sides of this account, any account balance must be due to differences between the standard and actual wage rates. This account therefore was closed out by entry (5):

(5)

Accrued Labor ................................... 2,180
    Labor Rate Variance ..........................          2,180

In this case the labor rate variance was favorable (credit balance), indicating that the average actual wage rate was less than the standard wage rates for the work done during the period.

## Completion of Intermediate and End Products

When a department completes a production order, the output is transferred to another department or to the finished goods storeroom. If the output is an intermediate product that is stored with the raw material, such as a batch of component parts, the transfer of the output is to the raw material stock room. These transfers are all recorded at standard cost, obtained from the file of standard product costs developed from the standard cost sheets illustrated in Exhibit 23–1.

In terms of procedure, the completion of a production order by a department is evidenced in the Landau Company by a *transfer slip* which identifies the item, the quantity transferred, the department that produced the item, and the department or inventory location to which the item was transferred. The accounting department refers to the standard product cost file to establish the standard labor and material cost per unit. The quantity transferred is then costed at these unit figures to establish the relevant totals.

The machining department in the Landau Company's factory transfers part of its completed production to the assembly department; the remainder, consisting of machined parts, is placed in the finished goods storeroom in the factory. The standard costs of the products completed by the machining department during September were as follows:

|  | Trans-ferred to Assembly Department | Transferred to Finished Goods Storeroom | Total Transfers |
|---|---|---|---|
| Materials ...................... | $52,050 | $5,200 | $57,250 |
| Labor........................ | 18,850 | 4,100 | 22,950 |
|     Total ..................... | $70,900 | $9,300 | $80,200 |

In summary form, the entries to record these transfers were as follows:

(6)

| | | |
|---|---|---|
| Material in Process—Assembly | 70,900 | |
| Finished Goods | 9,300 | |
|     Material in Process—Machining | | 57,250 |
|     Labor in Process—Machining | | 22,950 |

Notice that the *entire* standard cost of the items transferred to the assembly department was charged to the assembly department as *materials* costs. The reason is that the assembly department regards these items as materials. The assembly foreman neither knows nor cares whether labor cost in the machining department amounted to 10 percent or 90 percent of the total standard cost of these materials. If one of his operators destroys materials by careless handling, the cost of this loss is part of his materials quantity variance, not partly labor and partly materials. In other words, materials are materials whether received directly from outside vendors, transferred from other departments, or issued from the storeroom.

The assembly department, in turn, completed work on a number of jobs during the month and transferred the finished products to the finished goods stockroom. The standard costs of these items were:

| | |
|---|---|
| Materials | $ 98,400 |
| Labor | 26,300 |
| Total | $124,700 |

A summary entry to record these transfers would be:

(7)

| | | |
|---|---|---|
| Finished Goods | 124,700 | |
|     Material in Process—Assembly | | 98,400 |
|     Labor in Process—Assembly | | 26,300 |

## Deriving Usage Variances

After all of the machining department's transactions for the month had been recorded, its materials in process account showed the following:

Material in Process—Machining

| | | | | |
|---|---|---|---|---|
| Bal. 9/1 | 23,240 | (6) | | 57,250 |
| (2) | 53,200 | | | |
| | 76,440 | | | |
| Bal. 9/30 | 19,190 | | | |

As this shows, the department foreman was responsible for materials with a total standard cost of $76,440. By completing a number of jobs and transferring products to the assembly department or to the finished goods stockroom, he received credit for $57,250 in standard costs, leaving $19,190 unaccounted for. If the department had had no material in process at the end of the month, this would have indicated that the department had used $19,190 more material (at standard prices) than the standard material cost of the month's output.

The department manager would be quick to point out, however, that this calculation did not consider the material remaining in the department at the end of September. The extent to which the department's usage of material was above or below standard depends on the amount of material in process at the end of the month. As we saw earlier, the standard cost of the material in process in the machinery department at the end of September was $24,000. Therefore, the end-of-month material in process plus the material content of the goods finished is $24,000 + $57,250 = $81,250.

Comparing this with the total standard cost of the materials issued to the department during the month plus the materials in process in the department at the beginning of the month reveals a favorable materials quantity variance of $4,810. This is the same figure that we developed earlier, before introducing the use of accounts. The following entry served to record this variance and restore the Work in Process account to its correct end-of-month balance:

(8)

| | | |
|---|---|---|
| Material in Process – Machining | 4,810 | |
| Materials Quantity Variance | | 4,810 |

The credit to the variance account indicates that this particular variance was favorable.

All four departmental inventory accounts are shown in Exhibit 23–3. The standard costs of the other elements of the work in process on September 30 were found to be:

| | |
|---|---|
| Labor in process – machining | $ 8,400 |
| Material in process – assembly | 18,800 |
| Labor in process – assembly | 7,900 |

The quantity variances can be calculated by subtracting the balances in the accounts from the standard cost of the inventories

Exhibit 23–3

Landau Company

UNADJUSTED DEPARTMENT INVENTORY ACCOUNTS

September 30, 19x1

Material in Process — Machining

| | | | |
|---|---|---|---|
| Bal. 9/1 | 23,240 | (6) | 57,250 |
| (2) | 53,200 | | |
| | 76,440 | | |
| Bal. 19,190 | | | |

Material in Process — Assembly

| | | | |
|---|---|---|---|
| Bal. 9/1 | 31,300 | (7) | 98,400 |
| (2) | 15,800 | | |
| (6) | 70,900 | | |
| | 118,000 | | |
| Bal. 19,600 | | | |

Labor in Process — Machining

| | | | |
|---|---|---|---|
| Bal. 9/1 | 8,500 | (6) | 22,950 |
| (3) | 21,400 | | |
| | 29,900 | | |
| Bal. 6,950 | | | |

Labor in Process — Assembly

| | | | |
|---|---|---|---|
| Bal. 9/1 | 10,100 | (7) | 26,300 |
| (3) | 20,000 | | |
| | 30,100 | | |
| Bal. 3,800 | | | |

actually on hand at the end of the month. It may be helpful, however, to structure the variance calculations once again in the input/output format that we started with:

| | Machining Labor | Assembly Material | Assembly Labor |
|---|---|---|---|
| Output at standard cost: | | | |
| Completed production .............. | $22,950 | $98,400 | $26,300 |
| Increase (decrease) in work in process ...................... | (100) | (12,500) | (2,200) |
| Total output at standard cost.... | $22,850 | $85,900 | $24,100 |
| Input at standard prices.............. | 21,400 | 86,700 | 20,000 |
| Favorable (Unfavorable) Usage Variance .................... | $ 1,450 | $ (800) | $ 4,100 |

The entries which picked up the variances and restored the work in process accounts to their correct end-of-month balances were:

(9)

| | | |
|---|---|---|
| Labor in Process — Machining ...................... 1,450 | | |
| Labor Quantity Variance — Machining.......... | | 1,450 |

(10)

| | | |
|---|---|---|
| Material Quantity Variance — Assembly ............ 800 | | |
| Material in Process — Assembly................. | | 800 |

(11)

| | | |
|---|---|---|
| Labor in Process — Assembly ...................... 4,100 | | |
| Labor Quantity Variance — Assembly .......... | | 4,100 |

In other words, the assembly department used slightly more materials in the aggregate than the standards called for, while both departments were able to process their outputs with less than the standard quantities of labor.

### Transactions Summary

The cost flows in a basic plan standard costing system are summarized in Exhibit 23–4. Raw material is purchased and then issued to departments. Labor is used and charged to departments. Products are finished and their standard costs are transferred to the finished goods inventory account. Finally, variances are computed and transferred to variance accounts.

*Exhibit 23–4*

**DIRECT LABOR AND DIRECT MATERIALS COST FLOWS
IN A BASIC PLAN STANDARD COSTING SYSTEM**
(departmental detail and overhead costs omitted)

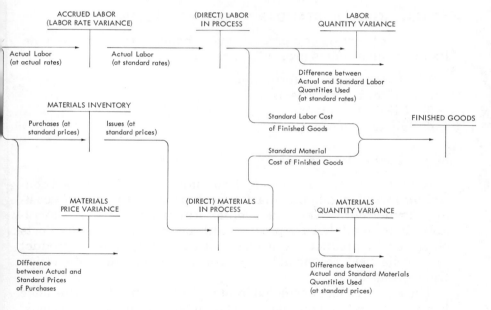

### Cost of Goods Sold under Standard Costing

Under standard costing, the finished goods inventories are measured at their standard costs. This means that when goods are sold, the amount transferred to the Cost of Goods Sold account will be the standard cost. In September, 19x1, these transfers totaled $119,300.

Reports summarizing operating results for management's information typically show not only the standard cost of goods sold but the variances as well. The total of all of these figures is sometimes called the actual cost of goods sold, but it may differ substantially from the cost of goods sold that would be recorded under an actual cost system. Under the basic plan standard cost system, the cost of goods sold for a month is the standard cost of goods sold, plus or minus: (1) the price variances on the material and labor *purchased* during the month; and (2) the usage variances on the *production* during the month.

The reason for this apparent contradiction is that management needs to be informed of the variances as soon after they take place as is feasible. For instance, if materials prices have gone up, management should be advised of their consequences for operations currently and not a few months later, as they would under most historical costing systems.

## ADVANTAGES OF STANDARD COSTING SYSTEMS

Standard costing can produce many benefits for management. Its main advantages are:

1. Better control information.
2. Better data for decisions.
3. Clerical economy.
4. Faster reporting.

### Better Control Information

Actual cost systems lack one important ingredient of good control information, a bench mark for comparison. In job order costing, furthermore, even when some form of bench mark is available, it is available by product and not by department. Costs classified by product are useless for control, because a product cannot be held responsible for or asked to explain a deviation from standard.

These defects are corrected by standard costing. The difference between actual and standard cost of goods manufactured is classified according to major areas of responsibility — materials price variance, wage rate variance, and labor and material usage variances. The last, in turn, are broken down to correspond to the department or individual immediately responsible for controlling the difference between actual and standard cost.

As long as variances are small, costs are deemed to be under control, *by definition*, and higher management need not concern itself with the subject. When substantial differences between actual and expected costs appear, however, they are automatically called to the attention of higher management, and that attention is directed to the place in the organization where the search for causes and corrective action should begin.

## Better Data for Decisions

It may be wondered how a standard cost system can be considered superior to an actual cost system in providing cost information for pricing and similar decisions. An actual cost system is continuously developing information on *actual* product costs. By contrast, the standard cost accounts can be said to provide no information on product costs, since actual costs are classified only by organization unit. The only product cost information in the accounts is standard product cost, and that is known before the production for the period is undertaken.[1]

The advantages of an actual cost system in this area are more apparent than real, however. Product cost analyses are useful only for pricing and other alternative choice decisions, and the information desired is what the cost *will be*, not what is *has been* during some prior period. The record of the actual cost the last time the item was produced may or may not provide this information.

In the first place, actual wage rates and material prices prevailing at that time may differ from those appropriate to the problem at hand. Consequently, unless the historical data are unusually detailed as regards quantity and price per unit of each class of labor and material used, it will be difficult, if not impossible, to translate them into current or expected prices. Second, because of the special conditions under which the job was produced, the actual quantities of labor and material used may be above or below what one might expect at present or in the future. If an attempt is made to correct any such unique condition by averaging costs over a number of prior jobs, the difficulty then encountered is that the data become less and less relevant as one goes back in time, and comprehensive adjustments for both price differences and technological change become necessary.

---

[1] This comment applies to the kind of standard costing system described in this chapter. Other, more complex systems can provide actual cost data by product as well as by department.

A further limitation on the usefulness of job cost information varies in importance from one firm to another but should in no case be underestimated. A department head regards his job as one of employing his men and material as efficiently as possible. Recording on each time slip and material requisition the job to be charged often appears a burdensome and senseless bookkeeping task which interferes with his primary responsibilities. He may therefore become lax in this regard, being careful only to charge each cost to *some* job, thereby keeping the bookkeepers from bothering him. The accuracy of usage data derived from job cost sheets is therefore always open to some question.

In short, the development of expected costs for decision problems from historical cost records may involve difficult and time-consuming analysis, and limitations in the organization and detail of the cost records may even then result in estimates that are far from satisfactory.

Standard cost systems, on the other hand, yield product cost information which may well be more useful than historical data. The standard cost sheet provides an estimate of what the product will cost broken down into the quantity and price for each factor: labor, material, and overhead. Insofar as current or expected labor and material prices differ from the standard prices, it is an easy task to substitute the expected values. The standard usages of labor and material are not distorted by abnormal conditions on some particular run, and therefore represent best estimates of expected usage.

### Clerical Economy

The previous description of a basic plan standard cost system indicates the main sources of clerical savings by comparison with an actual job cost system. First, an actual cost system requires raw material and finished goods ledgers with price and quantity information for each item of inventory. This information is required to cost material issues and goods sold. Because successive lots of a given item are likely to have different unit costs, the ledgers will have to keep track of separate lots (e.g., Fifo) or recompute average unit costs after each acquisition.

Under a standard cost system, no supporting ledgers are required for the raw material and finished goods accounts, since the debits and credits to these accounts are made at standard. Item inventory records can be kept in physical units only, to meet the needs of purchasing, production scheduling, and other staff departments. Debits and credits to the raw materials and finished goods accounts can be made simply by multiplying quantities in and quantities out by standard unit prices, This is simpler than maintaining an actual cost ledger, whether bookkeeping is done manually or by computer.

The second major savings in clerical cost arises from the elimination of the job cost sheets. To record actual material costs on job cost sheets, the material requisitions must be priced as described above, and then charged to individual jobs. For direct labor, the hours worked must be identified by job and the actual wage rates paid must be established and posted to the job cost sheets. This last set of operations is such a nuisance that many actual cost systems in fact charge jobs with actual hours at predetermined rates. A standard cost system just carries this to its logical conclusion. The actual material and labor used are costed at the more easily obtained standard prices, and the costs thus obtained are charged to departmental accounts only. The requisitions and time slips may or may not identify the job worked on, but the costs are not as a matter of routine classified by job.

These same features of standard costing can promote clerical cost savings in still another direction. Purchasing and production scheduling departments need up-to-date physical inventory records, as well as data on units on order or in production. The accounting department, on the other hand, needs inventory figures in monetary units to prepare external financial statements or to provide means of detecting loss and pilferage of materials and products. Actual-cost inventory ledgers, however, either cannot be updated rapidly enough to meet the needs of purchasing and production planners or are not readily accessible to nonaccounting personnel. Furthermore, they may be difficult to integrate with physical data on units on order or in production.

As a consequence of all this, purchasing and production planning often keep their own perpetual inventory records in physical terms, a costly duplication of clerical effort. Because standard costing eliminates the need for dollar figures in the ledgers used for routine financial reporting, one set of physical-unit ledgers can serve both purposes. The clerical savings from this kind of integration can be substantial.

### Faster Reporting

Standard costing can make another kind of contribution by enabling the accounting department to issue reports to management more promptly after the end of a reporting period. For example, when a job is finished, this fact can be recorded immediately without waiting for the complete posting of data from the requisitions and time tickets to the job cost sheet. Furthermore, with fewer clerical operations to be performed, the accounts themselves can be brought up to date more rapidly. If management can be more effective with a prompter feedback on the results of operations, the payoff from this feature can be great.

## IMPLEMENTATION PROBLEMS IN STANDARD COSTING

The successful use of standard costing requires the solution of a number of implementation problems. One is to achieve an appropriate balance between system benefits and system costs. We have already mentioned that basic plan systems are relatively cheap to operate because they sacrifice information. More elaborate systems can go so far as to provide variance reports daily, with quantity variances classified by machine center (group of similar machines), by individual machine, or even by individual operator. This added information is costly, of course, and management must decide whether it is worth the added cost.

Further discussion of this point can be found in more advanced texts, but three other kinds of problems are worth some discussion at the introductory level. One problem is to find appropriate data on which to base labor and material quantity standards. Related to this is the problem of dealing with inevitable inaccuracies in the quantity standards. Finally there is the necessity of anticipating and solving the behavioral problems that often arise in control systems. We shall deal briefly here with the problems of data gathering and data accuracy, leaving behavioral issues to the next chapter.

### Data for Quantity Standards

Standard usage rates are more difficult to derive than price standards. At the initial installation of a standard costing system, a firm may use its historical cost data, if these are reasonably well organized, to establish standard allowances for the material and labor content of each product. It is wise to supplement, or at least to check, such figures by consultation with production people in each department. Since the typical firm has developed and used this kind of product cost information for pricing purposes, it is usually readily available, and no great outlay of time and money is therefore needed to formulate workable standards.

However, the functions of a system based on such crude standards should be limited to reducing bookkeeping costs and shortening the time required for producing operating statements. Since many firms are well satisfied with systems which accomplish no more, one should not underestimate the practical importance of these objectives. As evidence of how little by way of accuracy may be required, some firms find it possible to revise standards as infrequently as once in five years. In such cases, top management continues to rely on observation and personal contact with department heads for incentives and control.

Once a standard cost system is installed, however, actual costs may no longer be classified by jobs, and job cost sheets can no longer be used to provide information on the cost of individual products. The material and labor usage variances for each department, which are generated by the system in operation, may tell management where the standards are unrealistic and require improvement, but they do not identify the products that are out of line.

When the variances in a department are persistently large and in one direction, or when the department head complains about certain of his standards, better figures are probably needed. One means of developing these is to accumulate job costs *for that department*. For the length of time needed to obtain accurate information on labor and material usage for each product, a job cost system is used in the department, and care is taken to insure that the costs are charged to the jobs as accurately as possible. The *actual labor and material quantities* charged to the department *at standard rates* are classified by jobs and the job cost sheets are then analyzed to establish actual usage rates on each product. The resultant information is more accurate and less expensive than data obtained by collecting job costs at actual prices for all products in all departments. As standards become obsolete because of changes in equipment or production methods or both, new standards may be developed in this manner.

So far, no mention has been made of the use of industrial engineering techniques for the development and maintenance of standards. These methods are generally considered the most accurate, and some firms bring in a battery of engineers to establish standards when they install a system. This is, however, both an expensive and a potentially dangerous approach to the problem. It is dangerous because the large outlay to develop accurate standards tends to generate false expectations with respect to what the system will accomplish for management. Experience indicates that the cost of time studying an operation *for the purpose of developing a standard* is rarely justified by the resultant benefits. Consequently, it is coming to be generally accepted that industrial engineering studies should be undertaken *for the purpose of discovering improved methods of production*. When studies are made for this purpose, accurate usage standards can be obtained as a by-product at little additional cost.

In other words, it is the authors' opinion that the adoption of a standard cost system will better precede than follow intensive work methods analysis. On installation of the system, existing information can be used to set temporary standards. Subsequently, the variances produced by the system in operation, the complaints of department heads, and the introduction of new operating methods will indicate to management which standards should be reviewed for possible revision. The improvement of usage standards should be a continuous process involving some combination of two methods: (1) accounting analyses of actual labor and material usage on jobs accomplished by taking samples of job costs (actual quantities at standard prices) as described above; and (2) industrial engineering studies undertaken primarily for the purpose of discovering better production methods. It follows, of course, that variances from standard costs must be used cautiously in evaluating performance until the standards have been proved reasonably accurate.

### Accuracy Required for Control

The big question now arises. What level of accuracy in standards is necessary to allow a management to use the system to control and evaluate performance? A management sometimes asks this question with another in mind, which is: What must we do in developing standards so that when a variance appears we know that the department head and not the standard is at fault? Unfortunately, standards of such accuracy are practically impossible.

For example, material usage and time standards may be very carefully developed for a steel mill's blast furnace department, which uses iron ore, coal, and limestone to make iron. Nevertheless, if the purchasing department buys ore with a different iron content or coal of a different grade from that assumed in the standard, usage variances will appear which are not the result of the department's performance.

The same kind of problem arises in the rolling mill, which receives steel ingots from the open hearths and rolls them into slabs. A standard rolling time and standard yield (percentage of ingot tons not scrapped) can be set for each dimension of the kind of steel and each width and thickness of the slab to be produced.

The rolling time and yield will also depend, however, on the mill on which the slabs are rolled, the size of the ingot, the ingot's quality, and the temperature of the ingot when it arrives at the mill (a function of the transit time from the open hearth furnace). Variances from these causes are clearly beyond the control of the rolling mill superintendent.

One solution is to establish allowances for nonstandard conditions. This is sometimes done for conditions that occur frequently and have a great impact on cost. Differences between the standard cost under normal conditions and the standard cost under the nonstandard conditions can then be charged or credited to appropriately titled variance accounts. In general, however, it is economically unfeasible or even impossible to do this. Management must be careful to recognize that departmental quantity variances will be affected by many factors beyond the department head's control, and that standards can never be accurate enough to relieve management of the job of managing.

## SUMMARY

Historical product costs ordinarily come too late for many planning purposes and fail to provide an adequate basis for cost control reporting. To remedy these defects, many companies have adopted standard cost systems. The primary feature of such systems is that they accumulate in the accounts differences or "variances" between actual and standard costs for the volume of operations achieved during a given time period. These variances are classified between rate or price variances and quantity or usage variances. The usage variances, in turn, are accumulated departmentally and are reported periodically to the executives responsible for departmental operations.

The central feature of the basic plan standard costing system described in this chapter is to charge each department with the standard cost of all the direct labor and direct materials used (inputs) and credit the department with the standard cost of all of the products it manufactures (outputs). The output of a given period consists of the amount of products completed during the period plus the increase (or minus the decrease) in the quantity of work in process between the beginning and the end of the period. The difference between input and output, measured in this way, is one measure of departmental efficiency during the period.

This system measures the quantity variances as departmental totals for the entire measurement period. It provides no further detail, and therefore is much cheaper to operate than other kinds of standard costing systems. It is appropriate whenever the need is primarily for scorecard information on overall results rather than for prompt, detailed information that will direct management's attention to specific problems that need immediate correction. To provide the latter kind of information, more detail has to be supplied, and at a greater cost.

## QUESTIONS AND PROBLEMS

1. What is a responsibility center? Might a responsibility center include two or more cost centers? Might a cost center include two or more responsibility centers?

2. What is management by exception? What kinds of actions might management take in implementing this concept?

3. In adopting a standard cost system, a firm hopes to achieve a reduction in its clerical costs and an improvement in management control. Describe how each of these objectives is expected to be realized.

4. What is the primary purpose of the bill of materials? The operations routing sheet? What other purposes do they serve?

5. How does the standard cost of goods completed differ from the standard cost of the work done?

6. What is a favorable variance? What is an unfavorable variance?

7. How is a quantity variance calculated? A price variance?

8. Why is it ordinarily regarded as unnecessary to classify materials price and labor rate variances by department?

9. What are the advantages of recognizing materials price variances at the time of purchase?

10. Why is a job cost sheet for each production order unnecessary under a standard cost system? For what purposes and under what circumstances would maintenance of the job cost sheet be desirable?

11. Assuming that standard costs can be prepared for each job entering a job shop, what additional control information can be obtained by incorporating these standard costs into the formal accounting records instead of merely listing them on the job order cost sheets and account-for actual costs by job order costing procedures?

12. Much of the bookkeeping economy achieved with a standard cost system is accomplished by giving up information obtained with an actual cost system. State three types of information lost under a basic plan standard costing system; indicate how giving up this information reduces bookkeeping costs; and discuss the problems connected with giving up the information.

13. "We don't use accounting reports for cost control. By the time a variance shows up in an accounting report, it is too late to control costs." Comment on this point of view.

*14. Materials can be purchased for $1 a pound. Under normal conditions, 10 percent by weight of the materials placed in production will be recovered as scrap, with a scrap value of $0.10 a pound. The remaining 90 percent of the materials shrinks to half its weight in processing. The final product weighs 6.3 pounds. What is the standard net materials cost per pound of finished product?

*15. Products A and B have standard labor requirements of two hours and three hours per unit, respectively. The standard wage rate is $3 an hour. During April, 1,500 units of product A and 4,000 units of product B were manufactured. Labor for the period totaled 14,500 hours and cost $44,000. Compute the labor variances.

16. The Hillman Company manufactures a single product known as Quik-Tite. Material A is the only raw material used in the manufacture of Quik-Tite. Transactions in material A for the month of June are as follows:

| | Standard | Actual |
|---|---|---|
| Units of Quik-Tite produced ..................... | | 61,000 |
| Pounds of material A required to produce one unit of Quik-Tite............................. | 1.6 lbs. | 1.5 lbs. |
| Cost of material A purchases during June ....... | $2.00/lb. | $2.05/lb. |
| Inventory of material A on June 1, costed at $2 a pound........................................ | | 4,000 lbs. |
| Material purchased during June ................ | | 95,000 lbs. |

Calculate and analyze the materials variances for the month.

*17. You have the following information about the operations of department Y during the month of March:

| | Product A | Product B |
|---|---|---|
| Units finished .................................... | 5,000 | 10,000 |
| Units in process: | | |
| March 1........................................ | 1,000 | 1,000 |
| March 31 ...................................... | 600 | 1,200 |
| Standard direct labor cost per unit .............. | $2 | $1 |

* Solutions to problems marked with an asterisk (*) are found in Appendix B.

Products in process on any date are presumed to be half-processed by department Y's labor force.

Direct labor cost in department Y amounted to $23,500 in March. The standard cost of this amount of labor totaled $22,000.

*a)* Compute the total direct labor cost variance for the month.
*b)* Analyze this variance in as much detail as you can and clearly label each component that you have identified.
*c)* Compute the standard direct labor cost of the inventory in process at the end of the month.

18. Follow the instructions given for each of the four exercises presented below. You should do these exercises in the sequence given.

*Exercise A:*

Tapscott Enterprises, Inc., reports materials and labor quantity variances to factory department heads each month. One of its departments worked on only two products during January. Its standard inputs and actual outputs were as follows:

|  | Standard Material Quantity per Unit (pounds) | Standard Labor Hours per Unit | Units of Product Manufactured During January |
|---|---|---|---|
| Product A .......................... | 6 | 4 | 2,000 |
| Product B ......................... | 10 | 2 | 3,000 |

The following quantities of materials and labor were used during January: materials, 44,000 pounds; labor, 13,500 hours.

*a)* Calculate materials and labor quantity variances for the month in terms of pounds of materials and hours of labor. Indicate whether each variance is favorable or unfavorable.
*b)* The standard materials price is $3 a pound. The standard wage rate is $5 an hour.
   (1) Calculate standard unit cost for each product in dollars.
   (2) Restate your quantity variances (from *a*) in monetary terms.

*Exercise B:*

Preston Pans, Ltd., manufactures cookware. All of its factory operations are performed in a single department. The department's facilities were used during February to manufacture the following three products:

|  | Standard Materials Quantity (pounds per unit) | | Standard Labor Hours per Unit | Units of Product Manufactured |
|---|---|---|---|---|
|  | Material X | Material Y | | |
| Product A ....... | 1 | 3 | 1 | 1,000 |
| Product B ....... | 2 | 1 | 1 | 3,000 |
| Product C ....... | 3 | 4 | 6 | 2,000 |

You have the following additional information:

(1) Standard materials prices: material X, $2 a pound; material Y, $5 a pound.
(2) Standard wage rate: $5 an hour.
(3) Direct materials purchased during February:
   Material X: 10,000 pounds, $21,000.
   Material Y: 15,000 pounds, $77,000.
(4) Direct material used during February:
   Material X: 12,600 pounds.
   Material Y: 15,000 pounds.
(5) Direct labor used during February: 16,800 hours, $80,000.

a) Calculate labor and materials variances, in dollars, in whatever detail you think is appropriate.
b) Indicate to whom each of your variances should be reported.

*Exercise C:*

Block Houses, Inc., manufactures prefabricated housing modules. The following information was collected for one department for the month of March:

(1) Inventory of work in process, March 1 (at standard cost):
   Materials: $28,000.
   Labor: $16,000.
(2) Direct materials with a standard cost of $22,000 were received in the department from the storeroom during the month.
(3) Direct labor cost for the month was $8,000 at actual wage rates and $7,500 at standard wage rates.
(4) The standard cost of products finished and transferred out of the department during the month was as follows:
   Standard direct materials cost: $21,200.
   Standard direct labor cost: $7,800.
(5) Inventory of work in process, March 31 (at standard cost):
   Materials cost: $24,000.
   Labor cost: $15,000.

a) Calculate the standard labor and materials costs of the work done during the month.
b) Calculate the labor and materials variances for the month.
c) Comment on the department head's cost control performance during the month.

*Exercise D:*

Anderson Products Company manufactures two products in a factory with three production centers—the preparing, bonding, and finishing departments. The head of each department is responsible for controlling the quantity of labor and materials used in his department.

Materials are issued from the storeroom to the preparing department. After processing there, they are transferred to the bonding department.

After bonding, they go to finishing and from finishing to the finished goods warehouse. You have the following additional information:

(1) Output of the preparing department ("intermediate products") during April:

|  | Product A | Product B |
|---|---|---|
| Standard cost per pound: |  |  |
| Materials ............................ | $2.00 | $5.00 |
| Labor ................................ | .50 | 2.00 |
| Pounds transferred to bonding ........... | 10,000 | 15,000 |

(2) Actual unit cost of intermediate product in preparing department during April:

|  | Product A | Product B |
|---|---|---|
| Materials .............................. | $2.05 | $5.20 |
| Labor ................................. | .50 | 2.10 |

(3) Standard costs per unit in bonding department:

|  | Product A | Product B |
|---|---|---|
| Intermediate product (from preparing department) .......................... | 1.1 lbs. | 1.5 lbs. |
| Direct labor (standard wage rate, $6 an hour) ........................... | 0.5 hrs. | 0.8 hrs. |

(4) Direct labor cost in bonding department during April: 13,000 hours, $80,000.

(5) Units completed and transferred to finishing department during April:
   Product A: 8,000 units.
   Product B: 10,500 units.

(6) Work in process inventories, bonding department, April 1 and April 30: negligible.

Calculate labor and materials quantity variances for the bonding department for the month of April.

19. You have the following information for a factory department for the month of September:

(1)

|  | Product X | Product Y |
|---|---|---|
| Units finished ......................... | 2,000 | 1,500 |
| Units in process: |  |  |
| September 1 .......................... | 1,000 | 500 |
| September 30 ......................... | 2,000 | 800 |
| Standard direct labor cost per unit (at $5 an hour) ...................... | $20 | $30 |

(2) One half of the required departmental direct labor had been performed on each unit in process on the indicated dates.

(3) Actual direct labor cost, month of September: 19,000 hours, $100,000.

a)  Calculate the standard direct labor cost of the work done in this department during September.
b)  Calculate the total direct labor cost variance for the month.
c)  Analyze this total variance. Which portion of the variance is likely to be subject to the department head's control?

**20.** The Mongol Company's factory contains 17 production departments. Products typically require processing in five or more of these departments. All products are subjected to final inspection before they are either placed in inventory or shipped to customers. Units rejected by the inspectors are sold immediately as seconds.

The company's industrial engineers have studied past experience with production rejects and have established the following standards: for products A, B, D, G, and H, rejects amount to 10 percent of the number of units placed in process; for all other products, rejects of 5 percent are regarded as normal.

During May, the production record was as follows:

| Product | No. of Good Units | No. of Re-jected Units |
|---|---|---|
| A | 470 | 50 |
| B | 820 | 60 |
| C | 1,460 | 110 |
| D | 320 | 40 |
| F | 540 | 40 |
| G | 990 | 60 |
| H | 80 | 20 |
| K | 3,400 | 300 |
| M | 650 | 70 |

a)  Prepare a report that will provide management with information on the effectiveness of quality control in the plant.
b)  What additional data would you regard as essential to good management information on this aspect of performance?
c)  If the company were to manufacture 1,000 different products each month, would you find it necessary to make changes in the report structure? Explain.

**21.** The Neptune Company operates a small factory which makes only one product. Four production operations are necessary, one in each of the factory's four departments. The company's engineers have determined that these operations should require the following labor-hour allowances under normal conditions:

| | Labor Hours per Unit of Product | | | |
|---|---|---|---|---|
| | Operation No. 1 | Operation No. 2 | Operation No. 3 | Operation No. 4 |
| Operators | 1.0 | 3.0 | 1.5 | 0.5 |
| Helpers | 0.5 | 2.5 | 2.0 | 0.1 |
| Handlers | 0.2 | 0.5 | 1.0 | 0.3 |

Operators are paid $6 an hour, helpers $4 an hour, and handlers $3 an hour.

During August, the factory's operations were:

|  | Operation No. 1 | Operation No. 2 | Operation No. 3 | Operation No. 4 |
|---|---|---|---|---|
| Units produced ... | 2,000 | 1,800 | 2,100 | 2,000 |
| Labor hours: |  |  |  |  |
| Operators....... | 1,100 | 5,200 | 3,400 | 980 |
| Helpers......... | 550 | 4,600 | 4,600 | 190 |
| Handlers ....... | 210 | 1,000 | 2,200 | 610 |

a) Prepare a report for management, summarizing labor operations for the month in terms of both hours and dollars, and write a brief paragraph commenting on the effectiveness of labor control during the month.

b) What advantages, if any, do you see in including dollar figures on this report? Explain.

22. The following material and labor cost variance report was prepared for a factory during July:

|  | ——Material—— |  | ——Labor—— |  |
|---|---|---|---|---|
| Raw material inventory, July 1 .... | $10,000 |  | $  — |  |
| Work in process inventory, July 1 .. | 4,000 |  | 4,500 |  |
| Materials purchased during July... | 24,000 |  | — |  |
| Labor used during July ........... | — |  | 45,000 |  |
| Total Cost to Be Accounted For . |  | $38,000 |  | $49,500 |
| Raw material inventory, July 31 ... | $ 8,000 |  | $  — |  |
| Work in process inventory, July 31 .. | 3,000 |  | 3,750 |  |
| Goods completed during July....... | 29,000 |  | 44,700 |  |
| Total Cost Accounted For...... |  | 40,000 |  | 48,450 |
| Variance.................... |  | $ 2,000 |  | $ (1,050) |

Additional data were as follows:

| Materials purchased during July: |  |
|---|---|
| At actual cost .............. | $24,000 |
| At standard cost ............ | 26,400 |
| Materials used during July: |  |
| At standard cost ............ | 28,400 |
| Labor used during July: |  |
| At actual cost .............. | 45,000 |
| At standard cost ............ | 44,250 |

a) Compute the price and quantity variances for materials and labor.

b) Suggest ways to improve the format of the variance report that is presented to the factory manager each month. What purpose would this report serve?

c) What action would you recommend as a result of the information revealed by your analysis of variance? The action might be to acquire certain additional information; in that case assume the necessary facts and then state what action should be taken on the basis of these facts.

*23. The Continental Company uses a basic plan system of standard costing. Its factory consists of a single department. Account balances relating to factory materials and labor were as follows on May 1:

|  | Dr. | Cr. |
|---|---|---|
| Raw materials | $29,460 | |
| Materials in process | 18,400 | |
| Labor in process | 9,650 | |
| Finished goods | 35,000 | |
| Accrued wages payable | | $1,620 |

The balance in the Finished Goods account represented the labor and materials cost of the goods on hand; overhead costs were accounted for separately and are not covered by this problem. All inventories were measured at their standard cost.

The transactions for the month were:

(1) Material costing $36,500 and with a standard cost of $37,900 was purchased.

(2) Material with a standard cost of $41,300 and an actual cost of $40,500 was put into process.

(3) Labor employed during the month at standard rates came to $28,400.

(4) The output transferred out of the department had the following standard costs:

   Material, $42,600
   Labor, $28,300

(5) Finished goods with a standard labor and materials cost of $79,200 were sold.

(6) The standard cost of the work in process at the end of the month was found by physical inventory to be:

   Material, $15,200
   Labor, $11,000

(7) The payrolls paid during the month came to $32,180, and there were no unpaid wages as of the end of the month.

Open T-accounts for the balances at the start of the month, account for the month's transactions, and make any entries necessary to adjust the inventory accounts to their correct level at the end of the month. Variances should be transferred to a Variance Summary account at the end of the month. Indicate the nature of each variance and state whether it was favorable or unfavorable.

24. The Jiffy Dinner Company manufactures 15 types of frozen dinners. A standard menu priced at predetermined food prices, labor rates, and standard processing times for each operation is the basis for a standard cost system in which the entire plant is treated as one department.

Work in process is small, and subject to little fluctuation from one month to the next. Therefore, to avoid the job of counting and costing it, the in-process inventory is assumed to be the same and equal to the following amounts at the end of each month:

Food, trays, etc., in process ................ $18,000
Labor in process............................    3,000

Actual overhead is charged to expense each month and is not included in product cost. The cost of goods and services purchased for factory use is credited to Accounts Payable; the cost of labor services used is credited to Accrued Wages Payable as the work is performed.

The firm's factory account balances on April 1 were as follows:

Cash ....................................... $34,000
Raw food and supplies ......................   33,000
Food, trays, etc., in process................   18,000
Labor in process............................    3,000
Frozen dinners.............................   67,000
Accrued wages payable ....................    1,800
Accounts payable ..........................   28,000

The transactions for the month were as follows:

(1)  Food and supplies purchased: actual cost $73,000, and standard cost, $70,300.
(2)  Direct labor cost: at standard wage rates, $26,400.
(3)  Payrolls paid, $25,000; accrued wages as of the end of the month, $1,300.
(4)  Actual overhead costs incurred, $42,000, including $4,000 of supplies at standard prices.
(5)  Food, trays, and other direct material transferred out of the storeroom: standard cost, $63,000.
(6)  Standard cost of frozen dinners produced:

Food, trays, etc. .................. $60,200
Direct labor ......................   27,500
Total .......................  $87,700

(7)  Standard cost of dinners sold: $115,000.

a)  Open T-accounts for the opening balances, account for the above transactions, and transfer all variances to the Cost of Goods Sold account. Identify and label each variance.
b)  How would the cost of goods sold have been different if the company had measured its inventory on a Fifo actual cost basis?
c)  Is a system of this kind likely to provide management with information that is detailed enough to be useful? What conditions must be present to justify an affirmative answer to this question?

**25.** The Glocken Steel Company has a standard cost system for direct labor and materials, the essentials of which as applied to the rolling mill are outlined below:

(1)  The rolling mill is charged with:

a) Ingots consumed at standard unit cost.
b) Actual direct labor hours at standard rates.
(2) The rolling mill is credited with or "earns":
a) Good product at standard unit cost.
b) Scrap at $54 a ton.
(3) The standard labor and material cost per ton of good product for each type (size, thickness, chemistry) of steel rolled is arrived at as follows:
a) The standard cost per ton of ingots is multiplied by the standard usage rate to obtain the gross material cost per ton of product. The standard scrap production per ton of good product at $54 a ton is deducted from the gross material cost to obtain the net material cost.
b) The standard rolling time per ton of good product is multiplied by $111, the standard direct labor cost per hour of mill operation, to obtain the standard direct labor cost per ton of product.
c) The standard labor and material cost per ton of good product is the sum of (a) and (b).
(4) The mill's "profit" or "loss" on labor and material in any month is the difference between its earnings and its costs, as defined above.

The operating data for the 8th month (the mill uses a 13-month year of four weeks each) are given below:

(1) Ingots consumed: 13,000 tons; standard cost, $975,000.
(2) Actual direct labor hours at standard rates: $44,160.
(3) Good product at standard cost:

| | | |
|---|---|---|
| Material | 10,500 tons | $856,080 |
| Labor | 410 mill hours | 45,510 |
| Total | | $901,590 |

(4) Scrap production: 2,500 tons.
(5) Including downtime caused by production interruptions, the mill operated 400 hours. The downtime was 14 hours. The actual direct labor time listed in (2) above included the costs of labor crews made idle by machine downtime.

a) Calculate the labor and materials cost variances for the month. Design a report that would be a useful summary of the mill's labor and materials cost performance during the month.
b) Set up appropriate T-accounts and record the month's transactions. Reconcile the account balances with your list of variances.

26. A factory has two production departments and a basic plan standard costing system. The inventories on May 1 had the following standard costs:

Raw materials........................ $40,000
Department A:
   Materials in process ................. 10,000
   Labor in process..................... 6,000
Department B:
   Materials in process ................. 8,000
   Labor in process..................... 9,000

The following transactions took place during May:

(1) Raw materials purchased: standard cost, $25,000; actual cost, $25,800.

(2) Materials issued (at standard cost):
   To Department A, $12,000.
   To Department B, $15,000.

(3) Direct labor cost (at standard wage rates):
   Department A, $11,000.
   Department B, $17,000.

(4) Actual direct labor payroll for the month, $30,100.

(5) Products completed by department A (at standard cost):

|  | Materials | Labor |
|---|---|---|
| Transferred to department B for further processing ............................. | $ 8,600 | $5,800 |
| Transferred to finished goods storeroom...... | 4,700 | 3,400 |
| Total................................. | $13,300 | $9,200 |

(6) Products completed by department B and transferred to finished goods storeroom (at standard cost): materials, $28,200; labor, $15,800.

(7) Work in process inventories on May 31, at standard cost:

|  | Materials in Process | Labor in Process |
|---|---|---|
| Department A........................... | $9,000 | $7,000 |
| Department B........................... | 9,000 | 8,000 |

a) Enter the opening balances in appropriately titled T-accounts, record the transactions, and make the necessary adjustments to restore the account balances to their correct December 31 levels.

b) Prepare a summary of the variances for the month.

# 24

# CONTROL OF
# OVERHEAD COSTS

WITH THE GROWTH of automation in the factory and the growing importance of the service sector of the economy, direct labor and direct materials costs account for an ever smaller percentage of total business costs. The problem of controlling overhead costs, both inside and outside the factory, therefore assumes greater and greater significance. The purpose of this chapter is to see what techniques might be useful in the control of overhead costs and how these tie into the accounting system.

## THE CONTROL OF DISCRETIONARY COSTS

Overhead costs can be divided into two broad classes: supportive overheads and discretionary overheads. Supportive overhead costs are incurred to enable the organization to fill demands that are placed on the system from outside. Like direct labor and direct materials, they are volume-determined—that is, they are necessary to service the volume of orders that have entered the system. Factory rent, factory supervision, and the costs of preparing customers' invoices are examples of supportive overheads.

Most of our discussion in this chapter will focus on supportive overheads. Before we turn to these, however, we must say a few words about discretionary overheads. As the name may imply, discretionary overheads are not incurred to meet the organization's commitment to deliver goods to its customers or to produce goods to keep inventories at adequate levels. Their purpose is to secure some future benefit or to meet some independent objective set by management. Many of them are incurred to obtain future sales—e.g., some kinds of advertising, research, and product development. Other examples are expenditures for community recreation programs, contributions to charitable organizations, and management consultants' fees.

### Planning Criteria

Discretionary costs are fixed costs—by definition, since only costs that vary in response to volume changes are variable costs. This being the case, most of the decisions that determine the level of discretionary costs are made when the budget is established. People are hired, commitments are made, and orders are placed on the strength of budget authorizations.

This means that the most crucial control process for discretionary overheads is budget review and approval. The basic criterion underlying these decisions is the cost-benefit criterion: do the anticipated benefits justify the cost? For activities such as research and development or advertising, benefits consist of positive future cash flows. Expenditures for community service activities may also be perceived in the same light, with benefits arising from better relations with employees and the public at large.

All of these are consistent with the notion of the firm as an organization seeking to maximize its present value. The problem is to quantify the anticipated monetary benefits. Not all discretionary costs are incurred to achieve direct monetary benefits, however. An increasing number of corporations are engaged in community relations programs, charitable activities, and other "good citizen" functions with neither the hope nor the expectation of reaping monetary benefits. In such cases cost and benefit cannot be measured in the same currency, and decision criteria may be even more difficult to derive than estimates of benefits.

Whether the managers of private business organizations should use corporate funds to support activities of no direct benefit to the corporation is beyond our scope here. Even on expenditures motivated by the expectation of corresponding corporate benefits, however, forecasting the benefits is subject to wide margins of error. Confronted with such uncertainty, management is often tempted to abandon the profitability approach and tie the appropriation to what others are doing or what has been done in the past. This places an even greater responsibility on the company's analytical staffs to attach profit estimates, even of the roughest sort, to appropriation requests. Errors of estimation are always present in managerial decision making, but it is better to have some indication of expected profitability, no matter how rough, than no guidance at all.

When management cannot or will not estimate future benefits, the practice is to use a rule of thumb such as $x$ percent of sales or $y$ dollars a year, to determine the overall appropriation. The possible projects or recipients of corporate largesse are then ranked qualitatively by one executive or a group of executives who apply their own subjective criteria. The expenditure pattern will then parallel the preference pattern of the responsible executives.

### Feedback Reporting

Feedback reporting is no less important than budgetary planning in the control of discretionary overhead costs. First, such costs are fixed in relation to output, but they are management decision costs as discussed in Chapter 20. A change in the firm's circumstances during the budgetary period may make it advisable to change the level or structure of these costs, and feedback reporting facilitates this process. Second, even without any change in management's plans, actual expenditures may deviate from the fixed budgets, and feedback reports call such deviations to management's attention.

This kind of reporting is not enough, however. It is easy enough to keep spending close to the amount budgeted – if window washing costs go up, for example, the budget line can be held by washing the windows less often. What is really important is what has been achieved for the money that has been spent. The accountant's problem is to find or develop measures of progress toward the objectives established by management.

It must be admitted that the accountant's success in solving this problem has been spotty. In many areas progress is difficult to measure in monetary terms, and accountants have shied from the task. Probably the best results have been achieved in reporting the results of marketing and research and development programs. We shall use a research and development example to show what can be done in feedback reporting when direct measures of monetary benefit are unavailable. Measures of marketing performance are generally profit-oriented, and we shall consider them at length in the next chapter.

### Reporting on Product Development Activities

The key to feedback reporting in product development and in many other discretionary activities is to break the overall objective down into a number of identifiable subobjectives. Product development projects, for example, ordinarily consist of a number of interrelated but separate activities. The actual cost of performing each of these activities can be compared with the estimated cost. Thus while overall project spending may be in line with the budget, the number of activities completed may be greater or smaller than the budget provided for.

To illustrate this idea, let us suppose that a project was started on March 1, with a scheduled completion date of October 31. Budgeted costs were as follows:

| Activity | Budgeted Completion | Budgeted Costs |
|---|---|---|
| Analysis........................................ | April 30 | $20,000 |
| Product specifications ......................... | May 15 | 6,000 |
| Blueprints..................................... | May 31 | 4,000 |
| Production specifications ...................... | June 30 | 8,000 |
| Prototypes..................................... | August 31 | 40,000 |
| Testing........................................ | September 30 | 10,000 |
| Final drawings and specifications ............. | October 31 | 9,000 |
| Total Cost ............................... | | $97,000 |

The analysis stage proceeded as planned, and was completed on April 30 at a cost of $19,500. Snags were encountered in the development of product specifications, however, and this activity was not completed until May 31, at a cost of $12,000. A performance report for the month of May might show the following:

| | This Month | Year to Date |
|---|---|---|
| Expenditure budget.......................... | $10,000 | $30,000 |
| Actual expenditures.......................... | 12,000 | 31,500 |
| (Over)/underexpended ................. | $ (2,000) | $ (1,500) |
| | | |
| Progress-adjusted budget .................... | $ 6,000 | $26,000 |
| Actual expenditures.......................... | 12,000 | 31,500 |
| (Overrun)/underrun .................. | $ (6,000) | $ (5,500) |

The expenditure budget figures shown on the first line are the amounts originally budgeted for the period through May 31, the first three figures in the previous table. The progress-adjusted budget, on the other hand, is the amount budgeted for the activities that have been completed, in this case only the first two in the earlier table.

It should be clear that for most managerial purposes the figures on the bottom line are better indicators of project performance. The work that has been done has cost the company $5,500 more than the approved budget provided for.

Reports of this kind focus exclusively on the past. Because discretionary activities can always be discontinued if the anticipated costs exceed the perceived benefits, a strong case can be made for incorporating revised forecasts of future costs and completion dates in the reports. Management can then decide whether to continue the project and, if so, whether to increase or decrease the rate of spending to advance or defer the estimated completion date.

Implementation of reporting schemes of this kind is not always as simple as this discussion might imply, and may in some cases be more costly than the results warrant. The time or cost involved in completing a research or development objective is extremely hard to forecast, and putting a number in a budget can alienate the personnel involved and impair their performance. Unless the behavioral problems, some of which are examined later in this chapter, can be solved adequately along with the informational and measurement problems, the system will be counterproductive.

## THE FLEXIBLE BUDGET

Supportive overheads are similar to factory direct labor and direct materials in that they are incurred to enable management to service the sales or production orders that are presented to it. They differ in other respects, however, and these differences call for a separate structure of feedback information. To keep this chapter from getting too long, we shall restrict ourselves to a discussion of factory overhead costs, leaving nonmanufacturing supportive overheads to more advanced texts.

### Structure of the Flexible Budget

Factory overhead costs in the typical case are neither constant per unit nor constant in total. Under these circumstances, no one budget is applicable to all possible operating volumes; instead, a series of alternative budgets must be prepared, one for each possible level of operating volume. This series of budgets is known collectively as the *flexible budget* or *semivariable overhead budget.* The applicable budget in any given period is the specific budget for the level of output achieved during that period.

An example of a flexible budget is shown in Exhibit 24–1. This shows the overhead budget for the molding department of the Lester Plastics Company. This department, consisting of 60 injection molding machines and certain auxiliary equipment, has a department head and a general foreman for each of the two shifts it operates. Each shift also has a section foreman who is responsible for supervising the operation of the department's manual machines. Supervision of the automatic machines is performed directly by the general forman on the shift. In addition, the department has a maintenance foreman to keep the machines in operation and a material control foreman to keep the machines supplied with material and to inspect and move the finished product out of the molding room.

Exhibit 24–1

Lester Plastics Company

MANUFACTURING OVERHEAD BUDGET

(Molding Department)

| Item | Monthly Fixed Cost | Variable Cost per Machine-Hour |
|---|---|---|
| Indirect labor: | | |
| Foremen and section foremen .......... | $2,941 | x |
| Floormen ............................. | x | $0.390 |
| Maintenance ......................... | 825 | 0.070 |
| Material control and testing ........... | 1,000 | 0.023 |
| Idle time ............................ | x | 0.043 |
| Overtime premium .................... | x | 0.050 |
| Other direct charges: | | |
| Employee benefits .................... | 424 | 0.160 |
| Indirect materials ................... | 365 | 0.280 |
| Machine setup........................ | 530 | 0.025 |
| Power .............................. | x | 0.093 |
| Depreciation......................... | 695 | x |
| Allocated service department costs ....... | 1,640 | x |
| Total .............................. | $8,420 | $1.134 |

The first column of Exhibit 24–1 lists the categories into which the department's overhead is classified; the second column shows the monthly fixed costs for each of these overhead items; and the third gives the variable cost per hour of machine operation. Machine-hours were selected as being the most accurate measure of production, on the basis of the criterion laid down in Chapter 21.

Notice that a linear cost-volume relationship is assumed in

this case—that is, the cost budget can be represented on a chart by a straight line, fitting a formula in the form:

Budgeted Cost = Fixed Costs + Variable Cost per Unit × Volume.

As Exhibit 24-1 shows, the department's estimated fixed cost is \$8,420 a month, while its variable cost is \$1.134 per machine-hour. The total budgeted overhead cost at any level of output for any month is found by substituting the number of machine-hours operated during the month for MH in the equation,

$$\text{Budgeted Cost} = \$8{,}420 + \$1.134 \times \text{MH},$$

and solving for budgeted cost. Since the department recorded 14,300 machine-hours during October, the total budget was:

$$\text{Budgeted Cost} = \$8{,}420 + \$1.134 \times 14{,}300 = \$24{,}636.$$

This is the figure that appeared on the bottom line of the first column of Exhibit 24-2. The budget allowance for any of the individual overhead items can be found in the same way.

Although it is almost always used for simplicity in textbook illustrations, the straight-line budget is not necessarily applicable in all cases. Budgeted overtime premium, for example, could be zero for all volumes up to 10,000 machine-hours a month, 50 cents an hour for the next 5,000 hours, and then \$1.50 an hour for all hours in excess of 15,000. The flexible budget allowances should conform to the anticipated facts and need not be squeezed out of shape to conform to some universally applicable formula.

### Sources of Budget Estimates

A variety of information sources are used to develop the budget amounts appearing in Exhibit 24-1. First, it is most helpful if the actual costs have been classified in the accounts in fine descriptive detail, since mere inspection of such data reveals many of the fixed costs. For certain of the variable and semivariable costs, however, engineering studies or statistical analyses of historical data obtained from the accounts must be used to establish the expected amounts at each level of output. Engineering studies may rely on informal observation or on very careful and extensive time studies. Analyses of historical data may rely on a very fine classification of costs and involve adjustments for changes in prices or production methods. The point at which increased effort ceases to pay off in greater accuracy is not easy to establish, but it cannot be ignored.

Valuable information on the variation of cost with output often can be obtained from another source, the departmental foreman. He usually knows his own operations better than anyone else, and his estimates of his needs for certain kinds of indirect manpower, services, and supplies may be far better than can be obtained from any statistical analysis of the past.

Many factory overhead costs have some of the characteristics of discretionary overheads. This is particularly true of staff activities such as personnel and industrial engineering. Neither analysis of historical cost records nor time studies can establish what these costs should be at any given volume. Substantial increases or decreases can be made without any really noticeable immediate effects on the factory's ability to meet delivery schedules efficiently.

The source of information for these costs is management. As we pointed out earlier, management must decide what it wants to achieve. It must try to appraise the benefits of such things as personnel management programs and decide how large an effort it wishes to make in each area. Once this has been done, historical analysis or discussions with authoritative personnel can be used to try to determine reasonable cost allowances to achieve management's objectives.

### Departmental Feedback Reports

Although preparation of the flexible budget has merit for its own sake, the primary payoff comes in periodic cost performance reporting. Some overhead cost reports are issued daily, some weekly, and some at longer intervals. A month is the typical reporting period for the main departmental cost summaries.

The monthly overhead cost summaries consist of *comparisons* of the actual costs for the month with the budget allowances appropriate to the volume actually achieved during the month. For example, the report shown in Exhibit 24–2 was issued to the head of the molding department, covering his department's operations for the month of October. During this month, the department operated at a volume of 14,300 machine-hours. This figure, applied to the budget formulas of Exhibit 24–1, provides the budget allowances shown in the "budget" column of Exhibit 24–2. Except for the allocated service department costs, the costs in the "actual" column are those which are recorded in the departmental accounts on the basis of requisitions, time tickets, and the like.

The differences between actual costs and the flexible budget allowances are most commonly referred to as *spending vari-*

Exhibit 24-2
Lester Plastics Company
FACTORY OVERHEAD COST REPORT

MONTHLY COST SUMMARY

Department   Molding                                      Month   October
Volume this month   14,300   machine-hours

| Item | Budget | Actual | (Over) Under |
|---|---|---|---|
| Indirect labor: | | | |
| Foremen and section foremen ........ | $ 2,941 | $ 2,985 | $ (44) |
| Floormen ........................... | 5,577 | 6,442 | (865) |
| Maintenance........................ | 1,826 | 2,306 | (480) |
| Material control and testing.......... | 1,329 | 1,188 | 141 |
| Idle time........................... | 615 | 942 | (327) |
| Overtime premium ................. | 715 | 1,293 | (578) |
| Other controllable direct charges: | | | |
| Employee benefits .................. | 2,712 | 2,922 | (210) |
| Indirect materials................... | 4,369 | 4,065 | 304 |
| Machine setup ..................... | 887 | 851 | 36 |
| Power............................. | 1,330 | 1,283 | 47 |
| Total Controllable Costs .......... | $22,301 | $24,277 | $(1,976) |
| Noncontrollable costs: | | | |
| Depreciation....................... | 695 | 705 | (10) |
| Allocated service department costs.... | 1,640 | 1,640 | – |
| Total Department Costs........... | $24,636 | $26,622 | $(1,986) |

ances, although other terms such as *budget variances* and *performance variances* are also used.

## The Controllability Criterion

The comparisons in Exhibit 24-2 are with the flexible budget allowances rather than with a budget that is independent of the month's output. The reason is that cost is *expected* to vary with output. The department head is not expected to operate at average normal cost when volume is far in excess of normal. Conversely, a fixed budget is likely to be too "loose" when volume is less than normal.

The department head's interest in this report centers on those items that he can influence. Notice that the costs charged to the molding department in Exhibit 24-2 are classified into controllable and noncontrollable costs. Depreciation, for example, was $10 higher than the budget allowed. Because the department head cannot influence this cost, it is shown "below the line" as a noncontrollable spending variance.

Controllability does not mean that the executive has all of the determinants of the cost within his grasp. Wage rates, for example, are seldom controllable at lower levels, but the quantity of labor may be very controllable. Multiplying a controllable quantity by a predetermined wage rate (standard wage rate) merely permits the controllable deviation to be measured in monetary terms without implying any control over the wage rate.

We should also emphasize that fixed overhead costs are just as likely to be controllable as variable overheads. The molding department uses substantial quantities of indirect materials, even at zero volume, and the manager is expected to be economical in his use of these materials. Without control, consumption of fixed input factors such as these can climb out of sight.

### Interdepartmental Cost Allocations

The final item in Exhibit 24–2 was for allocated service department costs. Production department burden rates, it will be recalled from Chapter 21, often include allowances for service department costs. Service cost allocations are also made after the fact in many cases, and thus appear on the overhead cost reports of the production departments.

In this case, the allocation was not only shown below the line, as a noncontrollable item, but the actual charge was exactly equal to the amount budgeted. This implies that the allocation method adopted by the Lester Plastics Company insures that no variance is ever reported in this item. The method is to charge production departments each month for a fixed amount of service department costs, exactly equal to the amount budgeted at the start of the year.

This should not be interpreted to mean that service cost allocations must always be equal to budget. If a department's use of a service department's services is variable, management may wish the cost records to reflect the history of service usage by each department. Furthermore, a charge for service should be made if the department's consumption is to some extent controllable by the department head. In the latter situation, however, the services should be billed to the department at a predetermined price; the production department manager cannot control the unit cost of operating the service department, and his charge for services should vary only as a result of variations in service quantities.

If allocations are made on this basis, the amounts charged to other departments will differ from the costs of the service center itself. Suppose, for example, that a maintenance department charges other departments for its services at a flat rate of $9 an hour. During September the department performed 1,000 hours of service and incurred $9,420 in costs. A summary T-account for the maintenance department would show the following:

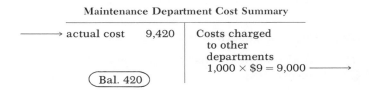

Maintenance Department Cost Summary

| ⟶ actual cost 9,420 | Costs charged to other departments 1,000 × $9 = 9,000 ⟶ |
| Bal. 420 | |

In other words, predetermining the rate at which other departments were charged for maintenance services left $420 of this department's costs unallocated. This is the service department's counterpart of the underabsorbed production department overhead that we first encountered in Chapter 19. It can be analyzed by the methods that we shall describe in the next section.

### Following Up the Reports

Cost reports of this type are only the first step in effective responsive control. Although the advantage of the flexible budget is that it adjusts the cost standard to current volume conditions, it cannot allow for changes in other factors such as wage rates, purchase prices, or manufacturing methods. Furthermore, management may deliberately incur excessive costs when volume is changing rapidly, to avoid even greater cost penalties in future periods.

The issuance of the report should be followed, therefore, by an attempt to identify the causes of major deviations. Whenever the deviations are unfavorable and the causes are controllable, corrective action should be initiated; other portions of the deviation are likely to call for replanning the future.

### ANALYSIS OF FACTORY OVERHEAD VARIANCES

Flexible budget allowances provide information that can be used to analyze the over- or underabsorbed factory overhead costs that we identified in Chapter 19. To illustrate, let us assume that the burden rate in the Lester Plastics Company's molding department was based on a normal volume of 20,000 machine-hours a month. The burden rate was:

$$\text{Burden rate} = \frac{\$8,420 + \$1.134 \times 20,000}{20,000} = \$1.555 \text{ an hour.}$$

From Exhibit 24–2 we find that the department operated 14,300 machine-hours during October. This means that the amount absorbed by production (charged to production orders) was:

$$\text{Overhead cost absorbed} = 14,300 \times \$1.555 = \$22,236.$$

Since the actual overhead cost for the month was $26,622, this left $4,386 unabsorbed.

### Reasons for Over- and Underabsorbed Overhead

Over- and underabsorbed overhead balances arise as a result of two phenomena:

1. Actual costs differ from the amounts that would normally be expected at the production volume actually achieved during the period.
2. Production volume during the period differs from the volume used to set the burden rate.

The amounts attributable to the first of these phenomena are the spending variances that we described earlier. These totaled $1,986 during October. The remainder of the unabsorbed overhead, or $2,400, was attributable to the difference between the 20,000-hour normal volume and the 14,300-hour actual volume for the month.

The reason why this is so is illustrated in Exhibit 24–3. The budget formula is represented by the line $BB'$. This shows budgeted overhead rising from $8,420 at zero volume to $24,636 at 14,300 machine-hours and $31,100 at 20,000 hours. The other line, $AA'$, indicates the amount of overhead cost that will be absorbed at different volumes by a burden rate of $1.555 an hour. This rises from zero at zero volume to $22,236 at 14,300 hours and $31,100 at 20,000 hours.

In other words, when volume is only 14,300 hours, management *expects* to underabsorb its overhead costs by $2,400 at this volume. This is represented on the diagram by the vertical distance between points $X$ and $Y$. It is due to the difference between actual and normal operating volume, and accountants call it the *volume variance*. If actual volume exceeds the normal volume, then the amount absorbed will exceed the amount budgeted and the volume variance will be favorable. A situation of this kind is

*Exhibit 24–3*

Lester Plastics Company

**BUDGETED VERSUS ABSORBED OVERHEAD**
(Molding Department)

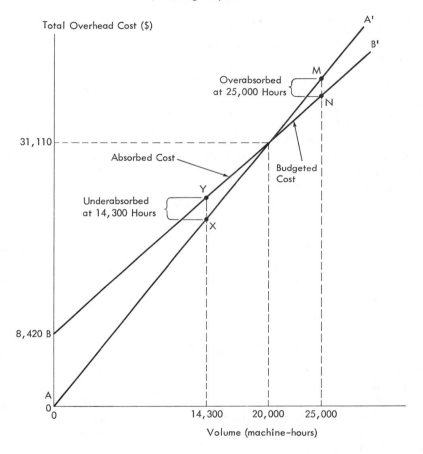

Total Overhead Cost ($)

Overabsorbed at 25,000 Hours

Absorbed Cost

Budgeted Cost

Underabsorbed at 14,300 Hours

31,110

8,420 B

A

0

14,300    20,000    25,000

Volume (machine-hours)

represented by the distance between points *M* and *N* in the diagram.

When budgeted fixed costs are the same at all production volumes, as they are in this illustration, the volume variance can be computed in another way. The fixed cost component of the burden rate in this case was $8,420/20,000 = $0.421. Volume in October was $20,000 - 14,300 = 5,700$ hours short of the normal level. The amount unabsorbed due to the low volume therefore was $5,700 \times$ $0.421 = $2,400$.

The entire analysis of the total overhead cost variance can be summarized as follows:

(1)  Costs charged to department..................... $26,622
(2)  Costs budgeted at actual volume................   24,636
     Spending variance (1) − (2) ..................             $(1,986)
(3)  Costs absorbed by production ...................   22,236
     Volume variance (2) − (3)...................              (2,400)
     Total Variance (1) − (3) ....................             $(4,386)

## Overhead Variance Analysis under Standard Costing

A company which uses standard costing for its direct labor and materials is likely to develop standard product costs for its factory overhead, too. The application of standard product costing to overhead costs changes the basis on which overhead costs are absorbed by production. The total amount of overhead absorbed in the illustration would be computed by multiplying the number of *standard* machine-hours by the burden rate.

For example, suppose that the molding department's output for October had a standard machine-hour content of 14,000 hours. (To provide this figure, each product's standard cost card would have to show the standard number of machine-hours required by that product.) The total amount absorbed by production would have been:

Overhead absorbed $= 14,000 \times \$1.555 = \$21,770.$

The total overhead variance therefore would be the difference between $21,770 and the $26,622 in actual overhead costs for the month, or $4,852.

The analysis of this variance into component parts depends on the anticipated pattern of cost behavior. In effect, the question is whether overhead cost performance should be judged against a budget appropriate to a volume of 14,300 hours or one for a volume of 14,000 hours.

The answer to this question depends on the answer to another: do overhead costs vary with *actual* input or with *standard* input? If overhead costs are governed by actual inputs, then the appraisal standard should be the fleixble budget allowances appropriate to the actual inputs. Otherwise, the allowances should be based on standard inputs.

This issue is outside the scope of an introductory text, and we shall take the simpler route of assuming that overhead costs always vary with standard inputs rather than with actual inputs. Based on this assumption, the flexible budget allowances for October in the molding department would be:

$$\text{Budget} = \$8,\!420 + 14,\!000 \times \$1.134 = \$24,\!296.$$

The analysis can now be summarized as follows:

(1)  Actual overhead costs........................... $26,622
(2)  Overhead costs budgeted at 14,000 standard
       machine-hours................................ 24,296
(3)     Spending variance ([1] − 2]).................             $(2,326)
(4)  Standard overhead costs absorbed .............. 21,770
(5)     Volume variance ([2] − [4])..................             (2,526)
(6)        Total Variance ([1] − [4]).................             $(4,852)

## Recording Standard Overhead Costs

The entries to recognize standard overhead costs add little to the previous discussion of standard costing and can be summarized quickly. Actual costs are recorded in departmental accounts, as before:

Factory Overhead—Molding ..................... 26,622
    Various Accounts (Accounts Payable, etc.)...        26,622

The amount absorbed is charged to the departmental overhead in process account:

Overhead in Process—Molding ................. 21,770
    Factory Overhead—Molding ................        21,770

The balance in the Factory Overhead—Molding account is thus the total overhead variance for the month. No overhead variance enters the overhead in process account. Furthermore, the figure obtained by multiplying actual machine-hours by the burden rate has no meaning in this system and *should not be calculated or recorded in the accounts.*

## BEHAVIORAL ISSUES IN COST CONTROL SYSTEMS

The technical problems encountered in the design and use of standard costs and flexible budgets for the control of overhead are small in comparison with the behavioral or human relations problems in employing such systems to aid management control in large organizations. Solutions to these problems are often elusive, and in any case space does not permit discussion of more than a few of them. We shall give brief attention to five questions:

1.  How can the accountant deal with shared responsibility for cost control?
2.  Do budgets serve automatically as operational objectives?

3. What is the role of participation in the budgeting process?
4. How far down in the organization should budget responsibility be pushed?
5. What problems can be created by poor system administration?

### Identifying Cost Responsibility

Assigning costs to organizational units whose managers are responsible for controlling them is not as easy as we may have implied. A cardinal rule in management is that a department head cannot be held responsible for personnel not under his supervision or for material or services that he has not requisitioned. For example, if men and material under the supervision of Jones are employed to provide a service used by Smith, Smith cannot be held responsible for the cost of providing the service. He may be held responsible for the usage of the service, but the primary point for control of the cost is Jones.

One problem is that actual authority and responsibility relationships typically depart in significant respects from those embodied in the formal organization structure. This cannot be blamed on management incompetence in establishing the organization structure, however. The fact is that organization charts are a gross oversimplification of reality. Even the plant manager has more than one boss, and to represent the connection between a staff worker or a department manager and other personnel in a company one would have to draw a number of lines upward, laterally, and at various angles. Furthermore, it is remarkable how many people in a plant work with everyone and are responsible to no one but the plant manager.

Despite these complexities, the accountant really has no alternative to assigning each cost to the individual with the day-to-day responsibility for requisitioning the material or supervising the personnel. For instance, maintenance material and personnel under the supervision of the maintenance manager are charged to him even though the work is done for the managers of other departments who have considerable influence on the level of maintenance costs.

Given this, it is especially important for all levels of management to recognize that (1) a department manager is not *solely* responsible for the costs assigned to him, and (2) he is not *without* responsibility for these costs. Once these points are recognized, it should be a simple matter to recognize that budgetary control systems should be used more to identify problem areas and effective actions than to assign absolute credit or absolute blame.

## Budgets as Operational Objectives

Responsibility accounting is built on the assumption that management at all levels will strive to reach or surpass budgeted performance levels. In this view, the budget identifies the goals of the organization and establishes a standard of performance which everyone will attempt to achieve.

Not everyone in a company is automatically motivated to achieve budgeted goals. The goals may or may not be shared by particular individuals, since a person's goals are based on his needs, and achieving budgeted performance may make little or no contribution to the satisfaction of these needs. An individual for whom this is true does not accept or *internalize* the budget. His aspiration level is below that required by the budget, and it does not motivate him. By contrast, when a manager internalizes the budget for his department, he accepts the organization's goals; we may say that *goal congruence* has been achieved.

Goal congruence is the most critical behavioral problem that management faces in the budgetary process. The prospect of promotion, incentive pay schemes, participation in setting the budget, and other means are employed to bring about goal congruence. Aspiration levels differ among individuals, however. Some value the "good life" and the approval of their subordinates more than organizational success. Policies that achieve goal congruence for one individual may not succeed for another. Changes in operating conditions or in a person's thinking as time goes by may influence his or her aspiration level. This makes it difficult to use aspiration levels as the basis for performance standards. The concept is important, however, and budgets which bear no relation to the aspiration levels of the personnel charged with implementing them will fail.

## Participation

One way to get a subordinate manager to internalize a performance standard is to have him participate in setting the standard. Participation means that decisions affecting a manager's operations are to some extent joint decisions of the manager and his superior. It does not mean that both must be in full agreement on every decision, but the subordinate must be convinced that he is given a fair shake.

Participation does not automatically insure the internalization of performance standards. The gap between the individual's goals and those of the organization may be too great to be bridged. Furthermore, conditions may be such that a more authoritarian managerial style will be more effective in raising the aspiration levels of subordinates. Even so, participation may be very useful. First, it can be used to strengthen the bonds among the members of the group by providing more effective communication. Second, it can increase the visibility of the progress that each member of the group is making toward internalization of organizational goals. The first of these increases the desire of the individual to share the goals of others in the group; the second increases his ability to do this.[1]

## Level of Budgetary Control

Another behavioral issue is how far down in the organization structure cost control responsibility should be pushed. For example, Lester Plastics Company's molding department could be treated as a single responsibility center or as four separate responsibility centers, one for each machine group in each of the two shifts the factory is operating. The choice between these two alternatives depends on answers to two questions:

1. Does the department head's day-to-day contact with the foremen provide adequate control over their areas, or is control and cost consciousness better served by putting each of the four foremen in direct contact with the budget?
2. Can the foremen operate from a budget, or is their ability limited to dealing with men and material, i.e., do budgets confuse and frighten them?

Since the variation in costs with output may differ between the two machine groups, or even between the two shifts of one machine group, budgets on the foreman's level may make better bench marks for control. Certain manufacturing costs, however, such as the costs of the department's maintenance staff, are

---

[1] For a more complete discussion of the role of participation in the budgeting process, see Selwyn Becker and David Green, Jr., "Budgeting and Employee Behavior," *Journal of Business,* October 1962, pp. 392–402; Andrew W. Stedry, "Budgeting and Employee Behavior: A Reply," *Journal of Business,* April 1964, pp. 195–202; and Selwyn Becker and David Green, Jr., "Budgeting and Employee Behavior: A Rejoinder to a 'Reply'," *Journal of Business,* April 1964, pp. 203–5. Additional discussion can be found in George J. Benston, "The Role of the Firm's Accounting System for Motivation," *Accounting Review,* April 1963, pp. 347–54. All four of these papers are reproduced in William J. Bruns, Jr., and Don T. DeCoster, *Accounting and Its Behavioral Implications* (New York: McGraw-Hill Book Company, 1969).

common to the whole department. To push control responsibility down to the foreman level, the maintenance men would either have to be split into four groups, which might not be economical, or would have to remain the responsibility of the department head in a separate cost center of their own. If costs of this kind are substantial, the overhead costs directly chargeable to each foreman and not common to the whole department may not be important enough to warrant the additional bookkeeping and other costs necessary to bring the budget down to the foreman's level.

Given these difficulties, it would not be surprising to find that the issue is sometimes resolved by a form of passing the buck. The manager at each level decides that he will meet the budget his superior gives him by converting it into a set of budgets for his subordinates. The buck-passing ends with the front-line foremen. If they are unable or unwilling to assume the responsibilities thrust upon them, the system collapses. A responsive control system is effective only to the extent that subordinates accept the responsibilities placed on them.

### System Administration

Behavioral problems are sometimes created or enhanced by the ways in which control systems are administered. One factor may be that the budget administrator regards his job as purely technical and is insensitive to the needs of the line executives. As a consequence he may create defensiveness, hostility, and conflict.

Another factor may be that higher management may misuse the budget, regarding it as a device to exert pressure on subordinates. The result is likely to be increased tension, interdepartmental warfare, resentment, and a good deal of other counterproductive behavior. The problem is a confusion of cost control with cost reduction. Cost control is the process of achieving planned performance under existing conditions; cost reduction is a process by which the underlying conditions of production are changed. Unless management recognizes the differences between these two processes, it will have difficulties with its budgetary control system.

### SUMMARY

Control of overhead costs, both in and out of the factory, can be even more important than control of factory direct labor and direct materials. For control purposes, overheads can be divided into two broad categories—discretionary costs and supportive costs. Supportive costs are made necessary by production orders or sales; discretionary costs are incurred to obtain sales orders or to achieve other benefits or objectives that are technologically independent of current volume levels.

Controlling discretionary costs is largely a matter of cost-benefit analysis, an essential ingredient of the budgetary planning process. This should be followed up by a system of feedback reporting that relates costs incurred to the amount of progress achieved toward the goals of the programs.

Control of supportive overheads requires the estimation of standard input/output relationships. Because many overhead costs are fixed in the short period, different input/output ratios are appropriate at different volumes. The set of alternative overhead budgets for different volume levels is known as the flexible budget. Differences between actual overheads and the flexible budget allowances for the volume actually achieved are known as spending variances. The remainder of the total overhead variance arises from the existence of fixed costs and the use of predetermined burden rates at nonstandard volumes. It is called a volume variance.

Use of standard costs and budgetary controls may increase or even create behavioral problems in the organization. Care must be taken to avoid misuse of the systems and to try to induce managers at all levels to internalize standards that represent good organizational performance.

## QUESTIONS AND PROBLEMS

1. Distinguish between supportive and discretionary overheads. What is the most important means of controlling discretionary overheads? Supportive overheads?

2. In what respects are supportive overheads similar to factory direct labor and direct materials from a cost control standpoint? In what respects are they different?

3. What is a progress-adjusted budget? How is it used and why is it important?

4. What is a flexible budget? How is it used and why is it important?

5. Should the overhead volume variance be reported to the department heads? Explain.

6. Does the use of departmental burden rates provide data that will help plant management control factory costs? Explain.

7. "The performance of a department in controlling overhead is measured satisfactorily by the over- or underabsorbed overhead account." Discuss.

8. Standard overhead cost per unit of product is not used in departmental cost control. Why is it computed?

9. What purpose do after-the-fact allocations of service department costs serve? How should these allocations be designed?

10. The volume variance arises because actual volume differs from normal or estimated volume, but it does not equal this volume difference multiplied by the burden rate. Explain why this is the case.

11. Does an unfavorable spending variance always measure poor cost control performance by the department head? Cite examples to support your position.

12. How does the use of flexible budgets realize the objectives of "management by exception"?

13. Some observers have suggested that control systems create such unfavorable behavioral responses that control systems ought to be abandoned entirely. How would you respond to this position? How might you test the validity of the comment?

14. The Sanders Electronics Company issues monthly cost reports to the head of each department. No detailed breakdown of costs is provided; each department head is merely notified of his total costs for the month, his budget, and the difference between the two. In support of this practice, the company's president stated: "We don't want our people to be pencil pushers. If costs are out of line, we expect them to know enough about their operations to find out what is wrong and to do something about it." Discuss this statement.

*15. A department's fixed costs are expected to be $12,450 a month, and the variable costs $1.15 per direct labor dollar. In arriving at a burden rate, it was estimated that the normal direct labor cost would be $15,000 a month.

During the month of March the actual direct labor cost was $17,600 and the actual overhead was $33,150.

Account for the department's overhead during March, using T-accounts, and develop the volume and spending variances for the month.

---

* Solutions to problems marked with an asterisk (*) are found in Appendix B.

**16.** Overhead costs in one of the Bastian Corporation's factory departments are expected to total $8,000 a month plus $1.40 per direct labor hour. The estimated average level of output is 11,000 direct labor hours a month.

During the month of June the actual overhead costs were $22,100 and the actual level of activity was 9,300 direct labor hours.

*a)* Establish a burden rate for the department.
*b)* Compute the volume and spending variances for the month.
*c)* Using T-accounts, show how these facts would be reflected in the factory accounts.

*17.* For each of the following, compute the number of hours on which flexible budget allowances should be based:

*a)* A job order cost system is used. The department's budget is based on actual machine-hours. The work completed by the department and transferred out of the department during the month had a machine-hour content of 15,000 machine-hours. Job orders in process in the department at the beginning of the month had already accumulated 3,000 machine-hours in previous months. Some 1,400 machine-hours had been accumulated on job orders still in process in the department at the end of the month.

*b)* A standard cost system is used. The department's budget is based on standard labor hours. Normal volume for the department is 20,000 standard labor hours per month, and the burden rate is $3 per standard labor hour. During the month, 21,300 actual labor hours were worked. The department finished and transferred to other departments during the month products with a standard overhead cost in this department of $69,000. The standard departmental overhead cost of work in process was $16,200 on the first of the month and $18,000 at the end of the month. Overhead cost fluctuations correlate more closely with product output than with direct labor input.

*18.* The Cotton Company uses a standard costing system and develops volume and spending variances in its overhead costs. You are given the following information for one of the company's factory departments:

(1) The opening balance in Overhead in Process was $6,680.
(2) The actual overhead for the month was $17,400.
(3) The overhead budget was $4,680 a month plus $1.15 per direct labor hour.
(4) The normal level of production was 9,000 direct labor hours.
(5) The department worked 10,800 direct labor hours during the month.
(6) The standard labor content of the products completed and transferred out of the department during the month was 10,500 hours.
(7) The standard labor content of the work in process was 4,000 hours at the start of the month and 3,600 hours at the end.
(8) Overhead costs are expected to vary with output rather than with actual direct labor hours.

*a)* What was the amount of overhead cost "earned" by this department during the month?

*b)* What is the correct month-end balance in the Overhead in Process account?

*c)* Develop the department's overhead spending and volume variances for the month.

19. A standard costing system is in use and standard factory overhead cost is $2 per direct labor hour. Overhead costs vary with the number of standard direct labor hours, according to the following formula:

Budgeted Costs = $11,000 per month + $0.90 per standard direct labor hour.

Actual overhead costs for October totaled $22,140, at an operating volume of 11,200 direct labor hours. Product standard cost and actual production volumes for October were:

| Product | Standard Overhead Cost per Unit | Units Produced, October |
|---|---|---|
| A | $ 5 | 100 |
| B | 6 | 500 |
| C | 10 | 1,000 |
| D | 3 | 1,200 |
| E | 2 | 2,000 |

*a)* Compute the total overhead variance, an overhead spending variance, and an overhead volume variance for the month. Indicate in each case whether the variance is favorable or unfavorable.

*b)* How, if at all, should the volume variance be reported to management? To what management level would you report it?

20. "What do you mean, I'm over my budget?" said Bob Dietz, shop foreman. "It says right here in the annual budget that my regular monthly indirect labor allowance is $3,300. You made up the budget, not me. I only spent $3,200, so where do you get off telling me I'm $200 over? Maybe it's those birds up in the accounting department, fouling me up again."

*a)* As Dietz's boss, how would you explain the situation to him? Was he right? Should he have had an allowance of $3,300?

*b)* If Dietz is typical of the shop foremen, what do you think should be done to strengthen the factory's overhead cost control system?

21. The Dearborn Company manufactures product X in standard batches of 100 units. A standard cost system is in use. The standard costs for a batch are as follows:

| | |
|---|---|
| Direct materials—60 pounds at $0.45 per pound | $ 27.00 |
| Direct labor—36 hours at $2.15 per hour | 77.40 |
| Overhead—36 direct labor hrs. at $2.75 per hour | 99.00 |
| Total Standard Cost per Batch | $203.40 |

Dearborn's normal monthly output is 240 batches (24,000 units). Factory fixed costs are budgeted at $4,752 a month.

The Dearborn Company's new president is worried by the size of the factory overhead costs, which make up almost half of the standard costs of product X. Accordingly, when he found that the actual overhead cost for April was down to $2.60 per actual direct labor hour, he felt somewhat encouraged.

Actual production in April amounted to 210 batches. Actual overhead cost totaled $20,592. Variable overhead costs vary with the number of standard direct labor hours.

a) Should Dearborn's president be encouraged by the reduction in average overhead cost? Prepare an analysis of the overhead costs in April that will help him understand the causes of the reduction.

b) Would average overhead cost per direct labor hour be a useful index of production efficiency for the factory manager? For the president? Comment.

**22.** David Rogers, head of the personnel department, wants to add four people to the employee training staff next year and two people to the recruiting staff. The personnel department now consists of 24 people with a combined annual budget of $1,000,000. Six of these employees are now engaged full time in employee training; three are in recruiting.

How would you evaluate this budget proposal? As a member of the top management budget review committee, what information would you ask for? Where would you expect this information to be found?

**23.** A research proposal called for the expenditure of $48,000, to be spread evenly over a six-month period. At the end of two months, $16,200 had been spent, the project was one-quarter complete, and management estimated that the project would be completed successfully seven months after it was begun, at a total cost of $60,000.

a) Present a brief financial report to the project manager's immediate superior, highlighting the financial performance of the project team.

b) What responses might management take in this situation? What criteria might it use in choosing among these? What data might it reasonably ask for to aid in this choice?

*24. A service department's budget includes the following summary figures:

Budgeted costs = $3,000/month + $7 × service hours.

Normal volume is 3,000 service hours a month.

The flexible budget for production department X allows for the use of 100 service hours a month and the manager is expected to control his usage of this service.

During August the service department provided 2,400 service hours to other departments at a cost of $22,000. Department X used 95 service hours this month.

*a)*  How much service department cost should be charged to department X for the month of August?

*b)*  What variance in service department costs should be reported to the manager of department X?

*c)*  What can you say about the cost performance of the service department manager during the month?


**25.** Department X is a factory service department. It provides labor services, on request, to all other factory departments.

Department X's flexible budget for overhead costs is $5,000 a month plus $4 per man-hour of service provided to other departments. Its normal volume is 5,000 man-hours a month.

Department A is a factory production department. Its normal monthly volume is 20,000 machine-hours. Its flexible budget includes a provision for department X services: 100 service man-hours a month plus one man-hour for every 50 department A machine-hours.

Each month, the factory accountants find department X's actual cost per service man-hour. Department A is then charged for its use of department X by multiplying this actual unit cost by the number of department X man-hours used in department A during the month.

During the month of June, department X recorded 4,500 man-hours, of which 500 were charged to department A. Operating costs in department X for the month totaled $24,300. Department A recorded 20,500 machine-hours during the month.

*a)*  What purpose, if any, is served by allocating service department costs to other departments? Is this likely to be a valid purpose in this case?

*b)*  Develop a department A budget formula from which flexible budget allowances, in dollars, can be derived for department A's consumption of department X services.

*c)*  Compute the amount of department X cost charged to department A for the month of June and compare this with the flexible budget allowance for department A derived from (*b*) above.

*d)*  Analyze the costs of department X and explain the reasons for the deviation between the allocated and budgeted cost.

*e)*  Suggest a way or ways by which the company's interdepartmental service cost allocation method could be improved.


*26.** M. B. Valence, Inc., uses a basic plan standard costing system in one of its manufacturing plants. Materials price variances are isolated at the time of purchase. Each department's work in process accounts are charged with actual quantities of direct labor and materials used, at standard wage rates and materials prices. These accounts are credited with the standard cost of the department's output. Variances are accumulated and reported monthly, and at the end of each month work in process inventories are restated at standard cost. Standard materials prices include an allowance for freight charges.

On January 1, 1961, selected factory inventory accounts showed the following balances:

| | |
|---|---|
| Materials inventory | $76,000 |
| Materials in process—department Y | 13,000 |
| Labor in process—department Y | 8,000 |
| Overhead in process—department Y | 12,000 |

The following transactions relating to department Y took place during the month of January, 1961:

(1) Purchased materials: actual prices, $48,000; standard prices, $50,000; and freight and delivery charges paid, $800.

(2) Accrued direct and indirect labor payrolls for department Y: actual direct labor hours at actual rates, $21,000; actual indirect labor hours at actual wage rates, $8,700.

(3) Actual direct labor hours, department Y, at standard wage rates, $20,000; indirect labor at standard wage rates, $9,000.

(4) Materials issued to department Y, at standard prices: direct materials, $17,000; indirect materials, $4,500.

(5) Overhead costs, other than indirect labor and indirect materials, charged to department Y, $15,000.

(6) Standard cost of work completed by department Y and transferred to finished goods warehouse during the month:

| | |
|---|---|
| Direct materials | $25,000 |
| Direct labor | 24,000 |
| Overhead | 36,000 |
| Total Standard Cost of Work Completed | $85,000 |

(7) Inventories in department Y on January 31 (at standard cost):

| | |
|---|---|
| Materials in process—department Y | $4,100 |
| Labor in process—department Y | 5,400 |
| Overhead in process—department Y | 8,100 |

(8) Overhead is absorbed at a rate of $1.50 per standard direct labor dollar.

(9) Budgeted monthly overhead costs for department Y are:

$$17,000 + \$0.50 \times \text{Standard Direct Labor Cost.}$$

a) Calculate standard direct labor cost for the month.
b) Prepare a schedule of the departmental variances for the month, distinguishing between those that should be reported to the department head and those that should not be reported to him.
c) Set up an appropriate set of T-accounts, enter the opening balances, record the month's transactions, and make entries to transfer all variances into a single Variance Summary account at the end of the month.

27. The Tumbler Company uses a system of departmental flexible budgets to provide overhead cost control information for its factory department managers. The machining department of this company's fac-

tory assigns overhead to products by means of a burden rate of $0.78 a machine-hour. The monthly flexible budget for the machining department is as follows:

| | Volume (machine-hours) | | | | |
|---|---|---|---|---|---|
| | 10,000 | 12,000 | 14,000 | 16,000 | 18,000 |
| Supervision.............. | $ 1,900 | $ 1,900 | $ 1,900 | $ 2,200 | $ 2,200 |
| Indirect labor............ | 2,000 | 2,200 | 2,400 | 2,600 | 2,800 |
| Supplies................. | 500 | 600 | 700 | 800 | 900 |
| Payroll taxes ............ | 1,210 | 1,430 | 1,660 | 1,930 | 2,210 |
| Overtime premiums ...... | 50 | 70 | 220 | 400 | 1,000 |
| Depreciation ............ | 800 | 800 | 800 | 800 | 800 |
| Floor space charges ...... | 3,000 | 3,000 | 3,000 | 3,000 | 3,000 |
| Engineering services ..... | 600 | 650 | 700 | 750 | 800 |
| Total ................ | $10,060 | $10,650 | $11,380 | $12,480 | $13,710 |

During May, this department operated at a rate of 16,000 machine-hours and was charged the following amounts:

| | |
|---|---|
| Supervision ......................... | $ 2,500 |
| Indirect labor ....................... | 2,710 |
| Supplies............................. | 720 |
| Payroll taxes ........................ | 2,000 |
| Overtime premium ................... | 900 |
| Depreciation ........................ | 850 |
| Floor space charges ................. | 2,700 |
| Engineering services ................. | 820 |
| Total ........................... | $13,200 |

The following additional information is available:

(1) The departmental supervision account is ordinarily charged for the straight-time wages earned by assistant foremen. Although these men are paid on an hourly basis, they usually work a full workweek. When the department head deems it necessary, a senior machinist is given additional supervisory duties and part of his wages are charged to the supervision account.

(2) The plant manager assigned a quality control supervisor to this department for one week during May to assist the department manager in the production of a long run of parts with very tight specifications. The departmental supervision account was charged $330 for the supervisor's services during this period.

(3) The indirect labor account is charged for the wages of departmental materials handlers and helpers, and also for the nonproductive time of machine operators. During May, machine operators were idle for approximately 100 hours because of machine breakdowns and delays in receiving work from other departments. The account was charged $420 for this idle time. The indirect labor budget figure includes an allowance for such costs in the amount of 1 cent per machine-hour.

(4) Departments are charged for payroll taxes on all departmental wages, both direct and indirect. Payroll taxes are charged to the departments at a predetermined rate per labor dollar. This rate is not changed during the year.

(5) Overtime work in each department is scheduled monthly by the production scheduling department, on the basis of scheduled production for the month. The department manager's primary responsibility is to meet the production schedule, and he may use whatever amount of overtime premium is necessary to accomplish this objective.

(6) The depreciation charge is computed monthly on the basis of the original cost of the equipment located in the department as of the first day of the month.

(7) Floor space charges are computed monthly by multiplying the number of square feet of floor space occupied by each department by the average cost of building depreciation, insurance, utilities, and janitorial and maintenance services for that month.

(8) Engineering services are provided to production departments by the factory engineering department. These services consist primarily of methods studies prepared at the request of the plant manager or on the initiative of the chief engineer. The charge for these services is based on a predetermined rate per engineering hour.

a) What is the normal operating volume for this department?

b) Compute the total overhead variance for this department for the month of May.

c) Prepare an analysis of the May overhead variance in as much detail as possible. Indicate what you would report to the department manager and why. Prepare a report for the department manager to show the format that you would use.

d) Would the figures for May seem to warrant any action by the department manager? By anyone else? Explain.

28. The Balfour Label Company prints labels, calendars, memo pads, and a variety of other similar products. Its factory consists of two production departments and one service department. The printing department lays out the work, sets type, and prints the products. The finishing department cuts and trims the printed sheets, boxes the finished products, packs the boxes in shipping cartons, and delivers the cartons to the loading dock for delivery to the finished goods warehouse.

A basic plan standard costing system is in use. Printing materials are taken into inventory at standard prices; these standard prices are also used to measure the cost of printing materials issued to the printing department. Direct labor is charged to the two production departments at actual hours and standard wage rates.

Actual overhead costs are accumulated in departmental overhead accounts, but the departmental overhead in inventory accounts reflect standard overhead costs only. The overhead costing rates reflected in the standard costs represent departmental full cost at normal volume. Service department overhead costs are charged to production department overhead accounts at predetermined rates.

The output of the printing department is transferred to the finishing department at standard cost. The standard cost of finished products is credited to the finishing department and charged to the finished goods inventory accounts.

You have the following additional information:

(1)  Budgeted monthly fixed costs were as follows:

|  | Printing | Finishing | Service |
|---|---|---|---|
| Supervision ............... | $ 1,500 | $1,900 | $1,800 |
| Indirect labor ............. | 800 | – | – |
| Equipment depreciation .... | 2,300 | 200 | 120 |
| Other traceable overhead... | 1,000 | 800 | 80 |
| Service department services ................ | 6,400 | 3,600 | – |
| Total ............... | $12,000 | $6,500 | $2,000 |

(2)  Budgeted variable overhead costs were:

|  | Printing (standard direct labor hours) | Finishing (standard direct labor hours) | Service (service hours) |
|---|---|---|---|
| Indirect labor .............. | $1.30 | $ .10 | $7.00 |
| Supplies.................... | .50 | .80 | .80 |
| Other ..................... | .20 | .10 | .20 |
| Total ............... | $2.00 | $1.00 | $8.00 |

(3)  Operating volume in a normal month was:
     Printing: 4,000 direct labor hours.
     Finishing: 6,500 direct labor hours.
     Service: 1,000 service hours.
(4)  Budgeted consumption of service hours:
     Printing: 640 service hours a month.
     Finishing: 360 service hours a month.
(5)  Printing materials inventory, May 1, at standard cost: $36,400.
(6)  Work in process inventory, May 1, at standard cost:

|  | Printing | Finishing |
|---|---|---|
| Materials in process..................... | $18,200 | $22,600 |
| Labor in process ....................... | 5,700 | 3,600 |
| Overhead in process .................... | 4,750 | 1,800 |

(7)  Printing materials purchased during May: actual cost, $37,492; standard cost, $36,100.

(8)  Printing materials issued to the printing department: standard cost, $31,900.

(9)  Direct labor used during the month:
Printing: $18,600 (3,100 hours at standard rates).
Finishing: $14,000 (3,500 hours at standard rates).

(10)  Payrolls paid in cash during the month: $31,500.

(11)  Accrued wages payable, May 1: $980. At the end of the month the direct labor hours worked but not yet paid were:
Printing: 300 hours.
Finishing: 550 hours.

(12)  Traceable overhead costs for the month were:

|  | Printing | Finishing | Service |
|---|---|---|---|
| Supervision ................ | $ 1,500 | $2,100 | $1,800 |
| Indirect labor ............. | 4,800 | 300 | 6,200 |
| Supplies.................... | 1,300 | 2,800 | 680 |
| Equipment depreciation .... | 2,300 | 200 | 120 |
| Other traceable overhead... | 1,800 | 600 | 100 |
| Total ................ | $11,700 | $6,000 | $8,900 |

(13)  Service department costs distributed, at predetermined rate:
To printing department: $5,900.
To finishing department: $3,200.

(14)  Jobs completed during the month, transferred out at standard cost:

|  | Printing | Finishing |
|---|---|---|
| Standard materials cost.................. | $32,700 | $60,800 |
| Standard labor cost ...................... | 16,800 | 15,200 |
| Standard overhead cost .................. | 14,000 | 7,600 |
| Total standard cost ............... | $63,500 | $83,600 |

(15)  Work remaining in process, May 31, at standard cost:

|  | Printing | Finishing |
|---|---|---|
| Material in process....................... | $17,600 | $25,900 |
| Labor in process ........................ | 6,600 | 3,000 |
| Overhead in process ..................... | 5,500 | 1,500 |

(16)  Equipment depreciation and supervision and service department utilization are regarded as noncontrollable by the heads of the three departments; all other costs are classified as controllable.

a)  Calculate standard direct materials cost, standard direct labor cost, and standard direct labor hours for the printing and finishing departments during May. Calculate budgeted overhead costs for the volume actually achieved in each of the three departments during the month.

b)  Determine the costs charged to each of the three departments during

May. (Do not overlook the transfer of work from the printing department to the finishing department.)

c) Prepare a cost summary for each of the three departments, in a form that the department head would find useful. Did the department heads control their costs satisfactorily?

d) Prepare a list of any variances that you did not include in your answer to (c). To whom would they be reported? What do they reveal?

e) Establish T-accounts for the departmental overhead and inventory accounts, enter the opening balances, record the month's transactions, and make the entries necessary to transfer the month's variances to appropriately titled variance accounts.

## Case 24–1: RUOHONEN OY.†

"These reports give me and my department heads what we need; any changes we make from now on will be very minor," said Mr. Arvo Simola, managing director of Ruohonen Oy., one of Finland's leading foundry companies. "I started working on the reporting system when I became managing director six years ago. The first set of reports I designed then was very different from the ones you see here, because we learned a lot as we went along. What we have now is as good a system as you'll see anywhere, and it doesn't cost us much, either."

The Ruohonen company employed 300 people in the foundry, plus another 70 on the administrative and clerical staff and a 7-man sales force. Net sales in 1968 exceeded 10 million Finmarks (Fmk.) and were growing.

### Preparing the Annual Factory Budget

The departmental reporting system began with the development of annual output, efficiency, and cost budgets for each department. Each autumn, Mr. Simola obtained a sales forecast from the marketing division showing estimated sales of each product for each month of the coming year. With this in hand, he met with his production scheduler and his cost accountant to work out tentative monthly production schedules for each department.

As soon as this task was completed, the cost accountant prepared a tentative forecast of average cost per unit for the scheduled production volume, assuming no change from the current year other than the change in volume. After examining these tentative cost estimates, Mr. Simola established tentative improvement targets for each department — that is, lower standard costs and higher yields than those of the current year.

---

† Copyright 1969 by l'Institut pour l'Etude des Méthodes de Direction de l'Entreprise (IMEDE), Lausanne, Switzerland. Adapted and reproduced by permission.

At this point, Mr. Simola called in his department heads one by one to discuss the new standards. He explained the basis on which he had adjusted the current-year figures and asked for comments. Whenever a department head was able to convince him that the proposed budget could not be achieved, the standard was revised.

Mr. Simola commented that the department heads were enthusiastic supporters of the new reporting system. Most of the department heads had been with the company for ten years or more. Although three of them had engineering degrees, few of the others had gone beyond secondary school. Most of them would probably remain in factory supervision until the time of retirement. Skeptical at first, they had come to value the opportunity to review their own performance and to work on methods improvement. Due in large measure to their help and cooperation, unit manufacturing costs had been cut almost in half between 1960 and 1968.

Once the final budget figures for the year were agreed upon, they were restated as daily averages. These averages were then regarded as cost and performance standards for the coming year. Total budgets for each month were obtained by multiplying the budgeted daily averages by the budgeted number of working days in that month.

## Monthly Departmental Performance Summaries

Mr. Simola's main control reports were prepared monthly. He received an income statement, a cost summary for the entire factory, and individual performance summaries for each of the foundry's 15 operating departments. "As you can see," he said, "most of the figures are on foundry operations. The reason is probably obvious: that's where most of our costs are and that's where we make money or lose it."

The departmental performance summaries were the key reports in the system. One copy of each report went to Mr. Simola; another went to the department head. Mr. Simola reviewed each of these reports personally and discussed unfavorable figures directly with the heads of the departments concerned.

The report illustrated in Exhibit 1 is typical of the reports that Mr. Simola received each month. This particular report was issued early in July, 1968, covering the operations of the foundry's Cupola department for the month of June. This department's task was to melt raw metals in prescribed proportions and deliver the molten metal at prescribed temperatures to other departments.

All of the figures in Exhibit 1 except those in items 8 and 9 represent physical data. Item 1, for example, shows the amount of raw metal or "charge" issued to the Cupola department during the month, in tons. Similarly, item 2 shows the amount of fuel (coke) used to melt the charge, expressed in tons and as a percentage of the amount of metal used.

Item 3 is more complex. The figure in column 5 of item 3A shows the amount of molten metal that the Cupola was scheduled to produce during the month of June, 630.5 tons. The amount shown for item 3B on the line below, 471.4 tons, is the daily average budgeted for the year, multiplied by the number of budgeted working days in June. The number of working days is shown in item 7C. Using these figures, the calculation for June is:

$$\text{Budgeted Yearly Output} \times \frac{\text{Budgeted Days in June}}{\text{Budgeted Days in 1968}}$$

$$= 5{,}793 \times \frac{24}{295} = 471.4 \text{ tons.}$$

Comparison of this figure with the one directly above on line 3B shows that the amount actually scheduled for June production was far in excess of the month's pro rata share of the budgeted annual output. Actual output tonnages for June, for May, and for the six months of January through June 1968, are then shown in columns 6, 7, and 8.

Finally, item 3C, the average daily output, is obtained by dividing the output figures in item 3B by the number of days shown on line 7C.

Item 4, the average yield, is the ratio of the output to the amount of the charge. The budget for June was calculated as follows:

$$\frac{\text{Output}}{\text{Charge}} = \frac{471.4}{724} = 65.1\%.$$

Similar calculations were performed on the actual monthly figures to derive the yields shown in columns 6, 7, and 8.

Item 5, labor hours, is straightforward. Departmental employees are divided into two groups, direct workers and indirect workers, and the number of labor hours is recorded separately for each group. Overtime hours are included in these totals, but a separate figure for total overtime hours for both groups of workers combined is shown on line 5D. Finally, the figures in line 5E are obtained by dividing the total labor hours for the month by the number of working days in the month.

The efficiency indexes shown in item 6 are obtained by dividing the output figures (line 3B) by total labor hours (line 5C) and direct labor hours (line 5A).

Item 7 consists of three sets of physical data that do not fall naturally into any of the items above. Line 7A shows the amount of the incentive bonus earned by departmental employees during the month, expressed as a percentage of their wages at basic straight-time rates. Item 7B shows the amount of the foundry's gross output that was found to be defective and had to be remelted, expressed as a percentage of good output. This percentage, it should be noted, is a foundry-wide figure — that is, it is the rejection rate for the foundry as a whole, not just for the Cupola department alone. An additional line was provided on the monthly reports of several departments, to show the specific rejection rates of those departments, but this item was not shown on the Cupola department's reports. Mr. Simola felt that rejects in the Cupola department were reflected in the yield percentage and that nothing would be gained by identifying them on a separate line.

*Exhibit 1*

## DEPARTMENTAL PERFORMANCE REPORT

Dept.  O1 – Cupola

Month   June, 1968

| Line | Description | Unit of Measure | Budgeted Year 1968 | Budgeted This Month | Actual Results This Month | Actual Results Last Month | Actual Results Year to Date | Indexes Col. 6 ÷ Col. 5 | Indexes Col. 8 ÷ Col. 4 | Actual Year 1967 |
|---|---|---|---|---|---|---|---|---|---|---|
| 1 | 2 | 3 | 4 | 5 | 6 | 7 | 8 | 9 | 10 | 11 |
| 1 | Charge (metal used) | Tons | 8,900 | 724 | 912 | 910 | 5,147.9 | 126.0 | 57.8 | 7,538 |
| 2 | Coke consumed | Tons | 1,080 | 87.9 | 112 | 106 | 624 | | 57.8 | 899 |
| | % of charge | % | 12 | 12 | 12.3 | 11.6 | 12.1 | | | 12 |
| 3A | Output: Prod. control dept. schedule | Tons | | 630.5 | 566.6 | 581.5 | 3,332.2 | | | |
| | Budget for year: | | | | | | | | | |
| 3B | Total | Tons | 5,793 | 471.4 | 566.6 | 581.5 | 3,332.2 | 120.2 | 57.5 | 4,759 |
| 3C | Average per day | Tons | 19.64 | 19.64 | 23.6 | 24.2 | 22.1 | | | 17.1 |
| 4 | Average yield (Output ÷ charge) | % | 65.1 | 65.1 | 62.1 | 63.9 | 64.7 | | | 63.1 |
| 5A | Labor hours: Direct | Hours | 27,260 | 2,217 | 2,390 | 2,298 | 14,394 | 107.8 | 52.8 | 26,113 |
| 5B | Indirect | Hours | 660 | 54 | 194 | 223 | 609 | | | 621 |
| 5C | Total (5A + 5B) | Hours | 27,920 | 2,271 | 2,584 | 2,521 | 15,003 | 113.8 | 53.7 | 26,734 |
| 5D | Overtime included in 5A & 5B | Hours | 1,300 | 106 | 248 | 270 | 1,209 | | | 1,485 |
| 5E | Average per day | Hours | 94.6 | 94.6 | 107.7 | 105 | 99.3 | | | 96.2 |

| | Description | Unit | | | | | | | | |
|---|---|---|---|---|---|---|---|---|---|---|
| | Efficiency indexes: | | | | | | | | | |
| 6A | Tot. hrs ÷ output | Hrs/ton | 4.82 | 4.82 | 4.56 | 4.34 | 4.50 | | | 5.62 |
| 6B | Dir. hrs ÷ output | Hrs/ton | 4.70 | 4.70 | 4.21 | 3.95 | 4.31 | | | 5.49 |
| 7A | Incentive bonus | % of base wage | 33 | 33 | 30.6 | 31 | | | | |
| 7B | Rejects in foundry | % of output | 8.4 | 8.4 | 9.3 | 8.1 | 8.2 | | | |
| 7C | Working days | Days | 295 | 24 | 24 | 24 | 151 | 100 | 51.2 | |
| | Monetary data: | | | | | | | | | |
| 8A | Avg. cost of output | Fmk./ton | 385.05 | 385.05 | 368.69 | 373.34 | 377.01 | | | |
| 8B | Total cost | Fmk.000 | 2,230.6 | 181.5 | 208.9 | 217.1 | 1,256.3 | | | |
| 8C | Total savings | Fmk.000 | | | 9.2 | 6.8 | 26.8 | | | |
| | Analysis of deviations: | | | | | | | | | |
| 9A | Efficiency of work | Fmk.000 | | | 1.769 | 2.819 | 8.237 | | | |
| 9B | External changes | Fmk.000 | | | -.454 | 92 | .134 | | | |
| 9C | Efficiency of indirect labor | Fmk.000 | | | 2.004 | .806 | 1.404 | | | |
| 9D | Changes of volume | Fmk.000 | | | 3.734 | 4.210 | 14.520 | | | |
| 9E | Efficient use of materials | Fmk.000 | | | 2.147 | -1.331 | 2.485 | | | |

Item 8 shows monthly cost data for the department in highly summarized form. Line 8B shows the total cost of operating the Cupola department during the month, including materials, labor and departmental overhead costs. Line 8A is this figure divided by total output for the month (from line 3B). Finally, item 8C is computed from the following formula:

Savings = Output × (Budgeted average cost − Actual average cost)

The final section of the report (item 9) is devoted to an analysis of the total cost savings figures shown on line 8C. In June, 1968, for example, Fmk.1,769 of the Fmk.9,200 total savings was due to work efficiency in the Cupola itself. This was offset to some extent by unfavorable changes arising outside the company (Fmk.454), but further savings resulted from above-normal levels of production volume (Fmk.3,734), low average indirect labor cost (Fmk.2,004), and efficient use of materials (Fmk.2,147).

## Overall Cost Summaries

Mr. Simola's staff also prepared a monthly summary report in the form illustrated in Exhibit 2. This report provided a summary breakdown of the operating costs in each of the 15 foundry departments, each line representing a single department. Additional lines were provided for two categories of nondepartmental manufacturing costs (lines 16 and 17) and for four categories of nonmanufacturing cost. All of the data in Exhibit 2 are expressed in thousands of Finmarks; no physical input or output data are shown. Furthermore, this report shows only cumulative data, reflecting experience for the year to date rather than for the current month only.

The first line of Exhibit 2, for example, summarizes the Cupola department's operations for the period January–June, 1968. The variance figure shown in the first column is the same as the "total savings" figure shown in column 8 or line 8C in Exhibit 1. The remaining columns then summarize the costs that were actually charged to the department during the period, classified into six different categories (columns 5 through 10). The total of these costs is shown in column 4.

Mr. Simola explained that the amounts shown for "materials burden" in column 6 represented an allocation of the costs of the Storage department. These costs included the costs of receiving and handling materials, including interest, warehousing labor, insurance, space charges, and inventory shrinkage costs. Mr. Simola felt that these costs should be charged to the factory departments so that the department heads would have an interest in keeping inventories low. The interest rate used for this purpose was the one used in the company's inventory control formula. The interest figure shown on line 21 was then the difference between the company's total interest charges for the period and the amounts charged to the Storage department.

Exhibit 2

# DEPARTMENTAL OPERATING COST SUMMARY

## January–June, 1968

### (in thousands of finmarks)

| Department | Variances Good | Variances Bad | Total Costs | Direct Materials | Materials Burden | Direct Labor | Other Direct Costs | Overhead Costs Variable | Overhead Costs Fixed |
|---|---|---|---|---|---|---|---|---|---|
| 1 | 2 | 3 | 4 | 5 | 6 | 7 | 8 | 9 | 10 |
| 01 Cupola | 26.8 |  | 1,256.3 | 890.5 | 43.7 | 93.1 |  | 89.3 | 139.7 |
| 02 Moulding Machines | 12.8 |  | 300.2 | 6.0 | 0.3 | 50.2 |  | 153.9 | 89.8 |
| 03 Bathtubs |  | 54.4 | 400.3 |  |  | 82.8 |  | 186.8 | 130.7 |
| 04 Frames |  | 6.5 | 31.9 |  |  | 7.5 |  | 9.4 | 15.0 |
| 05 Centrifugal Casting |  | 4.6 | 71.9 |  |  | 11.3 |  | 48.7 | 11.9 |
| 06 Floor Moulding | 15.3 |  | 345.6 | 12.0 | 0.7 | 106.3 |  | 150.6 | 76.0 |
| 07 Core Shop |  | 24.9 | 182.1 |  |  | 57.8 |  | 90.6 | 33.7 |
| 08 Fettling Shop | 19.6 |  | 355.2 | 15.0 | 0.8 | 152.3 |  | 106.0 | 81.1 |
| 09 Enamel Shop |  | 0.5 | 396.5 | 140.1 | 7.7 | 103.1 |  | 90.9 | 54.7 |
| 10 Pattern Shop |  |  | 90.4 | 10.0 | 0.5 | 47.9 |  | 2.1 | 29.9 |
| 11 Nonferrous Foundry |  |  | 425.5 | 298.4 | 15.3 | 41.6 |  | 38.3 | 31.9 |
| 12 Pumps | 3.2 |  | 114.9 | 37.0 | 2.0 | 45.6 |  | 3.4 | 26.9 |
| 13 Machining | 27.2 |  | 342.4 | 43.0 | 2.4 | 134.3 |  | 49.3 | 113.4 |
| 14 Engineering |  |  | 100.8 |  |  | 54.2 |  | 10.5 | 36.1 |
| 15 Plastics | 26.8 | 5.6 | 364.8 | 172.0 | 9.5 | 105.8 |  | 21.7 | 55.8 |
| 16 Subcontractors |  |  | 32.0 |  |  |  | 32.0 |  |  |
| 17 Miscellaneous |  |  | 50.0 |  |  |  | 50.0 |  |  |
| Total Factory | 131.7 | 94.5 | 4,860.8 | 1,624.0 | 82.9 | 1,093.8 | 82.0 | 1,051.5 | 926.6 |
| 18 Storage |  |  | 296.0 |  | (82.9) |  |  |  | 82.9 |
| 19 Administration |  |  | 162.0 |  |  |  |  |  | 296.0 |
| 20 Selling |  |  | 175.0 |  |  |  |  | 175.0 | 162.0 |
| 21 Interest |  |  |  |  |  |  |  |  |  |
| Total | 37.2 |  | 5,493.8 | 1,624.0 | — | 1,093.8 | 82.0 | 1,226.5 | 1,467.5 |

The amounts shown as overhead costs in columns 9 and 10 included both costs directly traceable to the department, such as supervision and depreciation on departmental equipment, and a pro rata share of the costs of operating the factory's service departments during the period. Mr. Simola preferred to put the service department costs here rather than show them on separate lines, mainly because the entire reporting system focussed on deviations from budgeted average unit cost in each of the production departments. Giving each service department a line of its own would have required the use of some composite measure of overall foundry output for these departments. Mr. Simola thought that this would be confusing and not very useful.

Cost details underlying the figures shown in Exhibit 2 were not reported to the department heads, nor were the flexible budget schedules. Mr. Simola had access to these figures at all times, but he felt that the department heads had no need for any figures other than those provided in the departmental performance summaries, such as the one illustrated in Exhibit 1. He himself, however, frequently had occasion to question one or more of the cost figures shown on Exhibit 2, and he usually asked his cost accountant for a further cost breakdown before he talked to the department head.

a) Study Exhibit 1 carefully. Make sure that you understand the relationships from line to line and from column to column.

b) Neither the flexible budget allowances nor detailed overhead cost figures are included in the monthly reports exemplified by Exhibit 1. Weigh the arguments for and against reporting these figures. Would reporting an "adjusted budget" figure for average cost per ton be likely to impair or enhance the value of the monthly performance reports?

c) What aspects of the measurement and reporting system would you change? Give your reasons.

d) This system seems to be working, in the sense that although budgeted unit costs were reduced year after year, most production departments managed to achieve favorable quantity or "efficiency" variances by the end of the year. Speculate on the factors that might have led to this improvement and indicate whether they are likely to persist in the future. What problems, if any, do you foresee? Discuss the method of deriving the annual and monthly budgets in this connection.

# 25

# REPORTING PROFITS
# TO MANAGEMENT

THE ANNUAL PROFIT PLAN played a relatively minor role in the kinds of feedback reporting discussed in the two previous chapters. In the final analysis, however, profit remains the main objective of the business corporation, the *sine qua non* for survival. Only profitable firms can afford costly efforts to reach other kinds of objectives.

Feedback information on profit performance therefore is of vital significance to top management and to others in the firm who have partial responsibility for part of the firm's profit generating activities. The purpose of this chapter is to see how internal profit reports can be used and how they may be constructed and interpreted.

## PURPOSES OF INTERNAL PROFIT REPORTING

As we indicated in Chapter 18, few companies are so narrowly based that a single company-wide profitability statement will give management the profit information it needs. Most companies have a number of relatively distinct product lines or geographical market areas, each with its own problems and its own opportunities.

Although ultimate profit responsibility rests with top management, at least some of this responsibility must be shared with managers at lower levels. The amount of responsibility and authority for profit performance that is delegated to a subordinate manager can range from very little to very much. In any case, the manager needs profit information on each segment for which he has some profit responsibility:

1.  To identify aspects of his operations that need attention.
2.  To find out how effective his efforts to generate profits have been.

For example, the monthly profit report may tell a branch manager that his branch has been generally successful in generating profits, but that two sales territories have fallen far below the performance level that he thinks they should have attained. The report of overall success should help him maintain his motivation or commitment to profit-oriented activity, while the detailed segment information should lead him to devote some time to finding out what went wrong in the low-yield territories and taking whatever action seems called for.

Higher management's interest in internal profit reports is similar but somewhat broader. At the very top, management is likely to use these reports in three ways:

1.  To evaluate the profit-generating performance of subordinate managers (*managerial evaluation*).
2.  To evaluate the profit-generating performance of the resources invested in individual segments (*investment evaluation*).
3.  To evaluate the methods used to generate profit in individual business segments (*operations evaluation*).

The reports are also intended to give top management the same kind of motivational reinforcement that they are designed to provide at lower levels.

Although the individual segments dealt with by top management are typically much larger than those identified by their subordinates, the major difference is that top management's decisions have greater scope. It can promote or remove subordinate executives, and can even decide to dispose of a segment entirely if its analysis of the investment points in this direction.

## PROFIT REPORTING FOR OPERATIONS EVALUATION

The most fundamental use of the internal profit report is to provide the profit-responsible executive with information that he can use in improving his own effectiveness in generating profits for the company. Four aspects of profit reporting for this purpose deserve discussion at this time:

1.  Measuring profit contribution.

2. Reporting segment investment.
3. Analyzing profit variances.
4. Choosing the aggregation level.

## Measuring Profit Contribution

The profit report for any given business segment should identify the amount the segment has contributed to total company profit. The question is how this contribution is to be measured.

Most reporting systems use one of the following two definitions:

1. *Profit contribution:* segment revenues, less the variable costs attributable to these revenues, less any fixed costs traceable to the segment.
2. *Net Profit:* profit contribution, less a pro rata share of all nontraceable fixed costs.

Exhibit 25–1 shows how the profit center concept may be used in reporting segment profit to the top management of a simple, two-segment firm. Separate columns are provided for each of the firm's two business segments: regular products and custom products. The top half of the statement summarizes the revenues and variable costs for each segment. Custom products, for example,

### Exhibit 25–1
### Saddler Products Corporation
#### PRODUCT PROFIT CONTRIBUTION STATEMENT
#### For the Month of March, 19x1

| | All Products | Regular Products Amount | % of Net Sales | Custom Products Amount | % of Net Sales |
|---|---|---|---|---|---|
| Net Sales | $2,000,000 | $1,640,000 | 100.0 | $360,000 | 100.0 |
| Variable costs (standard): | | | | | |
| Factory | $1,097,600 | $ 836,600 | | $261,000 | |
| Order filling | 65,100 | 52,600 | | 12,500 | |
| Total Variable Costs | $1,162,700 | $ 889,200 | 54.2 | $273,500 | 76.0 |
| Variable profit | $ 837,300 | $ 750,800 | 45.8 | $ 86,500 | 24.0 |
| Product-traceable fixed costs | $ 195,400 | $ 148,500 | | $ 46,900 | |
| Labor and materials variances | 7,900 | 10,600 | | (2,700) | |
| Profit contribution | $ 634,000 | $ 591,700 | 36.1 | $ 42,300 | 11.8 |
| Common fixed costs: | | | | | |
| Factory | $ 137,200 | | | | |
| Selling and administrative | 283,500 | | | | |
| Net Income before Tax | $ 213,300 | | | | |

had variable costs of $273,500, or 76 percent of the revenues for this segment. This left only $86,500 in variable profit and a variable profit/volume ratio $(P/V)$ of 24 percent, about half of that obtained from the company's regular products.

The next two lines show the amount of fixed costs specifically traceable to the individual segments, leading to the profit contribution figures on the line below. Other fixed costs, much larger in total, were not distributed between the two segments—that is, net income was calculated and reported only for the company as a whole. *Under the profit contribution approach, company net income is the sum of the segment profit contributions, less the total of the fixed costs not traceable to individual product-line segments.*

The argument for the profit contribution approach is that most allocations of the nontraceable fixed costs are to a large extent arbitrary. How much of the president's salary should be charged to regular products and how much to custom products is a question of metaphysics, not of management. Even when some apparently reasonable basis can be found for allocating nontraceable items, however, these allocations add nothing to the information content of the periodic reports. Profit contribution indicates the amount of profit generated by each individual business segment, the amount available to cover general fixed costs and provide a net profit for the company as a whole.

It should be emphasized that segment profit contribution does not necessarily measure the incremental profit stemming from that segment. For one thing, the segment's expenses may include depreciation and other allocations of historical costs that must be treated as sunk costs in any kind of incremental analysis. Second, increments refer to the future, not to the past, and the period covered by the profit contribution report may be highly unrepresentative of the results to be achieved in the future.

Third, segments are not totally independent of each other. The profit lost by abandoning one segment may be either greater or less than its profit contribution if its sales or operating costs are interdependent with those of another segment. Finally, although the unallocated fixed costs are not traceable to individual segments, elimination of an entire segment could very well lead to a restructuring of central supporting activities and to a reduction in nontraceable fixed costs.

These differences are relatively unimportant in operations evaluation. The objective of operations evaluation is to identify exceptionally good or exceptionally poor cost/benefit relationships. Deciding what action to take requires analysis of the causes of these conditions and estimates of the effectiveness of possible managerial responses. Reviewing the profit reports is only the first step in this process.

## Reporting Segment Investment

No reference was made in Exhibit 25–1 to the investment resources necessary to produce each segment's profit contribution. These resources are costly and should not be ignored in operations evaluation.

For example, suppose the investment in special equipment, inventories, and receivables for the custom products business was only $1 million, whereas a total investment of $20 million was directly traceable to the regular product lines. Suppose further that the cost of invested capital was 12 percent a year, or 1 percent a month. Under these circumstances it would be both reasonable and informative to deduct 1 percent of the traceable investment from the monthly profit contribution figure:

|  | Regular Products | Custom Products |
|---|---|---|
| Profit contribution | $591,700 | $42,300 |
| Interest on direct investment | 200,000 | 10,000 |
| Residual Profit Contribution | $391,700 | $32,300 |

This shows that both segments covered the implicit costs of the investment resources specifically devoted to them, but much of the profit contribution from regular products was consumed by the heavy capital requirements of that segment. At a minimum, management should have examined the investment structure to see whether the markets could be served effectively with a smaller capital commitment.

## Analyzing Profit Variances

The profit report shown in Exhibit 25–1 is of limited usefulness because it provides no comparison bench mark, but the profit contribution concept can be applied in comparative statements as well. Exhibit 25–2, for example, shows a comparative income statement for the regular products segment. Even a cursory examination of this report shows that the regular products line failed by a wide margin to meet its objectives during March. The cumulative performance for the year to date was also poor.

Exhibit 25–2

Saddler Products Corporation

Regular Products

COMPARATIVE PROFIT CONTRIBUTION REPORT

For the Month of March, 19x1

(000 omitted)

| | This Month | | | Year to Date | |
| --- | --- | --- | --- | --- | --- |
| | Actual Results | Budgeted Results | Variance Over/ (Under) | Actual Results | Variance Over/ (Under) |
| Net sales.................. | $1,640 | $1,800 | $(160) | $4,380 | $(520) |
| Variable costs (standard): | | | | | |
| Factory ................. | $ 837 | $ 900 | $ (63) | $2,123 | $(327) |
| Order filling............. | 52 | 54 | ( 2) | 158 | 21 |
| Total Variable Cost... | $ 889 | $ 954 | $ (65) | $2,281 | $(306) |
| Variable profit............. | $ 751 | $ 846 | $ (95) | $2,099 | $(214) |
| Product-traceable | | | | | |
| fixed costs............. | $ 148 | $ 144 | $ 4 | $ 450 | $ 18 |
| Traceable cost variances ... | 11 | 3 | 8 | 21 | 6 |
| Profit contribution......... | $ 592 | $ 699 | $(107) | $1,628 | $(238) |
| Interest on traceable | | | | | |
| investment............... | 200 | 180 | 20 | 515 | (5) |
| Residual Profit | | | | | |
| Contribution............. | $ 392 | $ 519 | $(127) | $1,113 | $(233) |

This statement shows that serious problems had arisen, so serious that they were likely to preclude achievement of the company's profit goals for the year. It says virtually nothing about the nature of these problems, however, or what the manager could do about them. To fill this void, most internal profit statements include some form of analysis or commentary on the deviations between actual and budgeted performance. The commentary may call attention to unusual events that had significant favorable or unfavorable effects on reported income during the period, and it may indicate whether these effects are expected to continue and what actions management is taking to cope with or capitalize on the situation.

These qualitative commentaries are often supported and supplemented by quantitative breakdowns of the aggregate profit variance in each segment of the business. For example, the analysis may identify the difference between actual and planned *selling prices* for the actual volume of business done. It may also measure a *sales volume* variance, measured by the deviation of physical sales volume from the planned volume, multiplied by the planned profit margin per unit.

Although the analytical techniques to provide this kind of information are too complex for explanation here,[1] one point deserves emphasis. If nontraceable fixed costs are allocated so that product-line reports show net profit, then the allocated fixed costs that are not traceable to individual product lines should be exactly equal to the amounts implicit in the product-line profit plan for the period. *Profit deviations should never result from changes in the basis on which allocations are made unless the allocations are designed to influence managerial behavior.* By accepting the division's profit plan for the year, top management has also agreed to incur fixed costs at the planned level. If these costs vary from the planned amounts, the variations are the result of head office rather than divisional activities. To put this another way, the place to analyze these variations is in the head office, where they arise, rather than at the various divisional offices. For this reason, the allocation should be a fixed quantity, unchanged from month to month throughout the year.

## Choosing the Aggregation Level

So far we have been dealing with what seems to be a very simple operating structure—only two business segments, with all profit responsibility assigned to top management. Even here, management would ordinarily want more detail. Subdivision of the regular products line into related product groups, classification of results by geographical areas, and a more complete descriptive classification of costs are all possible forms this additional detail might take.

In practice, additional detail is imperative because profit responsibility is shared with managers at a number of different levels. In this situation, the greatest amount of detail is usually provided only to managers at the lowest level of profit responsibility. Reports received routinely by top management show very little detail because responsibility for managing the details has been delegated to subordinates. Top management is likely to see detailed figures only when specific problems or opportunities call for top management attention.

Exhibit 25–3, for instance, shows a report that might be issued to the district sales manager as an overall summary of his district's profit contribution. The business segment in this case is the company's sales in its Boston district rather than company-wide sales of a specific product line as in Exhibit 25–2. The

---

[1] For one analytical scheme, see Gordon Shillinglaw, *Cost Accounting: Analysis and Control* (3d ed.; Homewood, Ill.: Richard D. Irwin, Inc., 1972), Chapter 24.

Exhibit 25–3

Carswell Corporation

DISTRICT PROFIT PERFORMANCE REPORT

Boston District — Month of January, 19x1

|  | Budget | Actual | Deviation | Actual % of Sales |
|---|---|---|---|---|
| Net sales billed .................. | $500,000 | $514,000 | $14,000 | 100.0 |
| Cost of sales ..................... | 375,000 | 381,000 | (6,000) | 74.1 |
| Gross margin .................... | $125,000 | $133,000 | $ 8,000 | 25.9 |
| District office costs: |  |  |  |  |
| Branch salaries................. | $   2,500 | $   2,500 | . . . | 0.5 |
| Sales salaries .................. | 25,000 | 25,500 | $   (500) | 5.0 |
| Travel ........................ | 8,000 | 6,800 | 1,200 | 1.3 |
| Entertainment.................. | 1,000 | 1,300 | (300) | 0.2 |
| Local advertising .............. | 500 | 500 | . . . | 0.1 |
| Storage and delivery ........... | 7,000 | 7,300 | (300) | 1.4 |
| Branch office expense.......... | 900 | 1,100 | (200) | 0.2 |
| Other ......................... | 600 | 700 | (100) | 0.1 |
| Total district cost ............. | $ 45,500 | $ 45,700 | $   (200) | 8.8 |
| District Profit Contribution........ | $ 79,500 | $ 87,300 | $ 7,800 | 17.1 |

format is the same, however, in that no allocations of head office fixed costs are charged against the individual district's revenues.

A glance at this report will tell the district manager that his actual sales volume was $514,000, that this gave him a gross margin $8,000 larger than his profit plan called for, and that his district profit contribution for the month was $7,800 greater than his profit objective.

While this kind of report is useful as an overall summary, it does not provide the district manager with any explanation of the *sources* of the main deviations. Another report that he might receive is shown in Exhibit 25–4, to permit him to monitor the performance of his individual salesmen. Although many companies limit such summaries to sales volume alone, the interjection of product costs and traceable fixed expenses can add a significant dimension to the sales figures. Salesman Kelly, for example, sold $4,000 more than Williams during the month but showed a $700 smaller profit contribution. Williams, on the other hand, failed to meet his profit objective for the period, as did three of the other salesmen.

The district manager might receive another report summarizing the same data but arranged as in Exhibit 25–5, if he is expected to influence product mix actively. Notice that in this exhibit a much smaller percentage of expenses is assigned to individual segments of the district's business. Salesmen's salaries and expenses are traceable to individual salesmen but not to individual product lines. Local advertising, on the other hand, in this instance is completely product-traceable and thus moves "above the line."

It is unnecessary, of course, to carry all reports down to the same final profit or variance figure. The tie-in has been made here, however, to emphasize that a single set of figures has been combined in several ways to illustrate different facets of the problem.

Profit reports for higher levels of marketing management are similar in structure to those just illustrated, but the level of

Exhibit 25–4

Carswell Corporation

### SALESMAN PERFORMANCE SUMMARY
Boston District — Month of January, 19x1

| Salesman | Net Sales Billed | Cost of Sales | Salary and Expenses | Profit Contribution Amount | Profit Contribution Budget Deviation | Profit Contribution % of Sales |
|---|---|---|---|---|---|---|
| Brown | $ 40,000 | $ 29,200 | $ 2,400 | $ 8,400 | $ (400) | 21.0% |
| Cannon | 31,000 | 24,300 | 3,200 | 3,500 | (900) | 11.3 |
| Evars | 63,000 | 42,700 | 4,100 | 16,200 | 3,700 | 25.7 |
| Johnson | 30,000 | 24,200 | 2,900 | 2,900 | (1,400) | 9.7 |
| Kelly | 54,000 | 40,100 | 4,200 | 9,700 | 200 | 18.0 |
| Lusso | 47,000 | 34,400 | 3,100 | 9,500 | 2,100 | 20.2 |
| McGregor | 76,000 | 56,000 | 3,800 | 16,200 | 4,000 | 21.3 |
| Nelson | 55,000 | 41,900 | 3,300 | 9,800 | 500 | 17.8 |
| Stern | 68,000 | 51,600 | 3,600 | 12,800 | 1,200 | 18.8 |
| Williams | 50,000 | 36,600 | 3,000 | 10,400 | (600) | 20.8 |
| Total | $514,000 | $381,000 | $33,600 | $99,400 | $8,400 | 19.4% |
| Other branch expenses | | | | 12,100 | (600) | 1.7 |
| District Profit Contribution | | | | $87,300 | $7,800 | 17.1% |

Exhibit 25–5

Carswell Corporation

### DISTRICT PRODUCT PROFIT CONTRIBUTION REPORT
Boston District — Month of January, 19x1

| Product Line | Net Sales Billed Actual | Net Sales Billed Variance | Cost of Sales | Other Product Expenses | Profit Contribution Actual | Profit Contribution Variance |
|---|---|---|---|---|---|---|
| White Shield | $204,000 | $26,000 | $136,000 | $500 | $ 67,500 | $14,000 |
| Red Label | 133,000 | (50,000) | 103,000 | — | 30,000 | (11,000) |
| Commercial | 177,000 | 38,000 | 142,000 | — | 35,000 | 5,000 |
| Total | $514,000 | $14,000 | $381,000 | $500 | $132,500 | $ 8,000 |
| Other branch expenses | | | | | 45,200 | (200) |
| District Profit Contribution | | | | | $ 87,300 | $ 7,800 |

aggregation is higher. For line management, the basic segmentation is typically along organizational lines, as in Exhibit 25–6. A product manager would receive a similar type of report, limited to his own product line.

Exhibit 25–6

Carswell Corporation

MARKETING DIVISION PERFORMANCE REPORT

For the Month of January, 19x1

(000 omitted)

| District | Net Sales Billed | Cost of Sales | District Selling Expense | District Profit Contribution | Budget Deviation | Contribution % of Sales |
|---|---|---|---|---|---|---|
| Boston ............... | $ 514 | $ 381 | $ 46 | $ 87 | $ 8 | 17.0% |
| New York ............ | 946 | 603 | 84 | 259 | 25 | 27.4 |
| Baltimore ............ | 472 | 365 | 51 | 56 | (33) | 11.9 |
| Atlanta............... | 348 | 260 | 42 | 46 | 5 | 13.2 |
| Pittsburgh........... | 588 | 434 | 63 | 91 | 3 | 15.5 |
| Cleveland ............ | 627 | 472 | 58 | 97 | (2) | 15.5 |
| Total ............... | $3,495 | $2,515 | $344 | $636 | $ 6 | 18.2% |
| Head office expense: | | | | | | |
| Management....... | | | | $ 40 | $ 1 | |
| Market research.... | | | | 26 | (1) | |
| Advertising......... | | | | 103 | 10 | |
| Other............... | | | | 23 | (3) | |
| Total head office expense ........ | | | | $192 | $ 7 | 5.5 |
| Net Marketing Margin | | | | $444 | $13 | 12.7% |

Sales management may also get routine or special profit reports on such bases as customer group or channel of distribution. Such reports are often restricted to gross sales or variable product profit unless the importance of other expenses is great enough to justify some form of distribution cost analysis.

It will be noticed that none of these performance reports has shown any factory cost variances. Manufacturing performance measures become an integral part of routine profit reports only at the level at which manufacturing and marketing responsibility are joined. In a straight line organization, this may be at the divisional or top-management level. When product managers are used, they may see the results of manufacturing as well as marketing operations. The product manager's report, however, should show manufacturing cost variances only if they depend at least partly on characteristics of the product line or methods of distribution. Excessive unfavorable factory cost variances, for example, may signify an ultraliberal product modification policy which may be worthy of the product manager's attention. Alternatively, if it shows that the factory cannot meet cost standards in a particular line, consideration may be given to changing product specifications, raising prices, or something else.

## INTERNAL PROFIT REPORTING FOR MANAGERIAL EVALUATION

Top management's second major use for periodic internal profit reports is in evaluating the ability of subordinate managers to generate profits, given the resources at their disposal and the environment in which they have to work. We shall look briefly at the evaluation of managerial profit performance in one specific kind of organization unit, the profit center.

### The Profit Center Concept

As we pointed out earlier, top management has a great deal of latitude in the amount of profit-determining decision authority it delegates to subordinate executives. Manufacturing managers, for example, are seldom given much direct power to decide such questions as what products to produce, how to market them, or what prices to set, although they may have a good deal of influence on these decisions. Sales managers, on the other hand, are typically responsible not only for bringing in orders from customers but also for emphasizing sales of the more profitable products while keeping the costs of sales solicitation within the bounds established by the benefits to be received.

Many companies go even farther and delegate virtually complete responsibility and authority for the profits generated by specific segments of the firm's operations. These segments are distinct units in the formal organization structure, and are usually referred to as *profit centers*. Whenever most of a company's economic activity is performed by profit centers, the company is said to be *decentralized*.

Ideally, each profit center should be completely independent of its sister divisions. To approach this, the divisional boundaries should be drawn so that each division has its own manufacturing and distributive facilities and relatively few transfers of product to other divisions. In short, decentralization is at its best whenever a division's operations come closest in scope and depth to those of separate independent companies. Under these circumstances, the profit reported by each division is largely independent of operating performance in other divisions of the company, thus facilitating the interpretation of reported profits.

Organization units that come closest to meeting these specifications are those that are responsible for the manufacture and sale of a single product line or a group of related product lines, although in some industries divisionalization on a regional basis is feasible.

## Reasons for Profit Decentralization

The creation of profit centers and the delegation of profit responsibility has three major objectives:

1.  To provide a basis for delegating portions of top management's decision-making responsibility to executives who have closer operating familiarity with individual products or markets.
2.  To bring subordinate executives into more direct contact with the ultimate profit objectives of the firm.
3.  To provide an integrated training ground for the top managers of the future.

Undoubtedly the most important of these is the first — to overcome the sheer weight of the decision-making responsibility in a large corporation. With operations spread over a vast geographical area and encompassing hundreds of products and thousands of customers, central management cannot hope to be completely and continuously in direct personal contact with every segment of the company's business. To provide flexibility and adaptability to changing conditions, it has become increasingly necessary to delegate substantial powers to executives who can maintain a closer, more detailed familiarity with individual products or markets. In other words, decentralization aims to recreate in the large organization the conditions that give life and flexibility to the small company without sacrificing the advantages of size.

## Standards for Managerial Evaluation

Standards to be used in evaluating the profit performance of profit center managers need to meet two major requirements: (1) current attainability; and (2) consistency with the degree of profit controllability by the profit center managers.

As to attainability, the real issue is not whether the profit standard actually can be reached but whether the manager thinks that he can reach it. The profit center manager, no less than anyone else, must internalize his goals if he is to be motivated by them. Regarding a profit standard as attainable is one giant step toward internalizing it.

Controllability, on the other hand, means the ability to influence an item of cost or revenue within limits. The importance of this criterion also stems from the need to insure that the profit center manager will accept the profit standard as a meaningful basis on which to evaluate his performance. If he feels that the determinants of his profits are out of his control, then he will not feel bound to meet the profit standard.

Because few if any variables are completely within a manager's control, controllability is a relative criterion. Variations in sales volume, for example, are an important dimension of managerial performance even though they may result in large part from changes in general business conditions. To define controllability so narrowly as to exclude this kind of variation would be to reduce profit comparisons to mere statements of cost variances. The profit center manager can influence sales volume and is expected to do so. The time to consider the impact of environmental shifts is in the analysis of differences between actual profit and the profit standard, not in the selection of the standard itself.

The profit standard that meets these criteria is the current profit plan. As we indicated earlier, most profit plans are established jointly by profit-responsible executives, their subordinates, and their immediate superiors. Once established, they become commitments – by the profit center manager to strive to carry them out, and by his superior to accept the achievement of planned results as satisfactory managerial performance. If the superior is unwilling to make this commitment, he should reject the plan and either demand a new one or find a new manager for the profit center.

This being the case, the inescapable conclusion must be that budgeted profit is the appropriate bench mark or standard against which managerial profit performance is to be judged.

This approach permits the manager himself to influence the criteria by which he will be judged. To reduce the likelihood that the manager will use this opportunity to set unrealistically low standards, top management must judge his performance at least as much by the quality of his budget proposals as by his success in carrying them out, and both parties must understand this clearly in advance. In addition, top management must carry out a rigorous, critical review of all budget proposals, usually with strong central staff participation. The conflicts between staff and division management that arise inevitably in this situation must be accepted as part of the cost of decentralization, and it is top management's responsibility to see that they are contained within reasonable limits.

### Measuring Profit Performance

In general, the profit measures that will serve for operations evaluation will serve for managerial evaluation as well. The only difference is the addition of the controllability criterion. This means that, whenever feasible, variances that are completely outside the control of the profit center manager should be excluded from the profit report.

Good examples of these are variances in the amount of head office expenses that are allocated to individual profit centers. Few variances are completely noncontrollable, however, and in general the noncontrollable elements must be identified in the process of variance analysis.

## INTERNAL PROFIT REPORTS FOR INVESTMENT EVALUATION

The main question in investment evaluation is whether the cash flows generated by a particular segment are adequate to justify continued investment of the company's funds. The answer to this question should be based on a comparison of the present value of the future cash flows from the segment with its present liquidation value. Since neither of these figures is likely to appear in the routine profit report, the function of the latter must be more limited, to signal the need for special cash flow studies.

Periodic routine reports on a segment of a firm provide realized net income and investment, both on a historical cost basis. Return on investment based on the relation between these two figures is a measure of the utilization of resources that is of interest to top management. Other things the same, any combination of higher income and reduced investment that increases return on investment is an improvement in performance.

Management must be extremely careful, however, in how it uses historical return on investment figures for a division or product line to evaluate divisional or product line performance. Many elements of cost and investment are centrally determined and centrally administered, and the allocations of these items to divisions or product lines are often highly arbitrary. The more important these elements are, the less reliance can be placed on the return on investment ratio.

Even so, as long as the reported return on investment is at

levels that management considers satisfactory, a more rigorous analysis of investment profitability is probably not necessary. Estimates of current liquidation values are costly and difficult to make, and they should be made only if management has some reason to believe that liquidation might be preferable to continued operation.

We shall leave further discussion of these questions to more advanced texts. In passing, however, we should note one hidden danger in return on investment reporting. Faced with persistently low return on investment ratios in some of its operations, management may find it extremely difficult to remember that the failure of these segments to meet minimum profitability standards is a suitable topic for investment evaluation, not managerial appraisal. The appropriate standard for managerial evaluation is planned profit, not the average or minimum acceptable percentage rate of return on investment. No manager should be rewarded for his good fortune in being placed in charge of a profitable operation or stigmatized for being assigned to activities that are inherently unprofitable.

## SUMMARY

Feedback information on the profit performance of individual company segments is of vital importance to management. It is used in evaluating the methods used to generate profit in the segment (operations evaluation), the performance of its management (managerial evaluation), and the profitability of the resources invested in it (investment evaluation).

Profit contribution figures — revenues minus variable expenses and traceable fixed costs — provide a useful basis for operations evaluation. The deduction of implicit interest on segment investment to produce residual profit contribution is a useful refinement. Allocations of nontraceable fixed costs and investments are unnecessary and may be misleading.

The same figures, classified between controllable and noncontrollable items, can be used for managerial evaluation. The appropriate standard for managerial evaluation is the profit plan, accepted both by those directly responsible for the segment and by top management. This is particularly true in the profit centers of decentralized companies in which the segment manager is given substantial authority over the determinants of profit. Deviations from profit plans must be scrutinized to separate those attributable to managerial actions from those arising from other sources.

Return on investment is the appropriate profit performance measure for investment evaluation. For management decisions, this should reflect estimates of present liquidation values and future cash flows. Estimates of liquidation values are too expensive to make routinely, however, and management generally makes them only when the historical return on investment figures are persistently low or negative. The historical figures are used in the interim to provide a rough index of the profitability of past investment decisions in the aggregate.

## QUESTIONS AND PROBLEMS

**1.** Distinguish among the operations evaluation, managerial evaluation, and investment evaluation uses of internal profit information.

**2.** How do top management's uses of internal profit information differ from those of lower management?

**3.** What is meant by "profit contribution"? How does it differ from net profit? From variable profit?

**4.** What is meant by residual profit contribution? Why might it be calculated?

**5.** What is the appropriate profit bench mark for use in managerial evaluation? For investment evaluation?

**6.** Should top management receive all of the profit reports issued to lower levels of management? What consequences might ensue if this were done?

**7.** What is a profit center? In what kinds of companies would you expect to find profit centers? Can a manufacturing division be a profit center?

**8.** What reasons can you suggest for initiating a policy of profit decentralization? Do you believe that these are good reasons?

**9.** A writer recently claimed that the only test of a manager's profit performance was his ability to maintain and raise the reported return on investment. Discuss this proposition.

**10.** To what kinds of decisions is investment evaluation directed? How, if at all, can historical return on investment figures be used for these decisions?

**11.** A marketing vice president received the following summary report on the operations of the company's sales districts during the month of October (in thousands of dollars):

| District | Sales Amount | Sales Over/(Under) Budget | Profit Contribution Amount | Profit Contribution Over/(Under) Budget |
|---|---|---|---|---|
| Boston............. | $ 220 | $ (10) | $ 59 | $ 4 |
| New York.......... | 380 | (20) | 110 | 1 |
| Pittsburgh ......... | 170 | (30) | 24 | (16) |
| Atlanta ........... | 340 | 20 | 91 | 6 |
| Chicago............ | 210 | (40) | 46 | (9) |
| New Orleans ....... | 140 | (10) | 18 | (6) |
| Denver ............ | 90 | (30) | 10 | – |
| Dallas ............. | 120 | – | 21 | 11 |
| Los Angeles........ | 290 | (10) | 66 | 6 |
| Seattle............. | 130 | (30) | 25 | (15) |
| Total......... | $2,090 | $(160) | $470 | $(18) |

Expenses other than those reflected in the district profit contribution figures averaged 12 percent of sales.

*a)* How would you expect the marketing vice president to use this report? What significant facts does it reveal?

*b)* What further information would you expect the marketing vice president to ask for? What managerial action would you expect to observe?

*12. The Dorsey Corporation has prepared the following performance summary for its industrial division for the month of December:

| | | |
|---|---|---|
| Net sales................................ | | $2,000,000 |
| Cost of goods sold: | | |
| Labor ................................. | $ 400,000 | |
| Materials ............................. | 100,000 | |
| Overhead (actual)...................... | 1,000,000 | |
| Costs incurred ....................... | $1,500,000 | |
| Overhead overabsorbed ................ | 100,000 | |
| Product costs ........................ | $1,600,000 | |
| Decrease in inventory.................. | 160,000 | |
| Cost of goods sold .................... | | 1,760,000 |
| Gross margin .......................... | | $ 240,000 |
| Less: Selling expenses .................... | $ 300,000 | |
| Administrative expenses ............ | 50,000 | 350,000 |
| Profit (loss) on sales.................... | | $ (110,000) |
| Add: Factory overhead overabsorbed ...... | | 100,000 |
| Net Income (Loss) before Taxes.......... | | $ (10,000) |

(1) Manufacturing overhead costs are all traceable to the division.

(2) At normal operating volumes, variable manufacturing overhead costs are approximately 30 percent of total manufacturing overhead costs in the industrial division. Variable overhead cost per labor dollar is not affected by fluctuations in production volume.

---

* Solutions to problems marked with an asterisk (*) are found in Appendix B.

(3) The volume variance in manufacturing overhead costs in the industrial division was favorable, amounting to $20,000.

(4) Variable selling expenses amount to 4 percent of industrial sales. All administrative expenses are fixed.

(5) $50,000 of fixed selling expense and $5,000 of administrative expense are traceable to the industrial division; all other fixed selling and administrative expenses come from allocations.

(6) An absorption costing system is in use in the factory. The ratio of the variable cost content of work in process and finished goods inventories to the total costs of these inventories is the same as the ratio of variable manufacturing cost to total "product costs" for the division for the period. Price level changes may be assumed to be negligible.

a) Compute the following:
  (1) Factory overhead spending variance.
  (2) Budgeted fixed manufacturing cost.
  (3) Variable profit ratio.

b) Prepare a profit contribution statement in good form, summarizing the results of the month's operations.

*13. A product manager received the following report on the profit performance of the product he was responsible for:

|  | Budget | Actual | Difference |
|---|---|---|---|
| Units sold | 10,000 | 11,000 | + 1,000 |
| Sales revenues | $60,000 | $60,500 | +$ 500 |
| Cost of goods sold: |  |  |  |
| Direct material | $10,000 | $11,200 | +$1,200 |
| Direct labor | 13,000 | 14,700 | + 1,700 |
| Factory overhead | 13,000 | 14,100 | + 1,100 |
| Total cost of goods sold | $36,000 | $40,000 | +$4,000 |
| Gross margin | $24,000 | $20,500 | −$3,500 |
| Selling and administrative expenses | 18,000 | 18,300 | +   300 |
| Net income | $ 6,000 | $ 2,200 | −$3,800 |

Additional information:

(1) Materials prices and wage rates were at budgeted levels.
(2) Production volume and sales volume were identical.
(3) Factory overhead was budgeted at $7,800 plus 40 percent of direct labor cost.
(4) All factory cost variances were included in the amounts reported on the income statement.
(5) Selling and administrative expenses were regarded as wholly fixed.

a) How much of the $3,800 difference between budgeted and actual net income was apparently due to the increase in the number of units sold? How much was due to changes in selling prices?

*b*) What explanation(s) can you give for the remainder of the profit difference?

**14.** Lee Merritt is manager of a division which has its own production facilities and its own sales force. He received the following monthly income statement on one of his product lines:

| | | |
|---|---:|---:|
| Sales revenues............................ | | $700 |
| Expenses: | | |
| Cost of goods sold...................... | $490 | |
| Marketing and distribution.............. | 70 | |
| Research and development.............. | 15 | |
| Administration......................... | 35 | 610 |
| Income before Taxes..................... | | $ 90 |

Surprised by the size of the income figure, Mr. Merritt has asked you to prepare a statement in a format that will help him see the impact of volume and other factors more readily. You are given the following additional information:

(1)  All of the products in this product line are manufactured in a single factory, which is devoted exclusively to this product line.
(2)  The $490 cost of goods sold included the following:

| | |
|---|---:|
| Standard direct materials ....................... | $ 95 |
| Standard direct labor........................... | 200 |
| Standard overhead .............................. | 160 |
| Factory overhead volume variance .............. | 30 |
| Factory overhead spending variance ............ | (5) |
| Price and wage rate variances .................. | (12) |
| Other factory cost variances ................... | 22 |
| Total...................................... | $490 |

(3)  Budgeted factory overhead = $90 + $0.50 × Standard direct labor cost.
(4)  Production volume was equal to sales volume during the month.
(5)  The marketing and distribution expenses were as follows:

| | |
|---|---:|
| Salesmen's commissions .......................... | $14 |
| Variable distribution costs......................... | 21 |
| Product-traceable fixed marketing costs ........... | 18 |
| Common marketing costs, allocated to product lines as a percentage of sales ................... | 17 |
| Total...................................... | $70 |

(6)  Research and development costs consisted of $3 in general research costs, allocated among the product lines as a percentage of sales, and $12 in the costs of projects for the development of new products for this line specifically.
(7)  Of the administrative expense, $5 was a fixed cost traceable to the product line, and the remainder consisted of allocated divisional and corporate headquarters expenses, entirely fixed.

*a*)  Prepare a profit contribution statement in good form. The bottom line on this statement should be the same as on the report originally submitted to Mr. Merritt. Factory cost variances other than the overhead volume variance should be classified as variable costs.

b) How would the product line's income before taxes be affected by a 10 percent decrease in sales and production volume? Prepare a revised profit contribution statement based on this assumption. Did the profit contribution format help you in any way?

15. George Ellis was the marketing manager for his company's cosmetics products. He reported to David Thompson, the firm's marketing vice president. Mr. Ellis supervised a field sales force engaged exclusively in marketing the cosmetics line. Factory operations, however, were within the jurisdiction of the manufacturing vice president. Many steps in the production process for the cosmetics products were performed on a job order basis by the personnel of factory departments also engaged in the manufacture of other company products.

Mr. Ellis received the following income statement for the cosmetics line for the month of August (in thousands of dollars):

|  | July Actual | August Actual | August Budget | August Variance |
|---|---|---|---|---|
| Sales | $1,000 | $1,300 | $1,200 | $100 |
| Standard cost of goods sold | 600 | 800 | 720 | (80) |
| Gross margin | $ 400 | $ 500 | $ 480 | $ 20 |
| Direct marketing expenses | 150 | 155 | 150 | (5) |
| Marketing margin | $ 250 | $ 345 | $ 330 | $ 15 |
| Favorable/(Unfavorable) factory variances: |  |  |  |  |
| Overhead volume variance | 10 | (50) | — | (50) |
| Overhead spending variance | 5 | ( 6) | — | ( 6) |
| Direct cost variances | (12) | (54) | — | (54) |
| Profit Contribution | $ 253 | $ 235 | $ 330 | $ (95) |

Inventories of cosmetics products remained constant and at budgeted levels throughout July and August.

Mr. Thompson called Mr. Ellis into his office shortly after this report was issued and told him that in view of his poor performance in August a scheduled promotion to the title of assistant vice president would be postponed. "We'll see how you do in September and October," he was told.

a) You are a consultant on retainer for this company and you happened to overhear this conversation. Draft a statement, outlining your evaluation of Mr. Ellis's performance. If you would like to have additional information, say what you would like to have, but you must give a tentative answer to this question before this additional information becomes available.

b) List changes, if any, that you would like to make in the company's measurement and reporting system and explain why?

**16.** Harry Keeler was the president of Anorak, Inc., a manufacturer of consumer goods. The income statements for the company's two divisions indicated that division A was highly profitable; division B was a break-even operation at best.

Mr. Keeler was due to retire soon, and the board of directors were examining the credentials of the two division managers. Both had been with the company for many years and had created enviable performance records in other positions before being named to head their respective divisions.

Both division managers seemed to have organizational ability, and employee morale in both divisions was extremely good. Both were well liked by the board members and seemed capable of representing the company effectively in dealings with outsiders.

The main difference between the two seemed to be that the manager of division A was able to generate profits, while the manager of division B could not. The following divisional income statements were prepared for the month of September:

| | Division A | | Division B | |
| --- | --- | --- | --- | --- |
| | Budget | Actual | Budget | Actual |
| Sales........................................ | $1,050 | $1,000 | $490 | $500 |
| Cost of goods sold........................ | 630 | 600 | 395 | 400 |
| Gross margin ........................... | $ 420 | $ 400 | $ 95 | $100 |
| Operating expenses: | | | | |
| Marketing and selling................. | $ 95 | $ 100 | $ 50 | $ 50 |
| Divisional administration ............. | 48 | 50 | 45 | 40 |
| Head office expense................... | 41 | 42 | 19 | 21 |
| Income taxes ......................... | 94 | 85 | (8) | (5) |
| Total operating expenses........... | $ 278 | $ 277 | $106 | $106 |
| Net Income (Loss) ...................... | $ 142 | $ 123 | $ (11) | $ (6) |

The following assets and liabilities were traced or assigned to these divisions at the end of September:

| | Division A | | Division B | |
| --- | --- | --- | --- | --- |
| | Budget | Actual | Budget | Actual |
| Directly traceable: | | | | |
| Accounts receivable.................... | $1,200 | $1,200 | $ 520 | $ 500 |
| Inventories .......................... | 1,100 | 1,100 | 860 | 800 |
| Plant and equipment (net) ............. | 700 | 700 | 300 | 300 |
| Accounts payable ..................... | (900) | (900) | (580) | (600) |
| Net traceable assets .............. | $2,100 | $2,100 | $1,100 | $1,000 |
| Allocated (% of sales): | | | | |
| Cash................................. | 380 | 400 | 190 | 200 |
| Headquarters buildings, furniture and equipment...................... | 300 | 300 | 150 | 150 |
| Net Assets ...................... | $2,780 | $2,800 | $1,440 | $1,350 |

Additional information:

(1) Each division is operated as a profit center. Each division manufactures all of its products in its own factories and sells them through its own sales force.

(2) The income statement comparisons for the year to date revealed a similar set of relationships to those in the statements for September.

(3) The company used a minimum after-tax rate of return on investment of 12 percent in evaluating new capital expenditure proposals.

(4) Head office expenses were allocated to product lines in proportion to actual sales.

(5) Market conditions for the products sold by both divisions were very close to those forecast at the beginning of the year.

(6) The market for division B's products appeared unlikely to show any major improvement for some time. Barring a radical change in the market or the introduction of a major new product, industry sales were likely to remain at or near their current levels for some time.

(7) The market for division A's products had been growing dramatically for several years, but the industry's growth had abated during this year, as anticipated.

Do these statements indicate that the manager of division A had a clearly superior profit performance in September? Prepare a summary report, showing insofar as you can the relative profit performance of the two managers, with your interpretation of the figures.

# Appendixes

# *Appendix A*

# COMPOUND INTEREST
# AND BOND TABLES

THE TABLES in this appendix contain the multipliers or conversion factors necessary to convert cash flows of one or more periods into their equivalent values at some other point in time. The basic explanation of the reasons for conversion is given in Chapter 10. Only the mechanical details of how the numbers in the tables should be used are explained here.

## Table 1: Future Value of $1

Each figure in Table 1 is the future value to which one dollar will grow by the end of $n$ periods at an interest rate $r$, compounded once per period. To obtain the future value of any sum:

1. Select a future date to serve as a reference date.
2. Determine the number of periods $(n)$ between the receipt or payment of cash and the reference date.
3. Determine the interest rate $(r)$ at which amounts are to be compounded.
4. Find the figure from Table 1 corresponding to these values of $n$ and $r$.
5. Multiply the cash sum by this figure.

For example, suppose that we have $10,000 now and expect to receive another $10,000 two years from now. We want to find the future values of these sums at a reference date five years from now, compounded annually at 10 percent.

The first of these sums will grow for 5 years, and the figure

741

from the 5-year row of the 10-percent column of Table 1 is 1.6105. This indicates that $1 now will grow to $1.6105 in five years. The future value of $10,000 therefore is 1.6105 × $10,000 = $16,105.

The second sum will have only 3 years to grow. The multiplier from the 3-year row of the 10-percent column is 1.3310, and the future value at the reference date is 1.3310 × $10,000 = $13,310.

These calculations can be summarized in a timetable of cash flows and future values:

| Years Before Reference Date | Cash Flow | Future Value Multiplier at 10% (Table 1) | Amount |
|---|---|---|---|
| 5 .............. | +$10,000 | 1.6105 | $16,105 |
| 3 .............. | + 10,000 | 1.3310 | 13,310 |
| Total ....... | | | $29,415 |

In using this table, care must be taken to insure that the *interest rate* is appropriate to the *period*. Thus, if an amount is compounded *semiannually* at r percent *per annum* for n years, the number of interest periods is 2n, and the interest rate per period is r/2. To illustrate, if interest is compounded *annually* at 6 percent, $10,000 now will grow to $32,071 by the end of 20 years. If interest is compounded *semiannually*, however, the future value is $32,620, reflecting interest at 3 percent per 6-month period for 40 periods.

### Extending Table 1

Table 1 can be extended easily to provide multipliers for any number of periods. For example, suppose that one wants to find the future value of $10,000 compounded annually at 6 percent for 21 periods. No 21-period row is in the table. However, it is known that at the end of 20 years, the future value will be $32,071. If reinvested for one more year at 6 percent, this sum will amount to 1.06 × $32,071 = $33,995. This is the future value of $10,000 21 periods hence at 6 percent per period.

Alternatively, $10,000 will grow to $17,908 in 10 years, and this sum will grow to $17,908 × 1.8983 = $33,995 in 11 additional years. (The 1.8983 figure comes from the 6 percent column, 11-period row of Table 1.) These relationships are shown in Figure 1.

Figure 1
FUTURE VALUES OF $10,000 AT 6%

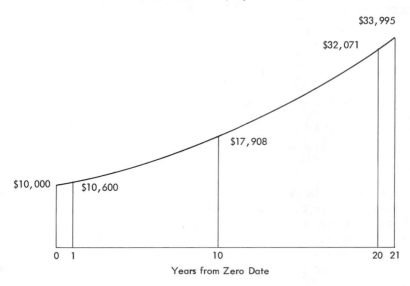

Years from Zero Date

In other words, the future value of a dollar at any time in the future can be obtained by multiplying together any two or more multipliers for which the number of periods adds up to the desired number. Thus, the multiplier for 21 periods can be obtained by multiplying the factors for 1 and 20 periods, or 3 and 18 periods, or any other combination of periods totaling 21.

### Table 2: Future Value of an Annuity of $1

The future value of a series of cash flows can always be determined with the aid of the multipliers in Table 1. This is time-consuming, however, and Table 2 has been developed for use as a computational short-cut whenever the cash flows in the series are identical in amount each period (an *annuity*).

The key to understanding this table is to realize that an annuity is really a combination of several cash flows, identical in amount and separated from each other by identical time intervals. Thus a two-year, $10,000 annuity is simply a series of two annual cash flows of $10,000 each. The future value of an annuity thus is simply the sum of the future values of the individual cash receipts or payments.

For example, the future value two years from now of $10,000 now and $10,000 a year from now, compounded annually at 6 percent, can be calculated with the aid of Table 1, as follows:

| Years Before Reference Date | Cash Flow | Future Value | |
|---|---|---|---|
| | | Multiplier at 10% (Table 1) | Amount |
| 2 .............. | +$10,000 | 1.1236 | $11,236 |
| 1 .............. | + 10,000 | 1.0600 | 10,600 |
| Total ....... | | | $21,836 |

The same answer can be found by multiplying the $10,000 annuity by the *sum* of the annual multipliers, 2.1836.

This is an example of an annuity *in advance* – that is, the cash flow took place at the *beginning* of each period. Suppose, instead, that the payments were made *in arrears* – that is, at the *end* of each period. The first payment would be made a year from now and would thus have only one year to grow before the two-year period ended. Thus, its future value would be only $10,600. The second payment, made at the end of the second year, would have no time at all to grow, and thus its future value would be $10,000.

The future value of a two-year, $10,000 annuity in arrears, compounded annually at 6 percent, therefore, is $10,600 + $10,000 = $20,600.

The multipliers in Table 2 are for annuities in arrears. The factor for a 2-year, 6-percent annuity in arrears is 2.0600. Multiplying this by the $10,000 annual cash flow produces a future value of $20,600, the same figure that we derived in the preceding paragraph.

## Converting Table 2 to Distant Future Equivalents

Table 2 consists of multipliers that can be used to calculate the future value of an annuity on the date the last payment is due to be made. Any multiplier in this table can also be translated into the multiplier that will determine future value as of some number of periods after the date of the final payment.

The procedure is to multiply the multiplier in Table 2 by the multiplier in Table 1 for the appropriate number of periods after the date of the last payment. For example, the future value 15 years from now at 8 percent of a series of ten annual payments of

$10,000 each, the first payment to be made one year from now, is calculated as follows:

$$\$10,000 \times 14.4866 \times 1.4693 = \$212,852$$

| (annuity) | (Table 2, | (Table 1, | (future value, |
|-----------|-----------|-----------|----------------|
|           | 10 years) | 5 years)  | 15 years)      |

The first multiplier determines the sum that $10,000 a year will build up to by the end of 10 years. Application of the second multiplier determines the amount that this sum will grow to in another 5 years.

### Converting Table 2 for Annuities in Advance

The multipliers in Table 2 can also be used to calculate the future values of annuities in advance. To do this, we need to recognize that the interval between each payment and the future date is one year longer than in an annuity in arrears. The first payment in a 3-year annuity in advance is made just 3 years before the future reference date. Since the first payment in a 4-year annuity in arrears is also made exactly 3 years before the reference date, a 3-year annuity in advance can be seen to be exactly the same as a 4-year annuity in arrears without the final payment.

Figure 2

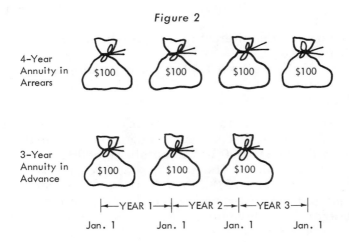

This relationship is diagrammed in Figure 2. Future value is to be calculated as of the end of year 3. From a vantage point at the end of year 3, the only difference between a 4-year annuity in arrears and a three-year annuity in advance is a single payment at the end of the third year. The calculation of the future value of a 3-year, $10,000 annuity in advance, compounded at 8 percent to a reference date three years in the future, is as follows:

$$\$10,000 \times 4.5061 - \$10,000 = \$35,061$$

| $10,000 | × 4.5061 | − $10,000 | = | $35,061 |
|---|---|---|---|---|
| (annuity, | (Table 2, | (omitted | | (future value |
| 4 years) | 4 years) | final | | 3 years hence) |
| | | payment) | | |

An identical result would be obtained by subtracting 1.0000 from the multiplier in Table 2:

$$(4.5061 - 1.0000) \times \$10,000 = 3.5061 \times \$10,000 = \$35,061.$$

The general rule is: to obtain the multiplier for the future value of an $n$-period annuity in advance, *take the multiplier from Table 2 for an annuity of* $(n + 1)$ *periods and subtract 1.0000.*

### Table 3: Present Value of $1

Each figure in Table 3 is the present value on a reference date of one dollar to be paid or received $n$ periods later. To obtain the present value of any sum:

1.  Select a date to serve as a reference date.
2.  Determine the number of periods $(n)$ between the reference date and the date on which the cash is to be paid or received.
3.  Determine the interest rate $(r)$ at which amounts are to be discounted.
4.  Find the figure from Table 3 corresponding to these values of $n$ and $r$.
5.  Multiply the cash sum by this figure.

For example, to find the present value of $10,000 to be received five years from now, discounted at a compound annual rate of 8 percent, multiply $10,000 by the number 0.6806 from the 8 percent column of Table 3. This says that $6,806 invested now at 8 percent will grow to $10,000 in five years if the interest is left on deposit and reinvested each year at 8 percent interest.

Once again, if compounding is to be semiannual, the factor should be taken from the column for an interest rate equal to $r/2$ and the row for a number of periods equal to $2n$. If quarterly compounding is used, use $r/4$ and $4n$ (e.g., 2 percent for 40 periods to show present value compounded quarterly at 8 percent a year for 10 years).

Furthermore, any column in the table can be extended by multiplying factors in the manner described earlier. Thus, $0.7473 is the present value of a dollar five years hence at 6 percent compounded annually; the present value of a dollar 10 years hence is 0.7473 times $0.7473 = $0.5585. This differs from the factor shown in the 10-period row of the 6 percent column of Table 3 by a rounding error which is immaterial in amount.

## Table 4: Present Value of an Annuity of $1 per Period

The present value of an annuity is the sum of the present values of each of the annuity payments (or receipts). For example, a series of three payments of $10,000 each, the first one a year from now, the second a year later, and the third a year after that, has a present value at 8 percent, compounded annually, as follows:

| Years After Reference Date | Cash Flow | Multiplier at 8% (Table 3) | Present Value at 8% |
|---|---|---|---|
| 1 . . . . . . . . . . . . . . . | $10,000 | 0.9259 | $ 9,259 |
| 2 . . . . . . . . . . . . . . . | 10,000 | 0.8573 | 8,573 |
| 3 . . . . . . . . . . . . . . . | 10,000 | 0.7938 | 7,938 |
| Total . . . . . . . | | | $25,770 |

The same result can be obtained more quickly with the aid of Table 4. The multiplier for a 3-year annuity at 8 percent is 2.5771. Multiplying this by the amount of the annuity, $10,000, produces a present value of $25,771, identical to the figure we derived above except for an insignificant rounding error. *Each multiplier in Table 4 is merely the sum of the multipliers in Table 3 for periods 1 through n.*

## Converting Table 4 to Earlier Equivalents

The multipliers in Table 4 are used to calculate the present value of a series of cash payments on a reference date that is exactly one period prior to the date of the first payment. To find the present value at a still earlier reference date, the present value of the annuity can be multiplied by the multiplier from Table 3 for the number of additional years desired.

For example, the present value at 8 percent of a 10-year, $10,000 annuity in arrears is:

$$\$10,000 \times 6.7101 = \$67,101.$$

Suppose, however, that the first payment in this annuity is 5 years from now and that we want to know its present value as of today. The $67,101 figure is the present value *one year before the first payment is made,* or 4 years from now. The present value today, therefore, can be obtained by multiplying $67,101 by the 4-year multiplier from Table 3:

$$\$67,101 \times 0.7350 = \$49,319.$$

The same figure can be derived in a different way. A 10-year annuity starting 5 years from now is the same as a 14-year annuity in arrears minus the first four payments. The multiplier in Table 4 for 14 years at 8 percent is 8.2442 and the multiplier for 4 years is 3.3121. The appropriate multiplier, therefore, is:

$$8.2442 - 3.3121 = 4.9321.$$

Multiplying this by the $10,000 annuity produces a present value of $49,321, which differs only by an insignificant rounding error from the answer we derived earlier.

### Converting Table 4 for Annuities in Advance

A somewhat similar procedure can be used to find the present value of an annuity in advance—that is, one in which the first payment is made on the date at which present value is to be calculated. A 10-year annuity in advance is simply a 9-year annuity in arrears plus one payment immediately. For $10,000 a year at 8 percent, the calculation is:

| $10,000 | + | $10,000 | × | 6.2469 | = | $72,469. |
|---|---|---|---|---|---|---|
| (immediate payment) | | (annuity, 9 years) | | (Table 4, 9 years) | | (present value, 10-year annuity) |

The general rule is: to convert a multiplier for the present value of an annuity in arrears to a multiplier for an annuity in advance, *take the multiplier for an interval one period shorter and add 1.0000.*

### Finding Equivalent Annuities

It is sometimes useful to find the annuity that is equivalent to a given present sum. This is a simple arithmetic operation, once the present sum and the interest rate are known. The formula for the present value of an annuity can be expressed as:

$$\text{Present value} = \text{Table 4 multiplier} \times \text{annuity}.$$

Turning this equation around, we find:

Annuity = Present value ÷ Table 4 multiplier.

The 10-year annuity in arrears that is equivalent at 8 percent interest to a present sum of $100,000 is:

Annuity = $100,000 ÷ 6.7101 = $14,903.

In other words, if someone wants to buy a 10-year annuity of $14,903 a year in an 8 percent market, he will have to pay $100,000 for it.

## Annuity Formulas

The equations for the future and present values of a single amount are:

$$F_n = P(1 + r)^n. \tag{1}$$

$$P = F_n(1 + r)^{-n}. \tag{2}$$

A brief derivation of these formulas is given in Chapter 10.

The formula for the future value of an annuity in arrears derives from equation (1). If $A$ represents a series of payments occurring at the *end* of each of $n$ periods, the first of such payments $(A_1)$ is compounded for $n - 1$ periods (see Figure 2) and has a future value of

$$F_{n-1} = A_1(1 + r)^{n-1}.$$

The future value of the second payment $(A_2)$ is

$$F_{n-2} = A_2(1 + r)^{n-2}.$$

By induction, the like value of the last, or $n$th, payment is

$$F_{n-n} = A_n(1 + r)^{n-n} = A_n(1 + r)^0 = A_n(1) = A_n.$$

The sum of the future values $(F_A)$ of all payments is

$$F_A = F_{n-1} + F_{n-2} + \ldots \ldots + F_{n-n}.$$

By substitution,

$$F_A = A_1(1 + r)^{n-1} + A_2(1 + r)^{n-2} + \ldots \ldots + A_n$$
$$= A[(1 + r)^{n-1} + (1 + r)^{n-2} + \ldots \ldots + 1]. \tag{3}$$

Multiplying equation (3) by $(1 + r)$, results in

$$(1 + r)F_A = A[(1 + r)^n + (1 + r)^{n-1} + \ldots \ldots + (1 + r)]. \tag{4}$$

By subtracting equation (3) from equation (4), the formula appearing at the head of Table 3 is obtained:

$$rF_A = A[(1 + r)^n - 1]$$
$$F_A = A\left[\frac{(1 + r)^n - 1}{r}\right]. \tag{5}$$

Formula (5) yields the values given in Table 3 where $A = \$1$.

The formula for the *present value* of an annuity in arrears derives from equation (2). The present value of the first payment $(A_1)$, discounted for one period, is

$$P = A_1(1 + r)^{-1} = \frac{A_1}{(1 + r)}.$$

The present value of the second payment $(A_2)$ is

$$P = A_2(1 + r)^{-2} = \frac{A_2}{(1 + r)^2}.$$

By induction, the like value of the last, or $n$th, payment is

$$P = A_n(1 + r)^{-n} = \frac{A_n}{(1 + r)^n}.$$

The sum of the present values $(P_A)$ of all payments is

$$P_A = \frac{A_1}{1 + r} + \frac{A_2}{(1 + r)^2} + \ldots + \frac{A_n}{(1 + r)^n}$$
$$= A\left[\frac{1}{1 + r} + \frac{1}{(1 + r)^2} + \ldots + \frac{1}{(1 + r)^n}\right]. \tag{6}$$

Multiplying equation (6) by $(1 + r)$, results in

$$(1 + r)P_A = A\left[1 + \frac{1}{1 + r} + \ldots + \frac{1}{(1 + r)^{n-1}}\right]. \tag{7}$$

Subtracting equation (6) from equation (7) results in the formula appearing at the head of Table 4:

$$rP_A = A\left[1 - \frac{1}{(1 + r)^n}\right] = A[1 - (1 + r)^{-n}]$$
$$P_A = A\left[\frac{1 - (1 + r)^{-n}}{r}\right]. \tag{8}$$

Formula (8) yields the values given in Table 4 where $A = \$1$.

## Bond Value Tables

Tables 5 through 13 give the present values at various yield rates of bonds bearing various coupon rates from 4 percent to 8 percent and of various terms from 6 months to 30 years. Values are stated in dollars per $100 of face value. To find the present value of any other face amount, multiply the face value by one one-hundredth of the factor shown in the table.

These tables are intended only as illustrative samples for use in connection with the problems in this book and are far less complete than the tables used in the investment banking community. Missing values can be derived, using Tables 3 and 4 in the manner prescribed in Chapter 14, but in practice it is more economical to obtain and apply more extensive published tables or work directly with standard computer programs.[1]

---

[1] For a more extensive set of commercially available tables, see Financial Publishing Company, *Investors Bond Value Tables* (Boston: Financial Publishing Company, 1962).

## Table 1
### FUTURE VALUE OF $1

$$F_n = P(1 + r)^n$$

| Pe-riods | 2% | 2½% | 3% | 4% | 5% | 6% | 8% | 10% |
|---|---|---|---|---|---|---|---|---|
| 1... | 1.0200 | 1.0250 | 1.0300 | 1.0400 | 1.0500 | 1.0600 | 1.0800 | 1.1000 |
| 2... | 1.0404 | 1.0506 | 1.0609 | 1.0816 | 1.1025 | 1.1236 | 1.1664 | 1.2100 |
| 3... | 1.0612 | 1.0769 | 1.0927 | 1.1249 | 1.1576 | 1.1910 | 1.2597 | 1.3310 |
| 4... | 1.0824 | 1.1038 | 1.1255 | 1.1699 | 1.2155 | 1.2625 | 1.3605 | 1.4641 |
| 5... | 1.1041 | 1.1314 | 1.1593 | 1.2167 | 1.2763 | 1.3382 | 1.4693 | 1.6105 |
| 6... | 1.1262 | 1.1597 | 1.1941 | 1.2653 | 1.3401 | 1.4185 | 1.5869 | 1.7716 |
| 7... | 1.1487 | 1.1887 | 1.2299 | 1.3159 | 1.4071 | 1.5036 | 1.7138 | 1.9488 |
| 8... | 1.1717 | 1.2184 | 1.2668 | 1.3686 | 1.4775 | 1.5938 | 1.8509 | 2.1436 |
| 9... | 1.1951 | 1.2489 | 1.3048 | 1.4233 | 1.5513 | 1.6895 | 1.9990 | 2.3589 |
| 10... | 1.2190 | 1.2801 | 1.3439 | 1.4802 | 1.6289 | 1.7908 | 2.1589 | 2.5938 |
| 11... | 1.2434 | 1.3121 | 1.3842 | 1.5395 | 1.7103 | 1.8983 | 2.3316 | 2.8532 |
| 12... | 1.2682 | 1.3449 | 1.4258 | 1.6010 | 1.7959 | 2.0122 | 2.5182 | 3.1385 |
| 13... | 1.2936 | 1.3785 | 1.4685 | 1.6651 | 1.8856 | 2.1329 | 2.7196 | 3.4524 |
| 14... | 1.3195 | 1.4130 | 1.5126 | 1.7317 | 1.9799 | 2.2609 | 2.9372 | 3.7976 |
| 15... | 1.3459 | 1.4483 | 1.5580 | 1.8009 | 2.0709 | 2.3966 | 3.1722 | 4.1774 |
| 16... | 1.3728 | 1.4845 | 1.6047 | 1.8730 | 2.1829 | 2.5404 | 3.4259 | 4.5951 |
| 17... | 1.4002 | 1.5216 | 1.6528 | 1.9479 | 2.2920 | 2.6928 | 3.7000 | 5.0545 |
| 18... | 1.4282 | 1.5597 | 1.7024 | 2.0258 | 2.4066 | 2.8543 | 3.9960 | 5.5600 |
| 19... | 1.4568 | 1.5987 | 1.7535 | 2.1068 | 2.5270 | 3.0256 | 4.3157 | 6.1160 |
| 20... | 1.4859 | 1.6386 | 1.8061 | 2.1911 | 2.6533 | 3.2071 | 4.6610 | 6.7276 |
| 22... | 1.5460 | 1.7216 | 1.9161 | 2.3699 | 2.9253 | 3.6035 | 5.4365 | 8.1404 |
| 24... | 1.6084 | 1.8087 | 2.0328 | 2.5633 | 3.2251 | 4.0489 | 6.3412 | 9.8498 |
| 26... | 1.6734 | 1.9003 | 2.1566 | 2.7725 | 3.5557 | 4.5494 | 7.3964 | 11.9183 |
| 28... | 1.7410 | 1.9965 | 2.2879 | 2.9987 | 3.9201 | 5.1117 | 8.6271 | 14.4211 |
| 30... | 1.8114 | 2.0976 | 2.4273 | 3.2434 | 4.3219 | 5.7435 | 10.0627 | 17.4495 |
| 32... | 1.8845 | 2.2038 | 2.5751 | 3.5081 | 4.7649 | 6.4534 | 11.7371 | 21.1140 |
| 34... | 1.9607 | 2.3153 | 2.7319 | 3.7943 | 5.2533 | 7.2510 | 13.6901 | 25.5479 |
| 36... | 2.0399 | 2.4325 | 2.8983 | 4.1039 | 5.7918 | 8.1473 | 15.9682 | 30.9130 |
| 38... | 2.1223 | 2.5557 | 3.0748 | 4.4388 | 6.3855 | 9.1543 | 18.6253 | 37.4047 |
| 40... | 2.2080 | 2.6851 | 3.2620 | 4.8010 | 7.0400 | 10.2857 | 21.7245 | 45.2597 |
| 42... | 2.2972 | 2.8210 | 3.4607 | 5.1928 | 7.7616 | 11.5570 | 25.3395 | 54.7643 |
| 44... | 2.3901 | 2.9638 | 3.6715 | 5.6165 | 8.5572 | 12.9855 | 29.5560 | 66.2648 |
| 46... | 2.4866 | 3.1139 | 3.8950 | 6.0748 | 9.4343 | 14.5905 | 34.4741 | 80.1804 |
| 48... | 2.5871 | 3.2715 | 4.1323 | 6.5705 | 10.4013 | 16.3939 | 40.2106 | 97.0182 |
| 50... | 2.6916 | 3.4371 | 4.3839 | 7.1067 | 11.4674 | 18.4202 | 46.9016 | 117.3920 |
| 60... | 3.2810 | 4.3998 | 5.8916 | 10.5196 | 18.6792 | 32.9877 | 101.2571 | 304.4846 |

## Table 2

### FUTURE VALUE OF ANNUITY OF $1 IN ARREARS

*recieved at end of the period*

$$\sum_{n=0}^{n} A(1+r)^{n} = F = A\left[\frac{(1+r)^n - 1}{r}\right]$$

*(finite)*

*$ in every period in the future*

| Pe-riods | 2% | 2½% | 3% | 4% | 5% | 6% | 8% | 10% |
|---|---|---|---|---|---|---|---|---|
| 1.. | 1.0000 | 1.0000 | 1.0000 | 1.0000 | 1.0000 | 1.0000 | 1.0000 | 1.0000 |
| 2.. | 2.0200 | 2.0250 | 2.0300 | 2.0400 | 2.0500 | 2.0600 | 2.0800 | 2.1000 |
| 3.. | 3.0604 | 3.0756 | 3.0909 | 3.1216 | 3.1525 | 3.1836 | 3.2464 | 3.3100 |
| 4.. | 4.1216 | 4.1525 | 4.1836 | 4.2465 | 4.3101 | 4.3746 | 4.5061 | 4.6410 |
| 5.. | 5.2040 | 5.2563 | 5.3091 | 5.4163 | 5.5256 | 5.6371 | 5.8666 | 6.1051 |
| 6.. | 6.3081 | 6.3877 | 6.4684 | 6.6330 | 6.8019 | 6.9753 | 7.3359 | 7.7156 |
| 7.. | 7.4343 | 7.5474 | 7.6625 | 7.8983 | 8.1420 | 8.3938 | 8.9228 | 9.4872 |
| 8.. | 8.5830 | 8.7361 | 8.8923 | 9.2142 | 9.5491 | 9.8975 | 10.6366 | 11.4360 |
| 9.. | 9.7546 | 9.9545 | 10.1591 | 10.5828 | 11.0266 | 11.4913 | 12.4876 | 13.5796 |
| 10.. | 10.9497 | 11.2034 | 11.4639 | 12.0061 | 12.5779 | 13.1808 | 14.4866 | 15.9376 |
| 11.. | 12.1687 | 12.4835 | 12.8078 | 13.4864 | 14.2068 | 14.9716 | 16.6455 | 18.5314 |
| 12.. | 13.4121 | 13.7956 | 14.1920 | 15.0258 | 15.9171 | 16.8699 | 18.9771 | 21.3846 |
| 13.. | 14.6803 | 15.1404 | 15.6178 | 16.6268 | 17.7130 | 18.8821 | 21.4953 | 24.5231 |
| 14.. | 15.9739 | 16.5190 | 17.0863 | 18.2919 | 19.5986 | 21.0151 | 24.2149 | 27.9755 |
| 15.. | 17.2934 | 17.9319 | 18.5989 | 20.0236 | 21.5786 | 23.2760 | 27.1521 | 31.7731 |
| 16.. | 18.6393 | 19.3802 | 20.1569 | 21.8245 | 23.6575 | 25.6725 | 30.3243 | 35.9503 |
| 17.. | 20.0121 | 20.8647 | 21.7616 | 23.6975 | 25.8404 | 28.2129 | 33.7502 | 40.5456 |
| 18.. | 21.4123 | 22.3863 | 23.4144 | 25.6454 | 28.1324 | 30.9057 | 37.4502 | 45.6001 |
| 19.. | 22.8406 | 23.9460 | 25.1169 | 27.6712 | 30.5390 | 33.7600 | 41.4463 | 51.1601 |
| 20.. | 24.2974 | 25.5447 | 26.8704 | 29.7781 | 33.0660 | 36.7856 | 45.7620 | 57.2761 |
| 22.. | 27.2990 | 28.8629 | 30.5368 | 34.2480 | 38.5052 | 43.3923 | 55.4568 | 71.4041 |
| 24.. | 30.4219 | 32.3490 | 34.4265 | 39.0826 | 44.5020 | 50.8156 | 66.7648 | 88.4989 |
| 26.. | 33.6709 | 36.0117 | 38.5530 | 44.3117 | 51.1135 | 59.1564 | 79.9544 | 109.1835 |
| 28.. | 37.0512 | 39.8598 | 42.9309 | 49.9676 | 58.4026 | 68.5281 | 95.3388 | 134.2119 |
| 30.. | 40.5681 | 43.9027 | 47.5754 | 56.0849 | 66.4388 | 79.0582 | 113.2832 | 164.4962 |
| 32.. | 44.2270 | 48.1503 | 52.5028 | 62.7015 | 75.2988 | 90.8898 | 134.2135 | 201.1402 |
| 34.. | 48.0338 | 52.6129 | 57.7302 | 69.8579 | 85.0670 | 104.1838 | 158.6267 | 245.4796 |
| 36.. | 51.9944 | 57.3014 | 63.2759 | 77.5983 | 95.8363 | 119.1209 | 187.1021 | 299.1302 |
| 38.. | 56.1149 | 62.2273 | 69.1594 | 85.9703 | 107.7095 | 135.9042 | 220.3159 | 364.0475 |
| 40.. | 60.4020 | 67.4026 | 75.4013 | 95.0255 | 120.7998 | 154.7620 | 259.0565 | 442.5974 |
| 42.. | 64.8622 | 72.8398 | 82.0232 | 104.8196 | 135.2318 | 175.9505 | 304.2435 | 537.6428 |
| 44.. | 69.5027 | 78.5523 | 89.0484 | 115.4129 | 151.1430 | 199.7580 | 356.9496 | 652.6478 |
| 46.. | 74.3306 | 84.5540 | 96.5015 | 126.8706 | 168.6852 | 226.5081 | 418.4261 | 791.8039 |
| 48.. | 79.3535 | 90.8596 | 104.4084 | 139.2632 | 188.0254 | 256.5645 | 490.1322 | 960.1827 |
| 50.. | 84.5794 | 97.4843 | 112.7969 | 152.6671 | 209.3480 | 290.3359 | 573.7702 | 1163.9209 |
| 60.. | 114.0515 | 135.9916 | 163.0534 | 237.9907 | 353.5837 | 533.1282 | 1253.2133 | 3034.8470 |

NOTE: To convert this table to values of an annuity in advance, take one more period and subtract 1.000.

## Table 3

### PRESENT VALUE OF $1

$$P = F_n(1 + r)^{-n}$$

| Periods (n) | 2% | 2½% | 3% | 3½% | 4% | 4½% | 5% | 6% | 7% | 8% | 9% |
|---|---|---|---|---|---|---|---|---|---|---|---|
| 1...... | 0.9804 | 0.9756 | 0.9709 | 0.9662 | 0.9615 | 0.9569 | 0.9524 | 0.9434 | 0.9346 | 0.9259 | .9174 |
| 2...... | 0.9612 | 0.9518 | 0.9426 | 0.9335 | 0.9246 | 0.9157 | 0.9070 | 0.8900 | 0.8734 | 0.8573 | .8417 |
| 3...... | 0.9423 | 0.9286 | 0.9151 | 0.9019 | 0.8890 | 0.8763 | 0.8638 | 0.8396 | 0.8163 | 0.7938 | .7722 |
| 4...... | 0.9238 | 0.9060 | 0.8885 | 0.8714 | 0.8548 | 0.8386 | 0.8227 | 0.7921 | 0.7629 | 0.7350 | .7084 |
| 5...... | 0.9057 | 0.8839 | 0.8626 | 0.8420 | 0.8219 | 0.8025 | 0.7835 | 0.7473 | 0.7130 | 0.6806 | .6499 |
| 6...... | 0.8880 | 0.8623 | 0.8375 | 0.8135 | 0.7903 | 0.7679 | 0.7462 | 0.7050 | 0.6663 | 0.6302 | .5963 |
| 7...... | 0.8706 | 0.8413 | 0.8131 | 0.7860 | 0.7599 | 0.7348 | 0.7107 | 0.6651 | 0.6227 | 0.5835 | .5470 |
| 8...... | 0.8535 | 0.8207 | 0.7894 | 0.7594 | 0.7307 | 0.7032 | 0.6768 | 0.6274 | 0.5820 | 0.5403 | .5019 |
| 9...... | 0.8368 | 0.8007 | 0.7664 | 0.7337 | 0.7026 | 0.6729 | 0.6446 | 0.5919 | 0.5439 | 0.5002 | .4604 |
| 10...... | 0.8203 | 0.7812 | 0.7441 | 0.7089 | 0.6756 | 0.6439 | 0.6139 | 0.5584 | 0.5083 | 0.4632 | .4224 |
| 11...... | 0.8043 | 0.7621 | 0.7224 | 0.6849 | 0.6496 | 0.6162 | 0.5847 | 0.5268 | 0.4751 | 0.4289 | .3875 |
| 12...... | 0.7885 | 0.7436 | 0.7014 | 0.6618 | 0.6246 | 0.5897 | 0.5568 | 0.4970 | 0.4440 | 0.3971 | .3555 |
| 13...... | 0.7730 | 0.7254 | 0.6810 | 0.6394 | 0.6006 | 0.5643 | 0.5303 | 0.4688 | 0.4150 | 0.3677 | .3262 |
| 14...... | 0.7579 | 0.7077 | 0.6611 | 0.6178 | 0.5775 | 0.5400 | 0.5051 | 0.4423 | 0.3878 | 0.3405 | .2992 |
| 15...... | 0.7430 | 0.6905 | 0.6419 | 0.5969 | 0.5553 | 0.5167 | 0.4810 | 0.4173 | 0.3624 | 0.3153 | .2745 |
| 16...... | 0.7284 | 0.6736 | 0.6232 | 0.5767 | 0.5339 | 0.4945 | 0.4581 | 0.3936 | 0.3387 | 0.2919 | .2519 |
| 17...... | 0.7142 | 0.6572 | 0.6050 | 0.5572 | 0.5134 | 0.4732 | 0.4363 | 0.3714 | 0.3166 | 0.2703 | .2311 |
| 18...... | 0.7002 | 0.6412 | 0.5874 | 0.5384 | 0.4936 | 0.4528 | 0.4155 | 0.3503 | 0.2959 | 0.2502 | .2120 |
| 19...... | 0.6864 | 0.6255 | 0.5703 | 0.5202 | 0.4746 | 0.4333 | 0.3957 | 0.3305 | 0.2765 | 0.2317 | .1945 |
| 20...... | 0.6730 | 0.6103 | 0.5537 | 0.5026 | 0.4564 | 0.4146 | 0.3769 | 0.3118 | 0.2584 | 0.2145 | .1784 |
| 21...... | 0.6598 | 0.5954 | 0.5375 | 0.4856 | 0.4388 | 0.3968 | 0.3589 | 0.2942 | 0.2415 | 0.1987 | .1637 |
| 22...... | 0.6468 | 0.5809 | 0.5219 | 0.4692 | 0.4220 | 0.3797 | 0.3418 | 0.2775 | 0.2257 | 0.1839 | .1502 |
| 23...... | 0.6342 | 0.5667 | 0.5067 | 0.4533 | 0.4057 | 0.3634 | 0.3256 | 0.2618 | 0.2109 | 0.1703 | .1378 |
| 24...... | 0.6217 | 0.5529 | 0.4919 | 0.4380 | 0.3901 | 0.3477 | 0.3101 | 0.2470 | 0.1971 | 0.1577 | .1264 |
| 25...... | 0.6095 | 0.5394 | 0.4776 | 0.4231 | 0.3751 | 0.3327 | 0.2953 | 0.2330 | 0.1842 | 0.1460 | .1160 |
| 26...... | 0.5976 | 0.5262 | 0.4637 | 0.4088 | 0.3607 | 0.3184 | 0.2812 | 0.2198 | 0.1722 | 0.1352 | .1064 |
| 27...... | 0.5859 | 0.5134 | 0.4502 | 0.3950 | 0.3468 | 0.3047 | 0.2678 | 0.2074 | 0.1609 | 0.1252 | .0976 |
| 28...... | 0.5744 | 0.5009 | 0.4371 | 0.3817 | 0.3335 | 0.2916 | 0.2551 | 0.1956 | 0.1504 | 0.1159 | .0895 |
| 29...... | 0.5631 | 0.4887 | 0.4243 | 0.3687 | 0.3207 | 0.2790 | 0.2429 | 0.1846 | 0.1406 | 0.1073 | .0822 |
| 30...... | 0.5521 | 0.4767 | 0.4120 | 0.3563 | 0.3083 | 0.2670 | 0.2314 | 0.1741 | 0.1314 | 0.0994 | .0754 |
| 40...... | 0.4529 | 0.3724 | 0.3066 | 0.2526 | 0.2083 | 0.1719 | 0.1420 | 0.0972 | 0.0668 | 0.0460 | .0318 |
| 50...... | 0.3715 | 0.2909 | 0.2281 | 0.1791 | 0.1407 | 0.1107 | 0.0872 | 0.0543 | 0.0339 | 0.0213 | .0134 |

| 10% | 12% | 14% | 15% | 16% | 18% | 20% | 25% | 30% | 40% | 50% |
|---|---|---|---|---|---|---|---|---|---|---|
| 0.9091 | 0.893 | 0.877 | 0.870 | 0.862 | 0.847 | 0.833 | 0.800 | 0.769 | 0.714 | 0.667 |
| 0.8264 | 0.797 | 0.769 | 0.756 | 0.743 | 0.718 | 0.694 | 0.640 | 0.592 | 0.510 | 0.444 |
| 0.7513 | 0.712 | 0.675 | 0.658 | 0.641 | 0.609 | 0.579 | 0.512 | 0.455 | 0.364 | 0.296 |
| 0.6830 | 0.636 | 0.592 | 0.572 | 0.552 | 0.516 | 0.482 | 0.410 | 0.350 | 0.260 | 0.198 |
| 0.6209 | 0.567 | 0.519 | 0.497 | 0.476 | 0.437 | 0.402 | 0.328 | 0.269 | 0.186 | 0.132 |
| 0.5645 | 0.507 | 0.456 | 0.432 | 0.410 | 0.370 | 0.335 | 0.262 | 0.207 | 0.133 | 0.088 |
| 0.5132 | 0.452 | 0.400 | 0.376 | 0.354 | 0.314 | 0.279 | 0.210 | 0.159 | 0.095 | 0.059 |
| 0.4665 | 0.404 | 0.351 | 0.327 | 0.305 | 0.266 | 0.233 | 0.168 | 0.123 | 0.068 | 0.039 |
| 0.4241 | 0.361 | 0.308 | 0.284 | 0.263 | 0.225 | 0.194 | 0.134 | 0.094 | 0.048 | 0.026 |
| 0.3855 | 0.322 | 0.270 | 0.247 | 0.227 | 0.191 | 0.162 | 0.107 | 0.073 | 0.035 | 0.017 |
| 0.3505 | 0.287 | 0.237 | 0.215 | 0.195 | 0.162 | 0.135 | 0.086 | 0.056 | 0.025 | 0.012 |
| 0.3186 | 0.257 | 0.208 | 0.187 | 0.168 | 0.137 | 0.112 | 0.069 | 0.043 | 0.018 | 0.008 |
| 0.2897 | 0.229 | 0.182 | 0.163 | 0.145 | 0.116 | 0.093 | 0.055 | 0.033 | 0.013 | 0.005 |
| 0.2633 | 0.205 | 0.160 | 0.141 | 0.125 | 0.099 | 0.078 | 0.044 | 0.025 | 0.009 | 0.003 |
| 0.2394 | 0.183 | 0.140 | 0.123 | 0.108 | 0.084 | 0.065 | 0.035 | 0.020 | 0.006 | 0.002 |
| 0.2176 | 0.163 | 0.123 | 0.107 | 0.093 | 0.071 | 0.054 | 0.028 | 0.015 | 0.005 | 0.002 |
| 0.1978 | 0.146 | 0.108 | 0.093 | 0.080 | 0.060 | 0.045 | 0.023 | 0.012 | 0.003 | 0.001 |
| 0.1799 | 0.130 | 0.095 | 0.081 | 0.069 | 0.051 | 0.038 | 0.018 | 0.009 | 0.002 | 0.001 |
| 0.1635 | 0.116 | 0.083 | 0.070 | 0.060 | 0.043 | 0.031 | 0.014 | 0.007 | 0.002 | |
| 0.1486 | 0.104 | 0.073 | 0.061 | 0.051 | 0.037 | 0.026 | 0.012 | 0.005 | 0.001 | |
| 0.1351 | 0.093 | 0.064 | 0.053 | 0.044 | 0.031 | 0.022 | 0.009 | 0.004 | 0.001 | |
| 0.1228 | 0.083 | 0.056 | 0.046 | 0.038 | 0.026 | 0.018 | 0.007 | 0.003 | 0.001 | |
| 0.1117 | 0.074 | 0.049 | 0.040 | 0.033 | 0.022 | 0.015 | 0.006 | 0.002 | | |
| 0.1015 | 0.066 | 0.043 | 0.035 | 0.028 | 0.019 | 0.013 | 0.005 | 0.002 | | |
| 0.0923 | 0.059 | 0.038 | 0.030 | 0.024 | 0.016 | 0.010 | 0.004 | 0.001 | | |
| 0.0839 | 0.053 | 0.033 | 0.026 | 0.021 | 0.014 | 0.009 | 0.003 | 0.001 | | |
| 0.0763 | 0.047 | 0.029 | 0.023 | 0.018 | 0.011 | 0.007 | 0.002 | 0.001 | | |
| 0.0693 | 0.042 | 0.026 | 0.020 | 0.016 | 0.010 | 0.006 | 0.002 | 0.001 | | |
| 0.0630 | 0.037 | 0.022 | 0.017 | 0.014 | 0.008 | 0.005 | 0.002 | 0.001 | | |
| 0.0573 | 0.033 | 0.020 | 0.015 | 0.012 | 0.007 | 0.004 | 0.001 | | | |
| 0.0221 | 0.011 | 0.005 | 0.004 | 0.003 | 0.001 | 0.001 | | | | |
| 0.0085 | 0.003 | 0.001 | 0.001 | 0.001 | | | | | | |

## Table 4
## PRESENT VALUE OF ANNUITY OF $1 IN ARREARS

$$P_A = A\left[\frac{1 - (1 + r)^{-n}}{r}\right]$$

| Periods (n) | 2% | 2½% | 3% | 3½% | 4% | 4½% | 5% | 6% | 7% | 8% |
|---|---|---|---|---|---|---|---|---|---|---|
| 1.... | 0.9804 | 0.9756 | 0.9709 | 0.9662 | 0.9615 | 0.9569 | 0.9524 | 0.9434 | 0.9346 | 0.9259 |
| 2.... | 1.9416 | 1.9274 | 1.9135 | 1.8997 | 1.8861 | 1.8727 | 1.8594 | 1.8334 | 1.8080 | 1.7833 |
| 3.... | 2.8839 | 2.8560 | 2.8286 | 2.8016 | 2.7751 | 2.7490 | 2.7232 | 2.6730 | 2.6243 | 2.5771 |
| 4.... | 3.8077 | 3.7620 | 3.7171 | 3.6731 | 3.6299 | 3.5875 | 3.5460 | 3.4651 | 3.3872 | 3.3121 |
| 5.... | 4.7135 | 4.6458 | 4.5797 | 4.5151 | 4.4518 | 4.3900 | 4.3295 | 4.2124 | 4.1002 | 3.9927 |
| 6.... | 5.6014 | 5.5081 | 5.4172 | 5.3286 | 5.2421 | 5.1579 | 5.0757 | 4.9173 | 4.7665 | 4.6229 |
| 7.... | 6.4720 | 6.3494 | 6.2303 | 6.1145 | 6.0021 | 5.8927 | 5.7864 | 5.5824 | 5.3893 | 5.2064 |
| 8.... | 7.3255 | 7.1701 | 7.0197 | 6.8740 | 6.7327 | 6.5959 | 6.4632 | 6.2098 | 5.9713 | 5.7466 |
| 9.... | 8.1622 | 7.9709 | 7.7861 | 7.6077 | 7.4353 | 7.2688 | 7.1078 | 6.8017 | 6.5152 | 6.2469 |
| 10.... | 8.9826 | 8.7521 | 8.5302 | 8.3166 | 8.1109 | 7.9127 | 7.7217 | 7.3601 | 7.0236 | 6.7101 |
| 11.... | 9.7868 | 9.5142 | 9.2526 | 9.0016 | 8.7605 | 8.5289 | 8.3064 | 7.8869 | 7.4987 | 7.1390 |
| 12.... | 10.5753 | 10.2578 | 9.9540 | 9.6633 | 9.3851 | 9.1186 | 8.8633 | 8.3838 | 7.9427 | 7.5361 |
| 13.... | 11.3484 | 10.9832 | 10.6350 | 10.3027 | 9.9856 | 9.6829 | 9.3936 | 8.8527 | 8.3577 | 7.9038 |
| 14.... | 12.1062 | 11.6909 | 11.2961 | 10.9205 | 10.5631 | 10.2228 | 9.8986 | 9.2950 | 8.7455 | 8.2442 |
| 15.... | 12.8493 | 12.3814 | 11.9379 | 11.5174 | 11.1184 | 10.7395 | 10.3797 | 9.7122 | 9.1079 | 8.5595 |
| 16.... | 13.5777 | 13.0550 | 12.5611 | 12.0941 | 11.6523 | 11.2340 | 10.8378 | 10.1059 | 9.4466 | 8.8514 |
| 17.... | 14.2919 | 13.7122 | 13.1661 | 12.6513 | 12.1657 | 11.7072 | 11.2741 | 10.4773 | 9.7632 | 9.1216 |
| 18.... | 14.9920 | 14.3534 | 13.7535 | 13.1897 | 12.6593 | 12.1600 | 11.6896 | 10.8276 | 10.0591 | 9.3719 |
| 19.... | 15.6785 | 14.9789 | 14.3238 | 13.7098 | 13.1339 | 12.5933 | 12.0853 | 11.1581 | 10.3356 | 9.6036 |
| 20.... | 16.3514 | 15.5892 | 14.8775 | 14.2124 | 13.5903 | 13.0079 | 12.4622 | 11.4699 | 10.5940 | 9.8181 |
| 21.... | 17.0112 | 16.1845 | 15.4150 | 14.6980 | 14.0292 | 13.4047 | 12.8212 | 11.7640 | 10.8355 | 10.0168 |
| 22.... | 17.6580 | 16.7654 | 15.9369 | 15.1671 | 14.4511 | 13.7844 | 13.1630 | 12.0416 | 11.0612 | 10.2007 |
| 23.... | 18.2922 | 17.3321 | 16.4436 | 15.6204 | 14.8568 | 14.1478 | 13.4886 | 12.3034 | 11.2722 | 10.3711 |
| 24.... | 18.9139 | 17.8850 | 16.9355 | 16.0584 | 15.2470 | 14.4955 | 13.7986 | 12.5504 | 11.4693 | 10.5288 |
| 25.... | 19.5235 | 18.4244 | 17.4131 | 16.4815 | 15.6221 | 14.8282 | 14.0939 | 12.7834 | 11.6536 | 10.6748 |
| 26.... | 20.1210 | 18.9506 | 17.8768 | 16.8904 | 15.9828 | 15.1466 | 14.3752 | 13.0032 | 11.8258 | 10.8100 |
| 27.... | 20.7069 | 19.4640 | 18.3270 | 17.2854 | 16.3296 | 15.4513 | 14.6430 | 13.2105 | 11.9867 | 10.9352 |
| 28.... | 21.2813 | 19.9649 | 18.7641 | 17.6670 | 16 6631 | 15.7429 | 14.8981 | 13.4062 | 12.1371 | 11.0511 |
| 29.... | 21.8444 | 20.4535 | 19.1885 | 18.0358 | 16.9837 | 16.0219 | 15.1411 | 13.5907 | 12.2777 | 11.1584 |
| 30.... | 22.3965 | 20.9303 | 19.6004 | 18.3920 | 17.2920 | 16.2889 | 15.3725 | 13.7648 | 12.4090 | 11.2578 |
| 40.... | 27.3555 | 25.1028 | 23.1148 | 21.3551 | 19.7928 | 18.4016 | 17.1591 | 15.0463 | 13.3317 | 11.9246 |
| 50.... | 31.4236 | 28.3623 | 25.7298 | 23.4556 | 21.4822 | 19.7620 | 18.2559 | 15.7619 | 13.8007 | 12.2335 |

| 9% | 10% | 12% | 14% | 15% | 16% | 18% | 20% | 25% | 30% | 40% | 50% |
|---|---|---|---|---|---|---|---|---|---|---|---|
| .9174 | 0.9091 | 0.893 | 0.877 | 0.870 | 0.862 | 0.847 | 0.833 | 0.800 | 0.769 | 0.714 | 0.667 |
| 1.7591 | 1.7355 | 1.690 | 1.647 | 1.626 | 1.605 | 1.566 | 1.528 | 1.440 | 1.361 | 1.224 | 1.111 |
| 2.5313 | 2.4869 | 2.402 | 2.322 | 2.283 | 2.246 | 2.174 | 2.106 | 1.952 | 1.816 | 1.589 | 1.407 |
| 3.2397 | 3.1699 | 3.037 | 2.914 | 2.855 | 2.798 | 2.690 | 2.589 | 2.362 | 2.166 | 1.849 | 1.605 |
| 3.8897 | 3.7908 | 3.605 | 3.433 | 3.352 | 3.274 | 3.127 | 2.991 | 2.689 | 2.436 | 2.035 | 1.737 |
| 4.4859 | 4.3553 | 4.111 | 3.889 | 3.784 | 3.685 | 3.498 | 3.326 | 2.951 | 2.643 | 2.168 | 1.824 |
| 5.0330 | 4.8684 | 4.564 | 4.288 | 4.160 | 4.039 | 3.812 | 3.605 | 3.161 | 2.802 | 2.263 | 1.883 |
| 5.5348 | 5.3349 | 4.968 | 4.639 | 4.487 | 4.344 | 4.078 | 3.837 | 3.329 | 2.925 | 2.331 | 1.922 |
| 5.9952 | 5.7590 | 5.328 | 4.946 | 4.772 | 4.607 | 4.303 | 4.031 | 3.463 | 3.019 | 2.379 | 1.948 |
| 6.4177 | 6.1446 | 5.650 | 5.216 | 5.019 | 4.833 | 4.494 | 4.192 | 3.571 | 3.092 | 2.414 | 1.965 |
| 6.8052 | 6.4951 | 5.988 | 5.453 | 5.234 | 5.029 | 4.656 | 4.327 | 3.656 | 3.147 | 2.438 | 1.977 |
| 7.1607 | 6.8137 | 6.194 | 5.660 | 5.421 | 5.197 | 4.793 | 4.439 | 3.725 | 3.190 | 2.456 | 1.985 |
| 7.4869 | 7.1034 | 6.424 | 5.842 | 5.583 | 5.342 | 4.910 | 4.533 | 3.780 | 3.223 | 2.468 | 1.990 |
| 7.7861 | 7.3667 | 6.628 | 6.002 | 5.724 | 5.468 | 5.008 | 4.611 | 3.824 | 3.249 | 2.477 | 1.993 |
| 8.0607 | 7.6061 | 6.811 | 6.142 | 5.847 | 5.575 | 5.092 | 4.675 | 3.859 | 3.268 | 2.484 | 1.995 |
| 8.3126 | 7.8237 | 6.974 | 6.265 | 5.954 | 5.669 | 5.162 | 4.730 | 3.887 | 3.283 | 2.489 | 1.997 |
| 8.5436 | 8.0216 | 7.120 | 6.373 | 6.047 | 5.749 | 5.222 | 4.775 | 3.910 | 3.295 | 2.492 | 1.998 |
| 8.7556 | 8.2014 | 7.250 | 6.467 | 6.128 | 5.818 | 5.273 | 4.812 | 3.928 | 3.304 | 2.494 | 1.999 |
| 8.9501 | 8.3649 | 7.366 | 6.550 | 6.198 | 5.877 | 5.316 | 4.844 | 3.942 | 3.311 | 2.496 | 1.999 |
| 9.1285 | 8.5136 | 7.469 | 6.623 | 6.259 | 5.929 | 5.353 | 4.870 | 3.954 | 3.316 | 2.497 | 1.999 |
| 9.2922 | 8.6487 | 7.562 | 6.687 | 6.312 | 5.973 | 5.384 | 4.891 | 3.963 | 3.320 | 2.498 | 2.000 |
| 9.4424 | 8.7715 | 7.645 | 6.743 | 6.359 | 6.011 | 5.410 | 4.909 | 3.970 | 3.323 | 2.498 | 2.000 |
| 9.5802 | 8.8832 | 7.718 | 6.792 | 6.399 | 6.044 | 5.432 | 4.925 | 3.976 | 3.325 | 2.499 | 2.000 |
| 9.7066 | 8.9847 | 7.784 | 6.835 | 6.434 | 6.073 | 5.451 | 4.937 | 3.981 | 3.327 | 2.499 | 2.000 |
| 9.8226 | 9.0770 | 7.843 | 6.873 | 6.464 | 6.097 | 5.467 | 4.948 | 3.985 | 3.329 | 2.499 | 2.000 |
| 9.9290 | 9.1609 | 7.896 | 6.906 | 6.491 | 6.118 | 5.480 | 4.956 | 3.988 | 3.330 | 2.500 | 2.000 |
| 10.0265 | 9.2372 | 7.943 | 6.935 | 6.514 | 6.136 | 5.492 | 4.964 | 3.990 | 3.331 | 2.500 | 2.000 |
| 10.1161 | 9.3066 | 7.984 | 6.961 | 6.534 | 6.152 | 5.502 | 4.970 | 3.992 | 3.331 | 2.500 | 2.000 |
| 10.1983 | 9.3696 | 8.022 | 6.983 | 6.551 | 6.166 | 5.510 | 4.975 | 3.994 | 3.332 | 2.500 | 2.000 |
| 10.2737 | 9.4269 | 8.055 | 7.003 | 6.566 | 6.177 | 5.517 | 4.979 | 3.995 | 3.332 | 2.500 | 2.000 |
| 10.7570 | 9.7791 | 8.244 | 7.105 | 6.642 | 6.234 | 5.548 | 4.997 | 3.999 | 3.333 | 2.500 | 2.000 |
| 10.9617 | 9.9148 | 8.304 | 7.133 | 6.661 | 6.246 | 5.554 | 4.999 | 4.000 | 3.333 | 2.500 | 2.000 |

NOTE: To convert this table to values of an annuity in advance, take one less period and add 1.0000.

## Table 5

### BOND VALUES — COUPON RATE OF 4 PERCENT

(semiannual interest payments; semiannual compounding)

| Annual Yield (%) | Years to Maturity | | | | | | | |
|---|---|---|---|---|---|---|---|---|
| | ½ | 1 | 5 | 10 | 15 | 19½ | 20 | 30 |
| 3.0 | 100.49 | 100.98 | 104.61 | 108.58 | 112.01 | 114.68 | 114.96 | 119.69 |
| 3.1 | 100.44 | 100.88 | 104.14 | 107.69 | 110.73 | 113.10 | 113.34 | 117.50 |
| 3.2 | 100.39 | 100.78 | 103.67 | 106.80 | 109.47 | 111.54 | 111.75 | 115.35 |
| 3.3 | 100.34 | 100.68 | 103.20 | 105.92 | 108.23 | 110.01 | 110.19 | 113.27 |
| 3.4 | 100.29 | 100.59 | 102.74 | 105.05 | 107.00 | 108.50 | 108.66 | 111.23 |
| 3.5 | 100.25 | 100.49 | 102.28 | 104.19 | 105.80 | 107.02 | 107.15 | 109.24 |
| 3.6 | 100.20 | 100.39 | 101.82 | 103.33 | 104.60 | 105.57 | 105.67 | 107.30 |
| 3.7 | 100.15 | 100.29 | 101.36 | 102.49 | 103.43 | 104.14 | 104.21 | 105.41 |
| 3.8 | 100.10 | 100.19 | 100.90 | 101.65 | 102.27 | 102.74 | 102.78 | 103.56 |
| 3.9 | 100.05 | 100.10 | 100.45 | 100.82 | 101.13 | 101.36 | 101.38 | 101.76 |
| 4.0 | 100.00 | 100.00 | 100.00 | 100.00 | 100.00 | 100.00 | 100.00 | 100.00 |
| 4.1 | 99.95 | 99.90 | 99.55 | 99.19 | 98.89 | 98.67 | 98.64 | 98.28 |
| 4.2 | 99.90 | 99.81 | 99.11 | 98.38 | 97.79 | 97.36 | 97.31 | 96.61 |
| 4.3 | 99.85 | 99.71 | 98.66 | 97.58 | 96.71 | 96.07 | 96.00 | 94.97 |
| 4.4 | 99.80 | 99.61 | 98.22 | 96.79 | 95.64 | 94.80 | 94.72 | 93.37 |
| 4.5 | 99.76 | 99.52 | 97.78 | 96.01 | 94.59 | 93.55 | 93.45 | 91.81 |
| 4.6 | 99.71 | 99.42 | 97.35 | 95.23 | 93.55 | 92.33 | 92.21 | 90.29 |
| 4.7 | 99.60 | 99.32 | 96.91 | 94.47 | 92.53 | 91.13 | 90.99 | 88.80 |
| 4.8 | 99.61 | 99.23 | 96.48 | 93.71 | 91.52 | 89.94 | 89.79 | 87.35 |
| 4.9 | 99.56 | 99.13 | 96.05 | 92.95 | 90.52 | 88.78 | 88.61 | 85.93 |
| 5.0 | 99.51 | 99.04 | 95.62 | 92.21 | 89.53 | 87.63 | 87.45 | 84.55 |
| 5.1 | 99.46 | 98.94 | 95.20 | 91.47 | 88.56 | 86.51 | 86.31 | 83.19 |
| 5.2 | 99.42 | 98.85 | 94.78 | 90.73 | 87.61 | 85.40 | 85.19 | 81.87 |
| 5.3 | 99.37 | 98.75 | 94.35 | 90.01 | 86.66 | 84.32 | 84.09 | 80.58 |
| 5.4 | 99.32 | 98.65 | 93.94 | 89.29 | 85.73 | 83.25 | 83.01 | 79.32 |
| 5.5 | 99.27 | 98.56 | 93.52 | 88.58 | 84.81 | 82.19 | 81.94 | 78.08 |
| 5.6 | 99.22 | 98.46 | 93.11 | 87.87 | 83.91 | 81.16 | 80.90 | 76.88 |
| 5.7 | 99.17 | 98.37 | 92.69 | 87.18 | 83.01 | 80.14 | 79.87 | 75.70 |
| 5.8 | 99.13 | 98.28 | 92.28 | 86.49 | 82.13 | 79.14 | 78.86 | 74.55 |
| 5.9 | 99.08 | 98.18 | 91.88 | 85.80 | 81.26 | 78.16 | 77.86 | 73.42 |
| 6.0 | 99.03 | 98.09 | 91.47 | 85.12 | 80.40 | 77.19 | 76.89 | 72.32 |
| 6.1 | 98.98 | 97.99 | 91.07 | 84.45 | 79.55 | 76.24 | 75.92 | 71.25 |
| 6.2 | 98.93 | 97.90 | 90.66 | 83.79 | 78.72 | 75.30 | 74.98 | 70.20 |
| 6.3 | 98.89 | 97.80 | 90.26 | 83.13 | 77.89 | 74.38 | 74.05 | 69.17 |
| 6.4 | 98.84 | 97.71 | 89.87 | 82.47 | 77.08 | 73.48 | 73.14 | 68.17 |
| 6.5 | 98.79 | 97.62 | 89.47 | 81.83 | 76.27 | 72.59 | 72.24 | 67.18 |
| 6.6 | 98.74 | 97.52 | 89.08 | 81.18 | 75.48 | 71.71 | 71.36 | 66.22 |
| 6.7 | 98.69 | 97.43 | 88.69 | 80.55 | 74.70 | 70.85 | 70.49 | 65.28 |
| 6.8 | 98.65 | 97.34 | 88.30 | 79.92 | 73.93 | 70.00 | 69.63 | 64.36 |
| 6.9 | 98.60 | 97.24 | 87.91 | 79.30 | 73.16 | 69.17 | 68.79 | 63.46 |
| 7.0 | 98.55 | 97.15 | 87.53 | 78.68 | 72.41 | 68.35 | 67.97 | 62.58 |
| 7.1 | 98.50 | 97.06 | 87.14 | 78.07 | 71.67 | 67.54 | 67.15 | 61.72 |
| 7.2 | 98.46 | 96.96 | 86.76 | 77.46 | 70.94 | 66.74 | 66.36 | 60.88 |
| 7.3 | 98.41 | 96.87 | 86.38 | 76.86 | 70.22 | 65.96 | 65.57 | 60.06 |
| 7.4 | 98.36 | 96.78 | 86.00 | 76.27 | 69.50 | 65.19 | 64.80 | 59.25 |

## Table 6
### BOND VALUES—COUPON RATE OF 4½ PERCENT
(semiannual interest payments; semiannual compounding)

| Annual Yield (%) | Years to Maturity | | | | | | | |
|---|---|---|---|---|---|---|---|---|
| | ½ | 1 | 5 | 10 | 15 | 19½ | 20 | 30 |
| 3.5.......... | 100.49 | 100.97 | 104.55 | 108.38 | 111.59 | 114.05 | 114.30 | 118.48 |
| 3.6.......... | 100.44 | 100.88 | 104.08 | 107.50 | 110.36 | 112.53 | 112.75 | 116.43 |
| 3.7.......... | 100.39 | 100.78 | 103.62 | 106.64 | 109.15 | 111.04 | 111.24 | 114.42 |
| 3.8.......... | 100.34 | 100.68 | 103.16 | 105.78 | 107.95 | 109.58 | 109.74 | 112.47 |
| 3.9.......... | 100.29 | 100.58 | 102.70 | 104.93 | 106.77 | 108.14 | 108.28 | 110.56 |
| 4.0.......... | 100.25 | 100.49 | 102.25 | 104.09 | 105.60 | 106.73 | 106.84 | 108.69 |
| 4.1.......... | 100.20 | 100.39 | 101.79 | 103.25 | 104.45 | 105.33 | 105.42 | 106.87 |
| 4.2.......... | 100.15 | 100.29 | 101.34 | 102.43 | 103.31 | 103.97 | 104.03 | 105.09 |
| 4.3.......... | 100.10 | 100.19 | 100.89 | 101.61 | 102.19 | 102.62 | 102.66 | 103.35 |
| 4.4.......... | 100.05 | 100.10 | 100.44 | 100.80 | 101.09 | 101.30 | 101.32 | 101.66 |
| 4.5.......... | 100.00 | 100.00 | 100.00 | 100.00 | 100.00 | 100.00 | 100.00 | 100.00 |
| 4.6.......... | 99.95 | 99.90 | 99.56 | 99.21 | 98.93 | 98.72 | 98.70 | 98.38 |
| 4.7.......... | 99.90 | 99.81 | 99.12 | 98.42 | 97.86 | 97.46 | 97.43 | 96.80 |
| 4.8.......... | 99.85 | 99.71 | 98.68 | 97.64 | 96.82 | 96.23 | 96.17 | 95.26 |
| 4.9.......... | 99.80 | 99.61 | 98.25 | 96.87 | 95.79 | 95.01 | 94.94 | 93.75 |
| 5.0.......... | 99.76 | 99.52 | 97.81 | 96.10 | 94.77 | 93.82 | 93.72 | 92.27 |
| 5.1.......... | 99.71 | 99.42 | 97.38 | 95.35 | 93.76 | 92.64 | 92.53 | 90.83 |
| 5.2.......... | 99.66 | 99.33 | 96.95 | 94.59 | 92.77 | 91.49 | 91.36 | 89.42 |
| 5.3.......... | 99.61 | 99.23 | 96.53 | 93.85 | 91.79 | 90.35 | 90.21 | 88.05 |
| 5.4.......... | 99.56 | 99.14 | 96.10 | 93.12 | 90.83 | 89.23 | 89.07 | 86.70 |
| 5.5.......... | 99.51 | 99.04 | 95.68 | 92.39 | 89.88 | 88.13 | 87.96 | 85.39 |
| 5.6.......... | 99.46 | 98.94 | 95.26 | 91.66 | 88.94 | 87.05 | 86.87 | 84.10 |
| 5.7.......... | 99.42 | 98.85 | 94.84 | 90.95 | 88.01 | 85.98 | 85.79 | 82.85 |
| 5.8.......... | 99.37 | 98.75 | 94.43 | 90.24 | 87.09 | 84.94 | 84.73 | 81.62 |
| 5.9.......... | 99.32 | 98.66 | 94.01 | 89.54 | 86.19 | 83.91 | 83.69 | 80.42 |
| 6.0.......... | 99.27 | 98.56 | 93.60 | 88.84 | 85.30 | 82.89 | 82.66 | 79.24 |
| 6.1.......... | 99.22 | 98.47 | 93.19 | 88.15 | 84.42 | 81.90 | 81.66 | 78.09 |
| 6.2.......... | 99.18 | 98.38 | 92.79 | 87.47 | 83.55 | 80.92 | 80.67 | 76.97 |
| 6.3.......... | 99.13 | 98.28 | 92.38 | 86.79 | 82.70 | 79.95 | 79.69 | 75.87 |
| 6.4.......... | 99.08 | 98.19 | 91.98 | 86.12 | 81.85 | 79.00 | 78.73 | 74.80 |
| 6.5.......... | 99.03 | 98.09 | 91.58 | 85.46 | 81.02 | 78.07 | 77.79 | 73.75 |
| 6.6.......... | 98.98 | 98.00 | 91.18 | 84.80 | 80.20 | 77.15 | 76.86 | 72.72 |
| 6.7.......... | 98.94 | 97.91 | 90.78 | 84.15 | 79.38 | 76.25 | 75.95 | 71.71 |
| 6.8.......... | 98.89 | 97.81 | 90.39 | 83.51 | 78.58 | 75.36 | 75.06 | 70.73 |
| 6.9.......... | 98.84 | 97.72 | 89.99 | 82.87 | 77.79 | 74.48 | 74.17 | 69.76 |
| 7.0.......... | 98.79 | 97.63 | 89.60 | 82.23 | 77.01 | 73.62 | 73.31 | 68.82 |
| 7.1.......... | 98.74 | 97.53 | 89.22 | 81.61 | 76.24 | 72.77 | 72.45 | 67.90 |
| 7.2.......... | 98.70 | 97.44 | 88.83 | 80.99 | 75.48 | 71.94 | 71.61 | 66.99 |
| 7.3.......... | 98.65 | 97.35 | 88.44 | 80.37 | 74.73 | 71.12 | 70.79 | 66.11 |
| 7.4.......... | 98.60 | 97.25 | 88.06 | 79.76 | 73.99 | 70.31 | 69.97 | 65.24 |
| 7.5.......... | 98.55 | 97.16 | 87.68 | 79.16 | 73.26 | 69.52 | 69.17 | 64.39 |
| 7.6.......... | 98.51 | 97.07 | 87.30 | 78.56 | 72.53 | 68.74 | 68.39 | 63.56 |
| 7.7.......... | 98.46 | 96.98 | 86.93 | 77.96 | 71.82 | 67.97 | 67.61 | 62.75 |
| 7.8.......... | 98.41 | 96.88 | 86.55 | 77.38 | 71.12 | 67.21 | 66.85 | 61.95 |
| 7.9.......... | 98.36 | 96.79 | 86.18 | 76.79 | 70.42 | 66.46 | 66.10 | 61.17 |

### Table 7

## BOND VALUES—COUPON RATE OF 5 PERCENT

### (semiannual interest payments; semiannual compounding)

| Annual Yield (%) | Years to Maturity | | | | | | | |
|---|---|---|---|---|---|---|---|---|
| | ½ | 1 | 5 | 10 | 15 | 19½ | 20 | 30 |
| 4.0......... | 100.49 | 100.97 | 104.49 | 108.18 | 111.20 | 113.45 | 113.68 | 117.38 |
| 4.1......... | 100.44 | 100.87 | 104.03 | 107.32 | 110.01 | 112.00 | 112.20 | 115.45 |
| 4.2......... | 100.39 | 100.78 | 103.57 | 106.48 | 108.84 | 110.58 | 110.75 | 113.57 |
| 4.3......... | 100.34 | 100.68 | 103.12 | 105.64 | 107.68 | 109.18 | 109.33 | 111.74 |
| 4.4......... | 100.29 | 100.58 | 102.67 | 104.81 | 106.54 | 107.80 | 107.93 | 109.94 |
| 4.5......... | 100.24 | 100.48 | 102.22 | 103.99 | 105.41 | 106.45 | 106.55 | 108.19 |
| 4.6......... | 100.20 | 100.39 | 101.77 | 103.18 | 104.30 | 105.11 | 105.19 | 106.47 |
| 4.7......... | 100.15 | 100.29 | 101.32 | 102.37 | 103.20 | 103.80 | 103.86 | 104.80 |
| 4.8......... | 100.10 | 100.19 | 100.88 | 101.57 | 102.12 | 102.51 | 102.55 | 103.16 |
| 4.9......... | 100.05 | 100.10 | 100.44 | 100.78 | 101.05 | 101.25 | 101.27 | 101.56 |
| 5.0......... | 100.00 | 100.00 | 100.00 | 100.00 | 100.00 | 100.00 | 100.00 | 100.00 |
| 5.1......... | 99.95 | 99.90 | 99.56 | 99.22 | 98.96 | 98.77 | 98.76 | 98.47 |
| 5.2......... | 99.90 | 99.81 | 99.13 | 98.46 | 97.93 | 97.57 | 97.53 | 96.98 |
| 5.3......... | 99.85 | 99.71 | 98.70 | 97.69 | 96.92 | 96.38 | 96.33 | 95.52 |
| 5.4......... | 99.81 | 99.62 | 98.27 | 96.94 | 95.92 | 95.21 | 95.14 | 94.09 |
| 5.5......... | 99.76 | 99.52 | 97.84 | 96.19 | 94.94 | 94.06 | 93.98 | 92.69 |
| 5.6......... | 99.71 | 99.42 | 97.41 | 95.45 | 93.96 | 92.94 | 92.84 | 91.33 |
| 5.7......... | 99.66 | 99.33 | 96.99 | 94.72 | 93.00 | 91.82 | 91.71 | 89.99 |
| 5.8......... | 99.61 | 99.23 | 96.57 | 93.99 | 92.06 | 90.73 | 90.60 | 88.69 |
| 5.9......... | 99.56 | 99.14 | 96.15 | 93.27 | 91.12 | 89.65 | 89.51 | 87.41 |
| 6.0......... | 99.51 | 99.04 | 95.73 | 92.56 | 90.20 | 88.60 | 88.44 | 86.16 |
| 6.1......... | 99.47 | 98.95 | 95.32 | 91.86 | 89.29 | 87.55 | 87.39 | 84.94 |
| 6.2......... | 99.42 | 98.85 | 94.91 | 91.16 | 88.39 | 86.53 | 86.35 | 83.74 |
| 6.3......... | 99.37 | 98.76 | 94.50 | 90.46 | 87.50 | 85.52 | 85.33 | 82.57 |
| 6.4......... | 99.32 | 98.66 | 94.09 | 89.78 | 86.63 | 84.53 | 84.33 | 81.43 |
| 6.5......... | 99.27 | 98.57 | 93.68 | 89.10 | 85.76 | 83.55 | 83.34 | 80.31 |
| 6.6......... | 99.23 | 98.48 | 93.28 | 88.42 | 84.91 | 82.59 | 82.37 | 79.21 |
| 6.7......... | 99.18 | 98.38 | 92.88 | 87.75 | 84.07 | 81.65 | 81.42 | 78.14 |
| 6.8......... | 99.13 | 98.29 | 92.48 | 87.09 | 83.24 | 80.72 | 80.48 | 77.09 |
| 6.9......... | 99.08 | 98.19 | 92.08 | 86.44 | 82.42 | 79.80 | 79.55 | 76.06 |
| 7.0......... | 99.03 | 98.10 | 91.68 | 85.79 | 81.61 | 78.90 | 78.64 | 75.06 |
| 7.1......... | 98.99 | 98.01 | 91.29 | 85.14 | 80.81 | 78.01 | 77.75 | 74.07 |
| 7.2......... | 98.94 | 97.91 | 90.90 | 84.51 | 80.02 | 77.14 | 76.87 | 73.10 |
| 7.3......... | 98.89 | 97.82 | 90.51 | 83.88 | 79.24 | 76.28 | 76.00 | 72.16 |
| 7.4......... | 98.84 | 97.73 | 90.12 | 83.25 | 78.47 | 75.43 | 75.15 | 71.23 |
| 7.5......... | 98.80 | 97.63 | 89.73 | 82.63 | 77.71 | 74.60 | 74.31 | 70.33 |
| 7.6......... | 98.75 | 97.54 | 89.35 | 82.02 | 76.96 | 73.78 | 73.49 | 69.44 |
| 7.7......... | 98.70 | 97.45 | 88.97 | 81.41 | 76.22 | 72.97 | 72.67 | 68.57 |
| 7.8......... | 98.65 | 97.36 | 88.59 | 80.80 | 75.49 | 72.18 | 71.87 | 67.72 |
| 7.9......... | 98.61 | 97.26 | 88.21 | 80.21 | 74.77 | 71.39 | 71.09 | 66.88 |
| 8.0......... | 98.56 | 97.17 | 87.83 | 79.61 | 74.06 | 70.62 | 70.31 | 66.06 |
| 8.1......... | 98.51 | 97.08 | 87.46 | 79.03 | 73.36 | 69.86 | 69.55 | 65.26 |
| 8.2......... | 98.46 | 96.99 | 87.09 | 78.45 | 72.67 | 69.12 | 68.80 | 64.48 |
| 8.3......... | 98.42 | 96.89 | 86.72 | 77.87 | 71.98 | 68.38 | 68.06 | 63.71 |
| 8.4......... | 98.37 | 96.80 | 86.35 | 77.30 | 71.30 | 67.66 | 67.33 | 62.95 |

*Table 8*

## BOND VALUES — COUPON RATE OF 5½ PERCENT
(semiannual interest payments; semiannual compounding)

| Annual Yield (%) | ½ | 1 | 5 | 10 | 15 | 19½ | 20 | 30 |
|---|---|---|---|---|---|---|---|---|
| 4.5.......... | 100.49 | 100.97 | 104.43 | 107.98 | 110.82 | 112.89 | 113.10 | 116.37 |
| 4.6.......... | 100.44 | 100.87 | 103.98 | 107.15 | 109.67 | 111.51 | 111.69 | 114.57 |
| 4.7.......... | 100.39 | 100.77 | 103.53 | 106.32 | 108.54 | 110.14 | 110.30 | 112.80 |
| 4.8.......... | 100.34 | 100.68 | 103.08 | 105.51 | 107.42 | 108.80 | 108.94 | 111.07 |
| 4.9.......... | 100.29 | 100.58 | 102.63 | 104.70 | 106.32 | 107.48 | 107.59 | 109.38 |
| 5.0.......... | 100.24 | 100.48 | 102.19 | 103.90 | 105.23 | 106.18 | 106.28 | 107.73 |
| 5.1.......... | 100.20 | 100.39 | 101.75 | 103.10 | 104.16 | 104.91 | 104.98 | 106.11 |
| 5.2.......... | 100.15 | 100.29 | 101.31 | 102.32 | 103.10 | 103.65 | 103.70 | 104.53 |
| 5.3.......... | 100.10 | 100.19 | 100.87 | 101.54 | 102.05 | 102.41 | 102.45 | 102.99 |
| 5.4.......... | 100.05 | 100.10 | 100.43 | 100.76 | 101.02 | 101.20 | 101.21 | 101.48 |
| 5.5.......... | 100.00 | 100.00 | 100.00 | 100.00 | 100.00 | 100.00 | 100.00 | 100.00 |
| 5.6.......... | 99.95 | 99.90 | 99.57 | 99.24 | 98.99 | 98.82 | 98.81 | 98.55 |
| 5.7.......... | 99.90 | 99.81 | 99.14 | 98.49 | 98.00 | 97.66 | 97.63 | 97.14 |
| 5.8.......... | 99.85 | 99.71 | 98.71 | 97.75 | 97.02 | 96.52 | 96.48 | 95.76 |
| 5.9.......... | 99.81 | 99.62 | 98.29 | 97.01 | 96.05 | 95.40 | 95.34 | 94.41 |
| 6.0.......... | 99.76 | 99.52 | 97.87 | 96.28 | 95.10 | 94.30 | 94.22 | 93.08 |
| 6.1.......... | 99.71 | 99.43 | 97.45 | 95.56 | 94.16 | 93.21 | 93.12 | 91.79 |
| 6.2.......... | 99.66 | 99.33 | 97.03 | 94.84 | 93.23 | 92.14 | 92.04 | 90.52 |
| 6.3.......... | 99.61 | 99.24 | 96.61 | 94.13 | 92.31 | 91.09 | 90.97 | 89.28 |
| 6.4.......... | 99.56 | 99.14 | 96.20 | 93.43 | 91.40 | 90.05 | 89.93 | 88.06 |
| 6.5.......... | 99.52 | 99.05 | 95.75 | 92.73 | 90.51 | 89.03 | 88.90 | 86.87 |
| 6.6.......... | 99.47 | 98.95 | 95.38 | 92.04 | 89.63 | 88.03 | 87.88 | 85.71 |
| 6.7.......... | 99.42 | 98.86 | 94.97 | 91.36 | 88.75 | 87.04 | 86.88 | 84.57 |
| 6.8.......... | 99.37 | 98.76 | 94.57 | 90.68 | 87.89 | 86.07 | 85.90 | 83.45 |
| 6.9.......... | 99.32 | 98.67 | 94.16 | 90.01 | 87.04 | 85.12 | 84.93 | 82.36 |
| 7.0.......... | 99.28 | 98.58 | 93.76 | 89.34 | 86.21 | 84.17 | 83.98 | 81.29 |
| 7.1.......... | 99.23 | 98.48 | 93.36 | 88.68 | 85.38 | 83.25 | 83.05 | 80.24 |
| 7.2.......... | 99.18 | 98.39 | 92.97 | 88.03 | 84.56 | 82.33 | 82.13 | 79.22 |
| 7.3.......... | 99.13 | 98.29 | 92.57 | 87.38 | 83.75 | 81.43 | 81.22 | 78.21 |
| 7.4.......... | 99.08 | 98.20 | 92.18 | 86.74 | 82.96 | 80.55 | 80.33 | 77.23 |
| 7.5.......... | 99.04 | 98.11 | 91.79 | 86.10 | 82.17 | 79.68 | 79.45 | 76.26 |
| 7.6.......... | 98.99 | 98.01 | 91.40 | 85.47 | 81.39 | 78.82 | 78.58 | 75.32 |
| 7.7.......... | 98.94 | 97.92 | 91.01 | 84.85 | 80.63 | 77.98 | 77.73 | 74.39 |
| 7.8.......... | 98.89 | 97.83 | 90.63 | 84.23 | 79.87 | 77.14 | 76.90 | 73.48 |
| 7.9.......... | 98.85 | 97.74 | 90.24 | 83.62 | 79.12 | 76.33 | 76.07 | 72.59 |
| 8.0.......... | 98.80 | 97.64 | 89.86 | 83.01 | 78.38 | 75.52 | 75.26 | 71.72 |
| 8.1.......... | 98.75 | 97.55 | 89.48 | 82.41 | 77.66 | 74.73 | 74.46 | 70.87 |
| 8.2.......... | 98.70 | 97.46 | 89.10 | 81.81 | 76.94 | 73.94 | 73.67 | 70.03 |
| 8.3.......... | 98.66 | 97.37 | 88.73 | 81.22 | 76.23 | 73.17 | 72.90 | 69.21 |
| 8.4.......... | 98.61 | 97.27 | 88.36 | 80.64 | 75.52 | 72.41 | 72.14 | 68.40 |

## Table 9

### BOND VALUES—COUPON RATE OF 6 PERCENT

(semiannual interest payments; semiannual compounding)

| Annual Yield (%) | Years to Maturity | | | | | | | |
|---|---|---|---|---|---|---|---|---|
| | ½ | 1 | 5 | 10 | 15 | 19½ | 20 | 30 |
| 4.5 | 100.73 | 101.45 | 106.65 | 111.97 | 116.23 | 119.34 | 119.65 | 124.56 |
| 4.6 | 100.68 | 101.35 | 106.19 | 111.12 | 115.05 | 117.90 | 118.18 | 122.66 |
| 4.7 | 100.64 | 101.26 | 105.73 | 110.28 | 113.88 | 116.48 | 116.74 | 120.80 |
| 4.8 | 100.59 | 101.16 | 105.28 | 109.44 | 112.73 | 115.09 | 115.32 | 118.98 |
| 4.9 | 100.54 | 101.06 | 104.83 | 108.61 | 111.59 | 113.71 | 113.92 | 117.20 |
| 5.0 | 100.49 | 100.96 | 104.38 | 107.79 | 110.47 | 112.37 | 112.55 | 115.45 |
| 5.1 | 100.44 | 100.87 | 103.93 | 106.98 | 109.36 | 111.04 | 111.20 | 113.75 |
| 5.2 | 100.39 | 100.77 | 103.48 | 106.18 | 108.26 | 109.73 | 109.87 | 112.09 |
| 5.3 | 100.34 | 100.67 | 103.04 | 105.38 | 107.18 | 108.45 | 108.57 | 110.46 |
| 5.4 | 100.29 | 100.58 | 102.60 | 104.59 | 106.11 | 107.18 | 107.28 | 108.86 |
| 5.5 | 100.24 | 100.48 | 102.16 | 103.81 | 105.06 | 105.94 | 106.02 | 107.31 |
| 5.6 | 100.19 | 100.38 | 101.72 | 103.03 | 104.02 | 104.71 | 104.78 | 105.78 |
| 5.7 | 100.15 | 100.29 | 101.29 | 102.26 | 103.00 | 103.50 | 103.55 | 104.29 |
| 5.8 | 100.10 | 100.19 | 100.86 | 101.50 | 101.99 | 102.32 | 102.35 | 102.83 |
| 5.9 | 100.05 | 100.10 | 100.43 | 100.75 | 100.99 | 101.15 | 101.17 | 101.40 |
| 6.0 | 100.00 | 100.00 | 100.00 | 100.00 | 100.00 | 100.00 | 100.00 | 100.00 |
| 6.1 | 99.95 | 99.90 | 99.57 | 99.26 | 99.03 | 98.87 | 98.85 | 98.63 |
| 6.2 | 99.90 | 99.81 | 99.15 | 98.53 | 98.07 | 97.75 | 97.73 | 97.29 |
| 6.3 | 99.85 | 99.71 | 98.73 | 97.80 | 97.12 | 96.66 | 96.62 | 95.98 |
| 6.4 | 99.81 | 99.62 | 98.31 | 97.08 | 96.18 | 95.58 | 95.52 | 94.69 |
| 6.5 | 99.76 | 99.52 | 97.89 | 96.37 | 95.25 | 94.52 | 94.45 | 93.44 |
| 6.6 | 99.71 | 99.43 | 97.48 | 95.66 | 94.34 | 93.47 | 93.39 | 92.21 |
| 6.7 | 99.66 | 99.33 | 97.07 | 94.96 | 93.44 | 92.44 | 92.35 | 91.00 |
| 6.8 | 99.61 | 99.24 | 96.66 | 94.26 | 92.55 | 91.43 | 91.32 | 89.82 |
| 6.9 | 99.57 | 99.14 | 96.25 | 93.58 | 91.67 | 90.43 | 90.32 | 88.66 |
| 7.0 | 99.52 | 99.05 | 95.84 | 92.89 | 90.80 | 89.45 | 89.32 | 87.53 |
| 7.1 | 99.47 | 98.96 | 95.44 | 92.22 | 89.95 | 88.48 | 88.35 | 86.42 |
| 7.2 | 99.42 | 98.86 | 95.04 | 91.55 | 89.10 | 87.53 | 87.38 | 85.33 |
| 7.3 | 99.37 | 98.77 | 94.63 | 90.89 | 88.27 | 86.59 | 86.44 | 84.26 |
| 7.4 | 99.32 | 98.67 | 94.24 | 90.23 | 87.44 | 85.67 | 85.50 | 83.22 |
| 7.5 | 99.28 | 98.58 | 93.84 | 89.58 | 86.63 | 84.76 | 84.59 | 82.20 |
| 7.6 | 99.23 | 98.49 | 93.45 | 88.93 | 85.82 | 83.86 | 83.68 | 81.19 |
| 7.7 | 99.18 | 98.39 | 93.05 | 88.29 | 85.03 | 82.98 | 82.79 | 80.21 |
| 7.8 | 99.13 | 98.30 | 92.66 | 87.66 | 84.25 | 82.11 | 81.92 | 79.25 |
| 7.9 | 99.09 | 98.21 | 92.28 | 87.03 | 83.47 | 81.26 | 81.06 | 78.30 |
| 8.0 | 99.04 | 98.11 | 91.89 | 86.41 | 82.71 | 80.42 | 80.21 | 77.38 |
| 8.1 | 98.99 | 98.02 | 91.50 | 85.79 | 81.95 | 79.59 | 79.37 | 76.47 |
| 8.2 | 98.94 | 97.93 | 91.12 | 85.18 | 81.21 | 78.77 | 78.55 | 75.58 |
| 8.3 | 98.90 | 97.84 | 90.74 | 84.58 | 80.47 | 77.96 | 77.74 | 74.71 |
| 8.4 | 98.85 | 97.74 | 90.36 | 83.98 | 79.74 | 77.17 | 76.94 | 73.85 |

*Table 10*

## BOND VALUES—COUPON RATE OF 6½ PERCENT
(semiannual interest payments; semiannual compounding)

| Annual Yield (%) | Years to Maturity | | | | | | | |
|---|---|---|---|---|---|---|---|---|
| | ½ | 1 | 5 | 10 | 15 | 19½ | 20 | 30 |
| 4.5 | 100.98 | 101.93 | 108.87 | 115.96 | 121.65 | 125.78 | 126.19 | 132.75 |
| 4.6 | 100.93 | 101.84 | 108.40 | 115.09 | 120.42 | 124.29 | 124.67 | 130.75 |
| 4.7 | 100.88 | 101.74 | 107.94 | 114.23 | 119.22 | 122.82 | 123.17 | 128.79 |
| 4.8 | 100.83 | 101.64 | 107.48 | 113.38 | 118.03 | 121.37 | 121.70 | 126.88 |
| 4.9 | 100.78 | 101.54 | 107.02 | 112.53 | 116.86 | 119.95 | 120.25 | 125.01 |
| 5.0 | 100.73 | 101.45 | 106.56 | 111.69 | 115.70 | 118.55 | 118.83 | 123.18 |
| 5.1 | 100.68 | 101.35 | 106.11 | 110.86 | 114.55 | 117.17 | 117.42 | 121.39 |
| 5.2 | 100.63 | 101.25 | 105.66 | 110.04 | 113.43 | 115.81 | 116.05 | 119.64 |
| 5.3 | 100.58 | 101.15 | 105.21 | 109.22 | 112.31 | 114.48 | 114.69 | 117.93 |
| 5.4 | 100.54 | 101.06 | 104.76 | 108.41 | 111.21 | 113.16 | 113.35 | 116.25 |
| 5.5 | 100.49 | 100.96 | 104.32 | 107.61 | 110.12 | 111.87 | 112.04 | 114.61 |
| 5.6 | 100.44 | 100.86 | 103.88 | 106.82 | 109.05 | 110.60 | 110.75 | 113.01 |
| 5.7 | 100.39 | 100.77 | 103.44 | 106.03 | 107.99 | 109.34 | 109.47 | 111.44 |
| 5.8 | 100.34 | 100.67 | 103.00 | 105.26 | 106.95 | 108.11 | 108.22 | 109.90 |
| 5.9 | 100.29 | 100.57 | 102.57 | 104.48 | 105.92 | 106.90 | 106.99 | 108.39 |
| 6.0 | 100.24 | 100.48 | 102.13 | 103.72 | 104.90 | 105.70 | 105.78 | 106.92 |
| 6.1 | 100.19 | 100.38 | 101.70 | 102.96 | 103.89 | 104.53 | 104.59 | 105.48 |
| 6.2 | 100.15 | 100.29 | 101.27 | 102.21 | 102.90 | 103.37 | 103.41 | 104.06 |
| 6.3 | 100.10 | 100.19 | 100.85 | 101.47 | 101.92 | 102.23 | 102.26 | 102.68 |
| 6.4 | 100.05 | 100.10 | 100.42 | 100.73 | 100.96 | 101.11 | 101.12 | 101.33 |
| 6.5 | 100.00 | 100.00 | 100.00 | 100.00 | 100.00 | 100.00 | 100.00 | 100.00 |
| 6.6 | 99.95 | 99.90 | 99.58 | 99.28 | 99.06 | 98.91 | 98.90 | 98.70 |
| 6.7 | 99.90 | 99.81 | 99.16 | 98.56 | 98.13 | 97.84 | 97.81 | 97.43 |
| 6.8 | 99.85 | 99.71 | 98.75 | 97.85 | 97.21 | 96.79 | 96.75 | 96.18 |
| 6.9 | 99.81 | 99.62 | 98.33 | 97.14 | 96.30 | 95.75 | 95.70 | 94.96 |
| 7.0 | 99.76 | 99.53 | 97.92 | 96.45 | 95.40 | 94.72 | 94.66 | 93.76 |
| 7.1 | 99.71 | 99.43 | 97.51 | 95.76 | 94.52 | 93.72 | 93.64 | 92.59 |
| 7.2 | 99.66 | 99.34 | 97.10 | 95.07 | 93.64 | 92.73 | 92.64 | 91.44 |
| 7.3 | 99.61 | 99.24 | 96.70 | 94.39 | 92.78 | 91.75 | 91.65 | 90.32 |
| 7.4 | 99.57 | 99.15 | 96.29 | 93.72 | 91.93 | 90.79 | 90.68 | 89.21 |
| 7.5 | 99.52 | 99.05 | 95.89 | 93.05 | 91.09 | 89.84 | 89.72 | 88.13 |
| 7.6 | 99.47 | 98.96 | 95.49 | 92.39 | 90.25 | 88.91 | 88.78 | 87.07 |
| 7.7 | 99.42 | 98.87 | 95.10 | 91.74 | 89.43 | 87.99 | 87.85 | 86.03 |
| 7.8 | 99.37 | 98.77 | 94.70 | 91.09 | 88.62 | 87.08 | 86.94 | 85.01 |
| 7.9 | 99.33 | 98.68 | 94.31 | 90.44 | 87.82 | 86.19 | 86.04 | 84.01 |
| 8.0 | 99.28 | 98.59 | 93.92 | 89.81 | 87.03 | 85.31 | 85.16 | 83.03 |
| 8.1 | 99.23 | 98.49 | 93.53 | 89.18 | 86.25 | 84.45 | 84.28 | 82.07 |
| 8.2 | 99.18 | 98.40 | 93.14 | 88.55 | 85.48 | 83.59 | 83.42 | 81.13 |
| 8.3 | 99.14 | 98.31 | 92.75 | 87.93 | 84.72 | 82.75 | 82.58 | 80.20 |
| 8.4 | 99.09 | 98.21 | 92.37 | 87.31 | 83.96 | 81.93 | 81.74 | 79.30 |
| 8.5 | 99.04 | 98.12 | 91.99 | 86.71 | 83.22 | 81.11 | 80.92 | 78.41 |
| 8.6 | 98.99 | 98.03 | 91.61 | 86.10 | 82.49 | 80.31 | 80.11 | 77.53 |
| 8.7 | 98.95 | 97.94 | 91.23 | 85.50 | 81.76 | 79.52 | 79.32 | 76.68 |
| 8.8 | 98.90 | 97.84 | 90.86 | 84.91 | 81.05 | 78.74 | 78.53 | 75.84 |
| 8.9 | 98.85 | 97.75 | 90.48 | 84.32 | 80.34 | 77.97 | 77.76 | 75.01 |

## Table 11

### BOND VALUES — COUPON RATE OF 7 PERCENT

(semiannual interest payments; semiannual compounding)

| Annual Yield (%) | Years to Maturity | | | | | | | |
|---|---|---|---|---|---|---|---|---|
| | ½ | 1 | 5 | 10 | 15 | 19½ | 20 | 30 |
| 5.0 | 100.98 | 101.93 | 108.75 | 115.59 | 120.93 | 124.73 | 125.10 | 130.91 |
| 5.1 | 100.93 | 101.83 | 108.29 | 114.74 | 119.75 | 123.30 | 123.65 | 129.03 |
| 5.2 | 100.88 | 101.73 | 107.84 | 113.90 | 118.59 | 121.89 | 122.22 | 127.19 |
| 5.3 | 100.83 | 101.63 | 107.38 | 113.06 | 117.44 | 120.51 | 120.81 | 125.40 |
| 5.4 | 100.78 | 101.54 | 106.93 | 112.24 | 116.31 | 119.15 | 119.42 | 123.64 |
| 5.5 | 100.73 | 101.44 | 106.48 | 111.42 | 115.19 | 117.81 | 118.06 | 121.92 |
| 5.6 | 100.68 | 101.34 | 106.03 | 110.61 | 114.08 | 116.48 | 116.72 | 120.23 |
| 5.7 | 100.63 | 101.25 | 105.59 | 109.81 | 112.99 | 115.18 | 115.40 | 118.58 |
| 5.8 | 100.58 | 101.15 | 105.14 | 109.01 | 111.91 | 113.90 | 114.10 | 116.97 |
| 5.9 | 100.53 | 101.05 | 104.70 | 108.22 | 110.85 | 112.64 | 112.82 | 115.39 |
| 6.0 | 100.49 | 100.96 | 104.27 | 107.44 | 109.80 | 111.40 | 111.56 | 113.84 |
| 6.1 | 100.44 | 100.86 | 103.83 | 106.66 | 108.76 | 110.18 | 110.32 | 112.32 |
| 6.2 | 100.39 | 100.76 | 103.39 | 105.90 | 107.74 | 108.98 | 109.10 | 110.84 |
| 6.3 | 100.34 | 100.67 | 102.96 | 105.14 | 106.73 | 107.80 | 107.90 | 109.38 |
| 6.4 | 100.29 | 100.57 | 102.53 | 104.38 | 105.73 | 106.63 | 106.72 | 107.96 |
| 6.5 | 100.24 | 100.48 | 102.11 | 103.63 | 104.75 | 105.48 | 105.55 | 106.56 |
| 6.6 | 100.19 | 100.38 | 101.68 | 102.89 | 103.77 | 104.35 | 104.41 | 105.20 |
| 6.7 | 100.15 | 100.29 | 101.26 | 102.16 | 102.81 | 103.24 | 103.28 | 103.86 |
| 6.8 | 100.10 | 100.19 | 100.84 | 101.43 | 101.86 | 102.14 | 102.17 | 102.55 |
| 6.9 | 100.05 | 100.10 | 100.42 | 100.71 | 100.93 | 101.06 | 101.08 | 101.26 |
| 7.0 | 100.00 | 100.00 | 100.00 | 100.00 | 100.00 | 100.00 | 100.00 | 100.00 |
| 7.1 | 99.95 | 99.91 | 99.59 | 99.29 | 99.09 | 98.95 | 98.94 | 98.77 |
| 7.2 | 99.90 | 99.81 | 99.17 | 98.59 | 98.18 | 97.92 | 97.90 | 97.55 |
| 7.3 | 99.86 | 99.72 | 98.76 | 97.90 | 97.29 | 96.91 | 96.87 | 96.37 |
| 7.4 | 99.81 | 99.62 | 98.35 | 97.21 | 96.41 | 95.91 | 95.86 | 95.21 |
| 7.5 | 99.76 | 99.53 | 97.95 | 96.53 | 95.54 | 94.92 | 94.86 | 94.07 |
| 7.6 | 99.71 | 99.43 | 97.54 | 95.85 | 94.68 | 93.95 | 93.88 | 92.95 |
| 7.7 | 99.66 | 99.34 | 97.14 | 95.18 | 93.84 | 92.99 | 92.92 | 91.85 |
| 7.8 | 99.62 | 99.24 | 96.74 | 94.52 | 93.00 | 92.05 | 91.96 | 90.78 |
| 7.9 | 99.57 | 99.15 | 96.34 | 93.86 | 92.17 | 91.12 | 91.03 | 89.72 |
| 8.0 | 99.52 | 99.06 | 95.94 | 93.20 | 91.35 | 90.21 | 90.10 | 88.69 |
| 8.1 | 99.47 | 98.96 | 95.55 | 92.56 | 90.55 | 89.31 | 89.19 | 87.67 |
| 8.2 | 99.42 | 98.87 | 95.16 | 91.92 | 89.75 | 88.42 | 88.30 | 86.68 |
| 8.3 | 99.38 | 98.78 | 94.77 | 91.28 | 88.96 | 87.54 | 87.42 | 85.70 |
| 8.4 | 99.33 | 98.68 | 94.38 | 90.65 | 88.18 | 86.68 | 86.55 | 84.75 |
| 8.5 | 99.28 | 98.59 | 93.99 | 90.03 | 87.42 | 85.83 | 85.69 | 83.81 |
| 8.6 | 99.23 | 98.50 | 93.61 | 89.41 | 86.66 | 85.00 | 84.85 | 82.88 |
| 8.7 | 99.19 | 98.40 | 93.22 | 88.80 | 85.91 | 84.17 | 84.02 | 81.98 |
| 8.8 | 99.14 | 98.31 | 92.84 | 88.19 | 85.17 | 83.36 | 83.20 | 81.09 |
| 8.9 | 99.09 | 98.22 | 92.46 | 87.59 | 84.43 | 82.56 | 82.39 | 80.22 |
| 9.0 | 99.04 | 98.13 | 92.09 | 86.99 | 83.71 | 81.77 | 81.60 | 79.36 |
| 9.1 | 99.00 | 98.04 | 91.71 | 86.40 | 83.00 | 80.99 | 80.82 | 78.52 |
| 9.2 | 98.95 | 97.94 | 91.34 | 85.81 | 82.29 | 80.23 | 80.04 | 77.70 |
| 9.3 | 98.90 | 97.85 | 90.97 | 85.23 | 81.59 | 79.47 | 79.28 | 76.89 |
| 9.4 | 98.85 | 97.76 | 90.60 | 84.66 | 80.91 | 78.73 | 78.53 | 76.09 |

*Table 12*

BOND VALUES — COUPON RATE OF 7½ PERCENT

(semiannual interest payments; semiannual compounding)

| Annual Yield (%) | Years to Maturity | | | | | | | |
|---|---|---|---|---|---|---|---|---|
| | ½ | 1 | 5 | 10 | 15 | 19½ | 20 | 30 |
| 5.5...... | 100.97 | 101.92 | 108.64 | 115.23 | 120.25 | 123.74 | 124.08 | 129.22 |
| 5.6...... | 100.92 | 101.82 | 108.19 | 114.40 | 119.11 | 122.37 | 122.69 | 127.46 |
| 5.7...... | 100.88 | 101.73 | 107.74 | 113.58 | 117.99 | 121.02 | 121.32 | 125.73 |
| 5.8...... | 100.83 | 101.63 | 107.29 | 112.76 | 116.88 | 119.70 | 119.97 | 124.04 |
| 5.9...... | 100.78 | 101.53 | 106.84 | 111.96 | 115.78 | 118.39 | 118.64 | 122.38 |
| 6.0...... | 100.73 | 101.44 | 106.40 | 111.16 | 114.70 | 117.11 | 117.34 | 120.76 |
| 6.1...... | 100.68 | 101.34 | 105.96 | 110.37 | 113.63 | 115.84 | 116.05 | 119.17 |
| 6.2...... | 100.63 | 101.24 | 105.52 | 109.58 | 112.58 | 114.59 | 114.78 | 117.61 |
| 6.3...... | 100.58 | 101.15 | 105.08 | 108.80 | 111.54 | 113.37 | 113.54 | 116.08 |
| 6.4...... | 100.53 | 101.05 | 104.64 | 108.03 | 110.51 | 112.16 | 112.31 | 114.59 |
| 6.5...... | 100.48 | 100.95 | 104.21 | 107.27 | 109.49 | 110.97 | 111.10 | 113.13 |
| 6.6...... | 100.44 | 100.86 | 103.78 | 106.51 | 108.49 | 109.79 | 109.92 | 111.69 |
| 6.7...... | 100.39 | 100.76 | 103.35 | 105.76 | 107.50 | 108.64 | 108.74 | 110.29 |
| 6.8...... | 100.34 | 100.67 | 102.93 | 105.02 | 106.52 | 107.50 | 107.59 | 108.91 |
| 6.9...... | 100.29 | 100.57 | 102.50 | 104.28 | 105.55 | 106.38 | 106.46 | 107.56 |
| 7.0...... | 100.24 | 100.47 | 102.08 | 103.55 | 104.60 | 105.28 | 105.34 | 106.24 |
| 7.1...... | 100.19 | 100.38 | 101.66 | 102.83 | 103.66 | 104.19 | 104.24 | 104.94 |
| 7.2...... | 100.14 | 100.28 | 101.24 | 102.11 | 102.72 | 103.12 | 103.15 | 103.67 |
| 7.3...... | 100.10 | 100.19 | 100.83 | 101.40 | 101.81 | 102.06 | 102.09 | 102.42 |
| 7.4...... | 100.05 | 100.09 | 100.41 | 100.70 | 100.90 | 101.02 | 101.04 | 101.20 |
| 7.5...... | 100.00 | 100.00 | 100.00 | 100.00 | 100.00 | 100.00 | 100.00 | 100.00 |
| 7.6...... | 99.95 | 99.91 | 99.59 | 99.31 | 99.11 | 98.99 | 98.98 | 98.82 |
| 7.7...... | 99.90 | 99.81 | 99.18 | 98.62 | 98.24 | 98.00 | 97.98 | 97.67 |
| 7.8...... | 99.86 | 99.72 | 98.78 | 97.94 | 97.37 | 97.02 | 96.99 | 96.54 |
| 7.9...... | 99.81 | 99.62 | 98.37 | 97.27 | 96.52 | 96.05 | 96.01 | 95.43 |
| 8.0...... | 99.76 | 99.53 | 97.97 | 96.60 | 95.68 | 95.10 | 95.05 | 94.34 |
| 8.1...... | 99.71 | 99.43 | 97.57 | 95.94 | 94.84 | 94.17 | 94.11 | 93.28 |
| 8.2...... | 99.66 | 99.34 | 97.18 | 95.29 | 94.02 | 93.24 | 93.17 | 92.23 |
| 8.3...... | 99.62 | 99.25 | 96.78 | 94.64 | 93.21 | 92.34 | 92.26 | 91.20 |
| 8.4...... | 99.57 | 99.15 | 96.39 | 93.99 | 92.40 | 91.44 | 91.35 | 90.19 |
| 8.5...... | 99.52 | 99.06 | 95.99 | 93.35 | 91.61 | 90.56 | 90.46 | 89.20 |
| 8.6...... | 99.47 | 98.97 | 95.60 | 92.72 | 90.83 | 89.69 | 89.58 | 88.23 |
| 8.7...... | 99.43 | 98.87 | 95.22 | 92.09 | 90.05 | 88.83 | 88.72 | 87.28 |
| 8.8...... | 99.38 | 98.78 | 94.83 | 91.47 | 89.29 | 87.98 | 87.87 | 86.34 |
| 8.9...... | 99.33 | 98.69 | 94.45 | 90.85 | 88.53 | 87.15 | 87.03 | 85.42 |
| 9.0...... | 99.28 | 98.60 | 94.07 | 90.24 | 87.78 | 86.33 | 86.20 | 84.52 |
| 9.1...... | 99.23 | 98.50 | 93.69 | 89.64 | 87.05 | 85.52 | 85.38 | 83.64 |
| 9.2...... | 99.19 | 98.41 | 93.31 | 89.04 | 86.32 | 84.72 | 84.58 | 82.77 |
| 9.3...... | 99.14 | 98.32 | 92.93 | 88.44 | 85.60 | 83.93 | 83.79 | 81.91 |
| 9.4...... | 99.09 | 98.23 | 92.56 | 87.85 | 84.88 | 83.16 | 83.01 | 81.07 |
| 9.5...... | 99.05 | 98.13 | 92.18 | 87.27 | 84.18 | 82.39 | 82.24 | 80.25 |
| 9.6...... | 99.00 | 98.04 | 91.81 | 86.69 | 83.48 | 81.64 | 81.48 | 79.44 |
| 9.7...... | 98.95 | 97.95 | 91.44 | 86.12 | 82.80 | 80.90 | 80.73 | 78.64 |
| 9.8...... | 98.90 | 97.86 | 91.08 | 85.55 | 82.12 | 80.16 | 79.99 | 77.86 |
| 9.9...... | 98.86 | 97.77 | 90.71 | 84.98 | 81.45 | 79.48 | 79.27 | 77.09 |

Table 13

BOND VALUES — COUPON RATE OF 8 PERCENT

(semiannual interest payments; semiannual compounding)

| Annual Yield (%) | Years to Maturity | | | | | | | |
|---|---|---|---|---|---|---|---|---|
| | ½ | 1 | 5 | 10 | 15 | 19½ | 20 | 30 |
| 5.5 | 101.22 | 102.40 | 110.80 | 119.03 | 125.31 | 129.68 | 130.10 | 136.53 |
| 5.6 | 101.17 | 102.30 | 110.34 | 118.19 | 124.14 | 128.26 | 128.66 | 134.68 |
| 5.7 | 101.12 | 102.21 | 109.89 | 117.35 | 122.98 | 126.86 | 127.24 | 132.88 |
| 5.8 | 101.07 | 102.11 | 109.43 | 116.52 | 121.84 | 125.49 | 125.84 | 131.11 |
| 5.9 | 101.02 | 102.01 | 108.98 | 115.69 | 120.71 | 124.14 | 124.47 | 129.37 |
| 6.0 | 100.97 | 101.91 | 108.53 | 114.88 | 119.60 | 122.81 | 123.11 | 127.68 |
| 6.1 | 100.92 | 101.82 | 108.08 | 114.07 | 118.50 | 121.50 | 121.78 | 126.01 |
| 6.2 | 100.87 | 101.72 | 107.64 | 113.27 | 117.41 | 120.21 | 120.47 | 124.38 |
| 6.3 | 100.82 | 101.62 | 107.20 | 112.47 | 116.34 | 118.93 | 119.18 | 122.79 |
| 6.4 | 100.78 | 101.53 | 106.76 | 111.68 | 115.28 | 117.68 | 117.91 | 121.22 |
| 6.5 | 100.73 | 101.43 | 106.32 | 110.90 | 114.24 | 116.45 | 116.66 | 119.69 |
| 6.6 | 100.68 | 101.33 | 105.88 | 110.13 | 113.20 | 115.23 | 115.42 | 118.19 |
| 6.7 | 100.63 | 101.24 | 105.45 | 109.36 | 112.18 | 114.04 | 114.21 | 116.72 |
| 6.8 | 100.58 | 101.14 | 105.02 | 108.61 | 111.17 | 112.86 | 113.01 | 115.27 |
| 6.9 | 100.53 | 101.05 | 104.59 | 107.85 | 110.18 | 111.70 | 111.84 | 113.86 |
| 7.0 | 100.48 | 100.95 | 104.16 | 107.11 | 109.20 | 110.55 | 110.68 | 112.47 |
| 7.1 | 100.43 | 100.85 | 103.73 | 106.37 | 108.22 | 109.42 | 109.54 | 111.11 |
| 7.2 | 100.39 | 100.76 | 103.31 | 105.63 | 107.27 | 108.31 | 108.41 | 109.78 |
| 7.3 | 100.34 | 100.66 | 102.89 | 104.91 | 106.32 | 107.22 | 107.30 | 108.47 |
| 7.4 | 100.29 | 100.57 | 102.47 | 104.19 | 105.38 | 106.14 | 106.21 | 107.19 |
| 7.5 | 100.24 | 100.47 | 102.05 | 103.47 | 104.46 | 105.08 | 105.14 | 105.93 |
| 7.6 | 100.19 | 100.38 | 101.64 | 102.77 | 103.54 | 104.03 | 104.08 | 104.70 |
| 7.7 | 100.14 | 100.28 | 101.23 | 102.07 | 102.64 | 103.00 | 103.04 | 103.49 |
| 7.8 | 100.10 | 100.19 | 100.82 | 101.37 | 101.75 | 101.99 | 102.01 | 102.31 |
| 7.9 | 100.05 | 100.09 | 100.41 | 100.68 | 100.87 | 100.99 | 101.00 | 101.14 |
| 8.0 | 100.00 | 100.00 | 100.00 | 100.00 | 100.00 | 100.00 | 100.00 | 100.00 |
| 8.1 | 99.95 | 99.91 | 99.60 | 99.32 | 99.14 | 99.03 | 99.02 | 98.88 |
| 8.2 | 99.90 | 99.81 | 99.19 | 98.65 | 98.29 | 98.07 | 98.05 | 97.78 |
| 8.3 | 99.86 | 99.72 | 98.79 | 97.99 | 97.45 | 97.13 | 97.10 | 96.70 |
| 8.4 | 99.81 | 99.62 | 98.39 | 97.33 | 96.62 | 96.20 | 96.16 | 95.64 |
| 8.5 | 99.76 | 99.53 | 98.00 | 96.68 | 95.81 | 95.28 | 95.23 | 94.60 |
| 8.6 | 99.71 | 99.44 | 97.60 | 96.03 | 95.00 | 94.37 | 94.32 | 93.58 |
| 8.7 | 99.66 | 99.34 | 97.21 | 95.39 | 94.20 | 93.48 | 93.42 | 92.58 |
| 8.8 | 99.62 | 99.25 | 96.82 | 94.75 | 93.41 | 92.60 | 92.53 | 91.60 |
| 8.9 | 99.57 | 99.16 | 96.43 | 94.12 | 92.63 | 91.74 | 91.66 | 90.63 |
| 9.0 | 99.52 | 99.06 | 96.04 | 93.50 | 91.86 | 90.89 | 90.80 | 89.68 |
| 9.1 | 99.47 | 98.97 | 95.66 | 92.88 | 91.09 | 90.04 | 89.95 | 88.75 |
| 9.2 | 99.43 | 98.88 | 95.28 | 92.26 | 90.34 | 89.21 | 89.11 | 87.83 |
| 9.3 | 99.38 | 98.79 | 94.89 | 91.65 | 89.60 | 88.40 | 88.29 | 86.94 |
| 9.4 | 99.33 | 98.69 | 94.52 | 91.05 | 88.86 | 87.59 | 87.48 | 86.05 |
| 9.5 | 99.28 | 98.60 | 94.14 | 90.45 | 88.13 | 86.79 | 86.68 | 85.19 |
| 9.6 | 99.24 | 98.51 | 93.76 | 89.86 | 87.42 | 86.01 | 85.89 | 84.33 |
| 9.7 | 99.19 | 98.42 | 93.39 | 89.27 | 86.71 | 85.24 | 85.11 | 83.50 |
| 9.8 | 99.14 | 98.32 | 93.02 | 88.69 | 86.01 | 84.48 | 84.34 | 82.67 |
| 9.9 | 99.09 | 98.23 | 92.65 | 88.11 | 85.31 | 83.72 | 83.59 | 81.87 |

## Table 14

### BOND VALUES — COUPON RATE OF 9 PERCENT

(semiannual interest payments; semiannual compounding)

| Annual Yield (%) | Years to Maturity | | | | | | | |
|---|---|---|---|---|---|---|---|---|
| | $\frac{1}{2}$ | 1 | 5 | 10 | 15 | $19\frac{1}{2}$ | 20 | 30 |
| 6.5..... | 101.21 | 102.38 | 110.53 | 118.17 | 123.73 | 127.41 | 127.76 | 132.82 |
| 6.6..... | 101.16 | 102.29 | 110.08 | 117.37 | 122.63 | 126.11 | 126.44 | 131.18 |
| 6.7..... | 101.11 | 102.19 | 109.64 | 116.57 | 121.55 | 124.83 | 125.14 | 129.57 |
| 6.8..... | 101.06 | 102.09 | 109.19 | 115.78 | 120.49 | 123.57 | 123.86 | 128.00 |
| 6.9..... | 101.01 | 102.00 | 108.75 | 114.99 | 119.43 | 122.33 | 122.60 | 126.46 |
| 7.0..... | 100.97 | 101.90 | 108.32 | 114.21 | 118.39 | 121.10 | 121.36 | 124.94 |
| 7.1..... | 100.92 | 101.80 | 107.88 | 113.44 | 117.36 | 119.90 | 120.13 | 123.46 |
| 7.2..... | 100.87 | 101.71 | 107.45 | 112.68 | 116.35 | 118.71 | 118.92 | 122.01 |
| 7.3..... | 100.82 | 101.61 | 107.02 | 111.92 | 115.34 | 117.53 | 117.74 | 120.58 |
| 7.4..... | 100.77 | 101.52 | 106.59 | 111.17 | 114.35 | 116.38 | 116.57 | 119.18 |
| 7.5..... | 100.72 | 101.42 | 106.16 | 110.42 | 113.37 | 115.24 | 115.41 | 117.80 |
| 7.6..... | 100.67 | 101.32 | 105.73 | 109.68 | 112.40 | 114.12 | 114.28 | 116.46 |
| 7.7..... | 100.63 | 101.23 | 105.31 | 108.95 | 111.45 | 113.01 | 113.16 | 115.13 |
| 7.8..... | 100.58 | 101.13 | 104.89 | 108.23 | 110.50 | 111.92 | 112.05 | 113.84 |
| 7.9..... | 100.53 | 101.04 | 104.47 | 107.51 | 109.57 | 110.85 | 110.97 | 112.56 |
| 8.0..... | 100.48 | 100.94 | 104.06 | 106.80 | 108.65 | 109.79 | 109.90 | 111.31 |
| 8.1..... | 100.43 | 100.85 | 103.64 | 106.09 | 107.73 | 108.75 | 108.84 | 110.08 |
| 8.2..... | 100.38 | 100.75 | 103.23 | 105.39 | 106.83 | 107.72 | 107.80 | 108.88 |
| 8.3..... | 100.34 | 100.66 | 102.82 | 104.69 | 105.94 | 106.71 | 106.78 | 107.70 |
| 8.4..... | 100.29 | 100.56 | 102.41 | 104.01 | 105.06 | 105.71 | 105.77 | 106.54 |
| 8.5..... | 100.24 | 100.47 | 102.00 | 103.32 | 104.19 | 104.72 | 104.77 | 105.40 |
| 8.6..... | 100.19 | 100.38 | 101.60 | 102.65 | 103.34 | 103.75 | 103.79 | 104.28 |
| 8.7..... | 100.14 | 100.28 | 101.20 | 101.98 | 102.49 | 102.79 | 102.82 | 103.18 |
| 8.8..... | 100.10 | 100.19 | 100.80 | 101.31 | 101.65 | 101.85 | 101.87 | 102.10 |
| 8.9..... | 100.05 | 100.09 | 100.40 | 100.65 | 100.82 | 100.92 | 100.93 | 101.04 |
| 9.0..... | 100.00 | 100.00 | 100.00 | 100.00 | 100.00 | 100.00 | 100.00 | 100.00 |
| 9.1..... | 99.95 | 99.91 | 99.61 | 99.35 | 99.19 | 99.09 | 99.09 | 98.98 |
| 9.2..... | 99.90 | 99.81 | 99.21 | 98.71 | 98.39 | 98.20 | 98.19 | 97.97 |
| 9.3..... | 99.86 | 99.72 | 98.82 | 98.07 | 97.60 | 97.32 | 97.30 | 96.99 |
| 9.4..... | 99.81 | 99.63 | 98.43 | 97.44 | 96.82 | 96.45 | 96.42 | 96.02 |
| 9.5..... | 99.76 | 99.53 | 98.05 | 96.82 | 96.04 | 95.60 | 95.56 | 95.06 |
| 9.6..... | 99.71 | 99.44 | 97.66 | 96.20 | 95.28 | 94.75 | 94.71 | 94.13 |
| 9.7..... | 99.67 | 99.35 | 97.28 | 95.58 | 94.53 | 93.92 | 93.87 | 93.20 |
| 9.8..... | 99.62 | 99.26 | 96.90 | 94.97 | 93.78 | 93.10 | 93.04 | 92.30 |
| 9.9..... | 99.57 | 99.16 | 96.52 | 94.37 | 93.04 | 92.29 | 92.23 | 91.41 |
| 10.0..... | 99.52 | 99.07 | 96.14 | 93.77 | 92.31 | 91.49 | 91.42 | 90.54 |
| 10.1..... | 99.48 | 98.98 | 95.76 | 93.17 | 91.59 | 90.70 | 90.63 | 89.68 |
| 10.2..... | 99.43 | 98.89 | 95.39 | 92.59 | 90.88 | 89.93 | 89.84 | 88.83 |
| 10.3..... | 99.38 | 98.79 | 95.02 | 92.00 | 90.18 | 89.16 | 89.07 | 88.00 |
| 10.4..... | 99.33 | 98.70 | 94.65 | 91.42 | 89.48 | 88.40 | 88.31 | 87.18 |
| 10.5..... | 99.29 | 98.61 | 94.28 | 90.85 | 88.79 | 87.66 | 87.56 | 86.38 |
| 10.6..... | 99.24 | 98.52 | 93.91 | 90.28 | 88.11 | 86.92 | 86.82 | 85.59 |
| 10.7..... | 99.19 | 98.43 | 93.55 | 89.71 | 87.44 | 86.19 | 86.09 | 84.81 |
| 10.8..... | 99.15 | 98.34 | 93.18 | 89.15 | 86.77 | 85.48 | 85.37 | 84.04 |
| 10.9..... | 99.10 | 98.24 | 92.82 | 88.60 | 86.12 | 84.77 | 84.66 | 83.29 |

# Appendix B

## SOLUTIONS TO SELECTED PROBLEMS

### Chapter 1

**1–7.**

**STATEMENT OF FINANCIAL POSITION**

| ASSETS | | LIABILITIES AND OWNERS' EQUITY | |
|---|---|---|---|
| *Current assets:* | | *Current liabilities:* | |
| Cash on hand and in banks............... | $ 9,000 | Accounts payable to creditors............. | $12,300 |
| Accounts receivable from customers...... | 6,900 | Notes payable to banks | 8,000 |
| Notes receivable from customers .......... | 3,900 | Total .............. | $20,300 |
| Inventory of | | Long-term debt.......... | 16,500 |
| merchandise......... | 29,100 | Total Liabilities.... | $36,800 |
| Total .............. | 48,900 | | |
| *Fixed assets:* | | Owners' equity .......... | 52,400 |
| Furniture and fixtures . | 4,200 | | |
| Delivery equipment.... | 9,600 | | |
| Building............... | 24,000 | | |
| Land ................... | 2,500 | | |
| Total ........... | $89,200 | Total ........... | $89,200 |

**1–10.** *a)*

**Dingy Dive Bar**

**STATEMENT OF FINANCIAL POSITION**
**January 21, 19x4**

| ASSETS | | LIABILITIES AND OWNERS' EQUITY | |
|---|---|---|---|
| *Current assets:* | | *Current liabilities:* | |
| Cash ................ | $ 1,500 | Note payable ....... | $11,500 |
| *Fixed assets:* | | Owners' equity: | |
| Bar equipment ...... | 1,000 | Mr. Robinson ........ | $ 1,500 |
| Buildings............ | 9,500 | Mr. Griffiths ......... | 1,500 |
| Improvements to | | Mr. Thorndike ....... | 1,500 |
| land............... | 2,000 | Total Owners' | |
| Land ................ | 2,000 | Equity......... | $ 4,500 |
| Total ........... | $16,000 | Total ........... | $16,000 |

*b)*                                   Dingy Dive Bar
### STATEMENT OF FINANCIAL POSITION
#### February 21, 19x4

| ASSETS | | | LIABILITIES AND OWNERS' EQUITY | | |
|---|---|---|---|---|---|
| *Current assets:* | | | *Current liabilities:* | | |
| Cash | $ 1,000 | | Wages payable | $ | 50 |
| Accounts receivable . | 150 | | Accounts payable.... | | 200 |
| Inventory............. | 300 | | Note payable........ | | 11,500 |
| Total Current | | | Total Current | | |
| Assets......... | $ 1,450 | | Liabilities ..... | | $11,750 |
| *Fixed assets:* | | | *Owners' Equity:* | | |
| Bar equipment ...... | 1,000 | | Mr. Robinson . | $1,400 | |
| Buildings............ | 9,500 | | Mr. Griffiths .. | 1,400 | |
| Improvements to | | | Mr. Thorndike | 1,400 | |
| land.............. | 2,000 | | Total Owners' | | |
| Land ............... | 2,000 | | Equity....... | | 4,200 |
| Total ......... | $15,950 | | Total ......... | | $15,950 |

*c)*   Since the partners have withdrawn a total of $600, it appears that the enterprise earned only $600 − $300 = $300 *before any charges for depreciation or any payments for services rendered by the proprietors.* The effect of the withdrawals has therefore been to reduce each partner's equity in the business.

# Chapter 2

**2–11.**                          INCOME STATEMENT

| | | |
|---|---|---|
| Revenue from sales................................. | | $1,000 |
| Cost of goods sold.................................. | | 700 |
| Gross margin ...................................... | | $  300 |
| Operating expenses: | | |
| Salaries and wages ............................ | $   120 | |
| Taxes......................................... | 20 | |
| Sundry........................................ | 60 | 200 |
| Net Income....................................... | | $  100 |

#### STATEMENT OF FINANCIAL POSITION

| ASSETS | | LIABILITIES AND OWNERS' EQUITY | |
|---|---|---|---|
| *Current assets:* | | *Current liabilities:* | |
| Cash.................... $ 100 | | Accounts payable....... $  250 | |
| Accounts receivable..... 300 | | Wages payable.......... 50 | |
| Inventories ............. 380 | | Taxes payable .......... 5 | |
| Prepaid rent ............ 40 | | Note payable........... 350 | |
| Total Current | | Total Current | |
| Assets ............ $ 820 | | Liabilities......... $  655 | |
| Furniture and fixtures .... 600 | | R. A. Copake, capital...... 765 | |
| Total.............. $1,420 | | Total.............. $1,420 | |

**2–16.**   (1)  Assuming that the equipment is equally useful in each of the 12 years, the annual depreciation should be $4,200/12 = $350. Since the furniture was purchased on July 1, only one-half year's depreciation, or $175, should be taken in 19x3.

(2)    The timing of the payments is irrelevant. The salesman worked 3 months in 19x3, and expense is 3 × $700 = $2,100.

(3)    The cost of goods sold is $220,000 and this is an expense, deductible from the revenues recognized in 19x3.

(4)    No expense. The payment merely canceled a liability that was assumed in 19x2.

(5)    Rent expense = 3 months' rentals = ³⁄₆ × $22,500 = $11,250.

2–20.  *a)*

|  | | Assets | | |
|---|---|---|---|---|
|  | Cash | Prepaid Rent | Equipment | Merchandise Inventory |
| (1) | $+300 | | | |
| (2) | − 45 | $+45 | | |
| (3) | −110 | | $+110 | |
| (4) | −100 | | | $+305 |
| (5) | +650 | | | −305 |
| (6a) | | −15 | | |
| (6b) | | | − 21 | |
| (7) | −205 | | | |
| Balance | $ 490 | $ 30 | $ 89 | $ — |

| | Liabilities | Owners' Equity | | | | |
|---|---|---|---|---|---|---|
| | Accounts Payable | Earl Holt, Proprietor | Sales Rev-enue (+) | Cost of Goods Sold (−) | Rent Ex-pense (−) | Depre-ciation Expense (−) |
| (1) | | $+300 | | | | |
| (4) | $+205 | | | | | |
| (5) | | | $650 | $305 | | |
| (6a) | | | | | $15 | |
| (6b) | | | | | | $21 |
| (7) | −205 | | | | | |
| Balance | $ — | $ 300 | $650 | $305 | $15 | $21 |

*b)*

### BALANCE SHEET, AS OF MONDAY NIGHT

| ASSETS | | LIABILITIES AND OWNER'S EQUITY | |
|---|---|---|---|
| Cash | $490 | Liabilities | None |
| Prepaid Rent | 30 | Owner's equity | $609 |
| Equipment | 89 | | |
| | | Total Liabilities and | |
| Total Assets | $609 | Owner's Equity | $609 |

*c)*

### INCOME STATEMENT FOR FIRST GAME

| | | |
|---|---|---|
| Sales revenue | | $650 |
| Less: Cost of goods sold | $305 | |
| Rent | 15 | |
| Depreciation | 21 | 341 |
| Net Income | | $309 |

## Chapter 3

**3–16.**

Owners' equity, end of year:  $140,000 − $28,000 = $112,000
Owners' equity, start of year: $120,000 − $24,000 =   96,000
  Increase in owners' equity during the year......$ 16,000
Additions and withdrawals by owners:
  Additions............................. $ 6,000
  Dividends............................   24,000
    Net withdrawals...................          18,000
    Net Income............................     $ 34,000

**3–18.** *a)* Since the costs of goods purchased were accumulated in other accounts, the balance in the inventory account must represent the cost of the inventory on hand at the beginning of the year. The $92,000 figure is the cost of the ending inventory. The $12,000 difference therefore represents the amount by which the cost of the ending inventory exceeded the cost of the beginning inventory.

*b)* The full cost of the items purchased includes the cost of delivering them to the company's premises:

Cost of goods purchased = $760,000 + $70,000 = $830,000

Cost of goods sold = $80,000 + 830,000 − $92,000 = $818,000.

**3–21.** *a)* Truck ..................................   4,000
            Cash ..............................          4,000

*b)* Depreciation Expense ...................   640
        Allowance for Depreciation..........          640

*c)* Cash .....................................   1,100
     Allowance for Depreciation..............   1,920
     Loss on Retirement......................    980
        Truck ..............................          4,000

**3–28.** (1) Merchandise Inventory................   5,000
             Notes Payable....................          5,000

(2) Cash ....................................   4,000
        Accounts Receivable ..............          4,000

(3) Accounts Payable .....................   6,000
        Cash ..............................          6,000

(4) Salaries Expense.....................   1,000
        Cash ..........................          1,000

(5) Cash .................................  50,000
        Note Payable.....................         50,000

(6) Accounts Receivable ..................   8,000
        Revenue from Goods Sold .........          8,000
    Cost of Goods Sold....................   6,000
        Merchandise Inventory...........          6,000

(7)  Land ................................. 7,000
        Cash ............................           7,000

(8)  Retained Earnings
        (Dividends Declared)................ 3,000
        Cash ............................           3,000

(9)  Office Supplies Expense..............    60
        Accounts Payable ................             60

(10)  Receivable from Insurance Company..   100
        Cash ............................            100

3–31.  *a)*  To save space, the journal entries are not listed here. They can easily be identified from the numerals in parentheses in the T-accounts below.

*b)*

**Cash**

| Bal. 9/1 | 2,510 | (3) | 4,480 |
|---|---|---|---|
| (1a) | 2,700 | (4) | 5,300 |
| (6) | 2,000 | | |
| (7) | 3,500 | | |

**Accounts Receivable**

| Bal. 9/1 | 3,060 | (7) | 3,500 |
|---|---|---|---|
| (1a) | 9,000 | | |

**Merchandise Inventory**

| Bal. 9/1 | 7,200 | (1b) | 6,700 |
|---|---|---|---|
| (2) | 4,630 | | |

**Equipment**

| Bal. 9/1 | 22,140 | | |
|---|---|---|---|
| (3) | 1,800 | | |

**Depreciation to Date**

| | | Bal. 9/1 | 7,120 |
|---|---|---|---|
| | | (5) | 160 |

**Accounts Payable**

| (4) | 5,300 | Bal. 9/1 | 5,180 |
|---|---|---|---|
| | | (2) | 4,630 |

**Salaries Payable**

| (3) | 140 | Bal. 9/1 | 140 |
|---|---|---|---|

**T. Square, Proprietor**

| | | Bal. 9/1 | 22,470 |
|---|---|---|---|
| | | (6) | 2,000 |

**Sales**

| | | (1a) | 11,700 |
|---|---|---|---|

**Cost of Goods Sold**

| (1b) | 6,700 | | |
|---|---|---|---|

**Salaries Expense**

| (3) | 1,340 | | |
|---|---|---|---|

**Rent Expense**

| (3) | 500 | | |
|---|---|---|---|

**Depreciation Expense**

| (5) | 160 | | |
|---|---|---|---|

**Other Expenses**

| (3) | 700 | | |
|---|---|---|---|

*c)*
### Handyman Tool Shop
### INCOME STATEMENT
#### For the Month of September, 19xx

| | | |
|---|---:|---:|
| Sales............................................ | | $11,700 |
| Less: Cost of goods sold................... | | 6,700 |
| Gross margin ............................. | | $ 5,000 |
| Less: Salaries............................. | $ 1,340 | |
| Rent ................................ | 500 | |
| Depreciation........................ | 160 | |
| Other expenses ..................... | 700 | 2,700 |
| Net Income............................. | | $ 2,300 |

### RECONCILIATION OF OWNER'S EQUITY

| | |
|---|---:|
| Owner's equity, August 31 ..... | $22,470 |
| Net income for the month...... | 2,300 |
| Additional investment.......... | 2,000 |
| Owner's equity, September 30.. | $26,770 |

### Handyman Tool Shop
### STATEMENT OF FINANCIAL POSITION
#### September 30, 19xx

| ASSETS | | LIABILITIES AND OWNERS' EQUITY | |
|---|---:|---|---:|
| *Current Assets:* | | *Current Liabilities:* | |
| Cash .......................... | $    930 | Accounts payable ... | $  4,510 |
| Accounts receivable .......... | 8,560 | | |
| Merchandise inventory ........ | 5,130 | *Owner's Equity:* | |
| Total Current Assets....... | $14,620 | T. Square, Proprietor | 26,770 |
| *Fixed Assets:* | | | |
| Equipment ................... | $23,940 | | |
| Less accumulated depreciation | 7,280 | | |
| Total Fixed Assets........ | $16,660 | | |
| Total ................... | $31,280 | Total ......... | $31,280 |

## Chapter 4

| | | |
|---|---|---:|
| 4–13. | Materials and Supplies.................... | 60,000 |
| | Accounts Payable.................... | |
| | | 60,000 |
| | Work in Process......................... | 80,000 |
| | Wages Payable, etc.................. | |
| | | 80,000 |
| | Work in Process......................... | 55,000 |
| | Materials and Supplies............... | |
| | | 55,000 |
| | Work in Process......................... | 30,000 |
| | Accounts Payable, etc................. | |
| | | 30,000 |
| | Finished Goods .......................... | 175,000 |
| | Work in Process...................... | |
| | | 175,000 |
| | Cost of Goods Sold ....................... | 167,000 |
| | Finished Goods ...................... | |
| | | 167,000 |

4–16.  (1)  Raw Materials Inventory.............    35,000
                  Accounts Payable................          35,000
             To record purchase of raw materials
             during April.

       (2)  Work in Process......................    48,400
                  Raw Materials ..................          48,400
             To record transfer of raw materials
             to work in process during April.

       (3)  Work in Process......................    26,000
                  Wages Payable..................          26,000
             To charge labor costs to April
             production.

       (4)  Work in Process......................    15,600
                  Accounts Payable, etc. ...........          15,600
             To record other factory costs for
             April; some of the credits, of course,
             would be to such accounts as Al-
             lowance for Depreciation or Sup-
             plies Inventory, but that informa-
             tion is not provided in this problem.

       (5)  Finished Goods...................... 109,000
                  Work in Process.................         109,000
             To record the cost of goods finished
             in April.

       (6)  Cost of Goods Sold ...................    97,000
                  Finished Goods..................          97,000
             To record the cost of goods sold dur-
             ing April.


4–17.  a)  Beginning receivables + sales − collections
                                      = ending receivables
              $80,000 + $500,000 − Collections = $100,000
                    Collections = $480,000
       b)  Beginning inventory + purchases − cost of goods sold
                                      = ending inventory
              $60,000 + Purchases − $300,000 = $70,000
                    Purchases = $310,000
       c)  Beginning payables + purchases + other expenses − payments
                                      = ending payables
              $50,000 + $310,000 + $100,000 − payments = $30,000
                    Payments = $430,000

       d)  Collections from customers ......................  $480,000
           Payments to suppliers, employees, and others .....   430,000
                  Cash provided by operations ...............  $ 50,000

*e)* To answer this, several more calculations are necessary:
  (1) Ending retained earnings = beginning retained earnings
      + net income − dividends
      $220,000 = $150,000 + $80,000 − Dividends
      Dividends = $10,000
  (2) Capital stock increased by $30,000.
  (3) The original cost of plant and equipment on hand increased by $60,000; the change in accumulated depreciation was equal to depreciation for the year, indicating that no plant and equipment was retired during the year. Therefore, plant and equipment purchases amounted to $60,000.

All of this can be summarized as follows:

Sources of cash:
Operations.............................. $50,000
Sale of stock........................... 30,000
    Total sources of cash .............. $80,000
Uses of cash:
Purchase of plant and equipment....... $60,000
Dividends............................. 10,000
    Total uses of cash.................. 70,000
Increase in cash balance................ $10,000

## Chapter 5

5-14. *a)* Accounts Receivable.................. 500,000
          Sales Revenues .................... 500,000

      Estimated Customer Defaults......... 5,000
          Allowance for Uncollectible
              Accounts...................... 5,000

      Cash................................. 510,000
          Accounts Receivable.............. 510,000

      Allowance for Uncollectible Accounts. 8,000
          Accounts Receivable.............. 8,000

  *b)* Accounts receivable, gross........................ $932,000
       Less: Allowance for uncollectibles .............. 22,000
       Accounts receivable, net......................... $910,000

  *c)* Customer defaults should be reported at $5,000 unless the company has evidence that its previous estimates were incorrect. The $8,000 write-off this month was the result of sales in previous months and was included in expense when these sales were made.

**5–15.**

Portion Estimated Uncollectible

| | | | |
|---|---|---|---|
| More than 60 days ........ | $     511 at | 100% | $   511 |
| 46–60 days............... | 12,552 at | 4 | 502 |
| 31–45 days............... | 52,110 at | 1 | 521 |
| 0–30 days............... | 283,615 at | 0.2 | 567 |
| Total................. | | | $2,101 |

This indicates that the balance in the Allowance for Uncollectible Accounts is $285 too low. The entry to correct the understatement is:

Estimated Customer Defaults................... 285
    Allowance for Uncollectible Accounts.......        285

**5–18.** *a)*  (1)  Accounts Receivable.......... 3,000,000
                    Sales Revenue............            3,000,000

(2)  Cash ........................ 2,800,000
        Accounts Receivable......            2,800,000

(3)  Product Guarantee Expense ..  60,000
        Liability under Product
            Guarantee.............            60,000
    (This recognizes an increase
    in the liability and a decrease
    in the owners' equity.)

(4)  Liability under Product
        Guarantee.................  53,000
        Cash ....................            53,000
    (This recognizes the use of an
    asset, cash, to eliminate a lia-
    bility, the obligation to correct
    product defects.)

*b)*

Liability under Product Guarantee

| | | | |
|---|---|---|---|
| (4) | 53,000 | Bal. 1/1 | 25,000 |
| | | (3) | 60,000 |
| | | Bal. 32,000 | |

The $32,000 ending balance in this account measures the estimated cost of meeting the company's obligations to correct defects in products it has already delivered to its customers.

**5–20.** *a)*  (1)  The profit on a unit is $25 − $12 − $6 = $7.
        (2)  The inventory would be shown at sale price less future selling costs, $25 − $6 = $19.
        (3)  Cash would be decreased by the amount of the manufacturing cost, $12.
        (4)  Owners' equity would increase by the amount of the

profit, $7, and this increase would be recognized when the unit is produced.

b)

|  | First Year | Second Year |
|---|---|---|
| Revenue | $1,500,000 | $1,875,000 |
| Cost of goods sold | $ 720,000 | $ 900,000 |
| Selling expense | 360,000 | 450,000 |
| Administrative expense | 200,000 | 200,000 |
| Net Income | $ 220,000 | $ 325,000 |

# Chapter 6

6-13.  (1)
| | | |
|---|---|---|
| Office Salaries Expense | 10,000 | |
| Sales Salaries Expense | 20,000 | |
| Warehouse Salaries Expense | 12,000 | |
| Income Tax Withheld | | 6,200 |
| F.I.C.A. Tax Payable | | 2,100 |
| Insurance Premiums Payable | | 956 |
| Cash | | 32,744 |

(2)
| | | |
|---|---|---|
| Office Payroll Tax Expense | 800 | |
| Sales Payroll Tax Expense | 1,600 | |
| Warehouse Payroll Tax Expense | 960 | |
| F.I.C.A. Tax Payable | | 2,100 |
| Unemployment Taxes Payable | | 1,260 |

6-17.  a)

PACIFIC

| Feb. 12 | Inventory | 1,000 | |
|---|---|---|---|
| | Accounts Payable | | 1,000 |
| Feb. 14 | Accounts Receivable | 600 | |
| | Revenue from Goods Sold | | 600 |
| | Cost of Goods Sold | 500 | |
| | Inventory | | 500 |
| Feb. 16 | Inventory | 150 | |
| | Loss from Damaged Merchandise | 100 | |
| | Cost of Goods Sold | | 250 |
| | Sales Returns (or Revenue from Goods Sold) | 300 | |
| | Accounts Receivable | | 300 |
| Feb. 23 | Accounts Payable | 100 | |
| | Loss from Damaged Merchandise | | 100 |
| | Accounts Payable | 900 | |
| | Purchases Discounts | | 18 |
| | Cash | | 882 |
| Feb. 28 | Cash | 300 | |
| | Accounts Receivable | | 300 |

JONES

| | | | |
|---|---|---|---|
| Feb. 14 | Inventory............................ | 600 | |
| | Accounts Payable ............. | | 600 |
| Feb. 16 | Accounts Payable ................ | 300 | |
| | Inventory...................... | | 300 |
| Feb. 28 | Accounts Payable ................ | 300 | |
| | Cash ......................... | | 300 |

b) Pacific's inventory is overstated by the amounts of discounts applicable to goods on hand on February 28. Its accounts receivable and accounts payable may also be overstated if both Pacific and its customers typically take the discounts that are available. Whether income statements are correct will depend on whether purchases equal goods sold and sales equal collections from customers. An adjustment for discounts available on accounts outstanding at month-end presumably should be made for the sake of accuracy if the effect is material. Similar comments could be applied to Jones Electric.

## Chapter 7

7–11. a) Wages paid in February................................. $4,200
Less: Amounts earned in January but included in wages
    paid in February :................................. 300
                                                        $3,900
Add: Amounts earned in February but not to be paid until
    March............................................ 500
        Total wages expense............................. $4,400

b) Accrued wages payable, February 28 = $500

| | | | |
|---|---|---|---|
| 7–12. | Sept. 15 | Cash ............................ 6,000 | |
| | | Note Payable................. | 6,000 |
| | Nov. 14 | Interest Expense ................. | 60 |
| | | Cash ......................... | 60 |
| | Dec. 14 | Interest Expense ................. | 30 |
| | | Interest Payable.............. | 30 |
| | | To accrue interest. | |

| | | | |
|---|---|---|---|
| | | Notes Payable.................... 4,000 | |
| | | Cash ........................ | 4,000 |
| | | To record repayment of loan. | |

| | | | |
|---|---|---|---|
| | | Notes Payable.................... 2,000 | |
| | | Interest Payable.................. 30 | |
| | | Note Payable................. | 2,030 |
| | | To record refinancing of note. | |

| | | | |
|---|---|---|---|
| | Dec. 31 | Interest Expense ................. 5.75 | |
| | | Interest Payable ............. | 5.75 |
| | | To accrue interest for 17 days . | |

**7–17.**

James Dandy Sales Company

## INCOME STATEMENT AND STATEMENT OF
## CHANGES IN RETAINED EARNINGS

For the Year Ended December 31, 19x3

| | | |
|---|---:|---:|
| Sales........................................ | | $700,000 |
| Less: Returns and allowances............ | | 14,000 |
| Net sales ................................. | | $686,000 |
| Less: Cost of goods sold.................. | | 480,000 |
| Gross margin ............................. | | $206,000 |
| Less: Operating expenses: | | |
| Wages and salaries ...................... | $100,000 | |
| Rent expense ........................... | 22,000 | |
| Office supplies used...................... | 5,000 | |
| Insurance expired........................ | 1,000 | |
| Depreciation............................. | 21,000 | |
| Income taxes ........................... | 3,000 | |
| Interest expense ......................... | 4,000 | |
| Other expenses ......................... | 9,000 | |
| Fire loss* .............................. | 34,000 | 199,000 |
| Net income ............................... | | $    7,000 |
| Add: Retained earnings, January 1........ | | 48,000 |
| Refund of prior years' income taxes... | | 8,000 |
| | | $ 63,000 |
| Less: Dividends declared.................. | | 3,000 |
| Retained Earnings, December 31 ........... | | $ 60,000 |

\* Note: Although the fire loss was very large, it probably would not be classified as an extraordinary item because the firm is always exposed to the risk of fire damage. The tax refund was credited directly to Retained Earnings because it arose entirely from the events of a previous year.

## STATEMENT OF FINANCIAL POSITION
December 31, 19x3

| | | |
|---|---:|---:|
| *Current Assets:*   ASSETS | | |
| Cash .............................. | | $ 20,000 |
| Accounts receivable .................. | $ 50,000 | |
| Less: Allowance for bad debts...... | 1,000 | 49,000 |
| Inventories.......................... | | 80,000 |
| Prepaid insurance.................... | | 2,000 |
| Total Current Assets.............. | | $151,000 |
| *Long-Term Assets:* | | |
| Furniture and fixtures................ | $200,000 | |
| Less: Allowance for depreciation ..... | 62,000 | |
| Total Long-Term Assets .......... | | 138,000 |
| Total Assets .................... | | $289,000 |

LIABILITIES AND STOCKHOLDERS' EQUITY

| | | |
|---|---:|---:|
| *Current Liabilities:* | | |
| Accounts payable..................... | | $ 70,000 |
| Accrued wages ....................... | | 2,000 |
| Taxes payable........................ | | 4,000 |
| Notes payable ....................... | | 30,000 |
| Total Current Liabilities.......... | | $106,000 |
| Mortgage payable ...................... | | 50,000 |
| Total Liabilities ................ | | $156,000 |
| *Stockholders' Equity:* | | |
| Capital stock ........................ | $ 73,000 | |
| Retained earnings.................... | 60,000 | |
| Total Stockholders' Equity........ | | 133,000 |
| Total Liabilities and Stock- | | |
| holders' Equity .............. | | $289,000 |

7-23.  *a*)  T-accounts take up more space than we have available here. The same information can be shown more compactly by placing the unadjusted balances in one pair of columns, entering the adjustments in a second pair of columns, and listing the ending balances in a third pair of columns, as follows:

| Accounts | Unadjusted Trial Balance | | Adjustments | | Adjusted Trial Balance | |
|---|---|---|---|---|---|---|
| | Dr. | Cr. | Dr. | Cr. | Dr. | Cr. |
| Cash...................... | 56,000 | | | | 56,000 | |
| Accounts receivable....... | 170,000 | | | | 170,000 | |
| Inventory ................ | 525,000 | | | (5)300,000 | 225,000 | |
| Furniture and fixtures .... | 200,000 | | | | 200,000 | |
| Allowance for depreciation | | 125,000 | | (1) 24,000 | | 149,000 |
| Prepaid insurance........ | 2,000 | | | (2)    800 | 1,200 | |
| Prepaid rent ............. | 1,000 | | | (3)  1,000 | | |
| Accounts payable ........ | | 100,000 | | | | 100,000 |
| Wages payable........... | | | | (4)  4,000 | | 4,000 |
| Capital stock............. | | 200,000 | | | | 200,000 |
| Retained earnings........ | | 117,000 | | | | 117,000 |
| Sales.................... | | 500,000 | | | | 500,000 |
| Wage expense........... | 20,000 | | (4)   4,000 | | 24,000 | |
| Rent expense ............ | 11,000 | | (3)   1,000 | | 12,000 | |
| Depreciation expense ..... | | | (1) 24,000 | | 24,000 | |
| Miscellaneous expenses... | 55,000 | | (2)    800 | | 55,800 | |
| Cost of goods sold........ | | | (5)300,000 | | 300,000 | |
| Dividends declared........ | 2,000 | | | | 2,000 | |
| Total.............. | 1,042,000 | 1,042,000 | 329,800 | 329,800 | 1,070,000 | 1,070,000 |

*b*)

**Robant Hardware Company**

**INCOME STATEMENT AND RECONCILIATION OF**

**RETAINED EARNINGS**

**For the Year Ended December 31**

| | | |
|---|---|---|
| Sales ................................... | | $500,000 |
| Cost of goods sold....................... | | 300,000 |
| Gross margin ........................... | | $200,000 |
| Less: Wage expense .................... | $24,000 | |
| Rent expense ..................... | 12,000 | |
| Depreciation expense............. | 24,000 | |
| Miscellaneous expense............. | 55,800 | 115,800 |
| Net income............................ | | $ 84,200 |
| Retained earnings, January 1............ | | 117,000 |
| | | $201,200 |
| Less: Dividends declared ............... | | 2,000 |
| Retained Earnings, December 31 ........ | | $199,200 |

## Robant Hardware Company
### STATEMENT OF FINANCIAL POSITION
#### December 31

| ASSETS | | | LIABILITIES AND STOCKHOLDERS' EQUITY | | |
|---|---|---|---|---|---|
| *Current assets:* | | | *Current liabilities:* | | |
| Cash................ | | $ 56,000 | Accounts payable... | | $100,000 |
| Accounts receivable | | 170,000 | Wages payable ..... | | 4,000 |
| Inventory........... | | 225,000 | Total current | | |
| Prepaid insurance... | | 1,200 | liabilities..... | | $104,000 |
| Total current | | | *Stockholders' equity:* | | |
| assets......... | | $452,200 | Capital stock..... | $200,000 | |
| *Long-life assets:* | | | Retained earnings | 203,200 | |
| Furn. & fixtures .... | $200,000 | | Total.......... | | 399,200 |
| Accum. depreciation | 149,000 | 51,000 | Total Liabili- | | |
| | | | ties and Stock- | | |
| Total Assets .... | | $503,200 | holders' Equity | | $503,200 |

7–24.  Again a columnar worksheet is provided here instead of T-accounts, for the reasons set forth in the solution to problem 7–23.

| Accounts | Trial Balance Dec. 31, 19x3 | | Adjustments | | | | Adjusted Trial Balance | |
|---|---|---|---|---|---|---|---|---|
| Cash.......................... | 28,800 | | | | | | 28,800 | |
| Temporary investments......... | 17,700 | | | | | | 17,700 | |
| Accounts receivable............ | 91,600 | | | | (7) | 890 | 90,710 | |
| Allowance for uncollectible | | | | | | | | |
| accounts.................... | | 1,500 | | | (8) | 650 | | 2,150 |
| Inventory of merchandise....... | 89,000 | | (5) | 344,500 | (5) | 347,060 | 87,415 | |
| | | | (6) | 975 | | | | |
| Prepaid insurance.............. | 1,900 | | | | (2) | 175 | 1,725 | |
| Other prepaid expense ......... | 1,340 | | | | | | 1,340 | |
| Land.......................... | 16,000 | | | | | | 16,000 | |
| Bldg. and equipment........... | 45,800 | | | | | | 45,800 | |
| Allowance for depreciation, | | | | | | | | |
| building and equipment....... | | 8,100 | | | (4) | 1,240 | | 9,340 |
| Accounts payable .............. | | 18,800 | | | (6) | 975 | | 19,775 |
| Mortgage on real estate ........ | | 45,000 | | | | | | 45,000 |
| Capital stock.................. | | 150,000 | | | | | | 150,000 |
| Retained earnings.............. | | 53,720 | | | | | | 53,720 |
| Sales.......................... | | 412,000 | | | | | | 412,000 |
| Sales discounts, returns | | | | | | | | |
| and allowances .............. | 12,000 | | (7) | 890 | | | 12,890 | |
| Estimated customer defaults.... | 2,100 | | (8) | 650 | | | 2,750 | |
| Interest income ................ | | 480 | | | | | | 480 |
| Purchases...................... | 344,500 | | | | (5) | 344,500 | | |
| Advertising :................... | 1,200 | | | | | | 1,200 | |
| Salaries and wages............. | 16,400 | | (3) | 240 | | | 16,640 | |
| Miscellaneous selling expense... | 5,800 | | | | | | 5,800 | |
| Property taxes................. | 3,300 | | | | | | 3,300 | |
| Insurance expense ............. | 525 | | (2) | 175 | | | 700 | |
| Miscellaneous general expense.. | 8,435 | | | | | | 8,435 | |
| Interest expense ............... | 3,200 | | (1) | 400 | | | 3,600 | |
| Accrued interest payable........ | | | | | (1) | 400 | | 400 |
| Accrued wages payable ......... | | | | | (3) | 240 | | 240 |
| Depreciation expense .......... | | | (4) | 1,240 | | | 1,240 | |
| Cost of goods sold ............. | | | (5) | 347,060 | | | 347,060 | |
| Total..................... | 689,600 | 689,600 | | 696,130 | | 696,130 | 693,105 | 693,105 |

### The Guyton Company
## INCOME STATEMENT
### For the Year Ended December 31, 19x3

| | | |
|---|---:|---:|
| Sales revenues | | $412,000 |
| Less: Discounts, returns, and allowances | $ 12,890 | |
| Estimated customer defaults | 2,750 | 15,640 |
| Net sales revenues | | $396,360 |
| Interest income | | 480 |
| Total revenue | | $396,840 |
| Expenses: | | |
| Cost of goods sold | $347,060 | |
| Salaries and wages | 16,640 | |
| Advertising | 1,200 | |
| Miscellaneous selling expense | 5,800 | |
| Insurance | 700 | |
| Depreciation | 1,240 | |
| Property taxes | 3,300 | |
| Miscellaneous general expenses | 8,435 | |
| Interest expense | 3,600 | 387,975 |
| Net Income | | $   8,865 |

### The Guyton Company
## STATEMENT OF FINANCIAL POSITION
### December 31, 19x3

#### ASSETS

| | | |
|---|---:|---:|
| *Current Assets:* | | |
| Cash | | $ 28,800 |
| Temporary investments | | 17,700 |
| Accounts receivable (net) | | 88,560 |
| Inventory of merchandise | | 87,415 |
| Prepaid insurance | | 1,725 |
| Other prepaid expenses | | 1,340 |
| Total Current Assets | | $225,540 |
| *Fixed Assets:* | | |
| Land | | 16,000 |
| Building and equipment | $ 45,800 | |
| Less: Allowance for depreciation | 9,340 | 36,460 |
| Total Assets | | $278,000 |

#### LIABILITIES AND STOCKHOLDERS' EQUITY

| | | |
|---|---:|---:|
| *Current Liabilities:* | | |
| Accounts payable | | $ 19,775 |
| Accrued interest payable | | 400 |
| Accrued wages payable | | 240 |
| Total Current Liabilities | | $ 20,415 |
| Mortgage on real estate | | 45,000 |
| Total Liabilities | | $ 65,415 |
| *Stockholders' Equity:* | | |
| Capital stock | $150,000 | |
| Retained earnings | 62,585 | |
| Total Stockholders' Equity | | 212,585 |
| Total Liabilities and Stockholders' Equity | | $278,000 |

## Chapter 8

8–18.  *a)*  Amount of sales billed is posted as a credit to Sales *and* as a debit to Accounts Receivable. Individual postings will also be made to the subsidiary customers' accounts. Amount of cost of goods sold is posted as a credit to Inventory *and* as a debit to Cost of Goods Sold.

   *b)*  Accounts Receivable certainly and Inventory probably.

8–21.  *a)*  The store should keep a petty cash book of some sort and should maintain a petty cash voucher system so that the fund will contain a given amount in some combination of cash and vouchers at all times.

   *b)*  Petty Cash ..................................... 300
          Cash ...................................... 300

   *c)*  Labor Expense (items No. 1 and 6)............ 124
          Miscellaneous General Expense
           (items No. 2, 3, 4, 5, and 7)................. 91
             Cash ...................................... 215
          The expenses may actually be accounted for
          in greater detail.

8–25.  (1)  (S) Accounts Receivable (John Jones)..... 1,000
                  Revenue from Sales .............. 1,000
             NOTE: If recorded at net price, the
             amount is $980.

   (2)  (VR) Delivery Equipment ................. 2,700
                  Vouchers Payable
                   (Speedy Motor Co.).............. 2,700

   (3)  (CR) Cash............................... 750
                  Revenue from Cash Sales........ 750
             NOTE: If it is desired to have a complete
             record of sales in the sales register, there
             would also be an additional entry of:
             (S) Revenue from Cash Sales ............. 750
                  Revenue from Sales .............. 750

   (4)  (CR) Cash............................... 980
             Sales Discounts..................... 20
                  Accounts Receivable (John Jones) 1,000

   (5)  (VR) Advertising Expense................. 100
             Prepaid Advertising.................. 80
                  Vouchers Payable (Texas Bugle). 180

        (CD) Vouchers Payable (Texas Bugle)..... 180
                  Cash............................ 180

(6)  (J) Depreciation Expense................    100
      Allowance for Depreciation,
      Delivery Equipment ..............    100

(7)  (J) Sales Salaries and Wages Expense.....    250
      Office Salaries and Wages Expense ....    200
      Accrued Wages Payable ...........    450

## Chapter 9

9–17.  *a*)  Return on assets $= \dfrac{\text{Earnings Before Interest and Taxes (EBIT)}}{\text{Total Assets}}$

Because this equation contains two unknowns, we must start by deriving one of them.

Return on common equity $= \dfrac{(\text{EBIT} - \text{Interest}) \times (1 - \text{tax rate})}{\text{Common Equity}}$

Again we have two unknowns, but we know that the common equity equals total assets minus total liabilities and that liabilities are 25 percent of the common equity. Putting these together, we find that:

Common equity = $100,000/1.25 = $80,000.

This permits the calculation of EBIT:

$$7.2\% = \frac{\text{EBIT} - \$2,000}{\$80,000} \times 0.55$$

EBIT = $10,473 + $2,000 = $12,473.

Return on assets (before taxes) = $12,473/$100,000 = 12.47%.
Return on assets (after taxes) = 12.47% × (1 − .45) = 6.86%.

*b*)  Since the after-tax return on assets is less than the return on common equity, the use of leverage succeeded in increasing the rate of return on the common equity.

|  | | *19x3* | *19x4* | *19x5* | *19x6* |
|---|---|---|---|---|---|
| 9–20. | *a*) Number of shares (000) ..... | 50,000 | 50,000 | 52,000 | 52,000 |
| | Earnings available for common stock (000) .......... | | $96,000 | $101,300 | $99,100 |
| | Earnings per share ......... | | $1.92 | $1.95 | $1.91 |
| | *b*) Book value per share ........ | $16.60 | $17.52 | $18.60 | $19.50 |
| | *c*) Average common equity (000) | | $853,000 | $921,650 | $990,850 |
| | Return on common equity ... | | 11.3% | 11.0% | 10.0% |

| | *Where Got* | *Where Gone* |
|---|---|---|
| 9–22. | | |
| From operations ........................ | $ 7,500 | |
| From long-term debt..................... | 10,000 | |
| From capital stock...................... | 5,000 | |
| To increase current assets .............. | | $ 9,000 |
| To acquire buildings and equipment ..... | | 8,500 |
| To acquire land.......................... | | 2,000 |
| To reduce current liabilities.............. | | 3,000 |
| Total................................ | $22,500 | $22,500 |

## Chapter 10

**10–19.** This an annuity in arrears:
$$F = \text{multiplier} \times A$$
The unknown is the amount of the annuity:
$$A = F/\text{multiplier}$$
$$= \$1,000,000/14.4866 = \$69,029.31$$

**10–20.** *a*)

| | |
|---|---:|
| Present value of outlay ........................... | −$ 35,000 |
| Present value of receipts: 0.322 × $100,000 = | + 32,200 |
| Net Present Value ........................... | −$ 2,800 |

*b*)

| | |
|---|---:|
| Present value of 1/1/75 outlay..................... | −$ 80,000 |
| Present value of 1/1/80 outlay: 0.567 × $20,000 = | − 11,340 |
| Present value of receipt of $10,000 per period for six periods: 4.111 × $10,000 = | + 41,110 |
| Present value of receipt of $20,000 per period for 10 periods starting six periods hence: (6.974 − 4.111) × $20,000 = | + 57,260 |
| Net Present Value ........................... | +$ 7,030 |

*c*)

| | |
|---|---:|
| Present value of outlay of $20,000 per period for 11 periods (annuity in advance): (5.650 + 1.000) × $20,000 = | −$133,000 |
| Present value of receipt of $250,000 at end of 12 periods: 0.257 × $250,000 = | + 64,250 |
| Net Present Value............................ | −$ 68,750 |

**10–21.** The key here is to find a 7-year annuity in advance that will have the same present value as a 5-year annuity in arrears which starts in year 4:

Present value of 5-year annuity =
$$(5.7466 − 2.5771) \times \$4,000 = \$12,678$$
Present value of 7-year annuity = $(4.6229 + 1.0000) \times$ Annuity
$$\text{Annuity} = \$12,678/5.6229 = \$2,255.$$

This can be checked by calculating the amount of interest accrued on the amount invested, and deducting the amounts repaid:

| Year | Cash Flow Before Interest | Amount Invested After Cash Flow | Interest @ 8% | Amount Invested One Year Later |
|---|---|---:|---:|---:|
| 0 | −2,255 | 2,255 | 180 | 2,435 |
| 1 | −2,255 | 4,690 | 375 | 5,065 |
| 2 | −2,255 | 7,320 | 586 | 7,906 |
| 3 | −2,255 | 10,161 | 813 | 10,974 |
| 4 | −2,255 + 4,000 {= +1,745} | 9,229 | 738 | 9,967 |
| 5 | +1,745 | 8,222 | 658 | 8,880 |
| 6 | +1,745 | 7,135 | 571 | 7,706 |
| 7 | +4,000 | 3,706 | 296 | 4,002 |
| 8 | +4,000 | 2* | 0 | 0 |

\* Rounding error.

The amounts invested, with interest, are just adequate to cover the five payments of $4,000 each.

**10-24.**   Future value = 36.7856 × Annuity = $100,000
Annuity = $100,000/36.7856 = $2,718.18

**10-27.**   The key to a solution of this problem lies in recognizing when the last payment will be made: 16 years from now, not 17 years from now. Once this has been realized, the solution can be obtained in a variety of equivalent ways.

Simplest approach:

| | |
|---|---|
| 16-year annuity factor (Table 4) ................ | 10.1059 |
| 6-year annuity factor (Table 4) ................ | 4.9173 |
| Annuity factor for years 7–16 ............... | 5.1886 |

Purchase price: $15,000 × 5.1886 = $77,829.

This leaves $22,171 for Mr. Hastings to spend.
Alternative: add interest factors (Table 3) for years 7–16
(= 5.1886).

Second alternative:

| | |
|---|---|
| 10-year annuity factor (Table 4)................ | 7.3601 |
| 6-year* present value factor (Table 3).......... | × .7050 |
| Annuity factor for years 7–16 .............. | 5.1889 |

* The 6-year figure is used because the 10-year annuity is an annuity in arrears. The present value of a 10-year annuity in arrears is as of a date one year before the first annuity payment—i.e., 6 years from zero date. The difference between 5.1889 and the factors derived above is due to rounding errors in the interest tables.

**10-34.**  *a)*

| Year | Cash Flow | Multiplier (Table 3) | Present Value |
|---|---|---|---|
| 1 .......... | $100,000 | .9434 | $ 94,340 |
| 2 .......... | 180,000 | .8900 | 160,200 |
| Total ......... | | | $254,540 |

*b)*

| | | | |
|---|---|---|---|
| 0 .......... | $100,000 | 1.0000 | $100,000 |
| 1 .......... | 180,000 | .9434 | 169,812 |
| Total ......... | | | $269,812 |

*c)*   Income = $269,812 − $254,540 = $15,272.
(This can also be obtained by taking 6% of $254,540 = $15,272.)

*d)*

| | |
|---|---|
| Present value, end of year 2 ........................... | $180,000 |
| Present value, beginning of year 2...................... | 169,812 |
| Income, Year 2 ...................................... | $ 10,188 |

# Chapter 11

**11-15.**  *a)*  Fifo inventory:

| | | | |
|---|---|---|---|
| 200 @ | $41.70 | = | $ 8,340 |
| 400 @ | 41.60 | = | 16,640 |
| 300 @ | 41.60 | = | 12,480 |
| 200 @ | 41.55 | = | 8,310 |
| 1,100 | | | $45,770 |

Lifo inventory (the year is the accounting period):

$$1,000 \text{ @ } \$41.00 = \$41,000$$
$$\underline{\phantom{1,}100} \text{ @ } \phantom{0}41.20 = \underline{\phantom{00}4,120}$$
$$1,000 \qquad\qquad \$45,120$$

b)  Assuming that Lifo was adopted at the start of the year, the opening inventory is the same under both methods, 1,000 @ $41. The Fifo reported earnings therefore are $650 greater than the Lifo earnings, the amount by which the closing Fifo inventory is greater than the closing Lifo inventory.

11–16.  a)

| | | |
|---|---|---|
| Beginning inventory: 1,600 @ $10 . . . . . . . | | $16,000 |
| Plus: Purchases . . . . . . . . . . . . . . . . . . . . . . . . | | 32,100 |
| Total Available . . . . . . . . . . . . . . . . . . . . . . | | $48,100 |
| Less: Ending inventory: | | |
| 1,400 @ $12 . . . . . . . | $16,800 | |
| 500 @ 13 . . . . . . . | 6,500 | 23,300 |
| Cost of Goods Sold . . . . . . . . . . . . . . . . . . . | | $24,800 |

b)  Moving weighted average method:

| Date | Receipts | Issues | Balances |
|---|---|---|---|
| 1 | | | 1,600 at $10.00 = $16,000 |
| 3 | | 900 at $10.00 = $ 9,000 | 700 at 10.00 = 7,000 |
| 5 | 800 at $11.00 = $ 8,800 | | 1,500 at 10.53 = 15,800 |
| 10 | | 800 at 10.53 = 8,427 | 700 at 10.53 = 7,373 |
| 20 | 500 at 13.00 = 6,500 | | 1,200 at 11.56 = 13,873 |
| 23 | | 700 at 11.56 = 8,093 | 500 at 11.56 = 5,780 |
| 31 | 1,400 at 12.00 = 16,800 | | 1,900 at 11.88 = 22,580 |
| | Total Cost of Goods Sold . . . . . . . . . . . . . . . . . . . . | $25,520 | |

c)  Market value is $12.

Ending inventory: 1,900 @ $12. . . . . . . . . . . . . . . $22,800
Cost of goods sold: $48,100 − $22,800 . . . . . . . . $25,300

11–17.  a)

| Year | Lifo Cost of Goods Sold | Lifo Ending Inventory |
|---|---|---|
| 19x1 | 55,000 × $3.10 = $170,500 | 10,000 × $3.00 = $ 30,000 |
| | | 5,000 × 3.10 = 15,500 |
| | | $ 45,500 |
| 19x2 | 68,000 × $3.50 = $238,000 | 10,000 × $3.00 = $ 30,000 |
| | | 5,000 × 3.10 = 15,500 |
| | | 2,000 × 3.50 = 7,000 |
| | | $ 52,500 |
| 19x3 | 80,000 × $3.75 = $300,000 | 10,000 × $3.00 = $ 30,000 |
| | | 5,000 × 3.10 = 15,500 |
| | | 2,000 × 3.50 = 7,000 |
| | | 10,000 × 3.75 = 37,500 |
| | | $ 90,000 |
| 19x4 | 70,000 × $3.80 = $266,000 | 10,000 × $3.00 = $ 30,000 |
| | 2,000 × $3.75 = 7,500 | 5,000 × 3.10 = 15,500 |
| | $273,500 | 2,000 × 3.50 = 7,000 |
| | | 8,000 × 3.75 = 30,000 |
| | | $ 82,500 |

| Year | Lifo Cost of Goods Sold | Lifo Ending Inventory |
|---|---|---|
| 19x5 | 75,000 × $4.00 = $300,000 | 10,000 × $3.00 = $ 30,000 |
| | | 5,000 × 3.10 = 15,500 |
| | | 2,000 × 3.50 = 7,000 |
| | | 8,000 × 3.75 = 30,000 |
| | | 5,000 × 4.00 = 20,000 |
| | | $102,500 |
| 19x6 | 70,000 × $4.25 = $297,500 | 10,000 × $3.00 = $ 30,000 |
| | 5,000 × 4.00 = 20,000 | 5,000 × 3.10 = 15,500 |
| | 5,000 × 3.75 = 18,750 | 2,000 × 3.50 = 7,000 |
| | $336,250 | 3,000 × 3.75 = 11,250 |
| | | $ 63,750 |
| 19x7 | 85,000 × $4.40 = $374,000 | 10,000 × $3.00 = $ 30,000 |
| | | 5,000 × 3.10 = 15,500 |
| | | 2,000 × 3.50 = 7,000 |
| | | 3,000 × 3.75 = 11,250 |
| | | 15,000 × 4.40 = 66,000 |
| | | $129,750 |
| 19x8 | 95,000 × $4.50 = $427,500 | (same as 19x7) = $129,750 |

b)

| Year | Fifo Cost of Goods Sold | Fifo Ending Inventory |
|---|---|---|
| 19x1 | 10,000 × $3.00 = $ 30,000 | 15,000 × $3.10 = $ 46,500 |
| | 45,000 × 3.10 = 139,500 | |
| | $169,500 | |
| 19x2 | 15,000 × $3.10 = $ 46,500 | 17,000 × $3.50 = $ 59,500 |
| | 53,000 × 3.50 = 185,500 | |
| | $232,000 | |
| 19x3 | 17,000 × $3.50 = $ 59,500 | 27,000 × $3.75 = $101,250 |
| | 63,000 × 3.75 = 236,250 | |
| | $295,750 | |
| 19x4 | 27,000 × $3.75 = $101,250 | 25,000 × $3.80 = $ 95,000 |
| | 45,000 × 3.80 = 171,000 | |
| | $272,250 | |
| 19x5 | 25,000 × $3.80 = $ 95,000 | 30,000 × $4.00 = $120,000 |
| | 50,000 × 4.00 = 200,000 | |
| | $295,000 | |
| 19x6 | 30,000 × $4.00 = $120,000 | 20,000 × $4.25 = $ 85,000 |
| | 50,000 × 4.25 = 212,500 | |
| | $332,500 | |
| 19x7 | 20,000 × $4.25 = $ 85,000 | 35,000 × $4.40 = $154,000 |
| | 65,000 × 4.40 = 286,000 | |
| | $371,000 | |
| 19x8 | 35,000 × $4.40 = $154,000 | 35,000 × $4.50 = $157,500 |
| | 60,000 × 4.50 = 270,000 | |
| | $424,000 | |

c) The difference in the amount of inventory profit in reported income equals the difference betweeen the inventory figures at December 31, 19x8:

Fifo inventory .............................. $157,500
Lifo inventory .............................. 129,750
   Cumulative difference in inventory profit ... $ 27,750

Comparable figures can be calculated for any year by comparing the two Cost of Goods Sold figures for that year.

11–25. *a)*

| Date | Inventory | | Year | Cost of Goods Sold | |
|---|---|---|---|---|---|
| | *Fifo* | *Lifo* | | *Fifo* | *Lifo* |
| January 1, 1972.....$1,875,000 | $1,875,000 | | | | |
| | | | 1972 | $12,175,000 | $12,350,000 |
| December 31, 1972.. 2,700,000 | 2,525,000 | | | | |
| | | | 1973 | 14,600,000 | 14,500,000 |
| December 31, 1973.. 700,000 | 625,000 | | | | |

*b)*  The involuntary liquidation increased reported profit before taxes by $125,000. The liquidation amounted to 15,000 tons, but the first 5,000 of these were liquidated voluntarily. The involuntary part of the liquidation caused the transfer of 10,000 tons at $125 from the Lifo inventory. The effect on reported income was:

10,000 tons at current price of $140 ............. $1,400,000
10,000 tons at inventory price of $125 ........... 1,250,000
   Net Effect on Reported Income ................ $ 150,000

*c)*  The effect is to increase the cost of the inventory by $200,000 over the level that would have prevailed if there had been no involuntary liquidation:

Base quantity, 5,000 tons ....................... $   625,000
1974 layer, 10,000 tons ........................ 1,450,000
   Total ........................................ $2,075,000
Lifo cost of 15,000 tons, 12/31/72 ............... 1,875,000
   Net Effect on Inventory....................... $ 200,000

# Chapter 12

12–17. *a)*  The sum of the years' digits = 55
Depreciation per digit = $16,500/55 = $300
Depreciation schedule:

| Year | Depreciation |
|---|---|
| 1 | 10 × $300 = $3,000 |
| 2 | 9 × $300 = 2,700 |
| 3 | 8 × $300 = 2,400 |
| Total | $8,100 |

*b)*  Straight-line depreciation for 3 years = 3 × $1,650 = $4,950
Adjustment = $8,100 − $4,950 = $3,150
This would be deducted from the balance in Accumulated

Depreciation and would be shown below any extraordinary items on the income statement for the year.

12–22.  a)   Correct depreciation = $2 \times 84\% \times \$200,000/6$......= \$56,000
Actual charges made = $40\% \times \$200,000$ ..........=   80,000
Overstatement.................................= \$24,000

b)   No adjustment would be made. Corrections of estimates are regarded as inevitable; only future charges will be affected. It can be argued, of course, that this will result in understating annual depreciation costs in the future, but the Accounting Principles Board decided that this is likely to be less confusing than the main alternative, restatement of prior years' statements every time a change in an estimate is made.

c)   New depreciation rate:

Depreciation amount: $\$200,000 - \$80,000 - \$32,000$
$= \$88,000$

Annual depreciation = $\$88,000/4 = \$22,000$.

12–24.  a)   19x0   Depreciation Expense ...........   9,000
Allowance for Depreciation..        9,000

19x1   Cash ...........................   1,000
Allowance for Depreciation......   4,000
Equipment .................        5,000
Depreciation ...................   8,550
Allowance for Depreciation..        8,550

19x2   Cash ...........................   3,000
Allowance for Depreciation......   7,000
Equipment .................        10,000
Depreciation ...................   7,650
Allowance for Depreciation..        7,650

b)   19x0   Depreciation Expense ........... 20,000
Allowance for Depreciation..        20,000

19x1   Cash ...........................   1,000
Allowance for Depreciation......   4,000
Equipment .................        5,000
Depreciation Expense ........... 15,800
Allowance for Depreciation..        15,800

19x2   Cash ...........................   3,000
Allowance for Depreciation......   7,000
Equipment .................        10,000
Depreciation Expense ........... 12,040
Allowance for Depreciation..        12,040

## Chapter 13

13–12.  These expenditures are basically in the nature of maintenance, designed to secure the previously anticipated economic life. Although unusual and nonrecurring, they should be reported as expense of the current year.

13–13.  The cost of the shares was 21,600 × $15 = $324,000. This figure is obviously a very poor measure of the amount of resources sacrificed by Experimental Company to obtain the new building in 1967. Instead, the company should have used either the current market value of the stock or the current market value of the building, whichever could have been measured more accurately.

A market price of $105 a share gives an indicated market value of 21,600 × $105 = $2,268,000. A sale of this magnitude might very well have depressed the market price of the Respirator stock, however, so the true market value of the 21,600 shares was probably lower. If the shares were traded actively, the amount of the price reduction would have been quite small; for small companies the reduction is often substantial.

Appraisal values, too, are often inaccurate, but urban building appraisals are usually quite reliable. Capitalization in the neighborhood of $2,000,000 would seem reasonable here. A gain of $2,000,000 − $324,000 = $1,676,000 should be recognized on this transaction.

13–14.  *Asset cost:*

|  | *Each Machine* | *All Machines* |
|---|---|---|
| Purchase price.................... | $16,250 | $ 97,500 |
| Freight .......................... | 700 | 4,200 |
| Handling ....................... | 200 | 1,200 |
| Installation: |  |  |
| Labor......................... | 480 | 2,880 |
| Materials ..................... | 100 | 600 |
| Total..................... | $17,730 | $106,380 |

If the bookkeeping system is loosely designed, the installation materials and perhaps even some of the installation labor might be expensed. In concept, however, they should be capitalized.

13–18.  *a)*  Paper Machine ........................... 6,000
       Cash ................................      6,000

   *b)*  Depreciation Expense ................... 2,875
        Allowance for Depreciation—
          Paper Machine ...................      2,875

The life of the machine has not been extended, and the $6,000 outlay is depreciated over the remaining 16 years of life.

c) Allowance for Depreciation—
Paper Machine...................... 12,000
Cash ............................         12,000

This presumes that the overhaul takes the form of renewal or replacement of component parts; thus a debit to the Paper Machine account would be double-counting.

d)    Asset account: $50,000 + $6,000 =              $56,000
Allowance account:
4 × $2,500 =                          $10,000
12 × $2,875 =                          34,500
Overhaul                              (12,000)    32,500
Book Value .................                    $23,500

$$\text{Depreciation} = \frac{\$23,500}{9} = \$2,611 \text{ a year.}$$

## Chapter 14

14-12. Because payments are semiannual, use 3½ percent rate, 20 six-month periods.

| Periods Hence | Cash Flows | Present Value Factor @ 3½% | Present Value |
|---|---|---|---|
| 1-20 ................ | $4/period | 14.2124 | $ 56.85 |
| 20 ................. | $100 | .5026 | 50.26 |
| Total value ........ | | | $107.11 |

14-15. a) Interest payments: 8% × $1,000 × 10 years .......... = $800.00
Less: amortization of bond premium............... =     34.70
Interest income, Net................................ = $765.30

b) From Table 13, 10-year column, figure of 103.47 is found in 7.5 row. The yield therefore is 7.5 percent.

14-17. a) The face value is $1 million, the payments each year will be $80,000, and the amount paid equals the present value of the future payments when the latter are discounted at 9 percent, or 4½ percent compounded semiannually.

b) $908,000, because the price must be less than the maturity value to produce a yield in excess of the coupon rate.

c) The term is 20 years (the factor of 90.80 is found in the 20-year column, 9.0 percent row, of Table 13).

d) Interest expense = 9%/2 × $908,000 = $40,860.
Entry:

Interest Expense . . . . . . . . . . . . . . . . . . . .  40,860
    Cash . . . . . . . . . . . . . . . . . . . . . . . . . . .            40,000
    Unamortized Bond Discount . . . .               860

e) Principal = \$908,000 + \$860 = \$908,860.
Interest expense = $9\%/2 \times \$908,860 = \$40,899$.
Entry:

Interest Expense . . . . . . . . . . . . . . . . . . . .  40,899
    Cash . . . . . . . . . . . . . . . . . . . . . . . . . . .            40,000
    Unamortized Bond Discount . . . .               899

f) Bonds payable, maturity value . . . . . . . . . . . . . .  \$1,000,000
Less: Unamortized bond discount . . . . . . . . .  90,241
Bonds payable, net . . . . . . . . . . . . . . . . . . . . . . . .  \$ 909,759

14–21. Income calculation:

| | | |
|---|---|---|
| Income before depreciation and taxes . . | | \$6,200,000 |
| Depreciation . . . . . . . . . . . . . . . . . . . . . . . . . . | | 850,000 |
| Income after depreciation . . . . . . . . . . . . . | | \$5,350,000 |
| Income tax: Current . . . . . . . . . . . . . . . . . . | \$2,475,000 | |
| Deferred . . . . . . . . . . . . . . . . . | 200,000 | 2,675,000 |
| Net Income . . . . . . . . . . . . . . . . . . . . . . . | | \$2,675,000 |

Entries:

Depreciation . . . . . . . . . . . . . . . . . . . . . .  850,000
    Allowance for Depreciation. . . .         850,000
Income Taxes . . . . . . . . . . . . . . . . . . . . .  2,675,000
    Income Taxes Payable . . . . . . . .         2,475,000
    Provision for Deferred
       Income Taxes . . . . . . . . . . . . . .         200,000

Current taxable income = \$4,950,000.

14–26. a) Annuity factor in advance at $12\% = 3.037 + 1.000 = 4.037$.
Capitalized amount = $4.037 \times \$2,000 = \$8,074$.

Asset: Rights to leased property . . . . . . . . . . . . . . . . . . . . . . .  \$8,074
Liability: Liability for future lease
    payments = \$8,074 − \$2,000. . . . . . . . . . . . . . . . .  6,074

b) Depreciation = $1/5 \times \$8,074$ . . . . . . . . . . . . . . . . . . . . . . . . . . .  \$1,615
Interest = $12\% \times \$6,074$ . . . . . . . . . . . . . . . . . . . . . . . . . . . . .  729
    Total . . . . . . . . . . . . . . . . . . . . . . . . . . . . . . . . . . . . . . . . . . .  \$2,344

c) Book value of asset = \$8,074 − \$1,615 = \$6,459.
Book value of liability = \$6,074 − (\$2,000 − \$729) = \$4,803.
NOTE: in practice, this method would not be used unless the
           lease payments entitled the lessee to virtually all of
           the lifetime service values of the leased equipment.

## Chapter 15

15–13.  Retained Earnings ........................ 30,000
       Common Stock...................... 10,000
       Additional Paid-In Capital............. 20,000

15–14.  1/4   Treasury Stock ....................... 3,000
        Cash............................. 3,000

      3/18  Cash................................. 4,000
        Treasury Stock ................... 3,000
        Additional Paid-In Capital ........ 1,000

15–15.  a)  Sinking Fund for Bond Retirement   800,000
        Cash ....................... 800,000
     b)  Retained Earnings .............. 1,000,000
        Retained Earnings Appropri-
        ated for Debt Retirement ... 1,000,000

15–16.  Cash .............................. 3,000,000
       Common Stock................... 2,000,000
       Additional Paid-In Capital........ 1,000,000

15–17.  *First year:*
      Retained Earnings...................... 10,000
       Retained Earnings Appropriated for
       Damage Suit .................... 10,000
      *Second year:*
      Retained Earnings Appropriated for
      Damage Suit ........................ 10,000
       Retained Earnings................. 10,000
      Loss on Damage Suit ................... 11,500
       Cash ............................. 11,500

15–25.  a)  Income available for common stock =
        $312,000 − $50,000 = $262,000.
      Undiluted earnings per share = $262,000/100,000 = $2.62.

     b)  Equivalent common shares = 100,000 + 2 × 10,000 = 120,000.
      Fully diluted earnings per share = $312,000/120,000 = $2.60.

15–28.  a)

|  | Present | Borrowing | Stock Sale |
|---|---|---|---|
| Estimated annual earnings: | | | |
| Before interest and taxes .. | $1,500,000 | $2,500,000 | $2,500,000 |
| Bond interest | | | |
| (8% × $5,000,000) ....... | — | 400,000 | — |
| Earnings before taxes ..... | $1,500,000 | $2,100,000 | $2,500,000 |
| Income taxes @ 45% ...... | 675,000 | 945,000 | 1,125,000 |
| Net Income............... | $ 825,000 | $1,155,000 | $1,375,000 |
| Shares outstanding ......... | 1,000,000 | 1,000,000 | 1,625,000 |
| Earnings per share.......... | $0.825 | $1.155 | $0.846 |

The great impact of debt financing is due in part to leverage (before-tax earnings of 20 percent, interest cost of only 8 percent), in part to the tax-deductibility of interest.

b) Other factors to be considered in reaching a decision:

1. Loss of some control of corporation if new voting stock is issued.
2. Effect of the issue of a large block of stock upon the market price of Randolph Corporation stock.
3. Company's future need for credit—and possibilities of getting it if bonds are issued now.
4. Risk associated with a large debt outstanding.

## Chapter 16

16–15.  a) The only items to appear would be:

Goodwill.......................................... $10,000
Retained earnings ................................. 15,000

The latter figure would be combined with the retained earnings of Wolfe Corporation, the combined total being shown as a single figure.

b) Capital Stock—Lamb Company ....... 100,000
Consolidation Goodwill*.............. 10,000
    Investment in Lamb Company ....     90,000
    Retained Earnings† ..............     20,000

* Or "Investments in consolidated subsidiaries in excess of equity in tangible assets acquired."
† Or "Deficit" if that account title were used in the Lamb Company's trial balance. Usually the account title is still Retained Earnings, but the debit balance is listed as Deficit on the balance sheet.

16–16.  a) Unconsolidated income.............................. $ 55,000
Less: Dividends from Y............................. 8,000
Plus: Income of Y ................................. 15,000
Consolidated income .............................. $ 62,000
Less: Minority interest in income.................... 3,000
Net income......................................... $ 59,000

b) Minority interest .................................... $ 21,000
Common stock ...................................... 100,000
Premium on common stock.......................... 20,000
Retained earnings.................................. 404,000

The total ownership equity would commonly be reported as $524,000. The minority interest would not be included.

16–18. *a*)   Consolidated balance sheet, January 1, 19x2:

| | |
|---|---:|
| Current assets | $ 6,300 |
| Plant and equipment, net | 8,700 |
| Total Assets | $15,000 |
| Current liabilities | $ 2,800 |
| Common stock | 2,500 |
| Additional paid-in capital | 3,500 |
| Retained Earnings | 6,200 |
| Total Liabilities and Owners' Equity | $15,000 |

*b*)   Consolidated net income = $1,000 − $100 + $180 = $1,080.

*c*)

| | |
|---|---:|
| Common stock | $ 2,500 |
| Additional paid-in capital | 3,500 |
| Retained earnings | 6,880 |
| Total Owners' Equity | $12,880 |

16–22.

Sumner Corporation and Acme Company
### CONSOLIDATED INCOME STATEMENT AND RECONCILIATION OF RETAINED EARNINGS
#### For the Year 19x1

| | |
|---|---:|
| Sales | $80,000 |
| Cost of goods sold | 58,000 |
| Gross margin | $22,000 |
| General expenses | 10,300 |
| Net operating income | $11,700 |
| Less: Minority interest in earnings | 825 |
| Consolidated net income | $10,875 |
| Dividends paid | 5,000 |
| Net addition to retained earnings | $ 5,875 |
| Retained earnings, December 31, 19x0 | 9,000 |
| Retained earnings, December 31, 19x1 | $14,875 |

Sumner Corporation and Acme Company
### CONSOLIDATED STATEMENT OF FINANCIAL POSITION
#### December 31, 19x1

| ASSETS | | | LIABILITIES AND STOCKHOLDERS' EQUITY | | |
|---|---:|---:|---|---:|---:|
| *Current Assets:* | | | *Current Liabilities:* | | |
| Cash | $ 5,850 | | Accounts payable | | $ 6,200 |
| Accounts receivable | 10,050 | | Minority equity in | | |
| Inventory | 13,400 | | subsidiary | | 6,575 |
| Total Current Assets | $29,300 | | *Stockholders' Equity:* | | |
| Fixed assets (net) | 30,350 | | Common stock | $35,000 | |
| Consolidation goodwill | 3,000 | | Retained earnings | 14,875 | 49,875 |
| Total | $62,650 | | Total | | $62,650 |

## Consolidation Work Sheet

| Accounts | Independent Statements | | | | Eliminations and Adjustments | | Consolidated Statements | |
|---|---|---|---|---|---|---|---|---|
| | Sumner Corp. | | Acme Company | | | | | |
| | Debit | Credit | Debit | Credit | Debit | Credit | Debit | Credit |
| *Balance Sheet Items.* | | | | | | | | |
| Cash ........................ | 3,450 | | 2,400 | | | | 5,850 | |
| Accounts receivable ......... | 6,500 | | 4,250 | | | (5) 700 | 10,050 | |
| Inventory.................... | 7,100 | | 6,500 | | | (4) 200 | 13,400 | |
| Investments................. | 21,000 | | | | | (3) 21,000 | | |
| Fixed assets (net) ........... | 15,500 | | 14,850 | | | | 30,350 | |
| Consolidation goodwill ...... | | | | | (3) 3,000 | | 3,000 | |
| Accounts payable............ | | 5,200 | | 1,700 | (5) 700 | | | 6,200 |
| Minority equity in subsidiary . | | | | | | (6) 6,000 | | 6,575 |
| | | | | | | (7) 575 | | |
| Capital stock ............... | | 35,000 | | 20,000 | (3) 15,000 | | | 35,000 |
| | | | | | (6) 5,000 | | | |
| Retained earnings........... | | 9,000 | | 4,000 | (3) 3,000 | | | 9,000 |
| | | | | | (6) 1,000 | | | |
| *Income Statement Items, Etc.* | | | | | | | | |
| Sales........................ | | 60,000 | | 30,000 | (1) 10,000 | | | 80,000 |
| Cost of goods sold ........... | 48,000 | | 19,800 | | (4) 200 | (1) 10,000 | 58,000 | |
| General expenses............ | 3,400 | | 6,900 | | | | 10,300 | |
| Other income................ | | 750 | | | (2) 750 | | | |
| Dividends paid .............. | 5,000 | | 1,000 | | | (2) 750 | 5,000 | |
| | | | | | | (7) 250 | | |
| Minority interest in earnings . | | | | | (7) 825 | | 825 | |
| Total ................... | 109,950 | 109,950 | 55,700 | 55,700 | 39,475 | 39,475 | 136,775 | 136,775 |

## Chapter 17

17-12. This question calls for either a statement of cash flows or an extended funds statement. A cash flow statement cannot be prepared because the problem does not state which purchases of equipment were made in cash. The extended funds statement is as follows:

*Sources of funds:*
    Operations:
        Net income ................................... $16,211,410
        Depreciation................................. 5,447,120
        Total ...................................... $21,658,530
    Decreases in accounts receivable ................ 2,214,497
    Reduction in cash balance ....................... 38,053
        Total Sources of Funds ................... $23,911,080

*Uses of funds:*
    Dividends....................................... $ 3,000,000
    Equipment purchases........................... 9,886,498
    Increase in inventory ........................... 6,098,642
    Increase in marketable securities ................ 800,000
    Decrease in accounts payable, etc................ 4,125,940
        Total Uses of Funds ....................... $23,911,080

**17–15.    Statement of Changes in Financial Position:**

*Sources of Funds:*
  From operations:
    Net income ............................ $8,203,000
    Add: Depreciation and amortization..... <u>5,501,000</u>   $13,704,000
  From sale of common stock ...............   12,547,000
  From borrowing..........................   7,000,000
  From sale of plant assets* ..............   <u>83,000</u>
    Total Sources of Funds ..............   $33,334,000

*Uses of Funds:*
  To purchase plant assets..................   $18,082,000
  To invest in associated companies ........   1,005,000
  To retire preferred stock ..................   224,000
  To pay preferred dividends................   40,000
  To increase working capital..............   <u>13,983,000</u>
    Total Uses of Funds ..................   $33,334,000

* Original cost of property retired, $400,000, accumulated depreciation on these assets, $317,000, leaving a book value of $83,000 at the time of retirement. In the absence of further information, sale price has been assumed equal to book value. The amount is immaterial.

**17–18.    Extended statement of changes in financial position:**

*Sources of funds:*
  From operations:
    Net income ........................... $410,000
    Add: Depreciation...................... 350,000
      Loss on sale of equipment ......... <u>100,000</u>  $  860,000
  From sale of equipment...................   107,000
  From reduction of accounts receivable*...   53,000
  From decrease of inventories ............   705,000
  From reduction of cash and marketable
    securities ...............................   <u>553,000</u>
    Total Sources of Funds ..............   $2,278,000

*Uses of Funds:*
  To purchase plant assets..................   $  894,000
  To reduce mortgage......................   500,000
  To pay dividends.........................   300,000
  To increase prepaid expenses .............   82,000
  To reduce accounts payable...............   104,000
  To decrease accrued taxes ...............   340,000
  To settle prior years' taxes ...............   <u>58,000</u>
    Total Uses of Funds..................   $2,278,000

* This is based on the concept that the amount of receivables is the net book value, not the gross value.

## Chapter 18

18–16.

| a) PROFIT PLAN | Division A | Division B | Division C | Total |
|---|---|---|---|---|
| Sales revenues | $1,000 | $3,000 | $2,100 | $6,100 |
| Divisional expenses: | | | | |
| Cost of goods sold | $ 650 | $1,650 | $1,260 | $3,560 |
| Marketing | 150 | 500 | 300 | 950 |
| Administrative | 150 | 300 | 200 | 650 |
| Total | $ 950 | $2,450 | $1,760 | $5,160 |
| Division margin | $ 50 | $ 550 | $ 340 | $ 940 |
| Headquarters expenses | | | | 400 |
| Net Income | | | | $ 540 |
| CASH BUDGET | | | | |
| Revenues | $1,000 | $3,000 | $2,100 | $6,100 |
| Less: Increase in receivables | 10 | 200 | 50 | 260 |
| Collections | $ 990 | $2,800 | $2,050 | $5,840 |
| Cost of goods sold | $ 650 | $1,650 | $1,260 | $3,560 |
| Add: Inventory increase | 50 | 100 | 50 | 200 |
| Purchases | $ 700 | $1,750 | $1,310 | $3,760 |
| Less: Increase in payables | 15 | 50 | 80 | 145 |
| Payments to suppliers | $ 685 | $1,700 | $1,230 | $3,615 |
| Division marketing costs | 150 | 500 | 300 | 950 |
| Division administration | | | | |
| (expense less deprec.) | 145 | 285 | 180 | 610 |
| Total divisional | | | | |
| disbursements | $ 980 | $2,485 | $1,710 | $5,175 |
| Division Cash Flow | $ 10 | $ 315 | $ 340 | $ 665 |
| Head office disbursements: | | | | |
| Central administration | | | | $ 390 |
| Equipment purchases | | | | 130 |
| Dividends | | | | 350 |
| Total head office | | | | |
| disbursements | | | | $ 870 |
| Net Decrease in Cash | | | | $ (205) |

b) Anticipated cash balance = $290 − $205 ................ = $ 85
Minimum cash balance = 5% × $6,100 ................. = 305
Cash shortage ................................... = $220

Since the company has only a $100 line of credit, the proposed plan is not financially feasible.

## Chapter 19

19–11.  a)  Unit Cost = $29,632/9,800 = $3.02 per Unit.

  b)  (1)  Work in Process – Job No. 103 ..... 13,860
            Raw Materials Inventory ......        13,860

|       |       |     |                                      |        |        |
|-------|-------|-----|--------------------------------------|--------|--------|
|       |       | (2) | Work in Process – Job No. 103 ..... | 8,300  |        |
|       |       |     | Accrued Wages ...............        |        | 8,300  |
|       |       | (3) | Work in Process – Job No. 103 ..... | 8,000  |        |
|       |       |     | Manufacturing Overhead......         |        | 8,000  |
|       |       | (4) | Raw Materials Inventory ........     | 528    |        |
|       |       |     | Work in Process – Job No. 103 .      |        | 528    |
|       |       | (5) | Finished Goods Inventory ........   | 29,632 |        |
|       |       |     | Work in Process – Job No. 103 .      |        | 29,632 |

19–13. *a)* (1) Materials...................... 16,000
             Accounts Payable ............        16,000
         (2) Work in Process ................. 18,000
             Materials..................        18,000
         (3) Work in Process ................. 47,000
             Wages Payable ..............        47,000
         (4) Manufacturing Overhead......... 17,000
             Accounts Payable, etc. ......        17,000
         (5) Work in Process ................. 20,000
             Manufacturing Overhead......        20,000
         (6) Finished Goods .................. 80,000
             Work in Process ............        80,000
         (7) Cost of Goods Sold............... 77,000
             Finished Goods ..............        77,000

   *b)* $20,000 + $80,000 − $23,000 = $77,000.
   *c)* $17,000 − $20,000 = $3,000 overabsorbed.
   *d)* $15,000 + $18,000 + $47,000 + $20,000 − $80,000 = $20,000.

19–18. *a)* (1) Materials Inventory .............. 50,000
             Accounts Payable ............        50,000
         (2) Work in Process ................. 35,000
             Materials Inventory ..........        35,000
             Manufacturing Overhead......... 12,000
             Materials Inventory ..........        12,000
         (3) Work in Process ................. 20,000
             Wages Payable ..............        20,000
         (4) Manufacturing Overhead......... 500
             Wages Payable ..............        500
         (5) Manufacturing Overhead......... 30,000
             Liabilities ..................        30,000
             Work in Process ................. 40,000
             Manufacturing Overhead......        40,000
         (6) Finished Goods .................. 86,000
             Work in Process ............        86,000

   *b)* Total debits to Manufacturing Overhead............... $42,500
        Credit to Manufacturing Overhead at $10 per direct
        labor hour ....................................... 40,000
        Underabsorbed Manufacturing Overhead........ $ 2,500

c)　Total debits to Manufacturing Overhead............... $43,000
　　Credit to Manufacturing Overhead ($10 × 4,200) ...... 42,000
　　　　Underabsorbed Manufacturing Overhead........ $ 1,000

Reduction in Underabsorbed Manufacturing Overhead:

$$\$2,500 - \$900 = \$1,600.$$

# Chapter 20

**20–11.** *a)*
$$\text{Break-even Volume} = \frac{\$38,000}{\$6.20 - \$4.50}$$
$$= 22,353 \text{ Units, or } \$138,589.$$

*b)*
$$\text{Desired Volume} = \frac{(\$160,000)(20\%) + \$38,000}{\$6.20 - \$4.50}$$
$$= 41,176 \text{ Units, or } \$255,291.$$

**20–12.**

|  | | *Revenue* | | *Cost* | | *Profit* |
|---|---|---|---|---|---|---|
| 75,000 units | at $2.50 | $187,500 | at $2.00 | $150,000 | | $37,500 |
| 50,000 units | at $3.00 | 150,000 | at $2.25 | 112,500 | | 37,500 |
| Incremental Revenue . | | $ 37,500 | | | | |

Incremental Cost ......................... $ 37,500
Incremental Profit .................................. $　　0

**20–14.** *a)*
$$\text{Break-even Volume} = \frac{\text{Total Fixed Costs}}{\text{Price} - \text{Variable Cost}}$$
$$= \frac{\$320,000}{\$3.20} = 100,000 \text{ Units.}$$

*b)*　Desired Profit = $220,000 + $22,000 = $242,000.
　　New Variable Profit Ratio = $3.20 per Unit.
$$\text{Target Sales Volume} = \frac{\$242,000 + \$320,000}{\$3.20} = 175,625 \text{ Units.}$$

**20–17.**　Expected value of open market purchases:

$$0.6 \times \$0.75 + 0.4 \times \$0.90 = \$0.81.$$

This is virtually identical to the proposed contract price. The contract would provide a modest saving of $1,000 in cost each month and would also give management an opportunity to devote its attention to other matters, without worrying about the cost of its supplies for the next year. The contract should be accepted.

**20-27.**

| | Sheets (Doz.) | Gray Goods |
|---|---|---|
| Labor (excluding fixed labor costs).......... | $2.2540 | $ 0.0614 |
| Manufacturing overhead (excluding fixed costs) ..................................... | 0.6762 | 0.0154 |
| Process material............................ | 0.4092 | 0.0018 |
| Raw material............................... | 2.8240 | 0.1131 |
| Freight ..................................... | 0.0895 | |
| Incremental Cost* ...................... | $6.2529 | $ 0.1917 |
| Selling price ................................ | 7.5095 | 0.2250 |
| Gain per unit ............................... | $1.2566 | $ 0.0333 |
| Number of units............................ | × 27,000 | 900,000 |
| Incremental Profit......................... | $33,928 | $ 29,970 |

* Selling and administrative costs are excluded on the grounds that such portions as are not fixed have already been incurred (sunk) by reason of the fact that the orders have been obtained.

## Chapter 21

**21-13.** First, calculate plantwide and departmental burden rates:

| | | Hours | | | |
|---|---|---|---|---|---|
| Product | Output | Dept. 1 | Dept. 2 | Dept. 3 | All Depts. |
| A | 40,000 | 80,000 | 40,000 | 40,000 | |
| B | 40,000 | | 80,000 | 80,000 | |
| C | 10,000 | 20,000 | 30,000 | 30,000 | |
| Total hours | | 100,000 | 150,000 | 150,000 | 400,000 |
| Overhead | | $400,000 | $300,000 | $100,000 | $800,000 |
| Burden rate | | $4.00 | $2.00 | $0.67 | $2.00 |

Then calculate unit overhead cost for each product:

| | Product A | | Product B | | Product C | |
|---|---|---|---|---|---|---|
| | Hours | Cost | Hours | Cost | Hours | Cost |
| Departmental rates: | | | | | | |
| Department 1 ....... | 2 | $ 8.00 | — | | 2 | $ 8.00 |
| Department 2 ....... | 1 | 2.00 | 2 | $4.00 | 3 | 6.00 |
| Department 3 ....... | 1 | .67 | 2 | 1.34 | 3 | 2.01 |
| Total Unit Cost.. | | $10.67 | | $5.34 | | $16.01 |
| Plantwide rate ........ | 4 | $ 8.00 | 4 | $8.00 | 8 | $16.00 |

As this shows, the effect on the unit costs of products A and B is substantial, and the departmental burden rates presumably indicate more accurately the amount of resources used to support production of the product. If production and sales are not equal, the difference will also affect reported income.

**21-14.** Full cost rate = $7,000/1,400 = $5.00/service hour.
Variable cost rate = ($7,000 − $700 − $1,750)/1,400 = $3.25/service hour.

Cost included in a unit of product X:

Full cost basis:
Department 1: (200 × $5/10,000) ×   5 = $0.50/unit
Department 2: (300 × $5/30,000) × 10 =   0.50/unit
Total................................. $1.00/unit

Variable cost basis:
Department 1: (200 × $3.25/10,000) ×   5 = $0.325/unit
Department 2: (300 × $3.25/30,000) × 10 =   0.325/unit
Total................................. $0.650/unit

**21–16.**

| | (1)<br>Fraction<br>of Total<br>Value | (2)<br>Cost<br>Allocation<br>(1) × $828,000 | (3)<br>Unit<br>Cost<br>(2) ÷ Yield |
|---|---|---|---|
| Aviation gasoline .......... | 100/920 | $ 90,000 | $11.25 |
| Motor gasoline ............. | 420/920 | 378,000 | 9.00 |
| Kerosene................... | 88/920 | 79,200 | 7.92 |
| Distillate fuels............. | 160/920 | 144,000 | 7.20 |
| Lubricants................. | 100/920 | 90,000 | 18.00 |
| Residual fuels ............. | 52/920 | 46,800 | 4.68 |
| Total................ | | $828,000 | |

**21–19.**

| | Allocation<br>Basis | Melting<br>and<br>Pouring | Molding | Core<br>Making | Cleaning<br>and<br>Grinding |
|---|---|---|---|---|---|
| Indirect labor ........ | Traceable | $1,000 | $300 | $100 | $300 |
| Supplies used ........ | Traceable | 50 | 50 | 200 | 100 |
| Taxes: | | | | | |
|   Machinery and | | | | | |
|     equipment ....... | % of cost | 4 | 1 | 3 | 4 |
|   Building .......... | Floor space | 3 | 12 | 3 | 6 |
| Compensation | | | | | |
|   insurance ........ | % of payroll | 20 | 15 | 6 | 24 |
| Power............... | Usage | 10 | x | 10 | 30 |
| Heat and light ....... | Floor space | 10 | 40 | 10 | 20 |
| Depreciation: | | | | | |
|   Building .......... | Floor space | 8 | 32 | 8 | 16 |
|   Machinery ........ | % of cost | 20 | 5 | 15 | 20 |
|     Total ............ | | $1,125 | $455 | $355 | $520 |

# Chapter 22

**22–15.** Present acquisition cost of part: 6,000 at $0.50 ................. $3,000
Proposed production cost (excluding depreciation) 6,000 at $0.20   1,200
  Annual savings .......................................... $1,800
Present value of annuity of $1 in arrears for seven periods
  at 16  ......................................................   4,039
Capitalized value of annual savings.......................... $7,489

Cost of new machine......................................... $7,000
Plus: Sale value of old machine ............................... 1,500
Investment Required to Produce Part......................... $8,500

The present value of the savings is less than the present value of the investment required. The part should continue to be purchased.

22–19. *a)* Cost of machine ......................................... $100,000
Less: Tax reduction on portion expensed ($50,000) ..... (25,000)
7% tax credit on portion capitalized .............. (3,500)
Plus: Working capital required ........................ 10,000
Net Present Outlay ............................. $ 81,500

*b)*

| | Year 1 | Year 2 |
|---|---|---|
| (1) Before-tax reduction in operating costs.... | $20,000 | $20,000 |
| (2) Cost subject to depreciation for tax purposes, beginning of year ............. | $46,500 | $34,875 |
| (3) Tax-allowed depreciation [25% of (2)] ..... | 11,625 | 8,719 |
| (4) Taxable saving [(1) − (3)]................. | 8,375 | 11,281 |
| (5) Tax [50% of (4)]......................... | $ 4,188 | $ 5,641 |
| (6) After-tax cash flow [(1) − (5)]............. | $15,812 | $14,359 |

22–20. *a)* Initial cash flows before tax:

| Invoice price of new machine ............... | | $39,000 |
|---|---|---|
| Incidental outlays, capitalized............... | | 5,000 |
| Incidental outlays, expensed ................ | | 10,000 |
| Total.................................. | | $54,000 |
| Less: Resale value, present machine ........ | | 5,000 |
| Net cash outlay before taxes ............ | | $49,000 |

Annual operating costs (excluding depreciation):

| At present.................................... | $17,400 | |
|---|---|---|
| After new installation...................... | 7,400 | |
| Annual cash savings before tax ......... | $10,000 | |
| Present value multiplier @ 16%......... | 4,833 | |
| Present value of future savings ............. | | 48,330 |
| Net Present Value Before Taxes.............. | | $ (670) |

This indicates that the proposal should be rejected.

*b)* Initial cash flows after tax:

| Acquisition costs, new machine ............. | $54,000 | |
|---|---|---|
| Less: Tax credit, expensed portion......... | (2,500) | $51,500 |
| Proceeds, old machine: | | |
| Resale value ........................... | $ 5,000 | |
| Tax basis: $55,000 − ($10,000 + $9,000 + $8,000) ..................... | 28,000 | |
| Tax loss................................. | $23,000 | |
| Tax credit at 50% ........................ | (11,500) | |
| After-tax proceeds...................... | | 16,500 |
| Incremental Cash Flow After Tax........... | | $35,000 |

## ANNUAL CASH OPERATING COSTS AFTER TAX

| Years from Now | (1) Tax Depreciation Present Machine | (2) New Machine | (3) Difference | (4) Taxable Income $10,000 − (3) | (5) Income Tax @ 50% | (6) After-Tax Cash Flow $10,000 − (5) | Multiplier | Present Value |
|---|---|---|---|---|---|---|---|---|
| 1 ..... | $7,000 | $8,000 | $1,000 | $9,000 | $4,500 | $5,500 | .9091 | $ 5,450 |
| 2 ..... | 6,000 | 7,200 | 1,200 | 8,800 | 4,400 | 5,600 | .8264 | 4,628 |
| 3 ..... | 5,000 | 6,400 | 1,400 | 8,600 | 4,300 | 5,700 | .7513 | 4,282 |
| 4 ..... | 4,000 | 5,600 | 1,600 | 8,400 | 4,200 | 5,800 | .6830 | 3,961 |
| 5 ..... | 3,000 | 4,800 | 1,800 | 8,200 | 4,100 | 5,900 | .6209 | 3,663 |
| 6 ..... | 2,000 | 4,000 | 2,000 | 8,000 | 4,000 | 6,000 | .5645 | 3,384 |
| 7 ..... | 1,000 | 3,200 | 2,200 | 7,800 | 3,900 | 6,100 | .5132 | 3,131 |
| 8 ..... | − | 2,400 | 2,400 | 7,600 | 3,800 | 6,200 | .4665 | 2,892 |
| 9 ..... | − | 1,600 | 1,600 | 8,400 | 4,200 | 5,800 | .4241 | 2,460 |
| 10 ..... | − | 800 | 800 | 9,200 | 4,600 | 5,400 | .3855 | 2,082 |
| Total .. | | | | | | | | $35,933 |

The present value of the future cash flows exceeds the incremental outlay by $933. Other things being equal, the proposal should be accepted.

22–22.  *a)*  Present outlay:

| | | |
|---|---|---|
| Cost of machine............................ | | $50,000 |
| Less: Sale value of old machine............ | $10,000 | |
| Tax reduction on retirement loss on old machine...................... | 10,000 | 20,000 |
| Net present outlay........................ | | $30,000 |
| Present value at 10% of after-tax future cash savings (see table below)................. | | 68,453 |
| Net Present Value...................... | | +$38,453 |

## CALCULATION OF DISCOUNTED CASH FLOWS FROM INVESTMENT DECISION

| (1) Years Hence | (2) Net Book Value of New Machine | (3) Tax Depreciation | (4) Depreciation on old Machine | (5) Increase in Depreciation | (6) Taxable Income | (7) Income Tax | (8) After-Tax Cash Flow | (9) Present Value at 10% |
|---|---|---|---|---|---|---|---|---|
| 1 ..... | $50,000 | $10,000 | $ 3,750 | $ 6,250 | $ 13,750 | $ 6,875 | $ 13,125 | $11,932 |
| 2 ..... | 40,000 | 8,000 | 3,750 | 4,250 | 15,750 | 7,875 | 12,125 | 10,020 |
| 3 ..... | 32,000 | 6,400 | 3,750 | 2,650 | 17,350 | 8,675 | 11,325 | 8,508 |
| 4 ..... | 25,600 | 5,120 | 3,750 | 1,370 | 18,630 | 9,315 | 10,685 | 7,298 |
| 5 ..... | 20,480 | 4,096 | 3,750 | 346 | 19,654 | 9,827 | 10,173 | 6,316 |
| 6 ..... | 16,384 | 3,277 | 3,750 | − 473 | 20,473 | 10,237 | 9,763 | 5,511 |
| 7 ..... | 13,107 | 2,621 | 3,750 | − 1,129 | 21,129 | 10,564 | 9,436 | 4,843 |
| 8 ..... | 10,486 | 2,097 | 3,750 | − 1,653 | 21,653 | 10,826 | 9,174 | 4,280 |
| 9 ..... | 8,389 | 1,678 | − | 1,678 | 18,322 | 9,161 | 10,839 | 4,597 |
| 10 ..... | 6,711 | 1,342 | − | 1,342 | } 13,289 | 6,645 | 13,355 | 5,148 |
| 10 ..... | 5,369 | 5,369 | − | 5,369 | | | | |
| Total .. | | $50,000 | $30,000 | $20,000 | $180,000 | $90,000 | $110,000 | $68,453 |

Derivation of amounts in columns (3) through (9):
  (3)  20% of col. 2.
  (4)  12.5% of $30,000 (remaining book value).
  (5)  Col. 4 less col. 3.
  (6)  $20,000 cash flow less increase in depreciation (col. 5).
  (7)  50% of col. 6.
  (8)  $20,000 less col. 7.
  (9)  Col. 8 × Table 3, Appendix A.

*b)*  To find the internal rate of return, discount the cash flows in column 8 above, first at 40% and then at 50%:

| Year | Cash Flow | Present Value | |
|---|---|---|---|
| | | at 40% | at 50% |
| 0 | −30,000 | −30,000 | −30,000 |
| 1 | +13,125 | + 9,371 | + 8,754 |
| 2 | +12,125 | + 8,657 | + 5,384 |
| 3 | +11,325 | + 4,122 | + 3,352 |
| 4 | +10,685 | + 2,778 | + 2,116 |
| 5 | +10,173 | + 1,892 | + 1,343 |
| 6 | + 9,763 | + 1,298 | + 859 |
| 7 | + 9,436 | + 896 | + 557 |
| 8 | + 9,174 | + 624 | + 358 |
| 9 | +10,839 | + 520 | + 282 |
| 10 | +13,355 | + 467 | + 227 |
| Total | | + 625 | − 6,768 |

The internal rate of return is thus approximately 40.8%.

## Chapter 23

23–14. Let $x$ be the quantity of material required to produce 6.3 lbs. of product:

$$(x - 0.1x)(0.5) = 6.3 \quad x = 6.3/0.45 = 14 \text{ lbs. of material}$$

Input: 14 lbs. at $1 ................................. $14.00
Less scrap: 1.4 lbs. at $0.10........................... 0.14
Net cost of 6.3 lbs. of product......................... $13.86
    Cost per pound....................................    $2.20

23–15.  Labor quantity variance:
    1500 units of A @ 2 hours = 3,000 hours @ $3.... $ 9,000
    4000 units of B @ 3 hours = 12,000 hours @ $3... 36,000
    Standard usage of labor ......................... $45,000
    Actual usage of labor: 14,500 hours @ $3......... 43,500
       Favorable quantity variance................. $1,500
  Labor rate variance:
    Standard cost of labor worked: 14,500 hours @ $3.. $43,500
    Actual payroll .................................. 44,000
       Unfavorable rate variance................... (500)
  Net Labor Variance .............................. $1,000

23–17.  a)

| | Product A | Product B | Total |
|---|---|---|---|
| Equivalent units: | | | |
| Finished units ................ | 5,000 | 10,000 | |
| Ending inventory .............. | 300 | 600 | |
| | 5,300 | 10,600 | |
| Beginning inventory .......... | 500 | 500 | |
| Total..................... | 4,800 | 10,100 | |
| Standard labor cost per unit...... | × $2 | × $1 | |
| Total standard labor cost......... | $9,600 | $10,100 | $19,700 |
| Actual labor cost................ | | | 23,500 |
| Total Labor Cost Variance . | | | $ 3,800 |

b)  Standard labor cost........................... $19,700
    Actual hours × standard rates ................. 22,000
        Labor quantity variance.................         $(2,300)
    Actual hours × actual rates................... 23,500
        Labor rate variance .....................         (1,500)

c)  **Ending inventory:**
    Product A: 600 × ½ × $2 .................... $  600
    Product B: 1,200 × ½ × $1................... __600__
        Total ............................... $1,200

## 23–23.

### Raw Materials and Supplies

| | | | |
|---|---|---|---|
| Bal. 5/1 | 29,460 | (2) | 41,300 |
| (1) | 37,900 | Bal. 6/1 | 26,060 |
| Bal. 6/1 | 26,060 | | |

### Material in Process

| | | | |
|---|---|---|---|
| Bal. 5/1 | 18,400 | (4) | 42,600 |
| (2) | 41,300 | (6a) | 1,900 |
| | | Bal. 6/1 | 15,200 |
| Bal. 6/1 | 15,200 | | |

### Labor in Process

| | | | |
|---|---|---|---|
| Bal. 5/1 | 9,650 | (4) | 28,300 |
| (3) | 28,400 | | |
| (6b) | 1,250 | Bal. 6/1 | 11,000 |
| Bal. 6/1 | 11,000 | | |

### Accrued Wages

| | | | |
|---|---|---|---|
| (7) | 32,180 | Bal. 5/1 | 1,620 |
| | | (3) | 28,400 |
| | | (8) | 2,160 |

### Finished Goods

| | | | |
|---|---|---|---|
| Bal. 5/1 | 35,000 | (5) | 79,200 |
| (4) | 70,900 | Bal. 6/1 | 26,700 |
| Bal. 6/1 | 26,700 | | |

### Material Price Variance

| | | | |
|---|---|---|---|
| (9a) | 1,400 | (1) | 1,400 |

### Cost of Goods Sold

| | |
|---|---|
| (5) | 79,200 |

### Material Quantity Variance

| | | | |
|---|---|---|---|
| (6a) | 1,900 | (9b) | 1,900 |

### Variance Summary

| | | | |
|---|---|---|---|
| (9b) MQV | 1,900 | (9a) MPV | 1,400 |
| (9d) WRV | 2,160 | (9c) LQV | 1,250 |
| (unfavorable) | | (favorable) | |

### Labor Quantity Variance

| | | | |
|---|---|---|---|
| (9c) | 1,250 | (6b) | 1,250 |

### Accounts Payable, Cash, etc.

| | | | |
|---|---|---|---|
| | | (1) | 36,500 |
| | | (7) | 32,180 |

### Wage Rate Variance

| | | | |
|---|---|---|---|
| (8) | 2,160 | (9d) | 2,160 |

# Chapter 24

**24–15.** Normal burden rate per direct labor dollar:

Fixed costs ($12,450/$15,000) = $0.83
Variable costs ................. 1.15
Total ..................... $1.98

Absorbed cost $17,600 × 1.98 ........... $34,848
Budgeted cost $12,450 + $17,600 × 1.15... 32,690
  Volume variance ...................        $2,158 favorable
Actual cost ........................... 33,150
  Overhead spending variance ........          460 unfavorable
Net Variance (Absorbed Minus Actual)..        $1,698 favorable

Various account structures are available. By using separate accounts for manufacturing overhead and manufacturing overhead absorbed, these accounts can serve to accumulate running totals of these separate quantities. At the end of each period, they can be used to segregate the spending and volume variances by entering the budgeted amounts as in entry (3) below:

| Sundry Accounts | | | | Manufacturing Overhead | | | |
|---|---|---|---|---|---|---|---|
| (1) | 33,150 | | | (1) | 33,150 | (3) | 32,690 |
| | | | | | | (4) | 460 |

| Overhead Absorbed | | | | Overhead in Process | | | |
|---|---|---|---|---|---|---|---|
| (3) | 32,690 | (2) | 34,848 | (2) | 34,848 | | |
| (5) | 2,158 | | | | | | |

| Overhead Volume Variance | | | | Overhead Spending Variance | | | |
|---|---|---|---|---|---|---|---|
| | | (5) | 2,158 | (4) | 460 | | |

**24–17.** *a)*  Machine-hours transferred out...................... 15,000  hours
  Add: Hours in process, end of month................  1,400
  Less: Hours in process, start of month .............  (3,000)
    Machine-Hours Worked during Month .......... 13,400  hours

*b)*  Standard hours transferred out: $69,000/$3......... 23,000  hours
  Add: Standard hours in process, end of month:
    $18,000/$3.......................................  6,000
  Less: Standard hours in process, start of month:
    $16,200/$3.......................................  (5,400)
    Standard Labor Hours Worked during Month ... 23,600  hours

**24–18.** *a)*  Burden rate = $.52 + $1.15 = $1.67 per direct labor hour.
  Overhead earned: (10,500 hrs. + 3,600 hrs. − 4,000 hrs.) × $1.67 = $16,867.

b) Month-end balance: 3,600 hrs. × $1.67 = $6,012.

c) 
| | | |
|---|---|---|
| Actual overhead .................. | $17,400 | |
| Budgeted at earned hours (10,100). | 16,295 | |
| Spending variance ............. | | $1,105 unfavorable |
| Earned.......................... | 16,867 | |
| Volume variance.............. | | 572 favorable |
| Total variance ........ | | $ 533 unfavorable |

24–24. a) A predetermined charging rate should be used so that changes in the monthly charge measure changes in consumption only. The rate in this case would be:

$$(\$3,000 + \$7 \times 3,000)/3,000 = \$8 \text{ an hour.}$$

At this rate, the charge for August would be:

$$95 \times \$8 = \$760.$$

b) The budget is $100 \times \$8 = \$800$. The manager is expected to control usage, and the variance is $\$800 - \$760 = \$40$. This would be regarded as favorable unless it merely represents postponement of necessary service.

c) Actual cost in the service department was $2,200 in excess of the flexible budget allowance and $2,800 in excess of the amount charged to other departments. Much of the $2,200 may have resulted from an inability to reduce costs quickly to adapt to a suddenly lower level of service demand. This may be economically and organizationally justifiable. What the variance does is identify an out-of-line situation which management must then decide to correct or live with.

24–26. a) 
| | |
|---|---|
| Direct labor cost transferred out ......................... | $24,000 |
| Plus: End-of-month balance ........................... | 5,400 |
| Less: Beginning-of-month balance....................... | (8,000) |
| Standard direct labor cost of work done ........... | $21,400 |

b) 
| | | |
|---|---|---|
| Materials price variance: | | |
| ($48,000 + $800) − $50,000 = | | $1,200  Fav. |
| Materials quantity variance: | | |
| Standard direct materials cost: | | |
| $25,000 + $4,100 − $13,000 = | $16,100 | |
| Actual direct materials at | | |
| standard prices...................... | 17,000 | (900) Unfav. |
| Labor rate variance: | | |
| Direct labor: $21,000 − $20,000 = | $ (1,000) | |
| Indirect labor: $8,700 − $9,000 = | 300 | 700 Unfav. |
| Labor quantity variance: | | |
| Standard direct labor cost .............. | $21,400 | |
| Actual hours × standard rate .......... | 20,000 | 1,400 Fav. |
| Overhead: | | |
| Actual: $9,000 + $4,500 + $15,000 = | $28,500 | |
| Budgeted: $17,000 + 0.5 × $21,400 = | 27,700 | |
| Spending variance ............... | | (800) Unfav. |
| Absorbed: $36,000 + $8,100 − $12,000 = $32,100 | | |
| Volume variance................. | | 4,400 Fav. |

Report only the materials quantity variance, the labor quantity variance, and the overhead spending variance to the department head.

*c*)

**Materials Inventory**

| | | | |
|---|---|---|---|
| Bal. 1/1 | 76,000 | (4) | 21,500 |
| (1) | 50,000 | Bal. 2/1 | 104,500 |
| Bal. 2/1 | 104,500 | | |

**Materials in Process — Dept. Y**

| | | | |
|---|---|---|---|
| Bal. 1/1 | 13,000 | (6) | 25,000 |
| (4) | 17,000 | (7a) | 900 |
| | | Bal. 2/1 | 4,100 |
| Bal. 2/1 | 4,100 | | |

**Overhead — Dept. Y**

| | | | |
|---|---|---|---|
| (3b) | 9,000 | (8) | 32,100 |
| (4) | 4,500 | | |
| (5) | 15,000 | | |
| (9) | 3,600 | | |

**Labor in Process — Dept. Y**

| | | | |
|---|---|---|---|
| Bal. 1/1 | 8,000 | (6) | 24,000 |
| (3a) | 20,000 | | |
| (7b) | 1,400 | Bal. 2/1 | 5,400 |
| Bal. 2/1 | 5,400 | | |

**Accrued Wages**

| | | | |
|---|---|---|---|
| (2) | 29,700 | (3a) | 20,000 |
| | | (3b) | 9,000 |
| | | (10) | 700 |

**Overhead in Process — Dept. Y**

| | | | |
|---|---|---|---|
| Bal. 1/1 | 12,000 | (6) | 36,000 |
| (8) | 32,100 | Bal. 2/1 | 8,100 |
| Bal. 2/1 | 8,100 | | |

**Accounts Payable, etc.**

| | | | |
|---|---|---|---|
| (6) | 85,000 | (1) | 48,800 |
| | | (2) | 29,700 |
| | | (5) | 15,000 |

**Variance Summary**

| | | | | | |
|---|---|---|---|---|---|
| (7a) MQV | 900 | (1) | MPV | 1,200 |
| (10) LRV | 700 | (7b) | LQV | 1,400 |
| (9) OHSV | 800 | (9) | OHVV | 4,400 |

# Chapter 25

**25–12.** *a*) (1)

| | |
|---|---|
| Actual ..................................... | $1,000 |
| Total variance ............................ | 100 favorable |
| Absorbed ................................ | $1,100 |
| Volume variance........................... | 20 favorable |
| Budget.................................... | $1,080 |
| Spending variance ......................... | 80 favorable |

(2) Budgeted fixed cost: $1,080 − 30% of $1,100 = $750

(3) Variable cost:

| | |
|---|---|
| Labor..................... | $400 |
| Materials ................. | 100 |
| Overhead (30%) .......... | 330 |
| Total .................. | $830 = 830/1,600 of product cost |
| 830/1,600 × $1,760 = | $913 |
| Selling expense (4%)...... | 80 |
| Total Variable .......... | $993 |

Variable profit = $2,000 − $993 = $1,007 = 50.35%.

*b)*
| | | |
|---|---|---|
| Sales......................................... | | $2,000 |
| Variable costs: | | |
| Manufacturing................................ | $913 | |
| Selling ........................................ | 80 | 993 |
| Variable profit.................................... | | $1,007 |
| Traceable fixed costs: | | |
| Manufacturing................................ | $750 | |
| Selling and administrative ..................... | 55 | 805 |
| Spending variance (favorable) ................... | | (80) |
| Profit Contribution ........................... | | $  282 |

**25-13.** The text does not provide a detailed explanation of how to separate the profit variance into component parts. This problem has been inserted to provide a brief introduction to the technique.

*a)*   Effect of variations in selling price:

| | |
|---|---|
| Actual volume at actual price......................... | $60,500 |
| Actual volume at budgeted price...................... | 66,000 |
| Selling price variance........................... | $ (5,500) |

Effect of volume:

| | |
|---|---|
| Budgeted gross margin per unit = $2.40 | |
| Increase in gross margin due to | |
| sale of 1,000 additional units: | |
| 1,000 × $2.40 ...................................... | $ 2,400 |
| But the increase in production volume by 1,000 units | |
| produces a favorable overhead volume variance: | |
| Fixed overhead per unit = $0.78 | |
| Increased absorption: 1,000 × $0.78.................. | 780 |
| Total effect of volume (favorable)............. | $ 3,180 |

*b)*   The other variances can be found by adjusting the original budget allowances for the effects of selling price and volume variations:

| | Original Budget | Adjust- ments | Adjusted Budget |
|---|---|---|---|
| Direct materials................... | $10,000 | +$ 1,000 | $11,000 |
| Direct labor ...................... | 13,000 | + 1,300 | 14,300 |
| Factory overhead.................. | 13,000 | + 520 | 13,520 |
| Selling and administrative | | | |
| expenses...................... | 18,000 | − | 18,000 |

Variance calculations:

| | Actual | Adjusted Budget | Variance |
|---|---|---|---|
| Materials quantity variance..... | $11,200 | −$11,000 | $ (200) |
| Labor quantity variance......... | 14,700 | − 14,300 | (400) |
| Overhead spending variance .... | 14,100 | − 13,520 | (580) |
| Selling and administrative | | | |
| expense variance.............. | 18,300 | − 18,000 | (300) |
| Total..................... | | | $ (1,480) |

The total variance is $5,500 + $1,480 − $3,180 = $(3,800).

# INDEX

813

*This book has been set in 10 point and 9 point Primer, leaded 2 points. Part and chapter numbers are 24 point and 36 point Baskerville italic; part and chapter titles are 24 point and 18 point Baskerville. The size of the type page is 27 by 45½ picas.*